HANDBOOK OF
AFFECT AND SOCIAL COGNITION

HANDBOOK OF
AFFECT AND SOCIAL COGNITION

Edited by

Joseph P. Forgas
University of New South Wales
Sydney, Australia

LEA LAWRENCE ERLBAUM ASSOCIATES, PUBLISHERS
2001 Mahwah, New Jersey   London

Lawrence Erlbaum Associates, Inc., Publishers
10 Industrial Avenue
Mahwah, NJ 07430

Cover design by Kathryn Houghtaling Lacey

Library of Congress Cataloging-in-Publication Data

Handbook of affect and social cognition / edited by Joseph P. Forgas.
    p.   cm.
  Includes bibliographical references and index.
  ISBN 0-8058-3217-3 (alk. paper)
  1. Affect (Psychology)   2. Cognition—Social aspects.   I. Forgas, Joseph P.

BF511.H34   2000
152.4—dc21   00-034779

Printed in the United States of America
10 9 8 7 6 5 4 3 2 1

Contents

Contributors   **xiii**

Preface   **xv**

1 Introduction: Affect and Social Cognition   **1**
  Joseph P. Forgas, University of New South Wales

  Philosophical and Speculative Theories Linking Affect and Cognition   6
  Some Early Empirical Evidence for Affective Influences on Cognition
      and Judgments   7
  Psychodynamic Approaches to Affect and Cognition   8
  Conditioning Approaches to Affect and Cognition   9
  The Emergence of a Cognitive Paradigm   12
  Major Areas of Contemporary Research on Affect and Social
      Cognition   15
    Affect and Cognition: Fundamental Issues and the Nature
        of the Relationship   16
    Affective Influences on the Content of Cognition   17
    Affect and Social Information Processing   18
    Affective Influences on Social Motivation and Intentions   19
    Affect, Cognition, and Interpersonal Behavior   19
    Personality and Individual Differences in Affectivity   20
  Conclusion   21
  References   22

I **THE RELATIONSHIP BETWEEN AFFECT
     AND COGNITION: FUNDAMENTAL ISSUES**

2 The Interaction of Affect and Cognition: A Neurobiological Perspective   **27**
  Ralph Adolphs and Antonio R. Damasio, University of Iowa

  Cognitive Affect   28
  Affective Modulation of Memory, Attention, and Decision Making
      in Animals   30
  Affect Modulates Declarative Memory   33
  Affect Modulates Decision Making   37
  Affect and Social Judgment   40

Conclusions   43
Acknowledgments   45
References   45

3   Affect and Attitudes: A Social Neuroscience Approach   **50**
    Tiffany A. Ito, University of Colorado, and John T. Cacioppo,
    University of Chicago

    Why Social Neuroscience?   51
    The Separability of Positive and Negative Affect   52
        The Evaluative Space Model   54
        Neural Substrates   57
        Negativity Bias   58
        Summary   59
    Rerepresentation of Evaluative Processes Across the Neuraxis   60
        Feeling without Knowing   63
        Applications to Implicit and Explicit Prejudice   65
        Different Evaluative Mechanisms or Decreased Activation
            with Practice?   67
        Summary   68
    Conclusion   69
    References   70

4   Affect and Cognitive Appraisal Processes   **75**
    Craig A. Smith, Vanderbilt University, and Leslie D. Kirby,
    University of Alabama at Birmingham

    Appraisal Theory: Its Purpose and Major Assumptions   77
    Structural Models of Appraisal   80
    Toward a Process Model of Appraisal   84
    Appraisal Theory, Affect, and Social Cognition   89
    References   90

**II AFFECTIVE INFLUENCES ON THE CONTENT
     OF COGNITION**

5   Mood and Social Memory   **95**
    Gordon H. Bower, Stanford University, and Joseph P. Forgas,
    University of New South Wales

    Affective Features of Social Episode Representations   96
    Memory for Emotional Episodes   98
    Affective Recall without Factual Recall   99
    Emotional Units in Associative Networks   103
    Mood-Dependent Retrieval   104
    Mood-Congruent Processing   108
    Limitations on Mood Congruity   110

Information-Processing Strategies that Moderate Mood Effects
on Memory   112
Summary and Conclusions   115
Acknowledgment   116
References   117

6   Affect as Information   **121**
    Gerald L. Clore, University of Illinois at Urbana-Champaign,
    Karen Gasper, Pennsylvania State University, and Erika Garvin,
    University of Illinois at Urbana-Champaign

Affect and Judgment   122
    Traditional Views   122
    The Affect-as-Information View   123
Mood and Processing   129
    Priming and Processing   133
Mood and Memory   136
Summary   139
Acknowledgments   140
References   141

7   Affective Influences on the Self-Concept: Qualifying
    the Mood-Congruency Principle   **145**
    Constantine Sedikides, University of Southampton,
    and Jeffrey D. Green, University of North Carolina at Chapel Hill

The Affect Infusion Model   147
    Type of Self-Conceptions   147
    Individual Differences   151
    Judgmental Task Features   154
Concluding Remarks   156
References   158

III **AFFECTIVE INFLUENCES ON SOCIAL
     INFORMATION PROCESSING**

8   Affective Influences on Social Information Processing   **163**
    Klaus Fiedler, University of Heidelberg

A Fundamental Processing Dichotomy   165
    Basic Assumptions, Methods, and Findings   166
    Mood-Congruency Effects   168
    Mood Effects on Information-Processing Style   169
    Boundary Conditions of Mood-Congruent Memory and Judgment   171
    Integrating the Evidence in Terms of Processing Differences:
        The Affect Infusion Model (AIM)   172
    The Processing Consequences of Affect   176

Affect, Cognition, and Adaptive Learning: Assimilation
    versus Accommodation   177
Summary and Conclusions   182
References   183

9 Promotion and Prevention Experiences: Relating Emotions
to Nonemotional Motivational States   **186**
E. Tory Higgins, Columbia University

Promotion and Prevention Focus Concerns   189
Promotion and Prevention: Nonemotional Motivational States   192
Promotion and Prevention: Emotional Experiences   195
Promotion and Prevention Experiences of Motivational Strength   200
Additional Implications of Promotion and Prevention for Emotion 203
Acknowledgments   208
References   208

10 The Role of Affect in Attitude Change   **212**
Richard E. Petty, Ohio State University, David DeSteno,
Northeastern University, and Derek D. Rucker,
Ohio State University

Attitude Structure   215
Attitude Change with Relevant Affect   216
  Affective versus Cognitive Appeals   216
  Fear Appeals   217
Attitude Change with Irrelevant (Incidental) Affect   218
  Effects of Emotional Factors Under Low-Elaboration Conditions   219
  Effects of Emotional Factors Under High-Elaboration Conditions 221
  Effects of Emotional Factors Under Moderate-Elaboration
    Conditions   223
  Mood-Correction Effects   226
Conclusion   228
References   228

IV **AFFECTIVE INFLUENCES ON MOTIVATION**
    AND INTENTIONS

11 The Role of Affect in Cognitive-Dissonance Processes   **237**
Eddie Harmon-Jones, University of Wisconsin—Madison

Overview of the Theory of Cognitive Dissonance   238
  Research Paradigms   239
  Role of Negative Affect   240
A Conceptualization of Why Dissonance Produces Negative Affect   240
Cognitive Discrepancy as an Antecedent of Negative Affect   241
  Dissonance and Physiological Responses   241

Dissonance and Self-Reported Negative Affect   242
Using Assessments of Negative Affect to Understand the Motivation
    Underlying Dissonance Reduction   242
Critical Evaluation   244
On the Causal Relation Between Dissonance, Affect, and Discrepancy
    Reduction   245
The Relation of Dissonance-Produced Affect to Discrepancy
    Reduction   245
Dissonance and Misattribution of Affect   247
Independent Sources of Affect and Discrepancy Reduction   249
Affective Consequences of Cognitive-Discrepancy Reduction   250
Does Discrepancy Reduction Decrease Physiological Responses?   251
Does Discrepancy Reduction Decrease Negative Affect?   251
Resolving Discrepant Findings for Physiological Responses
    and Reported Affect   252
Summary and Conclusions   252
Acknowledgments   252
References   253

12 Mood as a Resource in Processing Self-Relevant Information   **256**
    Yaacov Trope, Melissa Ferguson, and Raj Raghunathan,
    New York University

Mood as a Resource in Overcoming Defensiveness   257
Mood-Incongruent Information Search   258
Self-Induced Positive Mood   261
Mood as a Resource and Mood as a Goal   262
Research on Mood as a Resource versus a Goal in Feedback-Seeking
    Behavior   263
Mood as a Resource versus a Goal in Processing Persuasive Messages   267
Mood-Incongruent Recall   267
Affective Consequences of Processing   268
Attitudes and Behavioral Intentions   269
Conclusions   270
References   272

13 The Role of Motivated Social Cognition in the Regulation
    of Affective States   **275**
    Maureen Wang Erber, Northeastern Illinois University and Ralph
    Erber, DePaul University

The Search for Mood Repair   276
The Social Constraints Model of Mood Regulation and Processing   279
Mood Regulation: What and When   284
Research Supporting the Social Constraints Model:
    The Coolness Effect   285

Research Supporting the Appropriateness Hypothesis I:
   Strangers versus Romantic Couples   286
Research Supporting the Appropriateness Hypothesis II:
   Accepting versus Critical Others   287
Some Parting Thoughts   288
References   289

**V AFFECTIVE INFLUENCES ON COGNITIVELY
   MEDIATED SOCIAL BEHAVIORS**

14 Affect, Cognition, and Interpersonal Behavior: The Mediating
   Role of Processing Strategies   **293**
   Joseph P. Forgas, University of New South Wales

Affect Congruence in Interpersonal Behavior   295
Affect Infusion: A Question of Processing Style?   296
Affective Influences on Behavior Interpretation   300
Affect and Eyewitness Memory for Observed Interactions   302
Affective Influences on Spontaneous Interaction   303
Affect Infusion and Interpersonal Strategies: Making a Request   304
Affective Influences on Responding to Unexpected Social Situations   307
Affective Influences on Planned Strategic Encounters   308
Affective Influences on Persuasive Communication   311
The Interaction Between Affect and Cognitive-Processing Strategies   312
Summary and Conclusions   314
Acknowledgments   316
References   316

15 Affective Influences on Stereotyping and Intergroup Relations   **319**
   *Galen V. Bodenhausen, Thomas Mussweiler, Shira Gabriel,
   and Kristen N. Moreno, Northwestern University*

The Affective Context of Intergroup Relations   320
   Chronic Integral Affect   321
   Episodic Integral Affect   322
   Incidental Affect   324
Mechanisms of Affective Influence on the Stereotyping Process   326
   Category Identification   326
   Stereotype Activation   328
   Stereotype Application   330
   Stereotype Correction   336
Final Thoughts   337
References   338

16 Affect and Health-Relevant Cognition   **344**
   *Peter Salovey, Jerusha B. Detweiler, Wayne T. Steward,
   and Brian T. Bedell, Yale University*

Induced Mood and Thoughts about Health   346
Direct Effects of Mood on Illness: Findings from
    Psychoneuroimmunology   349
    Induced Mood and Immunologic Parameters   349
    Laughter and Immunity   350
Dispositional Links Between Mood and Health   351
    Optimism   351
    Hope   352
    Religiosity   353
    Mood-Regulatory Skills   354
    Hardiness   355
    Negative Affectivity   356
    Affect Intensity   357
Mood and Attentional Focus   358
Affect, Health-Relevant Cognition, and Social Support   359
Changes in Mood Motivate Health-Relevant Behaviors   361
Conclusion   362
Acknowledgments   363
References   363

VI   THE ROLE OF INDIVIDUAL DIFFERENCES
IN AFFECTIVITY

17   Personality as a Moderator of Affective Influences on Cognition   **371**
        Cheryl L. Rusting, State University of New York at Buffalo

        Personality Traits that Enhance Mood-Congruent Processing   375
            Extraversion and Neuroticism   375
            Other Negative Traits   378
        Personality Traits that Reverse Negative Mood-Congruent Processing 379
            Mood-Regulation   380
            Self-Esteem   382
        When Are Personality and Mood Effects on Cognition Present?   383
            Type of Mood Induction   384
            Motivations to Regulate Emotions   385
            Type of Cognitive Task   386
        Difficulties in Research on Personality, Mood, and Cognition   387
        References   388

18   Affect, Stress, and Personality   **392**
        Jerry Suls, University of Iowa

        The Big Five, Affective Experience, and Stress   394
        Neuroticism and Responses to Life Events   396
        Processes Contributing to the Neurotic Cascade   399
        Personality in the Context of Affective–Cognitive Networks   402

Person × Environment Fit: The Case of Agreeableness   403
Conclusions   405
Acknowledgments   406
References   406

19 Emotion, Intelligence, and Emotional Intelligence   410
John D. Mayer, University of New Hampshire

Putting Emotion and Cognition in Their Place   413
  The Trilogy of Mind   413
  Other Parts of Personality   415
  Emotional Traits   415
  Cognitive Traits   416
  Emotion and Cognition: What Is Intelligence and What Is Not? 417
The Theory of Emotional Intelligence   418
  Emotion as Information   418
  Emotional Perception   419
  Emotional Integration   420
  Understanding Emotion   421
  Management of Emotion   422
Emotional Intelligence as a Standard Intelligence   423
  Measuring Emotional Intelligence as an Ability   423
  A Description of the MEIS   424
  Scoring the MEIS   425
  Findings with the MEIS   425
Discussion and Conclusion   426
References   428

Author Index   **433**

Subject Index   **451**

Contributors

Ralph Adolphs, *Department of Neurology, University of Iowa*

Brian T. Bedell, *Department of Psychology, Yale University*

Galen V. Bodenhausen, *Department of Psychology, Northwestern University*

Gordon H. Bower, *Department of Psychology, Stanford University*

John T. Cacioppo, *Department of Psychology, University of Chicago*

Gerald L. Clore, *Department of Psychology, University of Illinois at Urbana-Champaign*

Antonio R. Damasio, *Department of Neurology, University of Iowa*

David DeSteno, *Department of Psychology, Northeastern University*

Jerusha B. Detweiler, *Department of Psychology, Yale University*

Maureen Wang Erber, *Department of Psychology, Northeastern Illinois University*

Ralph Erber, *Department of Psychology, DePaul University*

Klaus Fiedler, *Department of Psychology, University of Heidelberg*

Joseph P. Forgas, *School of Psychology, University of New South Wales*

Melissa Ferguson, *Department of Psychology, New York University*

Shira Gabriel, *Department of Psychology, Northwestern University*

Erika Garvin, *Department of Psychology, University of Illinois at Urbana-Champaign*

Karen Gasper, *Department of Psychology, Pennsylvania State University*

Jeffrey D. Green, *Department of Psychology, University of North Carolina at Chapel Hill*

Eddie Harmon-Jones, *Department of Psychology, University of Wisconsin-Madison*

E. Tory Higgins, *Department of Psychology, Columbia University*

Tiffany A. Ito, *Department of Psychology, University of Colorado at Boulder*

Leslie D. Kirby, *Department of Psychology, University of Alabama at Birmingham*

John D. Mayer, *Department of Psychology, University of New Hampshire*

Kristen N. Moreno, *Department of Psychology, Northwestern University*

Thomas Mussweiler, *Department of Psychology, Northwestern University*

Richard E. Petty, *Department of Psychology, Ohio State University*

Raj Raghunathan, *Department of Psychology, New York University*

Derek D. Rucker, *Department of Psychology, Ohio State University*

Cheryl L. Rusting, *Department of Psychology, State University of New York at Buffalo*

Peter Salovey, *Department of Psychology, Yale University*

Constantine Sedikides, *Department of Psychology, University of Southampton*

Craig A. Smith, *Department of Psychology and Human Development, Vanderbilt University*

Wayne T. Steward, *Department of Psychology, Yale University*

Jerry Suls, *Department of Psychology, University of Iowa*

Yaacov Trope, *Department of Psychology, New York University*

Preface

The quest to understand the role of affect in human affairs represents one of the most important tasks for psychology. Affect seems to influence every aspect of mental life. Our thoughts, judgments, memories, and decisions all seem to be profoundly influenced by how we happen to feel at the time. It is rather surprising that despite the long-standing fascination with the intriguing influence of feelings on thinking and behavior, much of the scientific research on this topic has been done only during the last two decades or so. As a result, the precise nature of affective influences on social thinking and the psychological mechanisms responsible for these effects have not been properly understood until quite recently.

Many philosophers, starting with Plato, have traditionally assumed that affect has a dangerous, invasive quality on rational thinking and behavior. This view has gained renewed currency thanks to the psychoanalytic speculations of Freud and his followers. Unfortunately, scientific psychology had relatively little to say about affective phenomena until quite recently. This was at least partly the consequence of the single-minded pursuit of first the behaviorist and later the cognitivist agenda in our discipline during most of the 20th century. The situation is now rapidly changing. Research on affect has become one of the most rapidly expanding areas in psychology. There is convergent evidence from such disparate fields as social cognition, neuropsychology, and psychophysiology demonstrating that affect is intimately involved in everything we think and do. As several contributions to this book illustrate, interest in affect and cognition thus provides an important new integrative focus across a variety of fields such as social, cognitive, personality, developmental, clinical, and neuropsychology.

This is a particularly fortuitous time then to present a comprehensive and integrative review of what has been accomplished. This new *Handbook of Affect and Social Cognition* surveys what we now know about the multifaceted role of affect in social thinking and behavior. The book features specially commissioned contributions from leading researchers who provide a comprehensive and up-to-date summary of the current state of knowledge in this field. The chapters featured in this handbook seek to contribute to our understanding of exactly how, when, and why affect will influence people's thinking and behaviors. They also convey some of the excitement that comes from finally coming to grips with these intriguing phenomena. Of course, no single book could possibly include everything that is interesting and exciting in contemporary affect-cognition research within its covers. The present volume features a comprehensive range of chapters that sample most of the key areas.

The book is organised into six substantive sections, corresponding to major areas of contemporary research on affect and social cognition. The introductory chapter sets the scene for much of what follows and presents a historical and philosophical overview of the intricate relationship between feeling and thinking, affect and cognition. The first section discusses some of the *fundamental issues* about the relationship between affect and cognition. These chapters highlight impressive recent neurobiological (Adolphs & Damasio) and psychophysiological (Ito & Cacioppo) evidence demonstrating the close interdependence of feeling and thinking, and discuss the critical role cognitive appraisal processes play in affective experience (Smith & Kirby). The second section looks at contemporary research on affective influences on the *content* of our thinking. These chapters discuss the role of affect in social memory (Bower & Forgas), the everyday use of affect as information (Clore, Gasper, & Garvin), and affective influences on self-conceptions (Sedikides & Green). The third section explores affective influences on the way we think—our *information processing strategies* (Fiedler). The links between affect and promotion vs. prevention-oriented thinking are discussed (Higgins), and the role of affect in attitude change and the processing of persuasive messages in particular is reviewed (Petty, DeSteno, & Rucker).

Of course, affect influences not only the content and the process of thinking, but also our *motivations and intentions* in social situations. The chapters in section four review the role of affect in cognitive dissonance processes (Harmon-Jones), the use of affect as a resource when dealing with threatening self-relevant information (Trope, Ferguson, & Raghunathan), and consider the role that motivational processes play in the regulation of affective states (Erber & Erber). Section five of the book discusses how affective states come to influence cognitively mediated *social behaviors* (Forgas), such as the role of affect in stereotyping and intergroup relations (Bodenhausen, Mussweiler, Gabriel, & Moreno) and in health-related cognition and behavior (Salovey, Detweiler, Steward, & Bedell). There are of course very important *individual differences* in temperament and affectivity between people, and this is the theme of the final, sixth section here. Personality characteristics play a very important role in moderating affective influences on social cognition (Rusting) and are especially critical when it comes to understanding how people manage aversive affective experiences such as stress (Suls). In recent years, "emotional intelligence" has been proposed as an omnibus term to describe fundamental individual differences in temperament and affectivity, and Mayer provides a much-needed critical review and scientific evaluation of this construct in the last chapter.

Given the comprehensive coverage of this book, it should be useful both as a basic reference book and as an informative textbook to be used in advanced courses dealing with affect and thinking. The main target audience for this book comprises researchers, students, and professionals in all areas of the behavioral sciences where affect is important, such as social, cognitive, clinical, counseling, personality, organizational, and applied psychology, as well as sociology, communication studies, and cognitive science. The book is written in a particularly readable and scholarly style, and students both at the undergraduate and at the graduate level should find it an engaging survey of the field. The book should thus also have significant textbook potential for the growing number of undergraduate and graduate courses dealing with affect.

A better understanding of how affect and social cognition are related should also be of considerable applied importance, as several of the chapters here emphasize. As affect is clearly one of the key influences of how we think and behave in social situations, understanding the interaction between affect and cognition necessarily lies at the heart of many professional applications of psychology. The Handbook should be of direct relevance to practitioners and professionals in a number of applied fields where understanding and dealing with the complexities of human thinking and interpersonal behavior is of interest. This includes such key applied domains as counselling and clinical psychology, organizational research, health psychology, and marketing and advertising research.

Producing a complex multi-authored book such as this Handbook is a prolonged and sometimes challenging task. Occasionally such projects suffer from excessive delays, and coordinating contributions from so many outstanding researchers can be a demanding task. By definition, it is the editor's lot to be the source of unwanted reminders to busy contributors—reminders to write the chapter, revise it, deal with the copyedited manuscript, and correct the page proofs are rarely welcome. I have been extremely fortunate in this instance to work with such an excellent and cooperative group of contributors. My first thanks must go to them. Because of their help and professionalism, we were able to finish this project without any delays and indeed, somewhat ahead of time. Past friendships have not frayed, and we are still all on speaking terms; indeed, I hope that working together on this book has been as positive an experience for them as it has been for me.

I am also indebted to many people and organizations who have helped to make this project possible. I want to express my gratitude to Judi Amsel at Lawrence Erlbaum Associates who has nurtured this project right from the beginning and has been amazingly helpful, efficient, supportive–and if the occasion demanded it, funny–through all the stages of completing this book. The production staff at Erlbaum, Robin Weisberg and Art Lizza, have also been extremely efficient and helpful. My special thanks are due to the production editor, Michie Shaw, who handled many of the day-to-day problems and queries with great efficiency and patience. I am also very grateful to my past and present colleagues, collaborators, and students at the Affect Research Laboratory at the University of New South Wales, Sydney who were extremely supportive and helpful at every stage of this project. Stephanie Moylan and Cheri Robbins in particular have given invaluable help at the production stage. At various times while working on this book I received financial support from the Australian Research Council (Special Investigator Award), the University of New South Wales, and the Alexander von Humboldt Foundation, Germany (Research Prize); this help was essential to get this project completed quickly and efficiently. Last, but not least, I am deeply grateful for the love and support of my wife, Letitia Jane and my children, Paul and Peter, who have shown great forbearance in putting up with me during the many months of this project.

—*Joseph P. Forgas*

1

Introduction: Affect and Social Cognition

Joseph P. Forgas

University of New South Wales
Sydney, Australia

Philosophical and Speculative Theories Linking Affect and Cognition   6
Some Early Empirical Evidence for Affective Influences on
      Cognition and Judgments   7
Psychodynamic Approaches to Affect and Cognition   8
Conditioning Approaches to Affect and Cognition   9
The Emergence of a Cognitive Paradigm   12
Major Areas of Contemporary Research on Affect and Social Cognition   15
    Affect and Cognition: Fundamental Issues and the Nature
      of the Relationship   16
    Affective Influences on the Content of Cognition   17
    Affect and Social Information Processing   18
    Affective Influences on Social Motivation and Intentions   19
    Affect, Cognition, and Interpersonal Behavior   19
    Personality and Individual Differences in Affectivity   20
Conclusion   21
References   22

Support from the Australian Research Council (Special Investigator Award) and by the Alexander von Humboldt Foundation Research Prize, Germany, is gratefully acknowledged. Please address all correspondence to Joseph P. Forgas, School of Psychology, University of New South Wales, Sydney 2052, Australia; email: JP.Forgas@unsw.edu.au; internet: http://www.psy.unsw.edu.au/staff/jforgas.htm

1

There can be little doubt that affect is one of the most important yet least understood influences on the way people think and behave in social situations. Although intuitively we all know that our feelings frequently have a profound influence on our thoughts, judgments, and interpersonal behaviors, in practice we do not yet fully understand how and why these influences occur. Somewhat disappointingly, empirical research by psychologists has, until quite recently, provided only glimpses into the delicate relationship among affect, cognition, and behavior. In fact, most of what we know about the role of affect in social cognition has only been discovered since the beginning of the 1980s. This is thus a particularly fortuitous time to review and summarize what has been achieved in this exciting field to date. The main objective of this book is to provide a comprehensive and integrated overview of what we now know about the role of affect in social cognition.

Of course, interest in this issue goes back much further than just a few decades. In fact, ever since the dawn of human civilization, artists, writers, and philosophers as well as laypersons have been fascinated by the delicate relationships between feeling and thinking, affect and cognition. Classic philosophers such as Aristotle, Socrates, Plato, Epicurus, Descartes, Pascal, Kant, and others devoted considerable attention to the role of affect in human affairs. Plato was one of the earlier representatives of a long line of thinkers who believed that affect constitutes a more primitive, animalistic mode of responding that is incompatible with reason, and has an invasive, dangerous influence on rational thinking and behavior. The basic idea that affective reactions "tend to overwhelm or subvert rational mental processes" (Elster, 1985, p. 379) has been echoed in many philosophical, social, and psychological theories throughout the ages: Tarde, LeBon, and Freud are just a few classic theorists who saw emotion as a dangerous influence. Others, such as Arthur Koestler (1978), even suggested that the inability of human beings to fully understand and control their affective states is due to a "fatal flaw" in the way our central nervous system evolved that may ultimately threaten the very survival of our species.

Although the disruptive nature of affect has received much attention in traditional theorizing, in recent years a fundamentally different view began to emerge. Largely as a result of important advances in social cognition, neuroanatomy, and psychophysiology during the 1990s, it is now increasingly recognized that affect is not necessarily a disruptive influence on social thinking. In fact, the opposite may well be true: affect is often a useful and even essential component of rational behavior (see chapters by Adolphs & Damasio, Ito & Cacioppo, this volume). Indeed, recent research seems to bear out the philosopher Blaise Pascal's prescient prediction from more than 350 years ago, that "the heart has its reasons which reason does not understand" (Pascal, 1643/1966, p. 113). Research by DeSousa (1987), Damasio (1994), and others confirmed that the ability to experience and take into account affect in social decisions is an essential part of adaptive functioning. Individuals who suffer certain kinds of brain damage to the prefrontal cortex that impairs affective reactions but leaves cognitive capacities intact tend to make disastrous social decisions, and their social relationships suffer accordingly, even though their intellectual problem-solving ability may be completely normal.

Ultimately, most of the evidence from social cognition research since the early 1980s suggests that affect is neither a universally beneficial nor a universally disruptive influence on social cognitive processes. Rather, the effects of affective states on social thinking appear to be highly context specific (Fiedler, 1991; Martin, 2000; Sedikides, 1995). Sometimes, affective states facilitate effective decision making without any apparent impairment in the quality of the outcome (Isen & Means, 1983). At other times, affective states may contribute to cognitive and judgmental errors and lead to suboptimal and mistaken judgments and decisions (Forgas, 1998a). Whether the effects are adaptive or maladaptive, functional or dysfunctional depends on the nature of the task, the kind of information-processing strategy used, and the characteristics of the person and the situation (see also chapters by Rusting, and Mayer, this volume). Several of the contributions to this volume report important advances in our understanding of the delicate mechanisms that are responsible for mediating affective influences on social cognition, judgments, and interpersonal behaviors.

The book is organized into six main sections to correspond to six major areas of contemporary affect cognition research, and each section contains three contributions. After this introductory chapter, the first section considers some basic *conceptual issues* about the relationship between affect and cognition. The three chapters here take different and complementary approaches. Adolphs and Damasio emphasize the fundamental interaction between affect and cognition and the adaptive importance of this relationship based on recent neurobiological evidence, and discuss how affective states may modulate cognitive processes involved in attention, memory, judgment, and decision making. Ito and Cacioppo take a complementary social neuroscience perspective and analyze the role of affect in social attitudes. The third chapter in this section, by Smith and Kirby, focuses on yet another crucial aspect of the interaction between cognition and affect. Their chapter offers a comprehensive review and an integrative theory of the role of cognitive appraisal processes in the way affective states are experienced and defined.

The second section of the book reviews evidence for the role of affective states in influencing the *content of social cognition*. Gordon Bower and Joseph Forgas survey almost two decades of research on the role of affect in social memory, and suggest that a revised associative network theory is capable of accounting for most of the evidence for mood-congruent memory effects. A major alternative to memory-based network models is outlined by Gerald Clore, Karen Gasper, and Erika Garvin, who suggest that in many situations the direct use of affect as information can account for affective influences on social thinking, judgments, and information-processing style. Constantine Sedikides and Jeffrey Green discuss and integrate extensive evidence for affective influences on the content of ideas about the self and the self-concept, and offer a new theoretical perspective explaining how variables such as individual differences, judgmental and task features, and different types of self-conceptions can mediate these effects.

The chapters in the third section address one of the key issues in affect–cognition research: how affect is implicated in the *processing of social information*. Klaus Fiedler reviews recent evidence linking affective states to different information-processing strategies and outlines an integrative dual-process theory describing how positive and negative affective states selectively facilitate a processing style that promotes either the assimilation of, or accommodation to social information. Tory Higgins describes a fundamental dichotomy between promotion- and prevention-oriented experiences and processing style, and reviews the intricate role that affective states play in these two basic modes of relating to the social world. The third chapter in this section, by Richard Petty, David DeSteno, and Derek Rucker, discusses the role of affective states in attitude change and how people process persuasive messages in particular as a function of high or low elaboration processing styles.

Part IV contains contributions that analyze the relationship between *affect and social motivation and intentions*. Eddie Harmon-Jones reviews decades of research on the role of affective states in cognitive dissonance processes, one of the most productive motivational theories in our discipline, and provides an integrative theoretical treatment of these findings. Positive and negative mood can also play a crucial motivational role in how people process potentially threatening self-relevant information, according to the work reviewed by Yaacov Trope, Melissa Ferguson, and Raj Raghunathan. These authors suggest that mood can serve as a motivational resource in social cognition when people deal with self-relevant feedback or persuasive messages. The third chapter in this section, by Maureen Wang Erber and Ralph Erber, argues that motivated social cognition plays an important role in the regulation of affective states. These authors describe studies showing that people will use motivated strategies to selectively search for and use social information that helps them to calibrate their affect to fit in with contextual requirements.

Part V discusses the role of affective states in explanations of *cognitively mediated social behaviors*. The chapter by Joseph Forgas argues that different information-processing strategies play a key role in determining whether and how affect influences interpersonal behaviors. The chapter also describes a number of recent experiments demonstrating affective influences on how people interact with each other in various social situations. Stereotyping, prejudice, and intergroup behavior are among the most important real-life issues investigated by social psychologists, and the next chapter, by Galen Bodenhausen, Thomas Mussweiler, Shira Gabriel, and Kristen Moreno, reviews the role of affect in these processes. Affective states play a particularly important role in health-related cognition and behaviors, a topic that is also of considerable applied importance according to the chapter by Peter Salovey, Jerusha Detweiler, Wayne Steward, and Brian Bedell.

The final section of the book discusses the critical role of *individual differences and personality characteristics in affectivity*. Cheryl Rusting reviews and integrates recent evidence suggesting that personality characteristics such as extraversion, neuroticism, self-esteem, and other traits are critically involved in mediating affective influences on social cognition. In the next chapter, Jerry Suls analyzes the intricate relationship between affect, stress, personality, and social cognition. In the final chapter of this book, Jack Mayer, one of the researchers who first coined the term *emotional intelligence* to describe the complex set of individual characteristics that makes people able to manage affective states effectively, reviews recent work in this area and describes the development of a new empirical measure of the emotional intelligence construct.

The aim of this introductory chapter is to provide some background to much of what follows. The history of early philosophical and speculative ideas about the relationship between affect and cognition is reviewed briefly. Next, psychological explanations of affective influences on cognition based on psychodynamic or conditioning theories and processes is considered. The final section of the chapter discusses the emergence of a social cognitive approach to studying affective processes since the 1980s and offers a brief overview of the main threads of contemporary affect–cognition research as represented in this volume.

PHILOSOPHICAL AND SPECULATIVE
THEORIES LINKING AFFECT
AND COGNITION

Long before the advent of empirical psychology, there was much speculative and philosophical theorizing about the relationship between affect
and cognition in human affairs. By and large, theories that emphasized the
dangerous and threatening aspects of affectivity have predominated until
quite recently. This concern with the invasive and uncontrollable aspects of
emotion can be traced throughout most of the Western philosophical tradition, from the work of Plato through St. Augustine and Descartes to Kant.
Freud's psychodynamic theories were among the first to define a range of
specific "defense mechanisms" that are involved in keeping threatening
emotional impulses under control. The psychodynamic view of affect as
a powerful force that must be under continuous pychological control by
various ego mechanisms has had and continues to have a widespread influence on popular views of affect and cognition. The hydraulic principle
suggests that managing and controlling affective states requires considerable countervailing psychological resources, and that cognitive attempts at
affect control are often ineffective and frequently result in unintended and
dysfunctional consequences.

Although Freud has done much to place affect and emotions back on
the cultural agenda, his influence on empirical psychology has been more
limited, and research on affect remained a relatively neglected field until
recently. One reason for this neglect is probably empirical psychology's
fundamental assumption that different components of the human mind, affect, cognition, and conation, can be adequately studied in separation from
each other rather than in their interactions (Hilgard, 1980). The idea that human mental life can be readily separated into three distinct and fundamental
faculties, affect, cognition, and conation (feeling, knowing, and willing),
first emerged in a concrete form in the philosophy of the Enlightenment
in the 18th century. As Hilgard (1980) suggests, it was probably Christian
Wolff (1714–1762) who first proposed a distinction between a *facultas
cognoscivita* and a *facultas appetiva*—knowing and desire. Soon afterward,
Moses Mendelssohn (1729–1789) introduced a more elaborate, threefold
classification of the fundamental faculties of soul—understanding, feeling,
and will.

Perhaps the most influential philosopher of this period, Immanuel Kant,
readily accepted this tripartite division of the human mental faculties and
incorporated it into his philosophical system. For Kant, "pure reason

corresponds to intellect or cognition, practical reason to will, action or conation, and judgment to feeling pleasure or pain, hence affection" (Hilgard,
1980, p. 109). In fact, Kant's main philosophical works clearly reflect his acceptance of the tripartite categorization of human mental life into cognition,
conation, and affect (*Critique of Pure Reason*, 1789; *Critique of Practical
Reason*, 1788; *Critique of Judgment*, 1790). This philosophical classification of psychology's subject matter into affect, cognition, and conation has
had a major influence on the eventual development of empirical psychology.

In early laboratory research by Wilhelm Wundt, Titchener, and others,
the tripartite division was used as a guide to the introspective assessments of
various experimentally manipulated psychological experiences. For these
researchers, a subject's self-reported affective, cognitive, and conative responses to a given stimulus had to be analyzed jointly, and were considered
to be providing equally valid and complementary windows into the nature of an underlying and unitary psychological experience. However, this
"unitary" approach to the psychological study of human experience did
not survive early introspectionist experimentation. For most of the 20th
century, affect, cognition, and conation were studied without reference to
each other, as independent and isolated entities, and affect was arguably
the most "neglected" member of the trilogy of mind, at least until recently
(Hilgard, 1980). This does not mean, however, that there were no empirical
investigations touching on the relationship between affect and cognition,
as discussed in the next section.

SOME EARLY EMPIRICAL EVIDENCE
FOR AFFECTIVE INFLUENCES ON
COGNITION AND JUDGMENTS

There are several early empirical experiments that suggested the close interdependence between affect and cognition. Most of these studies looked
at affective influences on judgments and were typically concerned with
demonstrating and explaining affect-congruent phenomena. One early
demonstration of this effect was reported by Razran (1940) in a study that
foreshadowed much later research on affect congruence. In this experiment,
positive or negative affective states were induced unobtrusively, by expos-
ing participants to highly aversive smells or providing them with a free
lunch (!). Results showed that these manipulations produced a significant
mood-congruent influence on subsequent social judgments. In another early
demonstration of affect congruence, Wehmer and Izard (1962) used the

manipulated behavior of the experimenter to induce a positive or negative affective state. This study also found that people who were made to feel good subsequently made more positive judgments than did individuals who experienced induced negative mood.

In later studies, Izard (1964) relied on the behavior of a confederate (a trained actress) to produce good or bad mood. This research also confirmed that both social judgments and performance were more positive after positive mood induction and more negative after negative mood induction. These affective influences were not limited to experimentally induced mood states. Researchers such as Wessman and Ricks (1966) demonstrated that people's judgments about various social activities were also positively correlated with self-rated mood over time, suggesting that affect congruence in thinking and judgments is a reliable everyday phenomenon. Similar conclusions were reached in more recent experimental studies based on naturally occurring moods by Jack Mayer (see also chapter by Mayer, this volume). Although this review of early empirical research on affect and judgments is by no means complete, it is clear that there was considerable if scattered evidence for affect congruence in a variety of domains. How were these effects theoretically explained? The next section considers two of the dominant early theoretical accounts linking affect and social cognition: the psychoanalytic account and the conditioning account.

PSYCHODYNAMIC APPROACHES TO AFFECT AND COGNITION

As noted, Freud's elaborate psychodynamic theory and the resulting burgeoning psychoanalytic literature played a very important role in emphasizing the importance of affect and emotion in psychological functioning. In terms of this dynamic, hydraulic theory, most emotional reactions were thought to be located within the id, and in seeking expression, they were assumed to operate through exerting "pressure" against the countervailing forces of rational and controlled ego mechanisms. Psychoanalytic theorizing—consistent with many earlier philosophical theories—thus suggests that affect has a dynamic and invasive force and will "take over" controlled, rational thinking and behavior unless adequate psychological resources are available to control and channel these dangerous impulses.

For a while, psychoanalytic theories also had an influence on empirical psychology, and several attempts were made to incorporate psychoanalytic ideas into mainstream theories (e.g., Murray, 1933). Psychoanalytic ideas also stimulated a variety of empirical attempts to demonstrate the dynamic character of affective influences on judgments and behavior. For example, in a well-known study, Feshbach and Singer (1957) tested the counterintuitive prediction derived from psychoanalytic theories that emotional states should invade unrelated cognitive judgments and that, paradoxically, these effects should be greater when people try to consciously suppress their feelings, and thus generate greater "pressure" for affect infusion. These predictions are, of course, consistent with the hydraulic principle of psychoanalytic thinking. As emotional expression is suppressed, the "pressure" should increase for the repressed emotional state to find an alternative expression in unrelated judgments or behaviors.

To test this hypothesis, Feshbach and Singer (1957) used electric shocks to induce the emotional state of fear and anxiety in their subjects. The second manipulation was that fearful subjects were instructed either to repress their fear or were not given such instructions. Finally, all subjects had an opportunity to make social judgments about a target person. Consistent with the principle of affect infusion, fearful subjects were in fact more likely to "perceive another person as fearful and anxious" (p. 286). Further, this affect infusion effect was significantly greater precisely when subjects were trying to suppress their fear. The results were explained by Feshbach and Singer (1957) as due to fearful subjects using the defense mechanism of "projection" to relieve affective pressure, and in so doing they allowed their judgments of others to be infused by their own emotional state. In their words, "suppression of fear facilitates the tendency to project fear onto another social object" (p. 286). Despite some interesting results, such as the results reported by Feshbach and Singer (1957), psychoanalytic theories suffered a rapid decline in importance in empirical psychology. This was partly due to Popper's devastating epistemological criticisms of psychoanalytic theory as fundamentally unscientific, as well as to the difficulties experienced in providing convincing empirical support for Freud's theories. Associationism and conditioning theories provided the major conceptual alternative for explaining how affect can become linked to cognitive and behavioral responses.

CONDITIONING APPROACHES TO AFFECT AND COGNITION

The radical behaviorist paradigm that dominated psychological theorizing during the first half of the 20th century explicitly excluded the study of mentalistic phenomena, such as thinking and feelings from psychology's legitimate research domain. Watson's radical behaviorism and his "little

Albert" experiments in particular suggested that all emotional phenomena can be reduced to just a few fundamental, wired-in affective reactions that simply become elaborated into the full repertoire of human emotions through successive associations with novel environmental stimuli. Most subsequent behaviorist research, if concerned with affect at all, focused either on the manipulation of easily controlled drive states, such as hunger and thirst, or studied simple emotions easily elicited by environmental manipulations, such as fear induced by electric shocks delivered to an animal. The limitation of this approach is well illustrated by the very restrictive operationalization of affect it allowed. I can still well recall an undergradute lab class in which our task was to carefully count the number of fecal droppings produced by a frightened rat as our operationalization of "affect." Ultimately, orthodox behaviorist experimentation contributed very little to our understanding of the functions and consequences of affect in social thinking and behavior.

However, for several decades, behaviorist ideas also had an important influence on social psychology. The notion that powerful associations may be created between preexisting affective reactions and new, previously neutral stimuli as a result of temporal and spatial contiguity alone, as originally demonstrated by Watson, could also be applied to complex social situations. In a series of experiments concerned with interpersonal attraction, Byrne and Clore (1970) and Clore and Byrne (1974) proposed that simple conditioning principles alone may help to explain how affective states triggered by unrelated events can influence responses to other people. According to this account, aversive or pleasant environments (the unconditioned stimuli) could be used to produce an affective reaction (the unconditioned response) while participants meet and interact with another person (the conditioned stimulus). Results typically showed that the unconditioned affective reaction elicited by the aversive environment produced a more negative evaluation (conditioned response) of a person incidentally encountered in that environment.

These findings were, of course, explained in terms of conditioning theories, as a result of simple temporal and spatial contiguity between the two stimuli. For example, in one experiment, Griffitt (1970) demonstrated that people in whom unconditioned negative affect was induced due to exposure to excessive heat and humidity made more negative judgments of a target person encountered in that environment. According to these associative principles, it appears that "evaluative responses are . . . determined by the positive or negative properties of the total stimulus situation" (Griffitt, 1970, p. 240). In other experiments using a similar approach, Gouaux

(1971) showed that mood-congruent effects on social judgments can be elicited as a result of prior exposure to happy or depressing films, suggesting that liking and attraction for another person "is a positive function of the subject's affective state" (p. 40). In later experiments, Gouaux and Summers (1973) demonstrated mood congruence in judgments using manipulated interpersonal feedback to induce good or bad mood in participants.

It is highly interesting that these experiments used mood manipulations and produced mood-congruent outcomes in almost exactly the same way as some more recent studies have done. The main difference lies in the theoretical explanations offered for these effects. The studies in the 1960s and 1970s largely relied on "blind" conditioning principles based on temporal and spatial contiguity alone to explain how and why incidental affect can influence judgments. In contrast, contemporary studies using very similar manipulations emphasize cognitive, information-processing mechanisms (such as the misattribution affect, and/or its use as a heuristic cue) to explain the observed infusion of affect into thinking and judgments. It is thus important to recognize that early associationist experiments paved the way for some of the more productive contemporary research paradigms (Berkowitz, Jo, & Troccoli, 2000; Clore, Schwarz, & Conway, 1994).

In particular, the idea that preexisting affect may be "misattributed" to a current judgmental target, as proposed by the affect-as-information model developed by Schwarz and Clore (1983), is very similar to the predictions derived from Clore and Byrne's (1974) earlier model. The main difference is in the explanatory language used: Clore and Byrne (1974) relied on passive, associationistic principles to explain mood congruence, without any assumptions about the underlying cognitive processes involved. The affect-as-information approach, in contrast, assumes an active search for meaning and information as judges seek to infer their reactions to a target and mistakenly use their mood as a heuristic cue (see also chapter by Clore et al., this volume).

Although both psychodynamically oriented and conditioning studies were thus successful in demonstrating basic mood-congruent effects on social judgments, the theoretical explanations offered for these findings remained less than fully convincing. The recurring problem with psychodynamic accounts as invoked by Feshbach and Singer (1957) is that the postulated mental operations involved in mechanisms such as "projection" could not be independently demonstrated. Conditioning explanations were also found wanting. For one thing, the assumption that spatial and temporal contiguity alone produces an invariable and universal association effect between affect and a response could clearly not be sustained. As we now know, affective influences on thinking and judgment are highly sensitive to contextual and processing differences, and are not always linked to environmentally induced circumstances (Fiedler, 1991; Forgas, 2000; Martin, 2000; Sedikides, 1995).

Associationistic accounts also imply that affect infusion can only occur if the affect eliciting stimulus (UCS) and the judgmental target (CS) are simultaneously present. In fact, we now know that affective states can often have a delayed, "lingering" effect on subsequent thoughts and judgments. Indeed, most research supporting the affect-as-information model explicitly shows that the original eliciting cause of the affective state must be absent and forgotten for affect to be misattributed to a subsequent judgmental target. Both psychodynamic and conditioning theories can also be criticized for their inability to explain how multiple sources of affective and nonaffective information can be combined and integrated as people produce a social judgment (Abele & Petzold, 1994; Kaplan, 1991).

Ultimately, these theories failed to provide a convincing and comprehensive explanation of the relationship between affect and social cognition because they lacked a well-articulated model of the precise mental operations involved. In contrast, more recent social cognitive research focused on the information-processing mechanisms responsible for linking affect and cognition, and was able to develop far more sophisticated and realistic models. It is quite interesting, however, that it was the psychodynamic approach proposed by Feshbach and Singer (1957) that probably came closest to anticipating contemporary thinking by suggesting that cognition may become "infused" with affect. Although we now know that such affect infusion is unlikely to be driven by dynamic processes, contemporary social cognitive theories still seek to provide an answer as to how and under what circumstances the "infusion" of affect into social cognition occurs.

THE EMERGENCE OF A COGNITIVE PARADIGM

Eventually, both conditioning and psychoanalytic theories lost their appeal as explanations of affective influences on cognition. By the late 1960s, a new and more eclectic cognitive paradigm emerged as the mainstream orientation accepted by most psychologists. Unfortunately, this alternative cognitive framework was also characterized, until about the early 1980s, by an avowed lack of interest in affect (Hilgard, 1980). Affective states, if studied at all, were considered only as a disruptive influence on "proper"—that is, cold and affectless—ideation. The assumption that "proper" thinking, perception, and judgments should be devoid of affect soon came under growing strain as cognitive research progressed. The "new look" studies pioneered by Bruner (1957) and his colleagues were among the first to show convincingly that feelings, values, and preferences inevitably influence even simple perceptual judgments. More recently, researchers concerned with naturalistic memory phenomena also acknowledged that affective states play a critical role in how people remember realistic social information (Neisser, 1982).

By the early 1980s, the time was ripe for affect once again to occupy center stage in psychological theorizing. Within social psychology, it was Robert Zajonc (1980) who in an influential article called our attention to the importance of affective influences on social judgments and behavior (see also Zajonc, 2000). Within cognitive psychology, Gordon Bower's (1981) associative network theory of affective influences on memory gave a major impetus to affect–cognition research. The chapter by Bower and Forgas (this volume) on affect and social memory reviews much of the evidence accumulated in the intervening years and provides an overview and update of the original affect-priming framework. This chapter shows that affective states appear to have a reliable and consistent influence on social memory, but only in circumstances that facilitate constructive processing and allow the incidental use of affectively primed information. When considered from a historical perspective, the recent boom in research linking affect and social cognition confirms that these mental faculties cannot be effectively studied in isolation from each other. All the chapters included in this book emphasize the close interdependence of feeling and thinking in human social life, and thus represent the latest contribution to an age-old quest to understand the relationship between the rational and the emotional aspects of human nature (Hilgard, 1980).

This does not mean, however, that there is anything like a complete agreement among researchers about such fundamental issues as whether affect should be seen as an integral part of the cognitive-representational system. Examples of a more cognitivist orientation are provided in the chapters by Bower and Forgas; Fiedler; Rusting; and Sedikides (this volume). The alternative view is that affect should be considered as a separate and, in some ways, primary response system in its own right. Theorists such as Zajonc (2000) have forcefully argued for a such a "separate-systems" view, proposing that affective reactions often precede and are psychologically and neuroanatomically distinct from cognitive processes. The chapters by Adolphs and Damasio; Clore et al.; Ito and Cacioppo; Mayer; Smith and

Kirby; and Trope are somewhat closer to this latter position. Many other researchers, however, espouse an essentially interactionist position in which neither affect nor cognition is seen as primary or dominant.

The key research question then becomes exactly how do these two basic response systems interact and influence each other? The chapters by Bodenhausen et al.; Forgas; Higgins; Petty et al.; Harmon-Jones; Erber and Erber; and Suls present examples closer to such an interactionist conceptualization. To some extent, how one responds to the question of affective vs cognitive primacy at least partly depends on how broadly the domain of cognition is defined. Affect can be considered a primary and separate response system if cognition is defined as excluding early attentional and perceptual processes inevitably involved in constructive stimulus identification (Lazarus, 1984). However, a broad definition of cognition that includes all interpretational processes beyond the sensory system implies that affect must by necessity be part of a postcognitive response.

Whatever position one occupies on the affect–cognition primacy debate, all researchers accept that affective states can fulfil an important informational role in inferential social thinking and judgments. This view is supported both by neuroanatomical and neuropsychological research (see, for example, Adolphs & Damasio, Ito & Cacioppo) as well as social cognitive experiments (see chapters by Bodenhausen et al.; Erber & Erber; Forgas; Higgins; Petty et al.; Salovey et al.; Rusting; Suls; and Trope). Indeed, there is a long tradition in psychological theorizing that explicitly recognizes the close interdependence of feeling, thinking, and behavior. These ideas can be traced to a number of influential philosophical analyses of the nature of the human mind (e.g., Kant), and are identified in some of the work of William James (1890) and the theoretical approaches advocated by early introspectionist experimenters such as Wundt and Titchener. According to most of the evidence now available, there is thus clearly a bidirectional rather than a unidirectional link between affect and cognition.

Specific evidence reviewed in this book suggests that on the one hand, affective states can influence attention, learning, memory, and associations (see especially chapters by Bodenhausen et al.; Bower & Forgas; Fiedler; Higgins; and Petty et al. for work illustrating this link). On the other hand, cognitive information-processing strategies also play a crucial role in regulating affective states and influencing the nature and extent of affect infusion into social cognition (see chapters by Erber & Erber; Forgas; Mayer; and Smith & Kirby). In fact, there is some initial evidence suggesting that subtle shifts in information-processing strategies play an important role in the spontaneous and homeostatic regulation of everyday moods (Forgas, in press).

There is also a growing recognition that there are different categories of affective phenomena and their role in social cognition is quite distinct. One crucial distinction is between emotions and moods. Both emotions and moods may have an impact on social cognition, but the nature of this influence is quite different. Emotions are usually defined as intense, short-lived, and highly conscious affective states that typically have a salient cause and a great deal of cognitive content, featuring information about typical antecedents, expectations, and behavioral plans (Smith & Kirby, 2000). The cognitive consequences of emotions such as fear, disgust, or anger can be highly complex, and depend on the particular prototypical representations activated in specific situations. As distinct from emotions, moods are typically defined as relatively low-intensity, diffuse, and endur-ing affective states that have no salient antecedent cause and therefore little cognitive content (such as feeling good or feeling bad, or being in a good or bad mood). As moods tend to be less subject to conscious monitoring and control, paradoxically their effects on social thinking, memory, and judgments tend to be potentially more insidious, enduring, and subtle.

Many of the contributors to this volume address the question of how non-specific moods influence social cognition (see especially chapters by Clore et al.; Bower & Forgas; Fiedler; Forgas; and Petty et al.). The conceptual distinction between emotion and mood is further indicated by the diver-gent directions taken by researchers interested in emotion rather than mood. Emotion researchers typically study the cognitive *antecedents* and appraisal strategies people use to trigger an emotional response (see, for example, the chapter by Smith & Kirby). In contrast, researchers interested in more subtle *mood* effects typically study the cognitive *consequences* of these nonspecific affective states for thinking, attention, memory, and judgments. Despite the differences between emotion and mood, there is little doubt that these affective states frequently interact and influence each other. Powerful emotions often leave a lingering mood state in their wake, and moods in turn can have an impact on how emotional responses are generated.

MAJOR AREAS OF CONTEMPORARY RESEARCH ON AFFECT AND SOCIAL COGNITION

With the rapid development of empirical research on the cognitive an-tecedents and consequences of affective states since the 1980, a number of major research paradigms and findings have emerged. These distinct approaches are also reflected in the organization of the contributions to

this volume into six sections that more or less correspond to the six major
research areas to be covered here.

Affect and Cognition: Fundamental Issues and the Nature of the Relationship

A paper by Robert Zajonc (1980) first posed many of the questions about the
relationship between affect and cognition that are still with us. Zajonc suggested that affective and evaluative reactions to social stimuli are not only
distinct from, but frequently are also primary to, cognitive responses. He
reviewed extensive evidence suggesting that evaluations, preferences, and
feelings about social situations are typically rapid and immediate, and are
often remembered longer than the actual details of the situation that elicited
them. He reviewed accumulated evidence since then (Zajonc, 2000), and
concluded that the evidence for the primacy of affect in social reactions is
stronger than ever.

Although there has been considerable debate about the validity of these
claims (Lazarus, 1984), Zajonc's arguments were highly influential in plac-
ing the study of affect into the focus of social psychological research. A
conflicting research tradition, mainly associated with appraisal theory, has
long been concerned with the cognitive antecedents of emotional experiences. The contributions here by Smith and Kirby and, to some extent,
by Clore survey the most recent developments in this research. Smith and
Kirby emphasize the role of prior cognitive appraisals in affective reactions
and present a new process model of affect appraisal. Smith and Kirby suggest that schematic processing is the key mechanism that allows memory
representations associated with affect to be primed, leading to the production of emotional reactions without conscious cognitive processing. This
work suggests that priming mechanisms represent an important integrative
link between studies of the cognitive antecedents of affect (appraisal research) and investigations of the cognitive consequences of affect (affect
congruent cognition).

The rapid development of neuropsychological and neurobiological research provided another source of evidence with direct bearing on this
question since the 1980s. The work of Damasio, DeSousa, and others convincingly showed that affect is an essential component of adaptive cognitive
responses to the social world. Adolphs and Damasio (this volume) review
the most recent evidence on this issue, and Ito and Cacioppo (this volume) survey important recent neuropsychological evidence indicating the
interdependence of affect and cognition.

Affective Influences on the Content of Cognition

As the previous review showed, most of the early experimental work linking affect and cognition was concerned with exploring the influence of affective states—often moods—on the *content* of thinking, memory, and judgments (Clore & Byrne, 1974; Griffitt, 1970; Razran, 1940). In particular, the demonstration of mood-congruity effects and their explanation were the focus of most affect–cognition theorizing. We may call these theories *informational theories* because their aim is to explain how affect may inform the content of people's thinking, judgments, and decisions. Two major kinds of such theories have been proposed to explain these effects: memory-based accounts (e.g., the affect priming model; see Bower & Forgas, this volume), and inferential models (e.g., the affect-as-information model (see Clore et al., this volume).

Mood-congruent memory research took a new direction with the publication of Gordon Bower's (1981) paper, proposing an associative network theory to account for these effects. Evidence in the early 1980s seemed to largely confirm these theoretically based predictions of mood congruity in social memory and judgments (Clark & Isen, 1982; Forgas, Bower, & Krantz, 1984; Isen, 1984, 1987). The associative network model suggests that the links between affect and cognition are neither motivationally based, as psychodynamic theories suggest, nor are they the result of merely incidental associations, as conditioning theories imply. Instead, affect and cognition are integrally linked within an associative network of mental representations. Material that is associated with the current mood is more likely to be activated, recalled, and used in constructive cognitive tasks.

The priming model assumes that affect is not an incidental but an integral part of how we see and represent the world around us. Recent evidence also suggests that these affect-priming effects cannot be reduced to simple semantic priming mechanisms (Niedenthal, personal communication, 1999). However, it soon became apparent that affect priming and mood congruity phenomena are also subject to important boundary conditions. Much subsequent research sought to identify the boundary conditions and the kinds of processing strategies that are most likely to produce affect congruence (Eich & Macauley, 2000; Forgas, 1995). It now appears that mood congruity is a robust and reliable effect in social cognition, as long as an open, constructive, and generative information-processing strategy is adopted that promotes the incidental use of affectively primed information (Forgas, 1995). Several chapters in this book (see especially chapters by Bower & Forgas; Fiedler; Forgas; and Sedikides) offer comprehensive reviews and theoretical integration of the affect congruity phenomenon.

An alternative explanation of affect congruity in evaluative judgments was proposed by Schwarz and Clore (1983), who argued that the misattribution of a prior affective state as informative about current evaluative reactions may also produce mood congruence. The affect-as-information model assumes that "rather than computing a judgment on the basis of recalled features of a target, individuals may . . . ask themselves: 'How do I feel about it?' [and] in doing so, they may mistake feelings due to a pre-existing state as a reaction to the target" (Schwarz, 1990, p. 529). Such "direct" affective influences were first demonstrated in associationist research in the 1960s and 1970s (see previous mention; also, Clore & Byrne, 1974). Such a "How-do-I-feel-about-it" heuristic could account for a range of mood-congruent phenomena, although this theory has also been subject to a number of important revisions and qualifications in recent years (see especially Martin, 2000). The chapter by Clore (this volume) offers an up-to-date overview of this orientation.

Affect and Social Information Processing

A second major development in affect–cognition research in the 1980s was the realization that in addition to influencing the content of cognition—informational effects—affect may also influence the *process* of cognition; that is, how people think about social information (see especially chapters by Erber & Erber; Fiedler; Higgins; and Petty et al.). It was initially thought that people in a positive mood tend to think more rapidly and perhaps superficially; reach decisions more quickly; use less information; avoid demanding and systematic processing; and are more confident about their decisions. Negative affect, in turn, was assumed to trigger a more systematic, analytic, and vigilant processing style (Clark & Isen, 1982; Isen, 1984, 1987; Schwarz, 1990). More recent work showed that positive affect can also produce distinct processing advantages, as people are more likely to adopt more creative, open, constructive, and inclusive thinking styles (Bless, 2000; Fiedler, 2000). It now appears that positive affect promotes a more schema-based, top-down, and generative processing style, whereas negative affect produces a more bottom–up and externally focussed processing strategy. This processing dichotomy has close links with the fundamental distinction between promotion-oriented vs prevention-oriented processing developed by Tory Higgins here, a distinction that has deep roots in evolutionary theorizing as well as classic conditioning accounts.

Affective Influences on Social Motivation and Intentions

Affective states are also heavily implicated in influencing people's social motives and intentions. Most theories dealing with goal-oriented behavior typically assign a critical role to positive and negative affective states as significant feedback signals about progress toward goal achievement (Carver & Scheier, 1998). There is strong evidence, however, suggesting that affective states also have an important independent influence guiding people's goals and social motivations, and that these effects are largely mediated by social cognitive processes. Cognitive dissonance theories represent one of the most successful and productive motivational paradigms in social research. Harmon-Jones (this volume) provides a timely integration and review of what we know about the role of affect in cognitive dissonance phenomena.

Another motivational consequence of affective states is that they may facilitate or hinder people's ability to deal with negative or threatening information. Yaacov Trope et al. (this volume) review extensive research evidence demonstrating the effects of mood on people's motivation to deal with adverse information. Affect itself can also be a source of specific motivation designed either to maintain a rewarding mood state (mood maintenance) or to improve an aversive state (mood repair; Clark & Isen, 1982). Erber and Erber (this volume) survey important evidence demonstrating the role of motivated cognitive processes in the regulation of affective states. Indeed, some recent theories suggest that mood management in everyday life is largely achieved through homeostatic cognitive mechanisms. According to this model, continuous and spontaneous changes in information-processing strategies increase or decrease the extent of affect infusion into thinking and judgments, and thus help to calibrate mood valence and intensity (Forgas, in press; see also chapter by Forgas, this volume).

Affect, Cognition, and Interpersonal Behavior

Skilled social behavior typically requires complex inferential processing strategies as social actors need to select, interpret, and make sense of the rich social information available to them (Heider, 1958). Social cognition is thus heavily implicated in the way people plan and execute interpersonal behaviors. To the extent that affect can influence social information processing strategies, subsequent social behaviors should also be influenced by affect infusion. The chapter by Forgas (this volume) emphasizes such an interactive relationship among affect, social cognition, and interpersonal behavior, based on the author's multiprocess Affect Infusion Model (AIM; Forgas, 1995). The chapter reviews a number of empirical studies stimulated by the AIM, demonstrating that different processing strategies mediate affect infusion into social cognition, and ultimately also influence strategic interpersonal behaviors.

One especially important category of interpersonal behavior that is likely to be influenced by affect is the way different social groups perceive and interact with each other. The chapter by Bodenhausen et al. (this volume) reviews recent research demonstrating the role of affect in intergroup relations, and proposes a distinction between affective states that are either incidental or integral to the intergroup situation. The role of affect in the cognitive mechanisms involved in categorizing and stereotyping group members receives particular attention. Another domain in which affective influences can be particularly important is health-related behavior and cognition. Salovey, Detweiler, Steward, and Bedell (this volume) consider the cognitive mechanisms that can explain how induced moods may influence health-related thoughts and judgments. Ultimately, affective influences on health related thinking also have an impact on health-related behaviors and the eventual course of the illness. Taken together, these contributions make a strong case for the important real-life behavioral consequences of affective influences on social cognition.

Personality and Individual Differences in Affectivity

The idea that enduring personality differences in temperament may have a significant influence on how people deal with short-term affective states has been around for a very long time. However, the systematic exploration of this relationship between state- and trait-aspects of affectivity and their links with social cognition has not been undertaken until quite recently. With the accumulation of experimental studies of affective influences on cognition, it became clear that many of these effects are highly dependent on personality and individual difference variables. For example, self-esteem and trait anxiety were found to have a marked influence on how people cognitively respond to short-term experiences of negative affectivity (Ciarrochi & Forgas, 1999). The chapter by Cheryl Rusting (this volume) provides a comprehensive review and integration of the available evidence about the role of personality characteristics in mediating affective influences on cognition. According to the work reviewed by Rusting, some traits serve to amplify affective reactions, whereas other traits tend to have exactly the opposite effect, attenuating and even reversing the cognitive consequences of affective states. Several recent experiments found that affect infusion into social cognition and behavior are significantly moderated by personality traits (Forgas, 1998b).

Big five personality characteristics such as extraversion and neuroticism appear to play a particularly important role mediating the affect–cognition relationship. The research reviewed in the chapter by Jerry Suls (this volume) analyzes the links affect, stress, and personality and discusses the cognitive mechanisms that are implicated in the "neurotic cascade." Emotional intelligence is the theme of the final chapter by Mayer (this volume). Peter Salovey and Jack Mayer (both contributors to this volume) were the first scientists to coin the term *emotional intelligence* to identify long-term individual patterns in affective reactions. The concept of emotional intelligence has become highly popular as an explanation for a number of affective differences between people. In his chapter, Mayer argues for the development of a comprehensive theory of emotional intelligence and also discusses the difficulties involved in developing a reliable and valid measuring instrument to assess this construct.

CONCLUSION

In conclusion, the chapters presented here show that research on affect and social cognition is now a thriving and successful enterprise. We know more about the interaction between feelings and social thinking, judgments, and behaviors than at any time previously, and most of this information has been obtained since the early 1980s. Many of the chapters included here review new evidence and contain new data and theories that point to the increasing sophistication of this research area. The theories and research presented here hold out the prospect of increasing theoretical integration between various branches of psychology such as social, cognitive, personality, and developmental research. Most of the contributions also demonstrate the applied importance of research on affect and social cognition. Affect plays a crucial role in our conception of ourselves, our personal relationships, and our working lives. Professional and applied psychologists working in areas such as organizational, counselling, clinical, marketing, advertising, and health psychology should find much of interest in these chapters. Thus, this is certainly an exciting time to be doing research on affect and social cognition. It is hoped that this volume will be helpful in promoting further theoretical integration, highlighting practical implications, and most of all, will be useful in generating further interest in this fascinating field.

REFERENCES

Abele, A., & Petzold, P. (1994). How does mood operate in an impression formation task? An information integration approach. *European Journal of Social Psychology, 24,* 173–188.

Berkowitz, L., Jaffee, S., Jo, E., & Troccoli, B. T. (2000). On the correction of feeling-induced judgmental biases. In J. P. Forgas (Ed.), *Feeling and thinking: The role of affect in social cognition.* New York: Cambridge University Press.

Bless, H. (2000). The interplay of affect and cognition: The mediating role of general knowledge structures. In J. P. Forgas (Ed.). *Feeling and thinking: The role of affect in social cognition.* New York: Cambridge University Press.

Bower, G. H. (1981). Mood and memory. *American Psychologist, 36,* 129–148.

Byrne, D., & Clore, G. L. (1970). A reinforcement model of evaluation responses. *Personality: An International Journal, 1,* 103–128.

Bruner, J. S. (1957). On perceptual readiness. *Psychological Review, 64,* 123–152.

Carver, C. S., & Scheier, M. F. (1998). Themes and issues in the self-regulation of behavior. In R. S. Wyer (Ed.), *Advances in social cognition* (pp. 1–106). Mahwah, NJ: Lawrence Erlbaum Associates.

Ciarrochi, J. V., & Forgas, J. P. (1999). On being tense yet tolerant: The paradoxical effects of trait anxiety and aversive mood on intergroup judgments. *Group Dynamics: Theory, Research and Practice, 3,* 227–238.

Clark, M. S., & Isen, A. M. (1982). Towards understanding the relationship between feeling states and social behavior. In A. H. Hastorf & A. M. Isen (Eds.), *Cognitive social psychology* (pp. 73–108). New York: Elsevier–North Holland.

Clore, G. L., & Byrne, D. (1974). The reinforcement affect model of attraction. In T. L. Huston (Ed.), *Foundations of interpersonal attraction* (pp. 143–170). New York: Academic Press.

Clore, G. L., Schwarz, N., & Conway, M. (1994). Affective causes and consequences of social information processing. In R. S. Wyer & T. K. Srull (Eds.), *Handbook of social cognition* (2nd ed.). New Jersey: Erlbaum.

Damasio, A. R. (1994). *Descartes' error.* New York: Grosste/Putnam.

De Sousa, R. J. (1987). *The rationality of emotion.* Cambridge, MA: MIT Press.

Eich, E., & Macauley, D. (2000). Fundamental factors in mood-dependent memory. In J. P. Forgas (Ed.), *Feeling and thinking: The role of affect in social cognition* New York: Cambridge University Press.

Elster, J. (1985). Sadder but wiser? Rationality and the emotions. *Social Science Information, 24,* 375–406.

Feshbach, S., & Singer, R. D. (1957). The effects of fear arousal and suppression of fear upon social perception. *Journal of Abnormal and Social Psychology, 55,* 283–288.

Fiedler, K. (1991). On the task, the measures and the mood in research on affect and social cognition. In J. P. Forgas (Ed.), *Emotion and social judgments* (pp. 83–104). Oxford: Pergamon.

Fiedler, K. (2000). Towards an integrative account of affect and cognition phenomena using the BIAS computer algorithm. In J. P. Forgas (Ed.), *Feeling and thinking: The role of affect in social cognition* New York: Cambridge University Press.

Forgas, J. P. (1995). Mood and judgment: The affect infusion model (AIM). *Psychological Bulletin, 117*(1), 39–66.

Forgas, J. P. (1998a). On being happy and mistaken: Mood effects on the fundamental attribution error. *Journal of Personality and Social Psychology, 75,* 318–331.

Forgas, J. P. (1998b). On feeling good and getting your way: Mood effects on negotiation strategies and outcomes. *Journal of Personality and Social Psychology, 74*, 565–577.

Forgas, J. P. (Ed.) (2000). *Feeling and thinking: The role of affect in social cognition.* New York: Cambridge University Press.

Forgas, J. P. (in press). Managing moods: Towards a dual-process theory of spontaneous mood regulation. *Psychological Issues.*

Forgas, J. P., Bower, G. H., & Krantz, S. (1984). The influence of mood on perceptions of social interactions. *Journal of Experimental Social Psychology, 20*, 497–513.

Gouaux, C. (1971). Induced affective states and interpersonal attraction. *Journal of Personality and Social Psychology, 20*, 37–43.

Gouaux, C., & Summers, K. (1973). Interpersonal attraction as a function of affective states and affective change. *Journal of Research in Personality, 7*, 254–260.

Griffitt, W. (1970). Environmental effects on interpersonal behavior: Ambient effective temperature and attraction. *Journal of Personality and Social Psychology, 15*, 240–244.

Heider, F. (1958). *The psychology of interpersonal relations.* New York: Wiley.

Hilgard, E. R. (1980). The trilogy of mind: Cognition, affection, and conation. *Journal of the History of the Behavioral Sciences, 16*, 107–117.

Isen, A. M. (1984). Towards understanding the role of affect in cognition. In R. S. Wyer & T. K. Srull (Eds.), *Handbook of social cognition* (Vol. 3, pp. 179–236). Hillsdale, NJ: Erlbaum.

Isen, A. M. (1987). Positive affect, cognitive processes and social behaviour. In L. Berkowitz (Ed.), *Advances in experimental social psychology* (Vol. 20, pp. 203–253). New York: Academic Press.

Isen, A. M., & Means, B. (1983). The influence of positive affect on decision making strategy. *Social Cognition, 2*, 18–31.

Izard, C. E. (1964). The effect of role-played emotion on affective reactions, intellectual functioning and evaluative ratings of the actress. *Journal of Clinical Psychology, 20*, 444–446.

James, W. (1890). *Principles of psychology.* New York: Holt.

Kaplan, M. F. (1991). The joint effects of cognition and affect on social judgment. In J. P. Forgas (Ed.), *Emotion and social judgment.* Oxford: Pergamon.

Koestler, A. (1978). *Janus: A summing up.* London: Hutchinson.

Lazarus, R. S. (1984). On the primacy of cognition. *American Psychologist, 39*, 124–129.

Martin, L. (2000). Moods don't convey information: Moods in context do. In J. P. Forgas (Ed.), *Feeling and thinking: The role of affect in social cognition.* New York: Cambridge University Press.

Murray, H. A. (1933). The effects of fear upon estimates of the maliciousness of other personalities. *Journal of Social Psychology, 4*, 310–329.

Neisser, U. (1982). Memory: What are the important questions? In U. Neisser (Ed.), *Memory observed.* San Francisco: Freeman.

Pascal, B. (1966/1643). *Pensees.* Baltimore: Penguin Books.

Razran, G. H. S. (1940). Conditioned response changes in rating and appraising sociopolitical slogans. *Psychological Bulletin, 37*, 481.

Schwarz, N. (1990). Feelings as information: Informational and motivational functions of affective states. In E. T. Higgins & R. Sorrentino (Eds.), *Handbook of motivation and cognition: Foundations of social behaviour* (Vol. 2, pp. 527–561). New York: Guilford Press.

Schwarz, N., & Clore, G. L. (1983). Mood, misattribution and judgments of well-being: Informative and directive functions of affective states. *Journal of Personality and Social Psychology, 45*, 513–523.

Sedikides, C., (1995). Central and peripheral self-conceptions are differentially influenced by mood: Tests of the differential sensitivity hypothesis. *Journal of Personality and Social Psychology, 69*(4), 759–777.

Smith, C., & Kirby, L. D. (2000). Consequences require antecedents: Towards a process model of emotion elicitation. In J. P. Forgas (Ed.), *Feeling and thinking: The role of affect in social cognition.* New York: Cambridge University Press.

Wehmer, G., & Izard, C. E. (1962). *The effect of self-esteem and induced affect on interpersonal perception and intellective functioning*. Nashville: Vanderbilt University.

Wessman, A. E., & Ricks, D. F. (1966). Mood and personality. *Experimental Aging Research, 10*, 197–200.

Zajonc, R. B. (1980). Feeling and thinking: Preferences need no inferences. *American Psychologist, 35*, 151–175.

Zajonc, R. B. (2000). Feeling and thinking: Closing the debate over the independence of affect. In J. P. Forgas (Ed.), *Feeling and thinking: The role of affect in social cognition*. New York: Cambridge University Press.

I

The Relationship Between Affect and Cognition: Fundamental Issues

2

The Interaction of Affect and Cognition: A Neurobiological Perspective

Ralph Adolphs
Antonio R. Damasio

*The University of Iowa
Department of Neurology
Division of Cognitive Neuroscience
Iowa City, Iowa*

Cognitive Affect	28
Affective Modulation of Memory, Attention, and Decision Making in Animals	30
Affect Modulates Declarative Memory	33
Affect Modulates Decision Making	37
Affect and Social Judgment	40
Conclusions	43
Acknowledgments	45
References	45

Although emotion and cognition have sometimes been viewed as two distinct components of human psychology (Zajonc, 1980; Zajonc & Kunst-Wilson, 1980), findings from animals and humans strongly support a modified view, in which emotion is an integral attribute of cognition. In fact, there is now good evidence that emotion modulates information processing in domains ranging from memory to reasoning to decision making. Not only does

Address for reply: Ralph Adolphs, Department of Neurology, University Hospitals and Clinics, 200 Hawkins Drive, Iowa City, IA 52242, USA. Electronic mail: ralph-adolphs@uiowa.edu emotion modulate other aspects of cognition, but is also in fact properly considered cognitive in its own right, insofar as it constitutes computations over representations: namely, representations of the organism's body state.

In this chapter, we review the influences of emotion on cognition and sketch a theoretical framework that treats affect as thoroughly cognitive. We review recent experimental findings from cognitive neuroscience, with an emphasis on findings from humans that elucidate how affective processing fits into the economy of cognitive processing. Specifically, we discuss three domains for which a role in affective modulation is clearest: memory, judgment, and decision making.

COGNITIVE AFFECT

Emotions color virtually all aspects of our lives. What we pay attention to, what we decide to do, what we remember, and how we interact with other people are all influenced by emotion. Despite the fact that emotions permeate our thoughts and our behavior, the topic of emotion is a relative newcomer to cognitive neuroscience, largely for historical reasons. Recent studies have made substantial progress in understanding how the brain encodes and stores knowledge about emotion, how emotional states influence other cognitive processes, such as memory and decision making, and how emotional states influence behavior.

We can begin by pointing out that affective processing is representational, contrary to what some researchers have proposed. There is now good evidence from neuroanatomy, comparative studies, and neurophysiological and neuropsychological studies that supports the view that emotion concerns representations of the organism's state of the body. In particular, affective representations map the relationship between current or future body states and past or baseline states, with respect to how such changes in body state relate to the organism's survival and well-being. That is, emotion ultimately concerns homeostasis, broadly construed (Damasio, 1994, 1999; Panksepp, 1998).

In addition to representing changes in the global body state of an organism, emotional processing typically represents the relationship between such body state changes and external sensory stimuli. For example, the neural correlates of anger directed at another individual would consist in multiple neural mappings that provide a comprehensive representation of the external stimulus (the sight of the other individual), of the organism's own body state (e.g., readiness to fight), and of the relationship between the two (that the latter is a response toward the former, and that the former may have triggered the latter). Such a comprehensive set of representations, which comprise the central state "anger," unfold in a complex fashion in time, an issue that has received attention in psychology from component-process theory (Scherer, 1984), and for which we can begin to sketch a rough outline of at least some of its anatomic components. First, perception of the external stimulus must in some way trigger relatively fast and automatic components of emotional response (e.g., changes in autonomic tone, heart rate). As these components of emotional response are unfolding in time, parallel components that rely more on retrieval of knowledge from declarative memory and reasoning, and that are more influenced by conscious volition, are triggered as well. Together, then, several different sets of emotional responses are triggered by the stimulus. They result in a dynamic change in somatosensory state of the body, somatovisceral function, endocrine and neuroendocrine function, autonomic tone, and global brain functioning, all adapted to maximize successful behavior in response to the stimulus.

Such an emotional response has several consequences that also unfold in a complex way in time. First, they directly engage, as well as indirectly modulate, the organism's automatic and planned behavior at all levels. Second, they are perceived and represented by the organism's brain as comprehensive changes in body and brain state, a component that results in the conscious experience of the emotion, or "feeling." Third, the organism's emotional behavior may be directed at the stimulus that triggered the emotional response in the first place, and may thus feed back onto the environment in an effort to promote homeostasis, survival, and well-being.

We can begin to sketch a neuroanatomic picture of the component structures involved in some of the above processes. There is now good evidence that the amygdala is critical in the triggering of rapid physiological changes in response to emotionally salient stimuli, as illustrated by its role in conditioned responses. The ventromedial prefrontal cortex, which has extensive anatomic connections with the amygdala and is likely to function in tandem with it, is important in the triggering of physiological changes under more complex circumstances in which behavioral decisions cannot be made solely by conditioned associations or by exhaustive reasoning. Thus, the amygdala and the ventromedial prefrontal cortex may be candidates for the roles of structures that trigger emotional responses very rapidly and after more complex processing, respectively. The physiological changes encompassed by an emotional response are represented in a variety of brainstem, midbrain, and cortical structures that map somatic inputs. For instance, insula and other somatosensory-related cortices, especially in right hemisphere, have been shown to be important for normal recognition of emotions from external stimuli, for normal awareness of one's own body state, and for normal emotional experience.

AFFECTIVE MODULATION OF MEMORY, ATTENTION, AND DECISION MAKING IN ANIMALS

Before our discussion of affect and cognition in humans, we first briefly review what is known about affective modulation of other cognitive processes from studies in animals.

The largest number of animal experiments have focused on the role of affect in associative memory. Lesion studies in rats have shown that structures such as the amygdala are required for the acquisition of conditioned behavioral responses to stimuli that have been previously paired with an intrinsically aversive event, a paradigm called *fear conditioning* (Davis, 1992a; Gewirtz & Davis, 1997; Le Doux, 1996; LeDoux, Cicchetti, Xagoraris, & Romanski, 1990). In such an experiment, an animal is presented with two different types of stimuli: a stimulus that has intrinsic emotional value to the animal (e.g., a rewarding stimulus, such as food; or an aversive stimulus, such as electric shock), and a stimulus that has no intrinsic value to the animal (e.g., the sound of a tone). When these two stimuli are presented together on several occasions, the animal learns that the presence of one can predict the presence of the other: if the tone sounds, it is likely that the shock (or the food) will also occur. This very basic form of associative emotional memory may be an important substrate for more complex forms of learning and motivated behavior. Although there is extensive processing within the amygdala (Pitkanen, Savander, & LeDoux, 1997), one can describe a rough flow of information from higher-order sensory neocortex into the basolateral amygdala, where stimuli can be associated, and then on to various other structures or nuclei within the amygdala, such as the central nucleus, which serves to link amygdala to emotional effector structures (such as the hypothalamus; see Davis, 1992b). Several different neuroanatomic structures in addition to the amygdala have been shown to be involved in emotionally motivated learning, depending on the details of the task: the amygdala (Davis, 1992a; Le Doux, 1996), the ventral striatum (Everitt & Robbins, 1992), and the orbitofrontal cortex (Gaffan, Murray, & Fabre-Thorpe, 1993; Rolls, 1999) all appear to play important roles and are likely to function as components of a distributed, large-scale neural system for associating stimuli with their rewarding or punishing contingencies.

Although many of the above structures are implicated in processing both reward and punishment, they appear to be disproportionately important along certain dimensions of emotion. For instance, the amygdala specifically mediates behaviors and responses correlated with arousal and stress, especially emotional arousal pertaining to negatively valenced, aversive situations (Davis, 1992b; Goldstein, Rasmusson, Bunney, & Roth, 1996; Kesner, 1992). A direct dissociation on the basis of arousal has been demonstrated in rats: amygdala lesions interfere with avoidance of water that has been paired with electric shock (a highly arousing, unpleasant stimulus), but do not inferfere with avoidance of water that has been made to taste bitter (an unpleasant but not highly arousing stimulus) (Cahill & McGaugh, 1990). The amygdala thus plays a role in the acquisition of information during emotionally arousing situations, and perhaps especially during situations that are both arousing and unpleasant. Animal studies suggest that the amygdala circuitry underlying the processing of aversive stimuli depends on the central nucleus of the amygdala, whereas processing of stimuli that are rewarding appears to depend on projections from the basolateral nucleus of the amygdala to frontal cortex and ventral striatum.

The detailed role that the amygdala plays in the emotional modulation of other aspects of cognition, such as attention and memory, are rather complicated. Although the human studies we review below speak of "the amygdala" as if it were a homogeneous structure, it is important to bear in mind that the amygdala is in fact a complex collection of nuclei that all subserve somewhat different functions (Swanson & Petrovich, 1998). Furthermore, the amygdala is merely one nodal structure in a very distributed network that can modulate cognition on the basis of affect, and there are multiple neurotransmitter systems within these structures that can carry out different functional roles. The complexity of the systems is illustrated in the effects of emotional processing on modulating motivated learning in animals. A large number of studies (Cahill & McGaugh, 1996; McGaugh, 1989; McGaugh, Cahill, & Roozendaal, 1996) have shown that aversively motivated learning can be modulated by multiple neurotransmitter systems acting within the amygdala. For instance, direct post-training injections into the amygdala of a variety of drugs that modulate GABAergic, noradrenergic, or opiate-mediated neurotransmission influence long-term memory for inhibitory avoidance training (Brioni, Nagahara, & McGaugh, 1989; Gallagher, Kapp, Pascoe, & Rapp, 1981). Recent data suggest that the amygdala can influence memory by modulating consolidation that actually takes place within other brain structures, such as the hippocampus and basal ganglia. In one set of experiments, reversible pharmacologic lesions of the amygdala with lidocaine showed that the amygdala-mediated enhancement of different types of memory depends on the hippocampus (for memory in a spatial task) or the caudate nucleus (for memory in a cued task). Increasing neural activity within the amygdala by injections of d-amphetamine directly into the amygdala immediately after training enhanced performance on both spatial and cued water-maze tasks, and lidocaine injections into either hippocampus or caudate were found to block the effects of d-amphetamine amygdala injections on the respective task, but leave the amygdala's enhancement of the other task unaffected (Packard, Cahill, & McGaugh, 1994; Packard & Teather, 1996). Multiple neurotransmitter systems within the amygdala thus can modulate memory mechanisms in a variety of other structures, providing one mechanism for how changes in neuromodulatory transmitters induced by affective states could also modulate memory neurochemically (see Cahill & McGaugh, 1996, 1998; McGaugh, 1989; McGaugh et al., 1996, for reviews).

In addition to its role in emotional memory, the amygdala, together with a collection of nuclei termed the *basal forebrain*, have been shown to make critical contributions to the effect that emotion has on attentional processes. The amygdala's role in attentional processes has also been investigated in several recent experiments in rats (Holland & Gallagher, 1999). One component of attention, orienting behavior toward cues that have become associated with rewarding contingencies, has been found to rely on a circuit involving the central nucleus of the amygdala and its connections with the substantia nigra and the dorsal striatum (Han, McMahan, Holland, & Gallagher, 1997). Another important component of attention, increased allocation of processing resources toward novel or surprising situations, appears to depend on the integrity of the central nucleus of the amygdala and its connections with cholinergic neurons in the substantia innominata and nucleus basalis, structures in the basal forebrain. Thus, the amygdala could modulate cholinergic neuromodulatory functions of the basal forebrain nuclei, and consequently modulate attention, vigilance, signal-to-noise, and other aspects of information processing that depend on cholinergic modulation of cognition (Everitt & Robbins, 1997). Although this latter function has been studied in animals specifically as an increased ability to learn emotional associations that are unexpected, a more general role has been proposed in humans in regard to general vigilance and in attention to stimuli about which more information could be obtained (Whalen, 1999). Through circuits including components of amygdala, striatum, and basal forebrain, emotion may thus help to select particular aspects of the stimulus environment for disproportionate allocation of cognitive processing resources; namely, an organism should be designed to preferentially process information about those aspects of its environment that are most salient to its immediate survival and well-being.

Finally, it is clear that structures in close association with the amygdala, notably the bed nucleus of the stria terminalis, are necessary for more prolonged emotional states that can influence information processing in a global and less stimulus-driven fashion. In rats, the bed nucleus of the stria terminalis, together with nuclei within the amygdala proper, appear to be involved in anxiety rather than in fear; moreover, specific neuropeptides, such as corticotropin releasing hormone, have dramatic effects specifically on the bed nucleus of the stria terminalis and on anxiety, but not on fear (Davis, 1992a,b, 1997; Davis, Walker, & Lee, 1997). Although the detailed neural structures involved in fear and anxiety remain to be fully elucidated in humans, the findings from animal studies point toward anatomically and pharmacologically dissociable systems for fear and anxiety, and suggest particular avenues for further research as well as for therapeutic intervention (Davis, 1992b).

AFFECT MODULATES
DECLARATIVE MEMORY

The role of the amygdala in fear conditioning as discussed previously is consonant with recent data from humans: subjects with amygdala lesions fail to show conditioned skin-conductance response to stimuli that have been paired with an aversive, loud noise (Bechara et al., 1995; LaBar, LeDoux, Spencer, & Phelps, 1995), and the amygdala, together with other limbic structures, is activated during emotional conditioning paradigms in functional imaging studies (Buechel, Morris, Dolan, & Friston, 1998; LaBar, Gatenby, Gore, LeDoux, & Phelps, 1998). However, the amygdala's most interesting contribution to memory in humans is in the modulation of what we remember as conscious facts—in the modulation of declarative knowledge.

Common experience, as well as a large literature from human cognitive psychology, leave little doubt that declarative memory and emotion are intimately connected (Schacter, 1996). We often remember emotional episodes in our own lives with exceptional vividness and detail. A particularly striking example are so-called flashbulb memories: emotional events, such as president Kennedy's assassination or the explosion of the *Challenger* space shuttle, are frequently remembered as highly detailed images (Winograd & Neisser, 1992).

Naturalistic studies of memory for emotional events have suggested that relevant, salient information can often be enhanced by emotional arousal, but that information can also be distorted or suppressed. For instance, subjects giving eyewitness testimony often remember details about a knife or gun while forgetting other information about the scene (the so-called weapon focus effect; Loftus, 1979; Maass, & Koehnken, 1989; Steblay, 1992). Recent studies have attempted to simulate the naturalistic situation in the laboratory. In one series of studies, subjects were shown 12 slides accompanied by a narrative that together told a story (the "Reisberg task"; Burke, Heuer, & Reisberg, 1992; Heuer & Reisberg, 1990). Parts of the story were highly emotional. Subjects remembered the most detail about those parts of the story that were the most emotional. The data provided support for a theory, whereby emotion facilitates memory for information about the most salient features of a stimulus, compared to emotionally neutral stimuli (Burke et al., 1992; Heuer & Reisberg, 1990; Reisberg & Heuer, 1992).

Studies have shown that stimuli are remembered better the more emotionally arousing they are (Bradley, Greenwald, Petry, & Lang, 1992; Hamann, Cahill, & Squire, 1997b). These findings have led to the hypothesis that it is emotional arousal, and not valence, that is the major factor contributing to how well material is encoded into declarative memory. This hypothesis has been directly tested by manipulating arousal, either pharmacologically (Cahill, Prins, Weber, & McGaugh, 1994; O'Carroll, Drysdale, Cahill, Shajahan, & Ebmeier, 1998) or through the use of a specific context (Cahill & McGaugh, 1995) in normal human subjects. Both these manipulations showed that increased emotional arousal resulted in better encoding of material into declarative long-term memory, as assessed by subsequent recall.

The amygdala is the primary structure in humans that has been examined specifically in regard to emotional memory. Emotional memory in humans is impaired by amygdala lesions (Adolphs, Cahill, Schul, & Babinsky, 1997; Cahill, Babinsky, Markowitsch, & McGaugh, 1995; Phelps, LaBar, Anderson, O'Connor et al., 1998), but is not disproportionately impaired by lesions of other structures that can cause amnesia, such as the hippocampus (Hamann, Cahill, McGaugh, & Squire, 1997a; Hamann et al., 1997b). Studies of subjects with bilateral amygdala lesions found specific impairments in declarative memory for emotional material, despite normal

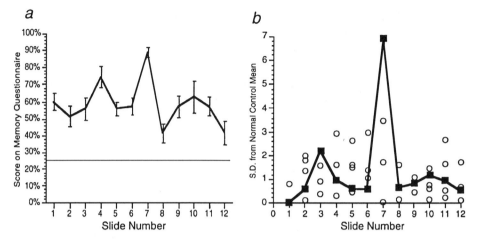

FIG. 2.1. Bilateral damage to the human amygdala impairs declarative memory for emotionally arousing material. Data are from seven normal control subjects, six brain-damaged control subjects who did not have damage to the amygdala, and from subject SM, who has complete bilateral damage to the amygdala. Subjects were shown a series of 12 slides that varied in emotional arousal. Slide 7 was the most arousing slide, showing surgically reattached legs of a car-crash victim. (a) Data from normal controls, showing memory score on a questionnaire about each slide. Chance is at 25% (*dotted line*). (b) Data from brain-damaged controls (*open circles*) and from subject SM (*black squares, solid lines*) plotted as differences from the normal control data. SM differed most from controls on the most emotional slide, an impairment not shown by any of the brain-damaged control subjects. The data suggest that the amygdala is important not for encoding memory in general, but specifically for enhancing the encoding of material into long-term declarative memory when such material is emotionally highly arousing. Modified from Adolphs, R., Cahill, L., Schul, R., & Babinsky, R. (1997). Impaired declarative memory for emotional material following bilateral amygdala damage in humans. *Learning and Memory, 4*, 291–300. Copyright © 1997, Cold Spring Harbor Laboratory Press.

declarative memory for neutral material (Fig. 2.1). These studies showed that the human amygdala enhances the encoding of material into declarative memory when the subject matter is unpleasant and emotionally arousing. Importantly, memory for neutral material was essentially normal in these patients: they just failed to show the normal facilitation when the subject matter was emotional. These findings from lesion studies are, in principle, consistent with two different interpretations. The amygdala may mediate the enhancing effects of emotion on the encoding of information into long-term memory, or it might mediate the enhancing effects of emotion on the subsequent retrieval of such information. Because emotional arousal of the subjects most likely occurred primarily when they first saw the stimuli during encoding, the former possibility is the most plausible. A confirmation has come from studies in normal subjects that used functional imaging during encoding.

A specific role for the amygdala in acquisition of declarative knowledge regarding emotionally arousing stimuli has been reported by recent imaging studies (Cahill et al., 1996; Canli, Zhao, Desmond, Glover, & Gabrieli, 1998; Hamann, Ely, Grafton, & Kilts, 1999). In one study (Cahill et al., 1996), amygdala activation at the time arousing unpleasant emotional stimuli (horror movies) were encoded into memory correlated significantly with how well the stimuli could subsequently be recalled; the authors argued that the amygdala is activated during the encoding of emotionally arousing material into declarative long-term memory. In another study (Hamann et al., 1999), amygdala activation correlated with encoding of either pleasant or unpleasant pictures into memory, as assessed by later recognition of the same stimuli. Taken together, both these imaging studies, as well as the findings from lesion studies, argue that the amygdala plays a critical role in modulating the encoding and the consolidation of knowledge during emotionally arousing circumstances.

It is interesting in this context to note that the human amygdala is also activated during REM sleep (Maquet et al., 1996), a finding consistent with a role for the amygdala in emotional memory because REM sleep typically involves emotional experiences and is likely to serve a function in consolidating emotional memory (Smith & Lapp, 1991). There are now several studies in humans that have confirmed a role for various stages of sleep in reorganizing and consolidating memory (Stickgold, 1999), consistent with single-unit neurophysiological findings from rats that have shown reprocessing of spatial information in the hippocampus during sleep (Wilson & McNaughton, 1994). These findings make it plausible that some of the amygdala's modulation of emotional memory occurs during sleep, and perhaps especially REM sleep.

All the previously discussed findings suggest a role for the amygdala in modulating the encoding and consolidation of long-term memory on the basis of the affective response and experience associated with the material that is being encoded. Of course, structures additional to the amygdala participate in such a process. Also, it remains to be explored how emotion may modulate memory retrieval, an issue that has received considerable attention from cognitive psychologists studying state-dependent memory

(Eich, 1995), but of which little is known regarding the neuroanatomic substrates.

A further question concerns the precise mechanisms by which emotional response can modulate declarative memory encoding. It is known that peripheral catecholamines modulate memory in part by neurotransmission of body-state information to central structures, such as the amygdala: vagotomized rats show a block of the normal potentiation of memory by peripheral catecholamines (Williams & Jensen, 1991), and direct stimulation of vagal afferents modulates memory (Clark et al., 1996). A recent study replicated this finding in humans who had vagal nerve stimulators implanted. Vagal nerve stimulation enhanced the acquisition and consolidation of memory (Clark, Naritoku, Smith, Browning, & Jensen, 1999), providing support for the idea that body-state information modulates cognitive processes, such as memory. The finding suggests that emotional responses to stimuli can modulate cognition not only directly, but also indirectly via the perception of body-state changes that have been triggered by the emotional response. In effect, the finding demonstrates that an emotional physiological response in the body has a direct effect on brain function. We take up this issue in more detail next, with respect to the effect of emotion on decision making.

AFFECT MODULATES DECISION MAKING

As with memory, common experience already suggests that our decisions are strongly influenced by affect. This has often been conceptualized as a case of emotion impairing decision making, but recent treatments have stressed the ecologically adaptive value of an emotional bias in guiding decision making under uncertainty (Damasio, 1994). Although, as one might predict, the amygdala also, at a basic level, participates in the modulation of decision making by emotion (e.g., Bechara, Damasio, Damasio, & Lee, 1999), the best studied structure in this regard is the ventromedial (VM) frontal cortex.

The VM frontal cortices have intimate connections with the amygdala, both directly and via the dorsomedial thalamus, and all these three structures appear to function as components of a distributed neural system for processing the rewarding or punishing contingencies of stimuli in relation to the animal's behavior (Gaffan & Murray, 1990; Gaffan et al., 1993; Schoenbaum, Chiba, & Gallagher, 1998; Tremblay & Schultz, 1999). In humans, the VM frontal cortex stands out as a structure indispensable to making decisions in complex environments, but not necessary for many other cognitive functions, such as those that contribute to working memory or general intelligence.

Clues about the functions of the VM frontal cortex date back to the late 1800s, as shown in the case of Phineas Gage. Gage suffered from a dramatic accident in which an iron rod was shot through his head as a result of an explosion. The injury resulted in a large bilateral lesion of VM frontal cortex (Damasio, Grabowski, Frank, Galaburda, & Damasio, 1994). It was surprising that he survived at all, but also intriguing was his changed personality after the accident. Whereas Gage had been a diligent, reliable, polite, and socially adept person before his accident, he had subsequently become uncaring, profane, and socially inappropriate in his conduct. This change in his personality remained a mystery until it could be interpreted in light of similar such patients in modern day: Like Gage, other subjects with bilateral damage to the VM frontal lobes show a severely impaired ability to function in society, despite an entirely normal profile on standard neuropsychological measures, such as IQ, language, perception, and memory.

The role of the VM prefrontal cortex in decision making has been explored in a series of studies by Antoine Bechara, who used a task in which subjects had to gamble in order to win money. As with gambling in real life, the task involved probabilistic contingencies that required subjects to make choices based on incomplete information. Normal subjects learned to maximize their profits on the task by building a representation of the statistical contingencies gleaned from prior experiences: In the long run, certain choices tend to pay off better than others. The key ingredient that distinguished the task of Bechara from other tasks of probabilistic reasoning is that subjects discriminated choices by feeling—they developed hunches that certain choices were better than others, and these hunches could be measured both by asking subjects verbally and by measuring autonomic correlates of emotional arousal, such as skin conductance response. Subjects with damage to the VM frontal cortex failed this task (Bechara, Damasio, Damasio, & Anderson, 1994), and they failed it precisely because they were unable to represent choice bias in the form of an emotional hunch (Bechara, Damasio, Tranel, & Damasio, 1997). Not only did subjects with VM frontal damage make poor choices on the task, they also acquired neither any subjective feeling regarding their choices (Bechara et al., 1997), nor any anticipatory autonomic changes (Bechara, Tranel, Damasio, & Damasio, 1996) (Fig. 2.2).

These findings are consonant with prior reports that subjects with VM frontal lobe damage do not trigger a normal emotional response to stimuli,

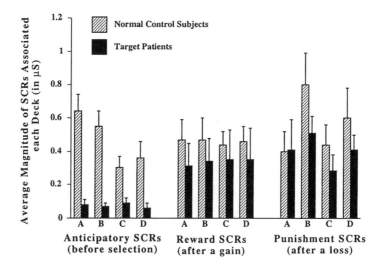

FIG. 2.2. Impaired ability to trigger emotional states during decision making following damage to ventromedial prefrontal cortex. Shown are mean (and SD) skin conductance responses from seven subjects with bilateral damage to the ventromedial (VM) prefrontal cortex (*solid black bars*) and from 12 normal controls (*striped bars*). Subjects participated in a gambling task (Bechara et al., 1996) in which they were asked to choose from four decks of cards (indicated as A, B, C, D on the *x*-axis) that were associated with different probabilities of winning and losing money. Decks A and B had the highest risk of losing money, and consequently normal subjects showed large changes in skin-conductance response (SCR) in anticipation as they chose cards from these decks, but subjects with damage to VM prefrontal cortex showed no such anticipatory index of emotional state (*left*; anticipatory SCRs). The discrepancy between control and target subjects became considerably less when examining their SCRs subsequent to having chosen a card from a deck as they were told how much money they had won or lost. Similar to controls, subjects with VM frontal damage did trigger SCRs when they received this news (*middle* and *right*: reward and punishment SCRs). The data thus indicate that the defect following damage to VM frontal lobe is not an inability to respond to reward or punishment per se, but to use the emotional state elicited by reward or punishment to trigger anticipation of future reward or punishment under similar circumstances, and to thus guide decision making on the basis of prior emotional experience. Modified from Bechara, A., Tranel, D., Damasio, H., & Damasio, A. R. (1996). Failure to respond autonomically to anticipated future outcomes following damage to prefrontal cortex. *Cerebral Cortex*, 6, 215–225. Copyright © 1996, Oxford University Press.

including socially relevant stimuli (Damasio, Tranel, & Damasio, 1990), and support a specific hypothesis that has been put forth by A. R. Damasio (1994, 1995, 1996): the somatic marker hypothesis. According to this hypothesis, the VM frontal cortex is a critical component of the neural systems by which we acquire, represent, and retrieve the values of our actions. This mechanism includes the generation of somatic states, or representations of somatic states, that correspond to the anticipated future outcome of decisions. Such a mechanism may be of special importance in the social domain, where the enormous complexity of the decision space precludes an exhaustive analysis.

AFFECT AND SOCIAL JUDGMENT

Affect and social behavior have long been believed to be related. Our interactions with other people typically involve affective reactions. The close relation between affect and social cognition was already exemplified in the previous section, in which we pointed out that emotion may be disproportionately important to guide decision making in the social domain.

It should come as no surprise then that many of the neural structures involved in processing emotion also play a key role in regulating social behavior. A recent set of studies of the human amygdala bear this out. Studies that have used functional neuroimaging in normal subjects (Breiter et al., 1996; Morris et al., 1996) and studies that have examined patients with damage to the amygdala (Adolphs, Tranel, Damasio, & Damasio, 1994; Adolphs et al., 1999; Young et al., 1995) provide something of a consensus that the amygdala is critical to the recognition of emotions from facial expressions, specifically certain negative emotions, especially fear (Adolphs et al., 1995; Broks et al., 1998; Calder et al., 1996). The findings have been broadly consonant with the amygdala's contribution to social behavior that was suggested by earlier lesion studies in animals (Kluver & Bucy, 1939; Weiskrantz, 1956), as well as with the large number of studies that have investigated the amygdala's role in fear conditioning (Davis, 1992a; Le Doux, 1996). All these different threads of research point to a disproportionately important role for the amygdala in processing stimuli related to danger and threat, both in the environment in general and in the social environment in particular. Given these findings, one might expect that the amygdala would make important contributions also to higher-level social cognition in humans, perhaps especially to those aspects of it that rely on recognizing social information from faces.

We investigated subjects' ability to judge how trustworthy or how approachable other people looked from perceiving their faces. In our study (Adolphs, Tranel, & Damasio, 1998), we found that three subjects who had bilateral amygdala damage all shared the same pattern of impairment: they judged to be abnormally trustworthy and approachable the faces of those people who are normally judged to look the most untrustworthy or most unapproachable (Fig. 2.3). Although the subjects with amygdala damage showed a general positive bias in judging all faces, they showed a disproportionate impairment when judging those faces normally given the most negative ratings. The amygdala's role in processing stimuli related to potential threat or danger thus appears to extend to the complex judgments on the basis of which we regulate our social behavior.

An issue of further interest is the specificity of the impairment to faces. Follow-up studies revealed that bilateral amygdala damage also impaired judgments for the preferences of nonsocial visual stimuli, such as color patterns or landscapes, although the effect was not as large. In this study (Adolphs & Tranel, 1999), subjects with amygdala damage liked pictures of nonsocial stimuli more than did control subjects. Thus, the amygdala's role does not appear to be entirely restricted to stimuli in the social domain, but may encompass a more general function that is of disproportionate importance to social cognition. A further experiment assessed social judgments that were made about other people on the basis of written descriptions of them. Judgments about people from such lexical stimuli were not impaired by amygdala damage (Adolphs et al., 1998). This latter finding suggests that the lexical stimuli provided sufficient explicit information such that normal task performance could result from reasoning strategies that did not necessarily require the amygdala. However, it is worth noting that there is evidence for the amygdala's importance in processing emotional stimuli that are lexical when such stimuli signal potential threat, danger, or other emotional arousal (Isenberg et al., 1999; Adolphs, Russell, & Tranel, 1999).

One would like also to extend the previously mentioned line of investigations to additional types of stimuli and additional types of social information that can be gleaned from such stimuli. Andrea Heberlein, a graduate student working with us, has begun such an investigation using visual motion cues to provide information about biological and psychological categories. In one experiment, subjects were shown a short video that depicts three geometric shapes moving on a plain, white background (Heider & Simmel, 1944). Although visual motion is the only available cue in this experiment, normal subjects have no difficulty interpreting the motion of the shapes in terms of social categories: The shapes are attributed psychological states,

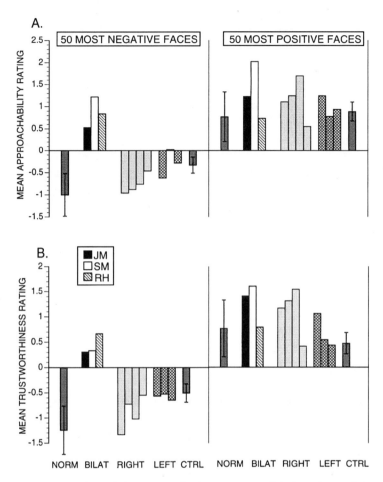

FIG. 2.3. Bilateral damage to the human amygdala impairs social judgment for faces. Shown are mean judgments of (*a*) approachability and (*b*) trustworthiness of the faces of 100 unfamiliar people. Data are broken down into those obtained from the 50 faces that received the most negative (*left*) and most positive (*right*) mean ratings from normal controls on each of these attributes. Each face was judged on a scale of −3 (very unapproachable or untrustworthy) to +3 (very approachable or trustworthy). Means and SD are shown for data from 46 normal controls (NORM). Individual means are shown for each of three subjects with bilateral amygdala damage (BILAT), four subjects with unilateral right (RIGHT), and three with unilateral left (LEFT) amygdala damage. Means and SEM are shown for seven brain-damaged controls with no damage to the amygdala (CTRL). Subjects with bilateral amygdala damage differed from all other groups in that they gave abnormally positive ratings to those faces that normally receive the most negative ratings. Modified from Adolphs, R., Tranel, D., & Damasio, A. R. (1998). The human amygdala in social judgment. *Nature*, 393, 470–474. Copyright © 1998, MacMillan Press.

such as goals, beliefs, desires, and emotions, on the basis of their relative motion. By contrast, a subject with selective bilateral amygdala damage did not make such automatic attributions (Heberlein et al., 1998). When shown the same stimulus, she described it in purely geometric terms, lacking the normal, automatic social interpretation. This finding suggests that our interpretation of the world around us is influenced by mechanisms for assigning emotional and social value, an ability that is clearly essential for survival in a complex social environment, but one that may also explain our tendency to anthropomorphize when misapplied.

The previously mentioned set of findings supports a role for the amygdala in mediating affective influences on social decision making and social judgment, in addition to a more general role in modulating cognition that may not be specific to the social domain. Similarly, the VM frontal cortices play a role in linking emotional associations to behavioral contingencies that go beyond social decision making. This raises the question of the specificity of affect in regulating social cognition, as compared with cognition in general. We believe that affect plays a disproportionately important role in social cognition, and it seems likely that the highly differentiated affective states of humans evolved to regulate social behavior (see Panksepp, 1998, for a detailed review of some of the neuroscientific support for this). In fact, a whole set of so-called social emotions pertain specifically to social situations (e.g., guilt, embarrassment, shyness, jealousy, shame). One might predict a need for highly differentiated affective responses precisely in guiding cognition and behavior in those domains with the greatest complexity, and surely the social domain is the most complex of all.

CONCLUSIONS

Although, for the sake of brevity, we have highlighted only a few neural structures about which we have clearest experimental evidence for a role in affective modulation of cognition, it should be clear that we envision a highly distributed system consisting of many distinct neuroanatomic components. Such a system would include the whole set of neural structures involved in representing somatic states, from brain stem nuclei, like the nucleus solitarius and the parabrachial nucleus, to neocortical structures, such as somatosensory cortices and insula. In fact, there is good evidence for the role of these structures in both emotion and social cognition. In addition to such representational structures, there are key nodal structures that link affect, or its somatic representation, to cognition and behavior—we have concentrated on the amygdala and VM frontal cortices. However, amygdala and VM frontal cortices are intimately connected with other structures that directly influence cognition: the basal forebrain cholinergic system, which contributes importantly to attention, as well as various neuromodulatory brain stem nuclei and dopaminergic nuclei in ventral tegmentum.

Together, all these neuroanatomic structures and neurochemical systems are in a position to modulate information processing globally in neocortical circuits that subserve perception, recognition, and memory consolidation. There is clear evidence from recent functional imaging studies that emotional states modulate activity in the neocortex globally: many higher sensory and association neocortices show a decrease in activation during highly emotional states, whereas other regions, such as the VM prefrontal cortices, show an increase (Drevets & Raichle, 1998). Likewise, there is evidence that mood states that are known to engage frontal cortex predominantly on either the left or the right side of the brain (Davidson & Hugdahl, 1995) in turn influence the cognitive functions subserved by that side of the frontal lobe. Thus, positive affect, which engages the left frontal cortex more than the right, facilitates verbal fluency, also a function attributable to the left frontal cortices. By contrast, negative affect, which engages the right frontal cortex more than the left, facilitates figural fluency, a function attributable to the right frontal cortices (Bartolic, Basso, Schefft, Glauser, & Titanic-Schefft, 1999). This affect-state dependence of cognition and its correlation with identified neural structures provide further evidence for the inseparable relation between emotion and other aspects of cognition. Our everyday experience also clearly shows that affect influences essentially all other aspects of cognitive functioning, including memory, attention, and decision making.

Despite such a global interrelation between affect and cognition, it is also the case that particular affective processes disproportionately influence certain types of knowledge structures. For example, as we reviewed previously, social judgments depend on affective circuitry involving the amygdala when such judgments are made on the basis of perceiving other people's faces, but not when they are made on the basis of explicit information provided in language. However, the reasons for this difference should be apparent: explicit, lexical information can bypass substantial information processing and can generate social judgment without requiring some of the intermediate representations that would be required in the case of faces. Subjects with bilateral damage to the amygdala are unable to generate the knowledge from seeing the person's face that person should be avoided; however, if told explicitly that the person is bad or dangerous to approach in some way, the same subjects have no difficulty in using this already supplied knowledge to guide their judgment.

In closing, it is worth considering the evolution of the relationship between affect and cognition, a topic already skirted at the beginning of this chapter. We consider affective processing to be an evolutionary antecedent to more complex forms of information processing; but higher cognition requires the guidance provided by affective processing (Damasio, 1994). The key ingredient offered by affect is a representation that incorporates the value of a stimulus or of an action to the organism. Biological value would provide an important bias not only to relatively fast, hard-wired stimulus–response processing in situations in which there is a premium on survival (running away from a bear), but would also permeate higher cognition. A key insight is that cognition must include not only representations of external sensory stimuli, but also representations of the organism that is perceiving those stimuli, including a representation of the biological value of those stimuli to the organism.

ACKNOWLEDGMENTS

We would like to thank our colleagues and collaborators, Hanna Damasio, Daniel Tranel, and Antoine Bechara. The research reported here was supported in part by a grant from NINDS to ARD, and grants from NIMH, the Sloan Foundation, and the EJLB Foundation to RA.

REFERENCES

Adolphs, R., Cahill, L., Schul, R., & Babinsky, R. (1997). Impaired declarative memory for emotional material following bilateral amygdala damage in humans. *Learning and Memory, 4*, 291–300.

Adolphs, R., & Tranel, D. (1999). Preferences for visual stimuli following amygdala damage. *Journal of Cognitive Neuroscience, 11*, 610–616.

Adolphs, R., Tranel, D., & Damasio, A. R. (1998). The human amygdala in social judgment. *Nature, 393*, 470–474.

Adolphs, R., Tranel, D., Damasio, H., & Damasio, A. (1994). Impaired recognition of emotion in facial expressions following bilateral damage to the human amygdala. *Nature, 372*, 669–672.

Adolphs, R., Tranel, D., Damasio, H., & Damasio, A. R. (1995). Fear and the human amygdala. *The Journal of Neuroscience, 15*, 5879–5892.

Adolphs, R., Tranel, D., Hamann, S., Young, A., Calder, A., Anderson, A., Phelps, E., & Damasio, A. R. (1999). Recognition of facial emotion in nine subjects with bilateral amygdala damage. *Neuropsychologia, 37*, 1111–1117.

Adolphs, R., Russell, J. A. & Tranel, D. (1999). A role for the human amygdala in recognizing emotional arousal from unpleasant stimuli. *Psychological Science, 10*, 167–171.

Bartolic, E. I., Basso, M. R., Schefft, B. K., Glauser, T., & Titanic-Schefft, M. (1999). Effects of experimentally induced emotional states on frontal lobe cognitive task performance. *Neuropsychologia, 37*, 677–683.

Bechara, A., Damasio, A. R., Damasio, H., & Anderson, S. W. (1994). Insensitivity to future consequences following damage to human prefrontal cortex. *Cognition, 50*, 7–15.

Bechara, A., Damasio, H., Tranel, D., & Damasio, A. (1997). Deciding advantageously before knowing the advantageous strategy. *Science, 275*, 1293–1295.

Bechara, A., Tranel, D., Damasio, H., Adolphs, R., Rockland, C., & Damasio, A. R. (1995). Double dissociation of conditioning and declarative knowledge relative to the amygdala and hippocampus in humans. *Science, 269*, 1115–1118.

Bechara, A., Tranel, D., Damasio, H., & Damasio, A. R. (1996). Failure to respond autonomically to anticipated future outcomes following damage to prefrontal cortex. *Cerebral Cortex, 6*, 215–225.

Bechara, A., Damasio, H., Damasio, A. R., & Lee, G. P. (1999). Different contributions of the human amygdala and ventromedial prefrontal cortex to decision-making. *The Journal of Neuroscience, 19*, 5473–5481.

Bradley, M. M., Greenwald, M. K., Petry, M. C., & Lang, P. J. (1992). Remembering pictures: Pleasure and arousal in memory. *The Journal of Experimental Psychology: Learning, Memory, and Cognition, 18*, 379–390.

Breiter, H. C., Etcoff, N. L., Whalen, P. J., Kennedy, W. A., Rauch, S. L., Buckner, R. L., Strauss, M. M., Hyman, S. E., & Rosen, B. R. (1996). Response and habituation of the human amygdala during visual processing of facial expression. *Neuron, 17*, 875–887.

Brioni, J. D., Nagahara, A. H., & McGaugh, J. L. (1989). Involvement of the amygdala GABAergic system in the modulation of memory storage. *Brain Research, 487*, 105–112.

Broks, P., Young, A. W., Maratos, E. J., Coffey, P. J., Calder, A. J., Isaac, C., Mayes, A. R., Hodges, J. R., Montaldi, D., Cezayirli, E., Roberts, N., & Hadley, D. (1998). Face processing impairments after encephalitis: Amygdala damage and recognition of fear. *Neuropsychologia, 36*, 59–70.

Buechel, C., Morris, J., Dolan, R. J., & Friston, K. J. (1998). Brain systems mediating aversive conditioning: An event-related fMRI study. *Neuron, 20*, 947–957.

Burke, A., Heuer, F., & Reisberg, D. (1992). Remembering emotional events. *Memory and Cognition, 20*, 277–290.

Cahill, L., Babinsky, R., Markowitsch, H. J., & McGaugh, J. L. (1995). The amygdala and emotional memory. *Nature, 377*, 295–296.

Cahill, L., Haier, R. J., Fallon, J., Alkire, M. T., Tang, C., Keator, D., Wu, J., & McGaugh, J. L. (1996). Amygdala activity at encoding correlated with long-term, free recall of emotional information. *Proceedings of the National Academy of Sciences (USA), 93*, 8016–8021.

Cahill, L., & McGaugh, J. L. (1990). Amygdaloid complex lesions differentially affect retention of tasks using appetitive and aversive reinforcement. *Behavioral Neuroscience, 104*, 532–543.

Cahill, L., & McGaugh, J. L. (1995). A novel demonstration of enhanced memory associated with emotional arousal. *Consciousness and Cognition, 4*, 410–421.

Cahill, L., & McGaugh, J. L. (1996). Modulation of memory storage. *Current Opinion in Neurobiology, 6*, 237–242.

Cahill, L., & McGaugh, J. L. (1998). Mechanisms of emotional arousal and lasting declarative memory. *Trends in Neurosciences, 21*, 294–299.

Cahill, L., Prins, B., Weber, M., & McGaugh, J. L. (1994). Beta-adrenergic activation and memory for emotional events. *Nature, 371*, 702–704.

Calder, A. J., Young, A. W., Rowland, D., Perrett, D. I., Hodges, J. R., & Etcoff, N. L. (1996). Facial emotion recognition after bilateral amygdala damage: differentially severe impairment of fear. *Cognitive Neuropsychology, 13*, 699–745.

Canli, T., Zhao, Z., Desmond, J., Glover, G., & Gabrieli, J. D. E. (1998). Amygdala activation at encoding correlates with long-term recognition memory for emotional pictures: An fMRI study. (From *Society for Neuroscience. Abstracts, 24*, page 935).

Clark, K. B., Naritoku, D. K., Smith, D. C., Browning, R. A., & Jensen, R. A. (1999). Enhanced recognition memory following vagus nerve stimulation in human subjects. *Nature Neuroscience, 2*, 94–98.

Clark, K. B., Smith, D. C., Hassert, D. L., Browning, R. B., Naritoku, D. K., & Jensen, R. A. (1996). Posttraining electrical stimulation of vagal afferents with concomitant efferent inactivation enhances memory storage processes in the rat. (From *Society for Neuroscience Abstract, 22*, Page 1877).

Damasio, A. R. (1994). *Descartes' error: Emotion, reason, and the human brain.* New York: Grosset/Putnam.

Damasio, A. R. (1995). Toward a neurobiology of emotion and feeling: operational concepts and hypotheses. *The Neuroscientist, 1*, 19–25.

Damasio, A. R. (1996). The somatic marker hypothesis and the possible functions of the prefrontal cortex. *Philosophical Transactions of the Royal Society (London) Series B, 351*, 1413–1420.

Damasio, A. R. (1999). *The feeling of what happens: Body and emotion in the making of consciousness.* New York: Harcourt Brace.

Damasio, A. R., Tranel, D., & Damasio, H. (1990). Individuals with sociopathic behavior caused by frontal damage fail to respond autonomically to social stimuli. *Behavioral Brain Research, 41*, 81–94.

Damasio, H., Grabowski, T., Frank, R., Galaburda, A. M., & Damasio, A. R. (1994). The return of Phineas Gage: Clues about the brain from the skull of a famous patient. *Science, 264*, 1102–1104.

Davidson, R. J., & Hugdahl, K. (1995). *Brain asymmetry.* Cambridge, MA: MIT Press.

Davis, M. (1992a). The role of the amygdala in conditioned fear. In J. P. Aggleton (Ed.), *The amygdala: Neurobiological aspects of emotion, memory, and mental dysfunction* (pp. 255–306). New York: Wiley-Liss.

Davis, M. (1992b). The role of the amygdala in fear and anxiety. *Annual Review of Neuroscience, 15*, 353–375.

Davis, M. (1997). Neurobiology of fear responses: The role of the amygdala. *Journal of Neuropsychiatry and Clinical Neurosciences, 9*, 382–402.

Davis, M., Walker, D. L., & Lee, Y. (1997). Amygdala and bed nucleus of the stria terminalis: Differential roles in fear and anxiety measured with the acoustic startle reflex. *Philosphical Transactions of the Royal Society (London) Series B, 352*, 1675–1687.

Drevets, W. C., & Raichle, M. E. (1998). Reciprocal suppression of regional cerebral blood flow during emotional versus higher cognitive processes: Implications for interactions between emotion and cognition. *Cognition and Emotion, 12*, 353–386.

Eich, E. (1995). Searching for mood dependent memory. *Psychological Science, 6*, 67–75.

Everitt, B. J., & Robbins, T. W. (1992). Amygdala–ventral striatal interactions and reward-related processes. In J. P. Aggleton (Ed.), *The amygdala: Neurobiological aspects of emotion, memory, and mental dysfunction* (pp. 401). New York: Wiley-Liss.

Everitt, B. J., & Robbins, T. W. (1997). Central cholinergic systems and cognition. *Annual Review of Psychology, 48*, 649–684.

Gaffan, D., & Murray, E. A. (1990). Amygdalar interaction with the mediodorsal nucleus of the thalamus and the ventromedial prefrontal cortex in stimulus–reward associative learning in the monkey. *Journal of Neuroscience, 10*, 3479–3493.

Gaffan, D., Murray, E. A., & Fabre-Thorpe, M. (1993). Interaction of the amygdala with the frontal lobe in reward memory. *European Journal of Neuroscience, 5*, 968–975.

Gallagher, M., Kapp, B. S., Pascoe, J. P., & Rapp, P. R. (1981). A neuropharmacology of amygdaloid systems which contribute to learning and memory. In Y. Ben-Ari (Ed.), *The amygdaloid complex.* Amsterdam: Elsevier.

Gewirtz, J. C., & Davis, M. (1997). Second-order fear conditioning prevented by blocking NMDA receptors in amygdala. *Nature, 388,* 471–474.

Goldstein, L. E., Rasmusson, A. M., Bunney, B. S., & Roth, R. H. (1996). Role of the amygdala in the coordination of behavioral, neuroendocrine, and prefrontal cortical monoamine responses to psychological stress in the rat. *The Journal of Neuroscience, 16,* 4787–4798.

Hamann, S. B., Cahill, L., McGaugh, J., & Squire, L. R. (1997a). Intact enhancement of declarative memory for emotional material in amnesia. *Learning and Memory, 4,* 301–309.

Hamann, S. B., Cahill, L., & Squire, L. R. (1997b). Emotional perception and memory in amnesia. *Neuropsychology, 11,* 104–113.

Hamann, S. B., Ely, T. D., Grafton, S. T., & Kilts, C. D. (1999). Amygdala activity related to enhanced memory for pleasant and aversive stimuli. *Nature Neuroscience, 2,* 289–293.

Han, J.-S., McMahan, R. W., Holland, P., & Gallagher, M. (1997). The role of an amygdalo-nigrostriatal pathway in associative learning. *The Journal of Neuroscience, 17,* 3913–3919.

Heberlein, A. S., Adolphs, R., Tranel, D., Kemmerer, D., Anderson, S., & Damasio, A. R. (1998). Impaired attribution of social meanings to abstract dynamic visual patterns following damage to the amygdala. (From *Society for Neuroscience Abstracts, 24,* p. 1176).

Heider, F., & Simmel, M. (1944). An experimental study of apparent behavior. *American Journal of Psychology, 57,* 243–259.

Heuer, F., & Reisberg, D. (1990). Vivid memories of emotional events: the accuracy of remembered minutiae. *Memory and Cognition, 18,* 496–506.

Holland, P. C., & Gallagher, M. (1999). Amygdala circuitry in attentional and representational processes. *Trends in Cognitive Sciences, 3,* 65–73.

Isenberg, N., Silbersweig, D., Engelien, A., Emmerich, S., Malavade, K., Beattie, M., Leon, A. C. & Stern, E. (1999). Linguistic threat activates the human amygdala. *Proceedings of the National Academy of Sciences (USA), 96,* 10456–10459.

Kesner, R. P. (1992). Learning and memory in rats with an emphasis on the role of the amygdala. In J. P. Aggleton (Ed.), *The amygdala: Neurobiological aspects of emotion, memory, and mental dysfunction* (pp. 379–400). New York: Wiley.

Kluver, H., & Bucy, P. C. (1939). Preliminary analysis of functions of the temporal lobes in monkeys. *Archives Neurological Psychiatry, 42,* 979–997.

LaBar, K. S., Gatenby, J. C., Gore, J. C., LeDoux, J. E., & Phelps, E. A. (1998). Human amygdala activation during conditioned fear acquisition and extinction: A mixed-trial fMRI study. *Neuron, 20,* 937–945.

LaBar, K. S., LeDoux, J. E., Spencer, D. D., & Phelps, E. A. (1995). Impaired fear conditioning following unilateral temporal lobectomy in humans. *The Journal of Neuroscience, 15,* 6846–6855.

Le Doux, J. (1996). *The emotional brain.* New York: Simon and Schuster.

LeDoux, J. E., Cicchetti, P., Xagoraris, A., & Romanski, L. M. (1990). The lateral amygdaloid nucleus: Sensory interface of the amygdala in fear conditioning. *The Journal of Neuroscience, 10,* 1062–1069.

Loftus, E. F. (1979). *Eyewitness testimony.* Cambridge, MA: Harvard University Press.

Maass, A., & Koehnken, G. (1989). Eyewitness identification. *Law and Human Behavior, 13,* 397–408.

Maquet, P., Peters, J.-M., Aerts, J., Delfiore, G., Degueldre, C., Luxen, A., & Franck, G. (1996). Functional neuroanatomy of human rapid-eye-movement sleep and dreaming. *Nature, 383,* 163–166.

McGaugh, J. L. (1989). Involvement of hormonal and neuromodulatory systems in the regulation of memory storage. *Annual Review of Neuroscience, 12,* 255–287.

McGaugh, J. L., Cahill, L., & Roozendaal, B. (1996). Involvement of the amygdala in memory storage: interaction with other brain systems. *Proceedings of the National Academy of Sciences (USA), 93,* 13508–13514.

Morris, J. S., Frith, C. D., Perrett, D. I., Rowland, D., Young, A. W., Calder, A. J., & Dolan, R. J. (1996). A differential neural response in the human amygdala to fearful and happy facial expressions. *Nature, 383,* 812–815.

O'Carroll, R. E., Drysdale, E., Cahill, L., Shajahan, P., & Ebmeier, K. P. (1998). Stimulation of the noradrenergic system enhances, and blockade reduces, memory for emotional material in man. (From *Society for Neuroscience Abstracts, 24*, p. 1523).

Packard, M. G., Cahill, L., & McGaugh, J. L. (1994). Amygdala modulation of hippocampal-dependent and caudate nucleus-dependent memory processes. *Proceedings of the National Academy of Sciences (USA), 91*, 8477–8481.

Packard, M. G., & Teather, L. A. (1996). Amygdala modulation of multiple memory systems. (From *Society for Neuroscience Abstracts, 22*, p. 1868.)

Panksepp, J. (1998). *Affective neuroscience*. New York: Oxford University Press.

Phelps, E. A., LaBar, K., Anderson, A. K., O'Connor, K. J., Fulbright, R. K., & Speucer, D. D. (1998). Specifying the contributions of the human amygdala to emotional memory: A case study. *Neurocase, 4*, 527–540.

Pitkanen, A., Savander, V., & LeDoux, J. E. (1997). Organization of intra-amygdaloid circuitries in the rat: An emerging framework for understanding functions of the amygdala. *Trends in Neurosciences, 20*, 517–523.

Reisberg, D., & Heuer, F. (1992). Remembering the details of emotional events. In E. Winograd & U. Neisser (Eds.), *Affect and accuracy in recall: Studies of "flashbulb" memories* (pp. 163–190). Cambridge, MA: Harvard University Press.

Rolls, E. T. (1999). *The brain and emotion*. New York: Oxford University Press.

Schacter, D. L. (1996). *Searching for memory: The brain, the mind, and the past*. New York: Basic Books.

Scherer, K. R. (1984). On the nature and function of emotion: A component process approach. In K. R. Scherer & P. Ekman (Eds.), *Approaches to emotion* (pp. 293–318). Hillsdale, NJ: Lawrence Erlbaum.

Schoenbaum, G., Chiba, A. A., & Gallagher, M. (1998). Orbitofrontal cortex and basolateral amygdala encode expected outcomes during learning. *Nature Neuroscience, 1*, 155–159.

Smith, C., & Lapp, L. (1991). Increases in number of REMs and REM density in humans following an intensive learning period. *Sleep, 14*, 325–330.

Steblay, N. M. (1992). A meta-analytic review of the weapon-focus effect. *Law and Human Behavior, 16*, 413–424.

Stickgold, R. (1999). Sleep: Off-line memory reprocessing. *Trends in Cognitive Sciences, 2*, 484–492.

Swanson, L. W., & Petrovich, G. D. (1998). What is the amygdala? *Trends in Neurosciences, 21*, 323–331.

Tremblay, L., & Schultz, W. (1999). Relative reward preference in primate orbitofrontal cortex. *Nature, 398*, 704–708.

Weiskrantz, L. (1956). Behavioral changes associated with ablation of the amygdaloid complex in monkeys. *Journal of Comparative Physiology and Psychology, 49*, 381–391.

Whalen, P. (1999). Fear, vigilance, and ambiguity: initial neuroimaging studies of the human amygdala. *Current Directions in Psychological Science, 7*, 177–187.

Williams, C., & Jensen, R. (1991). Vagal afferents: a possible mechanism for the modulation of memory by peripherally acting agents. In R. C. A. Frederickson, J. L. McGaugh, & D. L. Felten (Eds.), *Peripheral signalling of the brain: Role in neural-immune interactions, learning and memory*. Lewiston, NY: Hogrefe & Huber.

Wilson, M., & McNaughton, B. (1994). Reactivation of hippocampal ensemble memories during sleep. *Science, 265*, 676–679.

Winograd, E., & Neisser, U. (1992). *Affect and accuracy in recall: Studies of "flashbulb" memories*. Cambridge, MA: Harvard University Press.

Young, A. W., Aggleton, J. P., Hellawell, D. J., Johnson, M., Broks, P., & Hanley, J. R. (1995). Face processing impairments after amygdalotomy. *Brain, 118*, 15–24.

Zajonc, R. B. (1980). Feeling and thinking: Preferences need no inferences. *American Psychologist, 35*, 151–175.

Zajonc, R. B., & Kunst-Wilson, W. R. (1980). Affective discrimination of stimuli that cannot be recognized. *Science, 207*, 557–558.

3

Affect and Attitudes: A Social Neuroscience Approach

Tiffany A. Ito

Department of Psychology
University of Colorado

John T. Cacioppo

Department of Psychology
University of Chicago

Why Social Neuroscience?   51
The Separability of Positive and Negative Affect   52
   The Evaluative Space Model   54
   Neural Substrates   57
   Negativity Bias   58
   Summary   59
Rerepresentation of Evaluative Processes Across the Neuraxis   60
   Feeling without Knowing   63
   Applications to Implicit and Explicit Prejudice   65
   Different Evaluative Mechanisms or Decreased Activation with Practice? 67
   Summary   68
Conclusion   69
References   70

Evaluative and affective reactions are a ubiquitous and important aspect of everyday experience. At the extreme end, they aid in survival by helping to

Address for correspondence: Tiffany A. Ito, Department of Psychology, University of Colorado at Boulder. Muenzinger Psychology Building, Campus Box 345, Boulder, Colorado 80309-0345, USA. Email: tito@psych.colorado.edu determine which stimuli and environments should be avoided, and which should be approached. Even seemingly more mundane reactions, such as the pleasure experienced watching a puppy at play or the displeasure felt at the occurrence of an injustice, are important, because they infuse our lives with meaning. Affect can also have important influences on and be influenced by cognitive processes. For example, affective and emotional experiences may themselves arise from cognitive processes (Frijda, 1986; Ortony, Clore, & Collins, 1988; Scherer, 1984; Smith & Ellsworth, 1985), and cognitive processes such as decision making and memory are influenced by affective states (Forgas, 1995; Schwarz & Clore, 1983). Finally, affective states are also associated with a host of bodily changes that help meet current and expected metabolic demands (Cacioppo, Berntson, Larsen, Poehlmann, & Ito, 2000). A full understanding of the affect system therefore facilitates a more complete understanding of how we navigate in our social world.

In this chapter, we examine the affect system from a social neuroscience perspective. *Social neuroscience* refers to an integrative, multilevel analysis that extends from the neural to social level (Cacioppo & Berntson, 1992). Its goal is to broaden and stimulate research and theory through the application of findings at one level of analysis to inform, refine, and constrain inferences at another. This should not be interpreted as suggesting that research conducted within a single level of analysis is uninformative; nor are we implying that all research programs must span multiple levels of analysis. However, as we hope to illustrate in this chapter, we believe that insights can be gained through a consideration of findings and theories from other levels of analysis (see also Scherer, 1993). We focus in particular on two theoretical issues important to the study of affect and social cognition—the relation between positive and negative affect and the rerepresentation of evaluative mechanisms across different levels of the neuraxis.

WHY SOCIAL NEUROSCIENCE?

In addition to the possibility of new theoretical insights, a social neuroscience perspective is important in the context of current research emphasizing neural and genetic explanations. The growth of these disciplines appears to have encouraged reductionistic explanations by both scientists and the general public. People now talk about the "gene that causes" or the "gene for" depression, breast cancer, schizophrenia, homosexuality, and so on (for a discussion, see Anderson & Scott, 1999; Miller, 1996).

Such discussions often imply that the identification of a genetic marker is equivalent to a complete understanding of the phenomenon. Genetic research is clearly informative, but phenotypic expression is influenced by both the genotype and the social environment (Gottleib, 1998). An overreliance on reductionistic approaches will likely obscure important information contained in other levels of analysis.

The potential benefits of a social neuroscience perspective are also suggested by the complexity of the phenomena that interest psychologists, such as affect and social cognition. Cacioppo and Berntson (1992) describe three specific organizing principles that address these complexities. The first is the principle of *multiple determinism*, which states that a target event at one level of analysis may have multiple antecedents within or across structural levels of organization. This suggests that a single affective response, such as a self-report that one feels happy, may have multiple antecedents both within and across such diverse levels as the immediate social context, the larger cultural context, the individual's personal history, and constraints of the relevant neurophysiological systems, to name just a few.

The second principle, that of *nonadditive determinism*, states that properties of the whole are not always predictable from properties of the individual parts until properties of the whole have been studied and understood across levels of organization. That is, a phenomenon may not be fully comprehensible until it is viewed across multiple levels of organization. The relation of positive and negative affect, as we illustrate in the next section, may represent an instance in which the order in the data is more clearly revealed when findings on subjective experience are combined with findings on the underlying neural mechanisms.

Finally, the principle of *reciprocal determinism* states that factors operating at different levels of analysis can mutually influence one another. Reciprocal determinism suggests, for example, that we should consider not only how the neurophysiological substrates of the affect system work to produce subjective experience, but also how prior experience and cognitive appraisals may influence specific neurophysiological mechanisms. Together, these three principles reinforce the importance of examining affect from multiple levels of organization.

THE SEPARABILITY OF POSITIVE
AND NEGATIVE AFFECT

One of the more active areas of research on the affect system has concerned the structure of affective experience. Diener (1999) argues that this represents a fundamental question because its resolution has implications for such a wide range of issues, including the understanding of discrete emotions, personality, and cognition. At times, the discussion of the structure of affect has been viewed as a debate between psychologists who argue that affect is bipolar, and that positivity and negativity are reciprocally activated (e.g., Russell, 1979), and psychologists who argue that positivity and negativity are completely orthogonal factors (e.g., Diener & Emmons, 1985; Warr, Barter, & Brownbridge, 1983; Watson & Tellegen, 1985; Zevon & Tellegen, 1982). We believe that proponents on both sides of this debate are describing important but incomplete aspects of the affect system.

Any comprehensive theory of affect should be able to account for the large body of research showing that subjective affective experience and the language we use to describe our affective reactions can often be described by a single bipolar valence continuum, with high positive affect on one end and high negative affect on the other (e.g., Russell, 1979; Russell & Carroll, 1999; Russell & Feldman Barrett, 1999). In traditional bipolar models, positive and negative reactions are treated as operating in a reciprocal manner, such that increases in positivity are viewed as functionally equivalent to decreases in negativity, and vice versa. Most dimensional representations of subjective affective experience also include a second bipolar arousal or activation dimension, which refers to a subjective sense of mobilization or energy. Although researchers differ somewhat in the exact nature of the resulting valence × arousal circumplex (for reviews, see Larsen & Diener, 1992; Russell & Feldman Barrett, 1999), a bipolar valence dimension is common to all schemes.

At the same time, there is a large body of research suggesting that positive and negative affective reactions do not always operate in a reciprocal manner, and therefore can be separable. For example, reactions to political candidates reveal that disliking a candidate does not necessarily imply that the candidate is not also liked (Abelson, Kinder, Peters, & Fiske, 1982). Holbrook, Krosnick, Visser, Gardner, and Cacioppo (1999) analyzed cross-sectional (1972–1996) and longitudinal (1980–1996) National Election Study data. In both analyses, they found that the bipolar model (in which there is a single, linear valence dimension with positive and negative affect on opposite poles) did not provide a parsimonious account of voter sentiments or behavior. A study of undergraduate women's reactions to their dormitory roommates show similar results (Cacioppo, Gardner, & Berntson, 1997). Participants in this study rated how they felt toward their roommates using the Positive and Negative Affect Schedule (PANAS; Watson, Clark, & Tellegen, 1988), which provides separate self-report measures of positive and negative affective reactions. As with the reactions to political candidates, positivity and negativity elicited by the roommate were unrelated ($r = -.09$), suggesting stochastic independence. In addition, positivity and negativity appeared functionally independent; level of positivity but not negativity predicted the extent of friendship and amount of time spent with the roommate.

Separable motivational substrates have also been incorporated into a number of theories that deal with a range of affective and motivational issues. One example is work by Higgins and colleagues on regulatory focus, which suggests that behavior is guided by two motivational substrates labeled *promotion-focus* and *prevention-focus* (for a review, see Higgins, 1997). Chronic individual differences and situational fluctuations in these two motivations are thought to produce differences in sensitivity to positive and negative outcomes, with promotion-focus encouraging stronger approach than withdrawal motivations, and prevention-focus encouraging stronger withdrawal than approach motivations (Forster, Higgins, & Idson, 1998).

Separable positive and negative motivational substrates have also been observed or incorporated into explanations of phenomena as diverse as uplifts and hassles (Gannon, Vaux, Rhodes, & Luchetta, 1992; Zautra, Reich, & Gaurnaccia, 1990), self-knowledge (Showers, 1995; Showers & King, 1996), self-efficacy (Zautra, Hoffman, & Reich, 1997), personality processes (Costa & MacRae, 1980; Rusting & Larsen, 1998), achievement motivation (Elliot & Church, 1997; Elliot & Harackiewicz, 1996), organ donations (Cacioppo & Gardner, 1993), emotional expressivity (Gross & John, 1997), interpersonal relationships (Berry & Hansen, 1996), mood (Bradburn, 1969; Diener & Emmons, 1985; Goldstein & Strube, 1994; Warr, Barter, & Brownbridge, 1983; Watson & Tellegen, 1985; Zevon & Tellegen, 1982), and intergroup discrimination (Blanz, Mummendey, & Otten, 1997, Brewer, 1996; Katz & Hass, 1988).

The Evaluative Space Model

Cacioppo and colleagues (Cacioppo & Berntson, 1994; Cacioppo, Gardner, & Berntson, 1997) propose a general conceptual framework, termed the *evaluative space model* (ESM), within which to organize these divergent empirical findings. According to the ESM, a stimulus may simultaneously vary in terms of the strength of positive evaluative activation (i.e., positivity) and the strength of negative evaluative activation (i.e., negativity) it evokes. Thus, the activation of positivity and negativity at early stages of affective processing is conceptualized as potentially unfolding in parallel. The positive and negative activation functions are further conceived to be negatively accelerating functions with distinct coefficients, offsets, and exponents. Furthermore, although the consequences of positive and negative activation are generally antagonistic, a stimulus can evoke one of three modes of evaluative activation: (1) reciprocal activation, in which the same stimulus or environment has opposing effects on the activation of positivity and negativity; (2) uncoupled activation, in which the stimulus affects only positive or negative evaluative activation; and (3) coactivated or nonreciprocal activation, in which the same stimulus increases (or decreases) activation of both positivity and negativity. The three modes of activation are represented in the bivariate evaluative plane in Fig. 3.1.

Whereas the presence of two separate evaluative channels suggests an efficient system in which positive and negative information is simultaneously processed by the positive and negative motivational substrates, respectively, the affect system evolved to ultimately provide situation-appropriate

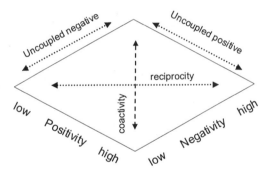

FIG. 3.1. The bivariate evaluative plane. The left axis represents the level of excitatory activation of positive evaluative processes (labeled "Positivity") and the right axis represents the level of excitatory negative evaluative processes (labeled "Negativity"). Along each axis, the level of activity increases with movement away from the front axis intersection. The dotted diagonal extending from the left to the right of the axis intersection depicts the diagonal of reciprocal control (labeled "Reciprocity"). The dashed diagonal extending from the back to the front axis intersection depicts the diagonal of nonrepirpocal control (labeled "Coactivity"). The arrows alongside the axes represent uncoupled changes in positive or negative evaluative processing. These diagonals and axes and vectors parallel to them illustrate major modes of evaluative activation. From "Relationship between attitudes and evaluative space: A critical review, with emphasis on the separability of positive and negative substrates," by J. T. Cacioppo & G. G. Berntson, 1994, Psychological Bulletin, 115, p. 402.

behavioral guides. Although it is possible to physically vacillate between approach and withdrawal, bivalent action tendencies are both the most efficient and adaptive. For this reason, stimulus processing continues after registration on the bivariate evaluative plane (Fig. 3.1) to include integration of the underlying evaluative substrates into a single net affective response or predisposition. Mapping of the underlying bivariate evaluative plane onto the associated net affective response surface is shown in Fig. 3.2. As noted previously, although positivity and negativity can be activated separately, they generally have antagonistic effects on response predispositions.

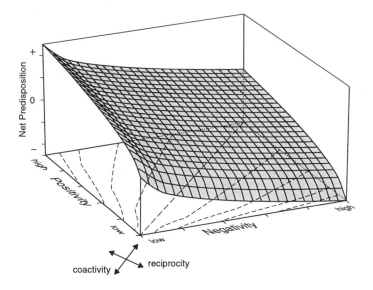

FIG. 3.2. The bivariate evaluative plane and its associated affective response surface. The surface represents the net affective predisposition of an individual toward (+) or away from (−) the target stimulus. Net predisposition is expressed in relative units. The point on the surface overlying the left axis intersection represents the maximally positive predisposition evoked by the target stimulus, and the point on the surface overlying the right axis intersection represents the maximally negative predisposition toward the target stimulus. The point on the surface overlying the left axis intersection represents the maximally positive disposition evoked by the target stimulus, and the point on the surface overlying the right axis intersection represents the maximally negative disposition toward the target stimulus. From "Relationship between attitudes and evaluative space: A critical review, with emphasis on the separability of positive and negative substrates," by J. T. Cacioppo & G. G. Berntson, 1994, Psychological Bulletin, 115, p. 412.

In addition to behavioral considerations, psychological factors also likely promote the integration of the two evaluative channels into a single, bipolar net affective response predisposition. When assigning psychological meaning, bipolar representations tend to be most stable and harmonious. For instance, the coactivation of positivity and negativity aroused by choosing between two equally desirable alternatives is often resolved though an exaggeration of the positive features of the chosen alternative and of the negative features of the unchosen alternative (Brehm, 1956; Schultz, Leveille, & Lepper, 1999).

The bipolar nature of the net affective response surface may account for the large number of findings suggesting that affective experience is bipolar; measures of subjective affective experience typically sample the net affective response predisposition surface. However, it is important to note that the affective response surface in Fig. 3.2 represents a behavioral or psychological endpoint, and not necessarily the underlying affective process. The ESM highlights the importance of distinguishing behavioral and psychological endpoints from the bivariate evaluative mechanisms that give rise to such endpoints.

Neural Substrates

Although the ESM is a model of the psychological operation of the affect system, these psychological processes are nevertheless ultimately achieved through the operation of underlying neurophysiological mechanisms. Research on the neural mechanisms associated with affect and emotion may therefore prove informative to psychological theories of affect. A review of neurochemical and neuroanatomic research reveals that separable positive and negative motivational substrates observed at the psychological level are likely the result of separable underlying positive and negative evaluative substrates at the neural level (cf. Lang, Bradley, & Cuthbert, 1990).

An approach/reward system has been associated with mesolimbic dopamine pathways, which originate in the ventral tegmentum and project to the nucleus accumbens. Research supporting this conclusion indicates that (1) animals self-stimulate to this pathway in proportion to the density of dopamine receptors surrounding the simulating electrode tip, (2) dopamine metabolism is also increased after such stimulation, and (3) dopamine antagonists decrease self-stimulation (Fibiger & Phillips, 1988; Fiorini, Coury, Fibiger, & Phillips, 1993; Wise & Rompre, 1989). In addition, the rewarding properties of some addictive drugs, such as cocaine and amphetamines, have been explained via their action in this pathway (Fibiger & Phillips,

1988; Hoebel, Herndandex, Mark, & Pothos, 1992; Wise, 1996; Wise & Rompre, 1989). Available human data is also consistent with the rewarding properties of the dopamine pathway. Trait levels of positivity are related to functional activity in dopamine systems, such that higher trait positivity has been associated with greater dopamine agonist reactivity, as measured by decreased prolactin secretion (Depue, Luciana, Arbisi, Collins, & Leon, 1994).

Whereas a dopaminergic system is implicated in appetitive motivation, an amygdala substrate has been implicated in aversion. In animals, lesions to the amygdala attenuate reactions to conditioned aversive stimuli (Davis, 1992a, 1992b; Hitchcock & Davis, 1986; LeDoux, Cicchetti, Xagoraris, & Romanski, 1990), and stimulation of the amygdala produces punishment effects (Halgran, 1982). In humans, functional neuroimaging reveals activation of the amygdala during the presentation of negative stimuli (Irwin et al., 1996; Whalen et al., 1998). There is also evidence that bilateral damage to the amygdala selectively impairs the ability to recognize facial expressions of fear and decreases perceptions their intensity (Adolphs, Tranel, Damasio, & Damasio, 1994, 1995).

Central nervous system mechanisms associated with the affect system are no doubt complex, and their full explication will likely reveal the involvement of other structures and neurochemical systems. Nevertheless, the extant neurochemical and neuroanatomic research is consistent with the separability of positive and negative motivational substrates at the psychological level. In addition to complementing analyses at more psychological levels of the affect system, neurophysiological analyses also provide insights that are not always possible with self-report data. Whereas self-reported affective experiences are particularly useful in describing conscious, subjective experience, they may not be the best indicators of the process or operations of the affect system. Direct measurements of physiological processes associated with the operation of the affect system can provide important insights into processes not unambiguously revealed in self-report data.

Negativity Bias

The complementary nature of self-report and neurophysiological assessments is illustrated by research on the negativity bias. A greater sensitivity to negative than to comparably extreme positive information has been demonstrated in a range of situations, including impression formation (Anderson, 1965; Fiske, 1980; Skowronski & Carlston, 1989) and risk-taking (Kahneman & Tversky, 1984). What is unclear from this corpus of self-reported reactions is the stage at which the negativity bias is introduced. To the extent that the negativity bias is an inherent property of the underlying affect system itself, as opposed to some form of response bias, it should be present early in evaluative processing. In order to assess this, Ito, Larsen, Smith, and Cacioppo (1998) recorded event-related brain potentials (ERPs) as participants made evaluations of a range of stimuli. A particular potential of the ERP, the late-positive potential (LPP), is sensitive to evaluative categorization processes but is relatively insensitive to response output operations (Cacioppo, Crites, Berntson, & Coles, 1993; Cacioppo, Crites, Gardner, & Berntson, 1994; Crites, Cacioppo, Gardner, & Berntson, 1995). In particular, the size of the LPP increases in response to changes in evaluation. For example, a positive stimulus embedded within a context of negative items (evaluative inconsistency) produces a larger LPP than a negative item in a negative context (evaluative consistency). Evidence of the negativity bias in the ERP responses would therefore suggest that it is introduced early in evaluative processing.

ERPs were recorded as participants viewed positive, negative, and neutral pictures embedded within sequences of other neutral pictures. Consistent with prior research showing the LPP's sensitivity to evaluative categorization processes, stimuli that were evaluatively inconsistent with the more frequently presented neutral stimuli were associated with larger LPPs. That is, both positive and negative stimuli were associated with larger LPPs than were evaluatively consistent neutral stimuli. However, the evaluative categorization of negative stimuli was associated with a larger amplitude LPP than was the evaluative categorization of positive stimuli, even though both were equally probable, evaluatively extreme, and arousing. These results suggest that the negativity bias is introduced early in evaluative processing. They also demonstrate how physiological measures can be used to assess the operation of psychological processes that would not be easily revealed with more traditional self-report measures.

Summary

This review of the structure of the affect system suggests a flexible and functionally adaptive system. At the level of underlying evaluative substrates, the presence of two separate channels allows for efficient parallel processing of both relevant safety- and threat-related cues. The system also accommodates important behavioral and psychological considerations through the integration of the bivariate evaluative plane into a single net affective response predisposition (Fig. 3.2). We should note that the net affective response surface represents only one of the two instances of bipolarity in the ESM. Bipolarity may also occur at the level of the underlying bivariate evaluative plane in the form of the reciprocal mode of evaluative activation. The presence of separable motivational substrates is therefore not inconsistent with demonstrations of bipolarity. Bipolarity is obtained from sampling the net affective response predisposition surface and/or sampling an instance in which reciprocal activation is occurring.

The challenge before us, as we see it, is to better understand what determines the underlying mode of activation. Also important is understanding consistency motives that work to produce bipolar psychological endpoints and instances in which inconsistency is not resolved to a bipolar endpoint. Such a state corresponds to ambivalence, and there are instances in which coactivation of positivity and negativity are maintained rather that resolved to a bipolar framework (Abelson et al., 1982; Bell & Esses, 1997; Katz & Hass, 1988; MacDonald & Zanna, 1998; Priester & Petty, 1996; Thompson, Zanna, & Griffin, 1995). The three modes of evaluative activation also have implications for understanding interactions among affective and cognitive processes, reminding us that positive and negative affective states should not necessarily be expected to produce reciprocal effects on cognition; the separability of positive and negative affective substrates indicates that each may be associated with distinguishable effects on cognition. To the extent that positive and negative affect operate in either an uncoupled of nonreciprocal mode, the effects of positive and negative affect on cognition should not be expected to mirror one another.

REREPRESENTATION OF EVALUATIVE PROCESSES ACROSS THE NEURAXIS

Research reviewed in the previous section suggests that the affect system is composed of separable positive and negative evaluative substrates. In this section, we discuss research suggesting that these evaluative mechanisms are rerepresented at different levels of the neuraxis. Stated differently, the ability to perform positive and negative evaluative categorizations is distributed across all levels of neural organization, from the spinal cord to higher cortical functions. This implies that both evaluations of the same stimulus or event and interactions among evaluative and cognitive processes can unfold simultaneously at multiple levels of the neuraxis.

The greatest flexibility and variability in evaluative mechanisms is shown at the highest levels of the central nervous system. Nevertheless, elementary evaluative mechanisms are present in the spinal cord, as seen in simple approach–withdrawal reflexes in animals and humans with spinal cord injuries (Grill & Berridge, 1985; Steiner, 1979). Although reflexive responses at this level can be modified via conditioning (Grill & Berridge, 1985; Berridge, 1991), a wider range of behavior, decreased stimulus dependence, and greater contextual sensitivity in evaluative mechanisms is observed at higher levels of the neuraxis. To illustrate, an animal with a lesion separating the brain from the spinal cord may show limb withdrawal from an aversive stimulus, but an intact animal may also display global escape behavior, vocalizations, or aggression. In addition, the behaviors may persist long after the limb is removed from the noxious stimulus in the form of agitation or escape attempts (see review by Berntson, Boysen, & Cacioppo, 1993) .

Berntson et al. (1993) note that this rerepresentation of evaluative mechanisms results in three important features. First, evaluative dispositions that arise from different levels of the neuraxis may be sensitive to only partially overlapping features of the environment. Thus, rather than representing an inefficient redundancy, the multiplicity of evaluative mechanisms produces a system in which lower-level processors are capable of responding to important classes of stimuli without intervention from higher-level functions. Whereas these low-level evaluative mechanisms may be relatively inflexible, they are efficient and place few burdens on higher-level processing operations. Pain processing provides an example of the efficiency of these lower-level mechanisms. In response to a painful stimulus, lower-level processing may predominate and produce a stereotyped yet efficient withdrawal of the limb. Involvement of higher levels of processing at this point is not necessary, and might serve only to delay the critical response.

A second important consequence of the rerepresentation of evaluative mechanisms is that evaluative processing at different levels of the neuraxis may influence different aspects of behavior. This suggests that different evaluative mechanisms may be best indexed by different types of measures. Returning to the example of pain perception, immediate limb response and later vocalizations are different behaviors that may derive from different evaluative mechanisms. In addition, these different aspects of behavior may be associated with differences in awareness of the source of an affective state. The relatively efficient and stereotypical processing of lower level evaluative mechanisms may allow them to operate largely outside of conscious awareness. Affective dispositions derived from lower evaluative mechanisms may therefore be consciously experienced, but their (true) source may not be appreciated (see also Gazzaniga & LeDoux, 1978; Nisbett & Wilson, 1977). Accurate awareness of the stimuli that elicit an affective reaction may be more likely with higher-level evaluative mechanisms.

Additional behavioral differences may also result through the use of diverging neural mechanisms at different neuraxial levels. This is seen in the control of facial musculature, where volitionally induced expressions are conveyed via the pyramidal tracts, whereas spontaneous emotional expressions use a separate, phylogenically older, extrapyramidal system (Rinn, 1984). Interesting behavioral dissociations are associated with damage to one but not the other pathway. Brain lesions that affect the extrapyramidal system compromise the ability to display spontaneous emotional facial responses but leave intact the ability to move facial muscles in response to verbal commands. Lesions to areas associated with the pyramidal tract can leave patients unable to voluntarily move the face on the side contralateral to the lesion. Contractions on this contralateral side will occur, however, in response to emotionally evocative stimulation (for a review, see Rinn, 1984).

The third implication of the rerepresented evaluative system is the potential for interactions among the mechanisms. Such interactions can be seen in an experiment in which evaluative preferences (attitudes) were created through classical conditioning (Cacioppo, Marshall-Goodell, Tassinary, & Petty, 1992). Familiar words and novel nonwords, matched for physical attributes and affective tone, served as stimuli. Electric shock was paired with either the words, nonwords, or with both words and nonwords. In a second block, the shocks were removed and participants rated their liking for all stimuli. A separate sample of participants received only a description of the experimental paradigm and were asked to predict their liking for the stimuli. These simulation participants predicted a simple conditioning effect in which stimuli that had been paired with shocks, whether they were words or nonwords, were disliked the most. By contrast, results from the main experiment revealed stronger conditioned negative reactions to nonwords than words. These results suggest that the evaluative dispositions previously associated with the words, and likely represented at higher levels of the neuraxis, attenuated conditioning effects operating at lower levels of the neuraxis.

Biasing effects of higher evaluative processes can also be seen in affective startle eyeblink modification. The eyeblink is one of the most reliable components of the startle response, which occurs following the presentation of intense and, unexpected stimuli. Although the eyeblink is a relatively obligatory aspect of the startle response, the intensity of the reflex can nevertheless be modified by higher-level evaluative processing. In particular, the size of the eyeblink varies as a function of one's current affective state.

Presentation of startle probes to participants as they view positive, negative, and neutral pictures reveals that negative states potentiate and positive states inhibit startle eyeblink relative to neutral states (Lang, Bradley, & Cuthbert, 1990, 1992; Lang, 1995).

Startle eyeblink modification following the presentation of hedonically toned stimuli has been explained by differential priming of the two motivational systems (Lang et al., 1990, 1992; Lang, 1995), which is thought to increase the likelihood and potential strength of responding of the activated system while simultaneously decreasing the likelihood and potential strength of responding for the nonengaged system. A negative stimulus that precedes a startle probe is therefore thought to activate the aversive system. The subsequent match between the already primed aversive system and the defensive startle reflex elicited by a startling stimulus results in potentiation of startle eyeblinks (reflex-affect match). By contrast, a positive affective foreground results in a mismatch between the valence of the affective foreground and the reflexive response, resulting in inhibition of startle eyeblinks (a reflex-affect mismatch).

Finally, although speculative, there are also implications of the rerepresentation of evaluative mechanisms for interactions between affect and cognition, suggesting that such interactions may occur at multiple levels of the neuraxis and with differing levels of awareness. Functionally, the multiple opportunities for affect and cognition to interact should maximally tune cognitive processes to the evaluative implications of the surrounding environment.

Feeling without Knowing

As we have noted, a theoretical implication of the multiplicity of evaluative mechanisms is that an individual may come to feel something without fully comprehending the source of those feelings. This was suggested in the conditioning experiment described above by the difference between expectations in the simulation experiment and actual results (Cacioppo et al., 1992). There have also been numerous other demonstrations of evaluative and affective processing outside of conscious awareness (e.g., Bargh, Chaiken, Govender, & Pratto, 1992; Fazio, Jackson, Dunton, & Williams, 1995; Fazio, Sanbonmatsu, Powell, & Kardes, 1986; Murphy & Zajonc, 1993; Wittenbrink, Judd, & Park, 1997; for a review, see Bargh, 1996; Wegner & Bargh, 1998).

Automatic affective and evaluative effects suggest that lower-level evaluative mechanisms automatically process stimuli and environmental contexts, even when we do not have an explicit evaluation goal. Consistent with this hypothesis, we obtained ERP (event-related brain potential) evidence of implicit evaluative categorizations (Ito & Cacioppo, in press). Recall that the LPP (late positive potential) is sensitive to changes in evaluative categorization. This same potential is also sensitive to changes in nonevaluative categorizations, such as the pitch of an auditory stimulus (Donchin, 1981; Donchin & Coles, 1988). Categorically inconsistent stimuli, such as a high-pitched tone embedded within a series of low-pitched tones, elicit a larger LPP than categorically consistent ones.

In order to assess implicit evaluative categorization processes, Ito and Cacioppo (in press) recorded ERPs as participants viewed photographs of stimuli that simultaneously varied both in valence (i.e., an evaluative categorization) and along a people–animal/objects dimension (i.e., a nonevaluative categorization). All participants viewed the same stimuli, but half were instructed to perform an evaluative categorization task by classifying stimuli as positive or negative. The other half of the participants performed a nonevaluative categorization task by classifying stimuli as showing people or animals and objects. No explicit mention was made of differences along the non-task-relevant dimension (e.g., differences along the people–animal/objects dimension were not mentioned to participants performing the evaluative categorization task).

Prior results led us to predict variations in the size of the LPP as a function of both the *explicit* evaluative and nonevaluative classifications, which were obtained. Among participants performing evaluative classifications, evaluatively inconsistent stimuli (e.g., a positive picture embedded within negative pictures) produced larger LPPs than evaluatively consistent stimuli (e.g., a positive picture embedded within positive pictures). Similarly, among participants performing nonevaluative classifications, nonevaluatively inconsistent stimuli (e.g., a picture with a person embedded within animal/object pictures) produced larger LPPs than nonevaluatively consistent stimuli (e.g., a picture with a person embedded within people pictures). However, we also obtained evidence of *implicit* evaluative categorization. Among participants explicitly instructed to categorize the stimuli along the people–animal/object dimension, the LPP was nevertheless sensitive to changes along the evaluative dimension.[1] These results suggest that lower-level evaluative mechanisms automatically process the

---

[1]There was also evidence of implicit nonevaluative categorization, such that the LPP was sensitive to variations in the people–animal/object dimension even among participants who were explicitly categorizing along the evaluative dimension.

environment in terms of its affective significance, even when higher-order processing goals are directing attention to other stimulus features. The implicit evaluative categorization even revealed evidence of a negativity bias, such that negative stimuli spontaneously received greater processing resources than positive ones. Coupled with the results of Ito et al. (1998), these results suggest that the negativity bias occurs early in evaluative processing, both when participants explicitly intend to evaluate stimuli in their environment and when evaluative categorizations occur more spontaneously. Such spontaneous dedication of greater processing resources to negative information (see also Pratto & John, 1991) may in turn help contribute to the more systematic, bottom-up processing that has been associated with negative affective states (Forgas, 1992, 1998; Schwarz, 1990).

Applications to Implicit and Explicit Prejudice

Implicit evaluative processes and the implications of multiple evaluative mechanisms may be especially relevant to issues of stereotyping and prejudice, and to research on implicit and explicit forms of prejudice in particular. Interest in implicit and explicit prejudice was stimulated by Devine (1989), who argued that an outgroup member can automatically activate negative, culturally transmitted stereotypical beliefs. At the same time, she noted, an individual may possess personal beliefs that are inconsistent with the negative stereotype. Devine suggested that these personal beliefs can result in inhibition of the negative automatic responses and initiation of new responses. Although inhibited from explicit expression, the automatically activated negative responses may nevertheless be detected on more automatic or implicit measures.

Cacioppo et al. (1992) elaborated on this theme by specifying a mechanism by which implicit negative associations with the outgroup could occur, and linking the maintenance of such associations in the face of more egalitarian personal beliefs to the rerepresentation of evaluative mechanisms. Their theorizing is based on their classical conditioning results, which, as previously discussed, revealed stronger conditioned affective associations to unfamiliar (nonword) than familiar (word) stimuli. In the domain of intergroup relations, racial outgroup members are typically less familiar than ingroup members (Linville, Fischer, & Salovey, 1989). These unfamiliar outgroup members may also be occasionally paired with negative or aversive cues such as a stereotypical negative portrayal in a movie. Even though ingroup members may also occasionally be paired with negative cues, the effects of familiarity on conditioning suggest that negative reactions are more likely to become associated with the racial outgroup members.

The inability of simulation participants in the Cacioppo et al. (1992) study to predict this familiarity effect suggests that differential racial conditioning could easily go unnoticed. Moreover, research on feelings without awareness indicates that individuals may confabulate reasons for affective arousal if the true source is unclear (Gazzaniga & LeDoux, 1978; Nisbett & Wilson, 1977). In the domain of prejudice, this suggests that we might construct rationalizations for classically conditioned prejudice, further obscuring the true source of the negative associations.

Like Devine (1989), Cacioppo et al. (1992) assume that individuals may develop more egalitarian personal beliefs that motivate them to control prejudiced responses. The most optimistic proposition is that the newer, more egalitarian personal beliefs and affective reactions will replace the older, negative beliefs and affective reactions. Behavior would then be influenced by only our more egalitarian beliefs. However, the multiplicity of evaluative mechanisms suggests that egalitarian personal beliefs and classically conditioned (negative) evaluative dispositions could easily coexist because they might operate at different levels of the neuraxis (Cacioppo et al., 1992).

Theorizing about implicit and explicit aspects of prejudice spurred the development of measures that are designed to assess the more automatic, implicit processes (e.g., Fazio et al., 1995; Wittenbrink et al., 1997). Comparisons between these and more traditional explicit measures (e.g., questionnaires) have yielded inconsistent results, with some studies reporting a dissociation between implicit and explicit measures (e.g., Banaji & Hardin, 1996; Dovidio, Kawakami, Johnson, Johnson, & Howard, 1997, studies 1 and 3; Fazio et al., 1995, Study 3; Greenwald, McGhee, & Schwartz, 1998, Study 3; Vanman, Paul, Ito, & Miller, 1997, studies 1 and 2) and others reporting associations between the two (e.g., Greenwald et al., 1998, Study 2; Dovidio et al., 1997, Study 2; Vanman et al., 1997, Study 3; Wittenbrink et al., 1997). On the surface, such inconsistencies are troubling. However, the first two features of a rerepresented evaluative system previously discussed—that different mechanisms may be sensitive to different stimulus features, and that different measures may index different mechanisms—anticipates this situation. The implicit and explicit measures may be indexing different evaluative mechanisms that are sensitive to different types of information.

The multiplicity of evaluative mechanisms suggests that we may therefore wish to recast our question from "Are implicit and explicit measures related?" to "*When* should we expect implicit and explicit measures to be related?" That is, when should we expect evaluative operations at different levels of the neuraxis to produce similar results and when should we expect divergence between the mechanisms? The answer to this question may depend on the types of measures being used, characteristics of the person, and features of the situation. In addition, as the number of different implicit measures increases, the issue of how different implicit measures relate to each other is increasingly raised. Just as implicit and explicit measures may index different levels of evaluative processing, so too may different implicit measures. Consequently, we should not necessarily expect relations between implicit measures, but we should make an effort to better understand what each is measuring.

Different Evaluative Mechanisms or Decreased Activation with Practice?

Our discussion of multiple evaluative mechanisms has suggested that implicit and explicit evaluative responses to outgroup members may represent evaluative mechanisms operating at different level of the neuraxis. Before leaving this topic, we should note an additional way in which implicit and explicit processes may differ. This suggestion comes from recent neuroimaging research investigating semantic repetition priming. In these studies, participants are required to retrieve certain semantic information multiple times, whereas other similar information is retrieved only once. For example, participants may be asked to judge whether words and pictures represent something that is living or nonliving, with some stimuli repeated multiple times and other stimuli presented only once (Wagner, Desmond, Demb, Glover, & Gabrieli, 1997). Behaviorally, repetition priming facilitates semantic encoding, as seen in faster decision times. Neurophysiologically, positron emission tomography (PET) and functional magnetic resonance imaging (fMRI) reveal a decrease in the activation of process-specific brain areas. Areas activated in initial task performance show a decrease in activation for repeated but not novel stimuli (Buckner, Raichle, Miezen, & Petersen, 1996; Gabrieli et al., 1996; Wagner et al., 1997). Such decreased activation suggests that repeated semantic processing of the same stimulus results in more efficient processing of that stimulus, achieved possibly through decreases in the duration and/or intensity of activity, compared to initial semantic encoding (Wagner et al., 1997).

These experiments used relatively simply semantic decisions (e.g., living/nonliving, abstract/concrete) and simple stimuli (e.g., words, line drawings) and examined repetition effects over relatively short retention intervals (e.g., minutes, days). Nevertheless, they suggest that repeated semantic associations produce changes in neurophysiological activation. To the extent that implicit and explicit prejudice differ in how well practiced they are (Devine, 1989), we might expect these processes to show similar differences in neurophysiological activation. These differences in activation could occur in addition to, or instead of, the differences in evaluative mechanisms suggested previously. It is clearly too early to determine the relative contribution of changes in neurophysiological activation and the rerepresentation of evaluative mechanisms to implicit and explicit prejudice, but this review does suggest future avenues for research. In addition, although we use prejudice as the specific example, the issues we discuss could apply more broadly to implicit and explicit evaluations in other domains.

Summary

The rerepresentation of evaluative mechanisms across levels of the neuraxis is a fundamental neurobehavioral organizing principle that also has important psychological consequences. One implication we discuss is that the same environment or stimulus may invoke different evaluative dispositions at different levels of the neuraxis. This is what may be occurring in studies of prejudice that reveal dissociations between implicit and explicit measures. In one such example, Vanman et al. (1997) had White participants imagine themselves in cooperative interactions with Black and White partners. Participants reported liking the Black partners more than the White partners, but facial electromyography revealed patterns of covert facial muscle activity indicative of greater negative affect toward Blacks than Whites. At first glance, these results seem inconsistent—how can the participants both like and dislike Black partners? The rerepresentation of evaluative mechanisms suggests that the measures may reflect different evaluative mechanisms and that, rather than thinking of a stimulus as producing a single affective response, it will be informative to study how evaluations of the same stimulus operate simultaneously across the neuraxis. An appreciation of the rerepresentation of evaluative mechanisms may also prove useful in understanding interactions between affect and cognition, suggesting that cognition may be influenced by multiple evaluative processes operating with differing levels of awareness at multiple neuraxial levels.

CONCLUSION

In our approach to the study of affect, we use findings from more bio-logical approaches to understand the operation of the affect system at the psychological level. This application of a social neuroscience perspective both provides useful insight and highlights potential important avenues for future research. When we look across levels of analysis, both psychologi-cal and more biological approaches converge in suggesting that separable positive and negative evaluative substrates underlie the affect system. It is important to distinguish these structural and functional aspects from behav-ioral and psychological endpoints. The latter are an important topic in their own right, but the structure of behavioral and psychological output does not unambiguously inform us about the structure and function of the sys-tem that produces them. The affect system has evolved to produce bipolar endpoints because they provide both clear bivalent action tendencies and harmonious and stable subjective experiences. This bipolar endpoint, how-ever, is derived from the activation of two intervening evaluative substrates that can operate in one of three different modes of evaluative activation: reciprocal, uncoupled, and coactivated. Measurement of the bipolar, net affective response carries important information but fails to reveal the rela-tionship between the underlying evaluative substrates. Moreover, sampling of only the affective endpoints does not allow us to address important is-sues about the bivariate evaluative activation, such as the antecedents and consequences of the different modes of activation. It may be especially informative to attend to how both the bipolar psychological and behav-ioral endpoints and the underlying bivariate activation impact on cognitive processing.

The rerepresentation of evaluative mechanisms across levels of the neu-raxis provides a second reason for greater attention to the structure and function of the affect system. Because evaluative dispositions that arise from different levels of the neuraxis may (a) be sensitive to only partially overlapping features of the environment, (b) influence different aspects of behavior, and (c) interact across levels of the neuraxis, the affect sys-tem is unlikely to be fully appreciated from measures that sample only a single endpoint. Advances in recording and measurement techniques, such as neuroimaging and reaction time–based implicit evaluation measures, should allow us greater insight into the multiple evaluative mechanisms, and in so doing foster a greater understanding of their interactions. As we more fully understand this multilevel system, we may also more fully appreciate the multiple levels at which interactions between affective and cognitive processing can occur.

REFERENCES

Abelson, R. P., Kinder, D. R., Peters, M. D., & Fiske, S. T. (1982). Affective and semantic components in political person perception. *Journal of Personality and Social Psychology, 42*, 619–630.

Adolphs, R., Tranel, D., Damasio, H., & Damasio, A. (1994). Impaired recognition of emotion in facial expressions following bilateral damage to the human amygdala. *Nature, 372*, 669–672.

Adolphs, R., Tranel, D., Damasio, H., & Damasio, A. (1995). Fear and the human amygdala. *Journal of Neuroscience, 15*, 5879–5891.

Anderson, N. B., & Scott, P. A. (1999). Making the case for psychophysiology during the era of molecular biology. *Psychophysiology, 36*, 1–13.

Anderson, N. H. (1965). Averaging versus adding as a stimulus–combination rule in impression formation. *Journal of Personality and Social Psychology, 2*, 1–9.

Banaji, M., & Hardin, C. (1996). Implicit gender stereotyping in judgements of fame. *Psychological Science, 7*, 136–141.

Bargh, J. A. (1996). Automaticity in social psychology. In E. T. Higgins & A. W. Kruglanski (Eds.), *Social psychology: Handbook of basic principles* (pp. 169–183). New York: Guilford Press.

Bargh, J. A., Chaiken, S., Govender, T., & Pratto, F. (1992). The generality of the automatic attitude activation effect. *Journal of Personality and Social Psychology, 62*, 893–912.

Bell, D. W., & Esses, V. M. (1997). Ambivalence and response amplification toward native peoples. *Journal of Applied Social Psychology, 27*, 1063–1084.

Berntson, G. G., Boysen, S. T., & Cacioppo, J. T. (1993). Neurobehavioral organization and the cardinal principle of evaluative bivalence. *Annals of the New York Academy of Sciences, 702*, 75–102.

Berridge, K. C. (1991). Modulation of taste affect by hunger, caloric satiety, and sensory-specific satiety in the rat. *Appetite, 16*, 103–120.

Berry, D. S., & Hansen, J. S. (1996). Positive affect, negative affect, and social interaction. *Journal of Personality and Social Psychology, 71*, 796–809.

Blanz, M. Mummendey, A., & Otten, S. (1997). Normative evaluations and frequency expectations regarding positive versus negative outcome allocations between groups. *European Journal of Social Psychology, 27*, 165–176.

Bradburn, N. M. (1969). *The structure of psychological well-being.* Chicago: Aldine.

Brehm, J. (1956). Post-decision changes in desirability of alternatives. *Journal of Abnormal and Social Psychology, 52*, 384–389.

Brewer, M. B. (1996). In-group favoritism: The subtle side of intergroup discrimination. In D. M. Messick & A. E. Tenbrunsel (Eds.), *Codes of conduct: Behavioral research into business ethics* (pp. 160–170). New York: Russell Sage Foundation.

Buckner, R., Raichle, M. E., Miezen, F. M., Petersen, S. E. (1996). Functional anatomic studies of memory retrieval for auditory words and visual pictures. *Journal of Neuroscience, 16*, 6219–6235.

Cacioppo, J. T., & Berntson, G. G. (1992). Social psychological contributions to the decade of the brain. *American Psychologist, 47*, 1019–1028.

Cacioppo, J. T., & Berntson, G. G. (1994). Relationship between attitudes and evaluative space: A critical review, with emphasis on the separability of positive and negative substrates. *Psychological Bulletin, 115*, 401–423.

Cacioppo, J. T., Berntson, G. G., Larsen, J. T., Poehlmann, K. M., & Ito, T. A. (2000). The psychophysiology of emotion. In M. Lewis, R. Wood, & J. M. Haviland-Jones (Eds.), *The handbook of emotions.* New York: Guilford Press.

Cacioppo, J. T., Crites, S. L. Jr., Berntson, G. G., & Coles, M. G. H. (1993). If attitudes affect how stimuli are processed, should they not affect the event-related brain potential? *Psychological Science, 4*, 108–112.

Cacioppo, J. T., Crites, S. L. Jr., Gardner, W. L., & Berntson, G. G. (1994). Bioelectrical echoes from evaluative categorizations: I. A late positive brain potential that varies as a function of trait negativity and extremity. *Journal of Personality and Social Psychology, 67*, 115–125.

Cacioppo, J. T., & Gardner, W. L. (1993). What underlies medical donor attitudes and behavior? *Health Psychology, 12,* 269–271.

Cacioppo, J. T., Gardner, W. L., & Berntson, G. G. (1997). Attitudes and evaluative space: Beyond bipolar conceptualizations and measures. *Personality and Social Psychology Review, 1,* 3–25.

Cacioppo, J. T., Marshall-Goodell, B. S., Tassinary, L. G., & Petty, R. E. (1992). Rudimentary determinants of attitudes: Classical conditioning is more effective when prior knowledge about the attitude stimulus is low than high. *Journal of Experimental Social Psychology, 28,* 207–233.

Costa, P. T., & Macrae, R. R. (1980). Influence of extraversion and neuroticism on subjective well-being: Happy and unhappy people. *Journal of Personality and Social Psychology, 38,* 668–678.

Crites, S. L. Jr., Cacioppo, J. T., Gardner, W. L., & Berntson, G. G. (1995). Bioelectrical echoes from evaluative categorizations: II. A late positive brain potential that varies as a function of attitude registration rather than attitude report. *Journal of Personality and Social Psychology, 68,* 997–1013.

Davis, M. (1992a). The role of the amygdala in conditioned fear. In J. P. Aggleton (Ed.), *The amygdala: Neurobiological aspects of emotion, memory, and mental dysfunction* (pp. 255–306). New York: Wiley Liss.

Davis, M. (1992b). The role of the amygdala in fear and anxiety. *Annual Review of Neuroscience, 15,* 353–375.

Depue, R. A., Luciana, M., Arbisi, P., Collins, P., & Leon, A. (1994). Dopamine and the structure of personality: Relation of agonist-induced dopamine activity to positive emotionality. *Journal of Personality and Social Psychology, 67,* 485–498.

Devine, P. G. (1989). Stereotypes and prejudice: Their automatic and controlled components. *Journal of Personality and Social Psychology, 56,* 5–18.

Diener, E. (1999). Introduction of the special section on the structure of emotion. *Journal of Personality and Social Psychology, 76,* 803–804.

Diener, E., & Emmons, R. A. (1985). The independence of positive and negative affect. *Journal of Personality and Social Psychology, 47,* 1105–1117.

Donchin, E. (1981). Surprise! . . . Surprise? *Psychophysiology, 18,* 493–513.

Donchin, E. & Coles, M. G. H. (1988). Is the P300 component a manifestation of context updating? *Behavioral and Brain Sciences, 11,* 357–374.

Dovidio, J. F., Kawakami, K., Johnson, C., Johnson, B., & Howard, A. (1997). On the nature of prejudice: Automatic and controlled processes. *Journal of Experimental Social Psychology, 33,* 510–540.

Elliot, A. J., & Church, M. A. (1997). A hierarchical model of approach and avoidance achievement motivation. *Journal of Personality and Social Psychology, 72,* 218–232.

Elliot, A. J., & Harackiewicz, J. M. (1996). Approach and avoidance achievement goals and intrinsic motivation: A mediational analysis. *Journal of Personality and Social Psychology, 70,* 461–475.

Fazio, R. H., Jackson, J. R., Dunton, B. C., & Williams, C. J. (1995). Variability in automatic activation as an unobtrusive measure of racial attitudes: A bona fide pipeline? *Journal of Personality and Social Psychology, 69,* 1013–1027.

Fazio, R. H., Sanbonmatsu, D. M., Powell, M. C., & Kardes, F. R. (1986). On the automatic activation of attitudes. *Journal of Personality and Social Psychology, 50,* 229–238.

Fibiger, H. C., & Phillips, A. G. (1988). Mesocorticolimbic dopamine systems and reward. *Annals of the New York Academy of Sciences, 537,* 206–215.

Fiorino, D. F., Coury, A., Fibiger, H. C., & Phillips, A. G. (1993). Electrical stimulation of reward sites in the ventral tegmental area increases dopamine transmission in the nucleus accumbens of the rat. *Behavioural Brain Research, 55,* 131–141.

Fiske, S. T. (1980). Attention and weight in person perception: The impact of negative and extreme information. *Journal of Personality and Social Psychology, 38,* 889–906.

Forgas, J. P. (1992). On bad mood and peculiar people: Affect and person typicality in impression formation. *Journal of Personanlity and Social Psychology, 62,* 863–875.

Forgas, J. P. (1995). Mood and judgment: The Affect Infusion Model (AIM). *Psychological Bulletin, 117,* 39–66.

Forgas, J. P. (1998). On being happy and mistaken: Mood effects on the fundamental attribution error. *Journal of Personality and Social Psychology, 75,* 318–331.

Forster, J., Higgins, E. T., & Idson, L. C. (1998). Approach and avoidance strength during goal attainment: Regulatory focus and the "goal looms larger" effect. *Journal of Personality and Social Psychology, 75,* 1115–1131.

Frijda, N. H. (1986). *The emotions.* New York: Cambridge University Press.

Gabrieli, J. D. E., Desmond, J. E., Demb, J. B., Wagner, A. D., Stone, M. V., Vaidya, C. J., & Glover, G. H. (1996). Functional magnetic resonance imaging of semantic memory processes in the frontal lobes. *Psychological Science, 7,* 278–283.

Gannon, L., Vaux, A., Rhodes, K., & Luchetta, T. (1992). A two-domain model of well-being: Everyday events, social support, and gender related personality factors. *Journal of Research in Personality, 26,* 288–301.

Gazzaniga, M. S., & LeDoux, J. E. (1978). *The integrated mind.* New York: Plenum Press.

Goldstein, M. D., & Strube, M. J. (1994). Independence revisited: The relation between positive and negative affect in a naturalistic setting. *Personality and Social Psychology Bulletin, 20,* 57–64.

Gottleib, G. (1998). Normally occurring environmental and behavioral influences on gene activity: From central dogma to probabilistic epigenesis. *Psychological Review, 105,* 792–802.

Greenwald, A. G., McGhee, D. E., & Schwartz, J. L. K. (1998). Measuring individual differences in implicit cognition: The Implicit Associations Test. *Journal of Personality and Social Psychology, 74,* 1464–1480.

Grill, H. J., & Berridge, K. C. (1985). Taste reactivity as a measure of the neural control of palatability. In J. M. Sprague & A. N. Epstein (Eds.), *Progress in psychobiology and physiological psychology* (Vol. II, pp. 1–16). Orlando, FL: Academic Press.

Gross, J. J., & John, O. P. (1997). Revealing feelings: Facets of emotional expressivity in self-reports, peer ratings, and behavior. *Journal of Personality and Social Psychology, 72,* 435–448.

Halgren, E. (1982). Mental phenomena induced by stimulation in the limbic system. *Human Neurobiology, 1,* 251–260.

Higgins, E. T. (1997). Beyond pleasure and pain. *American Psychologist, 52,* 1280–1300.

Hitchcock, J. M., & Davis, M. (1986). Lesions of the amygdala, but not of the cerebellum or red nucleus, block conditioned fear as measured with the potentiated startle paradigm. *Behavioral Neuroscience, 100,* 11–22.

Hoebel, B. G., Herndandex, L., Mark, G. P., & Pothos, E. (1992). Microdialysis in the study of psychostimulants and the neural substrates for reinforcement: Focus on dopamine and serotonin. *NIDA Research Monograph, 124,* 1–34.

Holbrook, A. L., Krosnick, J. A., Visser, P. S., Gardner, W. L., & Cacioppo, J. T. (1999). The formation of attitudes toward presidential candidates and political parties: An asymmetric nonlinear process. Manuscript under review.

Irwin, W., Davidson, R. J., Lowe, M. J., Mock, B. J., Sorenson, J. A., & Turski, P. A. (1996). Human amygdala activation detected with echo-planar functional magnetic resonance imaging. *Neuroreport, 7,* 1765–1769.

Ito, T. A., Larsen, J. T., Smith, N. K., & Cacioppo, J. T. (1998). Negative information weighs more heavily on the brain: The negativity bias in evaluative categorizations. *Journal of Personality and Social Psychology, 75,* 887–900.

Ito, T. A., & Cacioppo, J. T. (in press). Electrophysiological evidence of explicit and implicit categorization processes. *Journal of Experimental Social Psychology.*

Kahneman, D., & Tversky, A. (1984). Choices, values, and frames. *American Psychologist, 39,* 341–350.

Katz, I., & Hass, R. G. (1988). Racial ambivalence and American value conflict: Correlational and priming studies of dual cognitive structures. *Journal of Personality and Social Psychology, 55,* 893–905.

Lang, P. J. (1995). The emotion probe: Studies of motivation and attention. *American Psychologist, 50,* 372–385.

Lang, P. J., Bradley, M. M., & Cuthbert, B. N. (1990). Emotion, attention, and the startle reflex. *Psychological Review, 97,* 377–395.

Lang, P. J., Bradley, M. M., & Cuthbert, B. N. (1992). A motivational analysis of emotion: Reflex–cortex connections. *Psychological Science, 3,* 44–49.

Larsen, R. J., & Diener, E. (1992). Promises and problems with the circumplex model of emotion. *Review of Personality and Social Psychology, 13,* 25–59.

LeDoux, J. E., Cicchetti, P., Xagoraris, A., & Romaski, L. M. (1990). The lateral amygdaloid nucleus: Sensory interface of the sygdala in fear conditioning. *Journal of Neuroscience, 10,* 1062–1069.

Linville, P. W., Fischer, G. W., & Salovey, P. (1989). Perceived distributions of the characteristics of in-group and out-group members: Empirical evidence and a computer simulation. *Journal of Personality and Social Psychology, 57,* 165–188.

MacDonald, T. K., & Zanna, M. P. (1998). Cross-dimension ambivalence toward social groups: Can ambivalence affect intentions to hire feminists? *Personality and Social Psychology Bulletin, 24,* 427–441.

Miller, G. A. (1996). How we think about cognition, emotion, and biology in psychopathology. *Psychophysiology, 33,* 615–628.

Murphy, S. T., & Zajonc, R. B. (1993). Affect, cognition, and awareness: Affective priming with optimal and suboptimal stimulus exposures. *Journal of Personality and Social Psychology, 64,* 723–739.

Nisbett, R. E., & Wilson, T. D. (1977). Telling more than we can know: Verbal reports on mental processes. *Psychological Review, 84,* 231–259.

Ortony, A., Clore, G. L., & Collins, A. (1988). *The cognitive structure of emotions.* New York: Cambridge University Press.

Pratto, F., & John, O. P. (1991). Automatic vigilance: The attention-grabbing power of negative social information. *Journal of Personality and Social Psychology, 61,* 380–391.

Priester, J. R., & Petty, R. E. (1996). The gradual threshold model of ambivalence: Relating the positive and negative bases of attitudes to subjective ambivalence. *Journal of Personality and Social Psychology, 71,* 431–449.

Rinn, W. E. (1984). The neuropsychology of facial expression: A review of the neurological and psychological mechanisms for producing facial expression. *Psychological Bulletin, 95,* 52–77.

Russell, J. A. (1979). Affective space is bipolar. *Journal of Personality and Social Psychology, 37,* 345–356.

Russell, J. A., & Carroll, J. M. (1999). On the bipolarity of positive and negative affect. *Psychological Bulletin, 125,* 3–30.

Russell, J. A., & Feldman Barrett, L. (1999). Core affect, prototypical emotional episodes, and other things called emotion: Dissecting the elephant. *Journal of Personality and Social Psychology, 76,* 805–819.

Rusting, C. L., & Larsen, J. R. (1998). Personality and cognitive processing of affective information. *Personality and Social Psychology Bulletin, 24,* 200–213.

Scherer, K. R. (1984). On the nature and function of emotions: A component process approach. In K. R. Scherer & P. Ekman (Eds.), *Approaches to emotion* (pp. 293–317). Hillsdale, NJ: Erlbaum.

Scherer, K. R. (1993). Neuroscience projections to current debates in emotion psychology. *Cognition and Emotion, 7,* 1–41.

Schultz, T. R., Leveille, E., & Lepper, M. R. (1999). Free choice and cognitive dissoance revisited: Choosing "lesser evils" versus "greater gains." *Personality and Social Psychology Bulletin, 25,* 40–48.

Schwarz, N. (1990). Feelings as information: Informational and motivational functions of affective states. In E. T Higgins & R. M. Sorrentino (Eds.), *Handbook of motivation and cognition: Foundations of social behavior, Vol. 2* (pp. 527–561). New York: Guilford Press.

Schwarz, N., & Clore, G.L. (1983). Mood, misattribution, and judgments of well-being: Informative and directive functions of affective states. *Journal of Personality and Social Psychology, 45,* 513–523.

Showers, C. J. (1995). The evaluative organization of self-knowledge: Origins, processes, and implications for self-esteem. In M. Kernis (Ed.), *Efficacy, agency, and self-esteem* (pp. 101–120). New York: Plenum.

Showers, C. J., & King, K. C. (1996). Organization of self-knowledge: Implications for recovery from sad mood. *Journal of Personality and Social Psychology, 70,* 578–590.

Skowronski, J. J., & Carlston, D. E. (1989). Negativity and extremity biases in impression formation: A review of explanations. *Psychological Bulletin, 105,* 131–142.

Smith, C. A., & Ellsworth, P. C. (1985). Patterns of cognitive appraisal in emotion. *Journal of Personality and Social Psychology, 48,* 813–838.

Steiner, J. E. (1979). Human facial expression in response to taste and smell stimulation. *Advances in Child Development and Behavior, 13,* 237–295.

Thompson, M. M., Zanna, M. P., & Griffin, D. W. (1995). Let's not be indifferent about (attitudinal) ambivalence. In R. E. Petty & J. A. Krosnick (Eds.), *Attitude strength: Antecedents and consequences* (pp. 361–386). Mahwah, NJ: Lawrence Erlbaum Associates.

Vanman, E. J., Paul, B. Y., Ito, T. A., & Miller, N. (1997). The modern face of prejudice and structural features that moderate the effect of cooperation on affect. *Journal of Personality and Social Psychology, 73,* 941–959.

Wagner, A. D., Desmond, J. E., Demb, J. B., Glover, G. H., & Gabrieli, J. D. E. (1997). Semantic repetition priming for verbal and pictorial knowledge: A functional MRI study of left inferior prefrontal cortext. *Journal of Cognitive Neuroscience, 9,* 714–726.

Warr, P., Barter, J., & Brownbridge, G. (1983). On the independence of positive and negative affect. *Journal of Personality and Social Psychology, 44,* 644–651.

Watson, D., Clark, L. A., & Tellegen, A. (1988). Development and validation of brief measures of positive and negative affect: The PANAS scales. *Journal of Personality and Social Psychology, 54,* 1063–1070.

Watson, D., & Tellegen, A. (1985). Toward a consensual structure of mood. *Psychological Bulletin, 98,* 219–235.

Whalen, P. J., Rauch, S. L., Etcoff, N. L., McInerney, S. C., Lee, M. B., & Jenike, M. A. (1998). Masked presentations of emotional facial expressions modulate amygdala activity without explicit knowledge. *Journal of Neuroscience, 18,* 411–418.

Wegner, D. M., & Bargh, J. A. (1998). Control and automaticity in social life. In D. T. Gilbert, S. T. Fiske, & G. Lindzey (Eds.), *The handbook of social psychology* (Vol.1, pp. 446–496). New York: McGraw-Hill.

Wise, R. A. (1996). Addictive drugs and brain stimulation reward. *Annual Review of Neuroscience, 19,* 319–340.

Wise, R. A., & Rompre, P. P. (1989). Brain dopamine and reward. *Annual Review of Psychology, 40,* 191–225.

Wittenbrink, B., Judd, C. M., & Park, B. (1997). Evidence of racial prejudice at the implicit level and its relationship with questionnaire measures. *Journal of Personality and Social Psychology, 72,* 262–274.

Zautra, A. J., Hoffman, J., & Reich, J. W. (1997). The role of two kinds of efficacy beliefs in maintaining the well-being of chronically stressed older adults. In B. Gottlieb (Ed.), *Coping with chronic illness* (pp. 245–290). New York: Plenum.

Zautra, A. J., Reich, J. W., & Gaurnaccia, C. A. (1990). The everyday consequences of disability and bereavement for older adults. *Journal of Personality and Social Psychology, 59,* 550–561.

Zevon, M. A., & Tellegen, A. (1982). The structure of mood change: An ideographic/nomothetic analysis. *Journal of Personality and Social Psychology, 43,* 111–122.

4

Affect and Cognitive
Appraisal Processes

Craig A. Smith

*Department of Psychology and Human
Development, Vanderbilt University
Nashville, Tennessee*

Leslie D. Kirby

*Department of Psychology
University of Alabama at Birmingham
Birmingham, Alabama*

Appraisal Theory: Its Purpose and Major Assumptions	77
Structural Models of Appraisal	80
Toward a Process Model of Appraisal	84
Appraisal Theory, Affect, and Social Cognition	89
References	90

What does affect, or emotion, have to do with social cognition? If cognition is concerned with how people think, and social cognition concerns how people think about themselves and other people, what role is there for an analysis of how people *feel*? In the mid-1930s, the answer would have been, "Not much." In the wake of conflict theories of emotion (e.g., Angier, 1927; Claparède, 1928; Darrow, 1935; Young, 1936), which held emotion to be a disorganized and disorganizing response to difficult circumstances,

Address for correspondence: Craig A. Smith, Department of Psychology and Human Development, Vanderbilt University, Box 512 Peabody, Nashville, TN 37203, USA. Email: craig.a.smith@vanderbilt.edu the impact of emotion on cognition was seen primarily as a disruption of an otherwise logical (and preferred) mode of functioning. More recently, however, the dominant scientific view of emotion has shifted radically to one of emotions as highly organized and systematic responses to environmental demands that have evolved to serve adaptive functions (e.g., Arnold, 1960; Ekman, 1984; Izard, 1977; Plutchik, 1980; Scherer, 1984; Tomkins, 1962). Accompanying this philosophical shift, and after a long period of neglect, since the 1980s there has been a virtual explosion of research on affective phenomena, and especially on the interrelations between emotion and cognition. Through this work (much of which is summarized in this volume), we have learned that emotion is of critical importance to how we perceive (e.g., Derryberry & Tucker, 1994; Niedenthal, Setterlund, & Jones, 1994), evaluate (e.g., Keltner, Ellsworth, & Edwards, 1993), reason (e.g., Fiedler, Asbeck, & Nickel, 1991), remember (e.g., Bower, 1981; Forgas & Bower, 1987), and make decisions (e.g., Petty, Cacioppo, & Kasmer, 1988; Schwarz & Clore, 1983). In fact, there is no area of social cognition, or even "pure" cognition more broadly defined, where emotions have been shown not to have a significant impact.

Although recent work on emotions has gone a long way toward establishing the crucial importance of affect in social life, it has virtually ignored the nature of the emotions themselves and how they are generated. Thus, for instance, much of the work examining the effects of mood or emotion on a variety of cognitive processes has limited itself to an examination of pleasant versus unpleasant moods and emotions, with little regard to the nature of the specific emotions contributing to these pleasant or unpleasant states (but see Niedenthal et al., 1994, for an exception). Moreover, virtually all of this work began with individuals experiencing either naturally occurring or experimentally elicited emotions, and little attention has been directed toward the processes underlying the elicitation of these emotions or moods.

It is vital, however, that we develop clear and accurate models concerning both the nature and elicitation of emotion. First, a clearer understanding of the nature of emotional experience—how it is differentiated into a variety of distinct states, as well as the various functions served by these states—should allow us to more accurately predict the likely impact of these specific emotions on any of a variety of cognitive processes. Second, the development of models describing the elicitation of emotion should allow us to predict and understand when, under what conditions, and in whom different emotions are likely to be experienced. Without these types of understanding, the value of the knowledge we have gained regarding the effects of emotion on cognition is necessarily limited. Not only are our predictions of the effects on cognition of a particular emotion or set of emotions unlikely to be as specific as they might be, but we also have no way of predicting whether or when such emotions will arise.

In this chapter, we illustrate how appraisal theories of emotion step in to fill these gaps. First, we provide a brief overview of appraisal theory's perspective on emotion, as well as the major issues and problems appraisal theory was designed to address. Next, we discuss structural models of appraisal, which have been quite successful in delineating the relations between certain cognitions and the experience of specific emotions. We outline a structural model that we use in our research, based on Smith and Lazarus (1990), and demonstrate how such models go beyond the currently in-vogue two-dimensional models to describe the structure of emotions. Then we describe efforts to develop a process model of appraisal, designed to illustrate the mechanisms by which these cognitions are generated. Such process models are important complements to structural models of appraisal that can, by specifying the particular processes of emotion generation, account for certain phenomena that have been problematic for appraisal theory and emotion theory more generally in the past. Finally, we conclude by considering the ways in which the information about emotion and its antecedents provided by appraisal theory can be used to greatly enhance our study of the impact of emotion on social cognition.

APPRAISAL THEORY: ITS PURPOSE AND MAJOR ASSUMPTIONS

Having adopted early on the perspective that emotional reactions were organized and had evolved to serve largely adaptive functions, Magda Arnold was among the first of the contemporary emotion theorists to recognize the difficulty and importance of addressing the processes by which emotions occur. Arnold (1960) and virtually all subsequent appraisal theorists started with the assumption that different emotions served different adaptational functions that were called for under different sets of circumstances. The puzzle that appraisal theory set out to solve, then, was to describe the mechanism that had evolved to elicit the appropriate emotional reaction when a person was confronted with circumstances in which the function(s) served by that emotion were called for. This puzzle was complicated by the fact that, as Arnold (1960) recognized and subsequent appraisal theorists (e.g., Lazarus & Launier, 1978; Lazarus, 1991; Ortony, Clore, & Collins,

1988; Scherer, 1984; Smith & Lazarus, 1990) emphasized, emotions are not simple, reflexive responses to a stimulus situation. It is relatively easy to document that the same objective stimulus situation will evoke a broad range of emotions across individuals. Thus, an evaluative exam that might be anxiety producing to a person who doubts his abilities might be a welcome challenge to one who is confident of hers, and yet elicit indifference in one who is not invested in the outcome. Rather than assuming that this heterogeneity of response reflected a disorganized or chaotic system (as did the conflict theorists cited previously), beginning with Arnold (1960), appraisal theorists have assumed that emotional reactions are highly relational, in that they take into account not only the circumstances confronting an individual, but also what those circumstances imply for the individual in light of his or her personal hopes, desires, abilities, and the like. The elicitation mechanism Arnold (1960) proposed to give emotion this relational character was one of "appraisal," which she defined as an evaluation of the potential harms or benefits presented in any given situation. She then defined emotion as "the felt tendency toward anything intuitively appraised as good (beneficial), or away from anything intuitively appraised as bad (harmful)" (p. 182).

Beyond being relational, it is important to note that appraisal is also *meaning-based* and *evaluative*. The fact that appraisal combines both properties of the stimulus situation and of the person making the appraisal means that it cannot be a simple or reflexive response to the emotion-evoking stimulus. Instead, the appraisal is a reflection of what the stimulus means to the individual. Appraisal is also evaluative, in that it does not reflect a cold analysis of the situation, but rather, as Arnold (1960) emphasized, it is a very personal assessment of whether the situation is good or bad—is it (potentially) beneficial or harmful for me? That this evaluation is meaning based, rather than stimulus based, provides the emotion system with considerable flexibility and adaptational power. Not only will different individuals react to very similar situations with different emotions (as illustrated previously), but also objectively very different situations can elicit the same emotions if they imply the same meaning to the individuals appraising them. In addition, an individual can react very differently to the same situation across time if changes in his or her desires and abilities alter the implications of that situation for his or her well-being.

A further assumption is that appraisal occurs continuously. That is, a number of appraisal theorists have proposed that humans constantly engage in a meaning analysis in which the adaptational significance of their relationship to the environment is appraised, with the goal being to avoid, minimize, or alleviate an appraised actual or potential harm, or to seek, maximize, or maintain an appraised actual or potential benefit (e.g., Smith & Ellsworth, 1987; Smith & Lazarus, 1990). The reason for proposing that appraisal occurs continuously is that the emotion system is seen as an important motivational system that has evolved to alert the individual when he or she is confronted by adaptationally relevant circumstances. In order to serve this alerting function, the emotion-elicitation mechanism must be constantly "on guard" in order to be able to signal such circumstances when they arise. It is important to note that in making this assumption, appraisal theorists do not assert that the appraisal process need be conscious or deliberate; instead, they have consistently maintained that appraisal can occur automatically and outside of awareness (e.g., Arnold, 1960; Lazarus, 1968; Leventhal & Scherer, 1987; Smith & Lazarus, 1990). The importance and implications of this latter assumption is considered in more detail when we discuss process models of appraisal.

A final major assumption is that the emotion system is highly organized and differentiated. Appraisal theorists recognize that the same basic approach/avoid dichotomy associated with drives and reflexes (Cannon, 1929) and subscribed to by theorists endorsing two-dimensional conceptions of emotion, such as positive and negative affect (Watson & Tellegen, 1985), is fundamental to emotion. However, appraisal theorists describe emotion as being far more differentiated than a simple view of this dichotomy would allow. They argue that there are different major types of harm and benefit, and that these different types have different implications for how one might best contend with them. This is especially true for actual and potential harms, in which, depending on the circumstances, the most adaptive course might be to avoid the harmful situation, but could also range from active attack of the agent causing the harmful circumstances to reprimanding oneself if one caused the circumstances, to accepting and enduring the harmful circumstances if they cannot be avoided or repaired. Building on Arnold's (1960) definition of emotion mentioned previously, contemporary appraisal theorists tend to conceptualize different emotions as different modes of action readiness (Frijda, 1986), each of which is a response to a particular type of adaptationally relevant situation, and each of which physically and motivationally prepares and pushes the individual to contend with those circumstances in a certain way (e.g., to attack in anger, to avoid or flee in fear, to accept and heal in sadness; cf. Frijda, 1986; Izard, 1977). Within this differentiated system, the fundamental role of appraisal, again, is to call forth the appropriate emotion(s) when the individual is confronted with personally adaptationally relevant circumstances.

Intellectually, the construct of appraisal, as outlined previously, has considerable power and appeal. In the abstract, at least, it has the power to drive a highly flexible and adaptive emotion system. However, to be of practical theoretical utility, the construct must be fleshed out in at least two ways. First, the *contents* of appraisal need to be described. That is, specific models must be developed to detail the appraisals that are responsible for the elicitation of the different emotions. Second, the cognitive processes underlying these appraisals must also be described. This is especially important because, as alluded to, these processes are not thought to be necessarily conscious or deliberate, as critics of appraisal theory (e.g., Izard, 1993; Zajonc, 1980) have often assumed. Considerable effort has been devoted to the first issue, with the result being the development and testing of several different *structural models* of appraisal, which are the focus of the next section of this chapter. In addition, some appraisal theorists (e.g., Leventhal & Scherer, 1987; Smith & Kirby, 2000) have begun to attempt to develop *process models* of appraisal, and these efforts will be reviewed subsequently.

STRUCTURAL MODELS OF APPRAISAL

If appraisal involves an evaluation of a situation to determine potential harms or benefits as related to individual goals, then the first step in testing appraisal theory is to identify the dimensions along which evaluations are made, then test to see whether the identified dimensions do, in fact, elicit emotions in the predicted ways. Several such models have been proposed (e.g., Roseman, 1984, 1991; Scherer, 1984; Smith & Ellsworth, 1985; Smith & Lazarus, 1990), and a large body of research designed to test these models has been highly supportive of them. In particular, many studies have now asked subjects to report on both their appraisals and a wide array of emotions across a variety of contexts, including diverse retrospectively remembered experiences (Ellsworth & Smith, 1988a,b; Frijda, Kuipers, & ter Schure, 1989; Scherer, 1997; Smith & Ellsworth, 1985), hypothetical vignettes (e.g., Roseman, 1991; Smith & Lazarus, 1993), and even ongoing meaningful experiences (e.g., Griner & Smith, 2000; Kirby & Smith, 1999; Smith & Ellsworth, 1987). In each of these studies, not only have the experiences of different emotions been consistently found to be reliably and systematically associated with different appraisals, but the specific relations observed between the appraisals and the emotions have also largely been in line with the models being investigated.

Although the specific structural appraisal models proposed by various appraisal theorists (e.g., Lazarus, 1991; Ortony et al., 1988; Roseman, 1984; Scherer, 1984; Smith & Ellsworth, 1985; Smith & Lazarus, 1990) differ in a number of important respects (e.g., in some of the specific appraisal dimensions proposed to differentiate emotional experience; see Scherer, 1988, for an in-depth comparison of several of these models), far more telling is the fact that, overall, they are highly similar in the appraisal dimensions they propose and in the ways that outcomes along these dimensions are hypothesized to differentiate emotional experience. These similarities reflect the fact that the various appraisal theorists all set out to solve a common problem—to identify the set of evaluations that have evolved to link the various modes of action readiness, each serving different adaptational functions, to those circumstances in which those functions were called for—and that they happened to hit on similar solutions to that problem.

Thus, in one form or another, the existing appraisal models generally include some sort of evaluation of how important or relevant the stimulus situation is to the person, whether it is desirable or undesirable, whether and to what degree the person is able to cope with the situation, and who or what caused or is responsible for the situation (and thus toward what or whom one's coping efforts should be directed). Different patterns of outcomes along such dimensions are hypothesized to result in the experience of different emotions. Moreover, the specific pattern of appraisal hypothesized to result in the experience of a given emotion is conceptually closely linked to the functions proposed to be served by that emotion. To illustrate how these models are organized in this way, we draw on the model of Smith & Lazarus (1990), which is the model we use in our own research.

According to this model, situations are evaluated along seven dimensions: motivational relevance, motivational congruence, problem-focused coping potential, emotion-focused coping potential, self-accountability, other accountability, and future expectancy. *Motivational relevance* involves an evaluation of how important the situation is to the person; *motivational* is a key part of the term, however, in that the importance is appraised in a subjective, relational sense, evaluating the relevance of what is happening in the situation to the individual's goals and motivations. *Motivational congruence* is an appraisal of the extent to which the situation is in line with current goals, which again is relational—to the extent to which the circumstances are appraised as being consistent with one's goals, they are appraised as highly congruent or desirable, whereas to the extent to which they are appraised as inconsistent with those goals, they are appraised as incongruent or undesirable. *Problem-focused coping potential* is an assessment of the individual's ability to act on the situation to increase or maintain its desirability. In contrast, *emotion-focused coping potential* evaluates the ability to psychologically adjust to and deal with the situation should it turn out not to be as desired. *Self-accountability* is an assessment of the degree to which an individual sees her/himself as responsible for the situation, whereas *other accountability* is the extent to which the individual views someone or something else as responsible. Finally, *future expectancy* involves an evaluation of the degree to which, for any reason, the person expects the circumstances to become more or less desirable. According to the model, different patterns of outcomes along these dimensions (having different adaptational implications) result in the experience of different emotions (serving different adaptational functions). Thus, these appraisal dimensions are held to be responsible for the differentiation of emotional experience.

The first two dimensions, motivational relevance and motivational congruence, are relevant to every emotional encounter, and thus are sometimes referred to as dimensions of "primary appraisal" (e.g., Lazarus, 1991; Smith & Lazarus, 1990). By themselves they can distinguish between situations that are irrelevant to well-being (low motivational relevance), and thus are not emotionally evocative, and those that are either beneficial (high motivational relevance and motivational congruence) or stressful (high motivational relevance and motivational incongruence). In certain ways, these two dimensions of primary appraisal correspond closely to the dimensions present in many two-dimensional models of affect (e.g., Russell, 1980; Watson & Tellegen, 1985). Thus, the congruence dimension corresponds roughly to the valence dimension of Russell's (1980) and other's models, although one should note, as discussed later, emotions associated with motivational incongruence are not always unpleasant. In addition, the dimension of motivational relevance corresponds closely to the dimension of intensity, or activation, that accompanies valence in most two-dimensional models. Similarly, for those models that emphasize separate dimensions of approach (associated with positive affect) and withdrawal (associated with negative affect; e.g., Watson & Tellegen, 1985), the combined outcomes of these two appraisal dimensions to define one's circumstances as beneficial or stressful correspond well to those two dimensions of affect, respectively.

However, by including the additional appraisal dimensions concerning accountability and coping potential [often referred to as dimensions of "secondary appraisal" in the terminology of Lazarus (1991) and colleagues], appraisal theory is able to account for considerable further differentiation among emotional states in a way that the two dimensional models are not. For example, whereas anger and fear are essentially indistinguishable in almost all two-dimensional models, appraisal theory can readily handle them as the highly distinct physiological and motivational states that they are. Particularly in the case of stressful situations (i.e., those appraised as both motivationally relevant and motivationally incongruent), the dimensions of secondary appraisal allow for considerable differentiation of the emotional response to circumstances that can vary greatly in terms of their specific adaptational implications (see also Smith, 1991; Smith & Lazarus, 1990).

Thus, if a stressful situation is appraised as being brought about by someone else (other accountability), anger will result, which motivates the person to act toward the perceived cause to get that agent to stop what he or she is doing, and, perhaps, to fix the situation. If, however, the situation is appraised as being caused by oneself (self-accountability), shame or guilt results, which motivates the person to make amends for the bad situation and prevent the situation from happening again. If the situation is one that the person is unsure he or she can handle (low emotion-focused coping potential), then fear or anxiety results, which motivates the person to be cautious and to get rid of and avoid the potential harm, if at all possible. If the stressful situation is one in which the harm is perceived as unavoidable and irreparable (low problem-focused coping potential), then sadness results, which motivates the person to seek help and adapt to the inevitable harm. Finally, as mentioned previously, the emotional states associated with primary appraisals of stress are not always unpleasant or negative. If one is in a stressful situation in which one does not have something one wants, but perceives that with effort one can achieve one's goals (high coping potential), then a state of challenge results that motivates the person to stay engaged and persevere to achieve his or her goals. Even if problem-focused coping potential is low, hope might result if the person believes that, somehow, things might work out in the end (high future expectancy). In sum, different components of secondary appraisal combine with the same stress-related components of primary appraisal to yield a range of distinct emotional reactions that differ dramatically in their subjective, motivational, and physiological properties (see, for instance, Tomaka, Blascovich, Kelsey, & Leitten, 1993, for evidence of differences in physiological responses associated with appraisals of low versus high coping potential in response to the same stressor).

Structural models, like the one just outlined, by linking specific patterns of appraisal to specific emotions and the adaptational functions served by those emotions, can contribute much to our understanding of emotional experience and the roles that emotions play in social life. However, as noted previously, these structural models have been largely silent with respect to the cognitive processes responsible for producing the appraisals. We now turn our attention to issues surrounding the nature of these cognitive processes.

TOWARD A PROCESS MODEL OF APPRAISAL

Although the structural appraisal models described previously have been quite successful in describing cognitive antecedents of emotion, taken by themselves they create a potential problem for appraisal theory. By emphasizing that complex relational information is somehow drawn on in appraisal, this work could give the impression that appraisal is ponderous and slow. In fact, appraisal theory has often been criticized on just these grounds. Observers of appraisal theory have tended to interpret the structural descriptions of appraisal as implying that the process of appraisal is deliberate, slow, and verbally mediated. They then correctly note that such a process would fly directly in the face of common observations that emotions can be elicited very quickly, unbidden, often with a minimum of cognitive effort, and sometimes with little or no awareness of the nature of the emotion-eliciting stimulus (e.g., Izard, 1993; Zajonc, 1980). In addition, to the extent that appraisals are thought to be necessarily verbally mediated, it seems very difficult to apply one's appraisal-based theory to either preverbal infants or nonhuman vertebrates, as many appraisal theorists would like to do (e.g., Arnold, 1960; Lazarus, 1991; Scherer, 1984; Smith & Lazarus, 1990).

Appraisal theorists have been aware of these difficulties, and to our knowledge, none has claimed that appraisal need be performed consciously or that the information evaluated in appraisal need be represented verbally. To the contrary, beginning with Magda Arnold (1960), for whom appraisal was "direct, immediate, [and] intuitive" (p. 173), most appraisal theorists have explicitly maintained that appraisal can occur automatically and outside of focal awareness (e.g., Lazarus, 1968; Leventhal & Scherer, 1987; Smith & Lazarus, 1990). However, with few exceptions (e.g. Lazarus, 1991, ch. 4; Leventhal & Scherer, 1987; Robinson, 1998), there has been little effort to back up these claims with an explicit process model of appraisal that would explain how appraisals can occur in this manner. In the absence of such a model, theorists' claims regarding the potential automaticity of appraisal may not have been fully appreciated.

In response to the perceived need for a model of this type, we (Smith, Griner, Kirby, & Scott, 1996; Smith & Kirby, 2000) have begun working on the development of an explicit model of the cognitive processes underlying appraisal. Our goal has been to draw on our current understanding of cognitive processing to articulate a model that can allow appraisal to be information rich, relational, and inferentially based, as described previously, while at the same time allowing appraisals to elicit emotions quickly, automatically, and outside of conscious awareness. Below, we provide a brief sketch of our progress to date in developing such a model (for a more complete description of the model, its functioning, and its rationale, the reader is referred to Smith & Kirby, 2000). A diagram of this model is presented in Fig. 4.1.

Building, in part, on the earlier, seminal efforts of Leventhal (1984) and Leventhal and Scherer (1987), we propose that rather than a single unitary appraisal process, there are multiple appraisal processes that can occur in parallel and that involve distinct cognitive mechanisms. In particular, we highlight two distinct modes of cognitive processing we believe are especially important for understanding appraisal—*associative processing*, which involves priming and activation of memories and can occur quickly

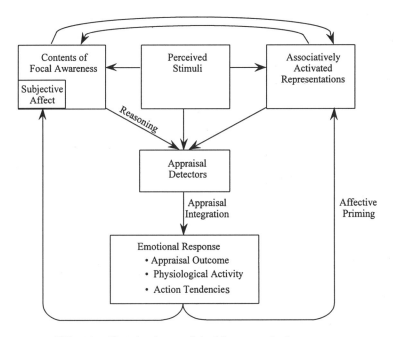

FIG. 4.1. Sketch of a model of the appraisal process.

and automatically, and *reasoning*, which involves a more controlled and deliberate thinking process that is more flexible than associative processing, but is relatively slow and attention intensive. Our distinction between these modes of processing is modeled closely after the distinction between schematic processing and conceptual processing discussed by Leventhal and Scherer (1987), and reflects a distinction between different types of cognitive processes that is quite common in the cognitive psychological literature (cf., Sloman, 1996).

A central, distinctive feature of this model is the existence of what we call "appraisal detectors." These detectors continuously monitor for, and are responsive to, appraisal information from multiple sources. The appraisal information they detect determines the person's emotional state. It should be noted that these detectors are not actively computing the appraisals, in the sense that they are performing an active evaluation of the person's relationship to the environment in terms of the various components of appraisal. Instead, they detect the appraisal information generated from different modes of processing (see description below). This information is then combined into an integrated appraisal that initiates processes to generate the various components of the emotional response, including an organized pattern of physiological activity, the action tendency, and the subjective feeling state.

As depicted in the figure, the appraisal detectors receive information from three distinct sources. First, some perceptual stimuli, such as pain sensations, looming objects, and possibly even certain facial expressions (e.g., McHugo & Smith, 1996; Öhman, 1986), may be preset to carry certain appraisal meanings that can be detected directly. For instance, all else being equal, painful sensations are inherently motivationally incongruent or undesirable. This pathway is akin to the perceptual-motor level of processing that Leventhal and Scherer (1987) include in their model. The bulk of the information processed by the appraisal detectors, however, is hypothesized to be generated through either associative processing or reasoning.

As noted previously, associative processing is a fast, automatic, memory-based mode of processing that involves priming and spreading activation (Bargh, 1989; Bower, 1981). Based on perceptual or conceptual similarities with one's current circumstances, or due to associations with other memories that are already activated, memories of prior experiences can become activated quickly, automatically, in parallel, outside of focal awareness, and using a minimum of attentional resources. As these memories are activated, any appraisal meanings associated with them are also activated, and when these meanings are activated to a sufficient degree, they can be recognized by the appraisal detectors and influence the person's emotional state.

Several assumptions we make about associative processing should be emphasized. First, we assume that anything that can be represented in memory, ranging from concrete representations of physical sensations, sounds, smells, tastes, and images up to representations of highly abstract concepts, is subject to this form of processing. That is, cues that can activate appraisal-laden memories include not only concrete stimuli, such as sensations, images, and sounds, but also highly conceptual stimuli, such as abstract ideas or the appraisal meanings themselves. Second, we assume that through principles of priming and spreading activation, full-blown appraisals associated with prior experiences can be activated very quickly and automatically. Thus, highly differentiated emotional reactions can be elicited almost instantaneously. Third, we assume that the activation threshold at which appraisal information becomes available to the appraisal detectors is somewhat less than the threshold at which the appraisal information and its associated memories become accessible to focal awareness and/or working memory. Through this assumption, it becomes possible that adaptationally relevant circumstances in one's environment, of which one is focally unaware, can activate memories and produce an emotional reaction. In this way, the first conscious indication to the person that he or she might be in an adaptationally relevant situation can be the perception of the subjective feeling state associated with the associatively elicited emotional reaction. Finally, we assume that the processes of memory activation, priming, and spreading activation occur continuously and automatically, just as the appraisal detectors monitor continuously for activated appraisal information. Thus, the person can be characterized as continuously appraising his or her circumstances for their implications for well-being, albeit not in a conscious, attention-intensive manner.

In contrast to associative processing, reasoning is a relatively slow, controlled process that is effortful, requires considerable attention and focal awareness, and is largely verbally mediated. Moreover, whereas associative processing is passive in the way that appraisal information is made available to the appraisal detectors (namely, appraisal information that happens to be sufficiently activated becomes available for detection), reasoning is a much more constructive process, whereby the contents of focal awareness are actively operated on and transformed to produce the appraisal meanings. In other words, what we are calling reasoning corresponds closely to the active posing and evaluating of appraisal questions that have sometimes been incorrectly assumed to encompass all of appraisal.

Because reasoning is active and highly resource intensive, it comes at a price. In addition to being relatively slow, we believe that this mode of processing is somewhat limited in the forms of information to which it can gain access. In contrast to associative processing, which can operate on any form of information stored in memory, we propose that only information that has been semantically encoded in some way is readily accessible to reasoning (Anderson, 1983; Paivio, 1971). That is, sensations, images, sounds, and so on are relatively inaccessible to reasoning unless and until they have been associated with some sort of semantic meaning. By implication, this means that although associative processing has access to all of the information to which the reasoning process has access, the reverse is not true.

Despite these limitations, reasoning is extremely important in that it enables the emotion system to use the full power of our highly developed and abstract thinking processes. Emotion-eliciting situations can be analyzed thoroughly and their meanings reappraised (Lazarus, 1968, 1991). Thus, initial associatively elicited appraisals that might not fully fit the current circumstances can be modified to provide a more appropriate evaluation and emotional response. New connections can be forged between one's present circumstances and potentially related previous experiences. It is even possible that appraisal meanings associated with previous experiences in memory can be reevaluated and changed. In addition, the "cognitive work" represented by reasoning—the results of the interpretation and reinterpretation of the emotion-eliciting situation—can be stored in memory as part of the emotion-eliciting event, and thus become available for subsequent associative processing. This last fact is vital, in that it provides a mechanism by which the emotion system can "learn," and through associative processing, can quickly and automatically produce the highly differentiated, information-rich signals that the motivational functions served by emotion seem to require.

The development of this model is still in its infancy. At a theoretical level, we are in the process of exploring the extent to which the model can account for phenomena, such as repression and the misattribution of arousal, that have traditionally caused problems for appraisal theory when appraisal has been conceptualized as a single, deliberative process (Smith & Kirby, 2000). In addition, we are in the process of generating testable, novel predictions from the model, particularly concerning how the two modes of appraisal, with their rather different properties, interact with one another. At an empirical level, work has just recently begun to demonstrate that the two modes of processing are both relevant to appraisal and emotion (e.g., van Reekum & Scherer, 1998).

APPRAISAL THEORY, AFFECT, AND
SOCIAL COGNITION

In his book *The Science of Emotion*, Cornelius (1996) summarizes the cognitive perspective on emotion as follows: "emotions require thought; in order to understand people's emotions, one must understand how people make judgments" (p. 115). We want to go further—in our view, if you want to understand people's judgments, you must understand people's emotions; emotions pervade social cognition.

In this volume, you encounter chapters on the impact of emotion on dissonance, self-concept, stereotyping, health, personality, and stress, among others. As you read through these chapters, we ask you to keep in mind both the process of emotion generation and the structure and function of the resulting emotions. Although current theories and techniques can document that being in an emotional state affects various cognitive processes in certain ways, appraisal theory is the only major theoretical approach to emotion that attempts to describe how the emotions themselves came about. In addition, in their efforts to link the antecedent appraisals in their models to the functions served by various emotions, appraisal theorists have called attention to the differentiated nature and function of emotion as much as any emotion theorists, and to a considerably greater degree than has typically been the case in the study of affect and social cognition.

We believe that both of these contributions of appraisal theory—a detailed description of the antecedents of emotion and a focus on the differential functions served by different emotions—have much to offer to our understanding of the influence of emotion on social cognition. First, knowledge of when, where, and under what conditions an individual is likely to experience this or that emotion is crucial for being able to predict the range of circumstances across which a given effect of emotion on cognition is likely to generalize and/or be especially relevant. Second, an appreciation that different emotions, such as sadness, anger, and fear, serve quite different motivational functions should encourage us to move beyond predicting differential effects of positive versus negative affect on cognitive processes to developing more emotion-specific models of those effects. The fact that in anger, the person is motivated to attack and remove a source of harm from his or her circumstances, whereas in fear, the person is motivated to be cautious and avoid the harm, whereas in sadness the person is motivated to give up and withdraw from the situation (cf. Izard, 1977; Smith & Lazarus, 1990) should have clear and differential implications as to what the person is likely to perceive and remember, as well as how he or she is likely to reason in those emotional states. Such differential effects can not be captured while considering the influences of "negative affect," because all three of these quite different emotions are subsumed under this super-ordinate construct. Drawing on appraisal theory to expand and develop our models of affect and social cognition in both of these ways should greatly enrich our appreciation and understanding of the importance of emotion in social life.

REFERENCES

Anderson, J. R. (1983). *The architecture of cognition.* Cambridge, MA: Harvard University Press.

Angier, R. P. (1927). The conflict theory of emotion. *American Journal of Psychology, 39,* 390–401.

Arnold, M. B. (1960). *Emotion and personality* (2 vols.). New York: Columbia University Press.

Bargh, J. A. (1989). Conditional automaticity: Varieties of automatic influence in social perception and cognition. In J. S. Uleman & J. A. Bargh (Eds.) *Unintended thought* (pp. 3–51). New York: The Guilford Press.

Bower, G. H. (1981). Mood and memory. *American Psychologist, 36,* 129–148.

Cannon, W. B. (1929). *Bodily changes in pain, hunger, fear, and rage* (2nd Ed.). New York: Appleton-Century.

Claparède, E. (1928). Feelings and emotions. In M. L. Reymert (Ed.), *Feelings and emotions: The Wittenberg Symposium* (pp. 124–139). Worcester, MA: Clark University Press.

Cornelius, R. (1996). *The science of emotion: Research and tradition in the psychology of emotions.* Upper Saddle River, NJ: Prentice-Hall.

Darrow, C. W. (1935). Emotion as relative functional decortication: The role of conflict. *Psychological Review, 42,* 566–578.

Derryberry, D., & Tucker, D. M. (1994). Motivating the focus of attention. In P. M. Niedenthal & S. Kitayama (Eds.), *The heart's eye: Emotional influences in perception and attention* (pp. 167–196). New York: Academic Press.

Ekman, P. (1984). Expression and the nature of emotion. In K. R. Scherer & P. Ekman (Eds.), *Approaches to emotion* (pp. 329–343). Hillsdale, NJ: Lawrence Erlbaum Associates.

Ellsworth, P. C., & Smith, C. A. (1988a). From appraisal to emotion: Differences among unpleasant feelings. *Motivation and Emotion, 12,* 271–302.

Ellsworth, P. C., & Smith, C. A. (1988b). Shades of joy: Patterns of appraisal differentiating pleasant emotions. *Cognition and Emotion, 2,* 301–331.

Fiedler, K., Asbeck, J., & Nickel, S. (1991). Mood and constructive memory effects on social judgement. *Cognition and Emotion, 5,* 363–378.

Forgas, J. P., & Bower, G. H. (1987). Mood effects on person perception judgements. *Journal of Personality and Social Psychology, 53,* 53–60.

Frijda, N. H. (1986). *The emotions.* New York: Cambridge University Press.

Frijda, N. H., Kuipers, P., & ter Schure, E. (1989). Relations among emotion, appraisal, and emotional action readiness. *Journal of Personality and Social Psychology, 57,* 212–228.

Griner, L. A., & Smith, C. A. (2000). Contributions of motivational orientation to appraisal and emotion. *Personality and Social Psychology Bulletin, 26,* 727–740.

Izard, C. E. (1977). *Human emotions.* New York: Plenum Press.

Izard, C. E. (1993). Four systems for emotion activation: Cognitive and noncognitive processes. *Psychological Review, 100,* 68–90.

Keltner, D., Ellsworth, P. C., & Edwards, K. (1993). Beyond simple pessimism: Effects of sadness and anger on social perception. *Journal of Personality and Social Psychology, 64,* 740–752.

Kirby, L. D., & Smith, C. A. (1999). *The person and situation in transaction: Antecedents of appraisal and emotion.* Manuscript submitted for publication. Vanderbilt University.

Lazarus, R. S. (1968). Emotions and adaptation: Conceptual and empirical relations. In W. J. Arnold (Ed.), *Nebraska Symposium on Motivation* (Vol. 16, pp. 175–266). Lincoln: University of Nebraska Press.

Lazarus, R. S. (1991). *Emotion and adaptation.* New York: Oxford University Press.

Lazarus, R. S., & Launier, R. (1978). Stress-related transactions between person and environment. In L. A. Pervin (Ed.), *Perspectives in interactional psychology* (pp. 287–327). New York: Plenum.

Leventhal, H. (1984). A perceptual motor theory of emotion. In K. R. Scherer & P. Ekman (Eds.), *Approaches to emotion* (pp. 271–291). Hillsdale, NJ: Lawrence Erlbaum Associates.

Leventhal, H., & Scherer, K. (1987). The relationship of emotion to cognition: A functional approach to a semantic controversy. *Cognition and Emotion, 1,* 3–28.

McHugo, G. J., & Smith, C. A. (1996). The power of faces: A review of John T. Lanzetta's research on facial expression and emotion. *Motivation and Emotion, 20,* 85–120.

Niedenthal, P. M., Setterlund, M. B., & Jones, D. E. (1994). Emotional organization of perceptual memory. In P. M. Niedenthal & S. Kitayama (Eds.), *The heart's eye: Emotional influences in perception and attention.* New York: Academic Press.

Öhman, A. (1986). Face the beast and fear the face: Animal and social fears as prototypes for evolutionary analyses of emotion. *Psychophysiology, 23,* 123–145.

Ortony, A., Clore, G. L., & Collins, A. (1988). *The cognitive structure of emotions.* New York: Cambridge University Press.

Paivio, A. (1971). *Imagery and verbal processes.* New York: Holt, Rinehart, and Winston.

Petty, R. E., Cacioppo, J. T., & Kasmer, J. A. (1988). The role of affect in the elaboration likelihood model of persuasion. In L. Donohew, H. E. Sypher, & E. T. Higgins (Eds.), *Communication, social cognition, and affect* (pp. 117–146). Hillsdale, NJ: Lawrence Erlbaum Associates.

Plutchik, R. (1980). *Emotion: A psychoevolutionary synthesis.* New York: Harper & Row.

Robinson, M. D. (1998). Running from William James' bear: A review of preattentive mechanisms and their contributions to emotional experience. *Cognition and Emotion, 12,* 667–696.

Roseman, I. J. (1984). Cognitive determinants of emotions: A structural theory. In P. Shaver (Ed.), *Review of Personality and Social Psychology* (Vol. 5, pp. 11–36). Newbury Park, CA: Sage.

Roseman, I. J. (1991). Appraisal determinants of discrete emotions. *Cognition and Emotion, 5,* 161–200.

Russell, J. A. (1980). A circumplex model of affect. *Journal of Personality and Social Psychology, 39,* 1161–1178.

Scherer, K. R. (1984). On the nature and function of emotion: A component process approach. In K. R. Scherer & P. Ekman (Eds.), *Approaches to emotion* (pp. 293–317). Hillsdale, NJ: Lawrence Erlbaum Associates.

Scherer, K. R. (1988). Criteria for emotion-antecedent appraisal: A review. In V. Hamilton, G. H. Bower, & N. H. Frijda (Eds.), *Cognitive perspectives on emotion and motivation* (pp. 89–126). Boston: Kluwer Academic Publishers.

Scherer, K. R. (1997). Profiles of emotion-antecedent appraisal: Testing theoretical predictions across cultures. *Cognition and Emotion, 11,* 113–150.

Schwarz, N., & Clore, G. L. (1983). Mood, misattribution and judgements of well-being: Informative and directive functions of affective states. *Journal of Personality and Social Psychology, 45,* 513–523.

Sloman, S. A. (1996). The empirical case for two systems of reasoning. *Psychological Bulletin, 119,* 3–22.

Smith, C. A. (1991). The self, appraisal, and coping. In C. R. Snyder & D. R. Forsyth (Eds.), *Handbook of social and clinical psychology: The health perspective* (pp. 116–137). New York: Pergamon Press.

Smith, C. A., & Ellsworth, P. C. (1985). Patterns of cognitive appraisal in emotion. *Journal of Personality and Social Psychology, 48,* 813–838.

Smith, C. A., & Ellsworth, P. C. (1987). Patterns of appraisal and emotion related to taking an exam. *Journal of Personality and Social Psychology, 52*, 475–488.

Smith, C. A., Griner, L. A., Kirby, L. D., & Scott, H. S. (1996, Abstract). Toward a process model of appraisal in emotion. *Proceedings of the Ninth Conference of the International Society for Research on Emotions* (pp. 101–105). Toronto, Ontario, Canada: International Society for Research on Emotions.

Smith, C. A., & Kirby, L. D. (2000). Consequences require antecedents: Toward a process model of emotion elicitation. J. Forgas (Ed.). *Feeling and thinking: The role of affect in social cognition* (pp. 83–106). Cambridge University Press.

Smith, C. A., & Lazarus, R. S. (1990). Emotion and adaptation. In L. A. Pervin (Ed.), *Handbook of personality: Theory and research* (pp. 609–637). New York: Guilford Press.

Smith, C. A., & Lazarus, R. S. (1993). Appraisal components, core relational themes, and the emotions. *Cognition and Emotion, 7*, 233–269.

Tomaka, J., Blascovich, J., Kelsey, R. M., & Leitten, C. L. (1993). Subjective, physiological, and behavioral effects of threat and challenge appraisal. *Journal of Personality and Social Psychology, 65*, 248–260.

Tomkins, S. S. (1962). *Affect, imagery, consciousness. Vol. I. The positive affects.* New York: Springer.

van Reekum, C. M., & Scherer, K. R. (1998, August). *Levels of processing in appraisal.* Paper presented at the 10th conference of the International Society for Research on Emotion. Würzburg, Germany.

Watson, D., & Tellegen, A. (1985). Toward a consensual structure of mood. *Psychological Bulletin, 98*, 219–235.

Young, P. T. (1936). *Motivation and behavior.* New York: Wiley.

Zajonc, R. B. (1980). Feeling and thinking: Preferences need no inferences. *American Psychologist, 35*, 151–175.

II

Affective Influences on the Content of Cognition

5

Mood and Social Memory

Gordon H. Bower
Stanford University

Joseph P. Forgas
University of New South Wales

Affective Features of Social Episode Representations 96
Memory for Emotional Episodes 98
Affective Recall without Factual Recall 99
Emotional Units in Associative Networks 103
Mood-Dependent Retrieval 104
Mood-Congruent Processing 108
Limitations on Mood Congruity 110
Information-Processing Strategies that Moderate Mood
    Effects on Memory 112
Summary and Conclusions 115
Acknowledgment 116
References 117

Our memory makes us who we are. People who have lost their memory, as happens to many victims of Alzheimer's disease, have also lost their personal identity. Just as we become unrecognizable to them, so do they

Gordon H. Bower is at the Department of Psychology, Stanford University, Stanford, CA 34305; email: gordon@psych.stanford.edu become unrecognizable to us. Major forces in shaping our memory are emotion and motivation: we remember better events that had motivational significance and about which we had intense feelings.

Recent investigation of how feelings influence memory have proceeded in two directions—toward exploring the biological substrates, and toward identifying the social causes and consequences of emotion. Neuropsychological investigations, reviewed in Chapter 2 by Adolphs and Damasio, have identified critical neuroendocrine and brain systems mediating enhanced memory for emotional compared to nonemotional events. We know, for example, that emotionally arousing events release a cascade of neuroendocrinal processes in catecholamine systems that have a major impact on the brain's amygdaloid complex, whose activity modulates consolidation of the memory of an emotional event (see Cahill, 1996; McGaugh & Cahill, 1997).

The other direction for research is toward exploring the social causes and consequences of emotion, and that is the major theme of this book. Many of the contributors to this book share the belief that for humans, it is social interaction that provides the predominant force that shapes an individual's emotional and affective life. In this chapter, we argue that people's affective states also play a key role in determining their memory for and processing of social information, their social judgments, and their social behaviors.

AFFECTIVE FEATURES OF SOCIAL EPISODE REPRESENTATIONS

We begin our discussion of affect and social memory by noting that most of our memory of everyday social interactions can be parsed into a collection of social episodes. These are the frequently recurring, well-rehearsed interaction routines of everyday life—chatting with a friend over coffee, purchasing a gift, sending messages by electronic mail, making a business phone call, taking the car in for repair, going out to a restaurant and movie, or attending a party. It is the routine nature of these interactions that makes social life predictable and generally unchallenging. Indeed, it may be said that shared knowledge about such episodes is what holds individuals, groups, and societies together (Forgas, 1981, p. 165).

When sufficiently routinized, such social episodes come to be represented in memory as abstracted stereotypes or social scripts (Abelson, 1981). Social scripts thus refer to stereotyped collections of actions having particular goals, standardized acts with some modest variations in quality and sequence, a set of social roles for the other participants, and a standardized way of proceeding. A particular episode (e.g., one's visit to-day to the dentist) can then be represented in memory as an instantiated version of the general script (see, e.g., Bower, Black, & Turner, 1979; Graesser, Woll, Kowalski, & Smith, 1980).

Studies by Magnusson (1971), Pervin (1976), and Forgas (1979, 1981) systematically explored how people think about and mentally represent standard social situations and episodes. These investigators treat social episodes as stimuli that can be judged, compared, and scaled according to their perceived features, just as persons are stimuli in studies of person perception. For example, Forgas (1979, 1981) analyzed the episode domains of several different subgroups ranging from Oxford housewives, university students, and academic staff to rugby teams. For each target subgroup, a collection of representative social episodes was sampled from interviews and diaries. These episodes were then rated for similarity, and these ratings submitted to multidimensional scaling.

A major finding of these studies is that people's mental representations of social episodes are largely dominated by the affective (connotative) characteristics of these encounters, rather than their actual descriptive features. Such characteristics as the pleasantness of the interaction, its intimacy, one's sense of personal involvement, and self-confidence in the situation seem to have emerged as key features defining episode representations in all such studies. In comparing episodes with one another, people tend to automatically rely on how they feel about the encounters in question, and pay little attention to the different settings, actors, props, and goals. As Pervin (1976) noted: "what is striking is the extent to which situations are described in terms of affects (e.g., threatening, warm, interesting, dull, tense, calm, rejecting) and organized in terms of similarity of affects aroused by them" (p. 471).

For example, a study of Oxford undergraduates' perceptions of social episodes showed that attending a tutorial, a formal wedding, and a psychology experiment were seen as highly similar. Why? Because the three situations involved very similar affective reactions—they are formal, strictly regulated, nonintimate, demanding, and slightly stressful situations, and are entered by the students with reduced self-confidence.

The principle that affective experiences play a key role in how social information is stored and represented in memory was further confirmed in a series of experiments by Niedenthal and Halberstadt (2000), who argue that affective reactions provide a basic and so far largely neglected source of cognitive categorization. According to Niedenthal and Halberstadt, social categories are almost never devoid of emotion, and affect often determines the use and the evaluation of categories of persons and situations. In fact, it was Bruner, Goodnow, and Austin (1956) who, in their seminal work, *A Study of Thinking*, first proposed that in social categorization of people, situations, and experiences, what holds them together and what leads one to say that some new experience "reminds one of such and such weather, people, and states" is the evocation of a defining affective response (p. 4). As Forgas (1979, 1981) and Niedenthal and Halberstadt (2000) found, apparently unrelated social stimuli can cohere and form a distinct category, even when they have nothing at all in common except for the similar emotional response they elicit.

Such results reinforce the position espoused by Zajonc (1980), among others, who advocated the primacy of affective reactions in social impressions. He wrote: "When we try to recall, recognize or retrieve an episode, a person, a piece of music, a story, a name . . . the affective quality of the original input is the first element to emerge" (p. 154).

The research demonstrating the strongly emotional character of social episodes and other social categories suggests that a person's current emotional state could also have a major impact on the way social events are attended to, interpreted, stored in memory, and subsequently retrieved. In a word, emotion and mood should have a profound impact on social memories and their reconstruction. This chapter reviews some of the research collected around this theme.

MEMORY FOR EMOTIONAL EPISODES

A well-established fact is that people's memory for social episodes is significantly influenced by the intensity of the emotion aroused by the episode. Emotional reactions play at least four important functional roles in directing how people learn and process such emotional events. First, emotional reactions frequently accompany failed expectations (and interruptions of goal strivings), and thus direct attention to the preceding and accompanying events as important items to be learned. Second, emotions mobilize attention to those features of an external situation that the learners judge to be significant or causative of the failed expectation and, in so doing, leads people to encode and learn about these features. Third, the inertial persistence of an emotional arousal and its slow decay (doubtless linked to endocrine discharges) facilitate the continued recycling, rehearsal, and continued consolidation of those encoded events that the person sees as causally belonging to the aroused emotion. Fourth, by their nature, highly emotional events are relatively rare, unusual, and distinctive amid the crowd of routine happenings of everyday life. Indeed, people arrange their daily world so that their goals are routinely satisfied and so they can avoid unpleasant surprises. The occasional upsets of people's social routines are not only emotionally arousing, but also rare; it is their rarity that makes them less subject to forgetting compared to the myriad routine happenings of their everyday life that are buried under massive interference from similar events.

The validity of this general analysis has been supported by considerable research, with both human and nonhuman subjects, both inside and outside the laboratory (for a review, see Bower, 1992; Christianson, 1992). Consider just one line of research relevant to social memory, namely, autobiographic memory. In several studies, subjects were recruited to record personal events in a daily diary and describe a number of their features (who, what, where, when, and how they felt about the event). After several weeks of recording, they turned in their diaries. Several days later, they were asked to recall or recognize the recorded incidents when given various cues about the incidents. Nearly all such studies have found that participants' recollections are higher for highly emotional events compared to nonemotional events. This result holds for both positive and negative events. Although the emotion felt is not an especially useful cue for a specific memory (who and where are better cues), the emotion felt at the time (and still felt when recollecting it) is a strong predictor of the recallability of the memory when given the effective cues.

AFFECTIVE RECALL WITHOUT FACTUAL RECALL

Robert Zajonc (1980, 2000) has long argued for the primacy of one's emotional reaction when asked to recollect some person or episode. After researching this topic since the 1980s (for a recent review, see Zajonc, 2000), there are now a large number of experiments that show that people tend to selectively remember their affective reactions to and evaluations of stimuli, even when they have no recollection of ever seeing that stimulus before, and have no memory for the reasons for their preferences. Indeed, it is a common experience in everyday life that we can recall how we felt about some person, place, happening, or attitude–object without being able to recall much in the way of specific supporting facts to justify our feelings.

A dramatic demonstration of this dissociation between evaluation and memory for supporting evidence occurred in a study of patients with severe memory impairments associated with Korsakoff's syndrome (Johnson, Kim, & Riff, 1985). Patients were shown a pair of photographs of neutral male faces and provided descriptions of prosocial (or antisocial) behaviors designed to make one man appear a likable "good guy" and the other a reprehensible "bad guy." Some days later, when shown each face, these amnesic patients were unable to recognize having seen the faces before or to recall any specific behavioral facts they had been told about these persons. Nonetheless, when asked to judge whether the photograph depicted someone who seemed like a nice or not-so-nice person, the patients' evaluations were consistent with the positive or negative descriptions they had heard earlier about each face, even though they had no recollection of any of the information that gave rise to the evaluation in the first place.

The demonstration with amnesic patients, illustrating the dissociation between storage of affective versus cognitive information, is just an extreme version of what often happens with all of us. This common observation turns out to have a simple explanation in associative network theories of the type long popular in cognitive psychology (see Anderson, 1983; Anderson & Bower, 1973). The basic idea (Fig. 5.1) is that as each fact (or belief with supporting evidence) about the person or place is encountered and thought about, our memory system stores a brief description of that information as well as a corresponding evaluation (positive, negative, or neutral) of it that is rendered automatically by the perceiver's affective appraisal system. As more episodes or facts about the object occur, each has just one fleeting opportunity to be learned, so the memory trace of the individual details (such as Positive Fact #1 and #7 in Fig. 5.1) is weak and easily forgotten. However, if each individual fact causes the same, for instance, positive evaluation, then a very strong association (labelled #1 in Fig. 5.1) is built up between the attitude–object and the positive valence node in memory. The more personally important a given fact is, the more it is thought about, and the more it causes a strengthening of the corresponding object-to-valence link. A given attitude–object, of course, may have a mixture of positive-, neutral-, and negative-valenced facts associated with it. The point is that the number and importance of these individual facts are accumulated and ultimately reflected in the strengths of the two object-to-valence links depicted in Fig. 5.1.

When the model is asked about the attitude–object ("What's your opinion of Harry?"), the various associations and memories come to mind (become available to consciousness) according to their relative strengths. The strongest one is likely to be the oft-repeated, oft-strengthened association to the predominant valence node. Thus, the model produces the primacy

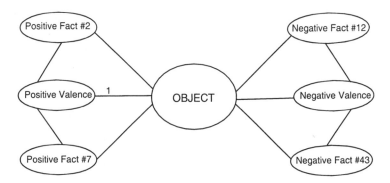

FIG. 5.1. Fragment of the associative network representing some person's beliefs (facts) and evaluations surrounding an attitude object, such as a person ("Harry") or a city ("New York"). Consideration of each valenced fact about this object causes simultaneous activation of and associations between the object and the corresponding valence node. Net evaluation of a concept depends on the strengths of its associations to the positive versus negative valence nodes. (Adapted from Bower, G. H., 1991. Mood congruity of social judgments. In J. P. Forgas (Ed.), *Emotion and social judgments* (pp. 31–53). Oxford: Pergamon Press.)

of affect phenomenon mentioned earlier. In fact, the model predicts that one should on some occasions be able to recall a strong evaluation without being able to recall any specific supporting facts (due to their weak traces). In terms of this analysis, there is no need to assume that affective reactions are somehow primary and separate from cognitive processes, as Zajonc (1980) proposed. Quite the opposite—it is the very close interdependence between how cognitive facts and affective evaluations are processed by the memory system that is largely responsible for the apparent primacy of affective evaluations.

When asked to give a balanced evaluation of a mixed attitude–object, the model essentially assesses the difference in strengths of associations from the object–node to the positive versus negative valence nodes. This can be achieved by activating the object concept ("thinking about Harry") and then checking to see how much activation accumulates at the positive versus negative valence nodes. A judgment may then be rendered depending on the difference in activation between the positive minus negative valence nodes. We should note that this valence-comparison process may well give rise to the phenomenologic experience of producing an evaluative response through the "How do I feel about it?" heuristic. Although several theorists argued that directly "consulting our feelings" involves no affect-priming and no memory-based processes (Clore, Schwarz, & Conway, 1994), our analysis suggests that the "How do I feel about it?" strategy may simply be the last and phenomenologically recognized stage in the kind of memory-based valence-comparison process we described here.

This associative network model provides the ingredients of an algebraic model of attitude and impression formation, like those proposed by Anderson (1974, 1996) and Fishbein and Ajzen (1975). As new beliefs are added (become associated with) to an existing attitude–object, the learner's judgment is shifted slightly in the evaluative direction of the new fact to a degree that depends on its personal significance (the intensity of emotional arousal it causes). The more facts that become known about a given attitude–object, the less in general is the impact of an additional fact on the summary judgment. This kind of algebraic model of information integration can also be elaborated to explain the effects of transient positive or negative moods on various evaluative judgments (see, for example, Abele & Petzold, 1994).

The network theory has several implications regarding social memory and social judgments. To begin with, the model implies that the extremity of an evaluative response should be greater, and the latency of its recall and expression should be shorter, to the extent that its association to one valenced node predominates over the other valence node. This relationship between decision latency and attitude extremity is well known in the survey and attitude-measurement literature. Several well-established models of recall and decision latency would predict this relationship between extremity of opinion and latency of judgment (see, e.g., Ratcliff, 1978).

A second implication of the associative network model is the existence of robust affective priming of the kind reported by Fazio, Sanbonmatsu, Powell, and Kardes (1986). The time subjects require to classify a given evaluative word such as *lovely* or *putrid* is reduced when these words are preceded by a matching positively or negatively valenced attitude item (such as *racist, abortion,* or *disarmament*). Positive judgments are speeded by positive primes, but are slowed by negative primes; negative judgments show the reverse pattern.

Such results flow naturally from the associative network model in Fig. 5.1. The evaluative decision about a target word is directly based on the strength of that word's long-term associations to the positive versus negative nodes in memory. The positive prime provides a headstart in activation accumulating at the positive valence node, so a positive target word (*pretty*) more quickly accumulates the differential activation needed to trigger a positive judgment. Conversely, a positive prime produces an initial handicap in valence that a negative target word (*putrid*) must overcome to reach the negative-judgment threshold—and this increases decision time for incongruous prime-target pairs of words.

EMOTIONAL UNITS IN
ASSOCIATIVE NETWORKS

The evaluation model outlined in Fig. 5.1 is one of a family of general network models proposed by the first author (Bower, 1981) and by Isen and associates (Clark & Isen, 1982; Isen, 1984; Isen et al., 1978) to account for mood effects on memory. This view is best summarized in Fig. 5.2, which depicts an emotion unit or node in an associative memory network (for example, #3 in Fig. 5.2 might correspond to anger or sadness). Bower presumed that there were about six (plus or minus two) "basic" emotion nodes that are biologically wired into the brain, each with several situational triggers, with each trigger becoming greatly elaborated and differentiated throughout the lifespan as a result of the person's socialization and cultural learning. Consistent with this view, Bower and Cohen (1982) proposed

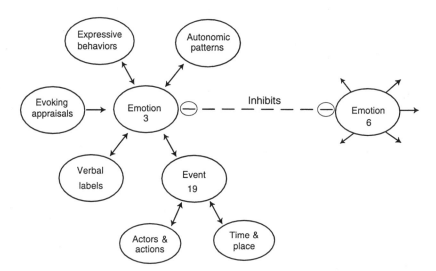

FIG. 5.2. A fragment of the associative network surrounding an emotion node in memory. For example, node 3 might represent sadness and inhibits emotion 6 for happiness. (Reproduced with permission from Bower, G. H., 1981. Mood and memory. *American Psychologist, 36,* 129–148.)

that the process of emotional elicitation could be modeled in terms of a collection of production rules that appraised and "recognized" particular situations calling for different emotional reactions. The specific content of such emotion production rules, and the cognitive mechanisms involved in emotion appraisal have been the subject of intensive research (see Smith and Kirby, 2000, for a review).

Once an emotion is aroused due to the person appraising an emotional situation, that node spreads excitation to a variety of indicators to which it is connected. These indicators include physiological and autonomic reactions characteristic of that emotion, facial and postural expressions, verbal labels for one's state, a collection of action tendencies, and a set of memories of episodes that had been associated with that emotion in the past. These would ordinarily be events that causally evoked (and "belonged to") that emotion. For example, assume that one event recorded in this memory structure is a description of a scene from a friend's funeral that caused a man to feel sad. If that man is later asked about his friend at a time when he is feeling sad, the funeral memory may receive more total activation from the retrieval cue plus his current emotion. As a result, this scene is more likely to come to mind and be reported than are other recollections about the friend (such as happy times spent together). This kind of summation of activation at the intersection between a retrieval cue and a current emotion node predicts that memory will be mood dependent or emotion dependent. In particular, the memory record of an event should be stored in association with the emotion evoked and experienced during that event. This implies that one efficient way for people to retrieve a memory later is for them to get back into the same (or similar) emotional or mood state as they were when they learned it.

MOOD-DEPENDENT RETRIEVAL

The story of research on mood-dependent retrieval began in the arid confines of standard laboratory investigations of context effects in human memory. In fact, these studies investigated memory for stimuli (lists of neutral, unrelated nouns) that were the very antithesis of realistic social episodes. In an early experiment of this kind, Bower, Monteiro, and Gilligan (1978) wondered whether a person's emotional mood would serve as a context to which the word lists would become associated. To this end, they conducted a two-phase experiment that has since become a prototype for such procedures. In a first phase, half the subjects were persuaded to get into a feeling state of happiness and the other half of the subjects were persuaded to get into a feeling state of sadness. In this first study, the mood induction consisted of having hypnotized college students replay slowly in their imagination some autobiographic events when they had felt happy or sad (these were typically interpersonal episodes). In later experiments, many different methods for inducing moods have been used, showing that the memory effects are not dependent on any particular mood induction technique.

Following a first mood induction, subjects studied then recalled a list of 16 unrelated nouns. Then a second, opposite mood was induced and subjects studied and recalled a second list of unrelated words. After a brief interpolated task, half the subjects were induced to feel happy and half to feel sad (via different remembered events than used initially) and were asked to free recall the first list of words, and then recall the second list. The order of learning and recall of the mood lists was counterbalanced over subjects. Results (Fig. 5.3) showed that subjects remembered the words

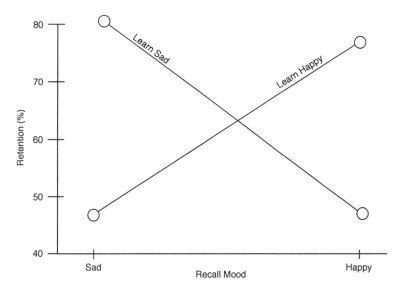

FIG. 5.3. Recall of lists of unrelated words learned earlier when subjects were happy or sad, and then recalled when they were feeling happy or sad. The better recall procured by matching of learning and recall moods is dubbed *mood-dependent retrieval*. (Reproduced with permission from Bower, G. H., Monteiro, K. P., & Gilligan, S. G., 1978. Emotional mood as a context for learning and recall. *Journal of Verbal Learning and Verbal Behavior*, 17, 573–585.)

better when their mood at recall matched the mood they were in when learning the list initially. The gist of this result was repeated in several other studies conducted around that time (Bower, 1981).

If such mood-dependent retrieval occurred only with unrelated word lists in the laboratory, it would be of limited interest. However, mood-dependent retrieval was soon shown also to arise in recall of autobiographic emotional episodes. When asked to recall events from their past, people recall a selected sample of memories whose valence agrees with their emotional state during recall. For example, when subjects were hypnotically induced to experience happy or sad moods and were asked to recall episodes from their childhood, their memories were predominantly consistent with their current mood. Happy subjects recalled more happy childhood episodes, and sad subjects remembered more sad episodes (Bower, 1981). In another experiment, recollections of emotional social events recorded in a diary were also significantly biased in the direction of subjects' current mood state (Bower, 1981). An experiment by Snyder and White (1982) illustrated similar mood-dependent biases in recall of recent autobiographic events. They induced their college-student subjects to feel happy or sad, then asked them to recall any autobiographic episodes from the previous 2 weeks. Figure 5.4

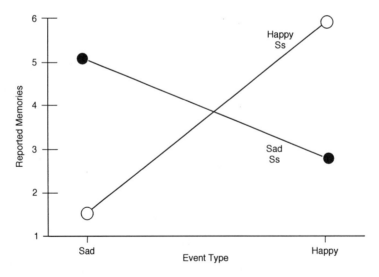

FIG. 5.4. Number of happy and sad memories of recent events reported by subjects made temporarily happy or sad. (Based on Snyder, M., & White, P., 1982. Moods and memories: Elation, depression and the remembering of the events of one's life. *Journal of Personality, 50,* 149–167. Adapted with permission.)

shows that when happy, subjects retrieved relatively more happy events; when sad, they retrieved more sad events. This result illustrates a mood-dependent retrieval pattern because presumably subjects felt appropriately happy or sad earlier when these events originally occurred in their lives.

A similar bias in recall also occurs for people who exhibit sadness as a long-term affective disorder. When recalling their recent past, psychiatrically depressed patients have a strong bias to recall mainly negative, depressing episodes (Lewinsohn & Rosenbaum, 1987). This mood-dependent recall bias contributes to the downward spiral of negative recollections feeding into a preexisting state of dysphoria, and is one of the obstacles to be overcome by effective psychotherapy. Similarly, highly anxious patients recall primarily frightening and/or threatening events from their past, often centered around some social area of particular concern to them (Burke & Mathews, 1992).

Research using implicit rather than explicit memory tasks (when subjects are not consciously trying to recall information) also provide convergent support for mood-dependent retrieval as predicted by network theories. For example, when asked to complete ambiguous word stems, depressed people tend to produce negative rather than positive words, consistent with the selective priming of negative information by their depressed mood (Ruiz-Caballero & Gonzalez, 1994). This mood-priming effect also influences the time it takes to retrieve emotional memories; it appears that depressed people take less time to retrieve unpleasant rather than pleasant memories, whereas nondepressed people show the opposite pattern (Lloyd & Lishman, 1975; Teasdale & Fogarty, 1979).

The original idea in proposing an explanation of such instances of mood-dependent retrieval was that an aroused emotion would become associated by temporal contiguity to whatever ideas or thoughts occupied short-term memory at the time. However, this simple and broad account relying on associations based on contiguity alone encountered some serious difficulties, and was later revised to restrict learning to associations between an episode and the emotional reaction that it caused. That is, for an association to occur, the person must causally attribute the emotional reaction to the episode that caused it (for a review, see Bower, 1992; Eich, 1995; Eich & Macauley, 2000). This is why, for example, mood-dependent retrieval occurs most reliably when happy or sad people recall autobiographic events. Remembering mood-congruent events is presumably easier because there is likely to be a causal link between the event and the mood elicited by it at the time.

Mood-dependent retrieval is also reliably obtained in many experiments looking at realistic social judgments (see Forgas & Bower, 1988). When the information to be encoded is about people, events, or complex social situations rather than word lists, subjects are more likely to perceive a degree of causal belonging between the material and their mood than would be the case with simple and personally uninvolving stimuli. Studies of social judgment provide subjects with a much richer and more elaborate set of encoding and retrieval cues than is the case in word-list experiments, increasing the likelihood that affective cues can effectively function as a useful and differentiating context in learning and recall.

MOOD-CONGRUENT PROCESSING

A second main effect of emotion implied by the network model in Fig. 5.2 is what has been called *mood-congruent processing*. This occurs when people become selectively sensitized to take in information that agrees with their prevailing emotional state. In an earlier paper, Bower (1983) wrote:

> When emotions are strongly aroused, concepts, words, themes, and rules of inference that are associated with that emotion will become primed and highly available for use by the emotional subject. We can thus expect the emotional person to use top-down or expectation-driven processing of his social environment. That is, his emotional state will bring into readiness certain perceptual categories, certain themes, certain ways of interpreting the world that are congruent with his emotional state; these mental sets then act as interpretive filters of reality and as biases in his judgments. (p. 395)

One implication of the associative network model is that mood-congruent material should become more salient, so that people should attend to it more and process it more deeply. This prediction has been verified several times (see Eich et al., in press). People who are made to feel happy versus sad spend more time looking at happy versus sad pictures, watch more happy versus sad television shows, listen more to happy versus sad music, and seek out more pleasant social activities versus somber solitary activities, respectively.

As a consequence of deeper processing of emotionally congruent material, subjects also tend to engage in greater associative elaboration of such information, and thus learn it better. Thus, when happy persons are exposed to a mixture of pleasant and unpleasant materials, they learn more about pleasant materials; when sad, they learn more about the unpleasant stimuli in their mixed environment. This result has been found in many studies. In one experiment that directly tested this effect, subjects read behavioral descriptions about target characters in an impression-formation experiment (Forgas & Bower, 1987). Participants in a happy mood spent longer reading and learning about positive characteristics and later remembered more of the positive, socially desirable behaviors and traits ascribed to a target stranger. Participants in a sad mood spent longer reading and remembered more of the socially undesirable behaviors and traits ascribed to the stranger. In a similar manner, depressed psychiatric patients show better learning and memory for depressive words (Watkins, Mathews, Williamson, & Fuller, 1992), a bias that disappears once the depressive symptoms are relieved (Bradley & Mathews, 1983). However, mood-congruent learning seems to be an evanescent phenomenon in patients suffering from anxiety (Burke & Mathews, 1992), possibly because anxious patients are particularly prone to use vigilant, motivated processing strategies designed to filter out anxiety arousing information (Mathews & MacLeod, 1994).

Mood congruence also arises when subjects produce free associations and imaginative fantasies. In free associations to ambiguous words like *my career*, *life*, or *future*, happy subjects tend to produce pleasant associations, whereas sad or angry subjects produce sad or unpleasant associations (Bower, 1981). A similar result occurs when subjects made temporarily happy or sad generate stories about inherently ambiguous social scenes depicted in Thematic Aperception Test (TAT) cards. Happy subjects tend to generate positive stories about success and romance; sad subjects produce negative stories about struggles, hardships, and failure. In terms of an associative network memory model, these mood-dependent effects arise because the emotion primes into readiness and facilitates the recall and use of mood-congruent valenced themes around which they begin to weave a story.

These associative effects also produce affect-congruent distortions in many real-life situations due to naturally occurring moods (Mayer & Volanth, 1985; Mayer et al., 1992). Mood congruence appears to be a reliable phenomenon when people recall and evaluate their possessions, their career, their marriage, their health status, their satisfaction with their lives, their prospects for the future, the likelihood of good or bad things happening in the near future, the acceptance of positive versus negative feedback about their personality, their manner of explaining their successes and failures, and estimates of their personal skills in social and nonsocial areas (for a review, see Eich et al., in press). Temporary happy or sad moods can also produce a marked congruent effect on many social judgments, such as perceptions of human faces (Schiffenbauer, 1974), impressions about people (Forgas, 1992; Forgas & Bower, 1987), attractiveness of verbally described characters (Gouaux, 1971; Gouaux & Summers, 1973), stereotypes of ethnic groups (Forgas & Moylan, 1991), and self-perceptions (Forgas, Bower, & Krantz, 1984; Sedikides, 1995).

LIMITATIONS ON MOOD CONGRUITY

Although there is substantial confirming evidence for affect priming and mood congruence, several studies found that mood congruence is sometimes absent or even reversed. Although the emotion network theory supposes that mood-congruent processing is the "natural tendency" whenever people experience a powerful emotion, it is clear that people can—and often do—overcome their natural tendencies. Indeed, socialization throughout childhood often requires learning to limit and even reverse natural emotional impulses. As a result, children do learn to sit still in school, even though they are excited; they learn to stifle giggles in church and suppress anger or sadness when such feelings are socially inappropriate. Most people have learned various cognitive tricks to control their emotional states and expressions—to suppress loud sobbing at the movies, to withstand the pain of the dentist's drill, to count to 10 when angered, to feign interest when bored, and to express gratitude for an unwanted gift. Such motivated strategies for controlling affect are an essential prerequisite for effective functioning within polite society. These cognitive tricks often make use of distractions and the imagined rehearsal of countervailing scenes, and selectively focusing on more positive thoughts. Momentarily depressed people usually know that they can improve their mood by watching comedies, talking to friends, and thinking over more pleasant times. In fact, these are the kinds of mental habits that many kinds of cognitive therapy seek to instill in clients suffering from chronic mood disorders such as depression.

Research has shown that to the extent that such mood-repair stratagems are likely to be activated, mood-congruity effects on memory, perceptions, and social judgments are ameliorated, eliminated, or occasionally reversed. Indeed, it seems that merely shifting attentional focus toward internal states seems sufficient to trigger motivated processing and eliminate mood congruence (Berkowitz et al., 2000). Of course, not all individuals are equally effective in engaging in such motivated mood control. For example, Smith and Petty (1995) found that the mood-congruent influence of a negative mood (after watching a film about cancer) on composing a brief fictional story was moderated by subjects' self-esteem. Subjects with low self-esteem showed simple mood congruity by writing sad stories. In contrast, subjects with high self-esteem were not influenced by their prevailing mood. In a similar vein, people who score high on traits such as machiavellianism and social desirability were also found to be more likely to engage in motivated processing, showing reduced mood-congruity effects in the way they perceived, planned, and performed in social encounters (Forgas, 1998). There is growing evidence that personality and individual differences play a critical role in moderating many affect-priming effects due to the targeted, motivated processing strategies they elicit (see Rusting, 1998, for a review of this issue).

It seems then that mood-congruent priming effects can be overridden when people have a clear motivation to do so (see Kunda, 1990). The occasional observations of mood-incongruent memory can perhaps be explained in this way. For example, Parrott and Sabini (1990) found mood-incongruent memory when students were asked to recall autobiographic events while being interviewed outdoors during a sunny versus an overcast day. People rated themselves as happier on the sunny day; yet, the first memory retrieved on an overcast day was more likely to be a pleasant one (even though later memories became more mood congruent). These mood-incongruent effects were explained by the authors as due to people trying to repair the bad mood that a rainy, overcast day instills.

These outcomes plus numerous other studies have suggested that affect priming and mood congruence are not a universal finding. Rather, affect priming effects vary widely depending on contextual factors such as the nature of the task, the complexity of the information, the personality and motivation of the subjects, and the features of the situation (Blaney, 1986; Fiedler, 1991; Forgas et al., 1984). For example, in experiments by Forgas (1992, 1994, 1995b, 1999), mood congruence was diminished as the targets to be judged became more clear-cut and thus required less constructive processing. Based on person-perception experiments showing variations in mood congruence, Fiedler (1991) had earlier suggested that mood congruence was best demonstrated when the subject's judgment or expression of opinion was about a somewhat ambiguous, vague, or amorphous topic that required some amount of open, constructive processing of information. Examples are such topics as satisfaction with one's life, career, marriage, or prospects for peace in some conflict arena. Constructing or arriving at an opinion about such vague topics requires the generation and use of previously stored and affectively primed information. In contrast, temporary affective states have less impact on memories and judgments when people express familiar, crystallized attitudes that they had stored previously, or when their responses are about a clear and strongly valenced stimulus that does not require cognitive elaboration. A further complication was reported by Schwarz (1990) and by Clore and coworkers (1994), who found that if the irrelevant source of a negative or positive mood was brought to the participant's attention, mood-congruity effects on life-satisfaction judgments were considerably weakened or even eliminated. These authors suggested that by bringing the current mood to subjects' attention, subjects could thereby discount its impact on their judgment.

INFORMATION-PROCESSING STRATEGIES THAT MODERATE MOOD EFFECTS ON MEMORY

The kind of associative network model of mood effects on memory discussed here (see also Figs. 5.1 and 5.2) is based on the assumption that people employ an open, unbiased search of their memory structures when producing a response. If a response can be generated in an alternate way that does not require the active and constructive search of preexisting memory representations, there is little reason to expect mood-congruity effects. The kind of information-processing strategy people adopt when dealing with a memory task may thus be critical to understanding why mood-congruent memory effects are obtained in some circumstances, but are absent in others. It was with this goal in mind that Forgas (1995a) proposed the affect infusion model (AIM; see also chap. 14, this volume), designed to specify the circumstances in which mood congruity is likely or unlikely to occur.

The AIM seeks to define and systematize what is now known about the boundary conditions of mood congruity effects as predicted by network theories. The AIM makes explicit what was, in fact, always an implicit assumption of the original network formulations: That it is only under conditions that lead to open and unbiased information search and processing strategies that the mood-congruent predictions of associative network models should arise. In effect, the AIM is a hybrid model that incorporates ideas from both cognitive and social psychology. Its key emphasis is on different information-processing strategies (a cognitive construct), but it predicts that these different information-processing styles are adopted in response to such social variables as the personal relevance of the topic, situational complexity, and the individual characteristics of the judge (e.g., expertise).

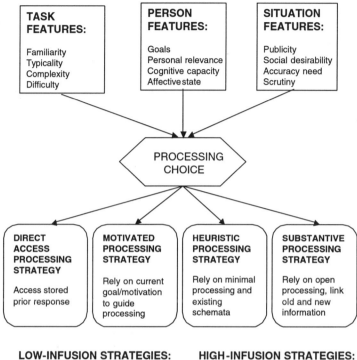

FIG. 5.5. Schematic outline of the multiprocess affect infusion model (AIM): Affect infusion in social cognition depends on which of four alternative processing strategies is adopted in response to target, judge, and situational features. The flowchart illustrates the hierarchical relationships among factors determining processing choices, and the multiple informational and processing effects influence of affect on judgments. (After Forgas, J. P., 1995a. Mood and judgment: The Affect Infusion Model (AIM). *Psychological Bulletin, 117,* 1–28.)

The AIM distinguishes among four distinct processing strategies, as depicted in Fig. 5.5. Two of these strategies (direct access and motivated processing) involve relatively closed, directed information-search processes that limit the opportunity for affect priming and affect infusion. The other two strategies (heuristic and substantive processing) require more constructive and open-ended thinking, which allows multiple avenues and opportunities for affect infusion. Affect priming is most likely in circumstances conducive to open, substantive processing. It is during substantive processing that people must constructively select, learn, interpret, and process information about a task and then relate this information to preexisting knowledge structures in memory. The AIM states that the likelihood of substantive processing is greater when the task is complex or atypical, personally relevant, and when subjects have adequate processing capacity but no specific countervailing motivational goal. Furthermore, the more extensive processing is required to compute a judgment, the more likely it is that affect infusion will influence the outcome.

This counterintuitive prediction—that more substantive processing should increase rather than reduce the extent of affect infusion—has been supported in several experiments (Fiedler, 1991; Forgas, 1992, 1993, 1994, 1995b). In these studies, happy or sad subjects encoded and later recalled and evaluated more or less typical others (Forgas, 1992), formed impressions about more or less well-matched dating couples (Forgas, 1993, 1995b; Forgas & Moylan, 1991), and explained more or less serious relationship conflicts (Forgas, 1994). In all cases, affect priming was observed mainly in circumstances conducive to substantive processing, as expected by the AIM. Furthermore, these studies also showed—consistent with associative network explanations—that the extent of mood congruity was directly related to the complexity and ambiguity of the task and to the extent that an open, constructive processing strategy was required to compose an opinion. Thus, judging atypical people, mismatched couples, and difficult marital conflicts took longer and produced greater mood congruity than did judging typical people, well-matched couples, and routine conflicts.

In terms of the AIM, rapid heuristic processing may also produce mood-congruent judgmental outcomes in circumstances in which subjects rely directly on their mood as a proxy to infer their evaluation of a topic. However, heuristic processing does not offer a plausible explanation for the kind of mood-congruent learning and memory effects discussed here, as it assumes the absence of extensive memory search processes.

Whether heuristic or substantive processing was used in producing a particular mood-congruent response can be evaluated empirically by recording latency of the opinion response, thus rendering the processing predictions of the AIM empirically falsifiable (Forgas & Bower, 1987). The evidence suggests that mood-congruent recall and judgment effects are greater when processing latency increases, a result suggesting that fast, heuristic processing is not producing these effects. In fact, affect priming typically occurs in the course of substantive, elaborate processing (when reaction times are slow) and disappears when other (heuristic, direct access, or motivated) processing strategies are used (Forgas, 1994, 1995b, 1998). Thus, the AIM provides a general framework within which the affect-priming influences on memory and judgments predicted by network theory can be delineated, and also explains the boundary conditions that limit affect priming.

SUMMARY AND CONCLUSIONS

Throughout history, philosophers, artists, and laypersons have long speculated about the close interdependence between feeling and thinking, and between affect and cognition (Hilgard, 1980). Associative network theories provide a conceptual framework for understanding the mechanisms that link affect and social cognition. These ideas have stimulated an impressive amount of research during the last few decades. The associative network model (Bower, 1981, 1991; Clark & Isen, 1982; Isen, 1984) explains how affect can facilitate access to related cognitions, and thus offers a simple and parsimonious explanation for a broad range of mood congruity effects on memory and judgments.

This chapter reviewed some of the basic explanations for affective influences on social memory and considered some of the empirical evidence supporting the associative network model. As accumulating research showed the absence or even reversal of mood-congruity effects on memory in occasional circumstances, a critical review of the network model has become necessary. Integrative theories such as the affect infusion model (AIM; Forgas, 1995a) seek to define the boundary conditions for the emotion network theory; AIM expects mood congruity to occur only when people adopt open, constructive, and substantive processing (Fiedler, 1991). Affect priming of social judgments is unlikely when heuristic, direct access, or motivated processing strategies are adopted. Such strategies preclude the open, constructive information processing that is a prerequisite for affect infusion (Forgas, 1995a).

Based on the available evidence, associative network theories continue to provide the most general and parsimonious explanation for the influence of affective states on memory and other cognitive processes. Specifically, counterintuitive results showing that more extensive, substantive processing enhances mood congruity provide particularly strong support for network models (Forgas, 1992, 1994, 1995b). The implications of network theories apply not only in the laboratory, but also in many real-life cognitive tasks. Numerous studies found affect-infusion effects on memory and thinking in organizational decisions, personnel selection choices, consumer preferences, clinical practice, and health-related judgments that support network theories (Bower, 1995; Eich et al., in press; Forgas, 2000; Mayer et al., 1992). Paradoxically, the more people need to engage in open, constructive processing in order to deal with a problem—that is, to "reason" about it—the more likely their affective state will influence their memory, judgments, and decisions. These effects can even influence such involved and complex tasks as remembering and seeking an explanation for difficult real-life relationship conflicts (Forgas, 1994).

Most of the evidence considered here deals with the cognitive consequences of affective states. However, associative network principles also describe how affective states are elicited as a result of the activation of emotion production rules that instantiate appraisal rules (Bower & Cohen, 1982). Indeed, recent theorizing within the emotional appraisal literature explicitly suggests that associative network models of memory provide the most promising integrative link between research concerned with the cognitive antecedents of emotion and research on the cognitive consequences of affect (Smith & Kirby, 2000).

To conclude, the associative network framework provides a general approach for understanding both affect-appraisal and affect-infusion effects. We now recognize that these effects depend on several aspects of the personal and social context. We believe that evidence suggesting the absence or even reversal of mood-congruity effects in some circumstances should not be interpreted as inconsistent with and disconfirming of associative network theory. The AIM approach offers an integrative framework for delineating the boundary conditions under which open and constructive memory search strategies are most likely to be used, so that affect-priming and mood-congruent outcomes should be obtained. By clarifying the characteristics and conditions of affective influences on social memory, we hope that this chapter will encourage further research in this important domain.

ACKNOWLEDGMENT

Preparation of this chapter was aided by an NIMH research grant, MH-47575, to the G. H. Bower from the National Institute of Mental Health. The research of J. P. Forgas was supported by an Australian Research Council

Special Investigator Award, and the Research Prize from the Alexander von Humboldt Foundation, Germany.

REFERENCES

Abele, A., & Petzold, P. (1994). How does mood operate in an impression formation task? An information integration approach. *European Journal of Social Psychology, 24,* 173–188.

Abelson, R. P. (1981). Psychological status of the script concept. *American Psychologist, 36,* 715–729.

Anderson, J. R. (1983). *The architecture of cognition.* Cambridge, MA: Harvard University Press.

Anderson, J. R., & Bower, G. H. (1973). *Human associative memory.* Washington DC: Winston & Sons.

Anderson, N. H. (1974). Information integration theory: A brief survey. In D. A. Krantz, R. C. Atkinson, R. D. Luce, & P. Suppes (Eds.), *Contemporary developments in mathematical psychology,* Vol. 2 (pp. 236–305). San Francisco: Freeman Press.

Anderson, N. H. (1996). *A functional theory of cognition.* Mahwah, NJ: Lawrence Erlbaum Associates.

Berkowitz, L., Jaffee, S., Jo, F., & Troccoli, B. T. (2000). On the correction of feeling-induced judgmental biases. In J. P. Forgas (Ed.), *Feeling and thinking: The role of affect in social cognition* (pp. 131–152). New York: Cambridge University Press.

Blaney, P. H. (1986). Affect and memory: A review. *Psychological Bulletin, 99,* 229–246.

Bower, G. H. (1981). Mood and memory. *American Psychologist, 36,* 129–148.

Bower, G. H. (1983). Affect and cognition. *Philosophical Transactions of the Royal Society of London B, 302,* 387–402.

Bower, G. H. (1991). Mood congruity of social judgments. In J. P. Forgas (Ed.), *Emotion and social judgments* (pp. 31–53). Oxford: Pergamon Press.

Bower, G. H. (1992). How might emotions affect learning? In F. A. Christianson, *The handbook of emotion and memory: Research and theory* (pp. 3–32). Hillsdale, NJ: Lawrence Erlbaum Associates.

Bower, G. H. (1995). Emotion and social judgments. Speech delivered at Capital Hill Sciences Seminar; paper published by the Federation of Behavioral, Psychological, and Cognitive Sciences, pp. 1–29, Washington, DC.

Bower, G. H., Black, J. B., & Turner, T. J. (1979). Scripts in memory for text. *Cognitive Psychology, 11,* 177–220.

Bower, G. H., & Cohen, P. R. (1982). Emotional influences in memory and thinking: Data and theory. In M. S. Clark & S. T. Fiske (Eds.), *Affect and cognition* (pp. 291–332). Hillsdale, NJ: Lawrence Erlbaum Associates.

Bower, G. H., Monteiro, K. P., & Gilligan, S. G. (1978). Emotional mood as a context for learning and recall. *Journal of Verbal Learning and Verbal Behavior, 17,* 573–585.

Bradley, P. P., & Mathews, A. M. (1983). Negative self schemata in clinical depression. *British Journal of Clinical Psychology, 22,* 173–181.

Bruner, J. S., Goodnow, J. J., & Austin, G. A. (1956). *A study of thinking.* New York: Wiley.

Burke, M., & Mathews, A. M. (1992). Autobiographical memory and clinical anxiety. *Cognition and Emotion, 6,* 23–35.

Cahill, L. (1996). The neurobiology of memory for emotional events: Converging evidence from infra-human and human studies. *Function and Dysfunction in the Nervous System, Symposium 61, LXI,* 259–264. Cold Spring Harbor: Harvard Press.

Christianson, F. A. (1992). *The handbook of emotion and memory: Research and theory.* Hillsdale, NJ: Lawrence Erlbaum Associates.

Clark, M. S., & Isen, A. M. (1982). Towards understanding the relationship between feeling states and social behavior. In A. H. Hastorf & A. M. Isen (Eds.), *Cognitive social psychology* (pp. 73–108). New York: Elsevier-North Holland.

Clore, G. L., Schwarz, N., & Conway, M. (1994). Affective causes and consequences of social information processing. In R. S. Wyer & T. K. Srull (Eds.), *Handbook of social cognition*, 2nd ed. (pp. 323–417). Hillsdale, NJ: Lawrence Erlbaum Associates.

Eich, E. (1995). Searching for mood dependent memory. *Psychological Science, 6*, 67–75.

Eich, E., & Macauley, E. (2000). Fundamental factors in mood dependent memory. In J. P. Forgas (Ed.), *Feeling and thinking: The role of affect in social cognition* (pp. 109–130). New York: Cambridge University Press.

Eich, E., Kihlstrom, J., Bower, G. H., Forgas, J. P., & Niedenthal, P. (in press). *Emotion and cognition.* New York: Oxford University Press.

Fazio, R. H., Sanbonmatsu, D. N., Powell, M. C., & Kardes, F. R. (1986). On the automatic activation of attitudes. *Journal of Personality and Social Psychology, 50*, 229–238.

Fiedler, K. (1991). On the task, the measures and the mood in research on affect and social cognition. In J. P. Forgas (Ed.), *Emotion and social judgments* (pp. 83–104). Oxford, MA: Pergamon Press.

Fishbein, M., & Ajzen. I. (1975). *Belief, attitude, intention, and behavior: An introduction to theory and research.* Redding, MA: Addison-Wesley.

Forgas, J. P. (1979). *Social episodes: The study of interaction routines.* London, New York: Academic Press.

Forgas, J. P. (1981). Affective and emotional influences on episode representations. In J. P. Forgas (Ed.), *Social cognition: Perspectives on everyday understanding.* London, New York: Academic Press.

Forgas, J. P. (1992). On bad mood and peculiar people: Affect and person typicality in impression formation. *Journal of Personality and Social Psychology, 62*, 863–875.

Forgas, J. P. (1993). On making sense of odd couples: Mood effects on the perception of mismatched relationships. *Personality and Social Psychology Bulletin, 19*, 59–71.

Forgas, J. P. (1994). Sad and guilty? Affective influences on the explanation of conflict episodes. *Journal of Personality and Social Psychology, 66*, 56–68.

Forgas, J. P. (1995a). Mood and judgment: The Affect Infusion Model (AIM). *Psychological Bulletin, 117*, 1–28.

Forgas, J. P. (1995b). Strange couples: Mood effects on judgments and memory about prototypical and atypical targets. *Personality and Social Psychology Bulletin, 21*, 747–765.

Forgas, J. P. (1998). Feeling good and getting your way: Mood effects on negotiating strategies and outcomes. *Journal of Personality and Social Psychology, 74*, 565–577.

Forgas, J. P. (1999). On feeling good and being rude: Affective influences on language use and request formulations. *Journal of Personality and Social Psychology, 76*, 928–939.

Forgas, J. P. (2000). (Ed.). *Feeling and thinking: The role of affect in social cognition and behavior.* New York: Cambridge University Press.

Forgas, J. P., & Bower, G. H. (1987). Mood effects on person–perception judgments. *Journal of Personality and Social Psychology, 53*, 53–60.

Forgas, J. P., & Bower, G. H. (1988). Affect in social judgements. *Australian Journal of Psychology, 40*, 125–145.

Forgas, J. P., & Moylan, S. J. (1991). Affective influences on stereotype judgments. *Cognition and Emotion, 5*, 379–397.

Forgas, J. P., Bower, G. H., & Krantz, S. (1984). The influence of mood on perceptions of social interactions. *Journal of Experimental Social Psychology, 20*, 497–513.

Gouaux, C. (1971). Induced affective states and interpersonal attraction. *Journal of Personality and Social Psychology, 20*, 37–43.

Gouaux, C., & Summers, K. (1973). Interpersonal attraction as a function of affective state and affective change. *Journal of Research in Personality, 7*, 254–260.

Graesser, A. C., Woll, F. B., Kowalski, D. J., & Smith, D. A. (1980). Memory for typical and atypical actions in scripted activities. *Journal of Experimental Psychology: Human Learning and Memory, 6*, 503–515.

Hilgard, E. R. (1980). The trilogy of mind: Cognition, affection and conation. *Journal of the History of the Behavioral Sciences, 16,* 107–117.

Isen, A. M. (1984). Toward understanding the role of affect in cognition. In R. S. Wyer & T. K. Srull (Eds.), *The handbook of social cognition,* (Vol. 3, pp. 179–236). Hillsdale, NJ: Lawrence Erlbaum Associates.

Isen, A. M., Shalker, T. E., Clark, M., & Karp, L. (1978). Affect, accessibility of material and memory, and behavior: A cognitive loop? *Journal of Personality and Social Psychology, 36,* 1–12.

Johnson, M. K., Kim, J. K., & Riff, G. (1985). Do alcoholic Korsakoff's syndrome patients acquire affective reactions? *Journal of Experimental Psychology: Learning, Memory and Cognition, 11,* 22–36.

Kunda, Z. (1990). The case for motivated reasoning. *Psychological Bulletin, 108,* 331–350.

Lewinsohn, P. M., & Rosenbaum, M. (1987). Recall of parental behavior by acute depressives, remitted depressives, and nondepressives. *Journal of Personality and Social Psychology, 52,* 611–619.

Lloyd, G. G., & Lishman, W. A. (1975). Effect of depression on the speed of recall of pleasant and unpleasant experiences. *Psychological Medicine, 5,* 173–180.

McGaugh, M. C., & Cahill, L. (1997). Interaction of neuromodulatory systems in modulating memory storage. *Behavioral Brain Research, 83,* 31–38.

Magnusson, D. E. (1971). An analysis of situational dimensions. *Perceptual and Motor Skills, 32,* 851–867.

Mathews, A. M., & McLeod, C. (1994). Cognitive approaches to emotion and emotional disorders. *Annual Review of Psychology, 45,* 25–50.

Mayer, J. D., & Volanth, A. J. (1985). Cognitive involvement in mood response system. *Motivation and Emotion, 9(3),* 261–275.

Mayer, J. D., Gaschke, Y. N., Braverman, D. L., & Evans, T. W. (1992). Mood congruent judgment is a general effect. *Journal of Personality and Social Psychology, 63,* 119–132.

Niedenthal, P., & Halberstadt, J. (2000). Grounding categories in emotional response. In J. P. Forgas (Ed.), *Feeling and thinking: The role of affect in social cognition* (pp. 357–386). New York: Cambridge University Press.

Parrott, W. G., & Sabini, J. (1990). Mood and memory under natural conditions: Evidence for mood incongruent recall. *Journal of Personality and Social Psychology, 59,* 321–336.

Pervin, L. A. (1976). A free response description approach to the study of person–situation interaction. *Journal of Personality and Social Psychology, 35,* 465–474.

Ratcliff, R. (1978). A theory of memory retrieval. *Psychological Review, 85,* 59–108.

Ruiz Caballero, J. A., & Gonzalez, P. (1994). Implicit and explicit memory bias in depressed and non-depressed subjects. *Cognition and Emotion, 8,* 555–570.

Rusting, C. L. (1998). Personality, mood, and cognitive processing of emotional information: Three conceptual frameworks. *Psychological Bulletin, 124(2),* 165–196.

Schiffenbauer, A. I. (1974). Effect of observer's emotional state on judgments of the emotional state of others. *Journal of Personality and Social Psychology, 30(1),* 31–35.

Schwarz, N. (1990). Feelings as information: Informational and motivational functions of affective states. In E. T. Higgins & R. Sorrentino (Eds.), *Handbook of motivation and cognition: Foundations of social behaviour* (Vol. 2, pp. 527–561). New York: Guilford Press.

Sedikides, C. (1995). Central and peripheral self-conceptions are differentially influenced by mood: Tests of the differential sensitivity hypothesis. *Journal of Personality and Social Psychology, 69(4),* 759–777.

Smith, C. A., & Kirby, L. D. (2000). Appraisal and memory: Toward a process model of emotion-eliciting situations. In J. P. Forgas (Ed.), *Feeling and thinking: The role of affect in social cognition* (pp. 83–108). New York: Cambridge University Press.

Smith, S. M., & Petty, R. E. (1995). Personality moderators of mood congruency effects on cognition: The role of self-esteem and negative mood regulation. *Journal of Personality & Social Psychology, 68,* 1092–1107.

Snyder, M., & White, P. (1982). Moods and memories: Elation, depression and the remembering of the events of one's life. *Journal of Personality, 50,* 149–167.

Teasdale, J. D., & Forgarty, S. J. (1979). Differential effects on induced mood on retrieval of pleasant and unpleasant events from episodic memory. *Journal of Abnormal Psychology, 88,* 248–257.

Watkins, T., Mathews, A. M., Williamson, D. A., & Fuller, R. (1992). Mood congruent memory in depression: Emotional priming or elaboration. *Journal of Abnormal Psychology, 101,* 581–586.

Zajonc, R. (1980). Feeling and thinking: Preferences need no inferences. *American Psychologist, 35,* 151–175.

Zajonc, R. (2000). Feeling and thinking: Closing the debate on the primacy of affect. In J. P. Forgas (Ed.), *Feeling and thinking: The role of affect in social cognition* (pp. 31–58). New York: Cambridge University Press.

6

Affect as Information

Gerald L. Clore

University of Illinois at Urbana-Champaign
Champaign, Illinois

Karen Gasper

Pennsylvania State University, University Park
Pennsylvania

Erika Garvin

University of Illinois at Urbana-Champaign
Champaign, Illinois

Affect and Judgment	122
Traditional Views	122
The Affect-as-Information View	123
Mood and Processing	129
Priming and Processing	133
Mood and Memory	136
Summary	139
Acknowledgments	140
References	141

Experience is something that can't be replaced. . . .
It's like describing what an orange tastes like.
You've got to eat an orange.

—Tango instructor Paul Pellicoro, as quoted by Scott, 1999: 8

Address for correspondence: Gerald L. Clore, Department of Psychology, University of Illinois at Urbana-Champaign, 603 East Daniel Street, Champaign, IL 61820, USA. Email: gclore@s. Psych.uiuc.edu

Philosophers during the enlightenment generally assumed that emotions contaminate reason, and that the proper goal of human intelligence is to elevate us above our animal passions. By contrast, current psychologists are beginning to depart from traditional views by entertaining such concepts as "emotional intelligence" (Salovey & Mayer, 1990). In the literature, affective influences are still often labeled as "affective biases." Increasingly, however, psychologists see affect and cognition as interdependent rather than as at odds. In a paper on the "emotional controls of cognition," Simon (1967) pointed out such interdependence, even as the cognitive revolution was being declared (Neisser, 1967). Since then, we have learned a good deal about how emotion exercises this control. In this chapter, we discuss the influence of mood on judgment, processing, and memory from the perspective of the affect-as-information hypothesis (e.g., Clore, 1992; Clore, Schwarz, & Conway, 1994; Schwarz, 1990; Schwarz, & Clore, 1983, 1988, 1996).

AFFECT AND JUDGMENT

Traditional Views

There have been two approaches to understanding the evaluative judgment process. One emphasizes beliefs about the positive versus negative attributes of the object of judgment, and the other emphasizes the experience of positive versus negative feelings by the person making the judgment. Traditional judgment theory assumed that evaluative judgments reflected evaluative beliefs. Thus, believing a person to be trustworthy, loyal, and friendly should make him or her more likable than believing him or her to be untrustworthy, disloyal, and unfriendly. In the 1960s and 1970s, quantitative models focused on rules describing how these attribute evaluations combine into overall impressions (Anderson, 1971) and attitudes (Fishbein & Ajzen, 1975).

When research on the cognitive effects of emotions and moods began to appear, some investigators looked to this same attribute-oriented approach for an explanation (Bower, Montiero, & Gilligan, 1978; Isen, Shalker, Clark, & Karp, 1978). They assumed that mood-congruent judgments would be based on mood-congruent attributes represented in memory. Activation spreading out from moods was expected to influence the retrieval of similarly valenced beliefs.

About this same time, investigators studying interpersonal attraction generated accounts that focused on affective reactions rather than beliefs

(Clore & Byrne, 1974). They showed that interpersonal attraction depended not only on attributes of the person judged, but also on how the person doing the judging reacted physiologically and emotionally to those attributes (Clore & Gormly, 1974). They maintained that such terms as "love" and "hate" and "like" and "dislike" refer to people's feelings about others rather than to their beliefs about others.

The difference between attribute views and affect views can be seen by considering how judgments of interpersonal attraction are made. Attribute-oriented approaches assume that one averages stored evaluations of individual beliefs about another person's attributes. Thus, to form a judgment about a woman named Beatrice, for example, one would reason that, "I must be attracted to Beatrice because I believe her to be friendly, courteous, and kind, and I know that these are likable attributes." This statement sounds odd, as if it might be made by an android in a science fiction film; real people are likely to be attracted to Beatrice because they find themselves enjoying her company not than because they know her to have positive attributes. Similarly, the affect-as-information view holds that they would like her when positive feelings in her presence are experienced as liking. Of course, they might also characterize her as friendly, courteous, and kind, and these attributions might be an insightful analysis of what makes her enjoyable. However, we would argue that if someone is attracted to Beatrice, the proximal cause of the liking is how she makes them feel. Thus, contrary to traditional accounts by judgment and decision theorists, we suggest an affect-as-information approach, which holds that people often make judgments by asking themselves (implicitly), "How do I feel about it?" (Schwarz & Clore, 1988).

The Affect-as-Information View

The affect-as-information view is more of an approach than a theory, an approach that a number of investigators have found compatible and to which many have made contributions and refinements. This plurality of inputs has ensured that the approach is a robust one that accounts for a variety of phenomena. In addition, just as multiple cooks generate variations on the same dish, there are variations on this basic explanatory approach (Martin & Clore, in press). However, there are also some common assumptions or principles underlying the general idea (Clore et al., in press; Wyer, Clore, & Isbell, 1999). We use some of these principles to organize our discussion.

The Experience Principle: The Cognitive Consequences of Affective States are Mediated by the Subjective Experience of Affect. Psychologists often reason that because humans and animals have a common emotion circuitry, any effects of emotion must be primitive and reflexive. A less popular starting point is the converse idea that subjective experiences mediate emotional influences and that such experiences are not uniquely human. In that context, results reported by Panksepp (1998) are especially intriguing. He discovered that the intensity of fear determines whether rabbits freeze or flee in response to threat. In addition, making high-frequency recordings of vocalizations in rats, he discovered that they laugh when tickled, an experience that they also greatly prefer to other forms of handling. In any case, our starting point is that one of the distinctive aspects of emotions is that they are felt, and that the experience of such feelings has important information-processing consequences.

Evidence comes from research on individual differences in emotional experience (Gohm & Clore, 2000). For example, in a study of mood and risk judgments (Gasper & Clore, 2000a), participants were divided according to their responses on the Attention to Emotion scale (Salovey, Mayer, Goldman, Turvey, & Palfai, 1994). Mood influenced risk judgments among individuals who said that they usually attended to their feelings, but mood was not related to risk judgments among those who said they did not attend to their feelings. These results suggest that attention to feelings mediate's mood effects on judgment. Also consistent is the fact that when individuals scoring low in attention were given instructions to attend to their feelings, they also began showing mood effects. We assume that affective feelings have such cognitive consequences because of the information they convey, as indicated in the Information Principle.

The Information Principle: Emotional Feelings Provide Conscious Information from Unconscious Appraisals of Situations. In information-processing theories, feelings are often pictured only as output arrows. Rarely are they also discussed as inputs or causal factors in subsequent processing. However, if emotions are reactions to the apparent significance of situations, as indicated in appraisal theories (e.g., Ortony, Clore, & Collins, 1988), it is reasonable to assume that emotional feelings represent that significance (Clore et al., 1994). Just as facial expressions of emotion convey emotional appraisals publicly (Ekman, 1982), we believe that emotional feelings convey such information privately. The affect-as-information approach assumes that emotional feelings serve as affective feedback that guides judgment, decision making, and information processing. Evidence consistent with this idea comes from studies of brain-damaged patients (Damasio, 1994) that suggest that the ability to detect and use such affective information may be necessary to pursue any goal-directed activity successfully.

It is important to note that the information to which we refer is experiential rather than conceptual information. For example, positive affect may be experienced as liking or success, as opposed to activating concepts about liking or success. However, by itself, the affect is simply an experiential form of goodness or badness. Its information value depends on the object to which this experience of goodness or badness is attributed. This process is the subject of the Attribution Principle.

The Attribution Principle: The Informativeness of Affect and Its Cognitive Consequences Depend on How the Experience of Affect is Attributed. The role of affect in judgment and decision making has long been obscured by the simple fact that feelings and beliefs generally move together. To determine whether feelings themselves play a role, it was necessary to vary affective experience independently of evaluative beliefs. To induce affective feelings in the laboratory, in one experiment Schwarz and Clore (1983) randomly assigned participants to write a description of either a happy or a sad event from their recent past. In a second experiment, they conducted a telephone survey on the first warm and sunny day of spring when people were naturally in positive moods, or on subsequent cold and rainy spring days when they felt less positively. In both cases, they found that ratings of life satisfaction were influenced by the momentary moods of respondents. They made higher ratings in happy moods than in sad moods.

However, feelings do not always affect judgment. Their influence depends on their being attributed to the object of judgment. When a cause other than the object of judgment was made salient, the mood effects disappeared. In the first experiment described above (Schwarz & Clore, 1983), the soundproof nature of a room in which participants worked (an incorrect cause) was made salient as a possible cause for their feelings, and in the second study, sunny or rainy weather (the correct cause) was made salient. In neither case did the attribution manipulation change how participants felt. Instead, it changed the apparent meaning or significance of the feelings, and hence their effects.

Such mood and attribution effects have frequently been replicated (e.g., Keltner, Locke, & Audrain, 1993; Schwarz, Servay, & Kumpf, 1985; Siemer & Reisenzein, 1994), but one experiment on the effects of trait as well as state affect yielded a surprising result (Gasper & Clore, 1998). Consistent with the usual finding, negative moods (state affect) produced heightened judgments of risk, and a manipulation that made salient an irrelevant cause resulted in the usual attribution effect (i.e., in elimination of most effects). However, the attribution effect occurred only for individuals who were low in trait anxiety. Individuals who were high in trait anxiety resisted the implication that their feelings were not relevant and showed no reduction in risk estimates in attribution conditions. The results suggest that individuals with chronically elevated affect may have difficulty discriminating when their feelings are and are not relevant.

Before leaving this topic, it might be of use to note that the value of such experiments is not as demonstrations that people make errors; rather, the purpose of misattribution experiments is to unconfound the roles of feelings and concepts in judgment. Two conclusions follow from them. First, that feelings do influence judgment independently of concepts; and second, that these influences are mediated by implicit attributions about their source. Such attributions provide an object that gives affective feelings their information value and, in some cases, their misinformation value. In real life, of course, most affective cues are not misattributed, because they are closely tied to current cognitive content, as indicated in the Immediacy Principle.

The Immediacy Principle: Affective Feelings Tend to Be Experienced as Reactions to Current Mental Content.

The Immediacy Principle: Affective Feelings Tend to Be Experienced as Reactions to Current Mental Content. The emotional system presumably evolved as an alarm system to facilitate coping with valuable opportunities and dangerous threats. To guide immediate action, the feelings must reflect current perceptual and cognitive content. One may regret the past, of course, but only by thinking about it in the present.

In addition to occasional emotions, minimal affective cues are available almost constantly in the form of feedback about progress toward minor subgoals, such as comprehending the instructions on a package, finding a number in the telephone book, having one's running shoe come untied, missing a stop light, and so on. We live in a stream of affective and other sensory feedback, the meaning of which is usually crystal clear. However, one can also be in a mood or have emotional feelings that result from background ideation of which one is only dimly aware. Without any fixed information value, these reactions are subject to misattribution. In that regard, the affective feelings caused by mood and the affective meaning caused by subliminally presented stimuli may both obey the same rules, as suggested by the Episodic Constraint Principle.

The Episodic Constraint Principle: Primed Concepts and Affective Feelings Should Have Similar Effects When the Obscurity of Their Sources Leaves Their Potential Meanings Similarly Unconstrained. We focus on the role of consciously accessible feelings, but some investigators focus on the unconscious priming of evaluative concepts (e.g., Bargh, 1997; Murphy & Zajonc, 1993). For example, Winkielman, Zajonc, and Schwarz (1997) presented happy or angry faces subliminally and masked them with Chinese ideographs (neutral stimuli). Participants did not report seeing the faces or feeling anything, but they did evaluate the ideographs more positively after happy than after angry faces. Such effects are no different that ordinary cognitive priming except that the visual mask interferes with awareness of the briefly exposed stimulus. However, it does not interfere with activation of the meaning of the prime, which is therefore cognitively accessible without any episodic constraints (Clore & Ketelaar, 1997; Clore & Ortony, 2000).

There is a fascinating parallel between the influences of such unconscious priming and the influences of mood (Clore & Parrott, 1991). Primed concepts and affective feelings should have similar effects when lack of awareness of their sources leaves their potential meanings similarly unconstrained. The resulting feelings and concepts are experienced as spontaneous personal reactions to whatever is in focus at the time. When the meaning of feelings or primed concepts is constrained by the salience of a specific source (through attribution manipulations or obvious priming), a reversal of the usual effects occurs.

The difference between the influence of affect that is and is not constrained by knowledge of its source is evident in experiments in which participants describe happy or sad events in ways that either do or do not induce a mood (e.g., Strack, Schwarz, & Gschneidinger, 1985). Hot descriptions of the events produce mood-congruent judgments, but cold cognitive descriptions produce the opposite, because the positivity of the event serves only as a point of comparison for subsequent judgments. Similarly, in studies of cognitive priming, conscious awareness of the priming produces the opposite of subtle or nonconscious priming (Lombardi, Higgins, & Bargh (1987).

We argue that the critical element in both mood studies and unconscious priming studies is the lack of constraint on the potential meanings of the subjective experiences of affect and ideas. For example, evaluative meaning may be the only thing that diverse primes have in common. As a result, positivity or negativity may become primed with no apparent source. Being unconstrained in this way, the primed evaluative meaning may be

TABLE 6.1
Object Specificity and Duration as Constraints on Experiential and
Conceptual Information

| | Sources of Affective Feeling | | Sources of Affective Meaning | |
	Current	Chronic	Current	Chronic
Salient object	Emotion	Attitude	Thought	Belief
No salient object	Mood	Temperament	Prime	Trait

experienced as a reaction to whatever is currently in focus, just as in the case of mood-based feelings. As one engages in self-monitoring, induced feelings or primed meaning may be misattributed to oneself. For example, positive mood or activated conceptual positivity might be experienced as self-confidence or well-being.

In line with these considerations, various forms of experiential and conceptual information can be differentiated in terms of constraints. Table 6.1 shows that attributions of affective feelings and affective meaning are both constrained by the duration of feelings and concepts and their apparent objects.

We assume, therefore, that the affect-as-information approach can accommodate affective concepts as well as affective feelings. The information conveyed by affective concepts and feelings both depend on attributions about their sources. Such attributions may be implicit and perceptual (rather than explicit and cognitive), and they may be determined by the proximity in time and space of concepts and feelings to their objects, as outlined by gestalt psychologists (e.g., Heider, 1958). Table 6.1 suggests that we have different labels for feelings and accessible concepts depending on whether they are dedicated to objects and whether they are current or chronic. Space does not permit full elaboration of the episodic constraint principle, which maintains that primed elements of meaning obey the same principles as mood-based affect. However, a useful exercise is to consider the claims in the subsequent sections with this hypothesis in mind.

We have discussed five assumptions underlying the affect-as-information approach. These are basic principles that have additional corollaries or implications. For instance, implicit in the immediacy principle is that the meaning and consequences of feelings (and primed concepts) depend not only on the specific object to which they are attributed, but also on the larger personal narrative within which affect is elicited or ideas are primed (e.g., Martin, Ward, Achee, & Wyer, 1993). So far, we have focused on how feelings and thoughts can affect judgment directly when experienced as reactions to objects of judgment. This can be summarized in the **Affective Judgment Principle: When one is object focused, affective reactions may be experienced as liking or disliking, leading to higher or lower evaluation of that object of judgment.** However, in cases in which one is not focused on an object with the goal of evaluating it, but on a problem with a goal of solving it or on a task with the goal of performing well, then affective reactions may have a different influence, as discussed next.

MOOD AND PROCESSING

Affective feelings are always experienced as evaluations, but the object that they imbue with value depends on one's focus of attention. Positive and negative affect may be experienced as liking or disliking when one is focused on an object, but when focused on a task, the same feelings may be experienced as feedback about one's ability to do the task. Thus, according to the **Affective Processing Principle, when one is task oriented, affective reactions may be experienced as confidence or doubt about cognitively accessible information, leading to greater or lesser reliance on one's own beliefs, expectations, and inclinations.** Evidence for the principle is that individuals in happy moods are more likely than those in sad moods to rely on accessible cognitions, including expectations and stereotypes (e.g., Bodenhausen, Kramer, & Susser, 1994). In a relevant study, participants read about a day in the life of a woman named Carol, who was initially described either as an introverted librarian or an extraverted sales representative (Isbell, Clore, & Wyer, 1999). The behaviors in the story about her were equally balanced between extraversion and introversion. Despite the balanced nature of the behaviors, happy participants relied on stereotyped expectations, judging Carol the librarian as introverted and Carol the sales representative as extraverted. By contrast, sad participants relied on Carol's behaviors, so that they judged her to be the same in both roles.

In addition to the use of stereotypes, individuals in happy moods also rely on other accessible information, including reliance on technical expertise (Isen, Rosenzweig, & Young, 1991), primacy information (Sinclair & Mark, 1992), behavioral scripts (Bless et al., 1996), and general categories (Dienes, 1996; Isen & Daubman, 1984; Kaplan, Kickul, & Reither, 1996).

The Processing Principle alluded to previously explains such effects by suggesting that affective feelings may serve as task-relevant feedback (see also Carver & Scheier, 1990). Other versions of the affect-as-information approach are similar, but differ in various ways. Schwarz (1990) proposed that affect serves as feedback about the external situation. He reasoned that if positive affect indicates that a situation is safe, people may see little need to expend cognitive effort (unless triggered by other currently active goals) so that they engage in heuristic processing. However, when negative affect indicates that a situation is problematic, it motivates more effortful and systematic processing. Schwarz assumes that cognitive-processing styles are tuned to meet the processing requirements signaled by one's affective state (see also Schwarz & Clore, 1996; Clore et al., 1994).

Bless (in press) proposed that mood effects on processing depend on implicit judgments about cognitive content, rather than on different kinds of processing. He also suggested that any reduced processing in positive moods simply means that the use of general knowledge in happy moods often makes extensive processing unnecessary, rather than that happy moods reduce the motivation for such processing. Bless et al. (1996) tested this hypothesis by examining performance on a secondary task. He found that during the period when they were relying on their general knowledge, participants in happy moods did better than sad participants on the secondary task. Rather than reflecting a desire to save effort, enhanced performance on the secondary task showed that the use of general knowledge in happy moods allowed attention to be devoted to the secondary task.

Whereas Schwarz (1990) focused on affect as information about the situation and its processing requirements, Martin et al. (1993) focused on affect as feedback about the adequacy of responses. They interpreted mood effects on processing as a consequence of judgments about response adequacy. Wyer, Clore, and Isbell (1999) extended this performance feedback interpretation. Martin et al. proposed that affective feedback serves as a basis for deciding whether to continue or to stop goal-directed processing, and Wyer et al. suggested that it serves as feedback about the strategy chosen to attain a particular objective. Thus, affect may be experienced as success or failure feedback about initial responses in task situations. Instead of focusing on the differences among formulations, we describe experiments designed to examine the reasonably general account offered by the processing principle in which positive and negative affect is believed to be experienced as confidence and doubt about one's own thoughts and inclinations (Clore et al., in press). According to this principle, affect should govern whether one assimilates incoming information to active concepts or accommodates concepts to incoming information from the environment. Thus, positive affect may serve as a cue or incentive to rely on internal thoughts, expectations, and inclinations, whereas negative affect should direct attention to new, external information. In a similar way, when a small food reward (or a shot of dopamine) is delivered to animals in the start box of an experiment, it elicits learned and accessible responses, whereas cues of punishment lead to gathering new information rather than reliance on prior learning (Hoebel, 1999).

We examined the processing proposition by studying the effect of mood on three classic phenomena (Gasper, 1999; Gasper & Clore, 2000a,b). The experiments used stimuli from the original demonstrations of mental schemas by Bartlett (1932), mental sets by Luchins (1942), and heuristic reasoning by Tversky and Kahneman (1973). Although the phenomena differ in content, they all depend on the use of accessible information during problem solving. As a result, if affective cues are experienced as feedback about the value of initially encountered and accessible information, we predicted that individuals in positive but not negative moods should show the classic effects.

In 1932, Bartlett devised the method of serial reproduction in which he showed a drawing of an African shield to his Cambridge undergraduates and asked them to draw it from memory. Their drawings were given to others, who subsequently tried to draw them from memory, and these were given to a third group to draw, and so on. The drawing (Fig. 6.1) was titled "Portrait of a man," and Bartlett showed that over trials, the reproductions were assimilated to the schema of a face. He used this experiment and others like it to establish his idea that memory is a constructive process.

Gasper and Clore (2000b) replicated Bartlett's study with mood to test the hypothesis that affect influences reliance on accessible information. To induce mood, we asked participants to write about a happy or sad event (Schwarz & Clore, 1983). As predicted, blind ratings showed that drawings done in happy moods looked more like a face than those in sad moods, suggesting again that positive affect promotes an internal focus on cognitively accessible information and negative affect promotes an external focus on new information.

As a second test of this hypothesis, we replicated a classic experiment by Luchins (1942) and showed that the induction of mental sets influences the problem solving of happy but not sad mood participants (Gasper & Clore, 2000b). In a third test, Gasper (1999) repeated one of Tversky and Kahneman's (1973) demonstrations of heuristic reasoning. On the well-known Linda problem, happy but not sad participants were led by initially

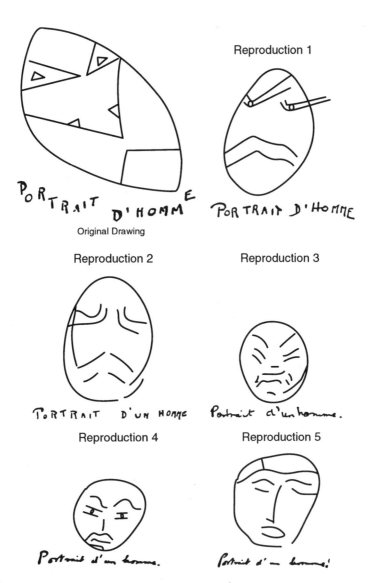

FIG. 6.1. Serial reproductions of drawings from Bartlett (1932) showing how a label, "Portrait of a man," serves as an organizing schema in reconstructing memories. (Gasper, K., & Clore, G. L., 2000b. *Paying attention to the big picture: Mood and the global vs. local processing of visual information.* Unpublished manuscript. University of Illionis at Urbana–Champaign.)

presented information to commit the conjunction fallacy by asserting that the conjunction of two events is more likely than either of the events alone. Specifically, background information about Linda's socially conscious political activity led respondents in happy but not in sad moods to conclude that the probability of Linda being both a feminist and a banker must be higher than that she is a banker only.

These three classic experiments all exploit the power of accessible cognitions, showing the effect of schemas on memory, mental sets on problem solving, and expectations on probabilistic reasoning. Consistent with the processing principle, positive affect led to the use of information that was cognitively accessible. In these particular problems, such accessibility effects led to errors; but for some problems, reliance on accessible categories (Dienes, 1996), knowledge (Isen, Rosenzweig, & Young, 1991), and associations (Isen, 1984) leads to superior performance.

Priming and Processing

Earlier, we proposed that subtly induced affective feelings and unconsciously primed affective concepts have parallel effects on evaluative judgment. We suggested that the informational and attributional principles governing the influence of feelings also apply to concepts. Mood-based feelings and unconsciously primed thoughts are both cognitively unconstrained so that they can be experienced as spontaneous, internally generated reactions to current stimuli. Most subliminal priming studies show effects on judgment, but data recently collected in our laboratory by Colcombe and Isbell suggest that primed affective meaning may influence processing in the same manner as induced affective feeling. Schematic smiley or frowny faces were presented subliminally just before participants completed the stereotyping task described earlier (Isbell et al., 1999). Consistent with the Episodic Constraint Principle, subliminal smiley faces appear to lead to greater reliance (and subliminal frowny faces to less reliance) on stereotypes when processing information about another person (for other research on the effects of smiles on processing, see Ottati, Terkildsen, & Hubbard, 1997). These data are consistent with the Affective Processing and Episodic Constraint principles. That is, the critical element in the cognitive consequences of affect is the experience of positive and negative thoughts and feelings as reactions that signal whether to "go" or "stop" using internal, accessible information. However, in addition, such top-down processing also appears to involve a focus on the global rather than the local aspects of stimuli, as described in the following paragraphs.

Affect and Level of Focus. To the extent that positive affect is experienced as an indication of the success of one's efforts and negative affect is experienced as evidence of a problem, there is reason to expect these affective cues to lead to differences in level of focus. In their work on action identification, Vallacher & Wegner (1985) showed that in the context of feedback about success, people characterize their behavior as relevant to higher-level, more abstract and encompassing goals, and with failure feedback to lower-level, more concrete and disconnected goals. On this logic, we (Clore et al., in press) have proposed a **Level of Focus Principle: Affect experienced as feedback about the likelihood of success or failure should also influence the global versus local focus of processing.**

Other versions of the affect-as-information approach have also emphasized the general versus specific distinction. Schwarz (1990) mentions that happy moods should be associated with reliance on general as opposed to detailed information, and Bless (in press) suggests that positive affect is associated with the use of general knowledge structures. Also, it is perhaps implicit in Fiedler's (in press) assimilation–accommodation view that general concepts assimilate more detailed data.

In addition, findings that individuals in positive moods rely more on expectations, stereotypes, and impressions than individuals in negative moods could also be interpreted as showing that positive mood leads to a global focus and negative mood to a local focus. The schemas, mental sets, and impressions formed in these experiments represent not only accessible information, but also global information.

A recent test of this hypothesis (Gasper & Clore, 1999c) used a global/local perceptual task (Kimchi & Palmer, 1982) to examine attentional focusing. Subjects were shown figures in which, for example, a triangle might be made of squares or a square of triangles. For each figure, they were to indicate which of two comparison figures (e.g., squares made of squares or triangles made of triangles) was most similar to the original (Fig. 6.2). Comparing the choices made across trials indicates whether a subject tends to focus at the global or local level in completing the task. The results show that individuals in happy moods did, in fact, focus at the global level to a greater extent than individuals in sad moods (see also Derryberry & Reed, 1998, who examined similar effects for trait affect).

We have focused on two kinds of processing effects—the role of mood in promoting reliance on accessible information and in adopting a global versus local focus. We have tended not to describe mood effects on processing in terms of amount of processing. We agree with Bless (in press) that evidence of less extensive processing in positive moods is not motivated by

FIG. 6.2. Sample item in a match-to-sample task assessing global versus local attentional focus. (Gasper, K., & Clore, G. L., 2000a. *Paying attention to the big picture: Mood and the global vs. local processing of visual information.* Unpublished manuscript. University of Illinois at Urbana–Champaign.)

a desire to reduce cognitive effort, but is a byproduct of the role of affect as feedback. In other words, if affective feedback indicates that one's current information is correct, then additional processing to find the correct answer is simply unnecessary.

Many of the basic affective phenomena are consistent with multiple hypotheses. However, the ability of attributional manipulations to alter or eliminate the effects implies that affect-as-information processes may be at work. Attributional manipulations typically do not alter affective feelings, but only their apparent meaning, significance, or information value. When a possible source is made salient that would render one's feelings nondiagnostic, then mood effects generally disappear (Dienes, 1996; Gasper, 1999; Isbell et al., 1999; Sinclair, Mark, & Clore, 1994). Such results strongly suggest that the active agent was the information value or experiential meaning of the affect.

We have reviewed briefly some of the research from the affect-as-information approach concerning the affective controls on processing. This work is guided by the idea that affect may be experienced as feedback about progress toward one's current goals. Therefore, the information value of affective feedback depends on the goal that is active. In this discussion, we have focused on situations in which we assume performance goals to be superordinate. When that is the case, positive affect is likely to lead to reliance on internally accessible information and negative affect to a focus on new information in the environment. However, a number of investigators have pointed out that people are sometimes focused on a goal of emotion regulation rather than performance (Erber & Erber, this volume). Under a goal to enjoy oneself, the same affective cues often have a different information value, as indicated in the Enjoyment Principle.

The Enjoyment Principle: When One is Emotion Focused, Affective Feelings May Be Experienced as Enjoyment or Displeasure, Leading to Greater or Lesser Persistence at an Activity. The Enjoyment Principle indicates that when engaged in activities just for fun, positive feelings may be experienced as feedback about enjoyment rather than about performance. Evidence that the information value of affect varies with the dominant goal comes from Martin et al. (1993; see also Wegener, Petty, & Smith, 1995). In one experiment, participants were given a stack of cards, each with a description of a behavior printed on it. They were to told to read the cards and either to continue as long as they were enjoying themselves or, in another condition, to stop as soon as they felt they had done enough. Martin et al., found that individuals in happy moods read more cards than those in sad moods when positive feelings were experienced as information that they were still enjoying themselves, but that they read fewer cards when positive feelings were experienced as information that they had done enough. The results show that the information value of affect may be different for enjoyment goals than for performance goals.

MOOD AND MEMORY

In addition to its effects on judgment and processing, mood is also widely believed to influence memory. This hypothesis also offers a powerful explanation for other phenomena (Bower, Montiero, & Gilligan, 1978; Isen, Shalker, Clark, & Karp, 1978). For example, judgment effects can be explained by assuming that moods bias the information available for judgment in a mood-congruent direction. However, the reliability of mood-congruent memory has always been an issue (Blaney, 1986). Commenting on their own difficulties replicating mood and memory effects, Bower and Mayer (1985) suggested that experimental inductions of mood might often be too weak to detect the effect. However, there are also theoretical reasons for questioning whether affect should function in that way. Indeed, Wyer et al. (1999) argue that, although affect may be conceptualized in terms of concepts from declarative memory, affect itself is not part of declarative memory.

The Affective Memory Principle: Affective Feelings May Activate Specific Concepts for Interpreting Them, but Such Affect is Not Itself Stored in Declarative Memory and Does Not Automatically Influence the Accessibility of Similarly Valenced Semantic Concepts and Declarative Knowledge (Clore et al., in press; Wyer et al., 1999). In our view, emotional feelings are an experiential representation of emotional significance. That emotional significance can also be represented symbolically in emotional concepts, which can prime related concepts and events in declarative memory. If one were sad, conceptualizing one's situation as "being sad" might make memories of other sad situations more accessible. However, that would not be an example of mood effects on memory, but simply of cognitive priming. Wyer et al. (1999) point out that we can interpret the experience of a chair by applying the concept "chair," and the experience of sadness by applying the concept "sad." However, there is no reason to assume that the sadness itself (as opposed to its conceptualization) exists in declarative memory any more than that the chair does, and hence there is no reason to assume that the experience of affect would necessarily activate similarly valenced memories, except perhaps as part of the conceptualization process. We propose, then, that when mood congruent memory does occur, it is a function of affective concepts rather than of affective feelings (Wyer et al., 1999).

Of course, happy and sad moods can influence memory to the extent that they involve the activation of relevant concepts. Thus, we are not suggesting that those claiming a relationship (Bower et al., 1978; Isen et al., 1978; Forgas, 1995) are necessarily incorrect. In general, clear distinctions have not been made between affective concepts and feelings, but the implication of their work has always been that affect itself activated affect-congruent material in memory. Wyer et al. (1999) suggest that this may turn out not to be the case. Whereas people do have concept-congruent lines of thought, they do not have affect-congruent lines of thought unless relevant concepts are active to do the priming. Feelings, by themselves, probably do not prime affectively similar concepts and memories. Thus, if one person tells a sad story, others may relate similar experiences. However, that would illustrate conceptual priming, not an effect of feeling on retrieval.

The behavioral economist Lowenstein (1996) observed that people routinely underestimate the role of emotional and other "visceral" experiences in decisions. He notes, but does not explain, that in judgments about one's own past behavior, forecasts of one's future behavior, and considerations of the behavior of others, people often fail to appreciate the role played by subjective experience. People are often especially bad at making decisions about alcohol, drugs, and sexual behavior, he says, because they underestimate the compelling nature of their own emotional experience. We suggest that this is so because one can store in memory only concepts about emotional experiences, not the actual experiences, and such symbolic representations of past bad outcomes are no match for the compelling nature of actual current experience.

The literature on fear conditioning might be thought to provide counterexamples of our claims about affect and memory. However, such conditioning does not work by storing the experience of fear to be elicited as a memory by the conditioned stimulus. It is not the fear response that is conditioned and hence remembered, but the threat meaning of the stimulus (Hebb, 1949). Subsequent fear reactions to the conditioned stimulus are new instances of fear triggered by the conditioned threat meaning, not old experiences that are retrieved from memory.

We are not suggesting that emotion is not important for memory. Emotional experience often causes memories to be quite indelible, and it presumably makes good evolutionary sense that we remember things that were emotionally significant. Indeed, aspects of traumatic situations may retain their ability to elicit unpleasant memories for a long time. However, these are not examples of feelings triggering memories but of events that are capable of eliciting feelings being memorable.

After a review of the literature, Wyer et al. (1999) and Wyer and Srull (1989) noted that studies of mood and memory generally involve explicit instructions to think of happy or sad events (Bower, 1981) or films with explicitly happy or sad themes. In contrast, Parrott and Sabini (1990) conducted a study in which the cause of mood had little cognitive content. They assessed students' moods on sunny and pleasant or rainy and unpleasant days and then asked them to recall events in their recent past. Mood-congruent memory was not found, except in a condition in which subjects were led to label their moods. Rothkopf and Blaney (1991) reported similar conclusions. Riskind (1989) also noted the ineffectuality of feelings as retrieval cues, focusing instead on the importance of cognitive priming in mood effects.

These considerations led Garvin (1999) to test the hypothesis that mood effects on memory involve conceptual rather than affective priming. Specifically, she examined the effects of happy versus sad feelings and happy versus sad primes on the recall of a story containing equal numbers of happy and sad events. Music was used to induce mood without activating mood concepts (Niedenthal & Setterlund, 1994). The priming task was a scrambled sentence test (Srull & Wyer, 1979). Participants underlined words that would make sentences in a series of four-word strings. Half of the 40 strings included a happy or a sad emotion word ("she disappointed crushed felt") and half were neutral ("turn go now left"). Participants then read a story (Bower, Gilligan, & Montiero, 1981) about a character named Paul who described an equal number of happy and sad events from childhood.

Garvin found, as predicted, that recall was congruent with the primes, but not with mood. However, mood did influence judgment, showing that the mood manipulation was effective. Consistent with the Affective Processing Principle, the concepts that had been made accessible through priming influenced judgment in positive moods and not in negative moods.

This is the first experiment (of which we are aware) that has varied priming and mood independently, and it serves as a strong test of the proposed principle. Replication is necessary, but it is noteworthy that this initial study used standard priming and mood induction procedures, and the original story from Bower et al. (1981).

SUMMARY

We have outlined the central assumptions of the feelings-as-information approach to affect and cognition (Clore, 1992; Clore et al., in press; Schwarz, 1990; Schwarz & Clore, 1983, 1988, 1996). In an attempt to make these explicit, we expressed them in 10 principles. The Experience and Information principles propose that emotional feelings are representations of unconscious appraisals, so that they are appropriately experienced as information about (one's view of) the objects of those appraisals. The Attribution and Immediacy principles propose that when the object of affective cues is unconstrained (e.g., when they arise from general moods and dispositions rather than from specific emotional appraisals), they are subject to misattribution to other accessible objects. The Episodic Constraint Principle proposes that the experience of (primed) concepts and (induced) feelings are governed by the same informational and attributional processes. Consistent with the Immediacy Principle, the influence of affect on information processing ultimately depends on the cognitive context in which the affect is experienced. The effects may differ, for example, depending on whether one focuses (1) on objects with the goal of evaluating them, (2) on tasks with the goal of performing well, or (3) on the feelings themselves with a goal of enjoyment.

The Judgment Principle indicates that when focused on objects with a goal of evaluating them, positive and negative affect may be experienced as liking and disliking, and may influence affective judgments and decisions. The Processing Principle is that when one is task oriented, affective reactions may be experienced as confidence or doubt about cognitively accessible information, leading to greater or lesser reliance on one's own beliefs, expectations, and inclinations. Thus, positive affect may promote top-down, theory-based processing in which one relies on cognitively accessible information (e.g., knowledge, beliefs, stereotypes, expectations, primed thoughts), and negative affect may promote bottom-up, data-based processing, in which one relies on data from the external environment rather than on internal cognitive constructions. Affect may thus play an important role in the constant cycle of data assimilation and schema accommodation. In addition, the Levels of Focus Principle suggests that affective feedback about goal-directed efforts should also influence the global versus local focus of processing, such that positive moods promote attention to the global, and negative moods to the local aspects of stimuli. A third possibility is that one can be focused on the feelings themselves with the goal of enjoyment. Then, according to the Enjoyment Principle, positive and negative affect may be experienced simply as enjoyment and lack of enjoyment, leading to greater and lesser persistence at an activity or task.

Finally, although it has traditionally been assumed that affect influences cognition indirectly through its effects on attention and memory, our emphasis on the direct influence of affect leads to a different view. According to the Memory Principle, affective feelings may activate specific concepts for interpreting them, but such affect is not itself stored in declarative memory and does not automatically influence the accessibility of similarly valenced semantic concepts and declarative knowledge. From this view, the literature on mood and memory may reflect the role in memory of activated concepts about mood rather than of feelings of mood.

ACKNOWLEDGMENTS

The writing of this chapter and much of the research reported was supported by NSF Grant SBR 96-01298. Thanks also to members of the Affect Group for their insights and contributions.

REFERENCES

Anderson, N. H. (1971). Integration theory and attitude change. *Psychological Review, 78*, 171–206.

Bargh, J. A. (1997). The automaticity of everyday life. In R. S. Wyer (Ed.), *Advances in social cognition* (Vol. 10, pp. 1–61). Mahwah, NJ: Lawrence Erlbaum Associates.

Bartlett, F. C. (1932). *Remembering.* Cambridge: Cambridge University Press.

Blaney, P. H. (1986). Affect and memory: A review. *Psychological Bulletin, 99*, 229–246.

Bless, H. (in press). Mood and the use of general knowledge structures. In L. L. Martin & G. L. Clore (Eds.), *Theories of mood and cognition: A user's handbook.* Mahwah, NJ: Lawrence Erlbaum Associates.

Bless, H., Clore, G. L., Schwarz, N., Golisano, V., Rabe, C., & Woelke, M. (1996). Mood and the use of scripts: Does being in a happy mood really lead to mindlessness? *Journal of Personality and Social Psychology, 71*, 665–679.

Bodenhausen, G. V., Kramer, G. P., & Susser, K. (1994). Happiness and stereotypic thinking in social judgment. *Journal of Personality and Social Psychology, 66*, 621–632.

Bower, G. H. (1981). Mood and memory. *American Psychologist, 36*, 129–148.

Bower, G. H., Gilligan, S. G., & Monteiro, K. P. (1981). Selectivity of learning caused by affective states. *Journal of Experimental Psychology: General, 110*, 451–473.

Bower, G. H., & Mayer, J. D. (1985). Failure to replicate mood-dependent retrieval. *Bulletin of the Psychonomic Society, 23*, 39–42.

Bower, G. H., Monteiro, K. P., & Gilligan, S. G. (1978). Emotional mood as a context of learning and recall. *Journal of Verbal Learning and Verbal Behavior, 17*, 573–585.

Carver, C. S., & Scheier, M. F. (1990). Origins and functions of positive and negative affect: A control-process view. *Psychological Review, 97*, 19–35.

Clore, G. L. (1992). Cognitive phenomenology: Feelings and the construction of judgment. In L. L. Martin & A. Tesser (Eds.), *The construction of social judgment* (pp. 133–164). Hillsdale, NJ: Lawrence Erlbaum Associates.

Clore, G. L., & Byrne, D. (1974). A reinforcement-affect model of attraction. In T. L. Huston (Ed.), *Foundations of interpersonal attraction* (pp. 143–170). New York: Academic Press.

Clore, G. L., & Gormly, J. B. (1974). Knowing, feeling, and liking: A psychophysiological study of attraction. *Journal of Research in Personality, 8*, 218–230.

Clore, G. L., & Ketelaar, T. (1997). Minding our emotions: On the role of automatic, unconscious affect. In R. S. Wyer (Ed.), *Advances in social cognition* (Vol. 10, pp. 105–120). Mahwah, NJ: Lawrence Erlbaum Associates.

Clore, G. L., & Parrott, W. G. (1991). Moods and their vicissitudes: Thoughts and feelings as information. In J. Forgas (Ed.), *Emotion and social judgment* (pp. 107–123). Oxford: Pergamon Press.

Clore, G. L., & Ortony, A. (1999). Cognitive in emotion: Never, sometimes, or always? In L. Nadel & R. Lane (Eds.), *The cognitive neuroscience of emotion* (pp. 24–61). New York: Oxford University Press.

Clore, G. L., Schwarz, N., & Conway, M. (1994). Affective causes and consequences of social information processing. In R. S. Wyer & T. K. Srull (Eds.), *Handbook of social cognition*, 2nd ed. (Vol. 1, pp. 323–417). Hillsdale, NJ: Lawrence Erlbaum Associates.

Clore, G. L., Wyer R. S., Dienes, B., Gasper, K., Gohm, C., & Isbell, L. (in press). Affective feelings as feedback: Some cognitive consequences. In L. L. Martin & G. L. Clore (Eds.), *Theories of mood and cognition: A user's handbook* (in press). Mahwah, NJ: Lawrence Erlbaum Associates.

Damasio, A. R. (1994). *Descartes' error.* New York: Putnam & Sons.

Derryberry, D., & Reed, M. A. (1998). Anxiety and attentional focusing: Trait, state, and hemispheric influences. *Personality and Individual Differences, 25*, 745–761.

Dienes, B. P. A. (1996). *Mood as information: Affective cues for cognitive processing styles.* Unpublished doctoral dissertation. University of Illinois.

Ekman, P. (1982). *Emotion in the human face*. New York: Cambridge University Press.

Erber, R. & Erber, M. W. (in press). Mood and processing: A view from a self-regulation perspective. In L. L. Martin & G. L. Clore (Eds.), *Theories of mood and cognition: A user's handbook* (in press). Mahwah, NJ: Lawrence Erlbaum Associates.

Fiedler, K. (in press). In L. L. Martin & G. L. Clore (Eds.), *Theories of mood and cognition: A user's handbook*. Mahwah, NJ: Lawrence Erlbaum Associates.

Fishbein, M., & Ajzen, I. (1975). *Belief, attitude, intention, and behavior*. Reading, MA: Addison-Wesley.

Forgas, J. P. (1995). Mood and judgment: The affect infusion model (AIM). *Psychological Bulletin, 117*, 39–66.

Garvin, E. (1999). *Mood and memory? Forget about it*. Unpublished Master's thesis, University of Illinois.

Gasper, K. (1999). *How thought and emotional awareness influence the role of affect in processing: When attempts to be reasonable fail*. Doctoral dissertation, University of Illinois at Urbana-Champaign.

Gasper, K., & Clore, G. L. (1998). The persistent use of negative affect by anxious individuals to estimate risk. *Journal of Personality and Social Psychology, 74*, 1350–1363.

Gasper, K., & Clore, G. L. (2000a). Do you have to pay attention to your feelings to be influenced by them? *Personality and Social Psychology Bulletin, 26*, 698–711.

Gasper, K., & Clore, G. L. (2000b). Mood and Mental Sets: Accessibility vs. Flexibility in Problem Solving. Unpublished manuscript. University of Illinois at Urbana-Champaign.

Gasper, K., & Clore, G. L. (2000c). *Paying attention to the big picture: Mood and the global vs. local processing of visual information*. Unpublished manuscript. University of Illinois at Urbana-Champaign.

Gohm, C., & Clore, G. L. (2000). Individual differences in emotional experience: A review of Scales. *Personality and Social Psychology Bulletin, 26*, 679–697.

Hebb, D. O. (1949). *The organization of behavior*. New York: Wiley.

Heider, F. (1958) *The psychology of interpersonal relations*. New York: Wiley.

Hoebel, B. G., Rada, P. V., Mark, G. P., & Pothos, E. (1999). Neural systems for reinforcement and inhibition of behavior: Relevance to eating, addiction, and depression. In D. Kahneman, E. Diener, & N. Schwarz (Eds.), *Well-being: The foundations of hedonic psychology* (pp. 560–574). New York: Russell Sage Foundation.

Isbell, L. M., Clore, G. L., & Wyer, R. S. (1999). *Mood-mediated uses of stereotyping in impression formation*. Unpublished manuscript, University of Illinois at Urbana-Champaign.

Isen, A. M. (1984). Toward understanding the role of affect in cognition. In R. S. Wyer & T. K. Srull (Eds.), *Handbook of social cognition* (Vol. 3, pp. 179–236). Hillsdale, NJ: Lawrence Erlbaum Associates.

Isen, A. M., & Daubman, L. A. (1984). The influence of affect on categorization. *Journal of Personality and Social Psychology, 47*, 1206–1217.

Isen, A. M., Rosenzweig, A. S., & Young, M. J. (1991). The influence of positive affect on clinical problem solving. *Medical Decision Making, 11*, 221–227.

Isen, A. M., Shalker, T. E., Clark, M. S., & Karp, L. (1978). Affect, accessibility of material in memory and behavior: A cognitive loop? *Journal of Personality and Social Psychology, 36*, 1–12.

Kaplan, M., Kickul, J., & Reither, A. (1996, May). *Mood and extent of processing plot and visual information about movies*. Paper delivered at Midwestern Psychological Association, Chicago.

Keltner, D., Lock, K. D., & Audrain, P. C. (1993). The influence of attributions on the relevance of negative feelings to satisfaction. *Personality and Social Psychology Bulletin, 19*, 21–30.

Kimchi, R., & Palmer, S. E. (1982). Form and texture in hierarchically constructed patterns. *Journal of Experimental Psychology: Human Perception and Performance, 8*, 521–535.

Loewenstein, G. (1996). Out of control: Visceral influences on behavior. *Organizational behavior and human decision processes, 65*, 272–292.

Lombardi, W. J., Higgins, E. T., & Bargh, J. A. (1987). The role of consciousness in priming effects on categorization: Assimilation versus contrast as a function of awareness of the priming task. *Personality and Social Psychology Bulletin, 13*, 411–429.

Luchins, A. S. (1942). Mechanization in problem solving: The effect of einstellung. *Psychological Monographs, 54*, 1–95.

Martin, L. L., & Clore, G. L. (Eds.) (in press). *Theories of mood and cognition: A user's handbook.* Mahwah, NJ: Lawrence Erlbaum Associates.

Martin, L. L., Ward, D. W., Achee, J. W., & Wyer, R. S. (1993). Mood as input: People have to interpret the motivational implications of their moods. *Journal of Personality and Social Psychology, 64*, 317–326.

Murphy, S., & Zajonc, R. B. (1993). Affect, cognition, and awareness: Affective priming with optimal and suboptimal stimulus exposures. *Journal of Personality and Social Psychology, 64*, 723–739.

Niedenthal, P. M., & Setterlund, M. B. (1994). Emotion congruence in perception. *Personality and Social Psychology Bulletin, 20*, 401–411.

Neisser, U. (1967). *Cognitive psychology.* Englewood Cliffs, NJ: Prentice-Hall.

Ortony, A., Clore, G. L., & Collins, A. (1988). *The cognitive structure of emotions.* New York: Cambridge University Press.

Ottati, V., Terkildsen, N., & Hubbard, C. (1997). Happy faces elicit heuristic processing in a televised impression formation task: A cognitive tuning account. *Personality and Social Psychology Bulletin, 23*, 1144–1156.

Panksepp, J. (1998). *Affective neuroscience: The foundations of human and animal emotions.* New York: Oxford University Press.

Parrott, G., & Sabini, J. (1990). Mood and memory under natural conditions: Evidence for mood and incongruent recall. *Journal of Personality and Social Psychology, 59*, 321–336.

Riskind, J. H. (1989). Will the field ultimately need a more detailed analysis of mood-memory? Comments on Ellis and Ashbrook. Special Issue: Mood and memory: Theory, research and applications. *Journal of Social Behavior & Personality, 4*, 39–43.

Rothkopf, J. S., & Blaney, P. H. (1991) Mood congruent memory: The role of affective focus and gender. *Cognition & Emotion, 5*, 53–64.

Salovey, P., & Mayer, J. D. (1990). Emotional intelligence. *Imagination, Cognition, and Personality, 9*, 185–211.

Salovey, P., Mayer, J. D., Goldman, S. L., Turvey, C., & Palfai, T. P. (1994). Emotional attention, clarity, and repair: Exploring emotional intelligence using the trait meta-mood scale. In J. Pennebaker (Ed.), *Emotion, disclosure, and health* (pp. 125–154). Washington, DC: American Psychological Association.

Schwarz, N. (1990). Happy but mindless? Mood effects on problem-solving and persuasion. In R. M. Sorrentino & E. T. Higgins (Eds.), *Handbook of motivation and cognition* (Vol. 2, pp. 527–561). New York: Guilford Press.

Schwarz, N., & Clore, G. L. (1983). Mood, misattribution, and judgments of well-being: Informative and directive functions of affective states. *Journal of Personality and Social Psychology, 45*, 513–523.

Schwarz, N., & Clore, G. L. (1988). How do I feel about it? Informative functions of affective states. In K. Fiedler & J. Forgas (Eds.), *Affect, cognition, and social behavior* (pp. 44–62). Toronto: Hofgrefe International.

Schwarz, N., & Clore, G. L. (1996). Feelings and phenomenal experiences. In E. T. Higgins & A. Kruglanski (Eds.), Social psychology: A handbook of basic principles. New York: Guilford Press.

Schwarz, N., Servay, W., & Kumpf, M. (1985). Attribution of arousal as a mediator of the effectiveness of fear-arousing communications. *Journal of Applied Social Psychology, 15*, 74–78.

Scott, J. (1999). "Flirting with the tango." *New York Times Weekend,* Friday, June 11, pp. 1, 8.

Siemer, M., & Reisenzein, R. (1994). Effects of mood on evaluative judgments: Influence of reduced processing capacity and mood salience. Manuscript under review.

Simon, H. A. (1967). Motivational and emotional controls of cognition. *Psychological Review, 74,* 29–39.

Sinclair, R. C., & Mark, M. M. (1992). The influence of mood state on judgment and action: Effects on persuasion, categorization, social justice, person perception, and judgmental accuracy. In L. L. Martin & A. Tesser (Eds.), *The construction of social judgments* (pp. 165–194). Hillsdale, NJ: Lawrence Erlbaum Associates.

Sinclair, R. C., Mark, M. M., & Clore, G. L. (1994). Mood-related persuasion depends on (mis)-attributions. *Social Cognition, 12,* 309–326.

Srull, T. K., & Wyer, R. S., Jr. (1979). The role of category accessibility in the interpretation of information about persons: Some determinants and implications. *Journal of Personality and Social Psychology, 37,* 1660–1672.

Strack, F., Schwarz, N., & Gschneidinger, E. (1985). Happiness and reminiscing: The role of time perspective, affect, and mode of thinking. *Journal of Personality and Social Psychology, 49,* 1460–1469.

Tversky, A., & Kahneman, D. (1973). Availability: A heuristic for judging frequency and probability. *Cognitive Psychology, 5,* 207–232.

Vallacher, R. R., & Wegner, D. M. (1985). *A theory of action identification.* Hillsdale NJ: Erlbaum.

Wegener, D. T., Petty, R. E., & Smith, S. M. (1995). Positive mood can increase or decrease message scrutiny: The hedonic contingency view of mood and message processing. *Journal of Personality and Social Psychology, 69,* 5–15.

Winkielman, P., Zajonc, R. B., & Schwarz, N. (1997). Subliminal affective priming resists attributional interventions. *Cognition and Emotion, 11,* 433–465.

Wyer, R. S., Clore, G. L., & Isbell, L. (1999). Affect and information processing. In M. Zanna (Ed.), *Advances in experimental social psychology* (pp. xxx). New York: Academic Press.

Wyer, R. S., & Srull, T. K. (1989). *Memory and cognition in its social context.* Hillsdale, NJ: Lawrence Erlbaum Associates.

7

Affective Influences on the Self-Concept: Qualifying the Mood-Congruency Principle

Constantine Sedikides
University of Southampton, Southampton, England

Jeffrey D. Green
University of North Carolina at Chapel Hill
Chapel Hill North Carolina

The Affect Infusion Model	147
Type of Self-Conceptions	147
Individual Differences	151
Judgmental Task Features	154
Concluding Remarks	156
References	158

The pivotal role of transient affect (i.e., mood) in human functioning is well established (Clore, Schwarz, & Conway, 1994; Fiedler & Bless, in press; Forgas, 1992, 1995). Mood influences judgment, memory, and behavior.[1]

---

[1] Our review excludes experiments that involve misattribution of mood states or experiments that manipulate the degree to which participants are aware of their mood states (e.g., Clore, Gaspar, & Garvin, chap. 6, this volume; Smith, chap. 4, this volume; Levine, Wyer, & Schwarz, 1994; Martin, Abend, Sedikides, & Green, 1997). Also, our review excludes experiments in which the mood-induction task was actually a failure or success experience based on task performance feedback (e.g., McFarland & Buehler, 1997, 1998).

Address for correspondence: Constantine Sedikides, Department of Psychology, University of Southampton, Highfield Campus, S017 1BJ Southampton, England, UK. Email: c.sedikides@soton. ac.uk

Specifically, mood states modify social judgments such as person and couple impressions, attributions for success or failure, and attitudes or beliefs. Moods affect memory and decision making (e.g., bargaining strategies), and change behavior, such as type of requests (i.e., polite or impolite) and intergroup discrimination. In addition, moods influence self-cognitions defined as judgments about the self (i.e., self-perceptions or self-evaluations), recall of autobiographical knowledge, or expectancies of self-relevant outcomes.

An earlier review of how experimentally induced mood states affect the valence (i.e., positivity–negativity) of self-cognitions focused exclusively on happy and sad moods (Sedikides, 1992). We adhere to tradition in this updated review—partly because of the historical prevalence of the affective valence dimension (e.g., Osgood, Suci, & Tannenbaum, 1957; Scherer, Koivumaki, & Rosenthal, 1972) and partly because additional affective states (e.g., anxiety, anger, stress) are covered by other contributions to this book (Bodenhausen, Mussweiler, Gabriel, & Moreno, chap. 15, this volume; and Suls, chap. 18, this volume).

The previously mentioned earlier review (Sedikides, 1992) pursued a general, unifying principle regarding the influence of happy and sad moods on the valence of the self-concept. The review concluded that this principle was mood congruency: happy moods augment the positivity of self-cognitions, whereas sad moods augment the negativity of self-cognitions.[2] For example, relative to sad moods, happy moods elicit favorable self-judgments, increase recall of positive self-referent information, and induce higher expectancies of positive self-relevant outcomes.

Research has continued to provide support for the mood congruency principle as it pertains to self-cognitions [e.g., Abele-Brehm & Hermer, 1993; Nasby, 1994 (judgment results); Nasby, 1996].[3] Most of the recent empirical efforts, however, have sought to qualify the mood-congruency principle. Our goal in the current review is to summarize these efforts. We review post-1992 research that qualifies the mood-congruency principle. We are guided theoretically in this selective review by Forgas' Affect Infusion Model (AIM; 1995, chap. 14, this volume).

---

[2] Another review (Mayer, Gaschke, Braverman, & Evans, 1992) established mood congruency as a general principle in the domain of non-self-relevant cognitions. For relevant discussions, see also: Bower & Forgas, chap. 5, this volume; Fiedler, chap. 8, this volume; Petty, DeSteno, & Rucker, chap. 10, this volume; and Salovey, Detwiler, Steward, & Bedell, chap. 16, this volume.

[3] For a nonreplication, see Cervone, Kopp, Schaumann, and Scott (1994, Experiments 1 and 2). These researchers reported null effects of mood on perceived self-efficacy.

THE AFFECT INFUSION MODEL

A key construct of the AIM is affect infusion, "the process whereby affectively loaded information exerts an influence on and becomes incorporated into the judgmental process, entering into the judge's constructive deliberations and eventually coloring the judgmental outcome" (Forgas, 1995, p. 39). Some kinds of processing strategies are characterized by low infusion potential. These are the direct-access strategy (i.e., when knowledge structures are retrieved from memory) and motivated-processing strategy (i.e., when processing is goal-driven). Other kinds of processing strategies involve relatively high infusion potential. One such strategy is heuristic processing, requiring an improvised judgment. Another strategy in which the judgment must be computed on-line is substantive processing. This strategy involves "the substantial transformation rather than the mere reproduction of existing cognitive representations, requiring a relatively open information search strategy, and a significant degree of generative elaboration of the available stimulus details" (Forgas, 1995, p. 39).

The AIM has important implications for the role of mood in the self-concept. The model predicts reasonably well the circumstances under which mood-congruency effects will or will not be obtained. These circumstances or moderators fall under three broad categories: type of self-conceptions, individual differences, and judgmental task features.

Type of Self-Conceptions

Does mood affect all aspects of the self-concept in a similar (i.e., valuatively congruent) manner? Alternatively, are mood congruency effects localized in a specific type of self-conceptions?

Central and Peripheral Self-Conceptions. Two types of self-conceptions have garnered the lion's share of the attention of self-concept theorists: central and peripheral self-conceptions (Gergen, 1968; Rosenberg, 1988; Stryker, 1980). These types of cognitive structures differ in several important ways, such as elaboration, certainty, positivity, and diagnosticity (Sedikides, 1995). Relative to peripheral ones, central self-conceptions contain higher amounts of detailed (i.e., elaborated) autobiographic knowledge, are held with higher certainty, are more positive, and are more likely to be thought of as representing the "true" self (Dunning, Perie, & Story, 1991; Sedikides, 1993). It is no surprise, then, that central self-conceptions are affirmed more strongly than peripheral ones (Markus, 1977; Pelham,

1991; Sedikides, 1993) through such mechanisms as selective attention to feedback, biased interpretation or explanation of feedback, reconstructive memory, and selective exposure to confirming social environments (Sedikides & Strube, 1997; Swann, 1990).

Based on the previously mentioned distinctions, Sedikides (1995) proposed that central and peripheral self-conceptions will be differentially sensitive to the influence of mood. Information pertaining to central and peripheral self-conceptions is likely to be processed via different AIM-specified strategies. Processing of information relevant to central self-conceptions likely has low infusion potential: such processing is either motivated by or presupposes the direct accessing of an already formed cognitive structure. However, processing of information relevant to peripheral self-conceptions likely has high infusion potential: such information requires the on-line computation of a judgment.

This analysis leads to differing hypotheses regarding the influence of mood on central versus peripheral self-conceptions. Mood will not affect central self-conceptions, but will affect peripheral self-conceptions in a valuatively congruent manner. Type of self-conceptions will qualify the mood-congruency principle.

Empirical Evidence. The differential sensitivity hypothesis has been tested in four experiments reported by Sedikides (1995). As a reminder, central and peripheral self-conceptions are likely to differ in four characteristics: valence, diagnosticity, certainty, and elaborative knowledge. In Experiment 1, Sedikides (1995) focused exclusively on the role of valence and diagnosticity.

Participants in the first experimental session generated four positive and four negative central traits, and four positive and four negative peripheral traits. The top three traits from each of the 16 categories were selected for subsequent use. Experimental assistants generated 12 high-diagnosticity behaviors for each trait. Diagnosticity was defined in terms of the likelihood of each behavior revealing whether the actor possessed the underlying trait. This pool of behaviors was rated by an independent sample in terms of diagnosticity. The result was the selection of 36 highly diagnostic behaviors (i.e., three behaviors per trait). Testing insured that the behaviors in all categories were approximately equal in diagnosticity and valence.[4]

---

[4]The central positive behaviors were rated significantly higher than the peripheral positive behaviors on valence. However, ancillary analyses ruled out differential valence as an explanation for the obtained findings.

Examples of the behaviors are: "I am the kind of person who would be able to complete both her Ph.D. and MD in 6 years" ("intelligent"—central positive trait); "I am the kind of person who would think and act funny around people I didn't know very well" ("socially awkward"—central negative trait); "I am the kind of person who would easily disappear for a week in the woods . . . just for kicks" ("carefree"—peripheral positive trait); and "I am the kind of person who would follow the advice of his parents for which professional or graduate school to attend" ("dependent"—peripheral negative trait).

Then, participants were telephoned and invited to a second laboratory session. Participants were put successfully into happy, neutral, or sad mood states through a guided imagery procedure. Participants in the happy mood condition imagined that a friend had won a free cruise to the Caribbean islands and also had won $1,000,000 in the lottery. Participants in the neutral mood condition imagined a friend watching television and riding the bus. Finally, participants in the sad mood condition imagined that a friend was burned in a fire and died. Next, participants rated themselves on the 36 behaviors. Participants completed their ratings one at a time and on a scale ranging from *definitely not me* to *definitely me*.

The results confirmed the differential sensitivity hypothesis. Mood did not influence the endorsement of behaviors that exemplified central traits. However, mood influenced in a congruent manner the endorsement of behaviors that exemplified peripheral traits. That is, compared to neutral mood, happy mood led to higher endorsement of peripheral positive behaviors but lower endorsement of peripheral negative behaviors. For example, happy participants considered the behavior "I am the kind of person who would easily disappear for a week in the woods . . . just for kicks" as more self-descriptive than neutral-mood participants, but considered the behavior "I am the kind of person who would follow the advice of his parents for which professional or graduate school to attend" as less self-descriptive than neutral-mood participants. The findings can be viewed from the perspective of the effects of sad mood. Compared to neutral mood, sad mood led to lower endorsement of peripheral negative behaviors but higher endorsement of peripheral positive behaviors. For example, in comparison to neutral-mood participants, sad participants considered the behavior "I am the kind of person who would easily disappear for a week in the woods . . . just for kicks" as less self-descriptive, but considered the behavior "I am the kind of person who would follow the advice of his parents for which professional or graduate school to attend" as more self-descriptive. Importantly, these findings generalized over valence and diagnosticity. The divergent effects of mood on the self could not be attributed to valence and diagnosticity differences between central and peripheral self-conceptions.

Could the mood effects be attributed to differences in certainty between central and peripheral self-conceptions? Experiment 2 sought to address this question. In the first experimental session, participants generated 16 traits: four central positive, four central negative, four peripheral positive, and four peripheral negative. Participants also rated these traits for valence and certainty of possession. Twelve traits were selected for subsequent use. (The mean valence ratings of these traits were approximately equal across the four categories.[5]) In the second experimental session, participants completed the dependent measure by rating the 12 traits for self-descriptiveness.

The results replicated the previous findings in bolstering the differential processing hypothesis. Mood did not alter the endorsement of central traits, but it did alter the endorsement of peripheral traits in a congruent manner. Happy participants were most likely to endorse peripheral positive traits and least likely to endorse peripheral negative traits. Importantly, these findings were due, in part, to certainty differences between central and peripheral traits. A reason that peripheral traits are more susceptible to the impact of mood than central traits is because peripheral traits are held with lower certainty.

Although the two experiments described are consistent with the AIM, they do not provide direct support for it. The purpose of Experiment 3 was to test the proposition of the AIM that affect is infused in the judgment (i.e., behavior or trait endorsement) to a greater degree when peripheral self-relevant information is processed, because in this case, substantive (rather than heuristic) processing takes place. If this proposition is correct, then judgmental latencies for the endorsement of peripheral traits would exceed endorsement latencies for central traits. Experiment 3 replicated the previous two experiments in showing that mood alters the valence of peripheral but not central self-conceptions. More importantly, however, Experiment 3 provided evidence for substantive processing of peripheral self-relevant information: Participants took more time to decide whether peripheral (as opposed to central) traits were self-descriptive, and this judgmental latency mediated their endorsement ratings. Another reason, besides certainty, for the differential influence of mood on peripheral versus central traits is that peripheral self-cognitions are less elaborated in autobiographic memory.

---

[5] As in Experiment 1, the central positive behaviors had significantly higher valence ratings than the peripheral positive behaviors. Supplementary analyses, however, ruled out differential valence as an explanation for the obtained findings.

Experiment 3 obtained mediational support for the notion that substantive processing is implicated in the case of peripheral traits. Experiment 4 sought direct support for this notion. Participants were induced into a happy, sad, or neutral mood state and were asked to complete self-descriptiveness ratings on three peripheral positive and three peripheral negative traits. Half of the participants were given low on-line elaboration instructions: They were asked to rate the traits at a rapid rate (i.e., 5 seconds per trait). The other half of the participants were placed in the high on-line elaboration condition: They were asked to think for 1 minute as to whether the trait was characteristic of them and then complete the trait rating. The results supported the proposition that mood affects the endorsement of peripheral self-cognitions through substantive processing. Mood congruency effects were stronger in the high than low on-line elaboration condition.

Summary. Type of self-conceptions is a potent moderator of the mood congruency principle. Mood influences peripheral self-cognitions in a valuatively congruent manner, but it has no effect on central self-cognitions.

Individual Differences

Another possible moderator of mood effects on the self is individual differences (Rusting, chap. 17, this volume). We are concerned, more specifically, with differences in level of self-esteem. Does mood affect persons with low and high self-esteem differently?

Self-Esteem. The construct of self-esteem continues to captivate social and personality psychologists (Baumeister, 1993, 1998). An important difference between persons with low and high self-esteem concerns the certainty or stability of self-knowledge. Persons with low self-esteem are less certain of who they are (Campbell et al., 1996) and are less stable over time in their self-views (Kernis & Waschull, 1996).

Capitalizing on this difference, the AIM offers interesting predictions. Mood influences persons with low self-esteem to a greater degree than persons with high self-esteem. That is, affect is infused to a greater degree in persons with low self-esteem given that these persons likely vacillate more in their self-judgments due to the uncertainty of their self-views.

Empirical Evidence. Smith and Petty (1995, Experiment 2) reported results relevant to the previously mentioned predictions. These researchers placed participants with low and high self-esteem in either sad or neutral mood states through video clips. Participants in the sad mood condition watched a clip of a boy dying of cancer, whereas participants in the neutral mood condition watched a clip on the social behavior of lions. Next, participants listed three memories from their high-school years. These memories were coded for degree of positivity by independent coders.

Smith and Petty (1995, Experiment 2) analyzed the results in terms of both first memory listed and total number of memories listed. The results were identical and supportive of the AIM. Specifically, participants with low self-esteem generated more memories in the sad than neutral mood condition. However, participants with high self-esteem generated an equivalent (i.e., nonsignificantly different) amount of memories in the two mood conditions. Stated somewhat differently, a mood-congruency effect was obtained only in the case of persons with low self-esteem.

Brown and Mankowski (1993) also examined the influence of mood on self-judgments of persons with low and high self-esteem. In Experiment 1, Brown and Mankowski placed participants with low and high self-esteem into a mood state through the Velten (1968) procedure. Participants in the happy mood condition read positively valenced self-referent statements (e.g., "I am cheerful and lively"). Participants in the sad mood condition read negatively valenced self-referent statements (e.g., "My life is so tiresome, the same old thing day after day depresses me"). Finally, participants in the neutral mood condition read statements that were neither valenced nor referenced (e.g., "Utah is the Beehive state"). Next, participants rated themselves on 16 adjectives, half of which were positive and half were negative.

Mood influenced the self-evaluations of persons with low self-esteem in a valuatively congruent manner. That is, compared to neutral mood, sad mood increased the negativity of self-ratings, whereas happy mood increased the positivity of self-ratings. However, mood had mixed effects with regard to the self-evaluations of persons with high self-esteem. The effects of happy mood did not differ significantly from the effects of neutral mood. These results can also be interpreted by comparing the effects of each mood state for persons with low and high self-esteem. Happy mood did not influence differentially persons with low and high self-esteem. However, sad mood did so, as it lowered the self-evaluations of persons with low, but not high, self-esteem.

In Experiment 2, Brown and Mankowski (1993) used only happy and sad mood conditions, and they induced mood through both the Velten procedure and musical selections (a jazz version of Bach's "Brandenburg Concerto No. 3" played by Hubert Laws in the happy mood condition, and Prokofiev's "Russia Under the Mongolian Yoke" played at half speed in the sad mood condition). Note that the two musical procedures yielded similar findings. These findings approximated the findings from Experiment 1. A statistically significant mood congruency effects was evident in the self-evaluations of persons with low self-esteem: Sad mood participants rated the self more negatively than happy mood participants. However, only a marginal mood congruency effect emerged in the case of the self-evaluations of persons with high self-esteem: Sad mood participants tended to rate the self more negatively than happy mood participants. Viewed from another angle, sad mood lowered substantially the self-evaluations of persons with low self-esteem, but it also lowered (significantly but less forcefully) the self-evaluations of persons with high self-esteem.

Taken together, the results of Smith and Petty (1995, Experiment 2) and Brown and Mankowski (1993, Experiments 1 and 2) are consistent with the AIM. Reliable congruency effects are observed with regard to the impact of mood on the self-perceptions of persons with low self-esteem. However, the effects of mood on the self-perceptions of persons with high self-esteem are rather inconsistent.

Summary. The individual difference of level of self-esteem emerged as a moderator of the mood-congruency principle. Mood influences in a valuatively congruent way how persons with low self-esteem view themselves, but it does not influence in a clear and systematic way how persons with high self-esteem view themselves.

How do the findings reviewed under the "Individual Differences" section relate to the findings reviewed under the "Type of Self-Conceptions" section? Sedikides (1995) reported mood effects on peripheral but not central self-conceptions. Were Smith and Petty (1995, Experiment 2) and Brown and Mankowski (1993, Experiments 1 and 2) concerned exclusively with peripheral self-conceptions? Although the latter two teams of researchers did not distinguish between types of self-conceptions, a perusal of their stimulus materials suggests that they used a mixture of peripheral and central self-conceptions. It is likely that the mood effects that these investigators reported were driven primarily by the endorsement patterns of peripheral self-conceptions. An important issue for future research is whether mood effects are an interactive function of type of self-conceptions and self-esteem. Are the central and peripheral self-conceptions of persons with low and high self-esteem influenced differentially by mood?

Judgmental Task Features

The third and final class of moderators of the mood congruency principle that we wish to consider involves features of the judgmental task. Three moderators have received empirical attention: affirmative versus nonaffirmative judgment, judgment of performance outcomes versus performance standards, and timing (immediate vs. delayed) of judgment.

Note that the relevancy of the AIM to this class of moderators is limited. The first moderator concerns the inhibitory effects of mood on encoding. The second and third moderators have to do, at least in part, with mood regulation. The AIM was not designed to address these issues. Nevertheless, the moderators are reviewed, as they place critical constraints on the mood-congruency principle.

Affirmative versus Nonaffirmative Judgment. Participants in Nasby's (1994) experiment were assigned into a happy, neutral, or sad mood state. Mood was induced through the Velten procedure. Next, participants were presented with 40 trait adjectives (20 positive and 20 negative) and were asked the question, "Does the following adjective describe you?" Participants completed both an affirmative (facilitatory) judgment and a nonaffirmative (inhibitory) judgment to each question. The affirmative judgment involved responding "Yes" to each question, whereas the nonaffirmative judgment involved responding "No" to each question. Following a filler task, participants were asked to recall the 40 trait adjectives.

The nature of the judgmental task moderated the effects of mood on recall. Mood-congruency effects were generally evident in the case of affirmative judgment. Compared to neutral mood, happy mood led to an increase in the recall of positive trait adjectives, although it did not decrease recall of negative trait adjectives. In a parallel manner, compared to neutral mood, sad mood lead to an increase in the recall of negative trait adjectives, although it did not reduce recall of positive trait adjectives. However, mood-congruency effects were eliminated in the case of nonaffirmative judgment. Mood had no influence on inhibitory encoding processes.

Although, as stated, Nasby's (1994) experiment does not necessarily constitute a direct test of the AIM (nor was it designed as such), the results are somewhat inconsistent with the tenets of AIM. Affirmative knowledge is well-established structurally in memory (Einhorn & Hogarth, 1978; Newman, Wolff, & Hearst, 1980) and likely is held with relatively high certainty. Nonaffirmative self-knowledge, however, likely is generated on external (e.g., experimental) demand, thus resembling an on-line judgment.

If these premises are correct, one would expect (based on AIM) the opposite pattern of results from that reported by Nasby: Mood-congruency effects on recall would be present in the case of nonaffirmative judgment, but absent in the case of affirmative judgment. Future research should explore more systematically the susceptibility of nonaffirmative encoding to the influence of mood.

Judgment of Performance Outcomes versus Performance Standards.

Cervone, Kopp, Schaumann, and Scott (1994, Experiment 3) distinguished between two kinds of performance expectancies: outcomes versus standards. *Performance outcomes* referred to participants' satisfaction with attaining a designated performance level. *Performance standards* referred to participants' minimum satisfactory level of performance.

Cervone et al. (1994, Experiment 3) induced either a sad or neutral mood through tape-recorded instructions. In the sad mood condition, participants imagined their best friend dying of cancer; in the neutral mood condition, participants visualized their room at home. Next, participants completed the dependent measures.

In the case of performance outcomes, participants rated how satisfied they would feel with themselves if they were to perform a task or an activity at a designated level. Participants rated 16 items, 10 of which pertained to academic tasks (e.g., "Present an oral report in front of a small class") or social tasks (e.g., "Tell a joke or a humorous anecdote at a party"). For these items, the designated level of performance was a level equal to that of the average individual. The remaining 6 items involved academic tasks (e.g., grade in introductory psychology, GPA), but the designated performance level was a specific numeric value. In the case of performance standards, participants rated the same 16 items, but with a different criterion in mind. Specifically, participants were asked to indicate the minimum level of performance that they would have to attain in order to be satisfied with how well they had done.

Mood affected performance outcomes in a congruent manner. Sad mood participants expressed lower evaluations of future outcomes than neutral mood participants. However, mood affected performance standards in an incongruent manner. Sad participants expressed higher personal standards than neutral mood participants. (For a replication of the latter finding, see Cervone et al., 1994, Experiments 1 and 2.)

There are at least two plausible explanations for the obtained mood incongruency results on performance standards. One explanation involves attributive processes (Clore, Gaspar, & Garvin, chap. 6, this volume;

Schwarz, 1990). Participants misattributed their sad mood to dissatisfaction with their performance and, hence, increased their performance standards in order to alleviate the feeling of dissatisfaction. A second explanation involves straightforward mood repair notions (Scheier & Carver, 1982; Erber & Erber, chap. 13, this volume). Participants in the sad mood condition elevated their standards in an effort to end their uncomfortable mood state.

Timing of Judgment. The mood repair notion has implication for an experiment reported by Sedikides (1994). Participants were placed into a happy, neutral, or sad mood state using guided imagery procedures similar to those of Sedikides (1995). Then, participants were handed a 40-page booklet and were asked to "tell us about yourself." Participants were instructed to write one open self-description on each page of the booklet and were allotted 6 minutes for the task. (Pilot testing had indicated that the duration of mood well exceeded the 6 minute mark.) After a 13-minute filler task, whose purpose was to ensure that the effects of mood had vanished, participants rated the valence of their listed self-descriptions.

Self-descriptions were divided up into halves and were entered in the analyses as a variable. Mood-congruency effects were obtained in the first half of self-descriptions. Sad mood participants described themselves in more negative terms than neutral mood participants; conversely, happy mood participants described themselves in more positive terms than neutral mood participants. However, a mixed pattern was obtained in the second half of self-descriptions. Although happy mood participants still described themselves more positively than neutral mood participants, neutral and sad mood participants did not differ in the positivity of their self-descriptions.

Timing, then, made a difference. In the first few (2–3) minutes following mood induction, mood affected self-descriptions in a congruent way. However, with the passage of time (after 3–4 minutes), sad mood ceased to influence the valence of self-views. Perhaps with the passage of time, mood repair processes became operative. Timing of self-judgment is a moderator of the mood-congruency principle.

CONCLUDING REMARKS

This chapter was concerned with the impact of mood states, specifically sad and happy states, on self-cognitions. The chapter built on an earlier review (Sedikides, 1992) that proposed that mood influences the self in a valuatively congruent manner. Although support for the mood-congruency principle continues to accumulate (e.g., Abele-Brehm & Hermer, 1993; Nasby, 1996), the current review engaged in a selective search for moderators of this general principle.

This review discussed research that used a variety of mood-induction procedures (e.g., guided imagery, musical selections, Velten) and several different dependent measures (e.g., self-evaluations, memory, judgments of future outcomes, self-descriptions). The review identified three moderators: type of self-conceptions, individual differences (i.e., self-esteem), and judgmental task features. Mood influences congruently the way in which individuals perceive themselves on peripheral self-conceptions, but mood does not affect self-perceptions on central self-conceptions. Mood affects congruently the self-evaluations of persons with low, but not necessarily persons with high, self-esteem. Finally, mood congruency effects are present (1) following facilitatory but not inhibitory encoding, (2) when judging performance outcomes but not performance standards, and (3) when the self is described in the immediate rather than distant future.

The AIM served as a useful integrative framework of much of the reviewed work. The AIM can explain reasonably well the confirmations and disconfirmations of the mood congruency principle with regard to the first two moderators, namely, type of self-conceptions and self-esteem. However, the AIM has difficulty accounting for the full spectrum of results concerning the third class of moderators, judgmental task features. Indeed, the experimental procedures relevant to testing this third class of moderators open up interesting new challenges for the AIM to explore. For example, why is it that affect is more likely to be infused in facilitatory as opposed to inhibitory encoding processes?

Future research will need to paint a more comprehensive picture of the circumstances under which mood-congruency effects versus mood-incongruency effects versus no mood effects are obtained. Indeed, research must move more assertively into pursuing interactive effects of mood and self-cognitions. For example, how does mood affect the peripheral self-conceptions of persons with high self-esteem who complete an inhibitory encoding task?

Another yet untested moderator of mood congruency effects on the self is the individual difference variable of affect intensity (Larsen & Diener, 1987). An example is provided by the work of Haddock, Zanna, and Esses (1994). These researchers split their sample into participants who were high versus low in affect intensity. After mood induction, participants expressed their attitudes and stereotypic beliefs toward social groups.

Mood-congruency effects were present only among high affect intensity participants. This pattern may be generalizable to self-judgments. In a somewhat similar vein, mood-congruency effects may be more prevalent among sensitizers than repressors (Epstein & Fenz, 1967; for relevant research, see McFarland & Buehler, 1997).

Research must also consider the consequences of mood for other facets of the self besides its valence. A relevant example is research of DeSteno and Salovey (1997), who examined the effects of mood on the structure of the self-concept. They found that neutral mood participants structured their self-conceptions around the dimensions of achievement and affiliation. However, the happy and sad participants organized their self-conceptions on the basis of the dimension of valence. Mood likely induces simplicity in the structure of the self-concept.

In summary, the present chapter has uncovered some intricate facets of the relation between mood and self-conception valence. Mood-congruency effects on the self are definitely less general than previously thought, and are limited by type of self-conceptions, trait self-esteem differences, and judgmental task features.

REFERENCES

Abele-Brehm, A., & Hermer, P. (1993). Mood influences on health-related judgments: Appraisal of own health versus appraisal of unhealthy behaviours. *European Journal of Social Psychology, 23,* 613–625.

Baumeister, R. F. (1993). *Self-esteem: The puzzle of low self-regard.* New York: Plenum Press.

Baumeister, R. F. (1998). The self. In D. T. Gilbert, S. T., Fiske, & G. Lindzey (Eds.), *The handbook of social psychology* (pp. 680–740). New York: Oxford University Press.

Brown, J. D., & Mankowski, T. A. (1993). Self-esteem, mood, and self-evaluation: Changes in the mood and the way you see you. *Journal of Personality and Social Psychology, 64,* 421–430.

Campbell, J. D., Trapnell, P. D., Heine, S. J., Katz, I. M., Lavallee, L. F., & Lehman, D. R. (1996). Self-concept clarity: Measurement, personality correlates, and cultural boundaries. *Journal of Personality and Social Psychology, 70,* 141–156.

Cervone, D., Kopp, D. A., Schaumann, L., & Scott, W. D. (1994). Mood, self-efficacy, and performance standards: Lower moods induce higher standards for performance. *Journal of Personality and Social Psychology, 67,* 499–512.

Clore, G. L., Schwarz, N., & Conway, M. (1994). Affective causes and consequences of social information processing. In R. S. Wyer, Jr., & T. K. Srull (Eds.), *Handbook of social cognition* (Vol. 1, pp. 323–417). Hillsdale, NJ: Lawrence Elrbaum Associates.

DeSteno, D. A., & Salovey, P. (1997). The effects of mood on the structure of the self-concept. *Cognition and Emotion, 11,* 351–372.

Dunning, D., Perie, M., & Story, A. L. (1991). Self-serving prototypes of social categories. *Journal of Personality and Social Psychology, 61,* 957–968.

Einhorn, H. J., & Hogarth, R. M. (1978). Confidence in judgment: Persistence of the illusion of validity. *Psychological Review, 85,* 395–416.

Epstein, S., & Fenz, W. D. (1967). The detection of areas of emotional stress through variations in perceptual threshold and physiological arousal. *Journal of Experimental Research in Personality, 2*, 191–199.

Fiedler, K., & Bless, H. (in press). In N. Frijda, A. Manstead, & S. Bem (Eds.), *The influence of emotions on beliefs.* Cambridge, London: Cambridge University.

Forgas, J. P. (1992). Affect in social judgments and decisions: A multi-process model. In M. Zanna (Ed.), *Advances in experimental social psychology* (Vol. 25, pp. 227–275). New York: Academic Press.

Forgas, J. P. (1995). Mood and judgment: The affect infusion model (AIM). *Psychological Bulletin, 116*, 39–66.

Gergen, K. J. (1968). Personal consistency and presentation of the self. In C. Gordon & K. J. Gergen (Eds.), *The self in social interaction* (Vol. 1, pp. 299–308). New York: Wiley.

Haddock, G., Zanna, M. P., & Esses, V. (1994). Mood and the expression of intergroup attitudes: The moderating role of affect intensity. *European Journal of Social Psychology, 24*, 189–205.

Kernis, M. H., & Waschull, S. B. (1996). The interactive roles of stability and level of self-esteem: Research and theory. In M. P. Zanna (Ed.), *Advances in experimental social psychology* (Vol. 27, pp. 93–141).

Larsen, R. J., & Diener, E. (1987). Affect intensity as an individual difference characteristic: A review. *Journal of Research in Personality, 21*, 1–39.

Levine, S. R., Wyer, R. S., & Schwarz, N. (1994). Are you what you feel? The affective and cognitive determinants of self-judgments. *European Journal of Social Psychology, 24*, 63–77.

Markus, H. (1977). Self-schemata and processing information about the self. *Journal of Personality and Social Psychology, 35*, 63–78.

Martin, L., Abend, T., Sedikides, C., & Green, J. D. (1997). How would I feel if . . . ?: Mood as input to a role fulfillment evaluation process. *Journal of Personality and Social Psychology, 73*, 242–253.

Mayer, J. D., Gaschke, Y. N., Braverman, D. L., & Evans, T. W. (1992). Mood-congruent judgment is a general effect. *Journal of Personality and Social Psychology, 63*, 119–132.

McFarland, C., & Buehler, R. (1997). Negative affective states and the motivated retrieval of positive life events: The role of affect acknowledgment. *Journal of Personality and Social Psychology, 73*, 200–214.

McFarland, C., & Buehler, R. (1998). The impact of negative affective on autobiographical memory: The role of self-focused attention to moods. *Journal of Personality and Social Psychology, 75*, 1424–1440.

Nasby, W. (1994). Moderators of mood-congruent encoding: Self-/other-reference and affirmative/nonaffirmative judgment. *Cognition and Emotion, 8*, 259–278.

Nasby, W. (1996). Moderators of mood-congruent encoding and judgment: Evidence that elated and depressed moods implicate distinct processes. *Cognition and Emotion, 10*, 361–377.

Newman, J., Wolff, W. T., & Hearst, E. (1980). The feature-positive effect in adult human subjects. *Journal of Experimental Psychology: Human Learning and Memory, 6*, 630–650.

Osgood, C. E., Suci, G. J., & Tannenbaum, P. H. (1957). *The measurement of meaning.* Urbana, IL: University of Illinois Press.

Pelham, B. W. (1991). On confidence and consequences: The certainty and importance of self- knowledge. *Journal of Personality and Social Psychology, 60*, 518–530.

Rosenberg, S. (1988). Self and others: Studies in social personality and autobiography. In L. Berkowitz (Ed.), *Advances in experimental social psychology* (Vol. 21, pp. 57–95). San Diego: Academic Press.

Scheier, M. F., & Carver, C. S. (1982). Cognition, affect, and self-regulation. In M. S. Clark & S. T. Fiske (Eds.), *Affect and cognition* (pp. 157–183). Hillsdale, NJ: Lawrence Erlbaum Associates.

Scherer, K. R., Koivumaki, J., & Rosenthal, R. (1972). Minimal cues in the vocal communication of affect: Judging emotions from content masked speech. *Journal of Personality and Social Psychology, 1*, 269–285.

Schwarz, N. (1990). Feelings as information: Information and motivational functions of affective states. In E. T. Higgins & R. M. Sorrentino (Eds.), *Motivation and cognition: Foundations of social behavior* (Vol. 2, pp. 527–561). New York: Guilford Press.

Sedikides, C. (1992). Changes in the valence of the self as a function of mood. *Review of Personality and Social Psychology, 14,* 271–311.

Sedikides, C. (1993). Assessment, enhancement, and verification determinants of the self-evaluation process. *Journal of Personality and Social Psychology, 65,* 317–338.

Sedikides, C. (1994). Incongruent effects of sad mood on self-conception valence: It's a matter of time. *European Journal of Social Psychology, 24,* 161–172.

Sedikides, C. (1995). Central and peripheral self-conceptions are differentially influenced by mood: Tests of the differential sensitivity hypothesis. *Journal of Personality and Social Psychology, 69,* 759–777.

Sedikides, C., & Strube, M. J. (1997). Self-evaluation: To thine own self be good, to thine own self be sure, to thine own self be true, and to thine own self be better. In M. P. Zanna (Ed.), *Advances in experimental social psychology* (Vol. 29, pp. 209–269). New York, NY: Academic Press.

Smith, S. M., & Petty, R. E. (1995). Personality moderators of mood congruency effects on cognition: The role of self-esteem and negative mood regulation. *Journal of Personality and Social Psychology, 68,* 1092–1107.

Stryker, S. (1980). *Symbolic interactionism.* Menlo Park, CA: Benjamin/Cummings.

Swann, W. B. Jr. (1990). To be adored or to be known? The interplay of self-enhancement and self-verification. In E. T. Higgins & R. M. Sorrentino (Eds.), *Handbook of motivation and cognition: Foundations of social behavior* (Vol. 2, pp. 408–448). New York: Guilford Press.

Velten, E. (1968). A laboratory task for induction of mood states. *Advances in Behavior Research and Therapy, 6,* 473–482.

III

Affective Influences on Social Information Processing

8

Affective Influences on Social Information Processing

Klaus Fiedler

University of Heidelberg
Heidelberg, Germany

A Fundamental Processing Dichotomy   165
  Basic Assumptions, Methods, and Findings   166
  Mood-Congruency Effects   168
  Mood Effects on Information-Processing Style   169
  Boundary Conditions of Mood-Congruent Memory and Judgment   171
  Integrating the Evidence in Terms of Processing Differences:
    The Affect Infusion Model (AIM)   172
  The Processing Consequences of Affect   176
  Affect, Cognition, and Adaptive Learning: Assimilation
    versus Accommodation   177
Summary and Conclusions   182
References   183

The systematic study of emotional influences on social information processing is a rather recent topic of research, even though its origins can be traced to the beginning of the 20th century. Among these precursors

Address for correspondence: Klaus Fiedler, Psychologisches Institut, Universität Heidelberg, Hauptst. 47–51, D-69117 Heidelberg, Germany. Email: kf@psi-sv2.psi.uni-heidelberg.de are Freud's (1915) notion of repressed memories for unpleasant materials, early emotion theories that emphasize the interrupt function of emotional reactions (cf. Frijda, 1986), the Yerkes–Dodson (1908) law that posits an inverted U-function between emotional arousal and cognitive performance, McDougall's (1928) emphasis on the communicative–informative function of emotions, and behaviorist research on conditioned emotional reactions (Watson & Rayner, 1920). Later, after World War II, important additional impulses came from Easterbrook's (1959) thesis that span of apprehension decreases with increasing arousal, and from Janis and Feshbach's (1953) seminal work on the disruptive effects of fear appeals in persuasive communication.

Although the lasting contribution of these studies is not clear and remains a matter for historical interpretation, there can be no doubt that elements of all of the previously mentioned ideas can be recognized in the modern research literature on affect and cognition. However, it is important to point out one noteworthy difference between these historical antecedents and the contemporary approaches to be reviewed in the present chapter. These pioneer researchers were concerned mainly with the ways in which emotions inhibit, restrict, interrupt, or interfere with perception, memory, and goal-directed action. Apart from this quantitative reduction in cognitive resources, early theorists were not interested in the influence of affect on cognitive processes and structures. Only after the ascent of the so-called cognitive revolution (Dember, 1974) in the 1960s and 1970s did new theoretical developments in cognitive psychology offer the concepts and research tools to investigate affective influences on cognitive functions under experimental control. In these studies, the focus was no longer on the disruptive cognitive side effects of emotions, but on the analysis of cognitive processes as a function of manipulated emotions or moods.

The present chapter presents an empirical overview and a theoretical integration of what we now know about the influence of affective states on social information processing (see also Clore, Schwarz, & Conway, 1994; Fiedler, 1990; Forgas, 1995; Martin & Clore, in press). It is argued that the fundamental links between affect and information processing are also relevant to a proper understanding of affect congruity effects in social thinking and judgments, topics that are covered in several other chapters in this book (see especially Bodenhausen, Mussweiler, Gabriel, & Moreno, chap.15, this volume; Bower & Forgas, chap. 5, this volume; Clore, Gasper, & Garvin, chap. 6, this volume; and Petty, DeSteno, & Rucker, chap.10, this volume).

A FUNDAMENTAL PROCESSING DICHOTOMY

In order to understand affective influences on social cognition, we must first understand on which dimension information-processing styles may differ. Consistent with past research, it is argued here that the influence of affect on social thinking can best be understood in terms of a fundamental processing dichotomy between accommodation and assimilation. *Accommodation* is an adaptive process in which the organism is focused on the demands of the external world; *assimilation*, in contrast, is a complementary process in which the organism actively adapts to the external world, relying on well-established internal structures and representations. In information-processing terms, accommodation requires the rather careful, exhaustive perception and conservation of stimulus information. Assimilation, in contrast, involves the active cognitive elaboration and transformation of stimuli using internal schemata and knowledge structures. In principle, every cognitive task involves both of these adaptive processing strategies, albeit in different proportions. We may thus distinguish between "conservation" problems, which require mainly accommodative processing, and "generative" problems, which involve active, creative information processing, "going beyond the information given" (Bruner, 1973).

This processing distinction is relevant because we now know that negative affect and aversive situations and stimuli facilitate and accommodative processing style. In contrast, positive affect promotes a more assimilative, creative, and top-down information-processing style (see also Bless, 2000). Considerable evidence now supports such a processing distinction. We know that high-level schemas and stereotypes are often more likely to be used in a positive mood (Bless, 2000). Happy people produce more creative and unusual associations (Isen, Johnson, Mertz, & Robinson, 1985); are better at encoding active, self-generated memories (Fiedler, Lachnit, Fay, & Krug, 1992); show stronger priming effects for personal characteristics (Bless & Fiedler, 1995); and show stronger congruence effects for self-generated rather than passivley received information (Fiedler et al., 1992). In contrast, people experiencing negative moods produce slower and less spontaneous and heuristic decisions (Isen & Means, 1983); are less likely to violate rules of transitivity (Fiedler, 1988); commit fewer constructive memory errors (Fiedler, Asbeck, & Nickel, 1991); and are more likely to produce attitudes and judgments based on a systematic evaluation of information (Bless, Bohner, Schwarz, & Strack, 1980;

Fiedler & Fladung, 1987). Extensive reviews of the relevant evidence can be found in Fiedler (1990, 1991), Forgas (1995, 2000), and Martin and Clore (2000).

It is argued that this fundamental distinction between accommodative and assimilative thinking can help us understand not only most of the available evidence for affective influences on information processing, but also extensive evidence showing affect congruence in memory and judgments under certain circumstances. We know that affect congruity effects are generally much stronger and more pronounced in positive than in negative mood states. As positive mood promotes constructive, assimiliative thinking, and assuming that affect congruence is largely driven by affect priming mechanisms that can only operate in the course of generative thinking, greater mood congruity in positive moods is consistent with the processing dichotomy suggested here. Such asymmetric mood effects thus partly reflect the asymmetric processing strategies that positive and negative moods stimulate. In the remainder of this chapter, empirical findings are reviewed that elucidate how affective influences on social information processing operate, and how these effects are related to affect congruence phenomena as well.

Basic Assumptions, Methods, and Findings

In order to investigate emotion influences on cognition, it is essential to manipulate emotions as an antecedent or independent variable and measure the consequent changes in dependent measures of cognitive performance. Most experiments have manipulated more or less enduring positive or negative *mood states*, rather than intense, short-term emotions. Relatively little is known about the impact of single qualitative emotions—such as anger, envy, fear, disgust, or hope—on cognitive functions. There are substantive as well as pragmatic reasons for this restriction. Unlike specific emotions, the origin of mood states is often diffuse and unclear. It is for this reason that the cognitive consequences of mood are more likely to be broad and general, spreading to diverse cognitive contents and strategies. The study of mood effects is thus more relevant to understanding everyday psychological processes than the study of intense emotions, because mood effects last longer, occur more frequently, and are less easily detected than are emotional influences. The concentration of research on positive (elated) versus negative (depressed) moods may thus be justified because it is these

TABLE 8.1

Overview of Different Procedures Used for the Experimental Induction of Moods

Type of Mood Induction Technique	Operationalized as[a]	Sample Reference	Restriction Potential Disadvantage
Experimenter suggestion	Hypnosis	Bower, Gilligan, & Monteiro (1981)	Only applicable to a minority of hypnotizable people
Autosuggestion	Recollecting pleasant vs. unpleasant memories	Fiedler & Stroehm (1986)	Induced mood confounded with priming of particular memory contents
Verbal self-instruction	Velten technique	Snyder & White (1982)	May induce demand effects rather than genuine mood states
Faked performance feedback	Feedback on high vs. low performance on a verbal intelligence test	Forgas & Bower (1987)	Violation of ethical norms
Mood induction by texts	Reading reports of sad events, in newspaper style	Johnson & Tversky (1983)	Priming of particular contents
Mood induction by films	Scenes from comedy series vs. film on death by cancer	Forgas (1992)	Individual differences in reactions to films
Mundane rewards	Free gift in a shopping mall	Isen et al. (1978)	Only applicable to positive mood May be too weak

[a] Examples given.

states that are likely to explain the greatest amount of variance in everyday changes in cognition.

Several procedures have been used to induce mood states under experimental control. Although all induction techniques have their virtues and vices (Table 8.1), there is now strong evidence that very similar effects can be produced by a variety of mood-induction methods. Naturally occurring moods appear to be more ecologically representative but are often confounded with many other factors (e.g., time of the day, eliciting conditions). Hypnotically induced moods are more intense than moods resulting from reading sad or happy text passages, but hypnosis is only applicable to a minority of people. Faked success versus failure feedback on task performance may also represent a natural source of mood. Fortunately, in spite of the heterogeneity of the manipulations employed, there is convergent evidence that the major empirical phenomena can be obtained with a variety of different mood-induction procedures.

The dependent measures used to operationalize mood effects on social information processing also impose important constraints on the possible empirical findings. By far the most frequently used dependent variables are direct memory tasks (typically free recall) and tests of indirect memory functions, such as judgments, based on previously presented stimulus information, decisions, or attitude change resulting from exposure to persuasive communications. Other, more refined measures directly assessing cognitive processes (e.g., response latencies, sorting tasks, priming effects, association tests) were used only exceptionally. It is no wonder, then, that the major empirical phenomena are based on evidence for the effects of mood on memory and evaluative judgments.

Most empirical findings of mood effects on social cognition relate either to mood-congruency effects or to mood-dependent changes in cognitive style. The main concern here is with the latter, processing effects. However, as the two classes of phenomena are theoretically related, a brief consideration of mood congruency effects is also necessary.

Mood-Congruency Effects

Mood congruency occurs when the individual's current mood facilitates the activation of mood-congruent concepts in memory and possibly inhibits the activation of concepts that are incongruent with the current mood. This basic prediction extends the general Gestalt notion of congruity or consistency to the affect-cognition domain. Controlled demonstrations of mood congruency include evidence for the mood-congruent recall of stories (Bower, Gilligan, & Monteiro, 1981), the better recall of mood-congruent words (Isen, Shalker, Clark, & Karp, 1978), and the production of mood-congruent judgments (Forgas, 1992, 1995). Further support for both encoding and retrieval mood effects was found in many subsequent studies, using various procedures to induce positive, neutral, and negative mood states (Fiedler & Stroehm, 1986). Moreover, the phenomenon was shown to generalize from recall tests to other memory-based cognitive functions, such as person-impression ratings (Forgas & Bower, 1987), risk appraisals (Johnson & Tversky, 1983), and judgments of well-being (Schwarz & Clore, 1988). If mood states serve to prime affectively congruent materials in memory, the selective accessibility of mood-congruent knowledge should not only affect recall performance, but knowledge-based judgments and decisions as well. The associative network model proposed by Bower (1981) explains most of these effects in terms of the affective priming of concepts and stored stimulus representations. This network metaphor highlights a basic associative assumption that is implicitly or explicitly shared by many other theories (see also Bower & Forgas, chap. 5, and Smith & Kirby, chap. 4, this volume).

Within an associative framework, mood-state dependency can also be understood as a special case of mood congruency. *Mood-state dependency* means that retrieval from memory is enhanced if the mood at the time of retrieval is the same as the mood at the time of learning (Bower, 1981; Eich, 1980). If one assumes that the same stimuli are subjectively encoded as more positive (negative) when a person is in a positive (negative) mood, then the same stimuli should be more easily retrieved in the same congruent mood.

One troubling issue is that mood-congruency effects are not equally powerful in positive and negative moods. Generally, congruency is stronger in positive moods and is often weak or absent in negative moods. Why should this be the case? To understand this asymmetry, we first must look at the effects of mood on information-processing strategies.

Mood Effects on Information-Processing Style

The second class of empirical phenomena show that people in different moods tend to adopt different cognitive styles. People in a negative mood tend to be more careful and sensitive to stimulus details, whereas people in a positive mood are characterized by a more creative, spontaneous, and top-down processing style (Bless, 2000; Clore et al., 1994; Fiedler, 2000; Isen, 1984). Unlike mood congruency, which suggests that people in good or bad mood selectively attend to pleasant and unpleasant information, the second phenomenon indicates that mood states make people differentially sensitive to different tasks. Negative mood creates an advantage on tasks that call for scrutiny and carefulness, whereas positive mood should benefit tasks calling for creative ideas and unconventional behavior.

Originally, this phenomenon was discovered in two areas, decision making and persuasion. Isen, Means, Patrick, and Nowicki (1982) were the first to demonstrate that consumer decisions were based on a more extensive search of information and a longer period of hesitation when participants were in a negative rather than positive state. The notion that people in a negative mood engage in more systematic information processing has also guided many persuasion experiments (Bless, Bohner, Schwarz, & Strack, 1980; Mackie & Worth, 1989; see also Petty et al., chap.10, this volume). When the recipients of a persuasive communication are in a negative mood, they are more sensitive to the quality of the presented arguments: strong arguments produce more attitude change than weak arguments. In contrast, those in positive mood are equally responsive to strong and weak arguments.

However, evidence for different processing styles comes from many different paradigms. Other studies demonstrated that people in a positive mood produce more unusual word associations (Isen, Johnson, Mertz, & Robinson, 1985), construct broader and more varied categories on sorting tasks (Isen & Daubman, 1984; Murray, Sujan, Hirt, & Sujan, 1990), show more flexibility in multiattribute decisions (Conway & Giannopoulos, 1993) and dilemma games (Hertel & Fiedler, 1994), and perform better on productive problem-solving tasks like Duncker's candle problem (Isen et al., 1982). Conversely, under negative mood, judgments remain closer to the stimulus input (Fiedler & Fladung, 1987), people produce less intransitivities on preference tasks (Fiedler, 1988), are less prone to optimistic biases and wishful thinking (Alloy & Abramson, 1979), and take longer to make decisions (Isen & Means, 1983).

It seems that the associative network metaphor that can explain most mood congruity effects cannot account for these changes in cognitive style. At first sight, the two classes of empirical phenomena appear to be fundamentally different and difficult to link within a common theoretical model. Mood effects on information processing strategies were thus typically explained within a fully independent theoretical framework. For example, Schwarz (1990) suggested that good or bad moods may convey evolutionary signals that trigger more or less vigilant processing, as if negative affect told us to "stop" and think before acting, whereas positive affect conveys a "go" signal (see Clore, Wyer, Dienes, Gasper, Gohm, & Isbell, 2000).

However, closer analyses of mood congruency reveal a number of boundary conditions that severely restrict the phenomenon. Several authors report failures to replicate congruency effects, or the effect turned out to be confined to specific experimental conditions pointing to important moderator variables (Bower & Mayer, 1985; Fiedler, 1990; Isen, 1984). It is these boundary conditions that led theorists to propose integrative explanations of the affect–cognition interface that finally demonstrate how the two phenomena may be linked. In other words, mood effects on cognitive style may play a critical role in congruency effects as well.

Boundary Conditions of Mood-Congruent Memory and Judgment

One challenging problem with the congruency effect is its asymmetry. The effect is usually much stronger for positive than for negative mood (Isen, 1984). This reduction or even reversal of congruency under negative mood is sometimes attributed to *mood repair*, suggesting deliberate attempts to improve one's own aversive affect. Another potent moderator of mood congruency is the demandingness or unusualness of the task. In the case of memory experiments, if the task is too easy because other, mood-independent associative pathways guarantee effective recall, little latitude is left for mood to influence performance. The same principle also applies to judgment tasks. Mood-related cues are more likely to influence social judgments if the target is unusual or strange than if the target is common or familiar. One pertinent investigation stems from Forgas (1995). Participants were induced into elated or depressed moods before watching images showing couples that appeared either normal or strange. Mood congruency on subsequent impression judgments was more pronounced for strange than for normal couples. Apparently, judgments of normal, prototypical couples arise so easy and with so little need for elaborative processing that mood-congruency effects have very little chance to intrude into the evaluation process. This conclusion is corroborated by a number of other experiments showing stronger mood influences for demanding, unstructured, novel tasks than for simple, highly prestructured, familiar tasks. This holds for mood congruency in recall (Fiedler & Stroehm, 1986) and in social judgments (Forgas, 1995, 1998) as well as for other types of memory effects (Eich, 1980; Ellis & Ashbrook, 1988).

The restriction of mood-congruent memory to recall as opposed to recognition tests (Bower & Cohen, 1982; Fiedler, 1990) may be understood as a special case of the same rule. A recognition test is highly prestructured, and the active search process is cut short by presenting the complete item and leaving only one bit of decision (i.e., to answer "old" or "new") for the participant to make. In such a restricted process, which is not driven by the individual's internal knowledge but by the presented recognition item itself, there is little chance for mood influences to intrude, unlike in the rich memory search that characterizes free recall. A further challenging finding is that affective influences on social judgments are sometimes stronger than, or independent of, a corresponding bias in memory tests (Mayer & Salovey, 1988; Schwarz & Clore, 1988). Thus, an up-to-date theoretical conception of affective influences on cognition must explain not only the basic congruency phenomena, but also these various moderator conditions. It turns out that different information-processing strategies seem to play a key role in explaining different patterns of mood congruency, as the next section suggests.

Integrating the Evidence in Terms of Processing Differences: The Affect Infusion Model (AIM)

One way of dealing with moderator effects and partially inconsistent findings is to divide the phenomena into separate categories representing qualitatively different psychological processes. With such an approach, different psychological laws apply to different subdomains, so that several theories of restricted scope can coexist but do not really conflict with each other. The Affect Infusion Model (AIM) by Forgas (1995) offers a rather refined solution of this kind, highlighting the role that different information-processing strategies play in producing different kinds of mood congruent outcomes. The AIM is based on a twofold distinction (Fig. 8.1) that has decisive implications regarding the nature of mood effects on cognitive process. First, the amount of effort expenditure (high vs. low) refers to the time and resources an individual is motivated to invest in a problem at hand, depending on such factors as personal involvement, time pressure, seriousness of consequences, familiarity, and task complexity. Although degree of effort determines the quantitative aspect of the cognitive strategy, the qualitative nature of the process depends on the second distinction. The task may be defined either as an open, constructive problem that calls for

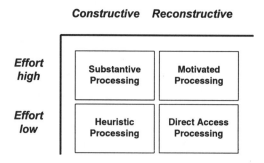

FIG. 8.1. The four processing strategies of the Affect Infusion Model. (Forgas, J. P., 1995. Mood and Judgment: The Affect Infusion Model (AIM). *Psychological Bulletin, 117,* 39–66.)

the transformation of the given input information into a new (yet unknown) solution. Conversely, the task may be defined as a closed, reconstructive problem, with a predetermined or inutitively apparent solution as a starting point that must be defended against the information given. The combination of these two distinctions, degree of effort and open versus closed problem, produces four basic processing strategies (see Fig. 8.1), for which Forgas (1995) coined the terms *substantive processing* (high effort/open), *motivated processing* (high effort/closed), *heuristic processing* (low effort/open), and *direct access* (low effort/closed). According to the AIM, the infusion of mood into cognitive performance is facilitated by open, constructive tasks—involving substantive or heuristic processing—but mood is unlikely to affect performance on closed, merely reconstructive tasks that call for motivated processing or direct access (see also Fiedler, 1990, 1991).

Direct Access. To illustrate the reasons underlying this central model assumption, consider the simplest case of direct access processing. Many everyday judgments and decisions are handled in a routinized fashion, based on fixed, predetermined solutions. People already know what products they purchase, what train they have to choose, or what they think about their partner or a political candidate. Given that standard reactions to such everyday topics are already preformed and stored in memory, a fixed solution can be retrieved easily and does not have to be created in an open process. It is no wonder that many mundane, routinized judgments are not affected by momentary mood states—nor indeed, by any other extraneous factor.

The failure of normal recognition tasks (Bower & Cohen, 1982) to produce mood congruency can also be explained in terms of direct access. Unlike free recall, a recognition task already provides the solution and only asks for the verification of an item as part of episodic memory. This is a very closed process, under strong semantic constraints, driven by the presented item and rather strict semantic and phonologic rules, leaving little room for mood infusion. It is interesting to note that when the normal recognition paradigm is modified to elicit a more open process—for example, by giving participants semantic cues to infer what recognition stimulus is gradually appearing behind a mask (Fiedler & Bless, 2000)—a typical mood-congruency effect reappears.

Motivated Processing. The consequences of motivated processing are less straightforward. Although this strategy is also closed or reconstructive, it need not be free of affect infusion. When there is only one reasonable motive (e.g., to repress an unpleasant memory; to support a favorite opinion; to promote a positive self- or group identity), and all cognitive activities serve such a predetermined goal, there is no reason to expect mood-dependent effects. Sometimes, however, there is more than one goal to fulfill, and individuals must make a choice between several motives. In one pertinent experiment, Forgas (1991) found that participants in happy, sad, and neutral moods were driven by different motives when they had to choose among eight people in a partner-selection task. Sad persons concentrated on interpersonal, affective information, obviously preferring socially rewarding choices. In contrast, happy persons gave more weight to task-related dimensions, preferring candidates with superior skills. In this case, greater personal relevance and negative mood combined to create a strong motivational goal—finding a rewarding partner.

Motivated processes are certainly relevant to explaining the asymmetry effect. The natural motivation to seek pleasant stimuli and avoid unpleasant experiences supports the associative impact of happy mood, but counteracts the consequences of depressed mood. Even when depressed mood makes unpleasant memories accessible, sad people are often motivated to avoid negative stimuli and repair their unpleasant state. Using such an effective metacognitive strategy (Wegener & Petty, 1997), they seek to overcome the unvoluntary congruency effect. Such theories conceive of motivated processes as responsible for correction effects that modify mood-congruent influences on associative memory. For example, Wegener, Petty, and Smith's (1995) *hedonic-contingency* view states that sad receivers engage in deeper processing of a persuasive message, but only when message processing serves the hedonic purpose of mood repair.

Heuristic Processing. The theory that most explicitly attributes mood-congruity effects to heuristic processing is Schwarz and Clore's (1983, 1988) mood-as-information approach. When the task is open and there is no predetermined solution, individuals may base their evaluative judgments on primitive rules of thumb, like the "How-do-I-feel-about-it?" heuristic. For example, when judging politicians during an election campaign, people may just ask themselves "How do I feel about it?" and use their momentary feelings as a basis for judgment. The feeling may be evoked by the target itself, but may also be due to some irrelevant source, like the weather or some recent event. To the extent that people use their momentary mood as a heuristic cue to produce a social judgment, affect infusion will occur.

ie - may have just read something with lots of words or

In a typical investigation by Schwarz and Clore (1983), participants were more satisfied with their lives on a sunny day than when the wheather was bad. Interestingly, the effect disappeared when respondents were sensitized to the weather as a potential source of bias (by the question "How is the weather today?" prior to the life satisfaction judgment). This discounting effect has been emphasized as a key prediction of the mood-as-information approach. If the informative value of mood for judgment is discredited because an external cause of the affective state (weather) is made salient, mood influences are predicted to disappear. For example, when attention was drawn to the unpleasantness of the tiny uncomfortable cubicle in which the experiment took place, negative mood could be attributed to this cause and its impact on judgments disappeared (Schwarz & Clore, 1983).

Although such projection of internal moods onto external judgment targets clearly contributes to many everyday mood effects, the generality of the phenomenon is limited in several ways. First, this theory is confined to an all-or-none effect, in which affect is either the sole source of information or is not used at all. Second, the mood-as-information model deals mainly with the consequences of misattributed affect. It is therefore restricted to dysfunctional situations in which the true origin of mood remains unknown. Once affective states are correctly attributed to external sources, their cognitive effects should disappear. However, this is not the case in the majority of experiments in which participants are fully aware of where their moods comes from. Third, the mood-as-information approach remains mute about the specific cognitive process itself by which features of the stimulus information come to be combined with existing knowledge structures.

Finally, it is important to note that the affect-as-information theory is not strictly in conflict with other process theories—such as associative network rules—and the elimination of mood effects through misattribution treatments does not strictly preclude that the original mood effects were caused by another process, such as affect priming (Berkowitz, Jaffee, Jo, & Troccoli 2000). In general, reliance on mood as a heuristic cue is most likely when other, nonheuristic processes are unlikely: when the task is of little personal relevance, when little other information is available, when problems are too complex to be solved systematically, and when time or attentional resources are limited.

Substantive Processing. If the problem is open and effort expenditure is high, a substantive-processing strategy is called for. Like heuristic processing, affect intrusion should be high in this case, but for different reasons.

Mood states should not be used directly as cues for judgmental inferences, but mood effects should operate indirectly, through selective facilitation of relevant information. Empirical support for this contention comes from numerous experiments showing that mood congruent memory and judgment increase with processing demands (Fiedler & Stroehm, 1986; Forgas, 1995). The more mental operations and transformations are needed, the more chances there are for mood infusion.

Research on productions of, and reactions to, polite versus impolite requests may illustrate the general principle (Forgas, 1998, 1999). In these experiments, the evaluation of requests was biased in a mood-congruent direction, with more benevolent reactions to speech acts in positive than negative mood. However, this effect was accentuated for impolite requests that were normatively unusual and required more coping activities and mental elaboration than polite requests (Forgas, 1998). Similar effects were obtained for request production (Forgas, 1999), such that sad mood enhanced and happy mood reduced request politeness. Recall analyses confirmed that these mood effects on verbal behavior increased with the degree of substantive processing. Such a mediating role for processing strategy in the production of mood-congruent memory and judgment biases is a defining feature of the substantive processing style.

The Processing Consequences of Affect

So far, we have seen that the four distinct processing strategies identified by the AIM play a critical role in accounting for the presence or absence of mood congruence in memory and judgments. However, affect itself also has a reverse influence on cognitive strategies, and it is this interaction between affect and information-processing styles that presents some of the greatest theoretical challenges in this field. What theoretical explanations are there for the information-processing consequences of affect? This issue is discussed in the next section.

Capacity Theories. Several theories suggest that the experience of affective states occupies significant cognitive resources. This reduction of capacity may be responsible for a shift from systematic to heuristic strategies. Worth and Mackie (1987) theorized that diminished resources and heuristic processing are characteristic of positive moods, because people use resources to enjoy, extend, and conserve happy situations. In their study, participants received either weak or strong arguments about controlling acid rain from either an expert or a nonexpert (the heuristic cue). Recipients in a positive mood were influenced by strong and weak arguments to a similar degree, suggesting that they did not process the information systematically. Recipients in a neutral mood showed more positive reactions to and changed their attitude more in response to strong rather than weak arguments. In contrast, people in a positive mood were more responsive to the manipulation of sender expertise, again suggesting more heuristic processing. Mackie and Worth (1989) also found that time pressure eliminated greater message elaboration in neutral mood as well.

Note that capacity reduction should impair the entire process across all capacity-demanding tasks. It does not matter whether mood states are attributed to judgment targets or to external causes, or whether the outcome of information processing is hedonically pleasant or unpleasant. Such strong and universal implications make a theory vulnerable and likely to conflict with other theories and to be falsified empirically. In fact, the assumption of lower capacity in positive than negative mood is incompatible with a number of findings. First, Ellis and Ashbrook (1988) have reviewed evidence for the reverse assumptions, that mental resources are reduced in depressive rather than elated states. Second, if capacity is generally reduced, it is hard to see how happy mood could facilitate creative thinking and cognitive flexibility as has been repeatedly found (Fiedler, 1988; Isen Means, Patrick, & Nowicki, 1982). Third, capacity reduction is not necessary to explain the previously mentioned findings. Even when argument strength does not influence attitude change in happy mood, happy people do nevertheless recognize the different quality of strong and weak arguments (Bless et al., 1990). Most critically, using a dual-task paradigm, Bless, Clore, Schwarz, Golisano, Rabe, and Woelk (1996) reported compelling evidence that the reduced processing of stimulus details in positive mood does not reflect a shortage of cognitive resources, but actually serves to win additional resources for enhanced performance on a secondary task (a concentration test).

Affect, Cognition, and Adaptive Learning: Assimilation versus Accommodation

The AIM as an organizing framework can thus be used to circumscribe the respective subdomains of different theories and to understand why affect infusion can be expected in some but not in other task situations. However, although the AIM predicts *when* affect infusion can be expected, it does not adequately explain *the causes and origins* of affective influences on information-processing strategies. Although the AIM assumes that affect infusion during substantive processing is due to affect priming effects, a number of substantial questions remain open.

For one, the model does not adequately discriminate between qualitatively different kinds of substantive-processing styles. We would expect that substantive processing that is accommodative in character and focuses on the external stimulus information should produce less affect congruency than assimilative processing. It is only when judges think substantively *and* rely on their own internal resources and knowledge structures to produce a response that affect priming and significant mood congruency would be expected to occur. The accommodation/assimilation processing dichotomy should also help us explore whether there is an intrinsic relationship between mood-congruency effects and mood effects on cognitive processing styles? Although a good deal of apparent inconsistency in the literature can be clarified when the four types of processing strategies are distinguished, the AIM does not fully reveal what actually happens in the affect–cognition interface.

This is further illustrated by evidence that shows that even holding the processing type constant—for example, substantive processing in a free-recall experiment—mood effects may nevertheless vary depending on whether stimuli are categorically structured (Fiedler & Stroehm, 1986). Likewise, the task may constantly involve heuristic judgments in the absence of rational criteria—such as intuitive perceptual judgments (Niedenthal & Setterlund, 1994)—but congruency effects will appear or disappear. Thus, in addition to disentangling the task conditions that make affect infusion more or less likely, a more refined process model is needed that helps to understand the mechanisms and reasons why mood intrudes into cognitive functions.

One pertinent theoretical approach is to consider affect and cognition from an adaptive learning perspective. In phylogenetic and ontogenetic development, positive and negative affective states can be associated with appetitive and aversive situations, respectively. A long tradition of behaviorist research (cf. Kimble, 1961) shows that performance in these situations is governed by different learning sets. The avoidance behavior that characterizes aversive settings must work reliably and error-free, without any reinforcement. A young child who is well adapted to dangerous traffic must have learned to be careful when crossing the street without being reinforced by occasional car accidents. This performance has to be perfectionist and stimulus driven—that is, it is essential to avoid mistakes and potentially

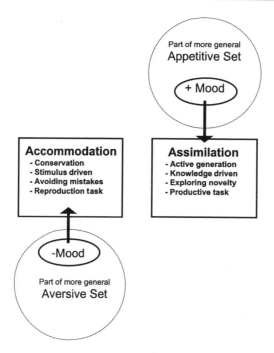

FIG. 8.2. Graphical illustration of assimilation and accommodation as two adaptive functions grounded in different learning sets, governing appetitive and aversive situations (Fiedler, 2000).

significant environmental stimuli must not be overlooked. In contrast to this aversive set, the appetitive set in positive situations is characterized by the rules of exploration behavior that gives more weight to curiosity than to safety and avoidance of mistakes (see also Higgins, chap. 9, this volume).

Borrowing two terms coined by Piaget (1954), these two learning sets, or complementary adaptive styles, can be termed *accommodation* and *assimilation*, respectively (Fig. 8.2). Accommodation is a bottom-up process by which the organism adapts to the affordances of the external stimulus world. Thus, *accommodation* means to stick to the facts, not to miss or loose potentially relevant stimuli, and to validly assess an actually given stimulus setting; in one word, its major function is *conservation*. In contrast, *assimilation* is the reverse adaptive function by which the organism imposes an internal cognitive structure on the external world. This is a top-down process whereby the stimulus input is transformed and enriched using internally activated knowledge structures. The function to be maximized here is *active generation*, rather than passive conservation.

The crucial assumption is that positive and negative mood states can be considered as special cases of appetitive and aversive settings, respectively (Fiedler, 2000; Fiedler & Bless, 2000). Therefore, positive mood states should support assimilative functions, whereas negative states should support accommodative functions, just like other (conditional) stimuli can trigger assimilation versus accommodation. In other words, positive mood should facilitate the top-down process of applying prior knowledge and successful internalized strategies to the active generation of new information. Negative mood should facilitate the bottom-up process of attending to and conserving given stimulus details. There is increasing consensus among several theorists on this issue (Bless, 2000; Clore et al., 1999).

In terms of how people process particular cognitive problems, the present theoretical approach predicts a pervasive interaction between mood (positive vs. negative) and the nature of the task (calling for assimilation vs. accommodation). Although both assimilation and accommodation must be present to some degree in every cognitive task, the performance on conservative tasks increases under negative mood, whereas positive mood benefits generative tasks. To test this central prediction, ideally we would need a method of scaling different tasks accurately on a conservative to generative continuum. Failing that, strong theoretical tests can be based on ranked tasks that clearly occupy different ordinal positions along this dimension. For example, given two cued-recall tasks, the active-generation component increases as the amount of cued information decreases. In word completion, the generative component increases as the proportion of missing letters increases. A judgment task becomes more generative as it becomes more ill-structured, or as the stimulus information becomes more complex and unusual (Forgas, 1995). It is also clear that free recall is a more generative memory task than recognition. Accordingly, it can be predicted and confirmed by the evidence reviewed previously that mood-congruence effects are stronger for free recall than recognition, for unstructured than prestructured judgment tasks (Forgas, 1995), or when cued recall involves minimal cues (Eich, 1980).

The assimilation–accommodation approach has considerable explanatory power, and it gives rise to novel and distinct implications. It provides a parsimonious integrative account of many affect and cognition phenomena in terms of common rules of adaptive learning. Moreover, both classes of empirical findings—concerning mood congruency and cognitive style—can be related within the same framework. Regarding cognitive style, the convergent evidence for careful processing under negative mood and enhanced creative performance under positive mood can be explained in terms of accommodative or assimilative cognitive styles. Regarding mood congruency, the essential prediction is that any selective influence on memory and judgments coming from the individual's affective state must arise in the assimilation component, for it is this component that is sensitive to influences coming from inside the individual. Accommodation by definition is driven by objective stimulus aspects rather than internal states. The origin of mood congruency can therefore be located in the assimilation component. This helps us to understand the two major boundary conditions of mood congruency: that it is stronger for ill-structured, open tasks (calling for assimilation); and asymmetrically stronger for positive than negative mood (because positive mood supports assimilation).

A more direct test of how mood congruency interacts with task conditions that vary in accommodation versus assimilation comes studies of memory for self-generated versus experimenter-provided information. In several experiments (Fiedler, 1991), funny or sad films were used to induce mood before the participants were exposed to positive versus negative stimulus words. Within each valence category, half of the words were presented in complete format (experimenter-provided), whereas several letters were missing in the remaining stimulus words, so that the meaning had to be generated by the participants themselves. Reading is obviously a more conservative (stimulus-driven) task than having to recreate a word despite missing letters. Consistent with the predictions, mood congruency on recall was pronounced for self-generated stimuli but was weak or absent for experimenter-provided stimuli. Moreover, the pattern was asymmetrical, such that generating positive (rather than negative) word meanings in positive mood enhanced subsequent recall, whereas negative mood had little effect. Several conceptual replications of this finding are now available (Fiedler, 1991, 2000).

Apart from simple mood congruency, positive mood also enhances the general recall advantage of self-generated over experimenter-provided information when stimuli are neutral in valence (Fiedler, Lachnit, Fay, & Krug, 1992; Slamecka & Graf, 1978). This finding is also consistent with the basic assumption that positive mood supports assimilative processes. Note that these findings are unlikely to be explained by alternative models. As the manipulation of self-generated and experimenter-provided stimuli is within participants, an absolute capacity restriction cannot be the cause of a congruency effect that is confined to one subset of stimuli. Also, it is hard to see why any heuristic tendency—to search for mood-congruent items in memory—should be restricted to the self-generated part only. As substantive processing (i.e., the same AIM slot) is characteristic of the entire recall task, the task-dependent variation within participants cannot be due to grossly different processing strategies.

One interesting corollary of this adaptive learning approach is that affective influences on cognition are not dependent on strong and intense emotions. Subtle affective cues and rather weak experiential states may be sufficient to produce the same effects. This could explain the intriguing fact that successful mood treatments are often very weak (Isen et al., 1978), and genuine mood variations may fail to produce the typical effects under natural conditions, when mood cues are easily overridden by stronger situational cues (Hasher, Rose, Zacks, Sanft, & Doren, 1985). At the same time, this view of affect as an informative cue (or a conditioned stimulus) that triggers different kinds of learning sets is less restrictive than the mood-as-information approach. It is compatible with countless experiments showing that mood effects need not disappear when affective states are obviously due to an experimental manipulation, and it can account for mood effects during both heuristic and substantive processing conditions.

SUMMARY AND CONCLUSIONS

The present chapter provided an overview of research on affective influences on social information-processing strategies. Based on an analysis of several research paradigms and their underlying assumptions, research evidence about two basic empirical phenomena was reviewed and illustrated, namely, mood congruency and affective influences on cognitive-processing styles. Several boundary conditions were identified that restrict the occurrence of these phenomena and theoretical approaches to account for the pattern of empirical evidence were outlined. Within the framework of the Affect Infusion Model (AIM), it was clarified that different theoretical approaches need not be incompatible, but may refer to different subdomains of findings. However, although the AIM predicts that affect infusion is generally more likely for substantive and heuristic processing than for motivated processing and direct access, it does not spell out important additional conditions for affect infusion to occur—that an open, assimilative, and top-down processing style be adopted. A more explicit process model was proposed, based on the adaptive distinction between assimilative and accommodative processing as the key to understanding the role of affective states in regulating cognitive-processing styles. This model is based on extensive evidence suggesting that opposite moods serve different adaptive functions: Positive moods facilitate assimilation, whereas negative moods facilitate accommodative processes. A variety of different research findings were reviewed and interpreted from this integrative perspective.

REFERENCES

Berkowitz, L., Jaffee, S., Jo, E., & Troccoli, B. T. (2000). On the correction of feeling-induced judgmental biases. In J.P. Forgas (Ed.). *Feeling and thinking. The role of affect in social cognition.* Cambridge University Press.

Bless, H. (2000). Mood and the use of general knowledge structures. In L. L. Martin & G. L. Clore (Eds.), *Mood and social cognition: Contrasting theories.* Mahwah, NJ: Lawrence Erlbaum Associates.

Bless, H., Bohner, G., Schwarz, N., & Strack, F. (1980). Mood and persuasion: A cognitive response analysis. *Personality and Social Psychology Bulletin, 16,* 331–345.

Bless, H., Clore, G. L., Schwarz, N., Golisano, V., Rabe, C., & Woelk, M. (1996). Mood and the use of scripts: Does happy mood make people really mindless? *Journal of Personality and Social Psychology, 71,* 665–679.

Bower, G. H. (1981). Mood and memory. *American Psychologist, 36,* 129–148.

Bower, G. H., & Cohen, P. R. (1982). Emotional influences in memory and thinking: Data and theory. In M. S. Clark & S. T. Fiske (Eds.), *Affect and cognition* (pp. 291–332). Hillsdale, NJ: Lawrence Erlbaum Associates.

Bower, G. H., Gilligan, S. G., & Monteiro, K. P. (1981). Selectivity of learning caused by affective states. *Journal of Experimental Psychology: General, 110,* 451–473.

Bower, G. H., & Mayer, J. D. (1985). Failure to replicate mood congruent retrieval. *Bulletin of the Psychonomic Society, 23,* 39–42.

Bruner, J. S. (1973). *Beyond the information given.* New York: Norton.

Clore, G. L., Schwarz, N., & Conway, M. (1994). Cognitive causes and consequences of emotion. In R. S. Wyer & T. K. Srull (Eds.), *Handbook of social cognition, 2nd ed.* (pp. 323–419). Hillsdale, NJ: Lawrence Erlbaum Associates.

Clore, G. L., Wyer, R. S., Dienes, B., Gasper, K., Gohm, C., & Isbell, L. (2000). Affective feelings as feedback: Some cognitive consequences. In L. L. Martin & G. L. Clore (Eds.), *Mood and social cognition: Contrasting theories.* Mahwah, NJ: Lawrence Erlbaum Associates.

Conway, M., & Giannopoulos, C. (1993). Dysphoria and decision making: Limited information use for evaluations of multiattribute targets. *Journal of Personality and Social Psychology, 64,* 613–623.

Dember, W. N. (1974). Motivation and the cognitive revolution. *American Psychologist,* 161–168.

Easterbrook, J. A. (1959). The effect of emotion on cue utilization and the organization of behavior. *Psychological Review, 66,* 183–201.

Eich, E. (1980). The cue dependent nature of state-dependent retrieval. *Memory and Cognition, 8,* 157–173.

Ellis, H. C., & Ashbrook, P. W. (1988). Resource allocation model of the effects of depressed mood states on memory. In K. Fiedler, & J. P. Forgas (Eds.), *Affect, cognition, and social behavior* (pp. 25–43). Toronto: Hogrefe.

Fiedler, K. (1988). Emotional mood, cognitive style, and behavior regulation. In K. Fiedler & J. P. Forgas (Eds.), *Affect, cognition, and social behavior* (pp. 100–119). Toronto: Hogrefe.

Fiedler, K. (1990). Mood-dependent selectivity in social cognition. In W. Stroebe & M. Hewstone (Eds.), *European Review of Social Psychology, Vol. 1* (pp. 1–32). New York: Wiley.

Fiedler, K. (1991). On the task, the measures, and the mood in research on affect and social cognition. In J. P. Forgas (Ed.), *Emotion and social judgments* (pp. 83–104). Cambridge: Cambridge University Press.

Fiedler, K. (2000). Affective states trigger processes of assimilation and accommodation. In L. L. Martin & G. L. Clore (Eds.), *Mood and social cognition: Contrasting theories.* Mahwah, NJ: Lawrence Erlbaum Associates.

Fiedler, K., & Bless, H. (2000). The formation of beliefs in the interface of affective and cognitive processes. In N. H. Frijda, A. K. R. Manstead, & S. Bem (Eds.), *Emotion and beliefs.* Cambridge: Cambridge University Press.

Fiedler, K., & Fladung, U. (1987). Emotionale Stimmung, Selbstbeteiligung und Empfänglichkeit für persuasive Kommunikation. (Emotional mood, self-involvement, and susceptiveness to persuasive communication.) *Zeitschrift fuer Sozialpsychologie, 18,* 169–179.

Fiedler, K., Lachnit, H., Fay, D., & Krug, C. (1992). Mobilization of cognitive resources and the generation effect. *Quarterly Journal of Experimental Psychology, 45A,* 149–171.

Fiedler, K., & Stroehm, W. (1986). What kind of mood influences what kind of memory: The role of arousal and information structure. *Memory and Cognition, 14,* 181–188.

Forgas, J. P. (1991). Mood effects on partner choice: Role of affect in social decisions. *Journal of Personality and Social Psychology, 61,* 708–720.

Forgas, J. P. (1992). On mood and peculiar people: Affect and person typicality in impression formation. *Journal of Personality and Social Psychology, 62,* 863–875.

Forgas, J. P. (1995). Mood and judgment: The Affect Infusion Model (AIM). *Psychological Bulletin, 117,* 39–66.

Forgas, J. P. (1995) Strange couples: Mood effects on judgments and memory about prototypical and atypical targets. *Personality and Social Psychology Bulletin, 21,* 747–765.

Forgas, J. P. (1998). Asking nicely: Mood effects on responding to more or less polite requests. *Personality and Social Psychology Bulletin, 24,* 173–185.

Forgas, J. P. (1999). On feeling good and being rude: Affective influences on language use and request formulations. *Journal of Personality and Social Psychology, 76,* 928–939.

Forgas, J. P., & Bower, G. H. (1987). Mood effects on person perception judgments. *Journal of Personality and Social Psychology, 53,* 53–60.

Frijda, N. (1986). *The emotions.* Cambridge: Cambridge University Press.

Freud, S. (1915). Instincts and their vicissitudes. In E. Jones (Ed.), *Sigmund Freud: Collected papers. Vol. 4.* New York: Basic Books, 1959.

Hasher, L., Rose, K. C., Zacks, R. T., Sanft, H., & Doren, B. (1985). Mood, recall, and selectivity effects in normal college students. *Journal of Experimental Psychology: General, 114,* 104–118.

Hertel, G., & Fiedler, K. (1994). Affective and cognitive influences in a social dilemma game. *European Journal of Social Psychology, 24,* 131–145.

Isen, A. M. (1984). Toward understanding the role of affect in cognition. In R. S. Wyer & T. K. Srull (Eds.), *Handbook of social cognition, Vol. 3, 2nd ed.* (pp. 179–236). Hillsdale, NJ: Lawrence Erlbaum Associates.

Isen, A. M., & Daubman, K. A. (1984). The influence of affect on categorization. *Journal of Personality and Social Psychology, 47,* 1206–1217.

Isen, A. M., Johnson, M. M. S., Mertz, E., & Robinson, G. (1985). The influence of positive affect on the unusualness of word association. *Journal of Personality and Social Psychology, 48,* 1413–1426.

Isen, A. M., & Means, B. (1983). The influence of positive affect on decision making strategy. *Social Cognition, 2,* 18–31.

Isen, A. M., Means, B., Patrick, R., & Nowicki, G. P. (1982). Some factors influencing decision-making and risk taking. In M. S. Clark, & S. T. Fiske (Eds.), *Affect and cognition* (pp. 243–261). Hillsdale, NJ: Erlbaum.

Isen, A. M., Shalker, T., Clark, M., & Karp, L. (1978). Affect, accessibility of material in memory and behavior: A cognitive loop? *Journal of Personality and Social Psychology, 36,* 1–12.

Janis, I. L., & Feshbach, S. (1953). Effects of fear-arousing communication. *Journal of Abnormal and Social Psychology, 48,* 78–92.

Johnson, E., & Tversky, A. (1983). Affect, generalization, and the perception of risk. *Journal of Personality and Social Psychology, 45,* 20–31.

Kimble, G. A. (1961). *Hilgard and Marquis' conditioning and learning*. New York: Appleton-Century-Crofts.

Mackie, D. M., & Worth, L. T. (1989). Cognitive deficits and the mediation of positive affect in persuasion. *Journal of Personality and Social Psychology, 57,* 27–40.

Martin, L. L. & Clore, G. L. (Eds.) (2000). *Mood and social cognition: Contrasting theories*. Mahwah, NJ: Lawrence Erlbaum Associates.

Mayer, J. D., & Salovey, P. (1988). Personality moderates the interaction of mood and cognition. In K. Fiedler, & J. P. Forgas (Eds.), *Affect, cognition, and social behavior* (pp. 87–99). Toronto: Hogrefe.

McDougall, W. (1928). *An outline of psychology*. New York: Scribner.

Murray, N., Sujan, H., Hirt, E. R., & Sujan, M. (1990). The influence of mood on categorization: A cognitive flexibility interpretation. *Journal of Personality and Social Psychology, 59,* 411–425.

Niedenthal, P. M., & Setterlund, M. B. (1994). Emotion congruence in perception. *Personality and Social Psychology Bulletin, 20,* 401–411.

Piaget, J. (1954). *The construction of reality in the child*. New York: Free Press.

Schwarz, N., & Clore, G. L. (1983). Mood, misattribution, and judgments of well-being: Informative and directive functions of affective states. *Journal of Personality and Social Psychology, 45,* 513–523.

Schwarz, N., & Clore, G. L. (1988). How do I feel about it? The informative function of affective states. In K. Fiedler & J. P. Forgas (Eds.), *Affect, cognition, and social behavior* (pp. 44–62). Toronto: Hogrefe.

Slamecka, N. J., & Graf, P. (1978). The generation effect: Delineation of a phenomenon. *Journal of Experimental Psychology: Learning, Memory and Cognition, 4,* 592–604.

Snyder, M., & White, P. (1982). Moods and memories: Elation, depression, and the remembering of events in one's life. *Journal of Personality and Social Psychology, 49,* 1076–1085.

Watson, J. B., & Rayner, R. (1920). Conditioned emotional reactions. *Journal of Experimental Psychology, 3,* 1–14.

Wegener, D. T., & Petty, R. E. (1997). The flexible correction model: The role of naive theories of bias in bias correction. In M. P. Zanna (Ed.), *Advances in experimental social psychology, Vol. 29* (pp. 141–208). New York: Academic Press.

Wegener, D. T., Petty, R. E., & Smith, S. S. (1995). Positive mood can increase or decrease message scrutiny: The hedonic contingency view of mood and message processing. *Journal of Personality and Social Psychology, 69,* 5–15.

Worth, L. T., & Mackie, D. M. (1987). Cognitive mediation of positive affect in persuasion. *Social Cognition, 5,* 76–94.

Yerkes, R. M., & Dodson, J. D. (1908). The relation of strengths of stimulus to rapidity of habit-formation. *Journal of Comparative Neurological Psychology, 18,* 459–482.

9

Promotion and Prevention Experiences: Relating Emotions to Nonemotional Motivational States

E. Tory Higgins
Columbia University, New York
New York

Promotion and Prevention Focus Concerns   189
Promotion and Prevention: Nonemotional Motivational States   192
Promotion and Prevention: Emotional Experiences   195
Promotion and Prevention Experiences of Motivational Strength   200
Additional Implications of Promotion and Prevention for Emotion   203
Acknowledgments   208
References   208

There are a variety of different emotions that people experience. How should differences in emotional experiences be characterized? What psychological variables account for them? To address these questions, it is necessary to divide emotions into a manageable set that researchers agree contains distinct types of experience. The following set of four types of emotions fulfills this requirement: (a) cheerfulness-related emotions, such as "happy," "elated," and "joyful"; (b) quiescence-related emotions, such

Address for correspondence: E. Tory Higgins, Columbia University, Department of Psychology, Schermerhorn Hall, New York, NY 10027, USA. Email: tory@psych.columbia.edu as "calm," "relaxed," and "serene"; (c) agitation-related emotions, such as "tense," "restless," and "nervous"; and (d) dejection-related emotions, such as "sad," "gloomy," and "disappointed." This set of different types of emotions provides a clear challenge to psychology concerning how best to characterize and account for differences in emotional experiences. I propose that our understanding of the differences among these types of emotional experience would be enhanced by a fuller consideration of the self-regulatory principles and motivational states that underlie them.

The self-regulatory principle that has received the most attention in theories of emotion is *self-regulatory effectiveness*. It has been suggested that the primary function of emotional experiences is to signal or provide feedback about self-regulatory success or failure (e.g., Frijda, 1986; Mandler, 1984; Simon, 1967). Both appraisal and circumplex models propose a basic dimension that distinguishes between pleasant and painful emotions (e.g., Diener & Emmons, 1984; Frijda, Kuipers, & ter Schure, 1989; Green, Goldman, & Salovey, 1993; Larsen & Diener, 1985; Ortony, Clore, & Collins, 1988; Roseman, 1984; Russell, 1978, 1980; Scherer, 1988; Smith & Ellsworth, 1985; see also Schlosberg, 1952; Wundt, 1896). Different models refer to the regulatory effectiveness that underlies this dimension in different ways. For example, it is referred to as *situational state* by Roseman (1984) (i.e., whether an event is consistent or inconsistent with personal motives) and as *goal conduciveness* by Scherer (1988) (i.e., whether an event blocks or helps achieve an organism's goals). Cybernetic-inspired models also postulate that emotions arise from feedback concerning self-regulatory success or failure (e.g., Carver, 1996; Pribram, 1970).

The principle of self-regulatory effectiveness distinguishes between pleasant emotional experiences when self-regulation succeeds and painful emotional experiences when it fails. It provides an important way to characterize the difference between emotions related to cheerfulness and quiescence versus agitation and dejection. Yet what about the difference between the pleasure of cheerfulness and the pleasure of quiescence, and the difference between the pain of agitation and the pain of dejection? How should differences between these emotional experiences be characterized?

Next to self-regulatory effectiveness, perhaps the variable that has received most attention in models of emotional experience has been *arousal* or *activation*. Some models include changes in autonomic arousal or excitation as a fundamental component of emotional experience (e.g., Lindsley, 1951; Mandler, 1984; Schachter & Singer, 1962; Wundt, 1896; Zillmann, 1978). Other models distinguish among different types of emotional experience in terms of their level of arousal or activation (e.g., Bush, 1973; Larsen & Diener, 1985; Reisenzein, 1994; Russell, 1978, 1980; Thayer, 1989; Watson & Tellegen, 1985; Watson, Clark, & Tellegen, 1988; Woodworth & Schlosberg, 1954). The variable of arousal or activation provides a way to characterize the differences between the pleasure of cheerfulness and the pleasure of quiescence, and between the pain of agitation and the pain of dejection. Experiences of emotions related to both cheerfulness and agitation involve relatively more arousal or activation than experiences of emotions related to quiescence and dejection (for a review, see Feldman Barrett & Russell, 1998).

It is possible, then, to distinguish among the emotional experiences of cheerfulness, quiescence, agitation, and dejection in terms of pleasure versus pain as a function of self-regulatory effectiveness and high versus low arousal or activation (see Feldman Barrett & Russell, 1998). Table 9.1 shows how these variables characterize the four types of emotional experience. According to Table 9.1, cheerfulness-related emotions involve a pleasant, high activation experience; quiescence-related emotions involve a pleasant, low activation experience; agitation-related emotions involve a painful, high activation experience; and dejection-related emotions involve a painful, low activation experience.

There is little question that these charaterizations of each type of emotional experience reflect important aspects of each experience. Any model of emotional experiences would need to account for these aspects. However, are these aspects sufficient to capture how these four types of emotional experience are similar and how they are different from one another?

TABLE 9.1

Distinguishing Among Emotions Related to Cheerfulness, Quiescence, Agitation, and Dejection as a Function of Self-Regulatory Effectiveness and Level of Activation

	Self-Regulatory Effectiveness	
	Success (Pleasure)	Failure (Pain)
Level of activation		
High	Cheerfulness	Agitation
Low	Quiescence	Dejection

Does agitation differ from dejection only by being higher in activation? Is cheerfulness more related to agitation than to dejection? Intuition suggests that something is missing. I believe that what is missing is a self-regulatory principle that distinguishes between different kinds of self-regulatory effectiveness. Specifically, I believe that models of emotion would benefit by including regulatory focus as a variable, and by relating emotional experiences to nonemotional motivational states.

This chapter begins by describing regulatory focus as a principle of self-regulation that distinguishes between promotion-focus concerns with advancement, growth, and accomplishment, and prevention-focus concerns with protection, safety, and responsibility. Differences between promotion focus and prevention focus in nonemotional motivational states are then discussed. The principles of regulatory focus and self-regulatory effectiveness are then combined to characterize the similarities and differences among the four types of emotional experience (see also Higgins, 1996; Higgins, Grant, & Shah, 1998). Next, the principles of regulatory focus and self-regulatory effectiveness are combined to account for the differences among these emotions in experiences of activation. The final section considers how the variable of regulatory focus and its relation to both emotional and nonemotional motivational states can increase our understanding of the nature and consequences of emotional experiences.

PROMOTION AND PREVENTION
FOCUS CONCERNS

An initial assumption of regulatory focus theory (Higgins, 1997, 1998) is that the hedonic principle of approaching pleasure and avoiding pain operates differently when serving the fundamentally different survival needs of *nurturance* (e.g., nourishment) versus *security* (e.g., protection). Regulatory focus theory proposes that nurturance-related regulation involves a promotion focus, whereas security-related regulation involves a prevention focus. Earlier papers on self-discrepancy theory (e.g., Higgins, 1987, 1989) describe how certain modes of caretaker–child interaction increase the likelihood that children will acquire strong desired end-states. These desired end-states represent either their own or significant others' hopes, wishes, and aspirations for them, referred to as *strong ideals*, or their own or significant others' beliefs about their duties, obligations, and responsibilities, referred to as *strong oughts*. Regulatory-focus theory proposes that ideal self-regulation involves a promotion focus, whereas ought self-regulation involves a prevention focus.

To illustrate this difference, let us briefly consider what children learn from interactions with caretakers that involve either a promotion focus or a prevention focus. Consider first caretaker–child interactions that involve a *promotion focus*. The child experiences the pleasure of the presence of positive outcomes when caretakers, for example, hug and kiss the child for his or her accomplishments. A child experiences the pain of the absence of positive outcomes when caretakers, for example, act disappointed when the child fails to fulfill the caretaker's hopes. Pleasure and pain from these interactions are experienced as *the presence or absence of positive outcomes*, respectively. The caretaker's message to the child in both cases is that what matters is attaining accomplishments or fulfilling hopes and aspirations (i.e., ideals). The promotion focus involves *a concern with advancement, aspirations, and accomplishment.*

Consider next caretaker–child interactions that involve a *prevention focus*. The child experiences the pleasure of the absence of negative outcomes when caretakers, for example, reassure the child by removing something the child finds threatening. The child experiences the pain of the presence of negative outcomes when caretakers, for example, criticize or punish the child when the child is irresponsible. Pleasure and pain from these interactions are experienced as *the absence or presence of negative outcomes*, respectively. The caretaker's message to the child in both cases is that what matters is ensuring safety, being responsible, and meeting obligations (i.e., oughts). The prevention focus involves *a concern with protection, safety and responsibility.*

A promotion or prevention focus, therefore, can become a chronic orientation depending on an individual's socialization history. Momentary situations are also capable of temporarily inducing either a promotion focus or a prevention focus. Just as the responses of caretakers to their children's actions provide promotion or prevention feedback, task feedback in general can communicate *gain/nongain* information (promotion) or *nonloss/loss* information (prevention). Task instructions concerning which actions produce which consequences can also communicate either gain/nongain (promotion) or nonloss/loss (prevention) information. Thus, the concept of regulatory focus is broader than just socialization of strong promotion-focus ideals or prevention-focus oughts, and regulatory focus theory is broader than self-discrepancy theory. Promotion focus and prevention focus

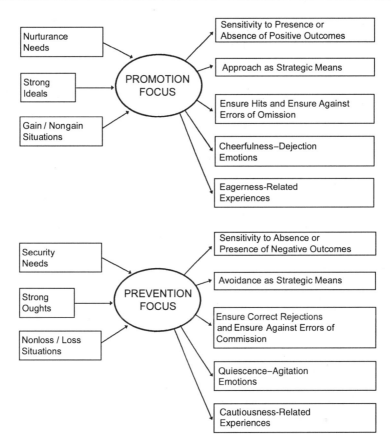

FIG. 9.1. Psychological variables with distinct relations to promotion focus and prevention focus.

are self-regulatory states that can be induced temporarily in momentary situations rather than being associated only with chronic self-regulation in relation to ideals and oughts.

The left side of Fig. 9.1 summarizes the different sets of psychological input variables that have distinct relations to promotion focus concerns and prevention focus concerns. Nurturance needs, strong ideals, and situations involving gain/nongain induce promotion-focus concerns with aspirations and accomplishments, whereas security needs, strong oughts, and situations involving nonloss/loss induce prevention-focus concerns with responsibilities and safety. The next section discusses how promotion focus and prevention focus also involve distinct motivational states and strategic inclinations.

PROMOTION AND PREVENTION: NONEMOTIONAL MOTIVATIONAL STATES

As discussed in the previous section, the promotion focus of ideal self-regulation is postulated to involve a sensitivity to the presence or absence of positive outcomes, whereas the prevention focus of ought self-regulation is postulated to involve a sensitivity to the absence or presence of negative outcomes. Higgins and Tykocinski (1992) tested this prediction by selecting participants who had either a strong promotion focus (operationalized as predominant actual/ideal discrepancies) or a strong prevention focus (operationalized as predominant actual/ought discrepancies). All participants read about everyday events in the life of another person that reflected either the presence or absence of positive outcomes (promotion succeeding or failing) and that reflected either the absence or presence of negative outcomes (prevention succeeding or failing). Ten minutes after reading the essay, the participants were asked to reproduce the essay word-for-word. The study found, as predicted, that events reflecting the presence or absence of positive outcomes were remembered better by promotion-focus than by prevention-focus participants, but the reverse was true for events reflecting the absence or presence of negative outcomes.

People are motivated to approach desired end-states, which could be either promotion-focus aspirations and accomplishments or prevention-focus responsibilities and safety. Within this general approach toward desired end-states, however, regulatory focus can induce either approach or avoidance strategic inclinations. Because a promotion focus involves a sensitivity to positive outcomes (their presence and absence), an inclination to approach matches to aspirations and accomplishment is the natural strategy for promotion self-regulation. In contrast, because a prevention focus involves a sensitivity to negative outcomes (their absence and presence), an inclination to avoid mismatches to safety or obligations is the natural strategy for prevention self-regulation.

In one study testing these predictions, Higgins, Roney, Crowe, and Hymes (1994) asked undergraduates to report on how either their hopes and goals have changed over time (activating ideal self-guides) or their sense of duty and obligation has changed over time (activating ought self-guides). To reveal strategic predilections, this study used a free-recall technique like that of Higgins and Tykocinski (1992). The participants read about several episodes that occurred over a few days in the life of another student. In each of the desired end-state episodes, the target used the strategy of either approaching a match or avoiding a mismatch. Consistent with predictions, the participants remembered desired end-state episodes that involved approaching a match better when ideal self-regulation was activated than when ought self-regulation was activated, whereas they remembered desired end-state episodes that involved avoiding a mismatch better when ought self-regulation was activated than when ideal self-regulation was activated.

Individuals in a promotion focus, with their inclination to approach matches, are eager to attain advancement and gains. In contrast, individuals in a prevention focus, with their inclination to avoid mismatches, are vigilant to assure safety and nonlosses. In signal detection terms (e.g., Tanner & Swets, 1954; see also Trope & Liberman, 1996), individuals in a state of eagerness from a promotion focus are motivated to ensure "hits" and ensure against errors of omission (i.e., a lack of accomplishment). In contrast, individuals in a state of vigilance from a prevention focus are motivated to ensure "correct rejections" and ensure against errors of commission (i.e., making a mistake). This regulatory difference has implications for decision making in signal detection tasks. Individuals in a promotion focus want to ensure recognizing a true target and ensure against omitting a true target, thereby producing an inclination to say "Yes" (a "risky" bias). Individuals in a prevention focus want to ensure rejecting a false distractor and ensure against failing to avoid a false distractor, thereby producing an inclination to say "No" (a "conservative" bias).

A study by Crowe and Higgins (1997) tested these predictions. The participants were told that they would first perform a recognition memory task and then would be assigned a second, final task. A liked and a disliked activity had been selected earlier for each participant to serve as the final task. The participants were told that which of the alternative final tasks they would work on at the end of the session depended on their performance on the initial recognition memory task. The relation between the initial memory task and the final task was described as contingent for everyone, but the framing varied as a function of both regulatory focus (promotion versus prevention) and valence [self-regulation succeeding (pleasure) versus self-regulation failing (pain)]. Valence was included to test whether regulatory focus influences decision making independent of participants' imagining pleasant versus painful outcomes (regulatory anticipation). The contingency framing was as follows: (a) Promotion Success: "If you do well on the word recognition memory task, you will get to do the [liked task] instead of the other task"; (b) Promotion Failure: "If you don't do well on the word recognition memory task, you won't get to do the [liked task] but will have to do the other task instead"; (c) Prevention Success:

"As long as you don't do poorly on the word recognition memory task, you won't have to do the [disliked task] and will do the other task instead"; and (d) Prevention Failure: "If you do poorly on the word recognition memory task, you will have to do the [disliked task] instead of the other task."

The study found, as predicted, that participants in the promotion-focus condition had a risky bias of saying "Yes" in the recognition memory task, whereas participants in the prevention-focus condition had a conservative bias of saying "No." Moreover, these regulatory focus effects were independent of the valence of framing (i.e., success versus failure framing), which itself had no significant effects. Using the same framing paradigm, Crowe and Higgins (1997) found in a second study that when individuals work on a task in which generating any number of alternatives is correct, those in a promotion focus generate more distinct alternatives (ensuring hits), whereas those in a prevention focus are more repetitive (ensuring against errors of commission).

A classic proposal for self-regulation in relation to desired end-states is that the motivational properties of the goal "loom larger" as one makes progress in attaining the goal, as reflected in a positive approach gradient (Lewin, 1935; Miller, 1994, 1959). Individuals in a promotion focus, therefore, should have stronger approach motivation as they work to achieve a goal. However, what about individuals in a prevention focus? Their general motivation would be to approach the goal, but their strategic inclination for doing so would be to avoid mismatches to goal attainment. If it is their strategic inclination that is responsive to the "goal looms larger" effect, then they should have a stronger avoidance motivation as they work to achieve a goal, as reflected in a positive avoidance gradient. This possibility was tested by Forster, Higgins, and Idson (1998) in one study in which regulatory focus was a chronic individual difference variable, and in another study in which it was experimentally manipulated using a framing manipulation conceptually similar to that used by Crowe and Higgins (1997) described earlier.

Both studies adapted a technique used previously as an independent variable to induce approach and avoidance motivations (see Cacioppo, Priester, & Berntson, 1993; Forster & Strack, 1997). These previous studies found that pressing downward on the top of a surface (arm extension) induces an avoidance motivation related to moving an object away from one's face and chest, whereas pressing upward on the bottom of a surface (arm flexion) induces an approach motivation related to bringing an object toward one's face and chest. Forster et al. (1998) used this same arm-pressure technique to serve as an on-line dependent measure of participants' approach and avoidance motivations. While solving one set of anagrams the participants pressed upward on the metal plate of a skin conductance machine attached to the bottom of a table. Pressing upward harder on the plate produced higher values on the machine's display, thereby measuring strength of approach motivation. While solving another set of anagrams the participants pressed downward on the plate of the machine attached to the top of the table, thereby measuring strength of avoidance motivation.

The participants were told that they were part of a physiological study using a newly invented skin conductance machine that measured emotions and motivation. They were told that for the machine to work, they needed to press one hand on the plate enough to maintain contact. Apart from supposedly measuring their physiology, the arm pressure was presented as incidental to the anagrams task. Both studies found, as predicted, that the approach gradient was steeper for participants with a promotion focus than those with a prevention focus, whereas the reverse was true for the avoidance gradient. Most significantly, both studies found a "goal looms larger" effect for avoidance motivations when participants had a prevention focus. A third study replicated this pattern of findings using persistence on the anagrams task, rather than arm pressure, as the measure of motivational strength.

The right side of Fig. 9.1 includes a summary of the different sets of psychological output variables discussed in this section that have distinct relations to promotion-focus concerns and prevention-focus concerns. A promotion focus yields sensitivity to the presence or absence of positive outcomes, approach as strategic means, inclinations to ensure "hits" and ensure against errors of omission, and motivational states related to eagerness. In contrast, a prevention focus yields sensitivity to the absence or presence of negative outcomes, avoidance as strategic means, inclinations to ensure correct rejections and ensure against errors of commission, and motivational states related to cautiousness or vigilance. How might these differences between promotion-focus motivation and prevention-focus motivation be used to characterize and account for the differences among cheerfulness, quiescence, agitation, and dejection emotional experiences? Let us turn now to this central question.

PROMOTION AND PREVENTION: EMOTIONAL EXPERIENCES

A review of the psychological literature (see Higgins, 1987) reveals evidence that people experience dejection-related emotions, such as disappointment, dissatisfaction, or sadness, when they fail to attain their hopes or ideals, whereas they experience agitation-related emotions, such as feeling uneasy, threatened, or afraid, when they fail to meet their obligations or responsibilities. Such evidence suggests that discrepancies from promotion-focus ideals, which represent the absence of positive outcomes, produce different types of pain than discrepancies from prevention-focus oughts, which represent the presence of negative outcomes. This possibility was directly investigated in a series of studies testing self-discrepancy theory (Higgins, 1987). Because these studies have been reviewed elsewhere (see Higgins, 1987, 1989, 1998), only a few illustrative studies are described here.

An early study by Strauman and Higgins (1988) used a latent variable analysis to test the hypothesis that promotion not working, as reflected in ideal discrepancies, predict different emotional problems than prevention not working, as reflected in ought discrepancies. One month after filling out the Selves Questionnaire measure of self-discrepancies, undergraduates filled out a battery of depression and social anxiety measures. Consistent with predictions, as the magnitude of participants' actual/ideal discrepancies increased, their suffering from depression symptoms increased, and as the magnitude of their actual/ought discrepancies increased, their suffering from social anxiety symptoms increased. Actual/ideal discrepancies were not related to social anxiety, and actual/ought discrepancies were not related to depression. Subsequent studies with clinically depressed and anxious persons have also generally found that depression is related to greater actual/ideal discrepancies, whereas anxiety is related to greater actual/ought discrepancies (e.g., Scott & O'Hara, 1993; Strauman, 1989).

It should also be possible to have momentary effects on dejection and agitation emotions by temporarily increasing the strength of people's promotion-focus ideals or prevention-focus oughts. This hypothesis was tested in a study by Higgins, Bond, Klein, and Strauman (1986, Study 2) that situationally primed ideals and oughts. Undergraduate participants completed the Selves Questionnaire weeks before the experiment. Individuals with either both ideal and ought discrepancies or neither type of discrepancy were recruited for the study. Half of the participants had their ideals primed when they described their own and their parents' hopes and aspirations for them. The other half of the participants had their oughts primed when they described their own and their parents' beliefs about their duties and obligations. This priming had no effect on participants' with neither type of discrepancy. However, the participants with both types of discrepancy experienced an increase in dejection-related emotions when ideals were primed and an increase in agitation-related emotions when oughts were primed.

Consistent with previous work on attitude accessibility (see Bassili, 1995, 1996; Fazio, 1986, 1995), Higgins, Shah, and Friedman (1997) conceptualized and operationalized the regulatory focus strength of ideals and oughts in terms of their accessibility. A computer measure of actual self and ideal and ought attributes was developed that was similar to the original Selves Questionnaire that has been used in most previous studies (see Higgins,1998). Promotion-focus strength of ideals was measured by response latencies in listing ideal attributes and giving extent ratings. Prevention-focus strength of oughts was measured by response latencies in listing ought attributes and giving extent ratings. Strength was operationalized as shorter response latencies. Actual/ideal and actual/ought discrepancies were measured by comparing the extent rating of each ideal or ought attribute with the extent rating of the actual self for that attribute.

Higgins et al. (1997) tested the relations among regulatory focus strength, self-discrepancies or self-congruencies, and the frequency that the undergraduate participants experienced different kinds of pleasant and painful emotions during the previous week. The emotions questionnaire included cheerfulness-related items such as "happy" and "satisfied," quiescence-related items such as "calm" and "relaxed," agitation-related emotions such as "on edge" and "tense," and dejection-related emotions such as "disappointed" and "sad." These studies found that: (a) the stronger the promotion focus (operationalized as highly accessible ideals), the more cheerfulness-related emotions are experienced when promotion succeeds (actual/ideal congruency) and the more dejection-related emotions are experienced when promotion fails (actual/ideal discrepancy); and (b) the stronger the prevention focus (operationalized as highly accessible oughts), the more quiescence-related emotions are experienced when prevention succeeds (actual/ought congruency) and the more agitation-related emotions are experienced when prevention fails (actual/ought discrepancy).

Higgins et al. (1997) further hypothesized that similar effects would be obtained for situational variability in strength of regulatory focus. The participants were given trigrams to memorize. A framing paradigm was used to manipulate promotion-focus strength (i.e., emphasizing gains and nongains) and prevention-focus strength (i.e., emphasizing nonlosses and losses), while keeping constant both the criterion and consequences of success on the task. For the promotion focus, the participants began with $5 and the instructions were about gains and nongains: "If you score above the 70th percentile, that is, if you remember a lot of letter strings, you will gain a dollar. Otherwise, you will not gain a dollar." For the prevention focus, the participants began with $6 and the instructions were about losses and nonlosses: "If you score above the 70th percentile, that is, if you don't forget a lot of letter strings, you won't lose a dollar. Otherwise, you will lose a dollar." After completing the task, the participants were given false feedback that they had either succeeded or failed. (Feedback-consistent emotional change is increasing positive and decreasing negative emotions following success, and decreasing positive and increasing negative emotions following failure.) The study found, as predicted, that feedback-consistent change on the cheerfulness/dejection dimension was greater for participants in the promotion than the prevention framing condition, whereas feedback-consistent change on the quiescence/agitation dimension was greater for participants in the prevention than the promotion framing condition (see also Brendl, Higgins, & Lemm, 1995; Roney, Higgins, & Shah, 1995).

Together, the results of these and other studies (see Higgins, 1997, 1998) suggest that it is possible to distinguish among the experiences of cheerfulness-related, quiescence-related, agitation-related, and dejection-related emotions in terms of self-regulatory effectiveness and promotion versus prevention focus (see also Higgins, 1996; Higgins, Grant, & Shah, 1998). Table 9.2 shows how these variables characterize the four types of emotional experiences. According to Table 9.2, cheerfulness-related emotions involve a pleasant experience of promotion success, quiescence-related emotions involve a pleasant experience of prevention success, agitation-related emotions involve a painful experience of prevention failure, and dejection-related emotions involve a painful experience of promotion failure.

Our understanding of the nature of these different types of emotional experiences is enhanced by characterizing them in terms of self-regulatory focus in combination with self-regulatory effectiveness, rather than just

TABLE 9.2
Distinguishing Among Emotions Related to Cheerfulness, Quiescence,
Agitation, and Dejection as a Function of Self-Regulatory Effectiveness
and Regulatory Focus

	Self-Regulatory Effectiveness	
	Success (Pleasure)	Failure (Pain)
Regulatory focus		
Promotion	Cheerfulness	Dejection
Prevention	Quiescence	Agitation

in terms of level of activation in combination with self-regulatory effectiveness. This increased understanding derives from the emotional experiences being related to the nonemotional motivational states associated with promotion focus and prevention focus. Regulatory focus differences in the nonemotional motivational states distinguish between cheerfulness and quiescence as pleasant emotional experiences and between agitation and dejection as painful emotional experiences beyond simply differences in level of activation.

One relation between the nonemotional motivational states and the emotional experiences concerns the psychological situation associated with each type of emotion. For pleasant emotional experiences, cheerfulness relates to the presence of positive outcomes, whereas quiescence relates to the absence of negative outcomes. For painful emotional experiences, agitation relates to the presence of negative outcomes, whereas dejection relates to the absence of positive outcomes.

A second relation between the nonemotional motivational states and the emotional experiences concerns the self-regulatory orientation associated with each type of emotion. For pleasant emotional experiences, cheerfulness relates to the success of eagerness, whereas quiescence relates to the success of cautiousness or vigilance. For painful emotional experiences, agitation relates to the failure of vigilance, whereas dejection relates to the failure of eagerness.

A third relation between the nonemotional motivational states and the emotional experiences concerns the strategic inclination associated with each type of emotion. For pleasant emotional experiences, cheerfulness relates to successful strategic approach, whereas quiescence relates to successful strategic avoidance. For painful emotional experiences, agitation relates to failed strategic avoidance, whereas dejection relates to failed strategic approach.

In sum, by relating the four different types of emotional experiences to promotion focus and prevention focus and their distinct nonemotional motivational states, we can deepen our understanding of the nature of these different emotional experiences. Thus, accounting for these different types of emotions in terms of regulatory focus (in combination with self-regulatory effectiveness) has some clear benefits. Yet what about the fact that people's experiences of these different types of emotions also vary in their level of activation? Is it necessary to have another variable to account for this aspect of people's experiences, or might it be possible to account for this aspect as well in terms of the combination of regulatory focus and self-regulatory effectiveness? The next section considers just how these two variables might account for this aspect of people's experiences as well by relating the different types of emotional experiences to their unique nonemotional motivational states.

PROMOTION AND PREVENTION EXPERIENCES OF MOTIVATIONAL STRENGTH

Level of arousal or activation as an aspect of emotional experience can be conceptualized as people's experience of the strength of the motivational state, that is, their determination, effort, energy output, associated with the emotion (see, for example, Feldman Barrett & Russell, 1998). People's experience of the strength of their motivational state, in turn, could be related to their experience of action readiness (see Frijda, 1986; Lang, 1995). Indeed, cheerfulness, quiescence, agitation, and dejection types of emotions have been distinguished in terms of the strength of their motivational approach or the strength of their motivational avoidance, such as the hyperactivation of motivational approach for joy and the hypoactivation for sadness (e.g., Frijda et al., 1989; Roseman, Wiest, & Swartz, 1994; Scherer, Walbott, & Summerfield, 1986). Can regulatory focus, in combination with self-regulatory effectiveness, account for level of activation as an aspect of emotional experience in terms of differences in underlying motivational strength? By relating the different types of emotional experiences to their unique nonemotional motivational states, there are several possible ways to do so.

The first possibility concerns the psychological situations associated with each type of emotion. There is considerable evidence that people perform better when dealing with information about something that has happened (the presence of some object or event) than when dealing with something that has not happened (the absence of some object or event); that is, the "feature-positive effect" (for a review, see Hearst, 1984; see also Ross, 1977). Motivation might also be stronger when a psychological situation concerns the presence versus the absence of an outcome. If so, then motivational strength and level of experienced activation should be stronger for cheerfulness-related emotions associated with the presence of positive outcomes than for dejection-related emotions associated with the absence of positive outcomes, and should also be stronger for agitation-related emotions associated with the presence of negative outcomes than for quiescence-related emotions associated with the absence of negative outcomes.

The second possibility concerns the self-regulatory orientations associated with each type of emotion. For the eagerness associated with promotion-focus self-regulation, one might expect that the eagerness associated with a promotion focus would be maintained or even increase when self-regulation is effective (e.g., making progress in accomplishing something), but that it would be reduced or even eliminated when self-regulation is ineffective (e.g., not making progress in accomplishing something). Thus, the experience of higher activation for cheerfulness than dejection emotions might reflect the fact that eagerness is higher for the former than the latter emotions. For the vigilance (or cautiousness) associated with prevention focus, one might expect that the vigilance would be maintained or even increase when self-regulation is ineffective (e.g., safety has not yet been attained), but that it would be reduced or even eliminated when self-regulation is effective (e.g., safety has been attained). Thus, the experience of higher activation for agitation than quiescence emotions might reflect the fact that vigilance is higher for the former than for the latter emotions.

For prospective emotions, there is a third possibility that concerns the strategic inclinations associated with each type of emotion. For the same goal, a promotion focus involves strategic approach, whereas a prevention focus involves strategic avoidance. Combining this difference in regulatory focus strategies with the difference between the motivation to approach success or avoid failure has implications for motivational strength. Table 9.3 shows how approach/avoidance compatibility varies as a function of regulatory focus and self-regulatory effectiveness. Promotion-focus strategic approach is more compatible with the prospect of approaching success than the prospect of avoiding failure. Thus, motivational strength

TABLE 9.3

Approach/Avoidance Compatibility as a Function of Regulatory Focus and
Self-Regulatory Effectiveness

	Self-Regulatory Effectiveness	
	Success (To Be Approached)	*Failure (To Be Avoided)*
Regulatory focus		
Promotion (strategic approach)	High compatibility	Low compatibility
Prevention (strategic avoidance)	Low compatibility	High compatibility

should be higher for prospective cheerfulness emotions than prospective dejection emotions. Prevention-focus strategic avoidance is more compatible with avoiding failure than approaching success. Thus, motivational strength should be higher for prospective agitation emotions than prospective quiescence emotions.

There is evidence from one of the Forster et al. (1998) studies that is consistent with this compatibility perspective on motivational strength underlying prospective emotions. Regulatory focus and self-regulatory effectiveness were crossed to create four framing conditions: (a) gain framing (promotion focus/success); (b) nongain framing (promotion focus/failure); (c) nonloss framing (prevention focus/success); and (d) loss framing (prevention focus/failure). Framing conditions (a) and (d) involve high compatibility, whereas framing conditions (b) and (c) involve low compatibility. Arm pressure, as discussed earlier, provides a direct measure of motivational strength. As shown in Table 9.4, motivational strength was higher for those conditions with high compatibility (promotion success and prevention failure) than those conditions with low compatibility (promotion failure and prevention success).

Another recent study by Idson, Liberman, and Higgins (2000) provides evidence that supports the general hypothesis that motivational strength as a function of regulatory focus and regulatory effectiveness underlies differences in emotional intensity. Participants who had either a predominant promotion focus or a predominant prevention focus worked on an anagrams task and then received either success or failure feedback. Following the feedback, all participants were asked about their experience of specific emotions belonging to each of the four different types of emotions on a scale of experienced intensity. The participants' reports of feeling

TABLE 9.4

Mean Arm Pressure as a Function of Regulatory Focus and Self-Regulatory Effectiveness Framing

	Self-Regulatory Effectiveness	
	Success (To Be Approached)	Failure (To Be Avoided)
Regulatory focus		
Promotion (strategic approach)	566	463
Prevention (strategic avoidance)	505	584

"happy" (following success) involved a higher intensity experience when their predominant focus was promotion than prevention, whereas their reports of feeling "tense" (following failure) involved a higher intensity experience when their predominant focus was prevention than promotion. The participants' reports of feeling "discouraged" (following failure) involved a lower intensity experience when their predominant focus was promotion than prevention, whereas their reports of feeling "relaxed" (following success) involved a lower intensity experience when their predominant focus was prevention than promotion.

These results support the following conclusions: (1) The high activation experiences normally associated with "happy" and "tense" occur when the motivational orientation of the relevant focus is maintained (i.e., "happy" for promotion-focus eagerness maintained by success; "tense" for prevention-focus vigilance maintained by failure); (2) The low activation experiences normally associated with "discouraged" and "relaxed" occur when the motivational orientation of the relevant focus is reduced (i.e., "discouraged" for promotion-focus eagerness reduced by failure; "relaxed" for prevention-focus vigilance reduced by success).

In sum, people's experience of high activation for emotions related to cheerfulness and agitation and their experience of low activation for emotions related to quiescence and dejection can be accounted for in terms of the combination of regulatory focus and self-regulatory effectiveness. Indeed, there are different ways to do so by relating the distinct emotional experiences to their unique nonemotional motivational states. A novel implication of this account is that the high and low activation experiences typically associated with different emotions depend on people having the relevant regulatory focus; that is, a promotion focus for cheerfulness and dejection, and a prevention focus for agitation and quiescence. Additional implications of regulatory focus for relating nonemotional motivational states to emotional experiences are considered next.

ADDITIONAL IMPLICATIONS
OF PROMOTION AND PREVENTION
FOR EMOTION

Differences among the experiences of emotions related to cheerfulness, quiescence, agitation, and dejection have been characterized in terms of pleasure versus pain as a function of self-regulatory effectiveness and high versus low arousal or activation (for a review, see Feldman Barrett & Russell, 1998). Cheerfulness emotions are characterized as pleasant, high activation experiences, quiescence emotions as pleasant, low activation experiences, agitation emotions as painful, high activation experiences, and dejection emotions as painful, low activation experiences.

As mentioned earlier, this now classic characterization concerns aspects of emotional experiences that any model must cover, but it also raises questions. One question is whether these aspects are sufficient to capture how these four types of emotional experiences are similar to and how they are different from one another. To the extent that these types of emotional experiences relate to different types of nonemotional motivational states, then this characterization is insufficient. The experience of agitation does not differ from the experience of dejection only by feeling higher in activation. Agitation relates to ineffective prevention and involves experiences of increased vigilance or cautiousness, whereas dejection relates to ineffective promotion and involves experiences of decreased eagerness or enthusiasm. Similarly, the experience of cheerfulness does not differ from the experience of quiescence only by feeling higher in activation. Cheerfulness relates to effective promotion and involves increased eagerness and enthusiasm, whereas quiescence relates to effective prevention and involves decreased vigilance and cautiousness.

There is another question about whether the classic characterization of the four types of emotional experiences sufficiently captures how they are similar and different from one another. One important form of similarity and difference concerns which pairs of these emotion types function as semantic opposites. *Roget's International Thesaurus* (1962) treats "excitability" and "inexcitability" as semantic opposites, and "cheerfulness" and "sadness" as semantic opposites. Excitability includes agitation-related emotions such as "agitated," "restless," "nervous," and "worried," and inexcitability includes quiescence-related emotions such as "quiet," "calm," "serene," and "tranquil." Cheerfulness includes such cheerfulness-related emotions as "cheerful," "joyful," "happy," and "elated." Sadness includes such dejection-related emotions as "dejected," "sad," "despondent," and "discouraged." These pairs of semantic opposites have also been reported by others (see, for example, Osgood, 1969; Russell, 1991).

How does the classic characterization of the emotional types account for these pairings? As noted by Feldman Barrett and Russell (1998), the pairs of semantic opposites are opposite on both valence (pleasant vs. painful) and activation (high vs. low). Restricted to only the classic characterization, then, cheerfulness and dejection would be semantic opposites because they are maximally different from one another, as quiescence and agitation would be. However, are semantic opposites maximally different from one another? If this were the case, then mother and nephew would be more likely to be semantic opposites than mother and father because there are more dimensions on which they differ (e.g., generation in addition to gender and family role). Giraffes are extremely different from seashells, but that does not make them strong semantic opposites.

For two things to be semantic opposites they must be comparable. They must be similar enough to be structurally alignable (see Markman & Gentner, 1993), such as belonging to the same basic category or dimension (e.g., mother and father are both parents). Thus, for cheefulness and dejection to be semantic opposites they must actually be the same in some important way, as must quiescence and agitation. Indeed, they are. Cheerfulness and dejection both involve a promotion focus, and quiescence and agitation both involve a prevention focus. They are opposites because cheerfulness is effective promotion, whereas dejection is ineffective promotion; and quiescence is effective prevention, whereas agitation is ineffective prevention. Regulatory focus is critical for understanding this aspect of emotional experiences.

Combining regulatory focus with self-regulatory effectiveness helps to distinguish among the emotional experiences of cheerfulness, quiescence, agitation, and dejection. Combining regulatory focus with other variables might help to distinguish between other types of emotional experiences as well (see also Higgins, 1996; Higgins, Grant, & Shah, 1998). From a self-regulatory perspective, for example, one would expect people to feel "angry" when they experience a barrier to their self-regulatory movements. Combining regulatory focus with self-regulatory impedance could help to distinguish between "frustration"-type anger for a promotion focus (experiencing a barrier to fulfilling aspirations or attaining accomplishments) and "resentment"-type anger for a prevention focus (experiencing a barrier to fulfilling responsibilities or attaining safety). The results of a study by Strauman and Higgins (1988) support this prediction. As another example, envy and jealousy both involve an inference that someone else has attained something one wants but does not have (or no longer has). Combining regulatory focus with perceived deprivation could help to distinguish between "envy" for a promotion focus (experiencing someone else attaining something one aspires to have) and "jealousy" for a prevention focus (experiencing someone else attaining something one believes one ought to have).

Our understanding of the similarities and differences among distinct types of emotional experiences can be increased by adding regulatory focus to the account. Our understanding of the nature and consequences of emotional experiences can be increased in other ways as well by considering the motivational properties of promotion and prevention focus. For example, regulatory focus contributes to the efficiency of emotional appraisals. People appraise attitude objects for functional reasons. People evaluate how much some attitude object serves their needs or fulfills their goals. They evaluate how they feel about an object. In a classic functional perspective on attitudes, Smith, Bruner, and White (1956) described the object-appraisal function of attitudes as providing guidelines for sizing-up objects and events in terms of a person's major interests and going concerns (see also Eagly & Chaiken, 1993).

Distinctions between types of positive and types of negative appraisals relevant to different types of concerns have received relatively little attention, however. Given that object appraisal serves the function of sizing-up attitude objects in relation to people's personal concerns, it would be adaptive for there to be different types of evaluations relevant to different types of concerns. Shah and Higgins (1998) predicted that people's emotional evaluations would be more efficient, and thus faster, when the type of evaluation they make is relevant to their promotion-versus-prevention concerns. Controlling for the extremity of participants' emotional responses, they found that individuals in a strong promotion focus were faster to answer how cheerful or how dejected an object made them feel, whereas individuals in a strong prevention focus were faster to answer how quiescent or how agitated an object made them feel. Thus, the efficiency of different types of emotional responses is related to people's regulatory focus concerns.

It is important to relate emotional experiences to underlying motivational states for another reason as well. Historically, psychologists have tended to contrast emotion with cognition—"hot" with "cold." Given this contrast, when studies control for cognitive determinants and find that different emotional states relate to differential responding on some task, there is a tendency to attribute the different responses to the effects of emotion. Our understanding of the true effects of emotions per se is hindered rather than helped by this tendency. Instead of contrasting emotion with cognition, we need to contrast emotions with nonemotional motivations that can also produce differential responding. People can experience motivational states such as difficulty or effort without currently experiencing an emotion. They can also be in a promotion state of eagerness or a prevention state of vigilance without currently experiencing emotions. In order to understand more fully the effects of emotion per se, it is necessary to contrast them with the effects of nonemotional motivational states because the motivational states themselves can produce differential responding. Let us consider a couple of examples.

As described earlier, Higgins and Tykocinski (1992) found in their study of biographic memory that events reflecting the presence or absence of positive outcomes were remembered better by promotion- than prevention-focus participants, but the reverse was true for events reflecting the absence or presence of negative outcomes. This study also found that this interaction was independent of participants' premood, postmood, or change in mood. Thus, emotional experiences during the study were not necessary for memory effects to occur. What influenced memory was the relevance of participants' chronic regulatory focus to the regulatory focus of the events. Such results raise the possibility that previous "mood and memory" studies may not have depended on emotional experiences per se. When studies manipulate emotional experiences with music, movies, gifts, or recollections of past events, it is possible that they manipulate nonemotional motivational states as well, such as promotion and prevention motivational states, and these motivational states might influence memory independent of emotions. Rather than emotions being necessary for the memory effects, what might be necessary is relevance between a person's regulatory focus and the regulatory focus that is represented in the to-be-remembered events (see Strauman, 1990).

There has been a special fascination among psychologists, especially clinicians, with how anxiety influences cognition. One major conclusion is that anxiety has negative effects on creativity. When people experience high (vs. low) anxiety, for example, they produce fewer subgroups in a sorting task, which is said to reflect concrete rather than abstract thinking (e.g., Mikulincer, Kedem, & Paz, 1990). Crowe and Higgins (1997), however, found that individuals with a prevention focus produce fewer subgroups in a sorting task than individuals with a promotion focus, and this effect was independent of the participants' emotional experiences during the study. Rather than emotions being necessary for the "creativity" effects to occur, it was a prevention focus that produced fewer subgroupings. It should be noted in this regard that participants in the high anxious group of previous studies (whether selected or induced) were likely to have been in a prevention focus.

In conclusion, our understanding of the nature and consequences of emotional experiences would benefit by relating emotional experiences to nonemotional motivational states. In particular, our understanding of the nature and consequences of the emotional experiences of cheerfulness, quiescence, agitation, and dejection would benefit by relating these experiences to the unique motivational states associated with a promotion focus and a prevention focus. Future research needs to disentangle the effects of the nonemotional motivational states of regulatory focus (e.g., eagerness vs. vigilance) from the effects of the emotions associated with regulatory success and failure. In this way, the unique contribution of emotions to psychological phenomena, beyond just their association with nonemotional motivational states, would become clearer. Hopefully, regulatory focus theory can contribute to this clarification.

ACKNOWLEDGMENTS

The research reported in this chapter was supported by National Institute of Mental Health Grant MH39429. I am grateful to the 1998 ISRE conference organizers, especially Nico Frijda and Fritz Strack, for the opportunity to first present the central themes of this chapter in an invited address and a symposium paper.

REFERENCES

Bassili, J. N. (1995). Response latency and the accessibility of voting intentions: What contributes to accessibility and how it affects vote choice. *Personality and Social Psychology Bulletin, 21*, 686–695.

Bassili, J. N. (1996). Meta-judgmental versus operative indices of psychological attributes: The case of measures of attitude strength. *Journal of Personality and Social Psychology, 71*, 637–653.

Brendl, C. M., Higgins, E. T., & Lemm, K. M. (1995). Sensitivity to varying gains and losses: The role of self-discrepancies and event framing. *Journal of Personality and Social Psychology, 69*,1028–1051.

Bush, L. E. II (1973). Individual differences multidimensional scaling of adjectives denoting feelings. *Journal of Personality and Social Psychology, 25*, 50–57.

Cacioppo, J. T., Priester, J. R., & Berntson, G. G. (1993). Rudimentary determinants of attitudes II: Arm flexion and extension have differential effects on attitudes. *Journal of Personality and Social Psychology, 65*, 5–17.

Carver, C. S. (1996). Some ways in which goals differ and some implications of those differences. In P. M. Gollwitzer & J. A. Bargh (Eds.), *The psychology of action: Linking cognition and motivation to behavior* (pp. 645–672). New York: Guilford Press.

Crowe, E., & Higgins, E. T. (1997). Regulatory focus and strategic inclinations: Promotion and prevention in decision-making. *Organizational Behavior and Human Decision Processes, 69*, 117–132.

Diener, E., & Emmons, R. A. (1984). The independence of positive and negative affect. *Journal of Personality and Social Psychology, 47*, 1105–1117.

Eagly, A. H., & Chaiken, S. (1993). *The psychology of attitudes*. New York: Harcourt Brace Jovanovich.

Fazio, R. H. (1986). How do attitudes guide behavior? In R. M. Sorrentino & E. T. Higgins (Eds.), *Handbook of motivation and cognition: Foundations of social behavior* (pp. 204–243). New York: Guilford Press.

Fazio, R. H. (1995). Attitudes as object-evaluation associations: Determinants, consequences, and correlates of attitude accessibility. In R. E. Petty & J. A. Krosnick (Eds.), *Attitude strength: Antecedents and consequences* (pp. 247–282). Mahwah, NJ: Lawrence Erlbaum Associates.

Feldman Barrett, L., & Russell, J. A. (1998). Independence and bipolarity in the structure of current affect. *Journal of Personality and Social Psychology, 74*, 967–984.

Forster, J., Higgins, E. T., & Idson, L. C. (1998). Approach and avoidance strength during goal attainment: Regulatory focus and the "goal looms larger" effect. *Journal of Personality and Social Psychology, 75*, 1115–1131.

Forster, J., & Strack, F. (1997). The influence of motor actions on retrieval of valenced information: A motor congruence effect. *Perceptual and Motor Skills, 85*, 1419–1427.

Frijda, N. H. (1986). *The emotions.* New York: Cambridge University Press.

Frijda, N. H., Kuipers, P., & ter Schure, E. (1989). Relations among emotion, appraisal, and emotional action readiness. *Journal of Personality and Social Psychology, 57*, 212–228.

Green, D. P., Goldman, S. L., & Salovey, P. (1993). Measurement error masks bipolarity in affect ratings. *Journal of Personality and Social Psychology, 64*, 1029–1041.

Hearst, E. (1984). Absence as information: Some implications for learning, performance, and representational process. In H. L. Roitblat, T. G. Bever, & H. S. Terrace (Eds.), *Animal cognition: Proceedings of the Harry Frank Guggenheim conference June 2–4, 1982* (pp. 311–332) Hillsdale, NJ: Erlbaum.

Higgins, E. T. (1987). Self-discrepancy: A theory relating self and affect. *Psychological Review, 94*, 319–340.

Higgins, E. T. (1989). Self-discrepancy theory: What patterns of self-beliefs cause people to suffer? In L. Berkowitz (Ed.), *Advances in experimental social psychology, Vol. 22* (pp. 93–136). New York: Academic Press.

Higgins, E. T. (1996). Emotional experiences: The pains and pleasures of distinct regulatory systems. In R. D. Kavanaugh, B. Zimmerberg, & S. Fein (Eds.), *Emotion: Interdisciplinary perspectives* (pp. 203–241). Mahwah, NJ: Lawrence Erlbaum Associates.

Higgins, E. T. (1997). Beyond pleasure and pain. *American Psychologist, 52*, 1280–1300.

Higgins, E. T. (1998). Promotion and prevention: Regulatory focus as a motivational principle. In M. P. Zanna (Ed.), *Advances in experimental social psychology* (Vol. 30, 1–46). New York: Academic Press.

Higgins, E. T., Bond, R. N., Klein, R., & Strauman, T. (1986). Self-discrepancies and emotional vulnerability: How magnitude, accessibility, and type of discrepancy influence affect. *Journal of Personality and Social Psychology, 51*, 5–15.

Higgins, E. T., Grant, H., & Shah, J. (1998). Self-regulation and quality of life: Emotional and nonemotional life experiences. In D. Kahneman, E. Diener, & N. Schwarz (Eds.), *Well-being: The foundations of hedonic psychology* (pp. 244–266). New York: Russell Sage.

Higgins, E. T., Roney, C., Crowe, E., & Hymes, C. (1994). Ideal versus ought predilections for approach and avoidance: Distinct self-regulatory systems. *Journal of Personality and Social Psychology, 66*, 276–286.

Higgins, E. T., Shah, J., & Friedman, R. (1997). Emotional responses to goal attainment: Strength of regulatory focus as moderator. *Journal of Personality and Social Psychology, 72*, 515–525.

Higgins, E. T., & Tykocinski, O. (1992). Self-discrepancies and biographical memory: Personality and cognition at the level of psychological situation. *Personality and Social Psychology Bulletin, 18*, 527–535.

Idson, L. C., Liberman, N., & Higgins, E. T. (2000). Distinguishing gains from non-losses and losses from non-gains: A regulatory focus perspective on hedonic intensity. *Journal of Experimental Social Psychology, 36*, 252–274.

Lang, P. J. (1995). The emotion probe: Studies of motivation and attention. *American Psychologist, 50*, 372–385.

Larsen, R. J., & Diener, E. (1985). A mutitrait–multimethod examination of affect structure: Hedonic level and emotional intensity. *Personality and Individual Differences, 6*, 631–636.

Lewin, K. (1935). *A dynamic theory of personality.* New York: McGraw-Hill.

Lindsley, D. B. (1951). Emotion. In S. S. Stevens (Ed.), *Handbook of experimental psychology* (pp. 473–516). New York: Wiley.

Mandler, G. (1984). *Mind and body: The psychology of emotion and stress.* New York: Norton.

Markman, A. B., & Gentner, D. (1993). Splitting the differences: A structural alignment view of similarity. *Journal of Memory and Language, 32*, 517–535.

Mikulincer, M., Kedem, P., & Paz, D. (1990). The impact of trait anxiety and situational stress on the categorization of natural objects. *Anxiety Research, 2*, 85–101.

Miller, N. E. (1944). Experimental studies of conflict. In J. McV. Hunt (Ed.), *Personality and the behavior disorders, Vol. 1* (pp. 431–465). New York: Ronald Press.

Miller, N. E. (1959). Liberalization of basic S-R concepts: Extensions to conflict behavior, motivation, and social learning. In S. Koch (Ed.), *Psychology: A study of a science Vol. 2. General systematic formulations, learning, and special processes* (pp. 196–292). New York: McGraw-Hill.

Osgood, C. E. (1969). On the whys and wherefores of E, P, and A. *Journal of Personality and Social Psychology, 12*, 194–199.

Ortony, A., Clore, G. L., & Collins, A. (1988). *The cognitive structure of emotions*. New York: Cambridge University Press.

Pribram, K. H. (1970). Feelings as monitors. In M. B. Arnold (Ed.), *Feelings and emotions* (pp. xxx). New York: Academic Press.

Reisenzein, R. (1994). Pleasure-activation theory and the intensity of emotions. *Journal of Personality and Social Psychology, 67*, 525–539.

Roget's International Thesaurus (3rd ed.). (1962). New York: Thomas Cromwell Company.

Roney, C. J. R., Higgins, E. T., & Shah, J. (1995). Goals and framing: How outcome focus influences motivation and emotion. *Personality and Social Psychology Bulletin, 21*, 1151–1160.

Roseman, I. J. (1984). Cognitive determinants of emotion: A structural theory. *Review of Personality and Social Psychology, 5*, 11–36.

Roseman, I. J., Wiest, C., & Swartz, T. S. (1994). Phenomenology, behaviors, and goals differentiate discrete emotions. *Journal of Personality and Social Psychology, 67*, 206–221.

Ross, L. (1977). The intuitive psychologist and his shortcomings: Distortions in the attribution process. In L. Berkowitz (Ed.), *Advances in experimental social psychology, Vol. 10* (pp. 173–220). New York: Academic Press.

Russell, J. A. (1978). Evidence of convergent validity on the dimensions of affect. *Journal of Personality and Social Psychology, 36*, 1152–1168.

Russell, J. A. (1980). A circumplex model of affect. *Journal of Personality and Social Psychology, 39*, 1161–1178.

Russell, J. A. (1991). Culture and the categorization of emotions. *Psychological Bulletin, 110*, 426–450.

Schachter, S., & Singer, J. E. (1962). Cognitive, social and physiological determinants of emotional state. *Psychological Review, 69*, 379–399.

Scherer, K. R. (1988). Criteria for emotion-antecedent appraisal: A review. In V. Hamilton, G. H. Bower, & N. H. Frijda (Eds.), *Cognitive perspectives on emotion and and motivation* (pp. 89–126). Norwell, MA: Kluwer Academic.

Scherer, K. R., Walbott, H. G., & Summerfield, A. B. (1986). *Experiencing emotions: A cross-cultural study*. Cambridge: Cambridge University Press.

Schlosberg, H. (1952). The description of facial expressions in terms of two dimensions. *Journal of Experimental Psychology, 44*, 229–237.

Scott, L., & O'Hara, M. W. (1993). Self-discrepancies in clinically anxious and depressed university students. *Journal of Abnormal Psychology, 102*, 282–287.

Shah, J., & Higgins, E. T. (1998). *Promotion and prevention appraisals: How functional relevance increases efficiency*. Unpublished manuscript, Columbia University.

Simon, H. A. (1967). Motivational and emotional controls of cognition. *Psychological Review, 74*, 29–39.

Smith, M. B., Bruner, J. S., & White, R. W. (1956). *Opinions and personality*. New York: Wiley.

Smith, C. A., & Ellsworth, P. C. (1985). Patterns of cognitive appraisal in emotion. *Journal of Personality and Social Psychology, 48*, 813–838.

Strauman, T. J. (1989). Self-discrepancies in clinical depression and social phobia: Cognitive structures that underlie emotional disorders? *Journal of Abnormal Psychology, 98*, 14–22.

Strauman, T. J. (1990). Self-guides and emotionally significant childhood memories: A study of retrieval efficiency and incidental negative emotional content. *Journal of Personality and Social Psychology, 59*, 869–880.

Strauman, T. J., & Higgins, E. T. (1988). Self-discrepancies as predictors of vulnerability to distinct syndromes of chronic emotional distress. *Journal of Personality, 56*, 685–707.

Tanner, W. P. Jr., & Swets, J. A. (1954). A decision-making theory of visual detection. *Psychological Review, 61*, 401–409.

Thayer, R. E. (1989). *The biopsychology of mood and activation.* New York: Oxford University Press.

Trope, Y., & Liberman, A. (1996). Social hypothesis testing: Cognitive and motivational mechanisms. In E. T. Higgins & A. W. Kruglanski (Eds.), *Social psychology: Handbook of basic principles* (pp. 239–270). New York: Guilford.

Watson, D., Clark, L. A., & Tellegen, A. (1988). Development and validation of brief measures of positive and negative affect: The PANAS scales. *Journal of Personality and Social Psychology, 54*, 1063–1070.

Watson, D., & Tellegen, A. (1985). Toward a consensual structure of mood. *Psychological Bulletin, 98*, 219–235.

Woodworth, R. S., & Schlosberg, H. (1954). *Experimental psychology* (rev. ed.). New York: Holt, Rinehart, & Winston.

Wundt, W. (1896). *Grundriss der psychologie* (C. H. Judd translation). Leipzig: Engleman.

Zillmann, D. (1978). Attribution and misattribution of excitatory reactions. In J. H. Harvey, W. J. Ickes, & R. F. Kidd (Eds.), *New directions in attribution research, Vol. 2* (pp. 335–368). Hillsdale, NJ: Lawrence Erlbaum Associates.

10

The Role of Affect in Attitude Change

Richard E. Petty
Ohio State University

David DeSteno
Northeastern University

Derek D. Rucker
Ohio State University

Attitude Structure	215
Attitude Change with Relevant Affect	216
Affective versus Cognitive Appeals	216
Fear Appeals	217
Attitude Change with Irrelevant (Incidental) Affect	218
Effects of Emotional Factors Under Low-Elaboration Conditions	219
Effects of Emotional Factors Under High-Elaboration Conditions	221
Effects of Emotional Factors Under Moderate-Elaboration Conditions	223
Mood-Correction Effects	226
Conclusion	228
References	228

Affect and persuasion have long been intertwined. Although not by any means a prerequisite for attitude change, the experience of emotion has been believed since the dawn of rhetoric to be one of many variables capable of influencing a message's persuasiveness. Cicero (55 BCE/1970) noted that

Address Correspondence to: Richard E. Petty, Department of Psychology, Ohio State University, 1885 Neil Avenue, Columbus, OHIO 43210, USA. email: petty.1@osu.edu successful orators of the classical world believed that one important method of persuasion involved the evocation of emotion among listeners. In more modern times, some of the earliest empirical studies of persuasion examined the role of emotional versus rational messages in producing attitude change (e.g., see Chen, 1933; Hartman, 1936). In reviewing much of the more contemporary scientific work regarding the ancient but enduring belief that emotions have an impact on persuasion, McGuire (1985) concurred in the assessment that affect can play an important role in attitude change. The specific question, of course, for philosophers and empiricists alike has centered around the exact role for affect in persuasion. Until very recently, the form of this question and the associated resulting theories reflected what could be termed a *main effect perspective*. That is, the majority of investigations sought to determine what the one effect of mood or emotion was on persuasion. For example, does positive mood produce more attitude change than negative mood?

The fruits of this inquiry from the origins of psychology until the late 1980s produced a plethora of findings suggesting that, in answer to that question, experiencing positive affect often resulted in greater persuasion than negative affect (e.g., Janis, Kaye, & Kirschner, 1965; Forgas & Moylan, 1987; Zanna, Kiesler, & Pilkonis, 1970; see McGuire, 1985; Petty, Gleicher, & Baker, 1991, for reviews). There were, however, dissenting voices suggesting the opposite was possible. Several studies found that increased persuasion could occur in negative states such as anger (Weiss & Fine, 1956) and fear (see Rogers, 1983). These contradictory findings continue in more recent persuasion research showing that the supposed general effect of positive mood on attitude change appears to be contingent on a variety of factors (e.g., Bless, Bohner, Schwarz, & Strack, 1990; Mackie & Worth, 1989; Wegener, Petty, & Smith, 1995). Thus, it is now quite clear that the preliminary conclusion that positive affect was good for persuasion and negative affect was bad was premature (McGuire, 1985).

What, then, is the role of emotion in attitude change? The relatively recent multiprocess theories of persuasion (e.g., Chaiken, Liberman, & Eagly, 1989; Petty & Cacioppo, 1986) offer a framework within which such varied, and sometimes contradictory, effects of affect can be more clearly understood. Accordingly, research from the 1990s has begun to chart the numerous ways in which emotional experiences can influence persuasion. The question no longer centers on finding the one effect of affect on persuasion, but reflects the more complex nature of the situation by examining the multiple ways in which affect helps or hinders persuasion.

Both the Elaboration Likelihood Model (ELM; Petty & Cacioppo, 1986; Petty & Wegener, 1999) and the Heuristic–Systematic Model (HSM; Chaiken et al., 1989) dictate that attitude change can occur through different mechanisms depending on the level of effort individuals exert when considering persuasive appeals. Therefore, the manner in which affect has an impact on persuasion also can vary as a function of individuals' levels of elaboration regarding the message at hand (Petty et al., 1993). According to the ELM, any variable, such as one's emotional state, can influence persuasion in one of several general ways: (1) it can serve as an item of issue-relevant information when processed as an argument; (2) it can influence attitudes by a peripheral mechanism (e.g., classical conditioning); (3) it can produce a bias to the ongoing information-processing activity; and (4) it can, itself, help to determine the levels of processing in which individuals engage. After a brief discussion of the definitions and structure of the constructs of interest, the remainder of this chapter focuses on explicating how emotional experiences can act in each of these ways depending on a person's motivation and ability to think about the persuasive message presented.

Before delving into a discussion of the ways in which emotional states can influence persuasion, it is useful to make explicit our definitions and conceptualizations of the key terms. In the present chapter, we use the term *affect* to encompass the broad range of experiences referred to as *emotions* and *moods*, in which emotions are understood as specific and short-lived internal feeling states, and moods are more global and enduring feeling states (cf. Schwarz & Clore, 1996). The term *attitude* denotes a general evaluation regarding some person, object, or issue (Fazio, 1986; Petty & Cacioppo, 1981). It is important to note that attitudes refer to valenced reactions to specific attitude objects and do not represent a global affective experience on the part of the individual. That is, the person does not experience the positivity or negativity of the attitude as a feeling or emotional state, but as an evaluative orientation toward an object. Therefore, a happy or sad person can, of course, possess both positive and negative attitudes.

To understand the role of affect in persuasion, it is sometimes useful to distinguish between what has been termed attitude *relevant affect* and *irrelevant affect* (Petty et al., 1991). *Relevant affect* implies that one's moods or emotions stem from consideration of the attitude object. For example, one's fear of death might be precipitated when considering an antismoking message. Likewise, an individual's attitude toward another person can appropriately be based on how he or she feels when interacting with this person. Affect, however, can be, and often is, *irrelevant* or incidental to the attitude object at hand. For example, the feelings induced by a television program are not really relevant to the merits of the advertisements placed within the program. In such cases, the origin of an individual's emotional state has nothing do with the attitude object he or she is considering at the moment. Nonetheless, a considerable body of evidence indicates that irrelevant affect can still exert a considerable influence on one's attitudes (Petty & Wegener, 1998; Schwarz & Clore, 1996; Wegener & Petty, 1996). In fact, much of the research from that on classical conditioning to today's multiprocess models examines and documents the impact of incidental affect on attitudes and persuasion.

ATTITUDE STRUCTURE

To better understand the role of affective factors in attitude change, it is helpful to understand the role of affect in the structure of an attitude. Both classic (Smith, 1947; Katz & Stotland, 1959; Rosenberg & Hovland, 1960) and more contemporary (Cacioppo, Petty, & Geen, 1989; Zajonc & Markus, 1982; Zanna & Rempel, 1988) treatments of attitudes view them as consisting of up to three evaluative bases: cognitive, behavioral, and affective. That is, although an attitude can contain all three elements, it can also be largely or solely based on one. The cognitive component of attitudes consists of one's thoughts or ideas, expressed as beliefs. For example, an individual might hold the belief that the president is doing a good job for the country. The behavioral component refers to observable behavior or intention to act. In relation to the president, supporters of the president might have a record of donating money to prior campaigns. Finally, the affective component of attitudes consists of feelings and emotions that individuals experience or have experienced regarding an attitude object. For example, thinking about the president might make one angry. All three components of an attitude can be measured across an evaluative continuum ranging from very negative to very positive. For instance, cognitions can range from perceiving the attitude object as worthwhile to worthless; behaviors can range from ones that foster approaching to avoiding the attitude object; and affect can range from adoration to disgust (e.g., see Crites, Fabrigar, & Petty, 1994; Eagly, Mladinic, & Otto, 1994; Kothandapani, 1971; Ostrom, 1969; Stangor, Sullivan, & Ford, 1991). One's overall evaluation (attitude) is based on some combination of one's affect, cognition, and behavioral tendencies toward the attitude object.

ATTITUDE CHANGE WITH
RELEVANT AFFECT

As noted earlier, the affect used in a persuasion setting can either stem directly from the attitude object or be completely incidental. We begin our review with the former type of affect and then address the latter. Regarding relevant affect, the vast preponderance of research has examined relevant affect that is part of the persuasive message itself. That is, the message invokes issue-relevant affect.

Affective versus Cognitive Appeals

When attempting to persuade another person, one can appeal to reason and provide information (cognitive appeal), one can provide attitude-relevant behavioral experience (behavioral appeal), or one can attempt to stir the passions (emotional appeal). Researchers have suggested that the initial primary basis of one's attitude (i.e., cognitive, affective, or behavioral) can moderate its susceptibility to subsequent persuasive appeals that are cognitively, affectively, or behaviorally based. Interestingly, the initial work on the links between attitude bases and message bases proved to be contradictory. Some researchers (Edwards, 1990; Edwards & von Hippel, 1995; Fabrigar & Petty, 1999) found more persuasion occurred when the basis of an attitude matched the type of persuasive appeal (e.g., to change an affectively based attitude, an affective appeal was more powerful than a cognitive appeal), whereas others found evidence for a mismatching effect (Millar & Millar, 1990). That is, more persuasion was found to result when persuasive appeals mismatched the basis of the original attitude.

Although the resolution of this discrepancy is uncertain at present, it is possible to generate plausible predictions concerning conditions that might foster matching versus mismatching effects (see Edwards, 1990; Edwards & von Hippel, 1995; Fabrigar & Petty, 1999; Millar & Millar, 1990; Petty, Gleicher, & Baker, 1991). For instance, one possibility is that matching should occur when it is possible to directly overwhelm the basis of the attitude. Thus, matching effects should occur when the basis of an attitude is relatively weak and/or the persuasive appeal is particularly strong because these are the conditions that would foster an undermining of the initial basis of the attitude. In contrast, if the basis of an attitude is extremely strong or the appeal is relatively weak, it is likely to be difficult to completely overwhelm the basis of an attitude with any single persuasive appeal. Indeed, a strong attitude basis might serve as a resource for counterarguing or resisting the appeal. In such cases, matching persuasion to bases could prove relatively ineffective. Thus, it might be more promising to use a mismatched persuasive appeal that provides novel information that does not directly challenge the existing basis. This analysis presumes people are actively analyzing the persuasive information presented. If this is not the case, other possibilities emerge. For example, some people may have a default preference for experiential/emotional messages, whereas other people may have a default preference for rational/logical messages (cf., Epstein & Rosemary, 1999).

Fear Appeals

Without a doubt, the most studied method of promoting attitude change with relevant affect is to incorporate fear-inducing material in the communication. When very strong negative consequences (e.g., cancerous lungs, death) are implied if an advocacy is not adopted, a fear appeal is being attempted, although it is not always certain if such material invokes a fearful state.[1] Based on expectancy-value theories (e.g., see Fishbein & Ajzen, 1975), it would appear that such appeals would be very effective because they depict extremely negative consequences as being likely to occur unless the recipient agrees with the message. In fact, a meta-analysis of the fear-appeals literature indicated that overall, increasing fear is associated with increased persuasion (Boster & Mongeau, 1984).

Yet, fear appeals are not invariably found to be more effective. In fact, one of the earliest studies on fear appeals suggested the opposite conclusion (Janis & Feshbach, 1953). There are several factors that militate against the effectiveness of fear appeals. First, even if people view the threatened negative consequence as horrific, they are often motivated by self-protection to minimize the likelihood that some frightening consequence might befall them (e.g., Ditto, Jemmott, & Darley, 1988; Ditto & Lopez, 1992). That is, they engage in "defensive processing." To the extent that this defensiveness can be minimized by encouraging objective processing, the effectiveness

---

[1] In fact, in the literature on fear appeals, a number of operationalizations are used. In some, the high fear message may include a greater number of negative consequences, or negative consequences of greater severity than in the low fear message, or the same consequences may be implied but are depicted more vividly, or are repeated more times in the high than low fear message. In still other studies, the same message is given, but recipient reactions are assessed to determine fear. Or, combinations of these features may be used to create high and low fear messages. Because of this complexity and confounding, some fear studies are open to simple (non-fear based) alternative interpretations (e.g., the high fear message was more persuasive because it included more or better arguments).

of a fear appeal can be increased (Keller & Block, 1995). Second, to the extent that the threat is so strong that it becomes physiologically arousing or distracting, message processing could be disrupted (Baron, Inman, Kao, & Logan, 1992; Jepson & Chaiken, 1990). This would reduce persuasion if the arguments were strong. Fear is especially likely to reduce message processing if recipients are assured that the recommendations are effective and the processing might undermine this assurance (Gleicher & Petty, 1992).[2]

The dominant theoretical perspective in the literature on fear appeals is Rogers' (1975; 1983) protection motivation theory. Consistent with expectancy-value notions, this model holds that fear appeals will be effective to the extent that the message convinces the recipient that some consequence is severe (i.e., is very undesirable) and very likely to occur if the recommended action is not followed. Importantly, this theory also holds that effective fear messages should also convey that the negative consequence can be avoided if the recommended action is followed and that the recipient has the requisite skills to take the recommended action (see also Beck & Frenkel, 1981; Sutton, 1982; Witte, 1992). Considerable evidence supports these predictions and has also shown that if people do not believe that they can cope effectively with the threat, then increasing threat tends to produce a boomerang effect, presumably as a consequence of attempting to restore control or reduce fear (e.g., Mullis & Lippa, 1990; Rippetoe & Rogers, 1987; Rogers & Mewborn, 1976). In sum, fear seems to be effective when the fear enhances the realization that some consequences are severe and likely, but can be overcome by following the recommendations. If fear is elicited in the absence of these cognitive processes, it is counterproductive.

ATTITUDE CHANGE WITH IRRELEVANT (INCIDENTAL) AFFECT

In the research on affective messages and fear appeals just described, the emotion is induced by and is part of the communication itself. That is, a persuasive appeal attempts to get people to feel happy about a soft drink by having them taste it (Edwards, 1990), or to feel fear about the consequences

---

[2]Some researchers argue that fear has opposite effects on some of the underlying processes of persuasion (e.g., reducing reception but enhancing yielding). If so, then an inverted-U relationship might be expected between fear and persuasion (e.g., Janis, 1967; McGuire, 1968). This has not generally been observed (Boster & Mongeau, 1984), but perhaps the high levels of fear needed to obtain it have not been present in the available research.

of not brushing their teeth by showing them rotting teeth (Janis & Feshbach, 1953). In other research, the effects of incidental affect are examined. For example, people are made to feel happy by watching an enjoyable television program (Petty et al., 1993), or winning some money (Worth & Mackie, 1987) prior to presentation of a message on a topic unrelated to the affect induction. The effects of these irrelevant affects have varied depending on whether people are exposed to them under conditions of low-, moderate-, or high-elaboration likelihood.

Effects of Emotional Factors Under Low-Elaboration Conditions

Under conditions of low elaboration, when individuals lack the motivation or ability to process a persuasive message, affect has been shown to function as a peripheral cue and to have an impact on attitudes in a manner consistent with its valence. Thus, positive mood tends to lead to more positive attitudes toward an object, but negative mood elicits more negative attitudes.

Early demonstrations of the effects of mood under conditions of low elaboration can be found in the extensive research on evaluative conditioning (e.g., Staats & Staats, 1958). Classical conditioning is, by nature, a process of simple association, rather than one involving scrutiny of message-relevant information. A number of studies using classical conditioning for studying emotional input (Gouaux, 1971; Griffitt, 1970; Razran, 1940; Zanna et al., 1970) demonstrated that emotions can influence attitudes by becoming directly associated with the attitude object. Repeatedly pairing an attitude object with stimuli that bring about positive feelings has led to more positive attitudes toward the attitude object compared to pairing an attitude object with stimuli that produce negative reactions.

An early demonstration of the effects of emotions using classical conditioning was conducted by Razran (1940). In this study, participants were presented with political slogans in one of two contexts: in the context of enjoying a free lunch or in the context of being exposed to noxious odors. Receiving a free lunch placed individuals in a positive affective state, whereas exposure to noxious odors placed individuals in a negative affective state. It was predicted that the message would become associated with the mood experienced by the individual, and therefore the message would be favored more when paired with the free lunch than with the noxious odors, and this was obtained. Individuals who received a free lunch had more positive attitudes toward the slogans than individuals who were exposed to noxious odors. The accumulated studies on classical conditioning are quite consistent, and relatively recent research suggests that such conditioning effects are strongest when the likelihood of elaboration of the attitude object is low (Cacioppo et al., 1992; Priester et al., 1996).

A second way emotions can influence attitudes under conditions of low elaboration is through the misattribution of one's emotional state to an attitude object (e.g., Zillmann, 1983). Rather than evaluating the merits of a message, one's emotional feeling is used as a simple cue to decide whether the message was good or bad (e.g., "If I'm feeling good, I must like or agree with the message"). Rather than being based on the merit of the message, an individual's attitude is based on the answer to the question "How do I feel about it?" (Schwarz, 1990; Schwarz & Clore, 1983; Srull, 1983; see Clore, Gasper, & Garvin, chap. 6, this volume).

In a pertinent example of the misattribution of mood, Sinclair, Mark, and Clore (1994) used changes in weather as an unobtrusive mood manipulation. College students were exposed to a message arguing for the implementation of comprehensive exams for seniors in one of two conditions. Half the participants were presented with the message when the weather was either pleasant (inducing positive mood), or when the weather was unpleasant (inducing negative mood). Sinclair and colleagues found that, even though mood induced by the weather was irrelevant to the message topic, individuals who were in a positive mood favored the implementation of comprehensive exams relative to individuals in a negative mood. Therefore, mood served as a simple cue that individuals used when forming an attitude toward the message.

Mood is especially likely to have these simple and direct cue effects when people are not inclined to be thinking about the message. Consistent with this, Petty et al. (1993) had participants view a series of commercials, one of which featured the attitude object of interest, a pen. Prior to viewing the commercials, participants' involvement with the target product was manipulated by informing them they would be allowed to choose a pen after seeing the commercials (high involvement) or another, unrelated product (low involvement). Participants' mood was manipulated by embedding the commercial in a television program that invoked either a positive or a neutral mood. After viewing the commercials, participant's attitudes toward the pen were assessed. Positive mood led to more favorable attitudes toward the pen. In addition, path analyses revealed that mood had a direct effect on attitudes when elaboration was low (the low-involvement condition), but had an indirect effect (by biasing thoughts generated) when elaboration was high (high-involvement condition). Similar effects have been observed when individual differences in propensity to think have been examined.

That is, when people are low in need for cognition (Cacioppo & Petty, 1982), moods have a direct impact on attitudes, but when people are high in need for cognition, moods influence attitudes by biasing thoughts (Batra & Stayman, 1990; Petty et al., 1993; see additional discussion below).

Effects of Emotional Factors Under High-Elaboration Conditions

As just noted, moods influence attitudes under high-elaboration conditions, but appear to do so in a different way than under low-elaboration conditions. Under high elaboration, people are carefully scrutinizing persuasive messages for merit. Emotional states themselves can also be scrutinized for their information value. Whereas under low elaboration, people might use their moods as an informative heuristic with relatively little thought ("If I feel good, I must like it"), under high elaboration, moods are subjected to greater scrutiny and can have an impact on attitudes if relevant to the attitude object under consideration. For example, if one's judgment concerns whether a person would make a suitable spouse, the feelings associated with the presence of that person are a central dimension of the merits of that potential companion (Petty & Cacioppo, 1986; Wegener & Petty, 1996). An empirical example of this was presented by Martin, Abend, Sedikides, and Green (1997). In their research, people in either a happy or sad mood were given either a happy or sad story and were asked to evaluate the story and their liking for it. In such a case (in which the "target" story was obviously meant to bring about a particular feeling), the emotion people felt when reading the story was likely to be perceived as a central merit of the story. Consistent with this notion, research participants' evaluations of and liking for the target stories were highest when the emotion before the story (and presumably during the story) matched rather than mismatched the intended effect of the story. When the purpose of the target story was to make people feel sad and people felt sad, the sad state actually led to higher ratings of the story than did a happy state.

Perhaps more often, when people are actively evaluating information about the target (i.e., when elaboration likelihood is high), mood can bias the interpretations of that information, especially if the information is ambiguous (Chaiken & Maheswaran, 1994; Petty, Gleicher, & Baker, 1991; see also Bower & Forgas, chap. 5, this volume). Forgas (1994) refers to this as an "affect infusion" effect (see Forgas, chap. 14, this volume). For example, positive moods might activate more positive interpretations of information than would negative moods (e.g., Bower, 1981; Breckler &

Wiggins, 1991; Isen, Shalker, Clark, & Karp, 1978). Regardless of whether one conceptualizes such activation in terms of associative networks (e.g., Anderson & Bower, 1973; Bower, 1981) or connectionist models (e.g., McClelland, Rumelhart, & Hinton, 1986; Smith, 1996), happy moods have often been found to make events or objects seem more desirable and/or more likely than the same events or objects appear when in sad or neutral moods (e.g., see Forgas & Moylan, 1987; Johnson & Tversky, 1983; Mayer, Gaschke, Braverman, & Evans, 1992). In addition, it has been shown that specific emotions have specific effects on the perceived likelihood of events such that angry emotional states make angering events seem more likely than sad ones, but sad emotional states make sad events seem more likely than angering ones (DeSteno, Petty, Wegener, & Rucker, 2000).

As noted earlier, explicit evidence of mood-biasing information processing was found by Petty et al. (1993). Under high-elaboration conditions in two experiments (i.e., when people were high in need for cognition or encountered information about a self-relevant product), mood-influenced judgments of the targets by influencing the cognitive responses to the information about the targets. That is, when effortful elaboration of judgment-relevant information was likely, positive mood produced greater positivity in thought content, which in turn influenced evaluations of the targets. Of course, mood would be less likely to exert a biasing impact on processing if there were salient and competing biasing factors operating—such as a strong prior attitude—or if the judgment-relevant information was completely unambiguous (see also Forgas, 1994).

It is also important to note that when moods bias processing, the mood state does not invariably lead to mood-congruent biases in overall evaluation (Petty & Wegener, 1991; Wegener et al., 1994). Using the expectancy (likelihood) × value (desirability) approach to attitude judgments (e.g., Fishbein & Ajzen, 1975), Wegener et al. (1994) found that differential framing of information about target actions led to different biasing effects of mood on assessments of those actions. Specifically, when the arguments in a persuasive message were framed to support the view that adopting the recommended position was likely to make good things happen, a happy mood was associated with more favorable views of the advocacy than a sad mood. However, when the arguments were framed such that failing to adopt the advocacy was likely to make bad things happen, a sad mood was associated with more favorable views of the advocacy than a happy mood. The reason for this was that a happy mood made the good things that would occur if the advocacy was adopted seem more likely, and the sad mood made the bad things that would occur if the advocacy was not adopted seem more likely. Consistent with the notion of this likelihood/desirability calculus being a relatively effortful activity, the likelihood mediation of mood effects on judgment only took place for people high in need for cognition. Of course, using this same likelihood/desirability view, one could also predict situations in which mood changes the perceived desirability of consequences of adopting the advocacy (thereby providing another means by which mood might bias the effortful assessment of the central merits of an advocacy; see Petty & Wegener, 1991, for additional discussion).

Effects of Emotional Factors Under Moderate-Elaboration Conditions

As mentioned at the outset of this chapter, according to the multiprocess theories that dominate the field of attitudes, variables can influence persuasion in many ways. Sometimes the variable serves as a central merit of consideration, but at other times it influences persuasion by invoking a more peripheral process (e.g., is used as a heuristic). In addition, sometimes variables bias the thoughts that come to mind. Finally, variables can also determine, either in isolation or in concert with other variables, the extent of processing a persuasive appeal receives. Therefore, in instances in which the level of elaboration a message receives is not constrained by other variables to be high or low, an individual's affective state can push processing along the elaboration continuum in one direction or another.

The majority of research in this area documents a general pattern. Individuals experiencing a positive mood have typically been less likely to engage in effortful processing of the information contained in a persuasive appeal in comparison to those experiencing a negative mood (Bless, Bohner, Schwarz, & Strack, 1990; Bohner, Crow, Erb, & Schwarz, 1992; Kuykendall & Keating, 1990; Mackie & Worth, 1989). A study by Bless et al. (1990) is illustrative. Participants in this experiment were asked to remember happy or sad experiences from their past. They were then presented with a message announcing a fee increase at their university. The message used either strong or weak arguments to bolster its point. In addition, participants were told that the study was concerned either with forms of language (a manipulation designed not to influence level of processing) or with the ability of people to evaluate message content (a manipulation designed to induce effortful processing). Results indicated that when the study was presented as examining language use, sad participants were more persuaded by strong than weak arguments, thereby indicating a relatively high level of processing. Happy participants, however, were equally persuaded by both messages, thereby indicating a relatively low level of message processing (cf., Petty, Wells, & Brock, 1976). This pattern did not emerge when the study was presented as involving message content; elaboration was constrained to be high in this condition. Thus, when elaboration is not determined by other variables, happiness seems to put people lower on the elaboration continuum, and thereby induce attitude change through more cue-based, or heuristic, mechanisms.

Currently, one of the most accepted theoretical explanations for the effects of affect on level of message elaboration is the feelings-as-information, or cognitive tuning, framework proposed by several researchers (Schwarz, Bless, & Bohner, 1991; Schwarz & Clore, 1988; see also Clore et al., chap. 6, this volume). Put simply, this theory postulates that individuals' moods and emotions serve as informational cues regarding the status of their environs and, consequently, influence motivation to engage in effortful cognitive processing. Specifically, negative affective states are theorized to inform individuals that their current environment is problematic, and therefore are believed to engender a relatively high level of effortful processing that would be appropriate to deal with such situations. Positive states are believed to produce a different motivational response—that the current situation is safe, and therefore does not require a high level of cognitive effort aimed at avoiding harm.

The rise of the feelings-as-information framework supplanted the previous explanation for the reduced effort levels associated with positive affect. Mackie and Worth (1989) originally had argued that the presence of a positive mood state might limit individuals' cognitive capacities and, thereby, inhibit their abilities to process information in an effortful manner. Experiments such as the one by Bless et al. (1990) cast some doubt that the elaboration decrement stems from limited capacity because the decrease in processing for happy participants was shown to be easily corrected as a function of motivation. However, given that Mackie and colleagues (1992) have suggested that capacity deficits are not all-encompassing, but, rather may be overcome with appropriate motivation, definitive support for one framework or the other is lacking.

Although negative emotional states might indeed signal that the world is a problematic place and induce greater processing, emotional states can have other motivational consequences as well. For example, the hedonic contingency model (Wegener & Petty, 1994) begins with the fairly obvious assumption that people prefer to keep their positive emotional states, but try to avoid their negative ones. The crux of the model hinges on the fact that as an individual's affective state becomes more and more positive, the actions in which he or she can engage that maintain or further elevate the mood state become increasingly limited. However, when an individual is sad, the majority of actions in which he or she can engage tend to elevate mood. Therefore, success in positive mood states (i.e., maintaining one's positive mood) is highly contingent on the consideration of the hedonic consequences of actions because only a small proportion serves to maintain or elevate one's affective state further. However, negative mood states require less vigilance because most activities serve to increase mood (see also Erber & Erber, chap. 13, this volume). Because of these contingencies, over time people become more sensitive to the hedonic consequences of their actions in positive rather than in negative emotional states.

In extending the hedonic contingency framework to the study of persuasion, Wegener, Petty, and Smith (1995) noted that the persuasive appeals used in past research examining the effect of emotional states on information processing were comprised largely of negative content (e.g., tuition increases, nuclear waste). Consequently, the lack of effortful consideration of such messages by individuals experiencing a positive mood state might represent a mood-management strategy as opposed to the utilization of a feelings-as-information motivational cue. Thinking about a tuition increase, after all, likely would not maintain an already pleasant affective state. Therefore, happy individuals should choose not to process the message in an effortful manner. Sad individuals, being less sensitive to hedonic contingencies, should devote more resources toward message processing. These predictions parallel those stemming from the feelings-as-information framework and are, therefore, in accord with much of the research in this area.

The critical test for the hedonic contingency view involves the case where effortful processing of a persuasive message could be considered a mood-enhancing endeavor. In such a situation, the hedonic contingency perspective predicts a relatively high level of effortful processing of the appeal. Importantly, this prediction would be at odds with that derived from the feelings-as-information framework. Positive mood, from that perspective, should always indicate safety and, consequently, a low need to expend cognitive effort. To test these competing predictions, Wegener et al. (1995) conducted a study in which affective states (happy vs. neutral), argument quality, and message framing were crossed. All participants read the same message, but it was introduced as being either one that tended to make people happy or as one that tended to make them sad. In accord with their predictions, Wegener et al. found that when the message was believed to cause sadness, happy individuals were less influenced by argument quality than sad individuals. However, when the message was believed to cause happiness, happy participants were more influenced by argument quality than sad individuals.

Although findings supporting the hedonic contingency model appear to contradict the feelings-as-information perspective, Schwarz and Clore (1996) state that attention to the hedonic qualities of activities may represent a rationale mood-management strategy, but one that individuals only have the luxury of engaging in when they first appraise their current environment as nonproblematic through the use of a feelings-as-information process (i.e., "The world is fine, so I think I'll stay happy by processing this message"). Consequently, they argue that the hedonic contingency model does not stand in opposition to the feelings-as-information perspective, but rather might be a secondary process that can further moderate the primary effect of positive mood.

One other process by which affective experience has been shown to influence attitude change stems from cognitive dissonance. As is well known, Festinger (1957) defined cognitive dissonance as a state in which two elements (e.g., cognitions, behaviors) are inconsistent. Such inconsistency is believed to be experienced as an aversive state by individuals and motivates actions aimed at reducing the dissonance. Decades of research have documented this phenomenon and the specific conditions under which it occurs (Cooper & Fazio, 1984) and therefore are not reviewed here. However, with regard to the link between emotion and persuasion, cognitive dissonance offers an important insight (see also Harmon-Jones, chap. 11, this volume).

Work by Zanna and Cooper (1974) clearly demonstrates that dissonance is experienced as an aversive state, much akin to tension. As Festinger (1957) notes, one way in which dissonance can be alleviated is through the changing of cognitions so that they no longer are discrepant. In support of this theory, much evidence has accumulated demonstrating that individuals' attitudes toward certain objects can change dramatically in response to dissonance manipulations that place their initial attitudes at odds with other thoughts or behaviors (for reviews, see Cooper & Fazio, 1984; Harmon-Jones, 1999). Consequently, cognitive dissonance can be understood to exert its influence on attitude change through a motivation to reduce inconsistencies that stems from the existence of an aversive affective state.

Mood-Correction Effects

In the vast majority of studies described in this chapter, the effects of emotion on attitudes can be considered to be implicit. That is, people are often not aware that their moods and emotions are coloring their judgments (e.g., that affect from a television program is influencing judgments of a product featured in an advertisement; Petty et al., 1993). Even when people explicitly consider their emotional states as relevant information, they are presumably not aware that the impact of the mood or emotional state was often produced by some stimulus irrelevant to the attitude object (e.g., good weather).

Some work, however, has examined what happens when people become aware of and wish to remove the irrelevant impact of affective states. Sometimes, when people become aware of the true source of their affect (e.g., the good weather rather than the attitude object), they discount their mood state as relevant information and thereby remove (or prevent) the mood bias (Schwarz & Clore, 1983). How do people remove or prevent this bias? According to the Flexible Correction Model (FCM; Petty & Wegener, 1993; Wegener & Petty, 1997), people's attempts at correction are guided by their theories of bias. For example, if people believe that how they feel is unduly affecting (or will unduly affect) their perceptions of a target, and if people are motivated and able to correct for these perceived biases, they can adjust assessments of the target in a direction opposite to the perceived bias in an attempt to characterize the target in an unbiased manner. If people overestimate the effect of their mood, then reverse effects can be obtained. That is, if a happy mood would have ordinarily made people more favorable toward a message than a sad mood, and people overestimate and correct for this unwanted bias, their final attitudes could be less favorable when happy than sad (DeSteno, Petty, Wegener, & Rucker, 2000; Petty, Wegener, & White, 1998).

Although corrections based on such naive theories of bias provide a potential means for lessening, removing, or reversing (if overcorrection occurs) the biasing effects of mood, a person's naive theories of bias can also introduce or augment existing mood-based biases. For example, if a person believes that happy mood makes them too positive toward an advocacy, but in fact happy mood led to a less positive view of the advocacy than a sad mood (e.g., Wegener et al., 1994; see also Martin et al., 1997), then corrections aimed at removing an undue influence of mood might actually exacerbate the effect that would have occurred without the correction. People could become aware of potential effects of mood (and might become motivated to remove those perceived effects) regardless of whether elaboration of judgment-relevant information is high or low (e.g., regardless of whether the perceived effect of mood was to bias active information processing or to influence perceptions through use as a decision rule or heuristic). Although theories of bias could guide corrections in both cases, it might be more difficult to correct effectively for mood-based biases on interpretation of many pieces of judgment-relevant information. If such an effortful correction occurs, however, it should be more likely to last than would a simpler "overall" correction, just as initial attitudes based on thought are more likely to persist (Petty, Haugtvedt, & Smith, 1995; see Wegener & Petty, 1997, for additional discussion of corrections for effects of mood).

CONCLUSION

In this chapter, we reviewed some of the ways in which affect can influence attitude change. A key point was that the influence of emotional factors, whether relevant or irrelevant to the attitude object, can occur through different primary mechanisms in different persuasion situations. That is, emotions can serve in multiple roles, and the effects of emotional factors appear to be quite diverse. Emotions can influence attitudes by peripheral mechanisms (such as classical conditioning), serve as items of issue-relevant information, bias message processing, and determine the extent of message scrutiny. Furthermore, under high-elaboration conditions, mood can not only encourage mood-congruent persuasion outcomes, but also produce mood-incongruent persuasion outcomes. The latter is most evident in the literature on fear appeals. Similarly, under relatively moderate elaboration conditions, positive moods can not only encourage reductions of message processing when compared with neutral and negative moods, but can also foster increases in message processing. Thus, the flexibilities in mood-based effects on persuasion that have been presented in this chapter help to more fully explain the psychological processes underlying the various effects of mood on attitudes.

REFERENCES

Anderson, J. R., & Bower, G. H. (1973). *Human associative memory*. Washington, DC: Winston.

Baron, R. S., Inman, M. L., Kao, C. F., & Logan, H. (1992). Negative emotion and superficial social processing. *Motivation & Emotion, 16*, 323–346.

Batra, R., & Stayman, D. M. (1990). The role of mood in advertising effectiveness. *Journal of Consumer Research, 17*, 203–214.

Beck, K. H., & Frankel, A. (1981). A conceptualization of threat communications and protective health behavior. *Social Psychology Quartely, 44*, 204–217.

Bless, H., Bohner, G., Schwarz, N., & Strack, F. (1990). Mood and persuasion: A cognitive response analysis. *Personality and Social Psychology Bulletin, 16*, 332–346.

Bohner, G., Crow, K., Erb, H. P., & Schwarz, N. (1992). Affect and persuasion: Mood effects on the processing of message content and context cues and on subsequent behavior. *European Journal of Social Psychology, 22*, 511–530.

Boster, F. J., & Mongeau, P. (1984). Fear-arousing persuasive messages. In R. N. Bostrom (Ed.), *Communication yearbook, Vol. 8* (pp. 330–375). Beverly Hills, CA: Sage.

Bower, G. (1981). Mood and memory. *American Psychologist, 36,* 129–148.

Breckler, S. J., & Wiggins, E. C. (1991). Cognitive responses in persuasion: Affective and evaluative determinants. *Journal of Experimental Social Psychology, 27,* 180–200.

Cacioppo, J. T., Marshall-Goodell, B. S., Tassinary, L. G., & Petty, R. E. (1992). Rudimentary determinants of attitudes: Classical conditioning is more effective when prior knowledge about the attitude stimulus is low than high. *Journal of Experimental Social Psychology, 28,* 207–233.

Cacioppo, J. T., & Petty, R. E. (1982). The need for cognition. *Journal of Personality and Social Psychology, 42,* 116–131.

Cacioppo, J. T., Petty, R. E., & Geen, T. R. (1989). Attitude structure and function: From the tripartite to the homeostasis model of attitudes. In A. R. Pratkanis, S. J. Breckler, & A. G. Greenwald (Eds.), *Attitude structure and function* (pp. 275–309). Hillsdale, NJ: Lawrence Erlbaum Associates.

Chaiken, S., Liberman, A., & Eagly, A. (1989). Heuristic and systematic information processing within and beyond the persuasion context. In J. S. Uleman & J. A. Bargh (Eds.), *Unintended thought: Limits of awareness, intention, and control* (pp. 212–252). New York: Guilford Press.

Chaiken, S., & Maheswaran, D. (1994). Heuristic processing can bias systematic processing: Effects of source credibility, argument ambiguity, and task importance on attitude judgment. *Journal of Personality and Social Psychology, 66,* 460–473.

Chen, W. K. (1933). The influence of oral propaganda material upon students' attitudes. *Archives of Psychology, 150,* 43.

Cicero, M. T. (1970). *De oratore* (J. S. Watson, Trans.). Carbondale, IL: Southern Illinois University Press. (Original work published in 55 BCE).

Cooper, J., & Fazio, R. H. (1984). A new look at dissonance theory. In L. Berkowitz (Ed.), *Advances in experimental social psychology, Vol. 17* (pp. 229–266). San Diego: Academic Press.

Crites, S. L., Fabrigar, L. R., & Petty, R. E. (1994). Measuring the affective and cognitive properties of attitudes: Conceptual and methodological issues. *Personality & Social Psychology Bulletin, 20,* 619–634.

Desteno, D., Petty, R. E., Wegener, D. T., & Rucker, D. D. (2000). Beyond valence in the perception of likelihood: The role of emotion specificity. *Journal of Personality and Social Psychology, 78,* 397–416.

Ditto, P. H., Jemmott, J. B., & Darley, J. M. (1988). Appraising the threat of illness: A mental representational approach. *Health Psychology, 7,* 183–201.

Ditto, P. H., & Lopez, D. F. (1992). Motivated skepticism: Use of differential decision criteria for preferred and nonpreferred conclusions. *Journal of Personality & Social Psychology, 63,* 568–584.

Eagly, A. H., Mladinic, A., & Otto, S. (1994). Cognitive and affective bases of attitudes toward social groups and social policies. *Journal of Experimental Social Psychology, 30,* 113–137.

Edwards, K. (1990). The interplay of affect and cognition in attitude formation and change. *Journal of Personality & Social Psychology, 59,* 202–216.

Edwards, K., & von Hippel, W. (1995). Hearts and minds: The priority of affective versus cognitive factors in person perception. *Personality and Social Psychology Bulletin, 21,* 996–1011.

Epstein, S., & Rosemary, P. (1999). Some basic issues regarding dual-process theories, from the perspective of cognitive–experiential self-theory. In S. Chaiken & Y. Trope (Eds.), *Dual-process theories in social psychology* (pp. 462–482). New York: Guilford Press.

Fabrigar, L. R., & Petty, R. E. (1999). The role of the affective and cognitive bases of attitudes in susceptibility to affectively and cognitively based persuasion. *Personality and Social Psychology Bulletin, 25,* 363–381.

Fazio, R. H. (1986). How do attitudes guide behavior? In R. Sorrentino & E. T. Higgins (Eds.), *The handbook of motivation and cognition* (pp. 204–243). New York: Guilford Press.

Festinger, L. (1957). *A theory of cognitive dissonance.* Palo Alto, CA: Stanford University Press.

Fishbein, M., & Ajzen, I. (1975). *Belief, attitude, intention, and behavior: An introduction to theory and research.* Reading, MA: Addison-Wesley.

Forgas, J. P. (Ed.). (1991). *Emotion and social judgments*. Oxford, England: Pergamon Press.

Forgas, J. P. (1994). The role of emotion in social judgments: An introductory review and an Affect Infusion Model (AIM). *European Journal of Social Psychology, 24*, 1–24.

Forgas, J. P., & Moylan, S. (1987). After the movies: Transient moods and social judgments. *Personality and Social Psychology Bulletin, 13*, 467–477.

Gleicher, F., & Petty, R. E. (1992). Expectations of reassurance influence the nature of fear-stimulated attitude change. *Journal of Experimental Social Psychology, 28*, 86–100.

Gouaux, C. (1971). Induced affective states and interpersonal attraction. *Journal of Personality and Social Psychology, 20*, 37–43.

Griffitt, W. B. (1970). Environmental effects on interpersonal affective behavior: Ambient effective temperature and attraction. *Journal of Personality and Social Psychology, 15*, 240–244.

Hartman, G. W. (1936). A field experiment on the comparative effectiveness of "emotional" and "rational" political leaflets in determining election results. *Journal of Abnormal and Social Psychology, 31*, 99–114.

Harmon-Jones, E., & Mills, J. (Eds.). (1999). *Cognitive dissonance: Progress on a pivotal theory in social psychology*. Washington, DC: American Psychological Association.

Isen, A. M., Shalker, T., Clark, M. S., & Karp, L. (1978). Affect, accessibility of material in memory, and behavior: A cognitive loop? *Journal of Personality and Social Psychology, 36*, 1–12.

Janis, I. L. (1967). Effects of fear arousal on attitude change: Recent developments in theory and experimental research. In L. Berkowitz (Ed.), *Advances in experimental social psychology, Vol. 3* (pp. 166–224). San Diego, CA: Academic Press.

Janis, I. L., & Feshbach, S. (1953). Effects of fear-arousing communications. *Journal of Abnormal and Social Psychology, 48*, 78–92.

Janis, I. L., Kaye, D., & Kirschner, P. (1965). Facilitating effects of "eating while reading" on responsiveness to persuasive communications. *Journal of Personality and Social Psychology, 1*, 181–186.

Jepson, C., & Chaiken, S. (1990). Chronic issue-specific fear inhibits systematic processing of persuasive communications. *Journal of Social Behavior and Personality, 5*, 61–84.

Johnson, E., & Tversky, A. (1983). Affect, generalization, and the perception of risk. *Journal of Personality and Social Psychology, 45*, 20–31.

Katz, D., & Stotland, E. (1959). A preliminary statement to a theory of attitude structure and change. In S. Koch (Ed.), *Psychology: A study of a science, Vol. 3* (pp. 423–475). New York: McGraw-Hill.

Keller, P. A., & Block, L. G. (1995). Increasing the persuasiveness of fear appeals: The effect of arousal and elaboration. *Journal of Consumer Research, 22*, 448–459.

Kothandapani, V. (1971). Validation of feeling, belief, and intention to act as three components of attitude and their contribution to prediction of contraceptive behavior. *Journal of Personality & Social Psychology, 19*, 321–333.

Kuykendall, D., & Keating, J. (1990). Mood and persuasion: Evidence for the differential influence of positive and negative states. *Psychology and Marketing, 7*, 1–9.

Mackie, D. M., Asuncion, A. G., & Rosselli, F. (1992). Impact of positive affect on persuasion processes. *Review of Personality and Social Psychology, 14*, 247–270.

Mackie, D. M., & Worth, L. (1989). Processing deficits and the mediation of positive affect in persuasion. *Journal of Personality and Social Psychology, 57*, 27–40.

Martin, L. L., Abend, T. A., Sedikides, C., & Green, J. (1997). How would I feel if...? Mood as input to a role fulfillment evaluation process. *Journal of Personality and Social Psychology, 73*, 242–253.

Mayer, J., Gaschke, Y., Braverman, D., & Evans, T. (1992). Mood-congruent judgment is a general effect. *Journal of Personality and Social Psychology, 63*, 119–132.

McClelland, J. L., Rumelhart, D. E., & Hinton, G. E. (1986). The appeal of parallel distributed processing. In D. E. Rumelhart, J. L. McClellan, & The PDP Research Group (Eds.), *Parallel distributed processing, Vol. 1* (pp. 3–44). Cambridge, MA: MIT Press.

McGuire, W. J. (1968). Personality and attitude change: An information-processing theory. In A. G. Greenwald, T. C. Brock, & T. M. Ostrom (Eds.), *Psychological foundations of attitudes* (pp. 171–196). New York: Academic.

McGuire, W. J. (1985). Attitudes and attitude change. In G. Lindzey & E. Aronson (Eds.), *The handbook or social psychology, 3rd ed., Vol. 2* (pp. 233–346). New York: Random House.

Millar, M. G., & Millar, K. U. (1990). Attitude change as a function of attitude type and argument type. *Journal of Personality and Social Psychology, 59*, 217–228.

Mulilis, J., & Lippa, R. (1990). Behavioral change in earthquake preparedness due to negative threat appeals: A test of protection motivation theory. *Journal of Applied Social Psychology, 20*, 619–638.

Ostrom, T. M. (1969). The relationship between the affective, behavioral and cognitive components of attitude. *Journal of Experimental Social Psychology, 5*, 12–30.

Petty, R. E., & Cacioppo, J. T. (1981). *Attitudes and persuasion: Classic and contemporary approaches.* Dubuque, IA: W.C. Brown.

Petty, R. E., Cacioppo, J. T., & Schumann, D. (1983). Central and peripheral routes to advertising effectiveness: The moderating role of involvement. *Journal of Consumer Research, 10*, 134–148.

Petty, R. E., & Cacioppo, J. T. (1986). The elaboration likelihood model of persuasion. In L. Berkowitz (Ed.), *Advances in experimental social psychology, Vol. 19* (pp. 123–205). New York: Academic Press.

Petty, R. E., Gleicher, F., & Baker, S. M. (1991). Multiple roles for affect in persuasion. In J. P. Forgas (Ed.), *Emotion and social judgments* (pp. 181–200). Oxford: Pergamon Press.

Petty, R. E., Haugtvedt, C., & Smith, S. M. (1995). Elaboration as a determinant of attitude strength: Creating attitudes that are persistent, resistant, and predictive of behavior. In R. E. Petty & J. A. Krosnick (Eds.), *Attitude strength: Antecedents and consequences* (pp. 93–130). Mahwah, NJ: Lawrence Erlbaum Associates.

Petty, R. E., Schumann, D. W., Richman, S. A., & Strathman, A. J. (1993). Positive mood and persuasion: Different roles for affect under high- and low-elaboration conditions. *Journal of Personality and Social Psychology, 64*, 5–20.

Petty, R. E., & Wegener, D. T. (1991). Thought systems, argument quality, and persuasion. In R. S. Wyer & T. K. Srull (Eds.), *Advances in social cognition, Vol. 4* (pp. 143–161). Hillsdale, NJ: Lawrence Erlbaum Associates.

Petty, R. E., & Wegener, D. T. (1993). Flexible correction processes in social judgment: Correcting for context-induced contrast. *Journal of Experimental Social Psychology, 29*, 137–165.

Petty, R. E, & Wegener, D. T. (1998). Attitude change: Multiple roles for persuasion variables. In D. T. Gilbert, S. T. Fiske, & G. Lindzey (Eds.), *The handbook of social psychology, 4th ed., Vol. 1* (pp. 323–390). New York: McGraw-Hill.

Petty, R. E., & Wegener, D. T. (1999). The elaboration likelihood model: Current status and controversies. In S. Chaiken, & Y. Trope (Eds.), *Dual-process theories in social psychology* (pp. 41–72). New York: Guilford Press.

Petty, R. E., Wegener, D. T., & White, P. (1998). Flexible correction processes in social judgment: Implications for persuasion. *Social Cognition, 16*, 93–113.

Petty, R. E., Wells, G. L., & Brock, T. C. (1976). Distraction can enhance or reduce yielding to propaganda: Thought disruption versus effort justification. *Journal of Personality and Social Psychology, 34*, 874–884.

Petty, R. E., Wells, G. L., Heesacker, M., Brock, T., & Cacioppo, J. T. (1983). The effects of recipient posture on persuasion: A cognitive response analysis. *Personality and Social Psychology Bulletin, 9*, 209–222.

Priester, J. R., Cacioppo, J. T., & Petty, R. E. (1996). The influence of motor processes on attitudes toward novel versus familiar semantic stimuli. *Personality & Social Psychology Bulletin, 22*, 442–447.

Razran, G. H. S. (1940). Conditioned response changes in rating and appraising sociopolitical slogans. *Psychological Bulletin, 37*, 481.

Rippetoe, P. A., & Rogers, R. W. (1987). Effects of components of protection–motivation theory on adaptive and maladaptive coping with a health threat. *Journal of Personality and Social Psychology, 52*, 596–604.

Rogers, R. W. (1975). A protection motivation theory of fear appeals and attitude change. *Journal of Psychology, 91*, 93–114.

Rogers, R. W. (1983). Cognitive and physiological processes in fear appeals and attitude change: A revised theory of protection motivation. In J. T. Cacioppo & R. E. Petty (Eds.), *Social psychophysiology: A sourcebook* (pp. 153–176). New York: Guilford Press.

Rogers, R. W., & Mewborn, C. R. (1976). Fear appeals and attitude change: Effects of a threat's noxiousness, probability of occurrence, and the efficacy of coping responses. *Journal of Personality and Social Psychology, 34*, 54–61.

Rosenberg, M. J., & Hovland, C. I. (1960). Cognitive, affective, and behavioral components of attitudes. In C. I. Hovland & M. J. Rosenberg (Eds.), *Attitude organization and change: An analysis of consistency among attitude components* (pp. 1–14). New Haven, CT: Yale University Press.

Schwarz, N. (1990). Feelings as information: Informational and motivational functions of affective states. In R. M. Sorrentino & E. T. Higgins (Eds.), *Handbook of motivation and cognition: Foundations of social behavior, Vol. 2* (pp. 527–561). New York: Guilford.

Schwarz, N., Bless, H., & Bohner, G. (1991). Mood and persuasion: Affective states influence processing of persuasive communications. In M. P. Zanna (Ed.), *Advances in experimental social psychology, Vol. 24* (pp. 161–199). New York: Academic Press.

Schwarz, N., & Clore, G. L. (1983). Mood, misattribution, and judgments of well-being: Informative and directive functions of affective states. *Journal of Personality and Social Psychology, 45*, 512–523.

Schwarz, N., & Clore, G. L. (1988). How do I feel about it? Informative functions of affective states. In K. Fiedler & J. Forgas (Eds.), *Affect, cognition, and social behavior* (pp. 44–62). Gottingen, Germany: Hogrefe.

Schwarz, N., & Clore, G. L. (1996). Feelings and phenomenal experiences. In E. T. Higgins & A. W. Kruglanski (Eds.), *Social psychology: Handbook of basic principles* (pp. 433–465). New York: Guilford Press.

Sinclair, R. C., Mark, M. M., & Clore, G. L. (1994). Mood related persuasion dependson (mis)attributions. *Social Cognition, 12*, 309–326.

Smith, E. R. (1996). What do connectionism and social psychology offer each other? *Journal of Personality and Social Psychology, 70*, 893–912.

Smith, M. B. (1947). The personal setting of public opinions: A study of attitudes toward Russia. *Public Opinion Quarterly, 11*, 507–523.

Srull, T. K. (1983). The role of prior knowledge in the acquisition, retention, and use of new information. *Advances in Consumer Research, 10*, 572–576.

Staats, A. W., & Staats, C. K. (1958). Attitudes established by classical conditioning. *Journal of Abnormal and Social Psychology, 57*, 37–40.

Stangor, C., Sullivan, L. A., & Ford, T. E. (1991). Affective and cognitive determinants of prejudice. *Social Cognition, 9*, 359–380.

Sutton, S. R. (1982). Fear-arousing communications: A critical examination of theory and research. In J. R. Eiser (Ed.), *Social psychology and behavioral medicine* (pp. 303–337). Chichester, England: Wiley.

Wegener, D. T., & Petty, R. E. (1994). Mood-management across affective states: The hedonic contingency hypothesis. *Journal of Personality and Social Psychology, 66*, 1034–1048.

Wegener, D. T., & Petty, R. E. (1996). Effects of mood on persuasion processes: Enhancing, reducing, and biasing scrutiny of attitude-relevant information. In L. L. Martin & A. Tesser (Eds.), *Striving and feeling: Interactions among goals, affect, and self-regulation* (pp. 329–362). Mahwah, NJ: Lawrence Erlbaum Associates.

Wegener, D. T., & Petty, R. E. (1997). The flexible correction model: The role of naïve theories of bias in bias correction. In M. P. Zanna (Ed.), *Advances in experimental social psychology, Vol. 29* (pp. 141–208). New York: Academic Press.

Wegener, D. T., Petty, R. E., & Klein, D. J. (1994) Effects of mood on high elaboration attitude change: The mediating role of likelihood judgments. *European Journal of Social Psychology, 24*, 25–43.

Wegener, D. T., Petty, R. E., & Smith, S. M. (1995). Positive mood can increase or decrease message scrutiny: The hedonic contingency view of mood and message processing. *Journal of Personality and Social Psychology, 69,* 5–15.

Weiss, W., & Fine, B. J. (1956). The effect of induced aggressiveness on opinion change. *Journal of Abnormal and Social Psychology, 52,* 109–114.

Witte, K. (1992). Putting the fear back into fear appeals: The extended parallel process model. *Communication Monographs, 59,* 329–349.

Worth, L. T., & Mackie, D. M. (1987). Cognitive mediation of positive affect in persuasion. *Social Cognition, 5,* 76–94.

Zajonc, R. B., & Markus, H. (1982). Affective and cognitive factors in preferences. *Journal of Consumer Research, 9,* 123–131.

Zanna, M. P., & Cooper, J. (1974). Dissonance and the pill: An attribution approach to studying the arousal properties of dissonance. *Journal of Personality and Social Psychology, 29,* 703–709.

Zanna, M. P., Kiesler, C. A., & Pilkonis, P. A. (1970). Positive and negative attitudinal affect established by classical conditioning. *Journal of Personality and Social Psychology, 14,* 321–328.

Zanna, M. P., & Rempel, J. K. (1988). Attitudes: A new look at an old concept. In D. Bar-Tal & A. W. Kruglanski (Eds.), *The social psychology of knowledge* (pp. 315–334). Cambridge, England: Cambridge University Press.

Zillmann, D. (1983). Transfer of excitation in emotional behavior. In J. T. Cacioppo & R. E. Petty (Eds.), *Social psychophysiology: A sourcebook* (pp. 153–176). New York: Guilford Press.

IV

Affective Influences on Motivation and Intentions

11

The Role of Affect in Cognitive-Dissonance Processes

Eddie Harmon-Jones
University of Wisconsin—Madison

Overview of the Theory of Cognitive Dissonance — 238
  Research Paradigms — 239
  Role of Negative Affect — 240
A Conceptualization of Why Dissonance Produces Negative Affect — 240
Cognitive Discrepancy as an Antecedent of Negative Affect — 241
  Dissonance and Physiological Responses — 241
  Dissonance and Self-Reported Negative Affect — 242
  Using Assessments of Negative Affect to Understand
      the Motivation Underlying Dissonance Reduction — 242
  Critical Evaluation — 244
On the Causal Relation Between Dissonance, Affect,
    and Discrepancy Reduction — 245
  The Relation of Dissonance-Produced Affect to Discrepancy Reduction — 245
  Dissonance and Misattribution of Affect — 247
  Independent Sources of Affect and Discrepancy Reduction — 249
Affective Consequences of Cognitive-Discrepancy Reduction — 250
  Does Discrepancy Reduction Decrease Physiological Responses? — 251

Address for correspondence: Eddie Harmon-Jones, University of Wisconsin—Madison, Department of Psychology, 1202 West Johnson Street, Madison, WI 53706, USA. Email: eharmonj@facstaff.wisc.edu

Does Discrepancy Reduction Decrease Negative Affect?   251
Resolving Discrepant Findings for Physiological Responses
    and Reported Affect   252
Summary and Conclusions   252
Acknowledgments   252
References   253

The theory of cognitive dissonance is based on the idea that inconsistency between elements of knowledge (cognitions) leads to a negative affective state that can motivate changes in elements of knowledge. The theory has generated considerable research aimed at better understanding, explaining, and predicting the formation and change of values, beliefs, attitudes, motivations, emotions, and behaviors. For instance, research derived from the theory has shown that dissonance processes can reduce hunger motivation, pain, and body weight; that dissonance processes can cause the internalization of values and the change of attitudes and beliefs about oneself; that dissonance processes can affect health behavior; and that dissonance processes can cause the formation and maintenance of religious beliefs (for reviews, see Beauvois & Joule, 1996; Harmon-Jones & Mills, 1999; Wicklund & Brehm, 1976; Zimbardo, 1969).

The cause of these important outcomes was, to the best of our knowledge, the result of dissonance, a motivational/emotional state aroused by the discrepancy between cognitions. Indeed, research has pointed to the importance of the emotive state of dissonance in determining cognitive and behavioral change. The bulk of the research on dissonance has focused on outcome variables of cognitive and behavioral change. However, some research has critically focused on determining the nature of this emotive state and how this state produces the cognitive and behavioral changes. In this chapter, research on the role of affect in dissonance processes is critically reviewed.

OVERVIEW OF THE THEORY
OF COGNITIVE DISSONANCE

The original statement of cognitive dissonance theory held that cognitive dissonance motivates individuals to attempt to reduce or eliminate the discrepancies between elements of knowledge or cognitions (Festinger, 1957). According to the theory, cognitions can be psychologically relevant or irrelevant to each other. If they are relevant to each other, they can exist in a relation of consonance, in which one cognition logically or psychologically follows from the other; or they can exist in a relation of dissonance, in which one cognition does not logically or psychologically follow from the other. The magnitude of dissonance aroused in regard to a particular cognition is a function of the number and importance of cognitions dissonant and consonant with this cognition. Cognitive dissonance can be reduced by adding consonant cognitions, subtracting dissonant cognitions, reducing the importance of dissonant cognitions, increasing the importance of consonant cognitions, or by using some combination of these routes. These modes of dissonance reduction may manifest themselves in attitude, belief, value, or behavior change. Dissonance reduction will typically be aimed at altering the cognition least resistant to change (see Harmon-Jones, 2000a, for a review).

Research Paradigms

In research paradigms used to test dissonance theory, the availability of the cognitions that serve to make the entire set of relevant cognitions more or less discrepant is manipulated. In the induced compliance paradigm, participants are induced to act contrary to an attitude, and if they are provided few consonant cognitions (few reasons or little justification) for doing so, they experience dissonance and reduce it, usually by changing their attitude to be more consistent with their behavior. For example, Festinger and Carlsmith (1959) found that participants given little justification for telling another "participant" that boring tasks were interesting later evaluated the tasks as more interesting than did participants given much justification for saying this counterattitudinal statement. In later research, dissonance was manipulated using perceived choice, assuming that having low choice to behave counterattitudinally is consonant with that behavior, whereas having high choice is not. These experiments found that participants who were given high choice, as opposed to low choice, to produce counterattitudinal statements changed their attitudes to be more consistent with their behavior (Brehm & Cohen, 1962).

In the free-choice paradigm, dissonance is aroused following a decision. Dissonance increases as the number and importance of the positive aspects of the rejected alternative and the negative aspects of the chosen alternative increase, because these cognitions are inconsistent with the decision. Similarly, dissonance decreases as the number and importance of the positive aspects of the chosen alternative and negative aspects of the rejected alternative increase, because these cognitions are consistent with the decision. To reduce dissonance, individuals may enhance the value of the chosen alternative and reduce the value of the rejected alternative (Brehm, 1956).

In the belief-disconfirmation paradigm, dissonance occurs when individuals' important and highly resistant-to-change beliefs are disconfirmed or contradicted by an external source. Individuals exposed to belief-disconfirming information may react to the dissonance by intensifying their beliefs (Festinger, Riecken, & Schachter, 1956).

Role of Negative Affect

Although the original theory of dissonance presumed negative affect to be the mediator of dissonance effects, relatively little research examined this presumption. In fact, not one of the previously mentioned classic studies included a measure of negative affect. The research that has attempted to provide this mediational evidence is reviewed. A review of this research not only assists in better understanding dissonance processes, but also assists in understanding the cognitive antecedents of motivation and affect, and how motivation and affect produce cognitive and behavioral changes.

A CONCEPTUALIZATION OF WHY DISSONANCE PRODUCES NEGATIVE AFFECT

Cognitive discrepancy may create negative affect in individuals because discrepancy among cognitions undermines the requirement for effective action. When perceptions about the environment or about oneself are dissonant, decisions cannot be implemented, and protective or facilitative action may be impeded (Harmon-Jones, 1999a, 2000a; Harmon-Jones et al., 1996; Jones & Gerard, 1967).[1]

According to this action-based model, the *proximal* motivation to reduce cognitive discrepancy stems from the need to reduce negative affect, whereas the *distal motivation* to reduce discrepancy stems from the requirement for effective action. When the maintenance of clear and certain

---

[1]Consistent with the action-based view, Festinger (1957) did note that cognition did more or less map reality, and that "it would be unlikely that an organism could live and survive if the elements of cognition were not to a large extent a veridical map of reality" (p. 10). When the "cognitions do not correspond with a certain reality which impinges, certain [dissonance reducing] pressures exist" (p. 11).

knowledge and thus the potential for effective action is threatened, negative affect results, which prompts attempts at the restoration of cognitions supportive of the action (i.e., cognitive discrepancy reduction). Therefore, the process of reducing dissonance is a motivated processing strategy that is guided by two goals—the need to reduce negative affect and the need to behave effectively. The motivation can lead persons to engage in information processing that may accomplish the goal of reducing negative affect and/or behaving effectively.

This view of dissonance fits with views of emotion that posit that emotional states serve adaptive functions. Following Darwin (1872), emotion scientists (e.g., Frijda, 1986; Izard, 1977) suggest that emotions serve the function of increasing chances of individual survival by organizing, motivating, and sustaining behavior in response to significant events. The emotion associated with dissonance may serve the function of motivating cognitive and behavioral changes that assist with the execution of effective behavior.

COGNITIVE DISCREPANCY AS AN ANTECEDENT OF NEGATIVE AFFECT

Does cognitive discrepancy cause increased negative affect? Most scientists working with dissonance theory assume that the cognitive and behavioral outcomes are the result of the motivation to reduce the uncomfortable dissonance. Research has tested the idea that cognitive discrepancy causes "arousal" by assessing physiological arousal, because Brehm and Cohen (1962) characterized dissonance as a drive state that is "tied to specific arousal" (p. 227). Other research has tested the idea that discrepancy causes increases in psychological discomfort (i.e., self-reported negative affect), because Festinger (1957) proposed that dissonance was "psychologically uncomfortable" (p. 3).

Dissonance and Physiological Responses

To provide direct evidence that cognitive discrepancy increased arousal, researchers have conducted experiments to assess whether discrepancy produces increased sympathetic nervous system activity. For instance, Elkin and Leippe (1986) found that participants who wrote counterattitudinal essays under high choice evidenced heightened electrodermal activity (which is associated with activation of sympathetic nervous system) in the minutes immediately following essay writing and changed their attitudes to align them with their behavior, whereas low-choice participants did not.

Dissonance and Self-Reported Negative Affect

Other research has demonstrated that individuals actually experience negative affect in response to cognitive discrepancy (e.g., Russell & Jones, 1980; Shaffer, 1975; Zanna & Cooper, 1974). Elliot and Devine (1994) noted that previous research had often assessed dissonance affect after participants had been given the opportunity to change their attitudes, used a conceptually or psychometrically unsound indicator of dissonance, and used methods that confounded dissonance with other causes of negative affect.

In their induced compliance experiment, Elliot and Devine (1994) found that participants who were given high choice to write a counterattitudinal essay reported more discomfort (uncomfortable, uneasy, bothered) than proattitudinal condition participants and baseline-condition participants, who completed the affect measure before being given low choice to write the counterattitudinal essay. High-choice participants also evidenced more attitude change than did other participants. No differences emerged between conditions in negative affect related to the self (disappointed with self, annoyed with self, guilty, self-critical) or in positive affect (good, happy, optimistic, friendly). Later research found that when persons are given high choice to act contrary to an extremely important attitude, they show increased reported negative affect but do not change their attitudes (reported in Devine, Tauer, Barron, Elliot, & Vance, 1999).

Using Assessments of Negative Affect to Understand the Motivation Underlying Dissonance Reduction

One of the most important questions for dissonance theory concerns the motivation underlying dissonance-produced cognitive and behavioral changes. Several revisions to the original theory have been proposed, and each of these proposes a different motivation as the source of dissonance effects (Harmon-Jones & Mills, 1999).

One of the most noted revisions of the original theory proposed that cognitive discrepancy was neither necessary nor sufficient to produce dissonance. Instead, this revision proposed that dissonance effects (e.g., attitude change) would emerge only when individuals felt personally responsible for producing foreseeable negative consequences (Cooper & Fazio, 1984). In this model, cognitive changes, such as attitude change, result because persons are motivated to render the consequences of their behavior non-aversive.

Using the paradigm in which most dissonance research has been conducted—the induced compliance paradigm—Harmon-Jones et al. (1996) found evidence that challenged the aversive consequences revision of dissonance theory. In three experiments, participants were given low or high choice to write counterattitudinal statements in private and with anonymity, and participants discarded the statements after they were written. Only high-choice participants showed dissonance-related attitude change. The participants did not cause an aversive consequence because, as Cooper and Fazio (1984) argued, "making a statement contrary to one's attitude while in solitude does not have the potential for bringing about an aversive event" (p. 232).

Using procedures similar to those used by Harmon-Jones et al. (1996), it was also found that participants given high choice to engage in the counterattitudinal behavior reported experiencing more negative affect (but not less positive affect) and changed their attitudes more than did participants given low choice to engage in the same behavior. A second experiment replicated these results using a different attitudinal object (Harmon-Jones, in press).

The results of these experiments cogently demonstrate that dissonance is associated with increased feelings of negative affect even in situations void of aversive consequences. Moreover, in the second experiment, it was found that writing the counterattitudinal statement did not significantly decrease state self-esteem. This finding does not conform to predictions derived from models of dissonance theory, which predict that " 'choosing' to write an essay against one's beliefs—makes one feel foolish, raises doubts about one's competence" (Steele, 1988, p. 278). These experiments strongly suggest that cognitive discrepancy per se can cause negative affect.

However, the finding on state self-esteem should not be interpreted to reflect that discrepancy never reduces state self-esteem, because Harmon-Jones (1999b) found state self-esteem to differ as a function of the magnitude of dissonance aroused in a free-choice paradigm. Whether dissonance decreases self-esteem probably depends on the cognitions involved in evoking the dissonance. If higher-order cognitions such as beliefs about one's own morality or competence are highly accessible and inconsistent with other cognitions, then self-esteem may temporarily decrease.

It is also possible that trait self-esteem may moderate responses to cognitive discrepancy. Indeed, research testing other theories has suggested that affective and cognitive responses are moderated by trait self-esteem, with high self-esteem persons being less affected by negative-affect inductions (e.g., Harmon-Jones et al., 1997) and being more able to regulate their affective states (e.g., Forgas & Ciarrochi, 1998). Theories of cognitive dissonance also posit that trait self-esteem should moderate responses to cognitive dissonance. Self-consistency theory (Aronson, 1969) predicts that high self-esteem persons should be more responsive than low self-esteem persons, whereas self-affirmation theory (Steele, 1988) predicts that low self-esteem persons should be more responsive than high self-esteem persons. Self-consistency derives its predictions from the idea that high self-esteem persons have higher standards for behavior than low self-esteem persons, and thus differences in the size of the cognitive discrepancy between high and low self-esteem persons should lead to more responsiveness by high self-esteem persons. In contrast, self-affirmation theory derives its predictions from the idea that self-esteem should serve as a buffer against the negative affect of dissonance, and thus high self-esteem persons should be better protected against the negative affect. Research supports predictions derived from each theory, and attempts at reconciliation have been proposed (Harmon-Jones, 2000b; Stone, 1999). Importantly, in the past research on these issues, it was assumed that the amount of dissonance affect, which was never measured, would directly relate to the amount of measured cognitive change, but as is discussed in following sections, this assumption is probably unwarranted.

Critical Evaluation

In the experiments by Elliot and Devine (1994) and Harmon-Jones (in press), reported positive affect was not found to decrease following counterattitudinal behavior. These results are consistent with other research that suggests positive and negative affect may, under some circumstances, be aroused independently (for a review, see Cacioppo & Gardner, 1999; Ito & Cacioppo, Chap. 3, this volume).

The research suggests that cognitive discrepancy causes an arousing and negatively valenced state. However, dissonance aroused by discrepancies between certain types of cognitive clusters may evoke specific types of negative affect. For instance, fear or anxiety may occur in response to belief disconfirmation, whereas regret may occur in response to a difficult decision. Indeed, research derived from self-discrepancy theory has demonstrated that individuals' perceived discrepancies between actual self-beliefs ("Who am I?") and two different self-guides evoke qualitatively distinct affective reactions. When persons experience a discrepancy between their actual self and their ought self-guide, which concerns their duties and obligations, they evidence agitation-related affects, such as anxiety. In contrast, when persons experience a discrepancy between their actual self and their ideal-self guide, which concerns their aspirations, they evidence dejection-related affects, such as depression (Higgins, 1989).

ON THE CAUSAL RELATION BETWEEN DISSONANCE, AFFECT, AND DISCREPANCY REDUCTION

According to the theory of cognitive dissonance, individuals are motivated to reduce discrepancies because of the psychological discomfort the discrepancies produce. Research assessing the correlation between indices of negative affect in response to discrepancy and discrepancy reduction and research using the misattribution paradigm have tested this hypothesis.

The Relation of Dissonance-Produced Affect to Discrepancy Reduction

In an induced-compliance experiment, Zanna and Cooper (1974) found a positive relation between discrepancy-produced negative affect (reported tension) and attitude change in the high-dissonance condition. However, Wixon and Laird (1976); Gaes, Melburg, and Tedeschi (1986); Elliot and Devine (1994); and Higgins, Rhodewalt, and Zanna (1979) assessed discrepancy-produced negative affect in induced-compliance paradigms and failed to find evidence or report evidence of a positive relation between attitude change and discrepancy-produced negative affect. The research assessing electrodermal activity has also failed to demonstrate consistent linear relationships between electrodermal activity and attitude change (Elkin & Leippe, 1986; Harmon-Jones et al., 1996; Losch & Cacioppo, 1990). Thus, these correlational results are ambiguous as to whether dissonance-related negative affect causes increases in discrepancy reduction.

Methodologic problems may account for this lack of a linear relation between measures of negative affect and attitude change. For instance, Wixon and Laird (1976) and Gaes et al. (1986) intended to assess dissonance-produced affect, but they measured self-reported negative affect after attitude change had occurred. Assessing negative affect after discrepancy reduction might yield less valid and reliable assessments because negative affect may decrease following discrepancy reduction. In addition, in several experiments, the lack of a pretest measure of attitude did not allow for a precise measure of attitude change, which might have attenuated the correlation between negative affect and discrepancy reduction.

In addition, there may be theoretical explanations for the lack of a linear relation between negative affect and attitude change. In fact, in the experiments examining the relation between affect and discrepancy reduction, only one measure of discrepancy reduction was assessed. However, as has been argued (e.g., Harmon-Jones, 2000a), when high levels of negative affect do not lead to increased attitude change, the attitude may be more resistant to change than the behavior. As a result, cognitive discrepancy may be reduced not by attitude change, but by maintenance or intensification of the original attitude, active forgetting of the discrepancy, reducing the commitment to the behavior, or reducing the importance of the behavior. Some induced-compliance research has found that persons for whom an attitude was extremely important reported increased negative affect, but did not change their attitudes (reported in Devine et al., 1999).

The lack of significant linear relations between reported negative affect and attitude change may be the result of other forces. For instance, discrepancy reduction may not occur and persons may simply live with the negative affect. Moreover, individuals may differ in their tolerance for dissonance (Festinger, 1957), and these individual differences may complicate relations between indices of dissonance and discrepancy reduction. Finally, as the experience of affect increases, so may awareness of affect, and once awareness of affect is increased, efforts at discrepancy reduction may not occur. This interpretation would fit with an interpretation advanced by Pyszczynski, Greenberg, Solomon, Sideris, and Stubing (1993), who hypothesized that expressing the negative affect associated with dissonance would reduce dissonance-related attitude change. They suggested that the negative affect associated with dissonance may not be available to conscious awareness, and that discrepancy reduction occurs to keep this negative affect out of consciousness. Furthermore, they suggested that if the dissonance affect were to appear in consciousness, persons would be less likely to engage in discrepancy reduction because "it may simply be too late for the defensive maneuver to fulfill its function," or "the individual may realize that he or she can tolerate such feelings" (p. 178). Results from their induced compliance experiment supported their analysis by showing that participants encouraged to express any emotions that resulted from writing the counterattitudinal essay changed their attitudes less than participants encouraged to suppress their emotions. Although several experiments provide evidence that persons have sufficient awareness of their negative affect to be able to report it, the level of awareness of the negative affect may relate directly to the intensity of the negative affect, so that persons who experience more negative affect may be more aware of it. This increased awareness of the dissonance-related negative affect may then decrease the discrepancy reduction.

Past research on dissonance in individuals high in the trait of repression is consistent with the research of Pyszczynski et al. (1993). For instance, Zanna and Aziza (1976) found that repressors evidenced more attitude change than sensitizers in a typical induced-compliance setting (see also Olson & Zanna, 1979). Research in other domains also supports the idea that once an affective state becomes the focus of conscious attention, its effects on cognition and behavior often diminish or disappear (Berkowitz, 1993; Forgas, 1995; Schwarz & Clore, 1983). It is important to note, however, that the dissonance effects may differ from these other effects in that with these other effects, persons are assumed to be aware that their affective states might infuse their judgments and behaviors, whereas with dissonance, persons are probably not aware that cognitive discrepancy would lead to cognitive changes (Nisbett & Wilson, 1977).

Dissonance and Misattribution of Affect

Research using the misattribution paradigm has addressed whether discrepancy reduction is motivated by the need to reduce negative affect. In the misattribution paradigm, participants are provided a stimulus (e.g., a placebo) that is said to cause specific side effects. Following Schachter and Singer (1962), researchers using this methodology assume that individuals may mistakenly attribute their dissonance arousal to this other source. Moreover, it is assumed that the individual makes this "misattribution" to the other source only when the side effects of the other source are similar to the state produced by dissonance. The nature of the internal state can then be inferred indirectly by determining the type of stimuli to which individuals misattribute the state aroused by dissonance. In the misattribution paradigm, participants are exposed to treatments that will or will not arouse dissonance, and then they are either provided or not provided a possible external cause for their experienced state.

Losch and Cacioppo (1990) used a misattribution source, prism goggles, that had been found to be novel, affectively malleable, and affectively neutral to assess the effects of positive and negative hedonic states on discrepancy reduction. Participants were told that the goggles would have the delayed effect of making them feel pleasantly excited or tense. Participants were then given high or low choice to write counterattitudinal essays. If discrepancy causes participants to feel tense, and participants change their attitudes to reduce this tension, then participants who believed the goggles would cause them to feel tense and who chose to write the counterattitudinal essay would misattribute the internal state induced by dissonance to the goggles, and consequently, they would not change their attitudes. However, attitude change should occur when participants believed that the goggles would cause them to feel pleasantly excited, because of the mismatch between the tension of dissonance and the pleasant excitement. Results supported these predictions. In addition, more electrodermal activity occurred in the high-choice than in the low-choice condition in the period after participants agreed to write the essay. This effect occurred regardless of misattribution cue. These results indicated that although the discrepancy produced heightened sympathetic activity, individuals engaged in discrepancy reduction to reduce the unpleasant state rather than to reduce undifferentiated arousal. Earlier experiments were consistent with the results of Losch and Cacioppo (1990), although in these earlier experiments, it was not clear whether dissonance was an undifferentiated arousal state that could be misattributed to positive stimuli (see reviews by Fazio & Cooper, 1983; Zanna & Cooper, 1976). The research by Losch and Cacioppo (1990) effectively addresses this question.

The research using the misattribution paradigm has provided cogent evidence that indicates that cognitive discrepancy reduction is motivated by negative affect. This research also suggests that the source of the negative affect produced by dissonance may not be well known to individuals experiencing it (at least in some cases) because in order for misattribution to occur, individuals should not know the source of their affect. Because the negative affect produced by discrepancy may have an unknown source, it may be misattributed or misapplied to other unpleasant or neutral stimuli. For instance, the affect associated with dissonance may be able to infuse other judgments and decisions not related to the dissonance-arousing event (Forgas, 1995). This would suggest that the affect associated with dissonance could cause affect infusion as well as affect control or motivated processing. In other words, the cognitive-discrepancy reduction evidence suggests that dissonance causes motivated processing, but no prior research has directly tested the idea that dissonance leads to affect infusion. In addition to the task, person, and situation factors that Forgas and colleagues (e.g., Forgas, Johnson, & Ciarrochi, 1998) suggest as being critical in determining whether affect control or affect infusion will occur, the ease of reducing the cognitive discrepancy may be a determinant.

Independent Sources of Affect and Discrepancy Reduction

If individuals reduce cognitive discrepancies because of the negative affect that discrepancies produce, alleviating negative affect that results from cognitive discrepancies in a manner other than the reduction of the discrepancies might reduce the motivation to reduce the discrepancies. Similarly, enhancing negative affect produced by cognitive discrepancies might enhance the motivation to reduce the discrepancies.

Modulation of Affect. Support for the idea that affect unrelated to dissonance can alter discrepancy reduction comes from an experiment by Rhodewalt and Comer (1979). In their experiment, participants wrote counterattitudinal statements while altering their facial expressions to form either a smile, frown, or neutral expression, which caused positive affect, negative affect, and neutral affect, respectively. Frowning and neutral expression participants changed their attitudes to align them with their behavior, whereas smiling participants did not. Moreover, frowning participants changed their attitudes more than did neutral expression participants. By showing that increased positive affect decreases discrepancy reduction and that increased negative affect increases discrepancy reduction, these findings support the hypothesis that discrepancy reduction is motivated by the need to reduce negative affect.[2]

Additional research on whether affect influences discrepancy reduction comes from experiments by Steele, Southwick, and Critchlow (1981), who found drinking alcohol eliminated discrepancy reduction, and by Kidd and Berkowitz (1976), who found that a positive mood induced by a humorous audio tape eliminated cognitive-discrepancy reduction.

---

[2]However, as Rhodewalt and Comer (1979) suggested, as compared with persons in the neutral expression condition, persons in the frown condition may have felt more committed to their counterattitudinal behavior, whereas persons in the smile condition may have felt less committed to their behavior. These differences in commitment to the behavior rather than the affective state may have caused the differences in cognitive-discrepancy reduction.

In addition, research on self-affirmation theory suggests that when persons reflect on an important self-relevant value unrelated to the dissonance-arousing event, they do not show cognitive-discrepancy reduction (Steele, 1988). Tesser and Cornell (1991) suggest that self-affirmations have this effect because self-affirmations decrease the negative affect associated with dissonance.

How Does Modulation of Affect Alter Discrepancy Reduction? The process by which independently increasing negative affect increases discrepancy reduction and independently increasing positive affect decreases discrepancy reduction is not yet understood. Increased negative affect may cause individuals to experience increased dissonance, which then causes the increased discrepancy reduction. The increased negative affect may cause individuals to be less tolerant of discrepancy, may decrease their ability to find routes other than the ones provided in the experiment to reduce the discrepancy, or may increase their attention to the dissonance or discrepancy. In contrast, increased positive affect may cause individuals to experience decreased dissonance, which then causes the decreased discrepancy reduction. The increased positive affect may allow individuals to live with the dissonance or discrepancy, may provide individuals more cognitive flexibility (see review by Isen, 1993) that allows them to find other routes to discrepancy reduction, or may simply distract individuals from the dissonance or discrepancy. The exact process by which independent sources of affect modulate discrepancy reduction must be understood. However, manipulated affect from a source other than cognitive discrepancy should alter discrepancy reduction only to the extent that the affective state adds or subtracts from the dissonance affect. If persons attribute their dissonance arousal to the other source of negative affect, then persons may not change their attitudes.

AFFECTIVE CONSEQUENCES OF COGNITIVE-DISCREPANCY REDUCTION

Although much research has examined whether dissonance produces increased physiological responses and negative affect and whether this state motivates discrepancy reduction, relatively less research has examined whether the reduction of discrepancy actually decreases physiological responses or negative affect.

Does Discrepancy Reduction Decrease Physiological Responses?

Two experiments designed to assess whether discrepancy reduction decreases electrodermal activity failed to find such an effect (Elkin & Leippe, 1986). In their first induced compliance experiment, high-choice participants evidenced increased electrodermal activity in the 3-min period following the attitude change opportunity. Harmon-Jones et al. (1996) replicated the finding of high-choice participants showing greater electrodermal activity than low-choice participants following discrepancy reduction.

In Elkin and Leippe's (1986) second experiment, results indicated that electrodermal activity remained elevated for 6 min after the attitude-change opportunity. Interestingly, when participants were not given an attitude-change opportunity and were instead given a magazine to read, their electrodermal activity decreased. Thus, being given the opportunity to change attitudes did not reduce arousal, whereas not reporting attitudes did. The attitude-change opportunity may have brought the discrepancy back into focus and caused increased arousal, and participants in the no-attitude change opportunity condition may have simply forgotten the discrepancy and were less aroused as a result.

Does Discrepancy Reduction Decrease Negative Affect?

In the Elliot and Devine (1994) experiments, high-discrepancy participants reported heightened negative affect following writing a counterattitudinal essay, and lowered negative affect following the attitude change opportunity. In their experiments, a negative correlation resulted between negative affect that occurred following attitude change and attitude change, suggesting that the more participants changed their attitudes, the less negative affect they reported. Higgins et al. (1979) also found reduced negative affect following discrepancy reduction, but did not report correlations between negative affect and degree of discrepancy reduction.

Burris, Harmon-Jones, and Tarpley (1997) extended the research on the relation between discrepancy reduction and negative affect. In their first experiment, religious individuals' beliefs were disconfirmed, and then they were given an opportunity to reduce dissonance by adding consonant cognitions that would explain the disconfirmation. Results indicated that endorsement of higher levels of discrepancy reduction related to lower levels of experienced negative affect. A second experiment conceptually replicated these results by demonstrating that when religious participants completed religious belief measures after reading the dissonance-provoking article, dissonance-related negative affect decreased relative to two comparison conditions.

Resolving Discrepant Findings for Physiological Responses and Reported Affect

The results for electrodermal activity and reported negative affect following the discrepancy reduction opportunity are inconsistent with each other, especially if it is assumed that electrodermal activity reflects negative affect. However, the electrodermal activity aroused during dissonance may reflect efforts at suppression of the negative affect. Indeed, results from research concerned with suppression of emotion suggests that emotional suppression increases electrodermal activity (e.g., Pennebaker, 1990). Thus, the increased electrodermal activity may reflect the suppression of negative affect associated with dissonance. This interpretation would fit with the research that suggests that repression relates to more discrepancy reduction (Zanna & Aziza, 1976) and that emotional expression relates to less discrepancy reduction (Pyszczynski et al., 1993).

SUMMARY AND CONCLUSIONS

Research spanning almost 50 years has pointed to the importance of the affective state of dissonance in motivating cognitive and behavioral adjustments. A critical review of the evidence testing the largely presumed role of dissonance affect in guiding these adjustments was presented. The evidence suggests that dissonance affect is involved in the adjustment process, but the exact mechanism by which it accomplishes these effects has yet to be determined.

ACKNOWLEDGMENTS

I would like to thank Joe Forgas and Cindy Harmon-Jones for providing useful comments on drafts of this paper.

REFERENCES

Aronson, E. (1969). The theory of cognitive dissonance: A current perspective. In L. Berkowitz (Ed.), *Advances in experimental social psychology, Vol. 4* (pp. 1–34). New York: Academic Press.

Beauvois, J. L., & Joule, R. V. (1996). *A radical dissonance theory.* London: Taylor and Francis.

Berkowitz, L. (1993). Towards a general theory of anger and emotional aggression: Implications of the cognitive-neoassociationistic perspective for the analysis of anger and other emotions. In R. S. Wyer & T. K. Srull (Eds.), *Perspectives on anger and emotion: Advances in social cognition, Vol. VI.* Hillsdale, NJ: Lawrence Erlbaum Associates.

Brehm, J. W. (1956). Postdecision changes in the desirability of alternatives. Journal of *Abnormal and Social Psychology, 52,* 384–389.

Brehm, J. W., & Cohen, A. R. (1962). *Explorations in cognitive dissonance.* New York: Wiley.

Burris, C. T., Harmon-Jones, E., & Tarpley, W. R. (1997). "By faith alone": Religious agitation and cognitive dissonance. *Basic and Applied Social Psychology, 19,* 17–31.

Cacioppo, J. T., & Gardner, W. L. (1999). Emotion. *Annual Review of Psychology, 50,* 191–214.

Cooper, J., & Fazio, R. H. (1984). A new look at dissonance theory. In L. Berkowitz (Ed.), *Advances in experimental social psychology, Vol. 17* (pp. 229–264). Orlando, FL: Academic Press.

Darwin, C. (1965). *The expression of emotions in man and animals.* Chicago: University of Chicago Press. (Original work published in 1872.)

Devine, P. G., Tauer, J. M., Barron, K. E., Elliot, A. J., & Vance, K. M. (1999). Moving beyond attitude change in the study of dissonance-related processes. In E. Harmon-Jones & J. Mills (Eds.), *Cognitive dissonance: Progress on a pivotal theory in social psychology* (pp. 297–323). Washington, DC: American Psychological Association.

Elkin, R. A., & Leippe, M. R. (1986). Physiological arousal, dissonance, and attitude change: Evidence for a dissonance-arousal link and a "don't remind me" effect. *Journal of Personality and Social Psychology, 51,* 55–65.

Elliot, A. J., & Devine, P. G. (1994). On the motivational nature of cognitive dissonance: Dissonance as psychological discomfort. *Journal of Personality and Social Psychology, 67,* 382–394.

Fazio, R. H., & Cooper, J. (1983). Arousal in the dissonance process. In J. T. Cacioppo & R. E. Petty (Eds.), *Social psychophysiology: A sourcebook* (pp. 122–152). New York: Guilford Press.

Festinger, L. (1957). *A theory of cognitive dissonance.* Stanford, CA: Stanford University Press.

Festinger, L., & Carlsmith, J. M. (1959). Cognitive consequences of forced compliance. *Journal of Abnormal and Social Psychology, 58,* 203–210.

Festinger, L., Riecken, H. W., & Schachter, S. (1956). *When prophecy fails.* Minneapolis: University of Minnesota Press.

Forgas, J. P. (1995). Mood and judgment: The affect infusion model (AIM). *Psychological Bulletin, 117,* 39–66.

Forgas, J. P., & Ciarrochi, J. (1998). *Mood congruent and incongruent thoughts over time: The role of self-esteem in mood management efficacy.* Manuscript submitted for publication.

Forgas, J. P., Johnson, R., & Ciarrochi, J. (1998). Mood management: The role of processing strategies in affect control and affect infusion. In M. Kofta, G. Weary, & G. Sedek (Eds.), *Personal control in action: Cognitive and motivational mechanisms* (pp. 155–195). New York: Plenum Press.

Frijda, N. H. (1986). *The emotions.* Cambridge: Cambridge University Press.

Gaes, G. G., Melburg, V., & Tedeschi, J. T. (1986). A study examining the arousal properties of the forced compliance situation. *Journal of Experimental Social Psychology, 22,* 136–147.

Harmon-Jones, E. (1999a). Toward an understanding of the motivation underlying dissonance effects: Is the production of aversive consequences necessary? In E. Harmon-Jones & J. Mills (Eds.), *Cognitive dissonance: Progress on a pivotal theory in social psychology* (pp. 71–99). Washington, DC: American Psychological Association.

Harmon-Jones, E. (1999b). *State self-esteem and cognitive dissonance.* Manuscript in preparation.

Harmon-Jones, E. (2000a). A cognitive dissonance theory perspective on the role of emotion in the maintenance and change of beliefs and attitudes. In N. H. Frijda, A. R. S. Manstead, & S. Bem (Eds.), *The effects of emotions upon the formation and strength of beliefs* (pp. 185–211). Cambridge: Cambridge University Press.

Harmon-Jones, E. (2000b). An update on dissonance theory, with a focus on the self. In A. Tesser, R. Felson, & J. Suls (Eds.). *Psychological perspectives on self and identity* (pp. 119–144). Washington, DC: American Psychological Association.

Harmon-Jones, E. (in press). Dissonance and affect: Evidence that dissonance-related negative affect occurs in the absence of aversive consequences. *Personality and Social Psychology Bulletin.*

Harmon-Jones, E., Brehm, J. W., Greenberg, J., Simon, L., & Nelson, D. E. (1996). Evidence that the production of aversive consequences is not necessary to create cognitive dissonance. *Journal of Personality and Social Psychology, 70,* 5–16.

Harmon-Jones, E., & Mills, J. (1999). *Cognitive dissonance: Progress on a pivotal theory in social psychology.* Washington, DC: American Psychological Association.

Harmon-Jones, E., Simon, L., Greenberg, J., Pyszczynski, T., Solomon, S., & McGregor, H. (1997). Terror management and self-esteem: Evidence that self-esteem reduces mortality salience effects. *Journal of Personality and Social Psychology, 72,* 24–26.

Higgins, E. T. (1989). Self-discrepancy theory: What patterns of self-beliefs cause people to suffer? In L. Berkowitz (Ed.), *Advances in experimental social psychology, Vol. 22* (pp. 93–136). San Diego: Academic Press.

Higgins, E. T., Rhodewalt, F., & Zanna, M. P. (1979). Dissonance motivation: Its nature, persistence, and reinstatement. *Journal of Experimental Social Psychology, 15,* 16–34.

Isen, A. M. (1993). Positive affect and decision making. In M. Lewis & J. M. Haviland (Eds.), *Handbook of emotions* (pp. 261–278). New York: Guilford Press.

Izard, C. E. (1977). *Human emotions.* New York: Plenum Press.

Jones, E. E., & Gerard, H. B. (1967). *Foundations of social psychology.* New York. Wiley.

Kidd, R. F., & Berkowitz, L. (1976). Effect of dissonance arousal on helpfulness. *Journal of Personality and Social Psychology, 33,* 613–622.

Losch, M. E., & Cacioppo, J. T. (1990). Cognitive dissonance may enhance sympathetic tonus, but attitudes are changed to reduce negative affect rather than arousal. *Journal of Experimental Social Psychology, 26,* 289–304.

Nisbett, R. E., & Wilson, T. D. (1977). Telling more than we can know: Verbal reports on mental processes. *Psychological Review, 84,* 231–259.

Olson, J. M., & Zanna, M. P. (1979). A new look at selective exposure. *Journal of Experimental Social Psychology, 15,* 1–15.

Pennebaker, J. W. (1990). *Opening up: The healing power of confiding in others.* New York: William Morrow and Company.

Pyszczynski, T., Greenberg, J., Solomon, S., Sideris, J., & Stubing, M. J. (1993). Emotional expression and the reduction of motivated cognitive bias: Evidence from cognitive dissonance and distancing from victims' paradigms. *Journal of Personality and Social Psychology, 64,* 177–186.

Rhodewalt, F., & Comer, R. (1979). Induced-compliance attitude change: Once more with feeling. *Journal of Experimental Social Psychology, 15,* 35–47.

Russell, D., & Jones, W. H. (1980). When superstition fails: Reactions to disconfirmation of paranormal beliefs. *Personality and Social Psychology Bulletin, 6,* 83–88.

Schachter, S., & Singer, J. E. (1962). Cognitive, social, and physiological determinants of emotional states. *Psychological Review, 69,* 379–399.

Schwartz, N., & Clore, G. L. (1983). Mood, misattribution, and judgments of well-being: Informative and directive functions of affective states. *Journal of Personality and Social Psychology, 45,* 513–523.

Shaffer, D. R. (1975). Some effects of consonant and dissonant attitudinal advocacy on initial attitude salience and attitude change. *Journal of Personality and Social Psychology, 32,* 160–168.

Steele, C. M. (1988). The psychology of self-affirmation: Sustaining the integrity of the self. In L. Berkowitz (Ed.), *Advances in experimental social psychology, Vol. 21* (pp. 261–302). San Diego: Academic Press.

Steele, C. M., Southwick, L. L., & Critchlow, B. (1981). Dissonance and alcohol: Drinking your troubles away. *Journal of Personality and Social Psychology, 41*, 831–846.

Stone, J. A. (1999). What exactly have I done? The role of self-attribute accessibility in dissonance. In E. Harmon-Jones & J. Mills (Eds.), *Cognitive dissonance: Progress on a pivotal theory in social psychology* (pp. 175–200). Washington, DC: American Psychological Association.

Tesser, A., & Cornell, D. P. (1991). On the confluence of self processes. *Journal of Experimental Social Psychology, 27*, 501–526.

Wicklund, R. A., & Brehm, J. W. (1976). *Perspectives on cognitive dissonance*. Hillsdale, NJ: Lawrence Erlbaum Associates.

Wixon, D. R., & Laird, J. D. (1976). Awareness and attitude change in the forced compliance paradigm: The importance of when. *Journal of Personality and Social Psychology, 34*, 376–384.

Zanna, M. P., & Aziza, C. (1976). On the interaction of repression-sensitization and attention in resolving cognitive dissonance. *Journal of Personality, 44*, 577–593.

Zanna, M. P., & Cooper, J. (1974). Dissonance and the pill: An attribution approach to studying the arousal properties of dissonance. *Journal of Personality and Social Psychology, 29*, 703–709.

Zanna, M. P., & Cooper, J. (1976). Dissonance and the attribution process. In J. H. Harvey, W. J. Ickes, & R. F. Kidd (Eds.), *New directions in attribution research, Vol. 1*. Hillsdale, NJ: Lawrence Erlbaum Associates.

Zimbardo, P. G. (1969). *The cognitive control of motivation: The consequences of choice and dissonance*. Glenview: IL: Scott, Foresman and Company.

12

Mood as a Resource in Processing Self-Relevant Information

Yaacov Trope, Melissa Ferguson, and
Raj Raghunathan

New York University

Mood as a Resource in Overcoming Defensiveness	257
Mood-Incongruent Information Search	258
Self-Induced Positive Mood	261
Mood as a Resource and Mood as a Goal	262
Research on Mood as a Resource versus a Goal in Feedback-Seeking Behavior	263
Mood as a Resource versus a Goal in Processing Persuasive Messages	267
Mood-Incongruent Recall	267
Affective Consequences of Processing	268
Attitudes and Behavioral Intentions	269
Conclusions	270
References	272

The present chapter examines the role of mood in determining how people seek and process information about themselves. We argue that positive mood may serve as a resource for achieving accurate self-assessment or as

Address for correspondence: Yaacov Trope, Department of Psychology, 6 Washington Pl. 7th Fl., New York University, New York, NY 10003, USA. Email: trope@psych.nyu.edu a goal in and of itself. As a resource, positive mood leads people to seek and process positive as well as negative information about themselves. As a goal, positive mood leads people to focus on positive information about themselves. Whether positive mood serves as a resource or as a goal depends on the value of the information. When the information is highly diagnostic of an important self-attribute, mood serves as a resource, but when the information is of low diagnostic value or when it pertains to an unimportant self-attribute, positive mood serves as a goal. We describe a series of studies designed to test these ideas. These studies demonstrate that positive mood leads people to seek negative self-relevant feedback when this feedback has high informational value, but not when the feedback has low informational value. The first set of studies examines search of ability-related information, whereas the second set of studies examines processing of health-related information.

MOOD AS A RESOURCE
IN OVERCOMING DEFENSIVENESS

Situations that offer individuals self-relevant information often create a motivational conflict. On the one hand, such new information may help individuals assess their skills, personality traits, or health and guide their future choices and self-improvement attempts (Taylor, Wayment, & Carrillo, 1996; Trope, 1975, 1983, 1986; Trope & Neter, 1994). On the other hand, self-relevant information may uncover individuals' liabilities, threatening their self-esteem and sense of well-being (Brown, 1990; Brown & Dutton, 1995; Pyscyzynski & Greenberg, 1987; Steele, 1988; Tesser, 1988; Tesser, Martin, & Cornell, 1996). The motivational conflict is particularly likely to arise in situations in which the information focuses on individuals' weaknesses rather than their strengths (see Sedikides & Strube, 1997). Such situations pose a self-control dilemma. Individuals may want to attain the long-term assessment benefits of negative feedback regarding self-relevant attributes. That is, they may want to know what skills they need to improve, what kinds of tasks to choose or avoid, and how much effort and preparation to invest in the tasks they choose. At the same time, individuals may be deterred by the emotional costs of negative feedback. These costs involve negative esteem-related feelings such as shame, dejection, and disappointment (see Weiner, 1986; Higgins, 1987). Indeed, research on task choice has found that people expect diagnostic failure to improve the accuracy of their self-knowledge, but also to make them feel shameful and dejected. In contrast, people expect diagnostic success to promote their self-knowledge as well as feelings of pride and gratification (see Trope, 1979, 1980; Trope & Brickman, 1975).

Thus, the decision to accept negative feedback that is diagnostic of self- relevant attributes entails a trade-off between long-term information gain and immediate emotional costs (Crocker & Major, 1989; Taylor, Wayment, & Carrillo, 1996). As argued by Trope (1986), this motivational conflict may be viewed as an instance of a general class of self-control dilemmas in which immediate emotional obstacles may prevent one from enacting a preferred course of action (see Carver & Scheier, 1990; Goll-witzer, 1990; Lazarus & Folkman, 1984; Lowenstein & Thaller, 1989; Kuhl, 1984; Metcalf & Mischel, 1999; Mischel, 1974, 1984; Schelling, 1984). Trope and Neter (1994) further proposed that the relative impor-tance of emotional costs and informational benefits of feedback depends on the individuals' mood when they decide whether to accept new feed-back. Positive mood presumably serves as a resource in buffering against the affective costs of negative feedback and enabling individuals to focus on the informational implications of the feedback. The weight of long-term information gains relative to the weight of immediate affective costs in feedback seeking should therefore be greater when people are in a positive mood rather than in a negative mood. As a resource, positive mood should thus increase the likelihood of accepting mood-incongruent negative feed-back regarding self-relevant attributes (see Aspinwall, 1998; Aspinwall & Taylor, 1997; Reed & Aspinwall, 1998).

Mood-Incongruent Information Search

Trope and Neter (1994) conducted two studies that examined the impact of mood on the ways in which participants subsequently searched for feedback information. They predicted that participants would show more interest in negative (rather than positive) feedback when they are in a positive (vs. neutral or negative) mood. In the first study, participants completed a spatial abilities test and were told either that they performed very well (in the top 10% of the student distribution: success condition) or very poorly (in the bottom 30% of the student distribution: failure condition). Participants in the control condition completed a similarity judgment task and were not given any feedback about their performance. A manipulation check indicated that those participants who received positive feedback about their spatial abilities reported a positive mood compared to those in the control and negative feedback conditions. Those who received negative feedback

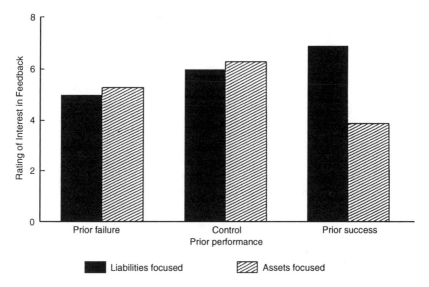

FIG. 12.1. Interest in assets-focused and liabilities-focused feedback as a function of prior outcomes on an unrelated task (Experiment 1).

reported being in a negative mood compared to those in the control and positive feedback conditions. All participants were then told that they would be taking a social sensitivity test, and were informed that detailed feedback about either their assets or liabilities in social sensitivity would be available on completion of the test. Participants were then asked to indicate which kind of feedback they would prefer.

As shown in Fig. 12.1, participants in the control and failure conditions preferred the feedback concerning their assets compared to the feedback concerning their liabilities. In contrast, those participants who had just received positive feedback concerning their spatial abilities significantly preferred feedback about their liabilities compared to their assets. These results seem to suggest that the positive experience of hearing about success acted as a buffer for participants, enabling them to handle the affective costs of listening to information concerning their weaknesses with regard to social sensitivity.

In the second study, positive or negative mood was induced by asking participants to recall prior life events. In the first part of the study, participants were asked to complete a social sensitivity test. In the second part, they were instructed to recall either positive or negative events from the past. Participants in the control condition were asked to complete a similarity judgment task. Then, in the third part of the study, participants were given feedback on the results of the social sensitivity test that they took in the first part of the experiment. They received positive feedback about some of the subscales of the test and negative feedback about the other subscales. They were then asked to indicate their interest in hearing more detailed and comprehensive feedback about each subscale. Trope and Neter predicted that those participants who had recalled positive life events would be more interested in negative feedback regarding their social sensitivity.

Participants who were asked to recall positive life events reported being in a more positive mood compared to participants in the control and negative life events conditions. Participants who recalled negative life events reported a more negative mood compared to participants in the control and positive life events conditions. As indicated in Fig.12.2, participants in the control condition and participants who recalled negative life events were more interested in positive (vs. negative) feedback about their social sensitivity. In contrast, participants who recalled positive life events were significantly more interested in negative (vs. positive) feedback. Similar to the results from the first study, participants who were in a positive mood were more likely to select information concerning their weaknesses rather than their strengths. The opposite pattern was found for participants who were

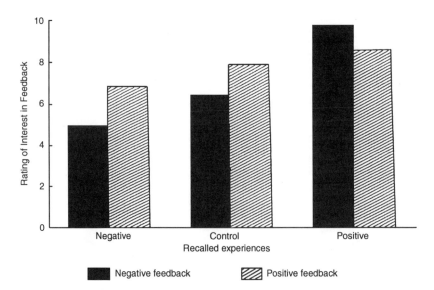

FIG. 12.2. Interest in detailed positive or negative feedback as a function of prior engagement in recall of positive or negative events (Experiment 2).

in the control condition or who were in a negative mood due to recalling negative experiences. Subsequent research by Trope and Pomerantz (1998) and by Aspinwall and colleagues (see Aspinwall, 1998; Reed & Aspinwall, 1998) provides further evidence showing that positive mood enhances people's preference for useful negative information about themselves.

In this research, mood influenced the perception of the offered feedback. Specifically, both the positive and negative feedback were perceived as more positive by the positive mood participants than by the neutral and negative mood participants. Consistent with extant models of mood effects on judgment, this finding indicates an assimilative effect of mood (Forgas, 1995; Forgas & Bower, 1987; Schwarz, 1990). However, positive mood did not diminish the perceived distinction between positive and negative feedback. That is, participants in a positive mood still viewed the positive feedback as quite positive and the negative feedback as quite negative. It seems that the offered feedback was sufficiently unambiguous to prevent more pronounced distortions. Therefore, the results cannot be explained by the negative feedback being construed as positive by those in a positive mood. Instead, these data suggest that positive mood acted as a resource in enabling participants to give more weight to the long-term benefits of negative feedback than to its short-term emotional cost in selecting feedback.

Self-Induced Positive Mood

The two feedback-seeking studies by Trope and Neter (1994) demonstrated that positive mood enhances individuals' ability to accept new negative feedback. The question is whether individuals will try to self-induce a positive mood when new negative feedback is made available to them. The mood-as-a-resource hypothesis would predict that when the offered feedback is useful for improving future decisions and performance, individuals may try to self-induce a positive mood in order to cope with the anticipated emotional costs of the feedback.

In order to test this prediction, Trope and Neter offered participants feedback regarding their intelligence, and unobtrusively measured how much time they spent reading positive personality feedback while waiting for the intelligence feedback. It was assumed that the amount of time spent reading the positive personality feedback reflects the degree to which participants' attempted to self-induce a positive mood prior to receiving the intelligence feedback. As predicted, the results showed that the more negative the anticipated intelligence feedback, the more time participants spent reading the positive personality feedback. Positive intelligence feedback was apparently easy to accept because it was both informative and emotionally gratifying. Individuals may feel capable of accepting such feedback without having first to boost their affective resources. As the anticipated feedback becomes more negative, the emotional threat increases and individuals may try to overcome this threat by attending to information that can improve their mood. This pattern of strategic mood regulation provides additional support for the idea that people use positive mood as a resource in coping with negative but useful information.

MOOD AS A RESOURCE AND MOOD AS A GOAL

Trope and Neter's finding that positive mood promotes search for negatively valenced information appears inconsistent with mood maintenance theories (e.g., Isen, 1984, 1993; Wegener & Petty, 1994). These theories suggest that people strive to maintain their positive moods and ameliorate their bad moods. People in a good mood attempt to avoid negative information or any information that might jeopardize their positive feelings. Furthermore, people in a bad mood attempt to focus on information or situations that might potentially rid them of their bad feelings and replace them with positive ones.

   The mood-as-a-resource hypothesis entails a resolution of this apparent disagreement. According to this hypothesis, people compromise their good moods in order to learn something about themselves with the assumed aim of improving their deficits. Therefore, they should only care about feedback that is accurate and reliable, and about feedback that addresses a domain that is important to them. For instance, if someone has a particular penchant for mathematics and finds out that she has the chance to receive some feedback about her weaknesses in the area of constructing proofs, she might be more interested in that feedback compared to hearing about an activity for which she does not care. She may not bother listening to negative feedback about her cross-country skiing ability if she does not plan on doing that activity in the future, or if she does not care about whether she is skilled at it. If feedback concerns a domain about which a person does not care, the person may well try to maintain her good mood by selecting positive versus negative feedback. In short, when there are no long-term learning benefits, people may adopt the goal of mood maintenance, which in turn may determine the search and processing of self-relevant information (see Aspinwall, 1998).

Similarly, the degree to which negative feedback can enable one to improve one's weaknesses in some area is contingent on the accuracy and reliability of the feedback. If feedback is unreliable, it may be unwise to incorporate the information into one's decisions about future choices and behavior. For example, when one is planning on going away for the weekend and listens to the weather channels for the prognosis of weekend weather, one will likely only make decisions about going away if the information is reliable and accurate. If one knows that local television channels are often inaccurate, one may decide to ignore the outlook. Likewise, if one knows that the boss is tired and stressed due to personal problems, one may not regard the boss's evaluation as diagnostic, accurate, or reliable. A realization of potential inaccuracy may lead one to forsake long-term learning goals in the interest of maintaining or repairing one's mood.

Whereas mood-maintenance and mood-repair theories do not make differential predictions on the basis of accuracy, reliability, and importance of domain, the tenets of the mood-as-a-resource hypothesis suggest that these variables will moderate the pattern of results. In particular, when the domain specified by the feedback is unimportant to the person, or when the feedback itself is unreliable and inaccurate, people are expected to regulate their behavior such that they attempt to maintain their positive mood and accordingly avoid negative feedback. However, when the domain is important and the feedback is reliable and accurate, people in a positive mood should have a buffer that allows them to select negative feedback in order to learn about their weaknesses. Such a positive mood should diminish the immediate affective costs of listening to negative feedback and increase the learning benefits of receiving this feedback.

RESEARCH ON MOOD AS A RESOURCE VERSUS A GOAL IN FEEDBACK-SEEKING BEHAVIOR

Research by Trope and Gervey (2000) tested these claims in a series of four studies. The first study manipulated the accuracy and reliability of the feedback, whereas the second study manipulated the importance of the domain that the feedback addressed. The third study recorded the amount of time that people exposed themselves to feedback as a function of their mood and the importance of the feedback. The fourth study introduced either a learning goal or a mood-maintenance goal within the experimental setting. The methodology and results from these four studies is discussed below.

In the first study, participants filled out a similarity judgment task if they were in the neutral mood condition or recalled positive memories if they were in the positive mood condition. After completing this task, they were told that they had completed a social sensitivity test as part of the battery in which all participants took part in the beginning of the semester. They then were told that the test was either highly reliable and accurate or rather new and untested in terms of its predictive value. Then they were given a sample of the feedback concerning liabilities and assets and were asked to indicate which types of feedback they would be interested in receiving at the end of the experiment.

When participants were told that the feedback was highly reliable and accurate, those in the positive mood condition, compared to those in the neutral mood condition, reported greater interest in receiving feedback concerning their weaknesses rather than their strengths. In contrast, when participants were told that the feedback was unreliable and probably inaccurate, those participants in the positive mood condition indicated greater interest in their strengths rather than their weaknesses. These data suggest that when the source of the feedback is not trustworthy, participants in a good mood adopted the goal of trying to maintain their positive mood by selecting positive feedback about themselves. Comparatively, when the source of the feedback was thought to be accurate, those in a positive mood seemed willing to withstand the immediate affective costs of receiving information about their weaknesses compared to their strengths. These data illustrate that people use their positive mood as a resource when feedback is accurate and reliable, and behave as though their positive mood is a goal in itself when the feedback is not very informative or trustworthy.

Data concerning participant's conceptions of the affective costs and informational value of the feedback were also collected in this study. Theoretically, the accuracy of the feedback and the mood of participants are expected to interactively determine interest in negative feedback through the change in the affective costs of the feedback and the perceived informational value of the feedback. A path analysis confirmed this prediction. When the feedback was accurate and participants were in a good mood, the affective costs of the negative feedback decreased and the informational value of the feedback increased. Also, the more the affective costs were diminished and the more the feedback was viewed as valuable, the more participants were interested in receiving negative feedback. When these changes in affective costs and informational value of feedback were controlled for, the interactive effect of positive mood and accuracy of feedback on interest in negative feedback vanished. That is, positive mood no longer increased interest in accurate negative feedback, nor did positive mood decrease interest in inaccurate positive feedback. The joint influence of accuracy of negative feedback and mood seemed to be mediated, then, by the perceived costs and informational benefits of this feedback. This process analysis lends support to the idea that positive mood enhances interest in accurate negative feedback by decreasing the impact of the immediate affective costs of this feedback and increasing the weight of its long-term learning benefits.

The second study was similar in methodology to the first study, except that participants were told that the feedback concerned a domain that was important or unimportant for future life satisfaction and success. When participants were told that the feedback was important, participants in a positive mood condition, compared to those in the neutral mood condition, indicated greater interest in receiving feedback concerning their weaknesses compared to feedback concerning their strengths. In contrast, when the domain was described as unimportant for future life satisfaction, those participants in a positive mood reported greater interest in receiving feedback regarding their strengths compared to their weaknesses.

It seems, then, that when the feedback was unimportant, participants behaved in a way that would have maintained their positive mood. Again, these results demonstrate the circumstances in which mood is a goal versus a resource. When feedback concerns an important domain, people seem to use their positive mood as a resource for helping them learn about themselves. In contrast, when feedback is irrelevant for the person's long-term interests, people seem to regulate their behavior in order to maintain their positive mood.

The methodology for the third study was very similar to that of the first and second studies, except that all participants viewed actual feedback about their strengths and weaknesses concerning their relationship abilities. Some of the aspects of the feedback were described as important, whereas others were described as unimportant. Participants then had the opportunity to see a sample of the feedback from the test. Participants had to indicate when they were finished reading each feedback item in order to get to the next item. The critical dependent measure for the third study was the time spent reading each feedback item.

For those feedback items that were described as important, those participants who were in a good mood spent more time reading about their weaknesses rather than their strengths. In comparison, for those items that had been identified as unimportant, those in a good mood spent more time reading about their strengths compared to their weaknesses. These data suggest that people process information about their weaknesses more carefully when the feedback is important, and they have the resources needed to diminish the affective costs of hearing negative self-relevant information.

In contrast, people who are in a good mood and who have the opportunity to view either positive or negative feedback about a domain that is unimportant process the positive feedback more carefully, thereby maintaining their good mood.

Theoretically, we are proposing that people adopt a learning motive and use their positive mood as a resource when the feedback is accurate, reliable, and important to them. Otherwise, people should adopt an affective goal and try to maintain their good mood when the feedback is not reliable, accurate, or important. The purpose of the fourth study was to test this assumption by experimentally inducing either a learning or an affective goal. If the pattern of results mimics the patterns of results from the first three studies, it would constitute support for the theoretical explanation for these self-regulatory behaviors.

The methodology of the fourth study was similar to that of the other three studies, with the exception that the accuracy and importance of the feedback was not manipulated. Instead, the feedback was described to all participants as important. Participants were instructed either to feel good about themselves or to learn about themselves. It was expected that those who had the learning motive and who were in a positive mood would be more interested in feedback concerning their weaknesses compared to their strengths. Participants who were instructed to feel good and who were in a positive mood were expected to express greater interest in their strengths versus their weaknesses, in line with maintaining their positive mood.

Of those participants who were instructed to learn about themselves, those who were in a positive mood reported greater interest in their weaknesses compared to their strengths. In contrast, of participants who were instructed to feel good, those who were also in a positive mood indicated greater interest in their strengths compared to their weaknesses. These results suggest that when a learning goal is adopted, positive mood serves as a resource in enabling people to cope with the emotional cost of negative feedback and focus on its long-term learning benefits of improving their deficits. When feeling good about oneself is the goal, people try to maintain a positive mood and avoid negative information about themselves. These results parallel those of the earlier studies and suggest that when people are offered diagnostic and important feedback, people who are in a positive mood adopt a learning goal (rather than an affective goal), which in turn leads them to engage in mood-incongruent (rather than mood-congruent) information search.

Together, the Trope and Gervey studies suggest that the degree to which a positive mood produces mood-incongruent versus congruent feedback seeking depends on people's goals. When the offered feedback is diagnostic and important, positive mood acts as a resource for attaining learning goals. The weight of affective cost of negative feedback is diminished, and the weight of its informational benefits is enhanced, thus enabling people to accept negative feedback about themselves. When the offered feedback is nondiagnostic or unimportant, positive mood becomes a goal in and of itself, and negative feedback is avoided.

MOOD AS A RESOURCE VERSUS A GOAL IN PROCESSING PERSUASIVE MESSAGES

Raghunathan and Trope (2000) tested the mood-as-a-resource hypothesis by examining participant's reactions to persuasive appeals concerning a self-relevant or irrelevant topic. It was predicted that when the persuasive appeal concerns a self-relevant (rather than irrelevant) topic, participants who are in a positive mood (rather than negative mood) would show greater elaboration of negatively valenced material. Positive mood is thus conceptualized as a resource because it is expected to enable people to process relevant, negative information extensively. Participants in a negative mood, however, do not have the affective resources to handle the negative information and therefore should process the positively valenced information extensively in order to ameliorate their bad moods. In a series of three studies, Raghunathan and Trope explored different aspects of participant's reactions to reading an essay on the effects of caffeine consumption that was adapted from research by Liberman and Chaiken (1992).

In all three studies, participants were told that the essay had appeared in a prestigious medical journal to ensure that they regarded the essay as credible. Also, the essay described positive, negative, and neutral consequences of ingesting caffeinated products. Finally, the self-relevance of the essay was determined on the basis of participant's reported level of caffeine consumption. For participants who reported a relatively large level of caffeine consumption, the essay was presumably of high self-relevance, whereas for participants who reported a relatively low level of caffeine consumption, the essay was presumably of low self-relevance.

Mood-Incongruent Recall

In the first study, Raghunathan and Trope examined participants' recall of the information contained in the essay. Participants were initially given positive, negative, or no feedback on a "Lateral Thinking Ability Test." Participants who were given positive feedback reported being in a positive mood compared to those who did not receive feedback; participants who heard negative feedback reported being in a negative mood compared to those who did not receive any feedback. All of the participants then read the essay, which contained an equal number of positive and negative pieces of information about caffeine consumption (i.e., some pieces of evidence suggested health benefits, whereas other evidence reported suggested health risks due to ingesting caffeine). Participants were then asked to recall as many of the pieces of evidence as possible.

Raghunathan and Trope predicted that for participants for whom the essay was relevant, those in a positive mood (vs. negative mood) should recall more negative (vs. positive) pieces of evidence. Participants in a negative mood, however, were expected to recall more positive (vs. negative) pieces of evidence. Consistent with these predictions, it was found that when the essay was personally relevant, participants who had a negative mood recalled more positive pieces of evidence compared to negative pieces. Participants who reported being in a positive mood, however, recalled both positive and negative pieces of evidence with a tendency to recall more negative than positive pieces of evidence. When the essay was personally irrelevant, positive mood and negative mood participants did not recall different proportions of positive and negative evidence.

These results suggest that for participants for whom the essay was relevant, a positive mood enabled a careful analysis of all information contained in the evidence rather than just the positive evidence. Such an impartial analysis of the essay might serve those participants well because they are attending to both health-affirming and health-harming information about a personally relevant topic. This suggests that their positive mood allowed an analysis of information that might benefit them in the future. After all, one would presumably want to know whether a daily habit might be injurious. Participants in a negative mood, in comparison, did not have the resources to process the negative evidence about the personally relevant issue. Instead, as indicated by their recall, they paid more attention to the positive evidence, perhaps in an attempt to alleviate their negative mood.

Affective Consequences of Processing

The second study examined whether participants' moods changed after reading the persuasive appeal. If positive mood produces elaborate processing of negatively valenced self-relevant arguments, then positive mood should be attenuated after reading the essay. Thus, Raghunathan and Trope predicted that when the essay was self-relevant, participants in a positive mood should report less of a positive mood after reading the essay compared to before reading the essay. Likewise, if participants in a negative mood are trying to alleviate their bad moods by concentrating on positive evidence, they should report more positive moods after reading the essay compared to before reading the essay.

Participants reported memories of either sad or happy events in their lives and then reported their moods. They then read the essay and were again asked to report their moods afterward. The results showed that in the positive mood condition, reading the essay decreased positive mood, whereas in the negative mood condition, reading the essay increased positive mood. Importantly, however, this pattern of mood changes was more pronounced when the essay was high rather than low in self-relevance.

Along with the results from the first study, this pattern of results suggests that when the essay was self-relevant, participants in a positive mood may have used their mood as a resource in order to manage processing the negative information. Participants who started with a positive mood felt worse after reading the essay, apparently because they attended to the negatively valenced information. In contrast, participants who started with a negative mood felt better after reading the essay, apparently because they attended to the positively valenced information.

Attitudes and Behavioral Intentions

The third study assessed the degree to which participants changed their attitudes and behavioral intentions regarding caffeine consumption after reading the essay. This study was conducted to provide substantive evidence that the different strategies of information processing identified in the earlier studies in fact yield different degrees of attitude and intention change. In addition, this study was also conducted in order to rule out an alternative explanation for the previously mentioned findings. Namely, those participants who were in a positive mood might have processed the negative information more effortfully in order to refute it (e.g., Isen & Simmonds, 1978).

The design of the third study was similar to that of the second study, except that participants' attitudes and intentions toward caffeine consumption were measured 1 month prior to the study and then again immediately after participants read the essay. It was predicted that when the essay was self-relevant, participants in a positive mood should demonstrate less favorable attitudes toward caffeine consumption and weaker intentions to ingest caffeine in the future. Participants in a negative mood, however, should report a more favorable attitude toward caffeine consumption and stronger intentions to ingest caffeine in the future.

The results showed that the effect of the essay on participants' attitudes and intentions depended on the induced mood state and the self-relevance of the essay. When the essay was self-relevant (rather than irrelevant), positive-mood participants developed less favorable attitudes and intentions toward caffeine consumption than did negative-mood participants. When the essay was self-irrelevant, there was no difference between positive and negative mood participants in their attitude toward caffeine consumption. Thus, positive mood (compared to negative mood) enabled high caffeine consumers to become less favorable toward caffeine consumption after reading the essay. These results argue against the interpretation that positive mood participants were merely trying to counter-argue self-relevant, negatively valenced arguments. Instead, as suggested by the mood-as-a-resource hypothesis, positive mood enhanced unbiased consideration and integration of various arguments in the essay into attitudes and intentions regarding caffeine consumption.

The findings of the Raghunathan and Trope studies demonstrate the operation of positive mood as a resource in processing persuasive messages. A variety of factors may give positively valenced arguments a processing advantage when people are in a positive mood state. The wish to maintain a positive mood may act against processing negatively valenced arguments (Wegener & Petty, 1994). Positive mood may signal to people that "Everything is OK," so that there is little need to extensively process information indicating the health hazards associated with one's daily habits (see Bless, Bohner, Schwarz, & Strack, 1990; Schwarz & Clore, 1996). Positive mood may also bias processing by making positively valenced material in memory more accessible and thus more readily processed compared to negatively valenced material in memory (Bower, 1981, 1991; Forgas, 1995; Isen, 1984, 1993). The present research suggests, however, that when the message contains unambiguous arguments regarding a highly self-relevant health issue, positive mood serves as a resource enabling people to engage in extensive processing of negatively valenced arguments. This processing strategy has short-term affective costs and comes at the expense of people's positive mood, but it also enables people to adopt healthier attitudes and intentions.

CONCLUSIONS

This chapter explores the role of mood states in the process of acquiring self-knowledge. Acquisition of such knowledge often requires seeking and processing of negatively valenced information, and thus poses a motivational dilemma. On the one hand, information about one's weaknesses and vulnerabilities has long-term value for future choice and self-improvement. On the other hand, such information is associated with immediate emotional costs. The mood-as-a-resource hypothesis suggests that mood influences how this conflict is resolved. Specifically, positive mood states may enable people to focus on the long-term value of negative information and better cope with its immediate emotional costs. Therefore, to the extent that important self-attributes can be diagnostically assessed, positive mood should enhance search, processing, and integration of mood-incongruent negative information.

The research reported in this chapter provides strong support for the mood-as-a-resource hypothesis. The studies by Trope and Neter (1994) and Trope and Pomerantz (1998) show that positive mood increases people's interest in receiving feedback about their weaknesses and liabilities in important performance domains. Participants in these studies knew that the offered feedback was negative. Nevertheless, they preferred this feedback to more positive feedback regarding their strengths.

The studies by Trope and Gervey (2000) further demonstrate that this mood-incongruent information search is conditional on the usefulness of the offered feedback. When the feedback was diagnostic of an important ability, participants who were in a positive mood preferentially solicited and extensively processed feedback regarding their weaknesses. However, when the offered feedback was nondiagnostic or when it pertained to an unimportant ability, participants who were in a positive mood preferred to receive feedback regarding their strengths rather than their weaknesses. Apparently, when the offered feedback was not very useful, participants were primarily motivated to maintain their positive mood and, therefore, preferred to hear positively valenced rather than negatively valenced information.

Raghunathan and Trope (2000) extended the test of the mood-as-a-resource hypothesis to processing of health-related persuasive messages. Their studies demonstrate that people in a positive mood not only selectively seek, but also better remember and accept negatively valenced arguments—arguments that specify the health risks associated with caffeine consumption. As this research showed, this processing strategy diminished participants' positive mood, but at the same time enhanced their willingness to give up unhealthy habits (see Aspinwall, 1998).

It seems, then, that instead of trying to maintain a positive mood, people are willing to exchange their positive mood for useful information about themselves. Research on mood as a prime (Forgas, 1995), as information

(Schwarz & Clore, 1996), and as a goal (Wegener & Petty, 1994) suggests that positive mood often favors a "rosy view" of the available information— a view that acts to perpetuate positive mood through mood-congruent information search and processing. Without denying the importance of these mechanisms, we claim that they represent only one side of the coin. The other side of the coin is that positive mood may also serve the function of enabling people to overcome their defensiveness and engage in extensive processing of negatively valenced information when this information can help people achieve their long-term goals. It is this adaptive aspect of positive mood states that our present program of research sought to illuminate.

REFERENCES

Aspinwall, L. G. (1998). Rethinking the role of positive affect in self-regulation. *Motivation and Emotion, 22*, 1–32.

Aspinwall, L. G., & Taylor, S. E. (1997). The effects of social comparison direction, threat, and self-esteem on affect, self-evaluation, and expected success. *Journal of Personality and Social Psychology, 64*, 708–722.

Bless, H., Bohner, G., Schwarz, N., & Strack, F. (1990). Mood and persuasion: A cognitive response analysis. *Personality and Social Psychology Bulletin, 16*, 331–345.

Bower, G. H. (1981). Mood and memory. *American Psychologist, 36*, 129–148.

Bower, G. H. (1991). Mood congruity of social judgments. In J. P. Forgas (Ed.), *Emotion and social judgments*. Oxford: Pergamon Press.

Brown, J. D. (1990). Evaluating one's abilities: Shortcuts and stumbling blocks on the road to self-knowledge. *Journal of Personality and Social Psychology, 50*, 149–167.

Brown, J. D., & Dutton, K. A. (1995). Truth and consequences: The costs and benefits of accurate self-knowledge. *Personality and Social Psychology Bulletin, 21*, 1288–1296.

Carver, S. C., & Scheier, M. F. (1990). Origins and functions of positive and negative affect. *Psychological Review, 97*, 19–35.

Crocker, J., & Major, B. (1989). Social stigma and self-esteem: The self-protective properties of stigma. *Psychological Review, 96*, 608–630.

Forgas, J. P. (1995). Mood and judgment: The Affect Infusion Model (AIM). *Journal of Personality and Social Psychology, 117*, 39–66.

Forgas, J. P., & Bower, G. H. (1987). Mood effects on person perception judgments. *Journal of Personality and Social Psychology, 53*, 53–60.

Gollwitzer, P. M. (1990). Action phases and mind-sets. In E. T. Higgins & R. M. Sorrentino (Eds.), *Handbook of motivation and cognition: Foundations of social behavior, Vol. 2* (pp. 53–92). New York: Guilford Press.

Higgins, E. T. (1987). Self discrepancy: A theory relating self and affect. *Psychological Review, 94*, 319–340.

Isen, A. M. (1984). Towards understanding the role of affect in cognition. In R. S. Wyer, Jr., & T. K. Srull (Eds.), *Handbook of social cognition, Vol. 3* (pp. 179–236). Hillsdale, NJ: Lawrence Erlbaum Associates.

Isen, A. M. (1993). Positive affect and decision making. In M. Lewis & J. Haviland (Eds.), *Handbook of emotion* (pp. 113–140). New York: Guilford Press.

Isen, A. M., & Simmonds, S. (1978). The effect of feeling good on a helping task that is incompatible with good mood. *Social Psychological Quarterly, 14*, 346–349.

Kuhl, J. (1984). Volitional aspects in achievement motivation and learned helplessness: Towards a comprehensive theory of action control. In B. A. Maher (Ed.), *Progress in experimental personality research, Vol. 12* (pp. 99–170). New York: Academic Press.

Lazarus, R. S., & Folkman, S. (1984). *Stress, appraisal, and coping.* New York: Springer.

Liberman, A., & Chaiken, S. (1992). Defensive processing of personally relevant health messages. *Personality and Social Psychology Bulletin, 18,* 669–679.

Lowenstein, G., & Thaller, R. H. (1989). Anomalies: Intertemporal choice. *Journal of Economic Perspectives, 3,* 181–193.

Metcalf, J., & Mischel, W. (1999). A hot/cool-system analysis of delay of gratification: Dynamics of willpower. *Psychological Review, 106,* 3–19.

Mischel, W. (1974). Processes in delay of gratification. In L. Berkowitz (Ed.), *Advances in experimental social psychology, Vol. 7* (pp. 249–292). New York: Academic Press.

Mischel, W. (1984). Convergences and challenges in the search for consistency. *American Psychologist, 39,* 351–364.

Pyszczynski, T. A., & Greenberg, J. (1987). Toward an integration of cognitive and motivational perspectives in social inference: A biased hypothesis-testing model. In L. Berkowitz (Ed.), *Advances in experimental social psychology, Vol. 20* (pp. 297–334). New York: Academic Press.

Raghunathan, R., & Trope, Y. (2000). Mood-as-a-resource in processing persuasive messages. Unpublished manuscript.

Reed, M. B., & Aspinwall, L. G. (1998). Self-affirmation reduces biased processing of health-risk information. *Motivation and Emotion, 22,* 99–132.

Schelling, T. (1984). Self command in practice, in theory and in a theory of rational choice. *American Economic Review, 74,* 1–11.

Schwarz, N. (1990). Feelings as information: Informational and affective functions of affective states. In E. T. Higgins & R. M. Sorrentino (Eds.), *Handbook of motivation and cognition: Foundations of social behavior, Vol. 2* (pp. 527–561). New York: Guilford Press.

Schwarz, N., & Clore, G. (1996). Feelings and phenomenal experiences. In E. T. Higgins & A. Kruglanski (Eds.), *Social Psychology: Handbook of Basic Principles* (pp. 250–296). New York: Guilford Press.

Sedikides, C., & Strube, M. J. (1997). Self-evaluation: To thine own self be good, to thine own self be sure, to thine own self be true, and to thine own self be better. In M. P. Zanna (Ed.), *Advances in experimental social psychology, Vol. 29* (pp. 209–270). New York: Academic Press.

Steele, C. M. (1988). The psychology of self affirmation: Sustaining the integrity of the self. In L. Berkowitz (Ed.), *Advances in experimental social psychology, Vol. 21* (pp. 249–292). New York: Academic Press.

Taylor, S. E., Wayment, H. A., & Carrillo, M. (1996). Social comparison, self-regulation, and motivation. In R. M. Sorrentino & E. T. Higgins (Eds.), *Handbook of motivation and cognition, Vol. 3* (pp. 3–37). New York: Guilford Press.

Tesser, A. (1988). Toward a self-evaluation maintenance model of social behavior. In L. Berkowitz (Ed.), *Advances in experimental social psychology, Vol. 21* (pp. 181–227). New York: Academic Press.

Tesser, A., Martin, L. L., & Cornell, D. P. (1996). On the substitutibility of self-protective mechanisms. In P. M. Gollwitzer & J. A. Bargh (Eds.) *The psychology of action: Linking cognition and motivation to behavior* (pp. 48–68). New York: Guilford Press.

Trope, Y. (1975). Seeking information about one's own ability as a determinant of choice among tasks. *Journal of Personality and Social Psychology, 32,* 1004–1013.

Trope, Y. (1979). Uncertainty-reducing properties of achievement tasks. *Journal of Personality and Social Psychology, 37,* 1505–1518.

Trope, Y. (1980). Self-assessment, self-enhancement and task preference. *Journal of Experimental Social Psychology, 16,* 116–129.

Trope, Y. (1983). Self-assessment in achievement behavior. In J. Suls & A. G. Greenwald (Eds.), *Psychological perspectives on the self, Vol. 2* (pp. 170–201). Hillsdale, NJ: Lawrence Erlbaum Associates.

Trope, Y. (1986). Self-enhancement and self-assessment in achievement behavior. In R. M. Sorrentino & E. T. Higgins (Eds.), *The handbook of motivation and cognition: Foundations of social behavior, Vol. 2* (pp. xxx). New York: Guilford Press.

Trope, Y., & Brickman, P. (1975). Difficulty and diagnosticity as determinants of choice among tasks. *Journal of Personality and Social Psychology, 31*, 918–925.

Trope, Y., & Gervey, B. (2000). Resolving conflicts among self-evaluative motives. *Paper presented at the Annual Convention of Workshop of Achievement and Task Motivation.* Thessaloniki, Greece.

Trope, Y., & Pomerantz, E. M. (1998). Resolving conflicts among self-evaluative motives: Positive experiences as a resource for overcoming defensiveness. *Motivation and Emotion, 22*, 53–72.

Trope, Y., & Neter, E. (1994). Reconciling competing motives in self-evaluation: The role of self-control in feedback seeking. *Journal of Personality and Social Psychology, 66*, 646–657.

Wegener, D. T., & Petty, R. E. (1994). Mood management across affective states: The hedonic contingency hypothesis. *Journal of Personality and Social Psychology, 66*, 1034–1048.

Weiner, B. (1986). Attribution, emotion, and action. In R. M. Sorrentino & E. T. Higgins (Eds.), *Handbook of motivation and cognition: Foundations of social behavior, Vol. 1* (pp. 281–312). New York: Guilford Press.

13

The Role of Motivated Social Cognition in the Regulation of Affective States

Maureen Wang Erber
Northeastern Illinois University

Ralph Erber
DePaul University

The Search for Mood Repair   276
The Social Constraints Model of Mood Regulation and Processing   279
Mood Regulation: What and When   284
Research Supporting the Social Constraints Model: The Coolness Effect   285
Research Supporting the Appropriateness Hypothesis I: Strangers versus
    Romantic Couples   286
Research Supporting the Appropriateness Hypothesis II: Accepting
    versus Critical Others   287
Some Parting Thoughts   288
References   289

So much of current American culture revolves around being happy: We quickly terminate unhappy marriages, we shirk difficult moral issues because they make us uncomfortable, we medicate ourselves and our children to alleviate the mildest depressions and slightest hints of hyperactivity, we

Address for correspondence: Maureen Wang Erber, Department of Psychology, Northeastern Illinois University, 5500 N. st. Louis Ave, Chicago, IL 60625, USA. Email: m-erber@neiu.edu are constantly bombarded with messages that consuming goods will bring us joy and make us happy. Quick fixes and easy outs. Thus, on surveying this cultural and moral landscape, it would be easy to conclude that the motive of modern man (and woman) is to seek pleasure and avoid pain. In emotional terms, this would translate into being motivated to maintain positive moods while avoiding or ridding ourselves of negative, unpleasant ones. Although hedonistic this principle is certainly a potent and undeniable one, (Bentham, 1789) we suggest that there is more to our emotional lives than this. This chapter presents our thinking and research in support of a broader, contextual model of mood regulation and processing.

The hedonistic principle has long pervaded theorizing in all areas of psychology. Furthermore, given the widespread application of hedonistic assumptions to explanations of human motivation and behavior (e.g., explanations of the self-serving bias, helping and altruism, person perception and impression formation), it is not surprising that these assumptions are even more prevalent in social psychological conceptions of how people regulate, manage, or control their emotional lives—including their moods. The generally accepted idea espoused by Isen (1984; see also Clark & Isen, 1982) and later echoed and amplified by Taylor (1991) is that positive affective states are sought and maintained because of their rewarding consequences, whereas negative affective states are avoided or repaired because of their unpleasantness. The mood-repair hypothesis became ubiquitous as an explanation for the failure of many studies to find effects for sad moods that would be mirror images of the effects of good moods. (Kirk to engine room: "We're not getting anything for the negative mood conditions." Engine room to Kirk: "Must be that we've got a bit of mood repair going on.") In fact, it is a more or less explicit component of many current models of mood and processing (e.g. Forgas, 1995; Wegener, Petty, & Smith, 1995). Therefore, let us explore our empirical challenges of this notion.

THE SEARCH FOR MOOD REPAIR

Presumably, the experience of mood entails a proclivity to entertain mood-congruent thoughts (Clark & Isen, 1982). Reasoning that moods might be attenuated if we could take sad participants' minds off their sad thoughts, we (Erber & Tesser, 1992) first put subjects into a sad mood through exposure to a depressing video (scenes from the movie "Sophie's Choice"). Subsequently, we asked them to solve a series of math problems. Some participants solved difficult problems (long division and multiplication) whereas other participants solved fairly simple problems (short division and multiplication) for 10 min. Participants in a control group solved no problems and instead waited an equal amount of time for the experimenter to return with the relevant questionnaire. At the end of that period, all participants reported their moods on a questionnaire, along with their general thoughts.

Just as we had expected, participants who had done the difficult math problems felt less sad than participants who had completed the simple problems and participants who just sat around for 10 min. Also, consistent with our hypothesis, participants who had solved difficult problems reported fewer thoughts related to either the depressing movie or their sad mood. What is interesting about these findings with regard to hedonism and mood repair is the observation that those participants who sat around for 10 min showed no evidence of attempting to repair the sad mood induced by the depressing video. This finding is troublesome for the mood-repair hypothesis, which, contrary to our results, predicts that in the absence of a suitable task provided by the experimenter, participants should generate strategies to attenuate their sadness on their own.

Additional findings from this study are equally troublesome (at least from a hedonistic approach). It just so happened that the design of the study included a group of participants who completed the math problems after being exposed to a cheerful video (comedy routines by Robin Williams and Billy Crystal). Doing the difficult problems attenuated the happy mood induced by the video in the same way that it attenuated the sad mood of those who had watched the depressing video. Doing the simple problems or just sitting around for 10 min preserved the happy mood, however. Again, these findings are difficult to handle by the mood-repair hypothesis because of its assumption of positive hedonism. If people preferred happiness to the extent predicted by theories based on the hedonism assumption, happy participants faced with the difficult math problems should have initiated strategies to counteract the mood-attenuating consequences of the task.

It is important to note that the findings from these studies are not simply an aberration or an exception to a more general "goody-goody" rule, as we have replicated them with different interventions and different affective states. In a series of studies, we (Erber & Therriault, 1994) had female participants engage in 10 min of step exercise or watch an exercise video ("Buns of Steel") for 10 min following a sad or happy mood induction. The results mimicked the findings of the previous study in that the happy and sad moods of participants were attenuated as a result of engaging in the exercise. Simply watching the exercise video did not result in mood attenuation compared to the control condition.

In another set of studies, we (Erber, Erber, Therriault, & Onesto, 1998) made some participants anxious by leading them to believe that they would be giving a speech on sexually transmitted diseases. In one study, participants believed that they would be making their presentation to a live audience, whereas in a second study, participants believed that their speech would be videotaped and then evaluated. Prior to giving the speech, participants were asked to solve a set of either easy or difficult anagrams. After several minutes of working on the anagrams, participants' blood pressure, pulse rate, and verbal responses were measured.

Results of both studies were as predicted and consistent with previous findings. Participants felt less anxious and reported fewer anxiety-related thoughts after solving the difficult anagrams and were much more anxious if they had worked on the easy anagrams. In other words, distraction alone (i.e., completion of the easy anagrams) was not enough to attenuate participants' anxiety. Instead, having been absorbed in trying to solve the difficult anagrams produced reductions in perceived anxiety.

Our research on the mechanisms underlying the attenuation of moods suggests that successful "mood repair" depends on both ability and motivation. It appears that it is most readily accomplished via cognitively taxing tasks, ostensibly because engaging in them detracts from mood-congruent thinking of any kind. It is worth noting that mood attenuation does not necessarily require engaging in tasks or activities whose valences are incongruent with one's currently experienced mood. In other words, sad people may be able to rid themselves of their mood by doing crossword puzzles or yardwork just as, if not more, successfully as they would from watching hours of side-splitting comedy. The research discussed thus far also suggests that mood itself is not the primary motivator for mood maintenance and "mood repair," as Isen (1984) and Taylor (1991) have suggested. If this were the case, our happy participants confronted with the difficult tasks should have initiated some type of strategy to counteract its mood-absorbing consequences. Similarly, our sad and anxious participants who had been deprived of a suitable task should have enacted some type of strategy to make themselves feel better, especially in light of the fact that they had nothing else to do.

Thus, despite the lack of empirical support for mood repair, hedonistically based models remain common and popular. Part of the allure of this type of thinking stems from its intuitive appeal, including its ready and easy application to many day-to-day events. It is indeed difficult to dismiss outright such "goody-goody theories" (Bower, Gilligan, & Monteiro, 1981), especially as they pertain to the regulation of moods. All else being equal, most people would probably prefer to be happy and content rather than sad and gloomy. However, at the same time, each of us can recall a time when we wallowed in sadness, enhancing and perpetuating a negative mood by listening to sad music or ruminating on morose thoughts. Conversely, there are also times when we find happy moods and thoughts intrusive and unwelcome: Thoughts, for example, of a new love interest or lottery jackpot that intrude on our efforts to console a sad friend or interfere with the completion of a manuscript. Thus, although we are certain that people can and do regulate their moods, the questions of when and how repair or regulation occur are more complex and intriguing. Indeed, when we first began to study mood regulation, it was important to determine not only *when* people would attempt to regulate their negative moods, but *how* they go about doing it as well—ambitious but crucial goals. Therefore, in the service of demonstrating that our model is more than a fiction concocted by a couple of eager social psychologists, we present both our most ideal theorizing as well as the empirical support for our notions.

THE SOCIAL CONSTRAINTS MODEL OF MOOD REGULATION AND PROCESSING

The social constraints model of mood regulation starts with the assumption that the effects of moods are context dependent. However, we would like to carry this a step further by suggesting that the experience of moods as a result of a mood-eliciting event may itself be context dependent. Context variables of any sort can often act as powerful constraints on our emotional experience and expression. In some cases they may even compel us to rid ourselves of inappropriate affect. Sometimes we work hard to hide and suppress signs of happiness when we have to deliver bad news to someone (Tesser & Rosen, 1975), and we often work just as hard not to look distressed or depressed as we join a birthday party, even though we may have been feuding with our partner or been at the receiving end of bad news. In other cases, situational constraints may suggest that we at least try to get into a certain type of mood (e.g., to be happy at weddings, to be sad at funerals) even though our present emotional state may not resemble the desired state. However, situations characterized by relative solitude may create a context to indulge in whatever mood we might be in at the time, *sad* or happy.

Thus, although many models (e.g., Isen, 1984) propose mood-congruent processing for positive moods and mood repair and mood incongruency

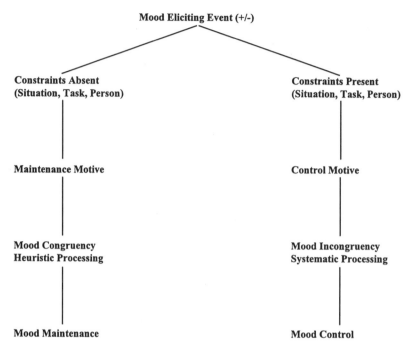

FIG. 13.1. The social constraints model of mood control and processing.

for negative moods, our model is one of the few to take a different path. For us, the consideration of context suggests a very different model of how mood regulation and processing operate. It is depicted in Fig. 13.1. First, it proposes that whether a mood-eliciting event leads to the experience of a corresponding mood does not solely or even primarily depend on the valence implications of the event. Instead, in the absence of specific constraints stemming from the situation, the task, or a disposition both positive and negative events will likely result in their respective mood states (cf. Erber & Erber, in press-a, for a more thorough discussion on the nature of social constraints). Furthermore, contrary to hedonistic assumptions, under such circumstances people may maintain even a *negative* mood for a number of reasons. One reason may be because the absence of a control motive leads to a passive priming of mood-congruent material. Other reasons may be because appropriate ways to get rid of negative moods may not be readily available (Erber & Tesser, 1992), or because the negative mood provides an opportunity to focus attention inward toward the self (Salovey, 1992; Wood, Saltzberg, & Goldsamt, 1990). As a consequence, processing may proceed in a mood-congruent

and perhaps heuristic fashion, which ultimately results in mood maintenance. Of course, this is not to say that moods will endure indefinitely in
the absence of social constraints. Instead, mood priming, just like any
other form of priming, is subject to natural decay. It is further possible that homeostatic processes come into play once the intensity of affect induced by mood priming reaches a certain threshold (Forgas, 1995).
However, in the short run, both positive and negative moods may be self-
perpetuating.

A very different picture emerges, however, when a mood-eliciting event
is encountered in the presence of situational constraints. In such cases, people may be compelled to control the implications of the event by accessing
mood-incongruent information, or by engaging in cognitively taxing tasks
in the ultimate service of mood control. Just why this would be the case
becomes clearer when one takes a closer look at the kinds of constraints
that may be present in a given situation. First, it is probably a basic fact
of life that we frequently find ourselves in the presence of others (e.g., at
work with colleagues, at home with family, at a ball game with strangers
of varying levels of intoxication). Because the real, imagined, and implied
presence of others has a profound impact on our thoughts, feelings, and
behavior (Allport, 1954), it stands to reason that the presence of others on
any level should influence our moods and our motivation to indulge in them
as well. Thus, our model suggests that given the proper set of constraints,
we could find ourselves giving up positive mood states. However, if left
to our own devices and in the absence of constraints to the contrary, we
would be likely to remain in whatever mood has been primed—even if it
is a negative one.

Perhaps an analogy for our model may be found in the physical sciences.
According to Newton's First Law, all bodies will continue in their state of
rest or uniform motion (i.e., a straight line) except insofar as they are
compelled to change that state by impressed force. Perhaps in the affective
world, moods remain at rest or in motion unless there is a reason to act on
them. In other words, individuals are likely to remain in whatever mood
they are in (positive, neutral, sad) unless they are compelled to change their
moods in light of perceived constraints.[1] That is, once set in motion, we
remain in whatever mood has been induced; however, when that mood is

---

[1]However, we are hesitant to embrace this position completely. Given the social nature of our
existence, there may be few cases when our emotional experience is completely unconstrained. Thus,
proposing defaults in the absence of constraints would come at the considerable and unnecessary
epistemic expense of deemphasizing the importance of context.

"challenged" by an event or context, we take action and amend our moods so that they are appropriate for the given situation.

Evidence for our social constraints model comes from a series of studies in which we (Erber, Wegner, & Therriault, 1996) made participants either happy or sad through exposure to cheerful or depressing music. Subsequently, participants were led to believe that they would be doing an unspecified task with either a stranger (i.e., another subject ostensibly doing the same experiment in the next room) or by themselves. All participants were then asked to indicate their preference for reading a set of newspapers that included headlines of humorous and uplifting, sad and depressing, or affectively neutral stories. As expected, participants who expected to complete the upcoming task by themselves preferred mood-congruent stories. In other words, happy participants, not surprisingly, preferred cheerful stories, whereas sad subjects (contrary to mood-repair predictions) preferred depressing stories. However, this preference for mood-congruent information shifted to a preference toward mood-incongruent information among those who expected to complete the task with a stranger. Happy participants preferred depressing stories, whereas sad participants preferred cheerful stories, ostensibly in order to regulate their mood for the anticipated interaction.

Preliminary evidence indicates that this preference for mood-incongruent material may in part be caused by concerns regarding the appropriateness of a happy or sad mood in social interactions. It appears to be most pronounced when it comes to real or imagined interactions with critical others. However, when the target of the anticipated interaction is a close other, mood congruency prevails (Commons & Erber, 1996).

Whether a mood-eliciting event results in the experience of a corresponding affective state may similarly be constrained by task-related variables to the extent that moods may have detrimental effects. Specifically, it appears that tasks that are perceived to be cognitively taxing (Erber & Erber, 1994) or require accuracy (Therriault, Erber, & Oktela, 1996) prompt attempts toward mood control. Finally, a number of individual differences may help to determine the extent to which mood-control motives may come into play. People with chronic proclivities to regulate negative moods are likely to respond to sadness with attempts toward control even in the absence of situational or task variables (Catanzaro & Mearns, 1990; Smith & Petty, 1995). Deliberative mind sets should promote a general tendency toward mood congruency and mood maintenance, whereas implemental mindsets may trigger a desire to rid oneself of one's mood (Gollwitzer, Heckhausen, & Steller, 1990). Similarly, ruminative self-focus may compel people to indulge in their moods, whereas reflective self-focus may lead to self-regulation efforts (Campbell et al., 1996).

In light of these considerations, it is important to note that the model we are proposing here is not an override model of mood regulation. Unlike mood-repair theories, which suggest that moods are repaired once they have been encountered, the present model proposes that we would evaluate the implications of a mood-eliciting event in light of situational or task-related constraints as well as constraints imposed by a disposition. The general principle suggested by these constraints is that people strive to attain moods that promote goal attainment. For example, we may try to enhance the impact of a positive event when we go to a party and enhance the impact of a negative event when we are about to go to a funeral. However, neutral moods may be particularly appropriate when we expect to meet a stranger or have to think clearly, and thus we work to attenuate the impact of a mood-eliciting event in light of these constraints. Why neutrality? There are several possibilities.

First, it may be that a neutral mood is a relatively good bet, particularly when we know little about how the person whom we are to meet is feeling. Unburdened, free from preoccupation with our feelings and its resulting distractions, a neutral mood allows us to be sensitive to multiple mood affordances suggested by the complexities of the social settings. This idea fits well with the observation that people frequently moderate their attitudes prior to discussing their attitudes with another person (Cialdini, Levy, Herman, & Levenbeck, 1973). Extrapolating from these findings, one would expect anticipatory mood control to follow similar principles. To the extent that people are inclined to regulate their mood in light of social constraints, the direction of such attempts should be toward relative neutrality, regardless of whether the initial mood is positive or negative.

Moreover, as we alluded to earlier, people may attempt to neutralize their moods under these circumstances to avoid being unfavorably evaluated for displaying potentially inappropriate moods. Just as singing show tunes off-key is perfectly all right in one's shower but not in a crowded subway car, the experience and display of moods may be similarly inappropriate in a public context.

Skeptics of our model often ask two questions. First, if neutral moods give us the most flexibility in confronting unknown people and situations, then why did our participants who did not anticipate future interaction with others maintain their positive or negative mood? One answer is that they had no reason to adjust their moods for the very fact that there were no situational constraints evident to them, and thus there was no impressed force to change their state. From this perspective, the model appears to suggest that maintaining a given mood regardless of its valence (positive, neutral, or negative) might indeed be the default, as long as there are no constraints present. Second, are there ever social constraints that would prompt people to seek a positive mood? The answer is a qualified "Yes." Whereas most social constraints call for a shift toward neutral, there are some that call for positive moods. For example, positive affect can increase one's willingness and ability to accept negative but useful feedback (Trope & Neter, 1994). Similarly, there is evidence that happy people engage in activities to bolster their moods when they expect to interact with a depressed other (Erber et al., 1996, Study 2). Presumably, positive affect can serve as a buffer against the consequences of interacting with someone who is feeling depressed (i.e., a shift toward sad mood).

In sum, our model is unique for a variety of reasons. First, rather than following the party line (i.e., positive moods lead to mood-congruent processing and negative moods yield to mood-incongruent processing), we propose that processing is not yoked to mood *per se*. Rather, both positive and negative moods can lead to either mood-congruent or mood-incongruent processing. Processing, then is tied not to mood, but depends instead on the presence or absence of situational constraints. A second notable feature of our model revolves around the issue of mood repair and regulation. Instead of assuming mood-repair as the default, we suggest that moods are intimately tied to their social contexts and that there are, likewise, no defaults *per se*. We also propose that characterizing our mood states as attempts to repair bad moods and attain good moods is simplistic and even wrong. Indeed, to date, we have amassed the strongest empirical support for the mood-regulation component of our model.

MOOD REGULATION: WHAT AND WHEN

Once we are thrust out of our isolated cocoons and into the vast ocean that makes up our social worlds, we may find that we are compelled to regulate our moods according to the demands of constantly changing situational constraints. Also, although some situations require the display and perhaps the experience of happiness (at one's birthday party) or sadness (hearing of a friend's misfortune), many situations require that we suspend or attenuate our moods to some extent. In fact, it has been argued (Goffman, 1963) that the ability to control socially inappropriate affect is what sets most of us apart from those incarcerated in mental hospitals.

As we have already suggested, we might consider the actual, imagined, or implied presence of others to act as the major social constraint on the kinds of moods we can reasonably experience. One reason why the presence of others acts as a constraint on our moods is because we often know little or nothing about other peoples' affective states; especially when they are strangers. Because of this, sad as well as happy moods may be a burden for a number of reasons. First, our preoccupation with mood-congruent thoughts may do little to promote and might actually interfere with the smoothness with which we interact with others. Moods may become burdensome if we fear that others look unfavorably on our happiness or sadness and their concomitant emotional displays. Or we may fear that a continued preoccupation with our moods may deprive us of a sense of composure. Consequently, we may be most likely to attempt attenuation of our happy and sad moods prior to interacting with a stranger.

RESEARCH SUPPORTING THE SOCIAL CONSTRAINTS MODEL: THE COOLNESS EFFECT

We conducted several studies to test the general idea of mood attenuation prior to social interaction with a stranger (Erber, Wegner, & Therriault, 1996). As discussed previously, after listening to either happy or depressing music, we told our now happy or sad participants that they would be completing a task either by themselves or with a stranger. Consistent with our expectations, participants who expected to complete the second part of the experiment by themselves preferred stories with headlines suggesting mood-congruent content: Sad participants indicated a preference for depressing stories, whereas happy participants preferred cheerful stories.

Also as expected, participants who expected to complete the second part of the experiment with a stranger preferred mood-incongruent stories. Specifically, sad participants preferred cheerful stories and (contrary to predictions made from hedonistic approaches) happy participants preferred depressing stories. According to our social constraints model, participants made these choices presumably as a means to attenuate their previously induced mood prior to meeting the stranger.

These results suggest that mood by itself does not serve as a primary motivational force in terms of the maintenance and attenuation of moods. Rather than using everything in their power to (1) maintain their happy mood and (2) repair their sad mood, our participants adopted strategies

designed to maintain both happy and sad moods in the absence of social constraints (that is, when there was no anticipated interaction with a
stranger). However, in the presence of social constraints, both happy and
sad participants relied on strategies that enabled them to extricate themselves from the mood we had previously induced.

Interestingly, participants' attempts at regulating their moods were aimed
at neutralizing both sad and happy moods. This was even the case when we
told participants in a second study that the person they were about to meet
was either happy or seemed somewhat depressed. The one notable exception was a tendency on the part of happy participants to bolster their mood
prior to interacting with a depressed stranger, presumably in preparation
for an interaction that would likely leave them somewhat depressed. However, even this finding could be considered an attempt at neutralization:
counteracting the affective consequences of spending a period of time with
someone who is depressed. However, we found no evidence that people
anticipate and try to adopt the moods of their future interaction partners.

Needless to say, it is difficult to account for these findings from models
based on hedonistic assumptions. Yet we must attempt to account for these
results and fill the vacuum left by hedonistic assumptions. Thus, we ask
how can we account for the seeming desire for attenuated moods prior to
entering into a social interaction with a stranger? Perhaps how we approach
our mood states has more to do with social appropriateness rather than
purely hedonistically driven goals.

RESEARCH SUPPORTING THE
APPROPRIATENESS HYPOTHESIS I:
STRANGERS VERSUS ROMANTIC
COUPLES

We completed several studies that support the idea that the "coolness effect"
may be mediated by concerns regarding the appropriateness of moods in
public contexts. In one study, we (Commons & Erber, 1996) recruited romantic couples for a "relationship study." Two couples signed up for each
time slot. Participants were then run through an experimental procedure
identical to the one employed by Erber et al. (1996), with one exception.
Rather than expecting to complete a second experiment either by themselves or with a stranger, participants were led to believe that they would
be doing this either with their romantic partner or with the opposite-sex
partner of the other couple (in essence, a stranger).

We predicted that participants who expected to do the second task with the stranger would once again show evidence of attempts toward regulating their happy and sad moods. However, among romantic couples, these concerns are, to some extent, superseded by norms prescribing self-disclosure that would render withholding one's feelings inappropriate. We expected those participants who anticipated doing the second task with their partner to show evidence of attempting to maintain both their happy and sad moods. This is exactly what we found. Whereas participants expecting to interact with a stranger preferred newspaper stories with a mood-incongruent content, participants expecting to interact with their partner preferred newspaper stories with a mood-congruent content. Again, these findings are difficult to explain from a hedonistic perspective. However, they make sense when one considers that concerns about the appropriateness of one's mood are of paramount importance in public contexts, yet largely irrelevant in the context of close relationships.

RESEARCH SUPPORTING THE APPROPRIATENESS HYPOTHESIS II: ACCEPTING VERSUS CRITICAL OTHERS

To the extent that anticipating interaction with a close other reverses our usual tendency to control our moods in the presence of a stranger, one would expect that the unique characteristics of the other would similarly predict different mood-regulation strategies. Others whom we perceive as accepting of us should trigger little in the way of controlling our mood because appropriateness concerns are of little importance. However, when the other is perceived as critical of us, mood control should become of paramount importance, as unaccepting others are most likely to respond to our potentially inappropriate moods with disapproval.

To test this idea, we adapted the research strategy reported by Baldwin, Carrell, and Lopez (1990) on the effects of imaginary audiences on self-evaluation. After inducing a sad or happy mood via having participants recall an appropriate autobiographic memory, we asked them to think of someone who was accepting or critical of them and write a short paragraph about that person. Subsequently, all participants indicated their preference for reading newspaper stories with a cheerful or depressing content. We expected that priming an accepting other through writing a paragraph about that person would not trigger much in the way of mood control. However, priming a critical other should highlight the evaluative nature of that person and consequently lead to an attempt toward controlling one's sad and happy moods as well. This is precisely what we found. Participants for whom an accepting other had been primed preferred mood-congruent stories, whereas participants in whom a critical other had been primed preferred mood-incongruent stories, presumably in an attempt to control their moods.

This finding provides further evidence for our theoretical claim that concerns about the appropriateness of one's mood contribute in important ways to our desire to control both our happy and sad moods. Moreover, it suggests that it does not require the actual or anticipated presence of others to instill a motive toward mood control. The finding that our participants attempted to regulate their mood in response to imagined others helps explain why we frequently manage to control our moods even though we may be by ourselves. It appears that under such circumstances, conjuring up images of critical others ("What would my mother say if she saw me like this?") may be what ultimately compels us to rid ourselves of the (inappropriate and unwanted) moods we are in.

SOME PARTING THOUGHTS

Our social constraints model, we feel, has something unique to offer to the understanding of moods and mood regulation. First, rather than base our model on hedonistic, pleasure–pain principles, we ground it instead in principles derived from Newton's First Law of Physics: Moods continue in their state unless they are acted on by some external force. Of course, like most metaphors, ours is far from perfect. Unlike physical objects, humans have motives and other dispositions that may act as agents of change. However, far from being our sovereign masters, many of them are activated by their social context (Martin, 1999). Thus, our model fits much better with the basic tenet of Lewinian Field theory than any analysis that relies exclusively on internal forces (e.g., pleasure seeking, pain avoidance). It also fits with what our research reveals about how we actually experience and manage our moods. That is, moods remain at rest or in motion unless there is reason to act on them. Individuals are likely to remain in whatever mood they are in unless appropriateness concerns brought on by perceived social constraints suggest a change.

Finally, although our model is first and foremost concerned with how people manage their moods, we believe that it has some obvious implications for understanding issues more generally related to mood and processing. In this regard, one of the unique contributions of our model is that it takes into account the mounting evidence that negative moods by themselves do not automatically trigger a repair model (cf, Erber & Erber, in press-a). This has led us to reject theoretical positions claiming that moods carry any sort of default mechanism or processes. Instead, by considering context and motivation early (i.e., when a potentially mood-eliciting stimulus is encountered), we were able to come up with a processing model that is considerably more parsimonious than models based on default-override principles. Although we believe in the power of our model to account for a number of diverse research findings, we also recognize that we have only just begun to push the boundaries of our model, both empirically and theoretically. Nonetheless, the progress we have made thus far might encourage others interested in the intersection of affect, motivation, and social cognition to engage in similar endeavours. As we noted elsewhere (Erber & Erber, in press-b), much of the research on motivated social cognition has worked from the assumption that pleasure and reward seeking along with pain and loss avoidance are the ultimate motivators of our thoughts and actions. Our research to date suggests that this is an oversimplification at best, and an epistemic dead-end at worst.

REFERENCES

Allport, G. H. (1954). The historical background of social psychology. In G. Lindzey (Ed.), *The handbook of social psychology, Vol 1*, 2nd ed. (pp. 3–56) Cambridge, MA: Addison-Wesley.

Baldwin, M. W., Carrell, S. E., & Lopez, D. F. (1990). Priming relationship schemas: My advisor and the pope are watching me from the back of my mind. *Journal of Experimental Social Psychology, 26*, 435–454.

Bentham, J. (1789). *An introduction to the principals of morals and legislation.* Oxford: Clarendon Press.

Bower, G. H., Gilligan, S. J., & Monteiro, K. P. (1981). Selectivity of learning caused by affective states. *Journal of Experimental Psychology: General, 110*, 451–473.

Campbell, J. D., Trapnell, P. D., Heine, S. J., Katz, I. M., Lavallee, L. F., & Lehman, D. R. (1996). Self-concept clarity, personality correlates, and cultural boundaries. *Journal of Personality and Social Psychology, 70*, 141–156.

Catanzaro, S. J., & Mearns, J. (1990). Measuring generalized expectancies for negative mood regulation: Initial scale development and implications. *Journal of Personality Assessment, 54*, 546–563.

Cialdini, R. B., Levy, A., Herman, C. P., & Levenbeck, S. (1973). Attitudinal politics: The strategy of moderation. *Journal of Personality and Social Psychology, 25*, 100–108.

Clark, M. S., & Isen, A. M. (1982). Toward understanding the relationship between feeling states and social behavior. In A. Hastorf & A. M. Isen (Eds.), *Cognitive social psychology* (pp. 73–108). New York: Elsevier North Holland.

Commons, M. J., & Erber, R. (1996, May). *Mood regulation in anticipation of social interaction: The case of strangers versus romantic partners.* Paper presented at the 69th annual meeting of the Midwestern Psychological Association. Chicago, IL.

Erber, M. W., Erber, R., Therriault, N., & Onesto, R. (1998). *On the puzzling nature of the self-regulation of anxiety: Absorption, anxiety, and anagrams*. Manuscript under preparation.

Erber, R., & Erber, M. W. (1994). Beyond mood and social judgment: Mood incongruent recall and mood regulation. *European Journal of Social Psychology, 24,* 79–88.

Erber, R., & Erber, M. W. (in press-a). Mood and processing: A view from a self-regulation perspective. In L. L. Martin & G. L. Clore (Eds.), *Theories of mood and information processing* (pp. xxx). Mahwah, NJ: Lawrence Erlbaum Associates.

Erber, R., & Erber, M. W. (in press-b). The self-regulation of moods: Second thoughts on the importance of happiness in everyday life. *Psychological Inquiry.*

Erber, R., & Tesser, A. (1992). Task effort and the regulation of mood: The absorption hypothesis. *Journal of Experimental Social Psychology, 28,* 339–359.

Erber, R., & Therriault, N. (1994, May). *Sweating to the oldies: The mood-absorbing qualities of exercise*. Paper presented at the 66th annual meeting of the Midwestern Psychological Association. Chicago, IL.

Erber, R., Wegner, D. M., & Therriault, N. (1996). On being cool and collected: Mood regulation in anticipation of social interaction. *Journal of Personality and Social Psychology, 70,* 757–766.

Forgas, J. P. (1995). Mood and judgment: The Affect Infusion Model (AIM). *Psychological Bulletin, 117,* 39–66.

Goffman, E. (1963). *Behavior in public places*. New York: Free Press.

Gollwitzer. P. M., Heckhausen, H., & Steller, B. (1990). Deliberative and implemental mind-sets: Cognitive tuning toward congruous thoughts and information. *Journal of Personality and Social Psychology, 59,* 1119–1127.

Isen, A. M. (1984). Toward understanding the role of affect in cognition. In R. S. Wyer, Jr. & T. Srull (Eds.), *Handbook of social cognition* (pp. 179–236). Hillsdale, NJ: Lawrence Erlbaum Associates.

Martin, L. L. (1999). I-D compensation theory: Some implications of trying to satisfy immediate-return needs in a delayed-return culture. *Psychological Inquiry, 10,* 195–208.

Salovey, P. (1992). Mood-induced self-focused attention. *Journal of Personality and Social Psychology, 62,* 699–707.

Smith, S. M., & Petty, R. E. (1995). Personality moderators of mood congruency effects on cognition: The role of self-esteem and negative mood regulation. *Journal of Personality and Social Psychology, 68,* 1092–1107.

Taylor, S. E. (1991). The asymmetrical effects of positive and negative events: The mobilization–minimization hypothesis. *Psychological Bulletin, 110,* 67–85.

Tesser, A., & Rosen, S. (1975). The reluctance to transmit bad news. In L. Berkowitz (Ed.), *Advances in experimental social psychology, Vol. 8* (pp. 193–232), New York: Academic Press.

Therriault, N., Erber, R., & Oktela, C. (1996). *Mood and self-perception in response to negative self-information: To ruminate or regulate*. Paper presented at the 68th annual meeting of the Midwestern Psychological Association. Chicago, IL.

Trope, Y., & Neter, E. (1994). Reconciling competing motives in self-evaluation: The role of self-control in feedback seeking. *Journal of Personality and Social Psychology, 66,* 646–657.

Wegener, D. T., Petty, R. E., & Smith, S. M. (1995). Positive mood can increase or decrease message scrutiny: The hedonic contingency view of mood and message processing. *Journal of Personality and Social Psychology, 69,* 5–15.

Wood, J. V., Saltzberg, J. A., & Goldsamt, L. A. (1990). Does affect induce self-focused attention? *Journal of Personality and Social Psychology, 58,* 899–908.

V

Affective Influences on Cognitively Mediated Social Behaviors

14

Affect, Cognition, and Interpersonal Behavior: The Mediating Role of Processing Strategies

Joseph P. Forgas
University of New South Wales
Sydney, Australia

Affect Congruence in Interpersonal Behavior   295
Affect Infusion: A Question of Processing Style?   296
Affective Influences on Behavior Interpretation   300
Affect and Eyewitness Memory for Observed Interactions   302
Affective Influences on Spontaneous Interaction   303
Affect Infusion and Interpersonal Strategies: Making a Request   304
Affective Influences on Responding to Unexpected Social Situations   307
Affective Influences on Planned Strategic Encounters   308
Affective Influences on Persuasive Communication   311
The Interaction Between Affect and Cognitive-Processing Strategies   312
Summary and Conclusions   314
Acknowledgments   316
References   316

Affect infuses every aspect of social life. Feelings, moods, and emotions constitute a critical part of how we perceive and judge ourselves and others,

Joseph P. Forgas is of the School of Psychology, University of New South Wales, Sydney 2052; email: jp.forgas@unsw.edu.au

293

and how we plan and execute interpersonal behaviors. This book bears eloquent testimony to the universality and importance of affective influences on social cognition. It is all the more surprising, then, to find that for most of the brief history of psychology as a scientific discipline, social cognition and behavior were studied as if affect was at best irrelevant, and at worst a source of bias and disruption. As Hilgard (1980) noted, one reason for this is probably the traditional division of psychology's subject matter into three fundamental "faculties of mind"—affect, cognition and conation—and the implicit assumption that these "faculties" can and should be studied independently of each other. Although cognition and conation have received intense attention in the past, affect has remained relatively neglected, as the introductory review in Chapter 1 suggests.

It was not until the early 1980s that a concentrated attempt was made to incorporate affective variables into psychological research on cognition and behavior. Parallel discoveries in social cognition as well as in neuroanatomy and neuropsychology confirmed that affect is an essential and indispensable component of social thinking and interpersonal behavior (see also chapters by Adolphs & Damasio, chap. 2, this volume; and Ito & Cacioppo, chap. 3, this volume). There can be little doubt that moods and emotions are a crucial and highly adaptive part of managing complex social relationships and situations. In an affective void, rational reasoning alone often leads to dysfunctional and maladaptive judgments and decisions.

How does affect influence the way people perceive, interpret, plan, and execute strategic interpersonal behaviors? The information available in the social world is typically unmanageably complex, indeterminate, and ambiguous. People must rely on highly generative and constructive information-processing strategies to select, interpret, learn, and remember social information. It is largely because social behavior requires highly constructive and generative processing strategies that affective states can either indirectly (through affect priming effects), or directly (through affect-as-information effects) influence the kind of information people pay attention to and the kind of processing strategies they adopt. Ultimately, affect infusion into social cognition also influences how individuals plan and execute interpersonal behaviors.

We have all experienced times when a positive mood spreads to and infuses everything we think and do. When we feel happy and satisfied, all seems to be well with the world: We are happy with our job, satisfied with our intimate relationships, and optimistic about the future. The research to be reviewed here shows that positive mood not only influences thoughts and judgments, but also promotes more cooperative, confident, and optimistic interpersonal behaviors. In contrast, bad mood produces an air of gloom that seems to spread over our thoughts and judgments: We are critical of our partners, pessimistic about the future, and become cautious and defensive in our interpersonal strategies (Forgas, 1994; Forgas, Levinger, & Moylan, 1994).

AFFECT CONGRUENCE IN INTERPERSONAL BEHAVIOR

There are several early experiments that suggest that affective states can significantly influence cognition and subsequent interpersonal behaviors. Fear and anxiety can produce more apprehensive and negative assessments of others, as Feshbach and Singer (1957) found in an early study. In another classic series of experiments, Schachter (1959) showed that induced anxiety can significantly influence realistic interpersonal preferences. People who were anxious sought to spend time with partners who were in the same predicament, and presumably most able to share (and alleviate) this aversive affective experience. Several experiments in the 1960s and 1970s found that evaluations of and reactions to others can be significantly influenced by a previously induced affective state (Griffitt, 1970). In these experiments, induced affective state became readily associated with evaluations of an interaction partner, and distorted subsequent judgments and behaviors in a mood-congruent direction.

Although affect congruence in thinking and judgments is commonly found both in laboratory experiments and in everyday life, this is by no means a universal phenomenon. Sometimes, affect fails to have a congruent influence on cognition, and frequently, an opposite, mood-incongruent effect is observed (Erber & Erber, chap. 13, this volume; Sedikides, 1994). To complicate matters even further, affective states do not only influence the content (positivity or negativity) of cognition (what people think), but also the process of cognition (the kind of information strategies used) (Bless, 2000; Fiedler, 2000; Schwarz & Clore, 1988). The task of a comprehensive theory of affect and social cognition is thus to explain when and how these different effects occur.

The main objective of this chapter is to argue that any understanding of affective influences on strategic interpersonal behaviors requires a careful analysis of the information-processing strategies that mediate these effects. People may adopt a variety of different information-processing styles when dealing with social information. Depending on the kind of processing strategies they use, we may observe affect congruence or incongruence, or perhaps no affective influences at all on their behaviors. This occurs because some processing styles invite and facilitate the constructive use of affect as a source of information in cognitive and behavioral tasks. In contrast, other processing styles inhibit affect infusion and even produce affect-incongruent outcomes. Of particular interest here is how temporary moods may influence interpersonal behaviors.

Moods may be defined as "low-intensity, diffuse and relatively enduring affective states without a salient antecedent cause and therefore little cognitive content (e.g., feeling good or feeling bad)" (Forgas, 1992a, p. 230). Unlike emotions, moods are typically not in the focus of our consciousness and have little cognitive content and structure. Yet it is precisely because of their low intensity and limited cognitive content that moods may often have a more long-lasting, subtle, and unconscious influence on people's thinking and social behaviors than do distinct emotions (Forgas, 1992a, 1993, 2000; Sedikides, 1995). One integrative theory, the multiprocess Affect Infusion Model (AIM; Forgas, 1995a) was developed to explain the subtle interaction between affect and cognition. The AIM assumes that affect can have both informational and processing effects on cognition, and assigns a central role to different processing strategies in the mediation of mood effects.

AFFECT INFUSION: A QUESTION OF PROCESSING STYLE?

One of the most productive affect-cognition theories was proposed by Bower (1981), who argued that affective states, once activated, can selectively prime and spread activation to associated cognitive constructs. As a result, affect-consistent ideas are more likely to reach threshold activation and be used in guiding selective attention, learning, associations, and recall. This theory continues to offer an elegant and parsimonious explanation of many affect-congruent phenomena. An alternative model was put forward by Schwarz and Clore (1988), who suggested that affect-congruence in some evaluative judgments may occur because people mistakenly rely on their prevailing affective state as information about their evaluative reactions to a target. This "How do I feel about it?" heuristic can explain some cases of mood congruence in judgments as long as the existing mood state is not already attributed to another cause.

A problem for both of these models is that affect congruence in thinking and behavior is not always observed. A comprehensive theory of affect infusion thus needs to be able to specify the circumstances when affect congruence should be expected and when it should be absent or even reversed. Furthermore, such a model must also explain the processing conditions likely to facilitate the use of affect priming, or the affect-as-information mechanisms in producing mood congruence. The AIM (Forgas, 1995a) was designed to fulfill this task. The AIM predicts that affect infusion is most likely whenever circumstances promote elaborate, open, and constructive information-processing style (Fiedler, 1991; Forgas, 1992b, 1995b). Only a brief overview of the AIM is included here, as a more detailed description of these ideas is available elsewhere (Forgas, 1992a, 1995a).

Affect infusion may be understood as the process whereby affectively loaded information becomes incorporated into and exerts a congruent influence on cognitive, judgmental, and behavioral processes (cf. Forgas, 1995a). However, such incidental incorporation of affectively loaded information into thinking and behavior is only likely to occur in circumstances when a social task can only be performed using constructive, generative, and highly elaborate information-processing strategies that allow and, indeed, facilitate the inadvertent use of affectively primed material. In contrast, tasks that call for the simple reproduction of a preexisting response, or are dominated by a particular motivational objective should be impervious to affect infusion. The AIM thus assumes that (a) the extent and nature of affect infusion should be dependent on the kind of processing strategy that is used, and (b) that all things being equal, people should use the least effortful and simplest processing strategy capable of producing a response.

The AIM identifies four alternative processing strategies: *direct access*, *motivated*, *heuristic*, and *substantive* processing. The first two of these strategies, direct access and motivated processing, involve highly targeted and predetermined patterns of information search and selection, strategies that limit the scope for incidental affect infusion. The *direct access strategy* simply involves the direct retrieval of a preexisting response. As people possess a rich store of preformed, crystallized responses to many social situations, they are likely to use this strategy whenever more extensive and constructive processing is not warranted. The AIM predicts that such direct access processing is most likely when the task is highly familiar, and when no strong cognitive, affective, situational, or motivational cues call for more elaborate processing.

The *motivated strategy* in turn involves highly selective and targeted information search that is directed by a particular motivational objective. Again, this strategy precludes the incidental use of affectively primed information, or the heuristic use of affect as information. Affective states may also trigger motivated processing in the service of mood maintenance or mood repair (Clark & Isen, 1982). A number of other goals have been identified that also produce motivated processing and result in the elimination or even reversal of affect infusion (see also Erber & Erber, chap. 13, this volume). Such social motives that limit affect infusion include self-evaluation maintenance, ego-enhancement, achievement motivation, affiliation, or in-group favoritism (Forgas, 1990, 1991; Forgas & Fiedler, 1996; Forgas, Bower, & Moylan, 1990).

Thus, both direct access and motivated processing tend to limit affect infusion effects. In contrast, the remaining two processing strategies, *heuristic* and *substantive* processing require more constructive and open-ended information-search strategies, and thus facilitate affect infusion. Heuristic processing should be used when there are no prior responses to access and no direct motivation that guides a response, and so people seek to compute a constructive response with minimal effort. In this case, individuals may rely on cognitive shortcuts or heuristics and consider only limited information when responding. This is most likely when the task is simple, familiar, of little personal relevance, and cognitive capacity is limited and there are no motivational or situational pressures for more detailed processing. Heuristic processing leads to affect infusion as long as people rely on affect as the heuristic cue, and adopt the "How do I feel about it?" heuristic to produce a response (Clore, Schwarz, & Conway, 1994; Schwarz & Clore, 1988).

When these simpler strategies are inadequate, people actually need to engage in *substantive processing* to deal with a social situation. Substantive processing requires individuals to select, encode, and interpret novel information and relate this information to their preexisting memory-based knowledge structures in order to respond. This kind of processing is most likely when the task is atypical, complex, or novel, there is adequate processing capacity, and there is no motivational goal to dominate processing. As substantive processing is an inherently constructive, generative strategy, affect may selectively prime access to and facilitate the use of related thoughts, ideas, memories, and interpretations. The AIM makes the interesting and counterintuitive prediction that affect infusion (and mood congruence) should be increased when more extensive and constructive processing is required to deal with more complex, demanding, or novel tasks. Several studies measuring processing latencies provided direct evidence showing a strong relationship between more substantive processing producing greater affect infusion (Forgas, 1992b, 1993, 1995b, 1998a,b; Forgas & Bower, 1987).

The AIM also specifies a range of contextual variables related to the *task*, the *person*, and the *situation* that influence processing choices. For example, greater task familiarity, complexity, and typicality should recruit more substantive processing. Personal characteristics that influence processing style include motivation, cognitive capacity, personality traits (see also Mayer, chap. 19, this volume; Rusting, chap. 17, this volume; and Suls, chap. 18, this volume) as well as affective state itself. Situational features that have an impact on processing style include social norms, public scrutiny, and social influence by others (e.g., Forgas, 1990). An important feature of the AIM is that it recognizes that affect itself can also influence processing choices. As several studies now show (e.g., Bless, 2000; Fiedler, 2000), positive affect typically generates a more top-down, schematic, and heuristic processing style, whereas negative affect triggers more piecemeal, bottom-up, and vigilant processing strategies. Such a positive–negative processing asymmetry can be explained in terms of cognitive capacity effects (Mackie & Worth, 1991), functional, evolutionary mechanisms, or motivational influences (Clark & Isen, 1982). The AIM highlights the need for a careful analysis of processing variables such as memory and processing latency measures, as it is only in this way that we can empirically link processing variables with the behavioral consequences of affect. The key prediction of the AIM is the *absence* of affect infusion when direct access or motivated processing is used, and the *presence* of affect infusion during heuristic and substantive processing, as the experimental evidence reviewed later in this chapter suggests.

In order to show that more or less constructive processing directly influences affect infusion, in a number of studies we explicitly varied the extent to which social tasks required more or less substantive processing. In several experiments, participants were asked to respond to more or less complex, atypical, and unusual versus simple and typical persons and situations. Unusual people and situations should require more constructive processing, and should thus produce greater affect infusion (Forgas, 1992b, 1993). An analysis of recall memory and processing latency data confirmed the process mediation of these mood effects. More atypical social information took longer to process, and there was correspondingly greater affect infusion into these judgments. Other studies used nonverbal stimuli (pictures of more or less complex, demanding targets) (Forgas, 1995b), and again found that affect infusion was significantly greater for unusual, atypical tasks. A mediational analysis specifically confirmed that processing strategy had a significant mediating effect on the extent of affect infusion.

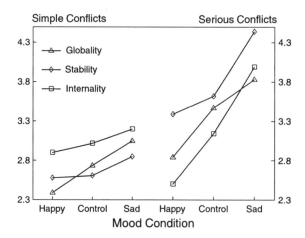

FIG. 14.1. The effects of mood on explanations for more or less serious conflicts in people's intimate personal relationships. Both positive and negative moods have a greater influence on the way more demanding, serious conflicts are explained, consistent with the more elaborate, substantive processing required to deal with this information. (Data based on Forgas, 1994.)

Somewhat surprisingly, similar effects were found when happy or sad persons made judgments about their own intimate relationships (Forgas, 1994; see also Fig. 14.1). In a counterintuitive pattern, these mood effects were consistently greater when more extensive, constructive processing was required to deal with more complex and serious rather than simple and everyday interpersonal issues. It seems then that even judgments about highly familiar people and events are more prone to affect infusion when a more substantive, constructive processing strategy is used. The principle, as predicted by the AIM, is that affect infusion in social cognition and behavior is greatest when people need to think more substantively to respond to a task. This is often the case when strategic interpersonal behaviors are planned and executed, as the next section suggests.

AFFECTIVE INFLUENCES
ON BEHAVIOR INTERPRETATION

Interacting with others requires constructive, generative information processing, as people must evaluate and plan their behaviors in inherently complex and uncertain social situations (Heider, 1958). To the extent that affective states may influence thinking and judgments, they should also influence subsequent social behaviors that are the outcome of constructive thinking. The on-line interpretation of observed behaviors is one of the most fundamental and automatic social–cognitive tasks people face in everyday life, and is likely to be a significant antecedent of behavioral responses. Does affect influence the outcome of such simple behavior interpretation tasks? As making sense of observed behaviors by definition requires some degree of inferential, substantive processing, there should be affect infusion into behavior interpretation.

This hypothesis was tested (Forgas, Bower, & Krantz, 1984) by providing happy or sad participants with a videotape of their own social interactions and asking them to monitor and rate their own and their partners' behaviors. There was a significant affective bias on behavior monitoring. Happy people "saw" significantly more positive and skilled and fewer negative and unskilled behaviors both in themselves and in their partners than did sad subjects. Objective observers who received no mood manipulation displayed no such monitoring biases. These results show that there is significant affect infusion into how interpersonal behaviors are monitored and interpreted, even when objective, videotaped evidence is readily available. In terms of the AIM, these effects occur because affect priming influences the kinds of interpretations, constructs, and associations that become available as people evaluate intrinsically complex and indeterminate social behaviors in the course of substantive, inferential processing. The same smile that is seen as "friendly" in a good mood may be judged as "awkward" when the observer is in a negative mood; discussing the weather could be seen as "poised" in good mood but "boring" when in a bad mood, and so on.

Later experiments confirmed these effects with more realistic judgments. People in a negative mood were also found to make more critical, self-deprecatory interpretations of their own behaviors, but people in a positive mood selectively looked for and found lenient and optimistic explanations for identical outcomes (Forgas, Bower, & Moylan, 1990). Rather surprisingly, such mood-induced distortions can also influence reactions to highly familiar, intimate events involving close partners (Forgas, 1994). In this study, partners in long-term intimate relationships were asked to evaluate behaviors in more or less serious interpersonal conflicts. Positive mood produced lenient, self-serving explanations. As suggested earlier, these mood effects became even stronger when the events judged were more complex and serious and thus required more constructive processing (Fig. 14.1). It seems then that affect tends to spontaneously infuse even such mundane tasks as the on-line monitoring of observed social behaviors, and these mood effects become stronger as the task becomes more complex and constructive.

AFFECT AND EYEWITNESS MEMORY FOR OBSERVED INTERACTIONS

People frequently witness various incidents in everyday life, and later rely on their memory to describe the event to others and to inform their own responses and interpersonal strategies. Such eyewitness memories play a very important role in interpersonal behavior, as well as in the legal system, where they are accorded special evidential status. However, as perceivers use highly constructive strategies to recall their experiences, eyewitness testimonies may well be contaminated by subsequent, unrelated information (Loftus, 1979). Recently, several experiments in our lab investigated the influence of affect on such eyewitness distortions. The events to be remembered were presented on videotapes. Some time later, participants were exposed to a mood induction, and then received some questions about the incidents that either included or did not include "planted" misleading details about the witnessed episodes. After a lengthy interval comprising several interference tasks, participants' recognition memory for the incidents was tested. We found that positive mood when the misleading information was presented significantly increased the mistaken incorporation of planted information into eyewitness memories, whereas negative mood decreased the same. It seems that the experience of positive affect produced a more top-down, superficial, and less attentive processing style, increasing the likelihood that false information suggested by the questioning will be incorporated into eyewitness memories. Negative affect in contrast triggered a more attentive bottom-up and externally focussed processing style, reducing the incidence of eyewitness errors. These effects were replicated in a naturalistic study, in which students were asked to recall a staged incident during a lecture. Once again, students feeling good while exposed to planted information were more likely to show incorrect memory, whereas negative affect reduced the incidence of such mistakes. These results—together with the evidence from other contributions to this book—confirm that even relatively mild, transient affective states can have a marked influence on the way people process, interpret and remember social information (see also Bower & Forgas, chap. 5; Clore, Gasper, & Garvin, chap. 6; Fiedler; Harmon-Jones, chap. 8; and Petty, DeSteno, &

Rucker, chap. 10, this volume). Does affect infusion also impact on actual interactive behaviors? This possibility was explored in several studies.

AFFECTIVE INFLUENCES
ON SPONTANEOUS INTERACTION

To the extent that the spontaneous on-line production of interactive behaviors also requires a degree of open, constructive information processing, we may expect that temporary mood should influence the responses people select. We may thus expect happy people to enact more friendly, likeable and rewarding interpersonal behaviors, while those in a sad mood may act and behave in a more constrained, unfriendly and less rewarding way, a prediction that was evaluated in a recent experiment carried out in collaboration with Anoushka Gunawardene (Forgas & Gunawardene, 1999). Female undergraduates were first induced into a positive or negative mood by watching happy or sad videotapes as part of an 'unrelated' study. Next, they participated in an interview about student life with a confederate, and their behavior was recorded by a hidden video camera.

The videotapes were subsequently watched and rated by trained observers blind to the manipulations who carefully recorded the valence, frequency and intensity of a wide variety of both verbal and nonverbal interactive behaviors, and also provided global ratings about the targets' behavior. There was a clear pattern of mood-congruence in these spontaneous behaviors. Happy participants displayed significantly more smiles, communicated more, disclosed more personal information about themselves and generally behaved in a more poised, skilled and rewarding manner. Sad participants were generally rated by observers as significantly more passive, uncomfortable, incompetent, shy, unfriendly, disinterested and tense than were happy participants (Figure 14.2)

It seems that even a minor affective experience such as watching a brief unrelated film has a highly significant and noticeable influence on subsequent interpersonal behaviors that can be readily detected by observers. It is remarkable that these behavioral effects occur reliably even in a highly structured interaction such as an interview. Mood should have an even more dramatic effect on social behaviors in open-ended, unstructured interactions. In addition to demonstrating such global affect infusion into interpersonal behaviors, we also need to assess the role of affect in the production and use of specific interpersonal behaviors, such as the

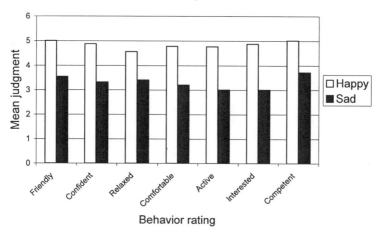

FIG. 14.2. Mood effects on spontaneous interpersonal behavior:
people experiencing happy mood behave in a more friendly, positive and confident way than people in a negative mood. (Data
based on Forgas & Gunawardene, 1999).

formulation of requests. This was undertaken in a series of recent studies
(Forgas, 1999a,b).

AFFECT INFUSION AND INTERPERSONAL
STRATEGIES: MAKING A REQUEST

Asking a person to do something for us—requesting—is one of most difficult and complex interpersonal tasks we face in everyday life (Gibbs, 1985).
When formulating a request, people are by definition uncertain of the outcome, and so must phrase their request with great care so as to maximize
the likelihood of compliance (by being more direct) without risking giving
offence (by not being *too* direct). Requesting is thus an interpersonal task
that is characterized by psychological ambiguity and requires constructive,
substantive processing to produce just the right degree of directness and
politeness.

In terms of the AIM, affective states should significantly influence requesting strategies. When in a positive mood, people should adopt a more
confident and direct requesting style as a result of the greater availability and
use of positively valenced thoughts and associations in their minds as they
constructively assess the situation (Forgas, 1998b, 1999a,b). Furthermore,

in terms of the AIM, these mood effects should be further magnified when the request situation is more complex and demanding, and requires more substantive and elaborate processing strategies.

This prediction was tested in several experiments. In one study, mood was induced by asking participants to recall and think about happy or sad autobiographical episodes in an allegedly separate task (Forgas, 1999a, Experiment 1). Next, participants were asked to identify more or less polite request forms they would prefer to use in an easy and in a difficult and demanding request situation. As predicted, participants in a happy mood used more direct, impolite requests, whereas sad persons preferred more cautious, indirect, and polite request alternatives. Results also showed that these mood effects on requesting strategies were much stronger when the request situation was more demanding and difficult, and required more extensive, substantive processing to evaluate.

In a follow-up experiment, happy or sad participants were asked to formulate their own open-ended requests, which were subsequently rated for politeness and elaboration (Forgas, 1999a, Experiment 2). Mood again had a significant influence. Those in a positive mood produced significantly more direct, impolite, and less elaborate requests than did individuals in a negative mood, and these mood effects were greater when the request situation was more difficult and problematic. In a further study, participants who were feeling happy or sad after watching videotapes were asked to select more or less polite request alternatives they would use in a variety of realistic social situations (Forgas, 1999b, Experiment 1). This time, results showed that affective influences on request preferences were greatest on decisions about using direct, impolite, and unconventional requests that most clearly violate cultural conventions of politeness, and should recruit the most substantive, elaborate processing strategies.

Overall, these results establish that affect has a significant influence on people's constructive interpretation of social situations and their subsequent interpersonal behaviors. The results also indicate that affective influences on social behaviors are highly process dependent. It appears that affect infusion is significantly increased or reduced depending on just how much open, constructive processing is required to deal with a more or less demanding interpersonal task.

Of course, the studies reported so far relied on laboratory procedures and hypothetical tasks. Are these effects also likely to occur in real-life interpersonal situations? In order to explore the ecological validity of this phenomenon, a further experiment was carried out using unobtrusive methods to explore affective influences on naturally produced requests (Forgas,

1999b, Experiment 2). Affect was induced by asking participants to view happy or sad films. Next, in an apparently impromptu development, the experimenter casually asked participants to get a file from a neighboring office while the next experiment was set up. All participants agreed. In fact, their actual words used in requesting the file were recorded by a concealed tape recorder in the neighboring office, and their requests were subsequently analyzed for politeness and other qualities.

Results confirmed that there was a significant affective influence on these naturally produced requests. Negative mood resulted in significantly more polite, indirect, friendly, and more elaborate request forms. Positive mood in turn produced less polite, more direct, and less elaborate requests (Fig. 14.3). Affective state also influenced the latency of the request: Those in a negative mood were more hesitant and delayed making their requests significantly longer than did control or happy persons. In order to assess the degree of elaborate processing involved in producing these requests, participants' recall memory for the exact words they used was also assessed later on. Results showed that recall accuracy—an index of elaborate processing—was positively related to the degree of affect infusion. This pattern supports the prediction of the AIM that greater mood effects should occur when more elaborate, substantive processing is used by a communicator. These results also confirm the findings reported earlier, and show that affect has a critical influence on strategic social behaviors in realistic social situations, with negative mood producing more polite, elaborate, and hedging request choices.

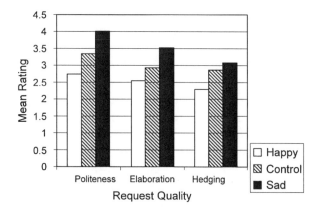

FIG. 14.3. Mood effects on the level of politeness, elaboration, and hedging in naturally produced requests: positive mood produces less polite, less elaborate, and less hedging request forms. (Data based on Forgas, 1998b).

AFFECTIVE INFLUENCES
ON RESPONDING TO UNEXPECTED
SOCIAL SITUATIONS

The previous experiments suggest that deliberative, planned interpersonal behaviors are subject to significant affect infusion effects, as long as some degree of elaborate, constructive processing is used. Frequently, however, we do not have the luxury to plan and deliberate about our social moves, but must respond almost instantaneously to a new social situation. To the extent that such rapid reactions also require some degree of constructive processing, responses should be subject to affect infusion effects. This prediction was evaluated in a series of recent field experiments (Forgas, 1998b). Being approached unexpectedly by another person with a request represents one of the simplest kinds of interpersonal tasks in which a rapid reaction involving constructive cognitive processing is required. In these studies, we assessed the role of induced affective states on how people evaluate and respond to such a situation.

The scene of the study was a university library. Affect was induced by leaving folders containing pretested pictures (or text) designed to induce positive or negative mood on some unoccupied library desks, with an instruction "Please open and consider this." Students entering the library and occupying the desks were surreptitiously observed to ensure that they fully exposed themselves to the mood induction. A few minutes later, they were approached by another student (in fact, a confederate) and received an unexpected polite or impolite request for several sheets of paper needed to complete an essay. Their responses were noted. A short time after the requesting incident, a second confederate approached the participants and explained that the request was in fact staged, and asked them to complete a brief questionnaire assessing their perception and evaluation of the request and the requester, and their recall of the request.

Consistent with the predictions, there was a clear mood-congruent pattern in how people behaved in this situation. Students who received the negative mood induction were significantly more likely to report a critical, negative evaluation of the request and the requester and were less inclined to comply than were positive mood participants. In a particularly interesting result, induced mood and the level of politeness of the request also had a significant interactive effect on people's responses. It turns out that mood effects were greater on the evaluation of and responses to impolite, unconventional requests that required more substantive processing. The more extensive processing recruited by impolite requests was also confirmed by better recall memory for these messages later on. Polite and conventional requests, however, were apparently processed less substantively, were less influenced by mood, and were also remembered less accurately later on.

These results confirm that affect infusion into the planning and execution of impromptu social behaviors is significantly mediated by the kind of processing strategy people employ. Of course, mood may not only influence reactions to unexpected social encounters. In terms of our theoretical framework, affect infusion should be even greater on strategically planned social encounters—such as a negotiating situation—that allow participants to adopt elaborate and extensive cognitive processing strategies to plan and execute their behaviors.

AFFECTIVE INFLUENCES ON PLANNED STRATEGIC ENCOUNTERS

Although many social situations call for rapid, impromptu responses like the ones investigated and described in the previous section, there are also numerous instances when social actors can deliberate and plan their interpersonal strategies well in advance. If affect infusion is a function of substantive, elaborate processing, we might expect affective states to play a particularly important role in such elaborately planned interpersonal encounters. In several experiments, we investigated affective influences on the planning and performance of complex behavior sequences such as negotiating encounters (Forgas, 1998a). Mood was induced by giving participants positive, negative, or neutral feedback about their performance on a verbal test.

After the mood induction, participants engaged in an informal, interpersonal and a formal, intergroup negotiating task with another team in what they believed was a separate experiment. The question we were interested in was how temporary moods might influence people's goals, plans, and, ultimately, their behaviors in this interaction. Results showed an interesting pattern. Those participants who were in an induced positive mood set themselves higher and more ambitious negotiating goals, formed higher expectations about the success of the forthcoming encounter, and also formulated specific action plans that were more optimistic, cooperative, and integrative than did control or negative mood participants. Those individuals who formulated more cooperative goals as a result of feeling good actually behaved more cooperatively and were more willing to use integrative strategies, and make and reciprocate deals than were those in a negative mood (Fig. 14.4).

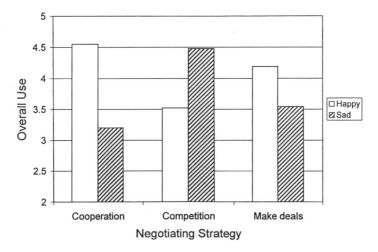

FIG. 14.4. Mood effects on bargaining and negotioation strategies: positive mood increases cooperation and deal-making, and
negative mood increases competitive strategies both in interpersonal and in intergroup negotiation. (Data based on Forgas,
1998a).

Surprisingly, these mood-induced differences in goal setting and bargaining behavior actually led to a significant difference in bargaining outcomes. Negotiators who experienced positive affect and were more cooperative and integrative achieved significantly better outcomes than did
those who were feeling bad. These findings clearly suggest that even slight
changes in affective state due to an unrelated prior event can influence the
goals that people set for themselves, the action plans they formulate, and
the way they ultimately behave in strategic interpersonal encounters.

What are the cognitive mechanisms responsible for these effects? In
terms of the AIM, mood effects on interpersonal behaviors that require
constructive processing can be explained as due to the operation of affect
priming mechanisms. When people face an uncertain and unpredictable
social encounter, such as a negotiating task, their thoughts and plans about
their bargaining strategies must be based on open, constructive, and inferential thinking. They must go beyond the information given and must
rely on their thoughts and memories to construct a response. Positive mood
should then selectively prime more positive thoughts and associations, and
the greater activation and accessibility of these ideas should ultimately lead
to the formulation of more optimistic expectations and the adoption of more
cooperative and integrative bargaining strategies. However, negative affect

should prime more pessimistic, negative memories and associations, and should lead to the planning and use of less optimistic, less cooperative, and, ultimately, less successful bargaining strategies.

Further experiments exploring this phenomenon also showed that mood effects on negotiation are subject to significant individual differences between negotiants. When we assessed participants in terms of their scores on individual difference measures such as machiavellianism and need for approval, we found that these measures significantly mediated mood effects. High macchiavellians and those high in need for approval were less influenced by temporary mood in formulating their plans and behaviors than were low scorers on these measures. Theoretically, as implied by the AIM, affect infusion should be constrained for individuals who habitually approach interpersonal tasks such as a bargaining encounter from a highly motivated, predetermined perspective. Such motivated processing should limit the degree of open, constructive thinking they employ when planning their strategies, and thus reduce the likelihood of affectively primed thoughts influencing their responses and their behaviors. It is almost as if high macchiavellians and those high in need for approval had their minds made up about what to do even before they started, thus limiting the extent of incidental affect infusion. There is now growing evidence suggesting that individual differences related to how people process social information play an important role in mediating affective influences on social cognition and behavior (see also Mayer, chap. 19; Rusting, chap. 17; and Suls, chap. 18, this volume).

It seems, then, that although some individuals are habitually open to affective influences, others may have a strong tendency to rely on motivated processing to control and limit their affective reactions to social situations. It turns out that there are a number of individual difference variables that mediate affect infusion into social judgments and behavior, and their effects can either increase or reduce affect dependence. For example, people who score high on traits such as Openness to Feelings (Costa & Macrae, 1985) seem to be significantly more likely to be influenced by affect in a mood-congruent direction in the way they perceive and evaluate information than are low scorers on this measure (Ciarrochi & Forgas, in press). Other studies showed that trait anxiety also significantly moderates the influence of negative affect on people's responses to a threatening outgroup (Ciarocchi & Forgas, 1999). Low trait-anxious people showed affect congruence and responded negatively to an outgroup. However, highly trait-anxious individuals displayed an opposite pattern: their reactions were more positive when they experienced negative mood. Such reversal of affect congruence in social reactions is consistent with the adoption of motivated processing by individuals who are especially anxious and defensive in social situations. These results confirm the general principle that affect congruence is significantly moderated by different processing strategies linked to enduring personality characteristics.

AFFECTIVE INFLUENCES ON PERSUASIVE COMMUNICATION

Although the evidence so far suggests that positive mood tends to promote more cooperative and successful interpersonal behaviors, not all strategic encounters function like this. Sometimes, the more cautious and situation oriented processing produced by bad moods can also produce distinct advantages. For example, producing high-quality persuasive messages to get others to agree with us may benefit from negative affect as aversive mood makes people pay greater attention to the demands of the situation and process their responses in a more careful, piecemeal fashion (Bless, 2000; Fiedler, 2000; Forgas, 1998a,b).

There has been a surprising dearth of work on affective influences on how persuasive messages are *produced*. Yet amateur persuaders—that is, all of us—must think on their feet, plan and produce their persuasive strategies on-line. This question was investigated in several recent unpublished experiments (Forgas, Ciarrochi, & Moylan, 2000). In the first study, videotapes were used to induce 59 volunteer student participants into positive or negative moods. Next, they were asked to write persuasive messages supporting or opposing (1) the proposition that student fees should be increased, and (2) the issue of Aboriginal land rights in Australia. Their arguments were subsequently rated for quality, persuasiveness, and valence by two judges who achieved an inter-rater reliability of .86. Mood had a strong influence on argument quality. Those in a negative mood produced significantly higher quality and more persuasive arguments than did happy persuaders on both issues and irrespective of the position they argued, indicating the cross-situational robustness of this result. Mood also influenced argument valence: happy persons produced more positive, and sad persons produced more negative arguments. Almost identical results were obtained in two follow-up experiments using different mood induction methods and different argument topics, confirming the reliability of these results.

A further experiment involved participants interacting with a 'partner' through a computer keyboard. This experiment also manipulated the motivation to be persuasive by offering some participants a significant reward (the chance to win highly desired movie passes). Two raters blind to the manipulations rated each argument for quality, complexity, persuasiveness, originality, and valence. There was a significant mood main effect: those in a negative mood produced significantly higher quality arguments than the neutral group who in turn did better than the positive group. This mood effect was partly dependent on the reward manipulation. Mood had a greater effect on argument quality in the low reward condition than the high reward condition. This finding is consistent with the Affect Infusion Model, and shows that mood effects on information processing—and subsequent social influence strategies—are likely to be strongest in the absence of motivated processing. The provision of a reward reduced mood effects on argument quality by imposing a strong external influence on how the task was approached and thereby presumably overriding more subtle mood effects.

These experiments thus provide convergent evidence that mood can produce profound behavioral differences in the quality and effectiveness of the persuasive arguments people produce. These effects were robust across a variety of situations and topics and using a range of different mood induction procedures. It appears then that negative affect can also produce certain strategic advantages in interpersonal behavior when a more careful, externally focused and bottom-up information processing style is adopted. Negative affect was previously found to lead to the elimination of some attribution errors and the reduction of eye-witness memory distortions (Forgas, 1998c).

THE INTERACTION BETWEEN AFFECT AND COGNITIVE-PROCESSING STRATEGIES

The studies reviewed so far suggest that affect has a strong influence on how people interpret and respond to social situations as long as some degree of open, constructive processing is required that allows affect infusion to occur. However, the relationship among affect, cognition, and behavior is not unidirectional. Just as processing strategies can mediate the nature and extent of affect infusion, affect in turn can influence information-processing style (Bless, 2000; Fiedler, 2000). The cognitive consequences of affect may play an important role in interpersonal behavior and judgments. We found that the kind of vigilant, systematic attention to stimulus details recruited by negative moods tends to reduce or even eliminate such common interpersonal biases as the fundamental attribution error (Forgas, 1998c). Furthermore, as we have seen, positive affect tends to increase and negative affect tends to reduce the likelihood of other kinds of cognitive mistakes in social thinking, such as the corruption of eyewitness recollections (Forgas, 1999c).

The tendency to ignore or underestimate situational influences on observed social behavior and focus on internal causes instead has been labeled the fundamental attribution error (FAE). One reason why the FAE occurs is because social actors are lazy information processors and seem to pay selective attention to the most conspicuous information—the person—and neglect important but less salient situational information (Gilbert & Malone, 1995). In other words, people seem to naturally assume a "unit relation" between the actor and his/her behavior, attributing causality internally, and may only correct for situational pressures subsequently, if at all (Heider, 1958). As we know, positive affect produces a more top-down, schematic and heuristic processing style that is less sensitive to situational information (Bless, 2000), it can be predicted that the additional consideration of external constraints necessary to avoid the FAE may be impaired in good moods, and improved in bad moods.

In these experiments, participants were provided with behavioral information about an actor (an essay written by a student participating in a debate) that expressed attitudes that were either freely chosen or assigned, and were either highly desirable or undesirable (Forgas, 1998c). The key finding was that people in a negative mood were less likely and those in a positive mood were more likely to commit the fundamental attribution error and assume that the observed behavior was internally caused, even when they were provided with clear evidence that the behavior was, in fact, coerced. This occurred most when the essays advocated a highly salient, unpopular protesting position. This effect was confirmed in further unobtrusive field studies. People who just saw happy or sad films made judgments about the writers of popular and unpopular essays in an ostensible "street survey." Again, positive affect increased and negative affect decreased the FAE. Subsequent mediational analyses (Forgas, 1998c, Experiment 3) established that these attributional biases were due to affect-induced differences in processing strategies. These studies show that affect has a significant influence on processing strategies and the way people explain the causes of desirable and undesirable social behaviors.

Research demonstrating the processing consequences of affect may also be relevant to explaining how people manage to calibrate and maintain a balanced mood state in interpersonal situations. Previous research suggests that affect management may involve selective exposure to mood-incongruent information (Erber & Erber, chap. 13, this volume; Forgas, 1992a), recall of mood-incongruent memories (Sedikides, 1994), engagin in mood-incongruent behaviors, interacting with rewarding partners (Forgas, 1991), or seeking distraction from the source of the mood (Rusting, chap. 17, this volume).

In several papers, we proposed a homeostatic model of spontaneous mood management that assumes that people automatically switch between substantive processing (producing affect infusion) and motivated processing (producing affect control) to maintain affective equilibrium (Forgas, in press; Forgas, Johnson, & Ciarrochi, 1998). Such a homeostatic affect management model predicts that once affect infusion reaches a threshold level as a result of substantive processing, an automatic switch toward motivated processing and mood-incongruent thinking should occur to restore affective homeostasis. Similar suggestions were made in some earlier studies by Clark and Isen (1982) and by Sedikides (1994).

We (Forgas & Ciarrochi, 2000) conducted several studies to test that affect infusion is eventually followed by a spontaneous switch to a motivated affect control strategy. In one study, participants who were feeling good or bad after thinking about happy or sad events from their past generated a series of trait adjectives. Mood initially produced mood-congruent adjectives, but over time, subjects spontaneously switched to recalling mood-incongruent adjectives. The same "first congruent, then incongruent" pattern of responses was repeated in two additional experiments. It appears, then, that once a threshold level of affect intensity was reached due to affect-infusion processes, people may spontaneously change their cognitive and behavioral strategies and turn to motivated, incongruent responses in order to control their mood. We also found that this ability to control moods by spontaneously switching from congruent to incongruent associations was particularly marked for high self-esteem people, consistent with the critical role of individual differences in mediating affective influences on cognition (see also Mayer, chap. 19; Rusting, chap. 17; and Suls, chap. 18, this volume). These studies suggest the intriguing possibility that fluctuating affective states can play an important role in producing spontaneous changes in cognitive and behavioral responses in order to maintain affective equilibrium over time.

SUMMARY AND CONCLUSIONS

This chapter argues that mild everyday affective states and moods have a significant influence on the way people perceive and interpret social behaviors, and the way they plan and execute strategic interactions. Furthermore, different information-processing strategies play a key role in explaining these effects. Multiprocess theories such as the Affect Infusion Model (AIM; Forgas, 1995a) offer a simple and parsimonious explanation of when and how affect infusion into social behaviors occurs. Several experiments found that more extensive, substantive processing enhances mood-congruity effects, consistent with the predictions of the AIM (Forgas, 1992b, 1994, 1995b). The chapter also reviews a number of empirical studies demonstrating how such principles can be translated into behavioral research, and how affective states can have an impact on both simple and complex interpersonal behaviors. The experiments described here show that affect can influence the formulation of and responses to requests (Forgas, 1998b, 1999a,b), the planning and execution of strategic negotiations (Forgas, 1998a), and the monitoring and interpretation of complex interactive behaviors (Forgas, 1994; Forgas et al., 1984, 1990). In contrast, affect infusion is absent whenever a social cognitive task could be performed using a simple, well-rehearsed direct access strategy or a highly motivated strategy. In these conditions, there is little need and little opportunity for incidentally primed mood-congruent information to infuse information processing (Fiedler, 1991; Forgas, 1995a).

Several of these experiments demonstrate that affect infusion occurs not only in the laboratory, but also in many real-life situations. Consistent with other chapters included in this book, affect can influence relationship behaviors, group behaviors, organizational decisions, consumer preferences, and health-related behaviors (Forgas & Moylan, 1987; Mayer et al., 1992; Salovey et al., 1991; Sedikides, 1992; see also Bodenhausen, Mussweiler, Gabriel, & Moreno, chap. 15; and Salovey, Detwiler, Steward, & Bedell, chap. 16, this volume). Even such highly involved and complex tasks as dealing with relationship conflicts can be subject to a mood-congruent bias (Forgas, 1994). Indeed, the tendency to alternate between substantive and motivated processing strategies, producing affect infusion and affect control, respectively, could be considered as part of an ongoing homeostatic strategy of controlled mood management (Forgas, in press; Forgas & Ciarrochi, 2000; Forgas, Johnson, & Ciarrochi, 1998). We still know relatively little about the homeostatic mechanisms that help us to maintain our affective states within relatively narrow limits, but it is highly likely that different information processing strategies play an important role in such a system.

Other research reviewed here also shows that positive and negative affective states have an important and asymmetric processing effect on cognition. We found that positive mood increases and negative mood decreases judgmental errors in how interpersonal behavior is explained, such as the fundamental attribution error (Forgas, 1998c). Mood also influences memory mistakes, such as the accuracy of eyewitness memory about observed interactions (Forgas, 1999c).

To conclude, this chapter emphasizes the closely interactive relationship between affective states and different information-processing strategies as the key to understanding affective influences on social cognition and interpersonal behavior. Theories such as the AIM offer a parsimonious account of the links between affect and cognition, and can explain the conditions likely to facilitate or inhibit affect-infusion processes. Much of the evidence reviewed here suggests that affect infusion is most likely in conditions requiring constructive, substantive processing. Other processing strategies such as direct access or motivated processing result in the absence or even reversal of affect infusion. Obviously, a great deal more research is needed before we can fully understand the multiple influences that affect has on interpersonal behavior. This chapter could do little more than review some of the recent evidence and, it is hoped, stimulate further interest in this fascinating area of inquiry.

ACKNOWLEDGMENTS

This work was supported by a Special Investigator award from the Australian Research Council, and the Research Prize by the Alexander von Humboldt Foundation to Joseph P. Forgas. The contribution of Joseph Ciarrochi, Stephanie Moylan, Patrick Vargas, and Joan Webb to this project is gratefully acknowledged. Please address all correspondence in connection with this paper to Joseph P. Forgas, School of Psychology, University of New South Wales, Sydney 2052, Australia; email *jp.forgas@unsw.edu.au*. For further information on this research project, see also website at *www.psy. unsw.edu.au/~joef/jforgas.htm*

REFERENCES

Bless, H. (2000). The interplay of affect and cognition: The mediating role of general knowledge structures. In J. P. Forgas (Ed.), *Feeling and thinking: The role of affect in social cognition* (pp. xxx). New York: Cambridge University Press.

Bower, G. H. (1981). Mood and memory. *American Psychologist, 36*, 129–148.

Ciarrochi, J. V., & Forgas, J. P. (1999). On being tense yet tolerant: The paradoxical effects of trait anxiety and aversive mood on intergroup judgments. *Group Dynamics: Theory, Research and Practice, 3*, 227–238.

Ciarrochi, J. V., & Forgas, J. P. (in press). The pleasure of possessions: Affect and consumer judgments. *European Journal of Social Psychology.*

Clark, M. S., & Isen, A. M. (1982). Towards understanding the relationship between feeling states and social behavior. In A. H. Hastorf & A. M. Isen (Eds.), *Cognitive social psychology* (pp. 73–108). New York: Elsevier-North Holland.

Clore, G. L., Schwarz, N., & Conway, M. (1994). Affective causes and consequences of social information processing. In R. S. Wyer & T. K. Srull (Eds.), *Handbook of social cognition*, 2nd ed. (pp. 323–417). Hillsdale, NJ: Lawrence Erlbaum Associates.

Costa, P. T., & McCrae, R. R. (1985). *The NEO Personality Inventory Manual.* Odessa, FL: Psychological Assessment Resources.

Damasio, A. R. (1994). *Descartes' error.* New York: Grosste/Putnam.

Feshbach, S., & Singer, R. D. (1957). The effects of fear arousal and suppression of fear upon social perception. *Journal of Abnormal and Social Psychology, 55,* 283–288.

Fiedler, K. (1991). On the task, the measures and the mood in research on affect and social cognition. In J. P. Forgas (Ed.), *Emotion and social judgments* (pp. 83–104). Oxford: Pergamon Press.

Fiedler, K. (2000). Towards an integrative account of affect and cognition phenomena using the BIAS computer algorithm. In J. P. Forgas (Ed.), *Feeling and thinking: The role of affect in social cognition* (pp. 223–252). New York: Cambridge University Press.

Forgas, J. P. (1990). Affective influences on individual and group judgments. *European Journal of Social Psychology, 20,* 441–453.

Forgas, J. P. (1991). Mood effects on partner choice: Role of affect in social decisions. *Journal of Personality and Social Psychology, 61,* 708–720.

Forgas, J. P. (1992a). Affect in social judgments and decisions: A multi-process model. In M. Zanna (Ed.), *Advances in experimental social psychology* (Vol. 25, pp. 227–275). New York: Academic Press.

Forgas, J. P. (1992b). On bad mood and peculiar people: Affect and person typicality in impression formation. *Journal of Personality and Social Psychology, 62,* 863–875.

Forgas, J. P. (1993). On making sense of odd couples: Mood effects on the perception of mismatched relationships. *Personality and Social Psychology Bulletin, 19,* 59–71.

Forgas, J. P. (1994). Sad and guilty? Affective influences on the explanation of conflict episodes. *Journal of Personality and Social Psychology, 66,* 56–68.

Forgas, J. P. (1995a). Mood and judgment: The affect infusion model (AIM). *Psychological Bulletin, 117*(1), 39–66.

Forgas, J. P. (1995b). Strange couples: Mood effects on judgments and memory about prototypical and atypical targets. *Personality and Social Psychology Bulletin, 21,* 747–765.

Forgas, J. P. (1998a). On feeling good and getting your way: Mood effects on negotiation strategies and outcomes. *Journal of Personality and Social Psychology, 74,* 565–577.

Forgas, J. P. (1998b). Asking nicely? Mood effects on responding to more or less polite requests. *Personality and Social Psychology Bulletin, 24,* 173–185.

Forgas, J. P. (1998c). Happy and mistaken? Mood effects on the fundamental attribution error. *Journal of Personality and Social Psychology, 75,* 318–331.

Forgas, J. P. (1999a). On feeling good and being rude: Affective influences on language use and request formulations. *Journal of Personality and Social Psychology, 76,* 928–939.

Forgas, J. P. (1999b). Feeling and speaking: Mood effects on verbal communication strategies. *Personality and Social Psychology Bulletin, 25,* 850–863.

Forgas, J. P. (1999c). *Mood effects on eyewitness accuracy.* Manuscript under review.

Forgas, J. P. (Ed.) (2000). *Feeling and thinking: The role of affect in social cognition.* New York: Cambridge University Press.

Forgas, J. P. (in press). Managing moods: Towards a dual-process theory of spontaneous mood regulation. *Psychological Issues.*

Forgas, J. P., & Bower, G. H. (1987). Mood effects on person perception judgements. *Journal of Personality and Social Psychology, 53,* 53–60.

Forgas, J. P., Bower, G. H., & Krantz, S. (1984). The influence of mood on perceptions of social interactions. *Journal of Experimental Social Psychology, 20,* 497–513.

Forgas, J. P., Bower, G. H., & Moylan, S. J. (1990). Praise or blame? Affective influences on attributions for achievement. *Journal of Personality and Social Psychology, 59,* 809–818.

Forgas, J. P., & Ciarrochi, J. (2000). Mood congruent and incongruent thoughts over time: The role of self-esteem in mood management efficacy. Manuscript submitted for publication.

Forgas, J. P. Ciarrochi, J. V., & Moylan, S. (2000). Affective influences on the production of persuasive massages. Manuscripts, University of New South Wales, Sydney, Australia.

Forgas, J. P., & Fiedler, K. (1996). Us and them: Mood effects on intergroup discrimination. *Journal of Personality and Social Psychology, 70,* 36–52.

Forgas, J. P., & Gunawardene, A. (1999). Mood effects on interpersonal behaviour. Manuscript, University of New South Wales, Sydney, Australia.

Forgas, J. P., Johnson, R., & Ciarrochi, J. (1998). Affect control and affect infusion: A multiprocess account of mood management and personal control. In M. Kofta, G. Weary, & G. Sedek (Eds.), *Personal control in action. Cognitive and motivational mechanisms* (pp. 155–189). New York: Plenum Press.

Forgas, J. P., Levinger, G., & Moylan, S. (1994). Feeling good and feeling close: Mood effects on the perception of intimate relationships. *Personal Relationships, 2,* 165–184.

Forgas, J. P., & Moylan, S. J. (1987). After the movies: The effects of transient mood states on social judgments. *Personality and Social Psychology Bulletin, 13,* 478–489.

Gibbs, R. (1985). Situational conventions and requests. In J. P. Forgas (Ed.), *Language and social situations* (pp. 97–113). New York: Springer.

Gilbert, D. T., & Malone, P. S. (1995). The correspondence bias. *Psychological Bulletin, 117,* 21–38.

Griffitt, W. (1970). Environmental effects on interpersonal behavior: Ambient effective temperature and attraction. *Journal of Personality and Social Psychology, 15,* 240–244.

Heider, F. (1958). *The psychology of interpersonal relations.* New York: Wiley.

Hilgard, E. R. (1980). The trilogy of mind: Cognition, affection, and conation. *Journal of the History of the Behavioral Sciences, 16,* 107–117.

Loftus, E. (1979). *Eyewitness testimony.* Cambridge: MIT Press.

Mackie, D., & Worth, L. (1991). Feeling good, but not thinking straight: The impact of positive mood on persuasion. In J. P. Forgas (Ed.), *Emotion and social judgments* (pp. 201–220). Oxford: Pergamon Press.

Mayer, J. D., Gaschke, Y. N., Braverman, D. L., & Evans, T. W. (1992). Mood congruent judgment is a general effect. *Journal of Personality and Social Psychology, 63,* 119–132.

Salovey, P., O'Leary, A., Stretton, M., Fishkin, S., & Drake, C. A. (1991). Influence of mood on judgments about health and illness. In J. P. Forgas (Ed.), *Emotion and social judgments* (pp. 241–262). Oxford: Pergamon Press.

Schachter, S. (1959). *The psychology of affiliation.* Palo Alto: Stanford University Press.

Schwarz, N., & Clore, G. L. (1988). How do I feel about it? The informative function of affective states. In K. Fiedler & J. P. Forgas (Eds.), *Affect, cognition, and social behavior* (pp. 44–62). Toronto: Hogrefe.

Sedikides, C. (1992). Changes in the valence of self as a function of mood. *Review of Personality and Social Psychology, 14,* 271–311.

Sedikides, C. (1994). Incongruent effects of sad mood on self-conception valence: It's a matter of time. *European Journal of Social Psychology, 24,* 161–172.

Sedikides, C. (1995). Central and peripheral self-conceptions are differentially influenced by mood: Tests of the differential sensitivity hypothesis. *Journal of Personality and Social Psychology, 69*(4), 759–777.

15

Affective Influences on Stereotyping and Intergroup Relations

Galen V. Bodenhausen, Thomas Mussweiler, Shira Gabriel, & Kristen N. Moreno

Northwestern University

The Affective Context of Intergroup Relations	320
Chronic Integral Affect	321
Episodic Integral Affect	322
Incidental Affect	324
Mechanisms of Affective Influence on the Stereotyping Process	326
Category Identification	326
Stereotype Activation	328
Stereotype Application	330
Stereotype Correction	336
Final Thoughts	337
References	338

A major theme of recent research on emotion has been the recognition of the intimate connections between feeling and thinking. Emotions have long been conceived of as arising from a functionally separate system that is at best orthogonal to or, more likely, at odds with effective reasoning and

Address for correspondence: Galen V. Bodenhausen, Department of Psychology, Northwestern University, 2029 Sheridan Road, Evanston, IL 60208-2710, U.S.A. Email: galen@nwu.edu intellectual functioning. This view has been supplanted by an emerging acknowledgment of the elaborately coordinated interactions and, indeed, indispensable collaboration between the cognitive and affective systems (e.g., Clore, Schwarz, & Conway, 1994; Damasio, 1994; Frijda, 1986; Zajonc & Markus, 1984). For example, Damasio (1994; see also Adolphs & Damasio, chap. 2, this volume) reports compelling evidence of the dysfunctions that arise when subjective feelings are no longer available to guide reactions, dysfunctions that are especially pronounced in the sphere of social functioning. As he notes, the "social domain is the one closest to our destiny and the one which involves the greatest uncertainty and complexity" (Damasio, 1994, p. 169), so it is perhaps not too surprising that it is in this domain that we most urgently need guidance from our "gut reactions" and subjective feelings.

In this chapter, we explore the role of affect in one particularly important social arena—namely, intergroup perception and behavior. Examination of the growing body of research directed at this topic reveals a complex but largely coherent picture of multiple pathways by which our subjective feeling states influence the way we perceive and respond to the members of stereotyped social groups. In many respects, the major findings challenge common preconceptions about the role of affect in intergroup relations, such as the notion that negative affect is uniformly associated with patterns of intergroup bias and discrimination, or the idea that positive affect is an all-purpose remedy for these same problems. Although perhaps initially surprising, the overall pattern of findings does accord with more general principles being uncovered by contemporary affect researchers.

THE AFFECTIVE CONTEXT
OF INTERGROUP RELATIONS

There have been three major contexts within which researchers have studied the effects of affective states on intergroup perception and behavior. Two of the domains have to do with affect that is elicited by the group itself and the social situations within which the group is experienced (termed *integral affect* by Bodenhausen, 1993). Research on *chronic integral affect* examined the impact of enduring affective reactions to the social group on attitudes and behavior toward the group and its members. Research on *episodic integral affect* examined the impact of affective reactions that are situationally created in intergroup settings, which may in principle be quite different from more chronic feelings about the group (as when one has a pleasant interaction with a member of an otherwise disliked group). The final domain involves affective states that arise for reasons having nothing to do with the intergroup context itself, but that are carried over from other events into an intergroup setting (termed *incidental affect* by Bodenhausen, 1993). In this section, we consider some of the common features and implications of research in each of these domains.

Chronic Integral Affect

Ever since Watson taught Little Albert to fear small furry objects (by consistently pairing them with noxious auditory stimulation), psychologists have known that, through experience, certain stimuli come to elicit consistent affective reactions. Although fear is undoubtedly the form of learned affective response that has been most extensively studied (e.g., Öhman, 1993), conditioning and other learning processes can clearly result in a range of chronic affective reactions to a variety of stimulus categories. Both positive and negative feelings have been experimentally produced via conditioning procedures (e.g., Zanna, Kiesler, & Pilkonis, 1970). Some theorists of intergroup relations (e.g., Gaertner & Dovidio, 1986; Katz, 1976) have argued that pervasive, culturally embedded forms of social conditioning tend to produce consistent patterns of affective reactions to certain social groups. To the extent that groups are culturally stigmatized or devalued, they tend to elicit a range of negative emotions such as contempt, disgust, discomfort, anger, or aversion. Groups that are socially valued and admired tend in contrast to elicit positive reactions. By being exposed consistently to social representations of social groups and their status within a given cultural system, participants in that system may come to hold corresponding affective predispositions toward the groups in question.

Most research examining the nature of chronic integral affect has been descriptive in nature. Researchers have mainly been interested in documenting which kinds of affective reactions are associated with various groups, as well as examining the relationships between intergroup affect on one hand and intergroup beliefs and attitudes on the other (e.g., Dijker, 1987; Haddock, Zanna, & Esses, 1993; Jackson & Sullivan, 1988; Jussim, Nelson, Manis, & Soffin, 1995; Stangor, Sullivan, & Ford, 1991). This research provides ample reason to believe that chronic integral affect plays a substantial role in intergroup attitudes (Cooper, 1959), but the theoretical message of these correlational studies remains fairly limited. We still know very little, for example, about the role played by chronic affect in cognitive representations of social groups and in the mental processes that operate on these representations. Fiske and Pavelchak (1986) provided one of the few attempts to construct a representational theory of intergroup affect. They proposed that memorial representations of social groups contain affective tags that can trigger the corresponding subjective feeling when the category representation is activated. Although the implications of this model were supported in some initial studies (Fiske, 1982), relatively little empirical attention has been devoted to this approach more recently.

Bodenhausen and Moreno (2000) reviewed a variety of issues pertaining to when chronic integral affect does or does not influence reactions to stereotyped group members. Extrapolating from other research on affect-based biases and their control, they proposed that such biases are likely to find expression when perceivers (a) are unaware that they are being influenced by their chronic background feelings about the group; (b) are unmotivated to correct such biases, as may be the case with high-prejudice persons; (c) lack the attentional resources that are necessary to suppress or correct for affective biases; or (d) convince themselves that their negative feelings are due to something other than the group's identity per se. Some initial findings are in line with this conceptualization (Moreno & Bodenhausen, in press), but in general, there is a noteworthy paucity of research examining the nature and consequences of chronic integral affect. One likely reason for this state of affairs is the simple fact that, in contrast to the other forms of intergroup affect, chronic integral affect must generally be treated as a (measured) subject variable rather than an experimentally manipulated one.

Episodic Integral Affect

Episodic integral affect refers to the affective states experienced in particular intergroup situations. It is dictated by the nature of the immediate interaction rather than by preexisting, chronic feelings per se. For example, one might generally experience negative feelings toward individuals with mental disorders, but an actual interaction with a person with such a disorder could turn out to be unexpectedly pleasant. In this case, the chronic affect is negative, but the episodic affect is positive. Of course, the chronic feelings we hold toward various groups are likely to provide a background context that can influence and constrain the nature of episodic affective reactions, but in principle the two can be quite distinct.

Most research on episodic integral affect has occurred within the context of studying the contact hypothesis (Allport, 1954; Amir, 1969; Brewer & Miller, 1996), which asserts that improved intergroup relations result from intergroup interactions. To the extent the problematic relations arise because of inaccurate preconceptions and a lack of familiarity with the outgroup, contact should provide the opportunity to remedy these inadequacies. Early research underscored the importance of positive episodic affect in producing improved intergroup relations (see Stephan & Stephan, 1996). Even though groups may chronically view one another with suspicion and general aversion, if contact episodes are structured in ways that create positive feelings, then they are likely to produce the intended benefits. Experiencing success in cooperative endeavors with outgroup members is a particularly auspicious antecedent of improved intergroup relations, perhaps in large part because of the good feelings it creates (Jones, 1997).

A question of considerable importance is exactly how such positive feelings exert their beneficial effects. Perhaps there is simply a direct conditioning process whereby the positive feelings become associated directly with the outgroup (e.g., Parish & Fleetwood, 1975). However, more recent research suggests that other mechanisms may be at work. Dovidio, Gaertner, Isen, Rust, and Guerra (1998) proposed that positive affective states tend to promote inclusive categorizations of stimuli (see also Isen, Niedenthal, & Cantor, 1992). As such, positive affect may promote a focus on broader categories that incorporate both the (former) outgroup and ingroup. For example, there may be a greater likelihood of conflict between Korean-Americans and African-Americans in a particular community if they define themselves in terms of their distinct ethnic identities. However, if they define themselves in terms of a shared superordinate identity (e.g., "resident of New York," "people of color," or simply "Americans"), there is a greater likelihood of positive relations (Gaertner, Dovidio, Anastasio, Bachman, & Rust, 1993). Research by Dovidio et al. (1998) suggests that positive affect increases the likelihood of these broader kinds of categorization.

Of course, not all intergroup episodes are positive, and much research attention has been devoted to the likelihood that people commonly experience anxiety in the context of intergroup interactions (Stephan & Stephan, 1985). There are several reasons why anxiety is likely to arise in intergroup contact situations, including (a) general uncertainty about unfamiliar situations, (b) negative stereotypic expectancies about the outgroup, and (c) concern about acting inappropriately or appearing to be prejudiced (Devine, Evett, & Vasquez-Suson, 1996). This kind of episodic anxiety can have a number of noteworthy effects. For example, Wilder and Shapiro (1989) report evidence suggesting that intergroup anxiety constrains processing capacity (cf. Darke, 1988), resulting in the tendency to view the outgroup in undifferentiated, stereotypic ways. They created contact situations in which some outgroup members behaved negatively, but one was quite positive. When anxiety was present, all outgroup members were viewed similarly, regardless of their behavior. In the low-anxiety condition, however, the positive outgroup member was differentiated from the others. One implication of this work is that anxiety may make people less likely to notice when outgroup members behave in positive, constructive ways. Anxiety, which is associated with sympathetic autonomic arousal, may also amplify dominant (stereotypic) responses to the outgroup (cf. Zajonc, 1965).

Intergroup anxiety can be viewed as both a dispositional/chronic form of integral affect as well as a consequence of a particular interaction episode. Some people may be chronically anxious about interacting with the members of certain groups (e.g., Britt, Boniecki, Vescio, Biernat, & Brown, 1996; Devine et al., 1996). Highly anxious persons are likely to experience contact anxiety regardless of the structure of the interaction, whereas low-anxiety persons are much more likely to respond to the nature of the contact setting. If the setting itself promotes anxiety, then even these dispositionally low-anxiety individuals may become susceptible to the negative consequences of negative episodic affect.

One other form of episodic integral affect has recently received some empirical scrutiny. Batson et al. (1997) examined the effects of situationally induced empathy in intergroup contact situations. Specifically, persons who had been induced to feel empathy for a particular member of a stigmatized social group whom they encountered (specifically, a person with AIDS or a homeless person) reported ultimately more favorable attitudes toward the group in question, relative to a low-empathy comparison group. So far, little is known about how empathy exerts its effects, including the question of whether it has any impact on relevant cognitive processes such as stereotyping.

Incidental Affect

Much recent research on the connections between affect and stereotyping has focused on incidental affect. This work addresses the question of how intergroup judgments are influenced by the perceiver's preexisting mood (or any other affective state that has arisen for reasons unrelated to the social group in question). Although there has been a substantial spate of empirical investigations into this question in recent years, it is certainly not a new question. Indeed, some of the oldest theories of prejudice and stereotyping emphasized the role of incidental affect. Frustration–aggression and scapegoating models of prejudice, for example, assume that the negativity that is often directed toward stigmatized outgroups most likely originated from sources unrelated to the targeted group, such as hard economic times (Dollard, Doob, Miller, Mowrer, & Sears, 1939). Some psychoanalytic approaches to prejudice argue that it arises, at least in part, from feelings of personal inadequacy and low self-esteem caused by inadequate parenting (Adorno, Frenkel-Brunswik, Levinson, & Sanford, 1950; Freud, 1921). In these approaches, negative feelings from unrelated sources are displaced onto social outgroups, resulting in harsh judgments and behaviors.

Although managing integral forms of intergroup affect unquestionably constitutes a core concern in improving intergroup relations, it is incidental affect that has received decidedly more attention more recently. There are undoubtedly several reasons for this focus, including the fact that incidental affect can be easily manipulated in experiments, as well as the rich and growing base of theoretical ideas concerning the impact of transient affective states on social-information processing. Initially, these theories focused on valence-based mood effects in which the focal comparisons were on the differential effects of negative versus neutral versus positive affective states. An implicit assumption of this approach is the notion that different types of affect within a particular valence (e.g., anger, sadness, fear) produce functionally equivalent effects. Based on the earliest work on incidental affect, one might expect to generally find that negative moods of any sort would be likely to promote greater use of negative stereotypes and more negative judgments of outgroups, whereas positive moods would have the opposite tendency. These commonsense intuitions have, however, proved to be incorrect. For one thing, it is becoming increasingly clear that one must look beyond valence to predict and explain the effects of incidental affect. For example, anger and sadness produce distinct effects (Bodenhausen, Sheppard, & Kramer, 1994b; Keltner, Ellsworth, & Edwards, 1993), as do anxiety and sadness (Raghunathan & Pham, 1999). Moreover, as we discuss momentarily, the general expectation of greater stereotyping in negative than in positive moods has simply not been supported. Indeed, another reason for the high level of interest in the question of incidental affect and stereotyping is the discovery of several relatively counterintuitive findings in this domain.

Given the number of studies that have addressed the connection between affect and stereotyping, there is currently a rather sizable number of conceptual approaches and empirical paradigms that have generated a variety of findings. It is unlikely that any single theoretical framework can provide a compelling, parsimonious account for all of these effects. Rather than attempting to construct such a model, in the subsequent section we attempt to identify major themes emerging in the literature, focusing on a variety of processing mechanisms that seem able to capture different functions of affect on information processing in intergroup contexts. In line with other researchers (e.g., Forgas, 1995; Hirt, Levine, McDonald, Melton, & Martin, 1997), we assume that multiple mechanisms are potentially operative when social cognition occurs in the context of pronounced background affect. A major goal for the next generation of research is the more precise specification of the boundary conditions under which each mechanism operates, as in Forgas's (1995) Affect Infusion Model (AIM).

MECHANISMS OF AFFECTIVE INFLUENCE ON THE STEREOTYPING PROCESS

The term *stereotyping* has come to have a variety of meanings in the research literature. We believe that stereotyping is best understood as a multistage process; affective states may influence each of the stages in a variety of ways. In this section, we consider four principal stages or aspects of the stereotyping process, expanding on distinctions originally proposed by Gilbert and Hixon (1991): *category identification* (i.e., assigning a stimulus person to a social category), *stereotype activation* (i.e., mental activation of attributes typically ascribed to the activated category), *stereotype application* (i.e., use of activated stereotypic concepts in construing the stimulus person), and *stereotype correction* (i.e., attempts to "undo" the effects of stereotype application). In each case, we highlight mechanisms whereby affective states may influence the outcome of that particular subcomponent of the stereotyping process.

Category Identification

Like most other entities, people can be categorized in a variety of ways (see Rosch, 1978). Along a "vertical" dimension, categories of increasing inclusiveness can be specified, such as "Black intellectual," "African American," "American," and "human being." In this scheme, each categorical identity constitutes a subset of the category above it in the hierarchy. Obviously, distinctly different stereotypes may be associated with these different levels of categorization. Along a "horizontal" dimension, a variety of orthogonal categories, each having a similar general level of inclusiveness, can be identified, such as "woman," "Jew," "middle-aged," and "professor." Of course, each of these "orthogonal" categories could be combined to form a more specific subtype within each of the more general superordinate categories, but in principle, these are distinct categories with distinct stereotypes that can be used separately and independently in organizing social perception. It has been argued that under many common circumstances, perceivers tend to identify other people in terms of only one of the numerous possible category identities to which they could potentially be assigned (Bodenhausen & Macrae, 1998; Macrae, Bodenhausen, & Milne, 1995). The selected category is likely to be affected by a variety of factors, including category accessibility (based on recency and frequency of use; e.g., Smith, Fazio, & Cejka, 1996), contextual salience (e.g., Biernat & Vescio, 1993), momentary goals and motivations (e.g., Sinclair & Kunda, 1999), and comparative and normative fit to the current situation (Oakes, Turner, & Haslam, 1991). The question of current focus is whether affective states can also influence which specific categories will be selected.

In general, it seems unlikely that affect will influence category selection along the horizontal dimension when there is a clear comparative or normative context for making the selection. In many real-life situations, there are strong contextual constraints on category selection (e.g., relying on occupational roles in business settings, or relying on gender types in a singles bar). In situations in which such constraints are weak or absent, affect may indeed play a role in category selection. One possibility is based on the mood-congruency effect, whereby affective states tend to make material of similar valence more salient or accessible (e.g., Forgas & Bower, 1987). Under positive moods, perceivers may be more likely to activate a positive categorical identity (e.g., "professor"), whereas they may be more likely to activate a negative categorical identity (e.g., "male chauvinist pig") when experiencing unpleasant affect. Affect-specific biases are also a distinct possibility. For example, when feeling anxious, perceivers may be sensitive to stimulus properties that are likely to evoke a threatening categorization (e.g., Matthews, 1990). By the same token, there is some evidence that feelings of threat can influence horizontal category selection in self-construals (Mussweiler, Gabriel, & Bodenhausen, in press), motivating perceivers to focus on the category that is most likely to ward off the ego threat. Similar processes may govern category selection in the perception of others during times of stress or threat (cf. Sinclair & Kunda, 1999). However, by and large there is very little evidence concerning the role affective states might play in the selection of horizontally competing categories.

There is some better evidence suggesting that affective states may influence the selection of social categories along the vertical dimension. Initial findings from Isen and Daubman (1984) suggested that positive moods may be associated with a tendency to form broader, more inclusive categories. A subsequent study by Dovidio, Gaertner, Isen, and Lowrance (1995) in the domain of social categorization confirmed that, compared to neutral-mood controls, participants who had been induced to experience incidental positive affect focused on categorical identities that were at higher (more superordinate) levels of the hierarchy. This tendency could be quite significant, because broader categories may be more likely to result in the perceiver and the target person(s) being grouped into a common, shared identity category (Dovidio et al., 1998). Intergroup bias and negative stereotyping should be markedly reduced under such conditions. Conversely, there is reason to believe that sad moods may lead perceivers to focus on lower levels of the hierarchy. Some theorists (e.g., Schwarz, 1990; Weary, 1990) have argued that sadness is associated with greater motivation to perceive the social environment accurately (presumably in order to resolve the problematic issues underlying their sadness). Along these lines, Pendry and Macrae (1996) have shown that accuracy-motivated perceivers tend to activate more specific, lower-level categories in forming social impressions. Taken together, these ideas suggest that sad people may tend to activate subtypes or other more fine-grained social categories, compared to their neutral and positive mood counterparts.

In general, researchers have tended to select empirical paradigms in which the options for social categorization are constrained or preselected by the researcher. As a result, we know rather little about the category identification process under unconstrained conditions of rich, multiply categorizable stimuli. Much remains to be discovered about the ways that affect might impinge on the assignment of competing categorical identities to the complex, multifaceted people we encounter in more naturalistic circumstances.

Stereotype Activation

Once a stimulus person has been assigned to particular social category, relevant stereotypes are highly likely to be automatically activated (for a review, see Macrae & Bodenhausen, 2000). Bargh (1999) argued in strong terms that automatic stereotype activation is inevitable. If so, then the perceiver's mood state should make little difference at this stage of the stereotyping process. In contrast to this position, several researchers have argued that stereotype activation can be moderated by a variety of factors, such as the availability of attentional resources (Gilbert & Hixon, 1991), prejudice levels (e.g., Wittenbrink, Judd, & Park, 1997), and momentary processing objectives (Macrae, Bodenhausen, Milne, Thorne, & Castelli, 1997). For example, Gilbert and Hixon report evidence suggesting that when perceivers are mentally busy or distracted, they may lack the necessary cognitive resources for activating stereotypes about persons they encounter. Although the generality of this conclusion has been questioned (see Bargh, 1999), if correct, it has some fairly clear implications concerning how affective states might influence stereotype activation. Specifically, certain affective states may produce sufficient distraction to interfere with cognitive operations that are conditional on the availability of adequate cognitive resources. Clearly, strong negative states such as terror or rage would be likely to preoccupy the mind, perhaps thereby preventing stereotype activation. To use one of Gilbert and Hixon's examples, in the panic of a house fire, perceivers may not get around to activating racial stereotypes concerning the firefighters on the scene. Although we know of no examples of research directly addressing the possibility that highly intense emotions might interfere with stereotype activation, it is certainly a generally plausible hypothesis.

Somewhat less intuitively, Mackie and Worth (1989) claimed that positive moods can also be resource depleting. They argued that when people are feeling good, they are distracted by numerous positive associations and thus have relatively little mental capacity left for effortful mental work, such as evaluating the validity of persuasive arguments. This conclusion has been questioned (e.g., Melton, 1995; Schwarz, Bless, & Bohner, 1991), but taken to its logical extreme, it suggests that positive moods might also impede stereotype activation. As shown later in this chapter, however, the available evidence does not support this idea. Undoubtedly, the resource requirements for stereotype activation are far more minimal than that required for effortful scrutiny of a persuasive essay, and the distraction potential of positive moods is unlikely to compromise resources sufficiently to block such activation.

Findings reported by Spencer, Fein, Wolfe, Fong, and Dunn (1998) provide a different challenge to Bargh's position that stereotype activation is inevitable. In their experiments, which built on Gilbert and Hixon (1991), they demonstrated that stereotype activation was likely to occur even among busy perceivers when such activation could contribute to their goal of coping with a threat to their self-image. By activating largely negative stereotypes about a stigmatized outgroup, ego-threatened persons were apparently able to engage in downward social comparison and thereby feel better about themselves. In line with scapegoating models previously described, this research suggests that stereotype activation can be one strategy for coping with negative affect. Indeed, one of the general themes in the affect and cognition literature is the notion of mood repair (see Erber & Erber, chap. 13, this volume). When perceivers are feeling bad, their cognitive processes may be biased in ways that are likely to eliminate these unwanted feelings and produce more palatable affective states. The work of Spencer et al. (1998) accords nicely with this possibility. It thus seems at least conceivable that stereotype activation might be moderated by the distracting and motivating properties of concurrent affective experience. Unfortunately, this is another possibility that has not yet received adequate empirical attention.

Stereotype Application

For most intents and purposes, *stereotype application* refers to situations in which judgments and behaviors about a social group and/or its members are assimilated toward stereotypic preconceptions.[1] Following category identification and stereotype activation, such preconceptions become mentally salient and can guide subsequent processing in several ways (see Bodenhausen & Macrae, 1998). Stereotypic beliefs can simply be added to the information that is otherwise available, or they may serve as a heuristic cue that provides a quick basis for making the type of judgment that is situationally required. For example, in judging whether a Latino convicted of criminal assault warrants parole, people may use general stereotypes ("Latinos are violent types") to conclude that the prisoner is still a menace to society and that parole would be unwise (Bodenhausen & Wyer, 1985). Of course, it is unlikely that judges would completely ignore other available information in reaching their final judgment, but the initial, stereotypic heuristic is likely to bias the processing of the subsequently encountered evidence (Bodenhausen, 1988; see also Chaiken &

---

[1]Biernat and colleagues (e.g., Biernat, Vescio, & Manis, 1998) documented situations in which stereotype application leads to contrast effects. Specifically, when stereotypes are activated and judges must make ratings on a subjective response scale, they may tend to shift the meaning of the scale in a stereotypic direction. For example, an assertive woman may be rated as more assertive than a comparably assertive man is because the response scale has been recalibrated in light of stereotypic expectancies (e.g., "She's very assertive, *for a woman*"). Thus, this kind of contrast effect still reflects the application of a group stereotype in the judgment process. To our knowledge, no research has addressed the influence of affective states on standard-shifting effects of this sort, so we restrict our discussion of stereotype application to the case of assimilation effects.

Maheswaran, 1994). To the extent that it is ambiguous, it will likely be assimilated to the implications of the activated stereotype (Duncan, 1976; Kunda & Sherman-Williams, 1993). In general, the activated stereotypic concepts serve to simplify and structure the process of social perception by providing a readymade framework for conceptualizing the target (for a review, see Bodenhausen, Macrae, & Sherman, 1999). This simplified processing strategy is preferred to the more arduous process of individuation, which requires bottom-up processing and integration of the concrete, specific information available about the target. Individuation is only likely to be pursued when (a) perceivers are highly motivated and able to engage in effortful processing, or (b) available individuating information provides an unambiguously poor fit to stereotypic expectations (Brewer, 1988; Fiske & Neuberg, 1990).

To what extent does the perceiver's affective state influence this process of stereotype application versus individuation? There is compelling evidence that moods do have a notable impact on relevant processes. In particular, positive moods appear to increase reliance on heuristics and generic knowledge structures of many sorts, including the availability heuristic (Isen & Means, 1983), source credibility heuristics (Schwarz et al., 1991; Worth & Mackie, 1987), simplistic political ideology schemas (Ottati, Terkildsen, & Hubbard, 1997), and scripts (Bless, Schwarz, Clore, Golisano, Rabe, & Wölk, 1996a). In addition, Hänze and colleagues (Hänze & Hesse, 1993; Hänze & Meyer, 1998) report evidence that automatic semantic priming effects are generally enhanced by positive moods. As a result of their tendency to rely on heuristics and simplified processing strategies, happy people also appear to render less accurate judgments in many common circumstances (Sinclair & Mark, 1995). In contrast, sadness seems to be associated with the avoidance or minimization of the use of heuristics, schemas, and other simplified processing strategies (e.g., Bless, Bohner, Schwarz, & Strack, 1990; Weary & Gannon, 1996). These findings clearly imply that happiness will likely be associated with greater reliance on stereotypes, whereas sadness may be associated with reduced reliance on them.

Much evidence accords with this expectation. Bodenhausen, Kramer, & Süsser (1994a) reported several experiments in which individuals in a positive mood were more likely than their neutral-mood counterparts to judge individual targets in ways that were stereotypic of their social groups. Category information has been found to exert a stronger effect on the judgments of happy than neutral or sad persons in several studies (e.g., Abele, Gendolla, & Petzold, 1998; Bless, Schwarz, & Wieland, 1996c). Blessum,

Lord, and Sia (1998) showed that happy people are less likely than controls to distinguish among gay targets based on their stereotypicality (instead viewing even atypical exemplars as relatively typical of the category). Along similar lines, Park and Banaji (in press) showed that happy people are less likely to discriminate accurately among different members of a stereotyped group. Instead, they tend to set a lower threshold for drawing stereotypic conclusions about group members, and hence they are more likely to incorrectly recall that specific group exemplars possess stereotypic traits. Finally, Forgas and Fiedler (1996) show that positive moods exacerbate reliance on a simple ingroup favoritism heuristic (so long as the personal relevance of the group was low).

With respect to sadness, there is less evidence, but the available studies are generally consistent with the idea that sad people do not rely much on generic knowledge. One study that contrasted sad and neutral participants found no differences in their tendency to rely on stereotypes (Bodenhausen et al., 1994b). Park and Banaji (in press, Experiment 3) found that sad persons were similar to neutral-mood persons in their sensitivity in distinguishing among category exemplars, and in fact, sad people were found to set a more stringent threshold for drawing stereotypic conclusions about group members than the neutral-mood controls. Although these findings fit well with the more general evidence suggesting that sad people are likely to focus more on the available concrete data and less on general preconceptions (e.g., Edwards & Weary, 1993; Schwarz, 1990), there is one set of studies that seems to contradict the idea that sad people render less stereotypic judgments. Esses and Zanna (1995) reported evidence from several studies indicating that negative moods result in the tendency to attribute negative stereotypes to certain ethnic minority groups. This finding may not be as incompatible with the previously discussed studies as it may first appear. First, the mood induction and manipulation checks in the studies made it somewhat ambiguous exactly what kind of negative moods had been created. Whereas sadness has specifically been theoretically and empirically linked to reductions in stereotyping, other types of negative affect do seem to promote greater stereotyping. For example, compared to neutral-mood controls, heightened stereotyping has been observed among both angry (Bodenhausen et al., 1994b) and anxious (Baron, Inman, Kao, & Logan, 1992) individuals. Second, the studies of Esses and Zanna (1995) did not actually suggest that negative moods result in greater use of heuristics or schemas per se; instead, their results showed that it was changes in the meaning ascribed to the traits associated with the ethnic groups that were effected by negative moods. When in a negative mood, participants tended to interpret the same stereotypic traits as having more negative connotations (i.e., a mood-congruency effect) than did people in neutral or positive moods. In contrast, there was no effect of negative mood on participants' tendency to make generalizations about the ethnic groups (in terms of the percentage of the group that was assumed to possess the stereotypic traits). Thus, these results suggest that the meaning attributed to social concepts tends to be assimilated to the perceiver's mood state, but this effect appears to be independent of any effect on more conventional indicators of stereotyping. Taken as a whole, the evidence suggests that sadness is *not* associated with increases in stereotyping.

The fact that positive moods can increase perceivers' reliance on simplistic social stereotypes seems at first blush to be fairly counterintuitive. After all, positive *integral* affect has been considered a key ingredient in the amelioration of intergroup antagonisms. Why, then, does positive *incidental* affect seem to promote reliance on longstanding stereotypes? As a result of the seeming perplexity of this state of affairs, a considerable amount of effort has been devoted to trying to explain the relationship between happiness and stereotyping. One initial idea was derived from the claim of Mackie and Worth (1989), in the persuasion domain, that positive moods may be distracting and hence may reduce perceivers' attentional resources. An extensive literature confirms that stereotypic responses are more likely to result when attentional resources are compromised (for a review, see Sherman, Macrae, & Bodenhausen, in press). Some evidence against this approach was provided by Schwarz et al. (1991), who found that happy people were quite able to engage in systematic processing if simply instructed to do so. Bodenhausen et al. (1994a) also showed that even happy moods that do not involve any potentially distracting cognitive content (e.g., moods arising from facial feedback) can promote greater stereotyping. Thus, the greater degree of stereotyping observed among happy-mood people does not seem attributable to simple distraction or an incapacity for more systematic and thorough modes of thought.

In addition to attentional capacity, stereotyping is moderated by perceivers' motivation for effortful thought. When such motivation is reduced or absent, they may be quite to content to rely on their stereotypic notions, when relevant, in judging the members of other groups. Perhaps happiness undermines processing motivation and hence promotes reliance on simplistic information-processing strategies, such as stereotyping. This general explanation has been favored by several theorists, although its specific form has varied over time. Schwarz (1990) and Schwarz and Bless (1991) proposed that happy moods may signal that "Everything is fine," and thus there is little need for careful analysis of the external environment. Consequently, happy people may generally prefer to conserve their mental resources rather than engaging in effortful, systematic thinking. Sad moods, in contrast, suggest to perceivers that their environment is problematic and may promote more detail-oriented, careful thinking. This line of argument gains some support from evidence that the superficial forms of thinking observed among happy people can be readily eliminated when the situation provides other motivational bases for effortful processing, such as relevance to personal outcomes (Forgas, 1989) or accountability of judgment to a third party (Bodenhausen et al., 1994a; see also Lerner, Goldberg, & Tetlock, 1998).

This approach was refined in light of an interesting empirical discovery by Martin, Ward, Achee, and Wyer (1993), who found that happy moods can both increase and decrease effortful processing, depending on how people are thinking about the cognitive task they are performing. When approaching a task from the standpoint of whether they have done enough, people experiencing a happy mood tend to use their positive feelings as evidence that they have indeed done enough mental work. Hence, they are likely to stop earlier, after having engaged in relatively less systematic processing. However, when approaching a task from the standpoint of whether they are enjoying it, people in a happy mood tend to use their positive feelings as evidence that they are indeed enjoying the task, so they persist in it. As a result, they are likely to keep thinking about it and may thus end up engaging in a more effortful, less simplistic analysis. This analysis suggests that mood is used as input into the "stop rules" that people invoke to determine whether they should continue or discontinue cognitive effort. Positive mood has different implications, depending on whether a performance-based or an enjoyment-based stop rule is being used (see also Hirt, Melton, McDonald, & Harackiewicz, 1996). If one makes the plausible assumption that participants in a psychological experiment on social perception often adopt a performance-based stop rule by default, then this model can readily explain the heightened level of stereotyping seen among happy people in such experiments. Their happy mood "informs" them that they have done enough after a relatively superficial, stereotypic analysis, and they go no further.

A related idea has been proposed by Bless and colleagues (Bless & Fiedler, 1995; Bless et al., 1996a; Bless, Schwarz, & Kemmelmeier, 1996b; Bless et al., 1996c). According to their approach, experiencing a positive mood is associated with greater confidence in, and hence greater reliance on, general knowledge structures. This approach does not assume that happy perceivers are *generally* unmotivated to engage in systematic thinking; rather, they are simply often content to rely heavily on their general knowledge and to use it as a basis for constructive elaboration (Fiedler, Asbeck, & Nickel, 1991), unless it proves to be inadequate for making sense of the object of judgment. In that case, perceivers are quite willing and able to engage in more detail-oriented processing. In the studies conducted by Bless et al. (1996c), for example, it was found that happy people did engage in greater stereotyping, unless the available individuating information was clearly and unambiguously counterstereotypic. Under such conditions, their judgments were clearly influenced by the counterstereotypic individuating information, reconfirming the importance of informational fit in the emergence of stereotyping effects (Fiske & Neuberg, 1990). Interpretations of the effects of positive mood under conditions of stereotype disconfirmation are complicated by the fact that stereotype-inconsistent information tends to be experienced as threatening (Förster, Higgins, & Strack, in press) and can itself create negative affect (Munro & Ditto, 1997). Nevertheless, this research makes it clear that initially happy perceivers do tend to process individuating information in enough detail to recognize whether their stereotypes seem to fit the individuating information. They simply seem to give greater weight to their global stereotypes, so long as they generally fit the data at hand.

Greater stereotype application under conditions of positive affect has thus been attributed to distraction, a general lack of epistemic motivation, the tendency to use a positive mood to infer that one has done enough work on the task after a relatively superficial analysis, and to a generally greater confidence in generic knowledge structures. Claims that happy people are generally unable or unwilling to engage in systematic thinking appear to be inaccurate. Rather, happy people appear to be flexible in their information-processing strategies (cf. Isen, 1993). Although often content to rely on efficient, simplified bases for judgment (such as stereotypes), they are quite capable of engaging in more detail-oriented processing if personally involved or otherwise motivated for more systematic thinking, or if simplified processing fails to provide a satisfactory basis for judgment, as is the case, for example, when individuating information contradicts the implications of an activated stereotype. The *lack* of stereotyping seen among sad persons may best be understood by considering the process of stereotype correction, to which we now turn our attention.

Stereotype Correction

Whether judgments and behaviors end up reflecting stereotypic bias is not only a function of stereotype application, but it is also crucially dependent on whether perceivers are motivated and able to try to correct for such bias. In contemporary society, many forms of stereotyping are frowned on, so perceivers may often want to avoid giving overt voice to stereotypic reactions (see Bodenhausen, Macrae, & Milne, 1998). To correct for stereotypic biases, perceivers can attempt to estimate the direction and extent of the bias, and make corresponding direct adjustments to their responses in the direction opposite to the presumed bias (Wegener & Petty, 1997; Wilson & Brekke, 1994). Alternatively, they may put aside their initial judgmental reaction and "recompute" their judgment, specifically laying aside the unwanted informational cues (Mussweiler & Strack, 1999). In both cases, the correction process is a controlled mental activity requiring perceiver intent and processing resources (e.g., Strack, 1992; Wilson & Brekke, 1994). Is the motivation and ability to engage in such corrective action influenced by the perceiver's affective state?

To date, research has examined the impact of two forms of affect on the tendency to engage in stereotype correction: sadness and guilt. As previously noted, there is some evidence that sad persons are less likely to engage in stereotyping. Research by Lambert, Khan, Lickel, and Fricke (1997) provides evidence that this tendency is likely to be attributable to sad people's greater tendency to engage in stereotype correction. Drawing on Schwarz's (1990) notion that sadness has alerting informational value in that it indicates that something is wrong in the environment, Lambert et al. argued that sadness should induce judges to scrutinize the use of stereotypes in the judgment process. Specifically, they assumed that sad judges should only use stereotypes in cases in which their use seems appropriate for the judgment to be made. In one study (Lambert et al., 1997, Experiment 3), participants were put into either a neutral or a sad mood and were then asked to play the role of a job interviewer and evaluate a particular candidate. The job opening was one for which a woman's physical attractiveness either was or was not an appropriate basis for the hiring decision. In the "inappropriate" condition, sad participants relied less on attractiveness than control participants did. In other studies, it was found that sad persons were more likely than controls to correct for negative stereotypes but not for positive stereotypes. Presumably, positive stereotypes were not considered an inappropriate or taboo basis for judgments, but negative stereotypes were. This kind of finding is consistent with the general idea that sad people are likely to be careful, systematic thinkers (e.g., Schwarz, 1990; Weary, 1990), applying stereotypes only when it seems appropriate to do so; otherwise, they seem to take pains to avoid letting such biases show in their judgments.

An extensive program of research by Devine and colleagues (Devine, Monteith, Zuwerink, & Elliott, 1991; Devine & Monteith, 1993) examined the impact of guilt arising in intergroup encounters on the tendency to engage in efforts to avoid subsequent stereotyping. In this case, the negative feelings are a form of episodic integral affect, arising from a failure to live up to one's personal standards for behavior in the intergroup context. Among low-prejudice persons who aspire to be free of stereotypic bias, the detection of such biases is likely to produce feelings of guilt and compunction. This negative self-related affect serves a warning function that induces people to be more careful with their responses and thus prompts them to behave in unprejudiced ways. Consistent with these assumptions, Monteith (1993) showed that among low-prejudice participants, inducing stereotype-related discrepancies produced feelings of guilt that resulted in greater subsequent carefulness in processing group-relevant information. They responded slowly and carefully, and they produced less stereotypic or prejudicial reactions toward the target group in question (i.e., gays). These findings indicate that, like sadness, negative self-related affect that is associated with the violation of internalized nonprejudiced standards can trigger attempts to correct for the influence of seemingly inappropriate stereotypes.

FINAL THOUGHTS

It appears that affect can influence all aspects of the stereotyping process, from the initial assignment of the target person to a particular category, to the activation of relevant stereotypes, to the application of those stereotypes to the case under consideration, and even the eventual undoing of this application in some cases. The picture defies some commonly held ideas about the linkages between affective experience and intergroup relations, because most of the research implicates a role of positive affect in heightened stereotyping while suggesting that some negative states (specifically, sadness) are associated with reductions or elimination of stereotypic biases. Yet the empirical phenomena that have been observed are largely interpretable in terms of more general theoretical ideas that have emerged in the literature on the affect–cognition interface (as documented in the other chapters of this volume).

Many avenues of investigation remain to be explored. For example, we need much more research on integral affect and its impact on social judgment and behavior. It remains unclear whether the growing body of findings involving incidental affect can provide much insight into the psychological consequences of integral affect. We must also understand much more about the potentially distinct effects of various discrete types of integral and incidental affect (e.g., guilt, pride, anger, resentment, envy, disgust). Research addressing the impact of affect on the earliest stages of person perception (i.e., category identification and stereotype activation) is clearly needed as well. As cognitive social psychology becomes "warmer and more social" (Schwarz, 1998), it will be imperative that we develop richer models of how our feelings about and around the members of other groups can influence and shape the course of intergroup relations.

REFERENCES

Abele, A., Gendolla, G. H. E., & Petzold, P. (1998). Positive mood and in-group-out-group differentiation in a minimal group setting. *Personality and Social Psychology Bulletin, 24*, 1343–1357.

Adorno, T. W., Frenkel-Brunswik, E., Levinson, D. J., & Sanford, R. N. (1950). *The authoritarian personality.* New York: Harper.

Allport, G. W. (1954). *The nature of prejudice.* Cambridge, MA: Addison-Wesley.

Amir, Y. (1969). Contact hypothesis in ethnic relations. *Psychological Bulletin, 71*, 319–342.

Bargh, J. A. (1999). The cognitive monster: The case against the controllability of automatic stereotype effects. In S. Chaiken & Y. Trope (Eds.), *Dual process theories in social psychology* (pp. 361–382). New York: Guilford Press.

Baron, R. S., Inman, M. L., Kao, C. F., & Logan, H. (1992). Negative emotion and superficial social processing. *Motivation and Emotion, 16*, 323–346.

Batson, C. D., Polycarpou, M. P., Harmon-Jones, E., Imhoff, H. J., Mitchener, E. C., Bednar, L. L., Klein, T. R., & Highberger, L. (1997). Empathy and attitudes: Can feeling for a member of a stigmatized group improve feelings toward the group? *Journal of Personality and Social Psychology, 72*, 105–118.

Biernat, M., & Vescio, T. K. (1993). Categorization and stereotyping: Effects of group context on memory and social judgment. *Journal of Experimental Social Psychology, 29*, 166–202.

Biernat, M., Vescio, T. K., & Manis, M. (1998). Judging and behaving toward members of stereotyped groups: A shifting standards perspective. In C. Sedikides, J. Schopler, & C. A. Insko (Eds.), *Intergroup cognition and intergroup behavior* (pp. 151–175). Mahwah, NJ: Lawrence Erlbaum Associates.

Bless, H., Bohner, G., Schwarz, N., & Strack, F. (1990). Mood and persuasion: A cognitive response analysis. *Personality and Social Psychology Bulletin, 16*, 331–345.

Bless, H., Clore, G., Schwarz, N., Golisano, V., Rabe, C., & Wölk, M. (1996a). Mood and the use of scripts: Does a happy mood really lead to mindlessness? *Journal of Personality and Social Psychology, 71*, 665–679.

Bless, H., & Fiedler, K. (1995). Affective states and the influence of activated general knowledge. *Personality and Social Psychology Bulletin, 21*, 766–778.

Bless, H., Schwarz, N., & Kemmelmeier, M. (1996b). Mood and stereotyping: Affective states and the use of general knowledge structures. In W. Stroebe & M. Hewstone (Eds.), *European review of social psychology* (Vol. 7, pp. 63–93). Chichester, England: Wiley.

Bless, H., Schwarz, N., & Wieland, R. (1996c). Mood and the impact of category membership and individuating information. *European Journal of Social Psychology, 26,* 935–959.

Blessum, K. A., Lord, C. G., & Sia, T. L. (1998). Cognitive load and positive mood reduce typicality effects in attitude-behavior consistency. *Personality and Social Psychology Bulletin, 24,* 496–504.

Bodenhausen, G. V. (1988). Stereotypic biases in social decision making and memory: Testing process models of stereotype use. *Journal of Personality and Social Psychology, 55,* 726–737.

Bodenhausen, G. V. (1993). Emotions, arousal, and stereotypic judgments: A heuristic model of affect and stereotyping. In D. M. Mackie & D. L. Hamilton (Eds.), *Affect, cognition, and stereotyping* (pp. 13–37). San Diego: Academic Press.

Bodenhausen, G. V., Kramer, G. P., & Süsser, K. (1994a). Happiness and stereotypic thinking in social judgment. *Journal of Personality and Social Psychology, 66,* 621–632.

Bodenhausen, G. V., & Macrae, C. N. (1998). Stereotype activation and inhibition. In R. S. Wyer, Jr. (Ed.), *Stereotype activation and inhibition: Advances in social cognition* (Vol. 11, pp. 1–52). Mahwah, NJ: Lawrence Erlbaum Associates.

Bodenhausen, G. V., Macrae, C. N., & Milne, A. B. (1998). Disregarding social stereotypes: Implications for memory, judgment, and behavior. In J. M. Golding & C. M. MacLeod (Eds.), *Intentional forgetting: Interdisciplinary approaches* (pp. 349–368). Mahwah, NJ: Lawrence Erlbaum Associates.

Bodenhausen, G. V., Macrae, C. N., & Sherman, J. W. (1999). On the dialectics of discrimination: Dual processes in social stereotyping. In S. Chaiken & Y. Trope (Eds.), *Dual-process theories in social psychology* (pp. 271–290). New York: Guilford Press.

Bodenhausen, G. V., & Moreno, K. N. (2000). How do I feel about them? The role of affective reactions in intergroup perception. In H. Bless & J. P. Forgas (Eds.), *The message within: The role of subjective states in social cognition and behavior.* Philadelphia: Psychology Press.

Bodenhausen, G. V., Sheppard, L. A., & Kramer, G. P. (1994b). Negative affect and social judgment: The differential impact of anger and sadness. *European Journal of Social Psychology, 24,* 45–62.

Bodenhausen, G. V., & Wyer, R. S., Jr. (1985). Effects of stereotypes on decision making and information-processing strategies. *Journal of Personality and Social Psychology, 48,* 267–282.

Brewer, M. B. (1988). A dual-process model of impression formation. In R. S. Wyer, Jr., & T. K. Srull (Eds.), *A dual process model of impression formation: Advances in social cognition* (Vol. 1, pp. 1–36). Hillsdale, NJ: Lawrence Erlbaum Associates.

Brewer, M. B., & Miller, N. (1996). *Intergroup relations.* Pacific Grove, CA: Brooks/Cole.

Britt, T. W., Boniecki, K. A., Vescio, T. K., Biernat, M., & Brown, L. M. (1996). Intergroup anxiety: A person × situation approach. *Personality and Social Psychology Bulletin, 22,* 1177–1188.

Chaiken, S., & Maheswaran, D. (1994). Heuristic processing can bias systematic processing: Effects of source credibility, argument ambiguity, and task importance on attitude judgment. *Journal of Personality and Social Psychology, 66,* 460–473.

Clore, G. L., Schwarz, N., & Conway, M. (1994). Cognitive causes and consequences of emotions. In R. S. Wyer, Jr., & T. K. Srull (Eds.), *Handbook of social cognition* (2nd ed., Vol. 1, pp. 323–417). Hillsdale, NJ: Lawrence Erlbaum Associates.

Cooper, J. B. (1959). Emotion in prejudice. *Science, 130,* 314–318.

Damasio, A. R. (1994). *Decartes' error: Emotion, reason, and the human brain.* New York: Putnam.

Darke, S. (1988). Anxiety and working memory capacity. *Cognition & Emotion, 2,* 145–154.

Devine, P. G., Evett, S. R., & Vasquez-Suson, K. A. (1996). Exploring the interpersonal dynamics of intergroup contact. In R. M. Sorrentino & E. T. Higgins (Eds.), *Handbook of motivation and cognition* (Vol. 3, pp. 423–464). New York: Guilford Press.

Devine, P. G., & Monteith, M. J. (1993). The role of discrepancy-associated affect in prejudice reduction. In D. M. Mackie & D. L. Hamilton (Eds.), *Affect, cognition, and stereotyping: Interactive processes in group perception* (pp. 317–344). San Diego: Academic Press.

Devine, P. G., Monteith, M. J., Zuwerink, J. R., & Elliot, A. J. (1991). Prejudice with and without compunction. *Journal of Personality and Social Psychology, 60*, 817–830.

Dijker, A. J. (1987). Emotional reactions to ethnic minorities. *European Journal of Social Psychology, 17*, 305–325.

Dollard, J., Miller, N. E., Doob, L., Mowrer, O. H., & Sears, R. R. (1939). *Frustration and aggression.* New Haven, CT: Yale University Press.

Dovidio, J. F., Gaertner, S. L., Isen, A. M., & Lowrance, R. (1995). Group representations and intergroup bias: Positive affect, similarity, and group size. *Personality and Social Psychology Bulletin, 18*, 856–865.

Dovidio, J. F., Gaertner, S. L., Isen, A. M., Rust, M., & Guerra, P. (1998). Positive affect, cognition, and the reduction of intergroup bias. In C. Sedikides, J. Schopler, & C. A. Insko (Eds.), *Intergroup cognition and intergroup behavior* (pp. 337–366). Mahwah, NJ: Lawrence Erlbaum Associates.

Duncan, B. L. (1976). Differential social perception and attribution of intergroup violence: Testing the lower limits of stereotyping of Blacks. *Journal of Personality and Social Psychology, 34*, 590–598.

Edwards, J. A., & Weary, G. (1993). Depression and the impression formation continuum: Piecemeal processing despite the availability of category information. *Journal of Personality and Social Psychology, 64*, 636–645.

Esses, V. M., & Zanna, M. P. (1995). Mood and the expression of ethnic stereotypes. *Journal of Personality and Social Psychology, 69*, 1052–1068.

Fiedler, K., Asbeck, J., & Nickel, S. (1991). Mood and constructive memory effects on social judgement. *Cognition and Emotion, 5*, 363–378.

Fiske, S. T. (1982). Schema-triggered affect: Applications to social perception. In M. S. Clark & S. T. Fiske (Eds.), *Affect and cognition: The 17th Carnegie symposium on cognition* (pp. 55–78). Hillsdale, NJ: Lawrence Erlbaum Associates.

Fiske, S. T., & Neuberg, S. L. (1990). A continuum of impression formation, from category-based to individuating processes: Influences of information and motivation on attention and interpretation. In M. P. Zanna (Ed.), *Advances in experimental social psychology* (Vol. 23, pp. 1–74). New York: Academic Press.

Fiske, S. T., & Pavelchak, M. A. (1986). Category-based versus piecemeal-based affective responses: Developments in schema-triggered affect. In R. M. Sorrentino & E. T. Higgins (Eds.), *Handbook of motivation and cognition* (Vol. 1, pp. 167–203). New York: Guilford Press.

Forgas, J. P. (1989). Mood effects on decision making strategies. *Australian Journal of Psychology, 41*, 197–214.

Forgas, J. P. (1995). Mood and judgment: The Affect Infusion Model (AIM). *Psychological Bulletin, 117*, 39–66.

Forgas, J. P., & Bower, G. H. (1987). Mood effects on person–perception judgments. *Journal of Personality and Social Psychology, 20*, 497–513.

Forgas, J. P., & Fiedler, K. (1996). Us and them: Mood effects on intergroup discrimination. *Journal of Personality and Social Psychology, 70*, 28–40.

Förster, J., Higgins, E. T., & Strack, F. (in press). Stereotype disconfirmation as personal threat. *Social Cognition.*

Freud, S. (1921). Group psychology and the analysis of the ego. In J. Strachey (Ed.), *Standard edition of the complete psychological works* (Vol. 18). London, Hogarth Press.

Frijda, N. (1986). *The emotions.* Cambridge: Cambridge University Press.

Gaertner, S. L., & Dovidio, J. F. (1986). The aversive form of racism. In J. F. Dovidio & S. L. Gaertner (Eds.), *Prejudice, discrimination, and racism* (pp. 91–125). San Diego: Academic Press.

Gaertner, S. L., Dovidio, J. F., Anastasio, P. A., Bachman, B. A., & Rust, M. C. (1993). The common ingroup identity model: Recategorization and the reduction of intergroup bias. In W. Stroebe & M. Hewstone (Eds.), *European review of social psychology* (Vol. 4, pp. 1–26). London: Wiley.

Gilbert, D. T., & Hixon, J. G. (1991). The trouble of thinking: Activation and application of stereotypic beliefs. *Journal of Personality and Social Psychology, 60,* 509–517.

Haddock, G., Zanna, M. P., & Esses, V. M. (1993). Assessing the structure of prejudicial attitudes: The case of attitudes toward homosexuals. *Journal of Personality and Social Psychology, 65,* 1105–1118.

Hänze, M., & Hesse, F. W. (1993). Emotional influences on semantic priming. *Cognition and Emotion, 7,* 195–205.

Hänze, M., & Meyer, H. A. (1998). Mood influences on automatic and controlled semantic priming. *American Journal of Psychology, 111,* 265–278.

Hirt, E. R., Levine, G. M., McDonald, H. E., Melton, R. J., & Martin, L. L. (1997). The role of mood in quantitative and qualitative aspects of performance: Single or multiple mechanisms? *Journal of Experimental Social Psychology, 33,* 602–629.

Hirt, E. R., Melton, R. J., McDonald, H. E., & Harackiewicz, J. M. (1996). Processing goals, task interest, and the mood-performance relationship: A mediational analysis. *Journal of Personality and Social Psychology, 71,* 245–261.

Isen, A. M. (1993). Positive affect and decision making. In M. Lewis & J. M. Haviland (Eds.), *Handbook of emotions* (pp. 261–277). New York: Guilford Press.

Isen, A. M., & Daubman, K. A. (1984). The influence of affect on categorization. *Journal of Personality and Social Psychology, 47,* 1206–1217.

Isen, A. M., & Means, B. (1983). The influence of positive affect on decision-making strategy. *Social Cognition, 2,* 18–31.

Isen, A. M., Niedenthal, P., & Cantor, N. (1992). An influence of positive affect on social categorization. *Motivation and Emotion, 16,* 65–78.

Jackson, L. A., & Sullivan, L. A. (1988). Cognition and affect in evaluation of stereotyped group members. *Journal of Social Psychology, 129,* 659–672.

Jones, J. M. (1997). *Prejudice and racism* (2nd ed.). New York: McGraw-Hill.

Jussim, L., Nelson, T. E., Manis, M., & Soffin, S. (1995). Prejudice, stereotypes, and labelling effects: Sources of bias in person perception. *Journal of Personality and Social Psychology, 68,* 228–246.

Katz, P. A. (1976). The acquisition of racial attitudes in children. In P. A. Katz (Ed.), *Towards the elimination of racism.* Elmsford, NY: Pergamon Press.

Keltner, D., Ellsworth, P. C., & Edwards, K. (1993). Beyond simple pessimism: Effects of sadness and anger on social judgment. *Journal of Personality and Social Psychology, 64,* 740–752.

Kunda, Z., & Sherman-Williams, B. (1993). Stereotypes and the construal of individuating information. *Personality and Social Psychology Bulletin, 19,* 90–99.

Lambert, A. J., Khan, S. R., Lickel, B. A., & Fricke, K. (1997). Mood and the correction of positive versus negative stereotypes. *Journal of Personality and Social Psychology, 72,* 1002–1016.

Lerner, J. S., Goldberg, J. H., & Tetlock, P. E. (1998). Sober second thought: The effects of accountability, anger, and authoritarianism on attributions of responsibility. *Personality and Social Psychology Bulletin, 24,* 563–574.

Mackie, D. M., & Worth, L. T. (1989). Processing deficits and the mediation of positive affect in persuasion. *Journal of Personality and Social Psychology, 57,* 27–40.

Macrae, C. N., & Bodenhausen, G. V. (2000). Social cognition: Thinking categorically about others. *Annual Review of Psychology, 51,* 93–120.

Macrae, C. N., Bodenhausen, G. V., & Milne, A. B. (1995). The dissection of selection in social perception: Inhibitory processes in social stereotyping. *Journal of Personality and Social Psychology, 69,* 397–407.

Macrae, C. N., Bodenhausen, G. V., Milne, A. B., Thorn, T. M. J., & Castelli, L. (1997). On the activation of social stereotypes: The moderating role of processing objectives. *Journal of Experimental Social Psychology, 33,* 471–489.

Martin, L. L., Ward, D. W., Achee, J. W., & Wyer, R. S., Jr. (1993). Mood as input: People have to interpret the motivational implications of their moods. *Journal of Personality and Social Psychology, 64,* 317–326.

Matthews, A. (1990). Why worry? The cognitive function of anxiety. *Behaviour Research and Therapy, 28,* 455–468.

Melton, R. J. (1995). The role of positive affect in syllogism performance. *Personality and Social Psychology Bulletin, 21,* 788–794.

Monteith, M. J. (1993). Self-regulation of prejudiced responses: Implications for progress in prejudice-reduction efforts. *Journal of Personality and Social Psychology, 65,* 469–485.

Moreno, K. N., & Bodenhausen, G. V. (in press). Intergroup affect and social judgment: Feelings as inadmissible information. *Group Processes and Intergroup Relations.*

Munro, G. D., & Ditto, P. H. (1997). Biased assimilation, attitude polarization, and affect in reactions to stereotype-relevant scientific information. *Personality and Social Psychology Bulletin, 23,* 636–653.

Mussweiler, T., Gabriel, S., & Bodenhausen, G. V. (in press). Shifting social identities as a strategy for deflecting threatening social comparisons. *Journal of Personality and Social Psychology.*

Mussweiler, T., & Strack, F. (1999, May). *Strategies of correction revisited: Theory-based adjustment versus recomputation.* Paper presented at the annual convention of the Midwestern Psychological Association, Chicago.

Oakes, P. J., Turner, J. C., & Haslam, S. A. (1991). Perceiving people as group members: The role of fit in the salience of social categorizations. *British Journal of Social Psychology, 30,* 125–144.

Öhman, A. (1993). Fear and anxiety as emotional phenomena: Clinical phenomenology, evolutionary perspectives, and information-processing mechanisms. In M. Lewis & J. M. Haviland (Eds.), *Handbook of emotions* (pp. 511–536). New York: Guilford Press.

Ottati, V., Terkildsen, N., & Hubbard, C. (1997). Happy faces elicit heuristic processing in a televised impression formation task: A cognitive tuning account. *Personality and Social Psychology Bulletin, 23,* 1144–1156.

Parish, T. S., & Fleetwood, R. S. (1975). Amount of conditioning and subsequent change in racial attitudes of children. *Perceptual and Motor Skills, 40,* 79–86.

Park, J., & Banaji, M. R. (in press). Mood and heuristics: The influence of happy and sad states on sensitivity and bias in stereotyping. *Journal of Personality and Social Psychology.*

Pendry, L. F., & Macrae, C. N. (1996). What the disinterested perceiver overlooks: Goal-directed social categorization. *Personality and Social Psychology Bulletin, 22,* 249–256.

Raghunathan, R., & Pham, M. T. (1999). All negative moods are not equal: Motivational influences of anxiety and sadness on decision making. *Organizational Behavior and Human Decision Processes, 79,* 56–77.

Rosch, E. (1978). Principles of categorization. In E. Rosch & B. Lloyd (Eds.), *Cognition and categorization.* Hillsdale, NJ: Lawrence Erlbaum Associates.

Schwarz, N. (1990). Feelings as information: Informational and motivational functions of affective states. In E. T. Higgins & R. M. Sorrentino (Eds.), *Handbook of motivation and cognition: Foundations of social behavior* (Vol. 2, pp. 527–561). New York: Guilford Press.

Schwarz, N. (1998). Warmer and more social: Recent developments in cognitive social psychology. *Annual Review of Sociology, 24,* 239–264.

Schwarz, N., & Bless, H. (1991). Happy and mindless, but sad and smart? The impact of affective states on analytical reasoning. In J. P. Forgas (Ed.), *Emotion and social judgments* (pp. 55–71). Oxford: Pergamon Press.

Schwarz, N., Bless, H., & Bohner, G. (1991). Mood and persuasion: Affective states influence the processing of persuasive communications. In M. P. Zanna (Ed.), *Advances in experimental social psychology* (Vol. 24, pp. 161–199). Orlando, FL: Academic Press.

Sherman, J. W., Macrae, C. N., & Bodenhausen, G. V. (in press). Attention and stereotyping: Cognitive constraints on the construction of meaningful social impressions. In W. Stroebe & M. Hewstone (Eds.), *European review of social psychology.* Chicester, England: Wiley.

Sinclair, L., & Kunda, Z. (1999). Reactions to a Black professional: Motivated inhibition and activation of conflicting stereotypes. *Journal of Personality and Social Psychology, 77,* 885–904.

Sinclair, R. C., & Mark, M. M. (1995). The effects of mood state on judgmental accuracy: Processing strategy as a mechanism. *Cognition and Emotion, 9,* 417–438.

Smith, E. R., Fazio, R. H., & Cejka, M. A. (1996). Accessible attitudes influence categorization of multiply categorizable objects. *Journal of Personality and Social Psychology, 71,* 888–898.

Spencer, S. J., Fein, S., Wolfe, C. T., Fong, C., & Dunn, M. (1998). Automatic activation of stereotypes: The role of self-image threat. *Personality and Social Psychology Bulletin, 24,* 1139–1152.

Stangor, C., Sullivan, L. A., & Ford, T. E. (1991). Affective and cognitive determinants of prejudice. *Social Cognition, 9,* 359–380.

Stephan, W. G., & Stephan, C. W. (1985). Intergroup anxiety. *Journal of Social Issues, 41*(3), 157–175.

Stephan, W. G., & Stephan, C. W. (1996). *Intergroup relations.* Boulder, CO: Westview Press.

Strack, F. (1992). The different routes to social judgments: Experiential versus informational strategies. In L. L. Martin & A. Tesser (Eds.), *The construction of social judgments* (pp. 249–275). Hillsdale, NJ: Lawrence Erlbaum Associates.

Weary, G. (1990). Depression and sensitivity to social information. In B. S. Moore & A. M. Isen (Eds.), *Affect and social behavior* (pp. 207–230). Cambridge: Cambridge University Press.

Weary, G., & Gannon, K. (1996). Depression, control motivation, and person perception. In P. M. Gollwitzer & J. A. Bargh (Eds.), *The psychology of action: Linking cognition and motivation to behavior* (pp. 146–167). New York: Guilford Press.

Wegener, D. T., & Petty, R. E. (1997). The flexible correction model: The role of naive theories of bias in bias correction. In M. P. Zanna (Ed.), *Advances in experimental social psychology* (Vol. 29, pp. 141–208). San Diego: Academic Press.

Wilder, D. A., & Shapiro, P. N. (1989). Role of competition-induced anxiety in limiting the beneficial impact of positive behavior by an outgroup member. *Journal of Personality and Social Psychology, 56,* 60–69.

Wilson, T. D., & Brekke, N. (1994). Mental contamination and mental correction: Unwanted influences on judgments and evaluations. *Psychological Bulletin, 116,* 117–142.

Wittenbrink, B., Judd, C. M., & Park, B. (1997). Evidence for racial prejudice at the implicit level and its relationship with questionnaire measures. *Journal of Personality and Social Psychology, 72,* 262–274.

Worth, L. T., & Mackie, D. M. (1987). Cognitive mediation of positive affect in persuasion. *Social Cognition, 5,* 76–94.

Zajonc, R. B. (1965). Social facilitation. *Science, 149,* 269–274.

Zajonc, R. B., & Markus, H. (1984). Affect and cognition: The hard interface. In C. Izard, J. Kagan, & R. B. Zajonc (Eds.), *Emotion, cognition, and behavior* (pp. 73–102). Cambridge: Cambridge University Press.

Zanna, M. P., Kiesler, C. A., & Pilkonis, P. A. (1970). Positive and negative attitudinal affect established by classical conditioning. *Journal of Personality and Social Psychology, 14,* 321–328.

16

Affect and Health-Relevant Cognition

Peter Salovey, Jerusha B. Detweiler,
Wayne T. Steward, & Brian T. Bedell

Yale University

Induced Mood and Thoughts about Health	346
Direct Effects of Mood on Illness: Findings from	
Psychoneuroimmunology	349
Induced Mood and Immunologic Parameters	349
Laughter and Immunity	350
Dispositional Links Between Mood and Health	351
Optimism	351
Hope	352
Religiosity	353
Mood-Regulatory Skills	354
Hardiness	355
Negative Affectivity	356
Affect Intensity	357
Mood and Attentional Focus	358
Affect, Health-Relevant Cognition, and Social Support	359
Changes in Mood Motivate Health-Relevant Behaviors	361
Conclusion	362

Address for correspondence: Peter Salovey, Department of Psychology, Yale University, PO Box 208205, New Haven, CT 06520-8205, USA. Email: peter.salovey@yale.edu

Acknowledgments 363
References 363

Hippocrates, the first physician, posited four body fluids ("humors") that when imbalanced produced various physical maladies. Hippocrates's theory, however, was more than just one that linked body fluids to diseases; it also included a role for emotion. The humoral imbalances thought to cause illness also, in his view, created characteristic and chronic emotional states—black bile led to sorrow, phlegm to sleepiness, blood to sanguine feelings, and yellow bile to anger—and thus Hippocrates linked affect and disease by virtue of their common antecedents. Hippocrates no doubt had the particulars wrong. Yet if we ignore the devil in the details and, instead, focus on the big picture, Hippocrates provides prescient guidance: He motivates us to look for connections between emotion and health.

Of course, physiologists more modern than Hippocrates have echoed this bit of wisdom. Harvard's Walter Cannon (1957) spent several decades in the early 20th century documenting what he called *voodoo death*, stories in various cultures about people who, because of some major emotional experience (often fright), suddenly died. Cannon even traced a reasonable pathophysiology that still sensibly provides an explanation for how a person literally could be scared to death.

The purpose of this chapter is to look at more modern research connecting emotional states to health cognition and, at times, to physical health outcomes. Pleasant (or unpleasant) affect may promote healthy (or unhealthy) perceptions, beliefs, and physical well-being. We review studies showing correlations between good moods and subjective health outcomes, and experimental research in which individuals report fewer physical symptoms and more salubrious health beliefs following happy as compared to sad mood induction. To understand these findings and suggest mechanisms linking pleasant feelings, salutary thoughts, and good health, research in other relevant domains is considered, including: (a) direct effects of affect on the immune system; (b) individual difference variables associated with both mood and health; (c) associations among emotional experiences, the focus of attention, and the perception of physical symptoms; (d) the antecedents and consequences of social support; and (e) the use of health-promoting or health-damaging behaviors as affect-regulation strategies. As anticipated by Hippocrates and Cannon, affect, health-relevant cognition, and health itself may be linked through multiple pathways.

INDUCED MOOD AND THOUGHTS
ABOUT HEALTH

We start with some observations from our laboratory in which individuals are led to experience different kinds of moods that subsequently affect the way they think about their health. Then, we review various ways in which feelings such as these could be connected to health outcomes.

Individuals suffering from psychological distress also report various physical symptoms (Katon, 1984; Maddox, 1962; Tessler & Mechanic, 1978). It seems rather obvious that the onset of physical illnesses with debilitating symptoms that interfere with pleasurable daily activities or cause considerable pain could result in depressed mood. Associations between illness and negative mood have been obtained in correlational and time-series analyses of daily diaries (Larsen & Kasimatis, 1991; Persson & Sjoberg, 1987), in clinical studies of pain patients who develop depressive disorders (Keefe, Wilkins, Cook, Crisson, & Muhlbaier, 1986; Turk, Rudy, & Stieg, 1987), in observations of individuals with other medical problems (Rodin & Voshart, 1986), and in studies of individuals experiencing academic or job stress (Griffin, Friend, Eitel, & Lobel, 1993; Repetti, 1993). The more interesting direction of causality that has not been explored as systematically concerns how ongoing moods produce changes in the evaluation of physical symptoms and in subsequent judgments about health and illness.

A relevant line of research concerns the induction of mood states in the laboratory followed by opportunities for individuals to report on beliefs about their physical health. The random assignment of participants to mood inductions allows for a more direct test of the hypothesis that mood shifts have an impact on health-related cognition. Croyle and Uretsky (1987), for example, found that perceived health status was mood-congruent; individuals who experienced sad moods reported more physical symptoms than those who experienced happy moods. These kinds of findings appear to be rather robust (e.g., Abele & Hermer, 1993; Knasko, 1992).

Salovey and Birnbaum (1989) asked college students who were experiencing cold or flu to participate in studies in which moods would be induced in the laboratory. In several different experiments, participants were assigned randomly to happy, sad, or neutral mood-induction conditions. After about 5 min, they were instructed to complete measures of health status. Participants' moods were verified using brief scales at several points during the experimental session. In the first experiment (Salovey &

Birnbaum, 1989), 66 sick undergraduates completed a standard physical symptom questionnaire (Wahler, 1968) and mood scales (McNair, Lorr, & Droppleman, 1971) both prior to and after the mood-induction procedure. These scales were included among a large variety of tasks in order to minimize experimental demand. As expected (because participants were randomly assigned to mood-induction conditions), there were no differences in mood or symptom reports prior to mood induction. However, after experiencing happy, sad, or neutral moods, participants reported symptoms of differing intensity and frequency. Individuals assigned to the sad mood condition reported nearly twice as many aches and pains as those assigned to the happy condition (even though both groups reported the same level of physical symptoms just prior to mood induction). Sad individuals reported more physical symptoms from the previous week, and they attributed greater discomfort to these symptoms than the individuals who were made happy (see Green, Salovey, & Truax, 1999, for further analyses of these data).

Perhaps more important in determining treatment seeking, however, are beliefs about one's capacity to engage successfully in salubrious behaviors and expectations that such behaviors will alleviate illness or maintain health: *self-efficacy* and *outcome efficacy* (Bandura, 1977, 1997). Self-efficacy beliefs are important predictors of diverse health behaviors such as smoking cessation, eating a healthy diet, and engaging in safer sex (reviewed in Salovey, Rothman, & Rodin, 1998). Individuals are unlikely to engage in health behaviors that they feel incapable of carrying out. Similarly, individuals are reluctant to engage in behaviors that they do not believe are health enhancing. These judgments also varied as a function of mood state. As compared with sad individuals, those who were happy perceived themselves as considerably more able to carry out health-promoting behaviors, and they were somewhat more likely to believe that these behaviors would relieve their illness (Salovey & Birnbaum, 1989).

Other important health-related beliefs that usually appear to be precursors of health behaviors are perceptions of vulnerability to future illnesses. Beliefs about risk likelihood and severity have been found to contribute to interest in risk-reducing behavior, such as seeking medical treatment when sick (Becker et al., 1977; Cummings, Jette, Brock, & Haefner, 1979; Kulik & Mahler, 1987; Turk, Rudy, & Salovey, 1984; Weinstein, 1982, 1983; but see also Gerrard, Gibbons, & Bushman, 1996). Individuals appear to be unlikely to take health-protective actions when they do not perceive themselves to be vulnerable to future illnesses (Janz & Becker, 1984).

Estimates of the likelihood of future positive and negative events have generally been among the most mood sensitive of all judgments (e.g., Forgas & Moylan, 1987; Johnson & Tversky, 1983; Mayer, Gaschke, Braverman, & Evans, 1992; Mayer & Volanth, 1985). We asked healthy undergraduates to submit to a happy, sad, or neutral mood induction. They then were administered a 14-item scale containing health-related outcomes, and requested to estimate the likelihood that each might happen in the (a) average student's lifetime and (b) in their own lifetime. For negative health outcomes (future diseases) but not positive health outcomes (maintaining good health), mood had a systematic and linear influence on probability estimates. Happy individuals thought that future diseases were considerably less likely to befall them than their classmates. This bias was almost completely eliminated among students made to feel sad (Salovey & Birnbaum, 1989).

Although this line of mood-induction research has produced some relatively stable and interesting findings, we still must speculate about the mechanisms that might account for such changes in physical symptom reporting and other health beliefs. The remainder of this chapter is devoted to exploring some possible mediators of mood's impact on health cognition. Some of these mechanisms are admittedly speculative and may be far removed from the kinds of studies we have just discussed. However, they are presented here as possible ways of understanding why happy individuals might report feeling good, whereas those experiencing sorrow might report feeling sick, in contexts more general than laboratory mood-induction experiments.

The first mechanism that we explore addresses the idea that pleasant and unpleasant moods may be associated with health outcomes because they have a direct influence on the immune system. Second, we look at whether mood and health are linked through common dispositional "third variables." The idea here is that there are individual difference characteristics that are associated with people's reports of happy or unhappy moods as well as health or illness, respectively. Thirdly, we delineate the associations among one's mood, focus of attention, and subjectively perceived health status. We then go on to discuss whether people who tend to express happier moods are better at eliciting social support from others which, in turn, may have positive health consequences. Finally, we explore whether chronic differences in mood are related to health-protective or health-damaging behaviors and, in particular, whether individuals prone to sad moods use health-damaging behaviors to regulate their moods. These alternative paths connecting feelings states to health beliefs and outcomes are illustrated in Fig. 16.1.

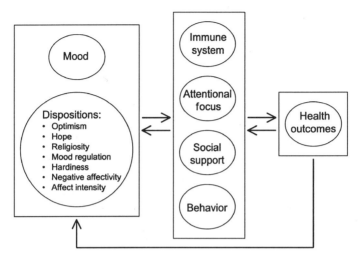

FIG. 16.1. Possible links among affective experiences, health cognition, and behavior.

DIRECT EFFECTS OF MOOD ON ILLNESS: FINDINGS FROM PSYCHONEUROIMMUNOLOGY

Induced Mood and Immunologic Parameters

A growing number of investigators have looked at whether mood can influence the immune system and disease susceptibility directly. In some studies, induced pleasant and unpleasant affective states are both associated with poorer immune function (Futterman, Kemeny, Shapiro, & Fahey, 1994; Knapp et al., 1992). However, the proliferative response to the mitogen phytohemagglutinin appears to be sensitive to the valence of the induced mood; it increases after positive moods and decreases after negative moods (Futterman et al., 1994; but see Futterman, Kemeny, Shapiro, Polonsky, & Fahey, 1992).

Other findings have been obtained by focusing on secretory immunoglobulin A (S-IgA), the antibody considered the first line of defense against the common cold, as the indicator of immune system functioning. Labott and colleagues (Labott, Ahleman, Wolever, & Martin, 1990) asked healthy college women to view two videos, one funny and one sad, and either to suppress their emotional reactions or to express their feelings as overtly as possible. Mood affected the release of S-IgA; levels increased after watching the humorous video, suggesting enhanced immune system activity. In contrast, they dropped after viewing the sad video, indicating suppressed immune system activity. These differences, however, were only found if participants had been instructed to express their mood overtly. Women who actively suppressed their moods showed little change in S-IgA levels. Although this study indicated that the expression of emotions can have immediate effects on some aspects of the immune system, it was not clear how long such effects might last and whether differences in chronic mood might lead to notable differences in disease resistance. Labott and Martin (1990) attempted to answer some of these questions by correlating coping styles with health outcomes. Older women who indicated that they frequently cried as a coping mechanism also reported a greater number of health problems than did older women who indicated that they cried less often.

Laughter and Immunity

There has long been popular belief in the health-enhancing effects of laughter (e.g., King Solomon suggested that "a merry heart doeth good like a medicine," Proverbs 17:22; Cousins, 1979, attributed his recovery from a life-threatening collagen disease to his active use of laughter). Research is now providing support for the idea that expressed humor has a positive impact on health. Recall that women who viewed a humorous video after being encouraged to laugh openly showed increased levels of S-IgA (Labott, Ahleman, Wolever, & Martin, 1990). Similarly, Dillon, Minchoff, and Baker (1985–1986) asked men and women to view two videos, one humorous and one with emotionally neutral content. These participants also showed enhanced levels of S-IgA after viewing the humorous video. In addition, initial levels of S-IgA were correlated with day-to-day coping through humor. Participants who indicated they more frequently used humor as a coping mechanism tended to show higher initial levels of S-IgA.

Humor may also enable a person to deal better with life stressors. Expression of humor appears to moderate associations between negative life events and mood disorders (Martin & Lefcourt, 1983; Nezu, Nezu, & Blisset, 1988). Similar findings have been reported for acute stressors; listening to a 20-min, laughter-inducing monolog enabled participants subsequently to tolerate higher levels of physical discomfort caused by increasing pressure from a blood-pressure cuff (Cogan, Cogan, Waltz, & McCue, 1987). Frequent laughing has also been associated with improved coping abilities (Keller, Shiflett, Schleifer, & Bartlett, 1994; Scheier et al., 1989) and increased perceptions of control (Fitzgerald, Tennen, Affleck, & Pransky, 1993). The physical act of laughter increases respiration, heart rate, and digestion, which could potentially lead to better health outcomes (Hafen, Karren, Frandsen, & Smith, 1996).

DISPOSITIONAL LINKS BETWEEN MOOD AND HEALTH

Several individual difference-level variables may be associated both with chronic moods and affective styles as well as with health beliefs and outcomes. These include optimism, hope, religiosity, mood regulatory skills, negative affectivity, hardiness, and affect intensity.

Optimism

The relationship between dispositional optimism and health has been studied extensively. Dispositional optimism is defined as the tendency to believe that one will experience good instead of bad outcomes in life, as measured, for example, by the Life Orientation Test (LOT; Scheier & Carver, 1985). Scheier and Carver (1992) reviewed research indicating that optimism can affect health positively in four ways. First, optimism may lead one to feel better about oneself or one's situation. For example, women with breast cancer showed an inverse relationship between distress and optimism (Carver et al., 1993). Second, optimism can also lead to more active, problem-focused coping. In a study of men recovering from coronary artery bypass surgery (Scheier et al., 1989), optimists coped differently from pessimists; optimists focused on postoperative goals whereas pessimists attempted to disengage from these goals. Third, optimism can relate to physical well-being. In the heart surgery study (Scheier et al., 1989), optimists showed fewer signs of perioperative myocardial infarction, achieved various markers of physical recovery more quickly, were judged by members of the cardiac rehabilitation team as evidencing a faster rate of recovery, and had a quicker return to different life activities by the time of the 6-month follow-up (see also Scheier et al., 1999). Finally, optimism can lead to better health behaviors. In a 5-year follow-up with the patients in the heart surgery study (Scheier et al., 1990), optimists reported healthier habits, such as regular use of vitamins, eating lunches with less fatty foods, and enrollment in a cardiac rehabilitation program. Some of these effects of optimism may be mediated by differences in perceptions of control (Fitzgerald et al., 1993).

Optimism also can have direct effects on immune system variables. Optimism, as measured by the LOT, is associated with higher levels of critical immune cells, including helper T-cells and natural killer cells (Segerstrom, Taylor, Kemeny, & Fahey, 1998). Reed, Kemeny, Taylor, Wang, and Visscher (1994) looked at "realistic acceptance" of death among gay men with AIDS. They found that men who were high in realistic acceptance died an average of 9 months earlier than those with lower levels of realistic acceptance. The authors hypothesized four potential explanations for this finding: Differential use of health behaviors, differential monitoring of health, existing but undetected differences in health, or actual immunological changes. Realistic acceptance may have led these men to become less optimistic about the future and, in turn, to experience fewer positive moods overall.

Hope

Optimistic individuals are also likely to be people who, in the face of aversive circumstances, hold out hope for positive outcomes. According to Snyder (1994, p. 10), "hope reflects a mental set in which we have the perceived willpower [desires] and waypower [pathways] to get to our destination [goal]." Snyder (1989, 1994) distinguishes hope from dispositional optimism in arguing that optimism implies that people possess a style of explaining events such that they minimize the impact of and distance themselves from current and potential failures. In contrast, hope implies that people undergo a process of linking themselves to potential successes. Whereas optimism creates a distance between the person and the potential for failure, according to Snyder, hope lessens the distance between the person and the potential for success.

Snyder and colleagues (1991) conceptualize hope as a stable cognitive set reflecting general expectancies about the future. The relationship between hope and positive mood is relatively straightforward. People who are hopeful tend to experience a more positive emotional state as they move toward goal-relevant activities. In contrast, people who are not as hopeful tend to experience a more negative emotional state when pursuing goals.

There is some support for the idea that experiencing hope leads to superior health outcomes. For instance, compared to those individuals with lower hope, people who have higher hope recover better from physical injury (Elliott, Witty, Herrick, & Hoffman, 1991). In this investigation, people who had experienced traumatic spinal cord injury, but had scored higher on a measure of hope, reported significantly less psychosocial impairment and lower levels of depression as compared to those low in hope.

Furthermore, hope was related to better adjustment in the month following the injury.

Correlational research further suggests that hopeful people may practice superior health-protective and maintaining behaviors than less hopeful people. In an investigation of hope and college women's cancer-related health practices, hopeful people appear to be more aware of the negative health effects of behaviors such as smoking (Irving, Snyder, & Crowson, 1998). Furthermore, hopeful individuals appear to be more willing to visit health professionals and to perform detection behaviors (such as skin cancer exams and breast examinations; Irving, Snyder, & Crowson, 1998). In addition, hopeful people may have more ideas as to how to take care of themselves when they do become sick (Snyder, 1994). Active participation in setting treatment goals and carrying out physicians' recommendations may, in part, be a result of perceived hope about regaining one's health in the future.

Up until this point, we have discussed hope as Snyder and colleagues have conceptualized it—primarily as a dispositional variable that leads people to experience positive moods when attempting to achieve their goals. Before closing our discussion on the relationship between hope, mood, and health, however, we would like to highlight the health-care worker's role as one who can inspire hope in others. Freud described that patients' expectancies, "colored by hope and faith," are "an effective force . . . in all our attempts at treatment and cure" (1953, p. 289). The link between such hopeful expectations and health outcomes becomes both clear and convincing though the investigation of placebo effects. Frank (1974) concluded that by raising the patient's level of hope, the health-care professional's positive expectations (even when administering a placebo) can influence the health of the patient.

Religiosity

For some, optimism, hopefulness, and positive mood are experienced through regular religious practice. Does religion have a positive impact on health? *Religiosity* is a vague term and is operationalized in a number of ways. Levin and Schiller (1987) reviewed more than 250 empirical studies with generally positive correlations between religiosity and various health outcomes. A study of patients recovering from open-heart surgery (Oxman, Freeman, & Manheimer, 1995) offers a good example. Patients who reported that they derived strength and comfort (positive affect) from religion and who participated in social groups had a survival rate that was higher than those who lacked both sources of support. Even without social support, religious people were more likely to survive than were nonreligious people.

If there is indeed an association between religion and health, how might this relationship be mediated? Levin (1994, 1996) outlined various paths through which religion could influence health. These include behavior, genetics, social support, ritual, belief, faith, and metaphysical effects such as supernatural blessings. Some of these possibilities obviously lend themselves to scientific investigation, whereas others are, by definition, outside the realm of science. A few of the possible pathways do not involve religious belief directly, but arise from situational characteristics associated with the practice of religion. For instance, certain religions encourage behaviors that promote health or discourage potentially health-damaging behaviors (e.g., alcohol or caffeine use). Religion can also build a supportive social network that would help buffer against stress, as discussed later in this chapter. Additional hypothesized pathways involve the psychological aspects of rituals, beliefs, and faith. Religious rituals may promote health by easing anxiety and inducing positive feelings of comfort and appreciation. Religious beliefs could also enhance health by giving people a sense of inner peace, self-confidence, and purpose. These psychological states may be associated with optimism, hope, and other salubrious feelings and belief systems.

Mood-Regulatory Skills

We now turn our discussion to the relationship between skills relevant to affect regulation and physical health. Affect regulation here refers to the individual's ability to terminate negative mood states and/or prolong positive ones (see also Erber & Erber, chap. 13, this volume, for another perspective on mood-repair processes). In other words, an individual who is inclined to repair or regulate his or her mood would have fewer, less negative thoughts in general, report more positive thoughts over time, and display greater control over negative moods (Salovey, Mayer, Goldman, Turvey, & Palfai, 1995). If, indeed, the relationship between positive mood and health is a stable one, we might hypothesize that individuals who are better able to regain and maintain positive mood states would experience better health outcomes than those individuals who are less able to implement such mood regulatory skills.

We believe that one of the more compelling pieces of evidence for the relationship between emotion regulation and health comes from an investigation carried out by Goldman, Kraemer, and Salovey (1996). In this investigation, 134 college students participated in a four-phase prospective study of mood regulatory skills, psychological stress, and illness reporting. The study was conducted over the course of an academic semester, with the objective of collecting health-related data during three relatively stressful periods. Participants in this investigation completed the Trait Meta-Mood Scale (TMMS; a 48-item self-report measure designed to assess a person's general beliefs about attention to mood, clarity of mood experiences, and efforts to repair mood states). Those individuals who said that they generally make an effort to achieve or maintain positive moods were less likely to report illnesses in the face of increasing stress levels than those individuals who described themselves as unlikely to engage in mood repair strategies. Individuals who did not believe that they could repair their moods were more likely to visit the university health center and to report that they had an illness than individuals who believed that they possessed the ability to repair their moods. Mood regulation appears to moderate the effect of stress on illness behaviors.

There are other investigators who have explored the link between emotion regulation and health. Catanzaro and colleagues conducted research investigating individuals' negative mood regulation expectancies. *Negative mood-regulation expectancies* (NMR) refer to individuals' beliefs concerning their ability to alleviate or terminate a negative mood state (Catanzaro & Mearns, 1990). Cross-sectional research suggests that NMR expectancies are positively associated with the use of active coping responses and inversely related to self-reported dysphoria and somatic symptoms, independent of coping behavior and negative life events (Kirsch, Mearns, & Catanzaro, 1990). Catanzaro and Greenwood (1994) hypothesized that individuals who hold an expectation that they can relieve negative moods are able to implement coping skills more effectively and report fewer somatic complaints during times of stress than those individuals who do not hold such expectations. The somatic symptoms that were targeted in this investigation included headaches, acne, and trouble sleeping (among others). NMR expectancies were negatively associated with somatic symptoms, even over the course of 6 to 8 weeks. Overall, individuals who have strong beliefs in their ability to regulate negative moods reported experiencing fewer somatic symptoms as compared to individuals who do not hold these beliefs.

Hardiness

We now turn our discussion to hardiness—another personality characteristic, likely related to the experience of positive affect that may, in fact, protect us from illness (Kobasa, 1979). Hardiness is made up of three specific dispositions: commitment (to one's self, work, and other values), control (over one's life), and challenge (i.e., a belief that change is stimulating). Kobasa hypothesized that this constellation of characteristics should act as a buffer against illness, particularly in times of stress. Several empirical investigations lend support to this hypothesis. Executives who faced stressful life events were less likely to show signs of illness if they were high in hardiness (Kobasa, 1979). In a prospective study, Kobasa, Maddi, and Kahn (1982) reported similar results. Although Kobasa and colleagues do not discuss the role of affect in this buffering process, we speculate that hardy individuals may possess two affective "legs up" in life. First, one's tendency to thrive in the face of challenge may indicate a proclivity toward success, and with this a preponderance of positive mood experiences. Second, a hardy individual's ability to perceive control over his or her life may reflect greater mood regulatory skills. Being able to maximize positive moods and minimize negative moods may have a direct impact on one's overall health status (as just argued). Taken together, these observations lead to a picture of individuals who are not only in charge of their lives, but also in charge of their emotions. We imagine that an individual high in hardiness may be someone who is able to utilize affect through fostering, maintaining, and maximizing positive mood experiences.

Negative Affectivity

Negative affectivity (NA) is a general dimension of subjective distress, including a broad range of negative mood states (Watson & Clark, 1984; Watson & Pennebaker, 1989; Watson & Tellegen, 1985). The personality characteristic most readily associated with NA is neuroticism, and as Costa and McCrae (1987) describe, this tendency to experience negative emotions is associated with subjective health complaints. Trait NA reliably correlates with many measures of subjective complaints and symptom reporting (Watson & Pennebaker, 1989). Despite this association, however, there is little evidence that NA leads to objective decrements in the individual's health status. It appears that individuals who are high in trait NA are likely to complain about their health, but do not necessarily experience greater health problems in the long run (Watson, 2000).

Although *trait* NA may be unrelated to actual physical symptoms, this null relationship may not hold for *state* NA. Cohen and colleagues (1995) carried out an investigation of the impact of state and trait NA on people's resilience to exposure to the rhinovirus and influenza virus. Individuals high in state NA (i.e., those people who were experiencing greater negative mood at the time of the investigation) developed a more severe illness in response to exposure to the respiratory viruses than those who were low in state NA (Cohen et al., 1995). Trait NA was unrelated to illness severity. As Cohen and colleagues (1995) suggest, although individuals high in trait NA may be particularly sensitive to the experience of symptoms (and, thus, would be more likely to report such symptoms), the experience of state NA is what drives objective health.

Affect Intensity

In concluding our discussion of the relationship between affective dispositions, health cognition, and illness itself, we would like to turn to the question of temperament. Does the intensity of positive and negative mood experiences—called *affect intensity* and generally thought to be an individual difference rooted in temperament—have an impact on people's health and overall well-being? Affect intensity is described as a stable individual difference in the strength with which people experience their emotions (Larsen & Diener, 1987). This stable characteristic is thought to generalize across emotions, such that individuals high in affect intensity experience very strong positive moods as well as very strong negative moods. Unlike emotionality (i.e., the tendency to move easily into a negative emotional state from a positive or neutral one; see Buss & Plomin, 1975), *affect intensity* refers to the tendency to experience strong emotions on a regular basis, across stimulus conditions and emotional domains (Larsen & Diener, 1987).

There has been some research suggesting a relationship between affect intensity and somatic disturbances (e.g., nausea, headaches, muscle soreness, shortness of breath). In two separate investigations (Diener, 1984; Larsen, Diener, & Emmons, 1985), individuals high in affect intensity reported more somatic problems than those low on the affect intensity dimension. Because the health-related data were subjective (i.e., the participants simply filled out symptom checklists), we cannot determine whether affect intensity is correlated with actual health problems. Interestingly, however, although affect intensity is significantly related to measures of somatic symptoms, it appears to be unrelated to indicators of psychological well-being (Larsen & Diener, 1987). Individuals who experience their emotions intensely may report a number of somatic and stress symptoms, but unlike the general population (wherein somatic distress is negatively correlated with overall well-being), their lifestyles and life satisfaction do not appear to suffer.

In the larger context of positive mood and health, this line of work is compelling in that it suggests that extremely positive moods may not always be markers of physical health. Individuals who intensely experience their moods (both positive and negative) may encounter more somatic distress throughout their lifetime than their more "mellow" (e.g., low affect intensity) counterparts. Because it is unclear as to whether these somatic symptoms translate into more serious health problems later in life, we feel that continuing to explore the impact of temperament on health is an endeavor well worth undertaking.

MOOD AND ATTENTIONAL FOCUS

Changes in mood are associated with shifts in attentional focus on to or away from oneself. Salovey and Rodin (1985) proposed that during all strong emotional experiences, especially negative ones, there is a tendency for individuals to focus their attention on themselves rather than on the external environment. In a variety of correlational studies, increased attentional focus on to the self has been associated with depressed moods (e.g., Ingram & Smith, 1984; Smith & Greenberg, 1981; for a review of this literature, see Ingram, 1990). Sadness-induced self-focusing has also been demonstrated experimentally (Salovey, 1992; Sedikides, 1992; Wood, Saltzberg, & Goldsamt, 1990). An association between positive states and self-focused attention has been more difficult to demonstrate (but see Fiedler, chap. 8, this volume, for a discussion of conditions under which positive affect might be associated with internally oriented thinking).

Pyszczynski and Greenberg (1987) have proposed that there is a self-focusing style that plays a role in the onset, maintenance, and exacerbation of depression. This theory builds on earlier work (Carver & Scheier, 1981; Duval & Wicklund, 1972) suggesting that allocation of attention on to the self serves a regulatory function and helps the individual to maintain goal-directed behavior (see also Berkowitz, 2000; Berkowitz & Troccoli, 1990). The depressive self-focusing style may in fact help to explain some of the more unusual effects that sadness has on judgments, such as increasing the accuracy of beliefs about the self, reducing self-inflating biases, and eliminating illusions of control (Taylor & Brown, 1988).

Nolen-Hoeksema (1991), who investigated self-focused rumination extensively, regards rumination as a particular style of responding to stressful events that tends to intensify and lengthen periods of depressed mood. Following the 1990 Loma Prieta earthquake in California, for example,

Nolen-Hoeksema and Morrow (1991) found that people who had a more ruminative response style before the earthquake were more depressed 10 days after the event. Similarly, newly bereaved men identified as ruminators prior to their loss experienced longer and more severe periods of depression after their partner's death (Nolen-Hoeksema et al., 1997). The deleterious effects of ruminative coping have been corroborated in a number of laboratory studies as well (e.g., Nolen-Hoeksema & Morrow, 1993). Self-focusing attention on the body, in particular, increases perceptions of symptoms and sensations (Pennebaker, 1982; Pennebaker & Lightner, 1980). For example, individuals who live in unstimulating environments—presumably that do not provide enough competition for internal cues—report more physical symptoms than individuals in stimulating environments.

The comorbidity of depression and physical symptoms may be understood because both appear to be related to self-focused attention. Of course, when one is self-focused, attention may be directed toward the mood-congruent ruminations of the conscious mind (as described in Bower & Forgas, chap. 5, this volume), or to the experiences of the body, or to both. We would expect, however, that when sad moods produce body-oriented self-focused attention, symptoms should be more likely noticed and, indeed, experienced more intensely. The greater salience of somatic cues may subsequently influence judgment about present and future health status as well. Likewise, happier individuals should be less likely to notice these somatic cues and should perceive their health more positively (Stretton & Salovey, 1998).

AFFECT, HEALTH-RELEVANT COGNITION, AND SOCIAL SUPPORT

Individuals who have minimal psychosocial resources appear to be more prone to illness and mood disturbances when faced with increased stress levels than individuals with considerable social support (DeLongis, Folkman, & Lazarus, 1988). The impact of social support on health is well established (Cohen & Syme, 1985; Stroebe & Stroebe, 1996). Social support is related to lower mortality (Berkman, 1985), greater resistance to physical diseases (Cohen, 1988), lower prevalence and incidence of coronary heart disease (Seeman & Syme, 1987), and faster recovery from heart disease and heart surgery (Ruberman, Weinblatt, Goldberg, & Chaudhary, 1984), for example. The relationship between social support and health may exist in part because of the mediating role of positive mood.

In the social support literature, there are two explanations for the relationship between social support and health (Cohen & Syme, 1985; Stroebe & Stroebe, 1996). The buffering hypothesis argues that social support protects people from the negative effects of stress. Social support may come into play by intervening between the stressful event and the stress experience, thus leading the individual to experience a lesser degree of stress in the face of a challenging situation. It may also come between the experience of stress and the negative health outcome by influencing other factors, such as health-relevant behaviors. For instance, social support networks may facilitate healthful behaviors such as exercise and proper nutrition in times of stress.

The direct effect hypothesis argues that social relationships promote health and well-being regardless of the individual's stress level. Social relationships may allow the individual to feel secure that help will be provided when and if necessary. The perception of others' helpfulness can lead to an experience of positive mood, which in turn allows the person to remain resilient to physical illness (Cohen & Syme, 1985). Of course, there are recursive influences of mood on thoughts of this kind as well. The effects of social support are experienced through two mechanisms: social influence and loneliness (Stroebe & Stroebe, 1996). Through social influence, members of the individual's reference group modify the health practices of the individual (regardless of stress levels). Loneliness is generally associated with somatic complaints, depression, and feelings of distress (Peplau, 1985). Medical students who described themselves as lonely had lower natural killer cell activity than less lonely students and responded with a weaker immune response to a hepatitis B vaccine than those with a larger social support network (Glaser et al., 1992; Kiecolt-Glaser & Glaser, 1992).

Social support can take a variety of forms, from friendships to familial relationships. One of the strongest potential sources of social support is marriage. Marital happiness contributes more to measures of overall happiness than friendships and work satisfaction (Glenn & Weaver, 1981), and unhappiness in marriage can lead to severe problems (including physical health problems; Renne, 1971). In an investigation of marital discord and immunological down-regulation, Kiecolt-Glaser et al. (1993) found that couples who were more hostile to one another during a 30-min interaction demonstrated greater immunologic changes relative to the couples who displayed little hostility. In addition, couples who expressed negative reactions to each other had larger and longer-lasting elevations in blood pressure than compatible couples.

Overall, higher levels of social support have been linked to lower negative affect (Cohen & Wills, 1985). There is less support for the relationship between social support and positive affect, however. Eckenrode, Kruger, and Cerkovnik (1986; in Cohen, 1988) demonstrated that positive mood is related to the perceived number of friends and family members who could be counted on and to the actual number of people who had provided help over the course of a year. In addition, neighborhood cohesion is associated with positive mood (Cohen et al., 1982). Although empirical support for the claim that the relationship between social support and health is mediated by positive mood is somewhat difficult to find, we feel confident that positive mood is a critical component of social interactions. We tend to agree with Cohen and Syme's (1985) suggestion that social support, through the stability, predictability, and control that it provides, leads people to feel positively about themselves and their environment. This feeling, in turn, leads people to want to take care of themselves, interact more positively with others, and demonstrate resilience in times of stress. The combined impact of all these variables leads to continued physical and psychological health, which results in further strengthening the individual's social network. Finally, and most relevant to the line of mood-induction experiments with which we opened this chapter, individuals who are happy may find it easier to develop a rich network of social support as compared with those who are more dour. We are likely attracted to people who are pleasant, thus providing them with the health benefits of social support.

CHANGES IN MOOD MOTIVATE
HEALTH-RELEVANT BEHAVIORS

Individuals may use behaviors relevant to their health as mood-regulation strategies. Examples of such behaviors might include eating, shopping, or drinking alcohol to cheer oneself after an upsetting event. Indeed, both anecdotal reports (e.g., Baumeister, 1991) and empirical findings (Leith & Baumeister, 1996) support a link between bad moods and behaviors presumably motivated by a desire to improve mood. For example, self-defined chocolate addicts and nonaddicts recorded their chocolate intake and the circumstances surrounding it for a week (Macdiarmid & Hetherington, 1995). The so-called addicts tended to eat more chocolate when reporting depressed moods. However, bad moods were not ameliorated by eating chocolate. Instead, the chocolate addicts experienced increased levels of guilt following its consumption. Similar results have been reported for alcohol consumption, which, although motivated by bad moods on occasion, does little to improve them (Gustafson, 1991).

If behaviors such eating or drinking do not actually improve mood, why are they used following an upsetting situation? Baumeister (1991) argues that a number of behaviors, including drinking, binge eating, masochistic sex, suicide attempts, and certain religious practices represent an escape from one's self. For example, a person suffering from *bulimia nervosa* may engage in binge eating following an upsetting event that reflects poorly on the self. During the binge, the person does not focus on the problems that led to the binge, nor does the person focus on the consequences of the excessive food consumption. Rather, attention is placed on the actual act of eating itself. For a brief time, eating is devoid of social meaning and thus devoid of the "self." The person only considers the consequences of these actions after the binge is over.

Baumeister (1991) presents evidence suggesting that during an escape from the self, a person also experiences a blunting of emotion, including any unpleasant emotions that elicited the need for escape. Thus, as was suggested by some research findings (e.g., Gustafson, 1991; Macdiarmid & Hetherington, 1995), many behaviors commonly thought to be mood altering do not actually induce new emotions. Instead, these behaviors may feel effective because they allow one to escape temporarily from negative emotions induced by unfavorable reflections on the self.

Although many of the behaviors described by Baumeister (1991) are effective as mood-alteration strategies because they turn off all emotions, including negative ones, other behaviors may work by actually inducing positive feelings. Physical activity can increase positive moods (Dyer & Crouch, 1988; Ewing, Scott, Mendez, & McBride, 1984; Steptoe & Cox, 1988). Measurement of mood changes immediately after exercise suggests that the physical activity only has an effect on positive moods (Ewing, Scott, Mendez, & McBride, 1984; Rudolph & Kim, 1996). However, a longitudinal study of people in exercise classes found a more positive mood profile and reduced negative emotions after several months (Dyer & Crouch, 1988).

CONCLUSION

To understand the links between affect, cognitive activities relevant to health, and health outcomes themselves, it is necessary to place these issues in a broader context than that which circumscribes most of the contributions to this book. Mood can influence thoughts about health quite directly, as laboratory mood-induction research has revealed. However, the mechanisms needed to explain the impact of mood on health cognition and behavior (and the recursive loops leading back to mood once again), require us to move beyond the domain of social cognition and consider variables at the level of immune system physiology, personality dispositions, social relationships, and consummatory behaviors. The excitement in studying links between affect and health cognition is that such work need not be constrained by laboratory technique or disciplinary thinking. Indeed, the most important discoveries in this field will be made by individuals least confined by these artificial boundaries.

ACKNOWLEDGMENTS

Preparation of this manuscript was facilitated by the following grants: American Cancer Society (RPG-93-028-05-PBP), National Cancer Institute (R01-CA68427), and National Institute of Mental Health (P01-MH/DA56826). We also acknowledge funding from the Ethel F. Donaghue Foundation Women's Health Investigator Program at Yale University.

REFERENCES

Abele, A., & Hermer, P. (1993). Mood influences on health-related judgments: Appraisal of own health versus appraisal of unhealthy behaviors. *European Journal of Social Psychology, 23*, 613–625.

Bandura, A. (1977). Self-efficacy: Toward a unifying theory of behavioral change. *Psychological Review, 84*, 191–215.

Bandura, A. (1997). *Self-efficacy: The exercise of control.* New York: W.H. Freeman.

Baumeister, R. F. (1991). *Escaping the self.* New York: Basic Books.

Becker, M. H., Haefner, D. P., Kasl, S. V., Kirscht, J. P., Maiman, L. H., & Rosenstock, I. M. (1977). Selected psychosocial models and correlates of individual health-related behaviors. *Medical Care, 15*, 27–46.

Berkman, L. F. (1985). The relationship of social networks and social support to morbidity and mortality. In S. Cohen & S. L. Syme (Eds.), *Social support and health* (pp. 243–262). Orlando, FL: Academic Press.

Berkowitz, L. (2000). *Feelings: Causes and consequences of positive and negative feelings.* New York: Cambridge University Press.

Berkowitz, L., & Troccoli, B. T. (1990). Feelings, direction of attention, and expressed evaluation of others. *Cognition and Emotion, 4*, 305–325.

Buss, A. H., & Plomin, R. (1975). *A temperament theory of personality.* New York: Wiley.

Cannon, W. B. (1957). "Voodoo" death. *Psychosomatic Medicine, 19*, 182–190.

Carver, C. S., Pozo, C., Harris, S. D., Noriega, V., Scheier, M. F., Robinson, D. S., Ketcham, A. S., Moffat, F. L., & Clark, K. C. (1993). How coping mediates the effect of optimism on distress: A study of women with early-stage breast-cancer. *Journal of Personality and Social Psychology, 65*, 375–390.

Carver, C. S., & Scheier, M. F. (1981). *Attention and self-regulation: A control-theory approach to human behavior*. New York: Springer.

Catanzaro, S. J., & Greenwood, G. (1994). Expectancies for negative mood regulation, coping, and dysphoria among college students. *Journal of Counseling Psychology, 41*, 34–44.

Catanzaro, S. J., & Mearns, J. (1990). Measuring generalized expectancies for negative mood regulation: Initial scale development and implications. *Journal of Personality Assessment, 54*, 546–563.

Cogan, R., Cogan, D., Waltz, W., & McCue, M. (1987). Effects of laughter and relaxation on discomfort thresholds. *Journal of Behavioral Medicine, 10*, 139–144.

Cohen, S. (1988). Psychosocial models of the role of social support in the etiology of physical disease. *Health Psychology, 7*, 269–297.

Cohen, S., Doyle, W. J., Skoner, D. P., Fireman, P., Gwaltney, J. M., & Newsom, J. T. (1995). State and trait negative affect as predictors of objective and subjective symptoms of respiratory viral infections. *Journal of Personality and Social Psychology, 68*, 159–169.

Cohen, S., Struening, E. L., Muhlin, G. L., Genevie, L. E., Kaplan, S. R., & Peck, H. B. (1982). Community stressors, mediating conditions, and well being in urban neighborhoods. *Journal of Community Psychology, 10*, 377–391.

Cohen, S., & Syme, S. L. (1985). Issues in the study and application of social support. In S. Cohen & S. L. Syme (Eds.), *Social support and health* (pp. 3–22). New York: Academic Press.

Cohen, S., & Wills, T. A. (1985). Stress, social support, and the buffering hypothesis. *Psychological Bulletin, 98*, 310–357.

Costa, P. T., Jr., & McCrae, R. R. (1987). Neuroticism, somatic complaints, and disease: Is the bark worse than the bite? *Journal of Personality, 55*, 299–316.

Cousins, N. (1979). *Anatomy of an illness*. New York: Norton.

Croyle, R. T., & Uretsky, M. D. (1987). Effects of mood on self-appraisal of health status. *Health Psychology, 6*, 239–253.

Cummings, K. M., Jette, A. M., Brock, B. M., & Haefner, D. P. (1979). Psychosocial determinants of immunization behavior in a swine influenza campaign. *Medical Care, 17*, 639–649.

DeLongis, A., Folkman, S., & Lazarus, R. S. (1988). The impact of daily stress on health and mood: Psychological and social resources as mediators. *Journal of Personality and Social Psychology, 54*, 486–495.

Diener, E. (1984). Subjective well-being. *Psychological Bulletin, 95*, 542–575.

Dillon, K. M., Minchoff, B., & Baker, K. H. (1985–1986). Positive emotional states and enhancement of the immune system. *International Journal of Psychiatry in Medicine, 15*, 13–17.

Duval, S., & Wicklund, R. A. (1972). *A theory of objective self-awareness*. New York: Academic Press.

Dyer, J. B., III, & Crouch, J. G. (1988). Effects of running and other activities on moods. *Perceptual and Motor Skills, 67*, 43–50.

Eckenrode, J., Kruger, G., & Cerkovnik, M. (1986, August). *Positive and negative affect: Life events and social support as predictors*. Paper presented at the annual meeting of the American Psychological Association, Washington, DC.

Elliott, T. R., Witty, T. E., Herrick, S., & Hoffman, J. T. (1991). Negotiating reality after physical loss: Hope, depression, and disability. *Journal of Personality and Social Psychology, 61*, 608–613.

Ewing, J. H., Scott, D. G., Mendez, A. A., & McBride, T. J. (1984). Effects of aerobic exercise upon affect and cognition. *Perceptual and Motor Skills, 59*, 407–414.

Fitzgerald, T. E., Tennen, H., Affleck, G., & Pransky, G. S. (1993). The relative importance of dispositional optimism and control appraisals in quality of life after coronary artery bypass surgery. *Journal of Behavioral Medicine, 16*, 25–43.

Forgas, J. P., & Moylan, S. (1987). After the movies: Transient mood and social judgments. *Personality and Social Psychology Bulletin, 13*, 467–477.

Frank, J. D. (1974). *Persuasion and healing: A comparative study of psychotherapy*. New York: Schocken Books.

Freud, S. (1953). *The complete psychological works of Sigmund Freud*, (Vol. 7). Edited and translated by J. Strachey. London: Hogarth Press & Institute of Psychoanalysis.

Futterman, A. D., Kemeny, M. E., Shapiro, D., & Fahey, J. L. (1994). Immunological and physiological changes associated with induced positive and negative mood. *Psychosomatic Medicine, 56,* 499–511.

Futterman, A. D., Kemeny, M. E., Shapiro, D., Polonsky, W., & Fahey, J. L. (1992). Immunological variability associated with experimentally-induced positive and negative affective states. *Psychology and Medicine, 22,* 231–238.

Gerrard, M., Gibbons, F. X., & Bushman, B. J. (1996). Relation between perceived vulnerability to HIV and precautionary sexual behavior. *Psychological Bulletin, 119,* 390–409.

Glaser, R., Kiecolt-Glaser, J. K., Bonneau, R., Malarkey, W., Kennedy, S., & Hughes, J. (1992). Stress-induced modulation of the immune response to recombinant hepatitis B vaccine. *Psychosomatic Medicine, 54,* 22–29.

Glenn, N. D., & Weaver, C. N. (1981). The contribution of marital happiness to global happiness. *Journal of Marriage and Family, 43,* 161–168.

Goldman, S. L., Kraemer, D. T., & Salovey, P. (1996). Beliefs about mood moderate the relationship of stress to illness and symptom reporting. *Journal of Psychosomatic Research, 41,* 115–128.

Green, D. P., Salovey, P., & Truax, K. M. (1999). Static, dynamic, and causative bipolarity of affect. *Journal of Personality and Social Psychology, 76,* 856–867.

Griffin, K. W., Friend, R., Eitel, P., & Lobel, M. (1993). Effects of environmental demands, stress, and mood on health practices. *Journal of Behavioral Medicine, 16,* 643–661.

Gustafson, R. (1991). Does a moderate dose of alcohol reinforce feelings of pleasure, well-being, happiness and joy? A brief communication. *Psychological Reports, 69,* 220–222.

Hafen, B. Q., Karren, K. J., Frandsen, K. J., & Smith, N. L. (1996). *Mind/body health: The effects of attitudes, emotions, and relationships*. Boston: Allyn & Bacon.

Ingram, R. E. (1990). Self-focused attention in clinical disorders: Review and a conceptual model. *Psychological Bulletin, 107,* 156–176.

Ingram, R. E., & Smith, T. W. (1984). Depression and internal versus external focus of attention. *Cognitive Therapy and Research, 8,* 139–152.

Irving, L. M., Snyder, C. R., & Crowson, J. J., Jr. (1998). Hope and coping with cancer by college women. *Journal of Personality, 66,* 195–214.

Janz, N. K., & Becker, M. H. (1984). The health beliefs model: A decade later. *Health Education Quarterly, 11,* 1–47.

Johnson, E. J., & Tversky, A. (1983). Affect, generalization, and the perception of risk. *Journal of Personality and Social Psychology, 45,* 20–33.

Katon, W. (1984). Depression: Relationship to somatization and chronic medical illness. *Journal of Clinical Psychiatry, 45,* 4–11.

Keefe, F. J., Wilkins, R. H., Cook, W. A., Crisson, J. E., & Muhlbaier, J. H. (1986). Depression, pain, and pain behavior. *Journal of Consulting and Clinical Psychology, 54,* 665–669.

Keller, S. E., Shiflett, S. C., Schleifer, S. J., & Bartlett, J. A. (1994). Stress, immunity and health. In R. Glaser & J. Kiecolt-Glaser (Eds.), *Handbook of human stress and immunity* (pp. xxx). New York: Academic Press.

Kiecolt-Glaser, J. K., & Glaser, R. (1992). Psychoneuroimmunology: Can psychological interventions modulate immunity? *Journal of Consulting and Clinical Psychology, 60,* 569–575.

Kiecolt-Glaser, J. K., Malarkey, W. B., Chee, M., Newton, T., Cacioppo, J. T., Mao, H., & Glaser, R. (1993). Negative behavior during marital conflict is associated with immunological down-regulation. *Psychosomatic medicine, 55,* 395–409.

Kirsch, I., Mearns, J., & Catanzaro, S. J. (1990). Mood-regulation expectancies as determinants of dysphoria in college students. *Journal of Counseling Psychology, 37,* 306–312.

Knapp, P. H., Levy, E. M., Giorgi, R. G., Black, P. H., Fox, B. H., & Heeren, T. C. (1992). Short-term immunological effects of induced emotions. *Psychosomatic Medicine, 54,* 133–148.

Knasko, S. C. (1992). Ambient odors effect on creativity, mood, and perceived health. *Chemical Senses, 17*, 27–35.

Kobasa, S. C. (1979). Stressful life events, personality, and health: An inquiry into hardiness. *Journal of Personality and Social Psychology, 37*, 1–11.

Kobasa, S. C., Maddi, S. R., & Kahn, S. (1982). Hardiness and health: A prospective study. *Journal of Personality and Social Psychology, 42*, 168–177.

Kulik, J. A., & Mahler, H. I. M. (1987). Health status, perceptions of risk, and prevention interest for health and nonhealth problems. *Health Psychology, 6*, 15–27.

Labott, S. M., Ahleman, S., Wolever, M. E., & Martin, R. B. (1990). The physiological and psychological effects of the expression and inhibition of emotion. *Behavioral Medicine, 16*, 182–189.

Labott, S. M., & Martin, R. B. (1990). Emotional coping, age, and physical disorder. *Behavioral Medicine, 16*, 53–61.

Larsen, R. J., & Diener, E. (1987). Affect intensity as an individual difference characteristic: A review. *Journal of Research in Personality, 21*, 1–39.

Larsen, R. J., Diener, E., & Emmons, R. A. (1985). Affect intensity and reactions to daily life events. *Journal of Personality and Social Psychology, 51*, 803–814.

Larsen, R. J., & Kasimatis, M. (1991). Day-to-day physical symptoms: Individual differences in the occurrence, duration, and emotional concomitants of minor daily illnesses. *Journal of Personality, 59*, 387–423.

Leith, K. P., & Baumeister, R. F. (1996). Why do bad moods increase self-defeating behavior? Emotion, risk taking, and self-regulation. *Journal of Personality and Social Psychology, 71*, 1250–1267.

Levin, J. S. (1994). Religion and health: Is there an association, is it valid, and is it causal? *Social Science and Medicine, 38*, 1475–1482.

Levin, J. S. (1996). How religion influences morbidity and health: Reflections on natural history, salutogenesis and host resistance. *Social Science and Medicine, 43*, 849–864.

Macdiarmid, J. I., & Hetherington, M. M. (1995). Mood modulation by food: An exploration of affect and cravings in 'chocolate addicts.' *British Journal of Clinical Psychology, 34*, 129–138.

Maddox, G. L. (1962). Some correlates of differences in self-assessment of health status among the elderly. *Journal of Gerontology, 17*, 180–185.

Martin, R. A., & Lefcourt, H. M. (1983). Sense of humor as a moderator of the relation between stressors and moods. *Journal of Personality and Social Psychology, 45*, 1313–1324.

Mayer, J. D., Gaschke, Y. N., Braverman, D. L., & Evans, T. W. (1992). Mood-congruent judgment is a general effect. *Journal of Personality and Social Psychology, 63*, 119–132.

Mayer, J. D., & Volanth, A. J. (1985). Cognitive involvement in the emotional response system. *Motivation and Emotion, 9*, 261–275.

McNair, D., Lorr, M., & Droppleman, L. (1971). *EDITS manual for the Profile of Mood States.* San Diego: Educational and Industrial Testing Service.

Nezu, A. M., Nezu, C. M., & Blisset, S. E. (1988). Sense of humor as a moderator of the relation between stressful events and psychological distress: A prospective analysis. *Journal of Personality and Social Psychology, 54*, 520–525.

Nolen-Hoeksema, S. (1991). Responses to depression and their effects on the duration of depressive episodes. *Journal of Abnormal Psychology, 100*, 569–582.

Nolen-Hoeksema, S., McBride, A., & Larsen, J. (1997). Rumination and psychological distress among bereaved partners. *Journal of Personality and Social Psychology, 72*, 855–862.

Nolen-Hoeksema, S., & Morrow, J. (1991). A prospective study of depression and posttraumatic stress symptoms after a natural disaster: The 1989 Loma Prieta earthquake. *Journal of Personality and Social Psychology, 61*, 115–121.

Nolen-Hoeksema, S., & Morrow, J. (1993). Effects of rumination and distraction on naturally occurring depressed mood. *Cognition and Emotion, 7*, 561–570.

Oxman, T. E., Freeman, D. H., & Manheimer, E. D. (1995). Lack of social participation or religious strength and comfort as risk factors for death after cardiac surgery in the elderly. *Psychosomatic Medicine, 57*, 5–15.

Pennebaker, J. W. (1982). *The psychology of physical symptoms.* New York: Springer.

Pennebaker, J. W., & Lightner, J. M. (1980). Competition of internal and external information in an exercise setting. *Journal of Personality and Social Psychology, 35,* 167–174.

Peplau, L. A. (1985). Loneliness research: Basic concepts and findings. In I. G. Sarason & B. R. Sarason (Eds.), *Social support: Theory, research, and applications* (pp. 269–286). The Hague: Martinus Nijhoff.

Persson, L.-O., & Sjoberg, L. (1987). Mood and somatic symptoms. *Journal of Psychosomatic Research, 31,* 499–511.

Pyszczynski, T., & Greenberg, J. (1987). Self-regulatory perseveration and the depressive self-focusing style: A self-awareness theory of depression. *Psychological Bulletin, 102,* 122–138.

Reed, G. M., Kemeny, M. E., Taylor, S. E., Wang, H. J., & Visscher, B. R. (1994). Realistic acceptance as a predictor of decreased survival time in gay men with AIDS. *Health Psychology, 13,* 299–307.

Renne, K. S. (1971). Health and marital experience in an urban population. *Journal of Marriage and Family, 23,* 338–350.

Repetti, R. L. (1993). Short-term effects of occupational stressors on daily mood and health complaints. *Health Psychology, 12,* 125–131.

Rodin, G., & Voshart, K. (1986). Depression in the medically ill: An overview. *American Journal of Psychiatry, 143,* 696–705.

Ruberman, W., Weinblatt, E., Goldberg, J. D., & Chaudhary, B. (1984). Psychosocial influences on mortality after myocardial infarction. *New England Journal of Medicine, 311,* 552–559.

Rudolph, D. L., & Kim, J. G. (1996). Mood responses to recreational sport and exercise in a Korean sample. *Journal of Social Behavior and Personality, 11,* 841–849.

Salovey, P. (1992). Mood induced self-focused attention. *Journal of Personality and Social Psychology, 62,* 699–707.

Salovey, P., & Birnbaum, D. (1989). Influence of mood on health-relevant cognitions. *Journal of Personality and Social Psychology, 57,* 539–551.

Salovey, P., Mayer, J. D., Goldman, S. L., Turvey, C., & Palfai, T. P. (1995). Emotional attention, clarity, and repair: Exploring emotional intelligence using the Trait-Meta-Mood Scale. In J. W. Pennebaker (Ed.), *Emotion, disclosure, and health* (pp. 125–154). Washington, DC: American Psychological Association.

Salovey, P., & Rodin, J. (1985). Cognitions about the self: Connecting feeling states and social behavior. In P. Shaver (Ed.), *Self, situations and social behavior: Review of personality and social psychology* (Vol. 6, pp. 143–166). Beverly Hills, CA: Sage.

Salovey, P., Rothman, A. J., & Rodin, J. (1998). Health behavior. In D. T. Gilbert, S. T. Fiske, & G. Lindzey (Eds.), *The handbook of social psychology* (4th ed., Vol. 2, pp. 633–683). New York: McGraw-Hill.

Salovey, P., & Singer, J. A. (1989). Mood congruency effects in recall of childhood versus recent memories. *Journal of Social Behavior and Personality, 4,* 99–120.

Scheier, M. F., & Carver, C. S. (1985). Optimism, coping, and health: Assessment and implications of generalized outcome expectancies. *Health Psychology, 4,* 219–247.

Scheier, M. F., & Carver, C. S. (1992). Effects of optimism on psychological and physical well-being: Theoretical overview and empirical update. *Cognitive Therapy and Research, 16,* 201–228.

Scheier, M. F., Matthews, K. A., Owens, J. F., Magovern, G. J., Lefebvre, R. C., Abbott, R. A., & Carver, C. S. (1989). Dispositional optimism and recovery from coronary artery bypass surgery: The beneficial-effects on physical and psychological well-being. *Journal of Personality and Social Psychology, 57,* 1024–1040.

Scheier, M. F., Matthews, K. A., Owens, J. F., Magovern, G. J., & Carver, C. S. (1990). Dispositional optimsism and recovery after 5 years from coronary artery bypass surgery. Unpublished raw data. [As cited in Scheier and Carver, 1992.]

Scheier, M. F., Matthews, K. A., Owens, J. F., Schulz, R., Bridges, M. W., Magovern, G. J., & Carver, C. S. (1999). Optimism and rehospitalization after coronary artery bypass graft surgery. *Archives of Internal Medicine, 159,* 829–834.

Sedikides, C. (1992). Mood as a determinant of attentional focus. *Cognition and Emotion, 6*, 129–148.

Seeman, T. E., & Syme, S. L. (1987). Social networks and coronary artery disease: A comparison of the structure and function of social relations as predictors of disease. *Psychosomatic Medicine, 49*, 341–354.

Segerstrom, S. C., Taylor, S. E., Kemeny, M. E., & Fahey, J. L. (1998). Optimism is associated with mood, coping, and immune change in response to stress. *Journal of Personality and Social Psychology, 74*, 1646–1655.

Smith, T. W., & Greenberg, J. (1981). Depression and self-focused attention. *Motivation and Emotion, 5*, 323–331.

Snyder, C. R. (1989). Reality negotiation: From excuses to hope and beyond. *Journal of Social and Clinical Psychology, 8*, 130–157.

Snyder, C. R. (1994). *The psychology of hope: You can get there from here.* New York: The Free Press.

Snyder, C. R., Harris, C., Anderson, J. R., Holleran, S. A., Irving, L. M., Sigmon, S. T., Yoshinobu, L. R., Gibb, J., Langelle, C., & Harney, P. (1991). The will and the ways: Development and validation of an individual-differences measure of hope. *Journal of Personality and Social Psychology, 60*, 570–585.

Snyder, C. R., Irving, L. M., & Anderson, J. R. (1991). Hope and health. In C. R. Snyder & D. R. Forsyth (Eds.), *Handbook of social and clinical psychology: The health perspective* (pp. 285–305). Elmsford, NY: Pergamon Press.

Steptoe, A., & Cox, S. (1988). Acute effects of aerobic exercise on mood. *Health Psychology, 7*, 329–340.

Stretton, M. S., & Salovey, P. (1998). Cognitive and affective components of hypochondriacal concerns. In W. F. Flack & J. D. Laird (Eds.), *Emotions in psychopathology: Theory and research* (pp. 265–279). New York: Oxford University Press.

Stroebe, W., & Stroebe, M. (1996). The social psychology of social support. In E. T. Higgins & A. W. Kruglanski (Eds.), *Social psychology: Handbook of basic principles* (pp. 597–621). New York: Guilford Press.

Taylor, S. E., & Brown, J. D. (1988). Illusion and well-being: A social psychological perspective on mental health. *Psychological Bulletin, 103*, 193–210.

Tessler, R., & Mechanic, D. (1978). Psychological distress and perceived health status. *Journal of Health and Social Behavior, 19*, 254–262.

Turk, D. C., Rudy, T. E., & Salovey, P. (1984). Health protection: Attitudes and behaviors of LPN's, teachers, and college students. *Health Psychology, 3*, 189–210.

Turk, D. C., Rudy, T. E., & Stieg, R. L. (1987). Pain and depression: 1. "Facts." *Pain Management, 1*, 17–26.

Wahler, H. J. (1968). The Physical Symptoms Inventory: Measuring levels of somatic complaining behavior. *Journal of Clinical Psychology, 24*, 207–211.

Watson, D. (2000). *Mood and temperament.* New York: Guilford Press.

Watson, D., & Clark, L. A. (1984). Negative affectivity: The disposition to experience aversive emotional states. *Psychological Bulletin, 96*, 465–490.

Watson, D., & Pennebaker, J. W. (1989). Health complaints, stress, and distress: Exploring the central role of negative affectivity. *Psychological Review, 96*, 234–254.

Watson, D., & Tellegen, A. (1985). Toward a consensual structure of mood. *Psychological Bulletin, 98*, 219–235.

Weinstein, N. D. (1982). Unrealistic optimism about susceptibility to health problems. *Journal of Behavioral Medicine, 5*, 441–460.

Weinstein, N. D. (1983). Reducing unrealistic optimism about illness susceptibility. *Health Psychology, 2*, 11–20.

Wood, J. V., Saltzberg, J. A., & Goldsamt, L. A. (1990). Does affect induce self-focus attention? *Journal of Personality and Social Psychology, 58*, 899–908.

VI

The Role of Individual
Differences in Affectivity

17

Personality as a Moderator of Affective Influences on Cognition

Cheryl L. Rusting
State University of New York at Buffalo

Personality Traits that Enhance Mood-Congruent
    Processing   375
  Extraversion and Neuroticism   375
  Other Negative Traits   378
Personality Traits that Reverse Negative Mood-Congruent Processing   379
  Mood-Regulation   380
  Self-Esteem   382
When Are Personality and Mood Effects on Cognition Present?   383
  Type of Mood Induction   384
  Motivations to Regulate Emotions   385
  Type of Cognitive Task   386
Difficulties in Research on Personality, Mood, and Cognition   387
References   388

To different minds, the same world is a hell, and a heaven.

—Ralph Waldo Emerson

Address for correspondence: Cheryl L. Rusting, Department of Psychology, 355 Park Hall, State University of New York at Buffalo, Buffalo, NY 14260-4110, USA. Email: crusting@acsu.buffalo.edu

371

It is generally believed that people react differently to the same life events and that these reactions have some emotional and cognitive consequences. Negative interpretations of events can lead to negative emotions, thoughts, and ideas. Positive interpretations, however, are likely to lead to positive emotions and thoughts. What causes people to make these positive or negative interpretations? In some cases an event is clearly positive (e.g., receiving an award) or negative (e.g., getting into a car accident). Other events, however, are more ambiguous and could be interpreted in a number of ways (e.g., Is that person smiling at me or smirking at me?). Our interpretations of these types of events are likely to result from our personality characteristics and from our current emotional states.

The idea that one's current emotional state can have an impact on cognitive processing has most commonly been described in the affect and cognition literature as the *mood congruency hypothesis. Mood congruency* refers to the notion that people selectively attend to, interpret, and remember information that is similar in emotional tone to their current mood state. That is, during a positive mood, people should be especially likely to retrieve positive memories and make positive judgments, and during a negative mood they should be especially likely to retrieve negative memories and make negative judgments.

This hypothesis dates back to Bower's (1981) associative network theory, which, in its original form, stated that memory is composed of a "network" of emotion nodes that are connected to emotion-relevant memories, ideas, and associations. When a specific emotion is experienced, the emotion node becomes activated and that activation spreads to all information that is connected to that emotion node. It follows from this model that emotional experiences should give rise to emotion-congruent thoughts and associations. When a person experiences a negative mood, he or she should be especially likely to retrieve negative memories and make negative judgments because those negative ideas have become activated in memory. During a positive mood, however, positive memories and judgments should be especially likely.

This hypothesis has been tested hundreds of times, and there is a good deal of evidence for the mood-congruency effect (for reviews, see Blaney, 1986; Forgas, 1994; Rusting, 1998; Singer & Salovey, 1988). However, there are a number of occasions in which mood-congruency effects are not obtained. For example, some researchers have found positive mood-congruency effects in the absence of negative mood-congruency effects (Isen, Shalker, Clark, & Karp, 1978; Nasby & Yando, 1982), other researchers have found no effects at all (Claeys, 1989; Gayle, 1997; Hasher,

Rose, Zacks, Sanft, & Doren, 1985; Kwiatkowski & Parkinson, 1994), and still other researchers found the opposite (people retrieve positive memories during a negative mood; Erber & Erber, 1994; Forgas, Burnham, & Trimboli, 1988; Parrott & Sabini, 1990; Rinck, Glowalla, & Schneider, 1992; Sedikides, 1994). Since the mid-1980s, much of the mood-congruency literature has centered around determining which subject and task characteristics are responsible for these different findings (e.g., Forgas, 1994, 1995; Isen, 1987; Rusting, 1998; Singer & Salovey, 1988).

Several theorists have suggested that motivational variables play a role in mood-congruent processing, and that the lack of attention to such variables in many studies has led to inconsistent results (Forgas, 1995; Isen, 1985, 1987; Parrott & Sabini, 1990; Sedikides, 1994; Singer & Salovey, 1988). For example, the asymmetrical and opposite effects obtained in some mood-congruency studies could be due to motivations to repair or eliminate negative moods. In other words, people might be motivated to eliminate negative moods, and do so by focusing on positive thoughts and retrieving positive memories and by avoiding negative thoughts and memories.

Other researchers have suggested that various methodological features have an impact on whether mood-congruency occurs (see Rusting, 1998, for a review). These include various problems such as small sample size, unreliable cognitive measures, and demand effects associated with mood inductions. These also include various features of the cognitive tasks used as dependent measures in individual studies. For example, a number of researchers have noted that tasks measuring constructive cognitive judgments (such as free association, probability estimates, or word completions) are more likely to elicit evidence for both positive and negative mood congruency than tasks measuring recall or recognition memory (Forgas, 1994; Rusting, 1998). Other researchers have suggested that self-reference plays an important role in obtaining mood-congruent results. When word lists are encoded as self-referent or when autobiographic memory tasks are used, researchers are more likely to obtain mood-congruent results (Blaney, 1986; Rusting, 1998). Still others have noted that characteristics of the mood state (whether a natural mood state is measured or a mood state is induced) have an impact on mood-congruency (Mayer, McCormick, & Strong, 1995; Hasher, Rose, Zacks, Sanft, & Doren, 1985; Parrot & Sabini, 1990).

All of these task characteristics no doubt play an important role in obtaining or not obtaining mood-congruency effects. In addition to examining task characteristics, however, it is also necessary to investigate how characteristics of the person have an impact on affect–cognition relations. That is, if we are to provide a realistic portrayal of the ways in which moods have an impact on cognitive processing, then it is necessary to also take into account the effects of individual differences in emotion and emotion-relevant personality traits on processing. Furthermore, the idea that motivations play an important role in mood congruency suggests that personality is especially relevant, because motivational variables have long been an integral part of the personality literature. More attention to personality variables, then, would greatly inform our understanding of mood and cognition relations and may help resolve some of the inconsistent findings in this literature.

In this chapter, I focus on the role that personality variables play in mood-congruent memory and judgment. I review some studies that have incorporated measures of both personality and mood, and provide some synthesis of the results of these studies with the theoretical literature. There are at least two ways in which personality can play a role in affect–cognition relations: (1) emotion-relevant personality traits can magnify or lessen mood-congruent processing, or (2) motivation-oriented traits can function to reverse negative mood-congruent processing (e.g., people experiencing negative moods might retrieve positive information as a means of mood repair). I review some of the existing literature within these two domains. Then, I discuss when personality versus mood effects on cognition should be present or absent (e.g., when are personality effects on cognition strongest and weakest?). As shown in Table 17.1, a number of task variables are likely to play a role in the strength of personality effects

TABLE 17.1
Variables the Influence Mood Congruent Processing

Personality variables that have an impact on mood-congruent processing
    Extraversion and neuroticism
    Trait anxiety
    Trait anger/hostility
    Mood-regulation expectancies
    Ruminative vs. distracting styles
    Self-esteem
Task variables that are likely to play a role
    Specificity of the mood induction
    Intensity of the mood induction
    Natural vs. induced mood
    Personal relevance
    Situations that reinforce or reduce motivations to regulate emotions
    Open-ended vs. close-ended tasks
    Ambiguous vs. nonambiguous judgment targets

on cognition. I conclude by highlighting some of the difficulties of doing research that incorporates both personality and mood variables, and with recommendations for future research.

PERSONALITY TRAITS THAT ENHANCE MOOD-CONGRUENT PROCESSING

One way in which personality variables may have an impact on mood-congruent processing is to strengthen or weaken the effect. Individuals may differ in the extent to which they show mood-congruent information processing, and these differences may be captured in emotion-relevant personality traits. That is, certain personality traits might moderate the strength of affect–cognition relations.

Extraversion and Neuroticism

A good deal of research within the personality literature has confirmed that people may be characterized as having certain emotional dispositions that make them differentially susceptible to positive or negative moods. Work by Watson and colleagues demonstrated that there are individual differences in the tendencies to experience positive and negative moods, and that these experiences are relatively stable over time (Ormel & Schaufeli, 1991; Watson & Slack, 1993; Watson & Walker, 1996). Even though moods fluctuate from day to day, people who score high on measures of positive emotionality tend to report more frequent and more intense positive moods than people who score low on positive emotionality. Likewise, people who score high on measures of negative emotionality tend to report more frequent and intense negative moods than those who score low on negative emotionality (Watson & Clark, 1984; Watson, Clark, & Tellegen, 1988).

A similar pattern has been found for the personality traits of extraversion and neuroticism. Extraverts report more frequent and intense positive emotions than introverts, and high-neuroticism individuals report more frequent and intense negative emotions than low-neuroticism individuals (e.g., Costa & McCrae, 1980; Gilboa & Revelle, 1994; Hepburn & Eysenck, 1989; Meyer & Shack, 1989; Rusting & Larsen, 1995; Tellegen, 1985; Watson & Clark, 1992). In addition to these correlational results, some researchers have shown that these traits actually represent propensities or susceptibilities to positive versus negative emotional states (Larsen & Ketelaar, 1989, 1991; Rusting & Larsen, 1997).

If personality and mood are so interrelated, then studies of mood congruency that leave out personality measures are missing at least part of the picture. One might expect that personality traits that are related to positive emotions should also enhance processing of positive information, and that these effects should be particularly pronounced when individuals who score high on such traits are also in a positive mood state. The same may be true for negative moods and traits: negative traits should enhance processing of negative information, especially during a negative mood state. In other words, both traits and moods might have an impact on cognition, and mood-congruency effects should be particularly strong when traits and moods match in emotional tone.

This prediction is consistent with the theoretical underpinnings of extraversion and neuroticism. According to Gray's (1981) theory, extraversion and neuroticism represent individual differences in the relative strengths of two motivational systems: the behavioral activation system (BAS) and the behavioral inhibition system (BIS). The BAS is thought to regulate behavior in the presence of signals of reward, and the BIS is thought to regulate behavior in the presence of signals of punishment. Gray suggested that neuroticism represents strong BIS activation, or an increased sensitivity to signals of punishment. Extraversion, according to this theory, represents strong BAS activation, or an increased sensitivity to signals of reward. A number of researchers have noted that these reward and punishment sensitivities may be related to emotional sensitivities, with positive affect resulting from exposure to signals of reward, and negative affect resulting from exposure to signals of punishment (e.g., Eysenck, 1987; Larsen & Ketelaar, 1991; Strelau, 1987). Extraverts, because of their increased sensitivity to signals of reward, should experience increased positive mood. Individuals high in neuroticism, because of their increased sensitivity to signals of punishment, should experience increased negative mood.

The same theory also provides a theoretical rationale for predicting trait and mood-congruent processing of information. If extraverts are sensitive to signals of reward, then they should be particularly likely to notice and remember positive information that indicates the presence of a reward. Likewise, if high-neuroticism individuals are sensitive to signals of punishment, then they should be particularly likely to notice and remember negative information that indicates the presence of a punishment. In other words, the cognitive networks for extraverted and neurotic individuals should contain a good deal of elaboration of positive and negative emotional concepts, because these individuals need to be able to notice and approach or avoid such rewarding or punishing information in their environments.

For the most part, the role that these traits play in mood-congruent processing remains to be tested. However, the work of Derryberry, Reed, and colleagues represents one beginning. Derryberry (1987) measured reaction times and errors in responding to affective cues. Following signals of reward, extraverts responded more rapidly and with a higher error rate (indicating that they were distracted by the rewarding signal) than introverts. Following signals of punishment, introverts responded more slowly than extraverts. Using a target-detection task, Derryberry and Reed (1994) found that extraverts were slower to shift attention away from the point where a positive incentive cue had been located, whereas introverts were slower to shift from the point where a negative incentive cue had been located. These biases were strongest in participants who scored high in neuroticism.

Other work on trait anxiety (a trait very similar to neuroticism) suggests that these types of effects are pronounced during negative mood states. MacLeod and Mathews (1988) measured trait anxiety and then compared individuals who were close to a major examination (high-state anxiety) to those who were not close to an examination (low-state anxiety). Individuals high in trait anxiety were especially likely to focus attention on threatening information, whereas individuals low in trait anxiety focused attention away from such information. These effects were particularly strong for the group of individuals in the high-state anxiety condition (close to the examination). MacLeod and Mathews concluded that, in predicting the attentional response to threatening stimuli, trait and state anxiety should be considered to function interactively.

In a series of studies, I tried to more directly test the hypothesis that extraversion and neuroticism moderate mood-congruency effects (Rusting, 1999). In the initial study, high- and low-extraversion and high- and low-neuroticism participants completed a mood measure and a series of memory and judgment tasks (free recall of positive and negative words, judgments of emotionally ambiguous scenarios, and story completion). In a second study I used the same procedure, except participants were randomly assigned to positive or negative mood-induction conditions instead of simply measuring their natural mood state. In both studies there was evidence for mood-congruency and trait-congruency effects. People who were in a positive or negative mood state were more likely to remember positive versus negative words and make positive versus negative judgments. In addition, extraverted individuals were particularly likely to remember positive words and make positive judgments, and individuals high in neuroticism were particularly likely to remember negative words and make negative judgments. In the second study, these main effects were qualified by a trait × mood interaction, which suggested that the mood-congruency effects were strengthened by individual differences in extraversion and neuroticism. Extraverted individuals who were in the positive mood condition recalled the highest proportion of positive words (and made the most positive judgments). Individuals high in neuroticism who were in the negative mood condition recalled the highest proportion of negative words (and made the most negative judgments). Taken together with the trait anxiety findings, these results support the notion that individual differences in emotion-relevant personality traits can influence the strength or weakness of mood-congruent memory and judgment.

Other Negative Traits

A number of other specific emotional traits also influence the strength of mood-congruent memory effects. These include studies of trait and state anxiety (described previously), subclinical depression, trait anger, and so on. Although the number of studies examining these effects is not large, the results of studies that do exist quite consistently show that such traits do in fact influence the strength of mood-congruency effects.

In one study, Richards, French, Johnson, Naparstek, and Williams (1992) induced an anxious mood in participants scoring high and low on trait anxiety, and measured performance on an attentional task. They found that high trait-anxiety individuals were less able than low trait-anxiety individuals to shift attention away from the threatening content of anxiety-related words. The same appears to be true for depressed individuals' attention to depressed-content words. For example, Gotlib and Cane (1987) measured depressed and nondepressed individuals' attention to depressed content words on two occasions, once before treatment (when depressed mood was high) and once after treatment (when depressed mood was low). Before treatment, the depressed individuals were slower than the nondepressed individuals to shift attention from depressed content words. After treatment, these effects were no longer apparent. These results suggest that the strength of mood-congruency effects are dependent on the emotion-relevant traits that individuals possess, and that the interactive effects of moods and traits on cognition occur for specific emotional contexts (anxiety/threatening and depressed content).

The same pattern of findings has been obtained in studies using recall measures to assess mood-congruent memory. For example, Ingram, Smith, and Brehm (1983) gave depressed and nondepressed people positive or negative feedback (as a mood manipulation), followed by a surprise free-recall test. They found that in the success (positive mood) condition, only nondepressed individuals showed the mood-congruency effect (they recalled more positive words than depressed individuals). Josephson, Singer, and Salovey (1996) found a similar effect for subclinically depressed and nondepressed individuals. They induced a sad or neutral mood state, and then asked participants to retrieve two "strongly positive or negative" personal memories. In the sad mood condition, depressed individuals were particularly likely to retrieve two sad memories, whereas nondepressed individuals were likely to retrieve a sad memory followed by a second happy memory. The same pattern of findings has been obtained in studies of the hostility component of the Type A personality. Moser and Dyck (1989) found that, after failure feedback, Type A individuals recalled more negative words than Type B individuals. Allred and Smith (1991) replicated this finding using a direct measure of hostility and a specific anger mood induction (a hostile social interaction). Following the hostile interaction, people high in trait hostility showed an increased recall of hostile and negative words. These studies all suggest that negative emotional traits moderate mood-congruent recall by amplifying mood-congruency effects.

To summarize so far, it appears that personality traits and mood states function interactively to impact cognitive processing. Extraversion and neuroticism, and more specific emotional traits (such as subclinical depression, trait hostility, Type A, and trait anxiety) appear to strengthen positive or negative mood-congruency effects. That is, those scoring high on positive traits (like extraversion) are particularly likely to show positive mood-congruent attention, memory, and judgment. Those scoring high on negative traits (like neuroticism, depression, anxiety, and hostility) are particularly likely to show negative mood-congruent attention, memory, and judgment. These personality variables, then, are particularly important to incorporate into studies of mood congruency.

PERSONALITY TRAITS THAT REVERSE NEGATIVE MOOD-CONGRUENT PROCESSING

Another way in which personality variables may have an impact on mood-congruent processing is to activate motivational processes, which then counteract the effect. Although there are certainly occasions in which people are prone to mood-congruent information processing, there are also occasions in which people may use motivational strategies designed to reduce or reverse such processing and the accompanying emotional state. For example, people might find negative states aversive, and might try to reduce them by attempting replace negative thoughts with positive ones. Personality traits that are related to such motivational tendencies should influence the positivity or negativity of postmood thoughts.

Mood-Regulation

One of the main criticisms of associative network models is that they do not account for the effects of motivation on mood-congruent memory and judgment (Singer & Salovey, 1988). There seems to be general agreement in the literature that motivational variables are important and can have an impact on whether mood-congruent or mood-incongruent results are obtained (Forgas, 1995; Isen, 1985, 1987; Parrott & Sabini, 1990; Sedikides, 1994; Singer & Salovey, 1988). According to this perspective, people are motivated to eliminate negative emotional states and maintain positive emotional states. When a negative mood is experienced, people may attempt to alleviate it by using one or more mood-regulatory strategies such as positive thinking, self-reward, or distraction (Frijda, 1988; Morris & Reilly, 1987; Thayer, Newman, & McClain, 1994). That is, individuals may try to repair negative mood states by focusing on pleasant thoughts or retrieving positive memories. Thus, situations in which those motivations are present should lead to more positive memory retrieval and judgment, even when the initial mood state was negative.

A number of studies suggest that people do not passively experience negative emotional states. People use a variety of strategies to regulate their emotions, attempting to either prolong positive states or attempting to reduce or eliminate negative states (Frijda, 1988; Morris & Reilly, 1987; Thayer, Newman, & McClain, 1994), and some strategies appear to be more effective than others. One strategy that has received a good deal of attention and that has a number of conceptual links to the affect and cognition literature is distraction, which usually involves active attempts to focus attention on something unrelated to the event causing the initial negative emotion, and it is usually most effective when it is absorbing or mildly pleasant (Nolen-Hoeksema & Morrow, 1993; Nolen-Hoeksema, Morrow, & Fredrickson, 1993; Rusting & Nolen-Hoeksema, 1998).

The use of certain strategies, such as distraction, should have an impact on the information that is activated within associative networks. Because distraction draws attention away from the event that caused the initial negative emotion and focuses attention on something else, it should interrupt the spreading of activation associated with the negative emotion and should activate other, more positive associations in memory. Traits that relate to the use of strategies such as distraction, then, should be associated with more positive thinking following a negative mood induction. That is, if an individual scores high on a measure of negative mood-regulation tendencies, then he/she is likely to use distraction (or some other effective strategy) whenever a negative mood is experienced. The use of that strategy should, in turn, interrupt the activation of negative concepts in memory and should activate more positive concepts. Thus, individuals who score high on traits related to negative mood regulation should be particularly likely to show reverse mood-congruency effects.

A similar argument could be made for individuals who typically respond to negative emotions by focusing on them (or ruminating about the emotions and the negative events that caused them). Some people respond to negative moods by focusing even more on the causes of their moods, perhaps as an attempt to better understand them (Nolen-Hoeksema, 1991). Work by Nolen-Hoeksema and colleagues suggests that there are individual differences in the tendencies to ruminate about negative emotions and negative events, and that these tendencies are associated with increased negative thinking and poor problem-solving skills (Lyubomirsky & Nolen-Hoeksema, 1993, 1994; Nolen-Hoeksema, 1991). Rumination about negative emotions and events should excite further negative associations in memory and should keep negative emotional concepts active. Thus, individuals who score high on trait measures of rumination should be particularly likely to show mood-congruency effects, at least relative to individuals who use more effective strategies (such as distraction).

In an effort to test these hypotheses, we ran a series of studies in which we manipulated the availability of distraction-oriented mood-regulation strategies and examined how these strategies had an impact on mood-congruent memory (Rusting & DeHart, 1999). After inducing a negative mood state, participants were asked to spend several minutes doing one of three tasks: thinking about their feelings and the event that caused their negative mood (rumination condition), thinking about a series of distracting thoughts provided to them (distraction condition), or freely listing their thoughts as they occurred (control condition). This manipulation was followed immediately by a short memory task.

We found that participants who focused on or ruminated about their negative mood recalled more negative memories than participants in the control condition. Participants who distracted, however, recalled more positive memories and fewer negative memories than participants in the control condition. An even more interesting finding was that the strength of these effects depended on the person's score on a measure of negative mood-regulation expectancies. This measure was designed to assess individual differences in beliefs about whether one is able to effectively regulate negative moods (Catanzaro & Mearns, 1990). Participants who scored high on this measure (who believed they were effective at mood regulation) recalled more positive memories than those who scored low. The high scorers' memories were most positive when they were also in the distraction condition. That is, of all of the groups of participants, those who were both high in negative mood-regulation expectancies and in the distraction condition retrieved the most positive memories (they showed the strongest mood-incongruent memory). Thus, personality traits related to mood regulation appear to interact with the use of particular motivational strategies to influence mood-congruent (or, in this case, mood-incongruent) memory.

Self-Esteem

Another individual difference variable that has an impact on mood-congruent memory is self-esteem. Although not commonly measured in studies of mood congruency, there is some evidence that self-esteem is linked to positive and negative mood experiences. Low self-esteem individuals have been shown to react to negative events with more negative affect than high self-esteem individuals (e.g., Moreland & Sweeney, 1984). They also respond with more negative self-evaluations than high self-esteem people following the induction of a negative mood, which suggests that low self-esteem people are more susceptible to negative self-relevant emotions (Brown & Mankowski, 1993). Research also suggests that high self-esteem individuals are more likely than low self-esteem individuals to respond to negative events with positive thoughts, perhaps as a means of reaffirming their self-concepts, and this strategy may in fact contribute to the maintenance of high self-esteem (Taylor & Brown, 1988). These findings suggest that high self-esteem individuals are more likely to use effective cognitive strategies for regulating negative emotions resulting from negative events. If so, then one would expect high self-esteem individuals to retrieve positive memories following the induction of a negative mood, whereas low self-esteem individuals should retrieve more negative memories following the induction of a negative mood.

In a series of studies, Smith and Petty (1995) tested this hypothesis. They induced negative and neutral moods in high and low self-esteem individuals, and then had participants complete free-recall and story-completion tasks. The main finding, which they replicated in three studies, was that there was an interaction between self-esteem and mood condition. Low self-esteem individuals showed mood-congruent recall; they recalled negative memories in the negative mood condition, and they recalled positive memories in the positive mood condition. High self-esteem participants, however, recalled *positive* memories in the *negative* mood condition. They interpreted these findings as evidence that individuals high in self-esteem retrieved positive information as an attempt to regulate the negative mood that had been induced. Self-esteem, then, appears to be an important individual difference variable to measure in studies of mood congruency. Depending on one's level of self-esteem, very different mood-congruent outcomes can result.

In summary, some personality variables can reverse or produce opposite mood-congruency effects. These variables include traits related to mood-regulatory tendencies, such as negative mood-regulation expectancies, distraction (verses ruminative) tendencies, and self-esteem. Individuals who are particularly adept at regulating negative moods (and who believe that they are effective) retrieve more positive memories than individuals who are not so adept at regulating negative moods. Individuals who ruminate about negative events are more likely to show typical mood-congruency effects than individuals who distract themselves from such events. The same is true for high versus low self-esteem individuals: low self-esteem individuals are more likely to show negative mood-congruency effects than high self-esteem individuals.

WHEN ARE PERSONALITY AND MOOD EFFECTS ON COGNITION PRESENT?

Although there are a number of cases in which personality traits interact with mood states to influence cognitive processing, such effects may be obtained only under certain conditions. In studies in which particularly strong mood inductions are used, or in which situational influences "overpower" individual difference variables, the effects of personality on affect and cognition may be somewhat remediated. At least three types of situations can influence whether personality effects on mood congruency may be detected: (1) the type of mood induction or mood measure used in the study, (2) whether motivations to regulate emotions are present, and (3) the type of cognitive task used to measure mood-congruent cognition.

Type of Mood Induction

Some researchers have noted that certain characteristics of mood-induction procedures can have an impact on whether mood-congruency effects are obtained (e.g., Laird, Cuniff, Sheehan, Shulman, & Strum, 1989; Mayer, Gayle, Meehan, & Haarman, 1990; Niedenthal, Setterlund, & Jones, 1994; Niedenthal & Setterlund, 1994; Rusting, 1998). For example, Laird et al. (1989) suggested that some of the failures to find mood-congruency effects for negative mood inductions occurred because the procedures used to induce mood have induced mainly sadness, and the effects of sadness may not be generalizable to other negative emotions. In a study designed to test this idea, they demonstrated that mood-congruency effects are emotion specific (happy people recall happy memories; angry people recall angry memories), and that such effects do not occur for sadness. The specificity of the induced mood may therefore determine the extent to which mood-congruency effects are obtained. The same pattern should emerge for the effects of specific personality traits on mood congruency, but this possibility remains to be tested. It may be the case that personality effects on mood congruency are stronger when the trait matches the mood and the cognitive material than when there is a discrepancy between the emotional tone of the trait and the mood.

Another potentially important characteristic of the mood induction that could influence the potential for personality to have an impact on mood congruency is its "intensity." Mood inductions that involve asking participants to experience an intense or extreme event could "wash out" any potential individual difference effects. For example, recruiting participants who have recently experienced the death of a spouse is likely to result in a sample with strong negative emotions. Because this type of event is "intense" (i.e., most people who experience the death of a spouse will have a strong negative emotional reaction), it is likely to override any potential individual differences in personality. It may be the case, then, that weaker or more "ambiguous" mood inductions are those in which individual differences are most likely to emerge, because those events allow for the maximum expression of personality. Many commonly used mood-induction procedures seem to fall into this category. For example, the use of film clips or guided imagery procedures are mild enough to allow for individual interpretations and reactions. These types of inductions should therefore be most amenable for the discovery of personality effects on affect and cognition.

It has also been well documented that mood-congruency effects are stronger when the material to be recalled is encoded as self-relevant or when the mood-induction procedure involves some sort of personal relevance (Blaney, 1986; Denny & Hunt, 1992; Derry & Kuiper, 1981; Kuiper, Olinger, MacDonald, & Shaw, 1985; Rusting, 1998). This self-relevance effect may be particularly meaningful for demonstrating the role that personality plays in the impact of mood on cognition. For example, some research within this approach has used autobiographic procedures, in which participants are asked to retrieve real-life positive or negative experiences and attempt to reexperience them as a means of inducing positive or negative mood. Such procedures allow for the expression of individual differences in personality because participants are not constrained into imagining an artificial situation.

Finally, one of the least constraining mood procedures to use is to use none at all and to simply measure participants' natural mood states. Natural mood studies tend to yield consistent evidence for positive and negative mood congruency (e.g., Mayer, Gaschke, Braverman, & Evans, 1992; Mayer & Volanth, 1985; Mayer, Mamberg, & Volanth, 1988). Because mood was not explicitly manipulated in these studies, the results may be due to stable personality variables that predispose individuals to experience the moods they experienced naturally. In light of the strong relationships between personality and emotion (i.e., extraversion and positive affect, and neuroticism and negative affect), studies using natural mood measures are perhaps coming closest to a realistic portrayal of relations among mood, personality, and cognition. Thus, one might expect the greatest contribution of personality variables to mood-congruent cognition when mood states are measured naturally rather than induced.

Motivations to Regulate Emotions

Another important set of variables that can have an impact on whether personality influences mood-congruent processing centers is the presence or absence of motivations to regulate emotional states. Earlier, I discussed the role that mood-regulatory strategies (and personality traits related to those strategies) play in reversing the mood-congruency effect. That is, certain distraction-oriented strategies tend to produce more positive memories during negative moods. It follows from this suggestion that when motivations to regulate emotions are not present, these reversal effects should also not be present. In other words, when individuals are motivated to regulate negative emotions, they should show mood-incongruent processing, but when they are not motivated to do so (or if they are motivated to prolong or intensify the emotion) they should show mood-congruent processing. The effects of personality traits related to the use of these strategies should only be present when the motivations to use those strategies are also present.

Forgas' (1994, 1995) Affect Infusion Model (AIM) highlights the role that motivated processing plays in mood-congruent processing. According to the model, when people are motivated to repair negative moods, they are unlikely to show mood-congruent judgment because they are attempting to counteract their initial negative feelings. Thus, in situations in which such motivations are especially salient (e.g., in certain occupational settings), one might expect stronger mood-incongruency effects than when such motivations are not present. Other situations might promote motivations to maintain or increase negative emotions (e.g., funerals), and these situations are likely to encourage mood-congruency effects. The motivational implications of certain settings might therefore interact with individual differences in personality traits related to the effective regulation of emotion to have an impact on mood-congruent or mood-incongruent processing. Although compelling, this particular idea has not yet been tested in the literature.

Type of Cognitive Task

A third characteristic that can have an impact on the extent to which personality traits interact with mood states to influence cognitive processing is the type of cognitive task that is used to measure mood-congruent cognition. Tasks that are open ended and involve interpretations of ambiguous stimuli are most likely to allow for the expression of personality. According to the AIM (Forgas, 1995), when faced with a complex or ambiguous judgment target, people should engage in more substantive processing, and mood-congruency effects should be more pronounced. It also stands to reason that personality variables should play a role in guiding such processing. Open-ended, ambiguous tasks allow people to place idiosyncratic interpretations onto stimuli that, to some extent, should be related to their personality traits.

It is also interesting to note that judgment tasks have yielded some of the most consistent evidence for mood congruency, whereas free-recall and other memory tasks that rely on standard word lists have not (see Rusting, 1998, for a review). Because they are more open ended, judgment tasks may be more amenable to the effects of individual difference variables. It may, in fact, be the case that the influence of individual differences in personality produces the consistent mood-congruent judgment effects obtained in these studies.

In summary, there are a number of variables that may have a potential impact on the role that personality plays in mood-congruent cognition. Personality effects may be more apparent in studies that involve personally relevant and "weak" mood inductions, and in studies that use cognitive tasks that are sensitive enough to capture the effects of individual difference variables on cognition. The presence or absence of motivations to repair or maintain negative mood states may also interact with mood-regulatory personality traits to have an impact on mood-congruent processing. Because very few studies have been conducted to test these propositions, they should be pursued in future research.

DIFFICULTIES IN RESEARCH ON PERSONALITY, MOOD, AND COGNITION

By now it should be evident that personality variables can have an impact on affect–cognition relations, at least under certain conditions. The next question, of course, is how these variables should be incorporated into studies of mood-congruent memory and judgment. Although it may seem quite easy to "throw in" a measure of personality into a study of affective influences on cognition, a number of difficulties in doing so become apparent. These difficulties range from standard methodologic issues to complex theoretical issues centering around the overlap and causal direction of the effects.

One very important issue that has not yet been addressed concerns the potential overlap in content between personality and mood variables. Because personality and mood measures tend to be correlated, it is very difficult to attempt to distinguish between effects on cognition that are due to transient mood and effects that are due to stable personality traits. Extraversion, for example, correlates with positive mood. Does this correlation mean that positive mood is a part of extraversion, or that the two are separate variables that happen to cooccur? In mood-congruency studies, when effects of both mood and personality are found, it is unclear whether these effects can really be attributed to separate mood and trait variables.

A related difficulty is that it is extremely difficult to tease apart the causal mechanism that underlies these effects. When different mood-congruency effects are obtained for individuals high and low on a particular trait, does this result mean that mood moderates personality effects on cognition, or that personality moderates mood effects on cognition? It is also possible that a mediating mechanism is occurring, whereby personality predisposes individuals to experience certain mood states, which then have an impact on cognitive processing. The picture quickly becomes complex when one considers the fact that all three variables (personality, mood, and cognition) are correlated with one another. Personality could predispose individuals to experience certain moods, but these moods then feed back to influence personality. Moods influence cognitive processing, but this cognitive processing also reinforces the mood. Which of these variables comes first? It is difficult, if not impossible, to attempt to specify one particular causal order.

Even though there are difficulties associated with this approach, it is crucially important to incorporate personality variables into studies of affect and cognition if we are to understand the ways in which affect and cognition are related. In fact, the complexities associated with incorporating personality variables into this literature suggest that inclusion of such variables probably brings us closer to a realistic portrayal of these processes.

If anything, research that has so far incorporated personality variables has shown that not every person shows mood-congruent processing to the same extent. High-neuroticism individuals and those who exhibit ruminative tendencies may be particularly prone to negative mood-congruent thinking. Extraverted individuals and those who are adept at regulating negative emotions through distraction (and other effective strategies) may be particularly prone to positive mood-congruent thinking. Thus, in order to arrive at a more realistic description of relationships between affect and cognition, the role that these traits play in information processing must be taken into account. More research is needed examining the conditions under which personality variables influence mood and cognition. Such research should shed some light on the complex interactions among personality, mood, and cognition, and should improve our understanding of individual differences in emotion and cognition.

REFERENCES

Allred, K. D., & Smith, T. W. (1991). Social cognition in cynical hostility. *Cognitive Therapy and Research, 15*, 399–412.

Blaney, P. H. (1986). Affect and memory: A review. *Psychological Bulletin, 99*, 229–246.

Bower, G. H. (1981). Mood and memory. *American Psychologist, 36*, 129–148.

Brown, J. D., & Mankowski, T. A. (1993). Self-esteem, mood, and self-evaluation: Changes in mood and the way you see you. *Journal of Personality and Social Psychology, 64*, 421–430.

Catanzaro, S. J., & Mearns, J. (1990). Measuring general expectancies for negative mood regulation: Initial scale development and implications. *Journal of Personality Assessment, 54*, 546–563.

Claeys, W. (1989). Social anxiety, evaluative threat and incidental recall of trait words. *Anxiety Research, 2*, 27–43.

Costa, P. T., & McCrae, R. R. (1980). Influence of extraversion and neuroticism on subjective well-being: Happy and unhappy people. *Journal of Personality and Social Psychology, 38*, 668–678.

Denny, E. B., & Hunt, R. R. (1992). Affective valence and memory in depression: Dissociation of recall and fragment completion. *Journal of Abnormal Psychology, 101*, 575–580.

Derry, P. A., & Kuiper, N. A. (1981). Schematic processing and self-reference in clinical depression. *Journal of Abnormal Psychology, 90*, 286–297.

Derryberry, D. (1987). Incentive and feedback effects on target detection: A chronometric analysis of Gray's model of temperament. *Personality and Individual Differences, 8*, 855–865.

Derryberry, D., & Reed, M. A. (1994). Temperament and attention: Orienting toward and away from positive and negative signals. *Journal of Personality and Social Psychology, 66*, 1128–1139.

Erber, R., & Erber, M. W. (1994). Beyond mood and social judgment: Mood incongruent recall and mood regulation. *European Journal of Social Psychology, 24*, 79–88.

Eysenck, M. W. (1987). Trait theories of anxiety. In J. Strelau & H. J. Eysenck (Eds.), *Personality dimensions and arousal* (pp. 79–97). New York: Plenum Press.

Forgas, J. P. (1994). The role of emotion in social judgments: An introductory review and an Affect Infusion Model (AIM). *European Journal of Social Psychology, 24*, 1–24.

Forgas, J. P. (1995). Mood and judgment: The Affect Infusion Model (AIM). *Psychological Bulletin, 117*, 39–66.

Forgas, J. P., Burnham, D. K., & Trimboli, C. (1988). Mood, memory, and social judgments in children. *Journal of Personality and Social Psychology, 54*, 697–703.

Frijda, N. H. (1988). The laws of emotion. *American Psychologist, 43*, 349–358.

Gayle, M. C. (1997). Mood-congruency in recall: The potential effect of arousal. *Journal of Social Behavior and Personality, 12*, 471–480.

Gilboa, E., & Revelle, W. (1994). Personality and the structure of affective responses. In S. H. M. Van Goozen, N. E. Van de Poll, & J. A. Sergeant (Eds.), *Emotions: Essays on emotion theory* (pp. 135–159). Hillsdale, NJ: Lawrence Erlbaum Associates.

Gotlib, I. H., & Cane, D. B. (1987). Construct accessibility and clinical depression: A longitudinal investigation. *Journal of Abnormal Psychology, 96*, 199–204.

Gray, J. A. (1981). A critique of Eysenck's theory of personality. In H. J. Eysenck (Ed.), *A model for personality* (pp. 246–276). New York: Springer.

Hasher, L., Rose, K. C., Zacks, R. T., Sanft, H., & Doren, B. (1985). Mood, recall, and sensitivity effects in normal college students. *Journal of Experimental Psychology: General, 114*, 104–118.

Hepburn, L., & Eysenck, M. W. (1989). Personality, average mood, and mood variability. *Personality and Individual Differences, 10*, 975–983.

Ingram, R. E., Smith, T. W., & Brehm, S. S. (1983). Depression and information processing: Self-schemata and the encoding of self-referent information. *Journal of Personality and Social Psychology, 45*, 412–420.

Isen, A. M. (1985). Asymmetry of happiness and sadness in effects on memory in normal college students: Comments on Hasher, Rose, Zacks, Sanft, and Doren. *Journal of Experimental Psychology: General, 114*, 388–391.

Isen, A. M. (1987). Positive affect, cognitive processes, and social behavior. In L. Berkowitz (Ed.), *Advances in Experimental Social Psychology* (Vol. 20, pp. 203–253). New York: Academic Press.

Isen, A. H., Shalker, T. E., Clark, M., & Karp, L. (1978). Affect, accessibility of material in memory, and behavior: A cognitive loop? *Journal of Personality and Social Psychology, 36*, 1–12.

Josephson, B. R., Singer, J. A., & Salovey, P. (1996). Mood regulation and memory: Repairing sad moods with happy memories. *Cognition and Emotion, 10*, 437–444.

Kuiper, N. A., Olinger, L. J., MacDonald, M. R., & Shaw, B. F. (1985). Self-schema processing of depressed and nondepressed content: The effects of vulnerability to depression. *Social Cognition, 4*, 77–93.

Kwiatkowski, S. J., & Parkinson, S. R. (1994). Depression, elaboration, and mood congruence: Differences between natural and induced mood. *Memory and Cognition, 22*, 225–233.

Laird, J. D., Cuniff, M., Sheehan, K. Shulman, D., & Strum, G. (1989). Emotion specific effects of facial expressions on memory for life events. *Journal of Social Behavior and Personality, 4*, 87–98.

Larsen, R. J., & Ketelaar, T. (1989). Extraversion, neuroticism, and susceptibility to positive and negative mood induction procedures. *Personality and Individual Differences, 10*, 1221–1228.

Larsen, R. J., & Ketelaar, T. (1991). Personality and susceptibility to positive and negative emotional states. *Journal of Personality and Social Psychology, 61*, 132–140.

Lyubomirsky, S., & Nolen-Hoeksema, S. (1993). Self-perpetuating properties of dysphoric rumination. *Journal of Personality and Social Psychology, 65*, 339–349.

Lyubomirsky, S., & Nolen-Hoeksema, S. (1994). Effects of self-focused rumination on negative thinking and interpersonal problem-solving. *Journal of Personality and Social Psychology, 69*, 176–190.

MacLeod, C., & Mathews, A. (1988). Anxiety and the allocation of attention to threat. *Quarterly Journal of Experimental Psychology, 40A*, 653–670.

Mayer, J. D., Gaschke, Y. N., Braverman, D. L., & Evans, T. W. (1992). Mood-congruent judgment is a general effect. *Journal of Personality and Social Psychology, 63*, 119–132.

Mayer, J. D., Gayle, M., Meehan, M. E., & Haarman, A. (1990). Toward better specification of the mood-congruency effect in recall. *Journal of Experimental Social Psychology, 26*, 465–480.

Mayer, J. D., Mamberg, M. H., & Volanth, A. J. (1988). Cognitive domains of the mood system. *Journal of Personality, 56*, 453–486.

Mayer, J. D., McCormick, L. J., & Strong, S. E. (1995). Mood-congruent memory and natural mood: New evidence. *Personality and Social Psychology Bulletin, 21*, 736–746.

Mayer, J. D., & Volanth, A. J. (1985). Cognitive involvement in the mood response system. *Motivation and Emotion, 9*, 261–275.

Meyer, G. J., & Shack, J. R. (1989). Structural convergence of mood and personality: Evidence for old and new "directions." *Journal of Personality and Social Psychology, 57*, 691–706.

Moreland, R. L., & Sweeney, P. D. (1984). Self-expectancies and reactions to evaluations of personal performance. *Journal of Personality, 52*, 156–176

Morris, W. N., & Reilly, N. P. (1987). Toward the self-regulation of mood: Theory and research. *Motivation and Emotion, 11*, 215–249.

Moser, C. G., & Dyck, D. G. (1989). Type A behavior, uncontrollability, and the activation of hostile self-schema responding. *Journal of Research in Personality, 23*, 248–267.

Nasby, W., & Yando, R. (1982). Selective encoding and retrieval of affectively valent information: Two cognitive consequences of children's mood states. *Journal of Personality and Social Psychology, 43*, 1244–1253.

Niedenthal, P. M., & Setterlund, M. B. (1994). Emotion congruence in perception. *Personality and Social Psychology Bulletin, 20*, 401–411.

Niedenthal, P. M., Setterlund, M. B., & Jones, D. E. (1994). Emotional organization of perceptual memory. In P. M. Niedenthal & S. Kitayama (Eds.), *The heart's eye: Emotional influences in perception and attention* (pp. 87–113). New York: Academic Press.

Nolen-Hoeksema, S. (1991). Responses to depression and their effects on the duration of depressive episodes. *Journal of Abnormal Psychology, 100*, 569–582.

Nolen-Hoeksema, S., & Morrow, J. (1993). Effects of rumination and distraction on naturally-occurring depressed moods. *Cognition and Emotion, 7*, 561–570.

Nolen-Hoeksema, S., Morrow, J., & Fredrickson, B. L. (1993). Response styles and duration of depressed moods. *Journal of Abnormal Psychology, 102*, 20–28.

Ormel, J., & Schaufeli, W. B. (1991). Stability and change in psychological distress and their relationship with self-esteem and locus of control: A dynamic equilibrium model. *Journal of Personality and Social Psychology, 60*, 288–299.

Parrott, W. G., & Sabini, J. (1990). Mood and memory under natural conditions: Evidence for mood incongruent recall. *Journal of Personality and Social Psychology, 59*, 321–336.

Richards, A., French, C. C., Johnson, W., Naparstek, J., & Williams, J. (1992). Effects of mood manipulation and anxiety on performance of an emotional Stroop task. *British Journal of Psychology*, *83*, 479–491.

Rinck, M., Glowalla, U., & Schneider, K. (1992). Mood-congruent and mood-incongruent learning. *Memory and Cognition*, *20*, 29–39.

Rusting, C. L. (1998). Personality, mood, and cognitive processing of emotional information: Three conceptual frameworks. *Psychological Bulletin*, *124*, 165–196.

Rusting, C. L. (1999). Personality × mood interaction effects in emotion-congruent memory and judgment. Manuscript submitted for publication.

Rusting, C. L., & DeHart, T. L. (1999). Retrieving positive memories to regulate negative mood: Consequences for mood-congruent judgment and memory. Manuscript submitted for publication.

Rusting, C. L., & Larsen, R. J. (1997). Extraversion, neuroticism, and susceptibility to positive and negative affect: A test of two theoretical models. *Personality and Individual Differences*, *22*, 607–612.

Rusting, C. L., & Larsen, R. J. (1995). Moods as sources of stimulation: Relationships between personality and desired mood states. *Personality and Individual Differences*, *18*, 321–329.

Rusting, C. L., & Nolen-Hoeksema, S. (1998). Regulating responses to anger: Effects of rumination and distraction on anger. *Journal of Personality and Social Psychology*, *74*, 790–803.

Sedikides, C. (1994). Incongruent effects of sad mood on self-conception valence: It's a matter of time. Special Issue: Affect in social judgments and cognition. *European Journal of Social Psychology*, *24*, 161–172.

Singer, J. A., & Salovey, P. (1988). Mood and memory: Evaluating the network theory of affect. *Clinical Psychology Review*, *8*, 211–251.

Smith, S. M., & Petty, R. E. (1995). Personality moderators of mood congruency effects on cognition: The role of self-esteem and negative mood regulation. *Journal of Personality and Social Psychology*, *68*, 1092–1107.

Strelau, J. (1987). Emotion as a key concept in temperament research. *Journal of Research in Personality*, *21*, 510–528.

Taylor, S. E., & Brown, J. D. (1988). Illusion and well-being: A social psychological perspective on mental health. *Psychological Bulletin*, *103*, 193–210.

Tellegen, A. (1985). Structures of mood and personality and their relevance to assessing anxiety, with an emphasis on self-report. In A. H. Tuma & J. D. Maser (Eds.), *Anxiety and the anxiety disorders* (pp. 681–706). Hillsdale, NJ: Lawrence Erlbaum Associates.

Thayer, R. E., Newman, J. R., & McClain, T. M. (1994). Self-regulation of mood: Strategies for changing a bad mood, raising energy, and reducing tension. *Journal of Personality and Social Psychology*, *67*, 910–925.

Watson, D., & Clark, L. A. (1984). Negative affectivity: The disposition to experience aversive emotional states. *Psychological Bulletin*, *96*, 465–490.

Watson, D., & Clark, L. A. (1992). On traits and temperament: General and specific factors of emotional experience and their relation to the five-factor model. *Journal of Personality*, *60*, 441–476.

Watson, D., Clark, L. A., & Tellegen, A. (1988). Development and validation of brief measures of positive and negative affect: The PANAS Scales. *Journal of Personality and Social Psychology*, *54*, 1063–1070.

Watson, D., & Slack, A. K. (1993). General factors of affective temperament and their relation to job satisfaction over time. *Organizational Behavior and Human Decision Processes*, *54*, 181–202.

Watson, D., & Walker, L. M. (1996). The long-term stability and predictive validity of trait measures of affect. *Journal of Personality and Social Psychology*, *70*, 567–577.

18

Affect, Stress, and Personality

Jerry Suls
University of Iowa

The Big Five, Affective Experience, and Stress   394
Neuroticism and Responses to Life Events   396
Processes Contributing to the Neurotic Cascade   399
Personality in the Context of Affective–Cognitive Networks   402
Person × Environment Fit: The Case of Agreeableness   403
Conclusions   405
Acknowledgments   406
References   406

The general consensus among emotion researchers is that mood is a function of both top-down and bottom-up influences (e.g., David, Green, Martin, & Suls, 1997; Feist, Bodner, Jacobs, Miles, & Tan, 1995). Situational factors, such as the occurrence of major and minor events, comprise a critical element of the bottom-up influence. Negative events tend to produce increases in negative affect, whereas positive events are associated with

---

Address for correspondence: Jerry Suls, Department of Psychology, University of Iowa, Iowa City, Iowa 52242, USA. Email: jerry-suls@uiowa.edu

positive affect. There are also top-down influences, which include personality dispositions to experience certain forms of affect, and which also predispose people to interpret and cope with life events in particular ways (Diener, Smith, & Fujita, 1995). In this chapter, I review relevant evidence concerning individual differences in response to life stressors using contemporary personality theory as a framework. As I describe, certain dispositions make people more emotionally reactive to stressors, partly because of the interactive roles of affect and cognition.

When the demands made by life events exceed the individual's resources, negative emotional responses tend to be elicited (DeLongis, Coyne, Dakof, Folkman, & Lazarus, 1982; Holmes & Rahe, 1967; Lazarus & Folkman, 1984; Suls & Mullen, 1981), but some people experience very aversive reactions to stressful life events, whereas others do not. If, for example, an individual appraises a life event as a challenge rather than as a threat, then negative reactions may not result (Lazarus & Folkman, 1984; Blascovich & Tomaka, 1996). Both the bottom-up and top-down influences alluded to earlier contribute to this variation. Differences in reactivity, appraisal, and coping may be explained by cognitive–emotional predispositions from the Five-Factor Model of Personality (FFM; Costa & McCrae, 1985; Goldberg, 1992). The operation of certain dispositional tendencies within a general affective–cognitive system is hypothesized to be responsible for the exaggerated affective effects, as described later in the chapter.

A comment about the weight that I place on basic traits in this paper may be appropriate at this point. Considerable attention has been devoted to a wide range of specific individual differences and their roles in coping and adaptation to stress. These include locus of control (Parkes, 1994), optimism (Scheier & Carver, 1987), and Type A behavior (Dembroski & Costa, 1987). My focus, however, is on basic dispositional traits, particularly those in the FFM (Costa & McCrae, 1985; Goldberg, 1992), rather than specific, narrow-band, individual differences. The FFM represents an attempt to classify trait characteristics as comprehensively and parsimoniously as possible. In this scheme, traits are ordered hierarchically. The "Big Five" represent higher-order superfactors, existing at the summit of this hierarchy. Because their scope is broader and more encompassing than narrow-band traits, such as locus of control, they are likely to provide a more general representation of how dispositions are associated with exaggerated enotional reactivity to stress. A second reason for my emphasis on basic traits is that I am concerned with whether there are individual differences that render people more vulnerable to problems of any kind, as opposed to particular kinds of negative life events. As I describe later, the FFM identifies one trait as especially likely to qualify in that regard.

THE BIG FIVE, AFFECTIVE EXPERIENCE, AND STRESS

Since the early 1980s, there have been considerable advances in the development of a systematic, consensual structure of personality. One taxonomy is called the "Big Three," which grew out of the work by Eysenck and Eysenck (1975), and the other is the "Big Five," which originated with Allport and Odbert (1936), and more recently developed by Cattell (1945), Norman (1963), Goldberg (1981), and Costa and McCrae (1985). The Big Three consists of neuroticism, extraversion, and psychoticism (perhaps more appropriately described as "disinhibition"). The Big Five is comprised of neuroticism, extraversion, conscientiousness, agreeableness, and openness to experience. Although these two taxonomic systems emerged from different conceptual and methodologic traditions, they are actually quite similar (Digman, 1990; Watson, David, & Suls, 1999). In fact, the FFM can be seen as a expanded version of the Big Three. For example, psychoticism represents a complex combination of conscientiousness and agreeableness. Several instruments such as the self-rating scales developed by Costa and McCrae (1985), the lexical markers of Goldberg (1992), and other inventories (John, 1990) provide continuous scores indicating a person's standing for each of the five dimensions.

The relevance of the FFM for emotional reactivity becomes clear when one considers that only certain dimensions of the Big Five are consistently associated with affective experience (e.g., Watson & Clark, 1992). Despite the commonsense notion that positive affect is the opposite of negative affect, factor-analytic evidence has emerged to indicate that self-reported mood tends to fall along two relatively independent dimensions, positive affect and negative affect (Watson & Tellegen, 1985). Thus, people can experience both positive and negative emotions at the same time.[1] Research has shown that certain personality dispositions consistently relate

---

[1] Whether positive and negative affect are independent dimensions or bipolar in nature is controversial (Russell & Carroll, 1999; Watson & Clark, 1997; see also Ito & Cacioppo, chap. 3, this volume). However, this controversy is less pertinent to the subject of this chapter—individual differences that predispose some individuals to experience more aversive reactions to stressful events. The independence approach assumes that stress would increase negative affect, but has no influence on positive affect. The bipolarity view would argue that stress creates negative, as opposed to positive affect.

to affective experience across situations. Persons scoring high in neuroticism tend to experience more frequent and more intense negative affects (such as fear, sadness, and anger; Watson & Clark, 1992; Diener et al., 1995; David et al., 1997). Higher levels of extraversion are associated with more frequent and intense episodes of positive emotional experience (joy, interest, enthusiasm). The other three traits in the FFM tend to be unrelated to experienced affect, or show relationships that are much weaker. An exception may be Openness to Experience. For example, Ciarrochi and Forgas (1999) found that those scoring high in Openness were significantly more influenced by mood when evaluating their possessions. However, even acknowledging some exceptions, the role of personality in understanding stress effects is mostly limited to neuroticism. This is understandable because the other dimensions are not affective in nature, but are more focused on behavior than affectivity. In other words, particular kinds of affect do not seem to be intrinsically related to status on these other three dimensions.

The preceding comments suggest that the neuroticism dimension may be most closely linked to negative stress reactions. The other Big Five dimensions should be unrelated to responses to stressful life events. (Of course, persons high in extraversion should respond more positively to favorable or pleasurable events, but that is beyond the purview of this chapter.) Indeed, Hans Eysenck (1967) proposed that more neurotic individuals have a stronger sensitivity to signals of punishment or negative events (see also Gray, 1981; Strelau, 1987). There is a possibility of confusion here, however, because persons characterized as "neurotic" or "negatively affective" (Watson & Clark, 1984) presumably already have a higher baseline for negative affect than do persons low in neuroticism. However, the question is whether more neurotic persons show an exaggerated reactivity to stressors or respond with the same intensity as other persons, but simply start at a higher baseline of negative affect.

In a review of the empirical literature, Watson and Clark (1984) found considerable evidence that persons scoring high in neuroticism on conventional inventories also reported higher levels of global satisfaction, anxiety, fear, depression, and irritability, and more negative responses to laboratory stressors. However, because of earlier researchers' failure to control for baseline differences in affect, available evidence was ambiguous about whether neurotics exhibited *differential* reactivity to stress. Recent evidence has more directly examined factors, including reactivity, that contribute to the high levels of negative affect reported by neurotic individuals. This research is reviewed later in the chapter.

Although I describe evidence from the stress literature, there is relevant research that has examined the role of personality in the processing of emotion-congruent information. In a review, Rusting (1998) showed how personality, and more specifically neuroticism, may contribute to mood effects on cognition and judgments in at least three ways (see also Rusting, chap. 17, this volume). Rusting (1998) notes that the traditional approach proposes that neuroticism has a direct, independent effect on emotional processing whereby negative affectivity "colors" perception, attention, interpretation, and memory (Watson & Clark, 1984). Another route of influence, the moderation approach, maintains that neuroticism moderates the relationship between mood states and emotional processing. As a consequence, some individuals may exhibit mood-congruent processing of emotional cues, but others may exhibit mood-incongruent processing depending on their personality traits. A third route, the mediational approach, proposes that the effect of neuroticism on emotional processing may be indirect; neuroticism predisposes people to experience certain mood states, which then influence emotional processing, which may account for why personality may influence emotional processing. Rusting (1998) finds evidence for all three mechanisms in the literature on processing of emotion-congruent information across a variety of cognitive tasks. The fact that neurotics process hedonic information differentially (e.g., Bradley & Moog, 1994; Rusting & Larsen, 1998; Young & Martin, 1989) has implications for the research that I review from the stress literature, as shown later in the chapter.

NEUROTICISM AND RESPONSES TO LIFE EVENTS

As noted previously, studies of neuroticism and reactivity conducted prior to 1984 tended to use suboptimal statistical controls or failed to assess changes in affect. A series of studies have corrected these flaws. In a laboratory experiment, Gross, Sutton, and Ketelaar (1998) manipulated affective states with film clips in persons varying in neuroticism. Both pre- and postfilm measures of mood were taken. Gross et al. (1998) found that more neurotic participants showed higher levels of negative affect across the pre- and postinduction phases; in other words, they exhibited a higher tonic level of negative feelings (i.e., affect-level differences). They also showed larger increases in negative emotions in response to the films (affect-reactivity differences). In a 7-year, three-wave study of life events changes and distress, Ormel and Wohlfarth (1991) found that neuroticism measured 7 years earlier had a strong effect on psychological distress, independent of the effect of life events. In addition, persons higher in neuroticism were more prone to be effected (negatively) by the occurrence of life problems; in other words, there was evidence of exaggerated reactivity. Neurotics also tended to report more life difficulties, but the effect of reactivity on subsequent distress remained even after controlling for the number of problems.

Other studies have used intensive measurement of everyday experience. In a naturalistic study of reactions to examination stress, Bolger (1990) found that students scoring higher in neuroticism reported more subsequent distress even after controlling for prior mood. In two subsequent studies, one with married adults (Bolger & Schilling, 1991) and another with college students (Bolger & Zuckerman, 1995), respondents kept daily diaries about the occurrence of interpersonal conflicts across several days or weeks. Both studies showed that more neurotic respondents were more upset by conflicts, as indicated by their mood at the end of the day.

Although recordings about stress and mood at the end of the day are more precise than global reports, such procedures are still subject to recall biases. To obtain an *in situ* assessment, Marco and Suls (1993) and Suls, Green, and Hillis (1998) had community residents, who previously had completed personality measures, report on the occurrence of problems and mood several times during the day on several successive days. Marco and Suls (1993) used experience sampling (via special signal watches at random intervals), whereas Suls et al. (1998) had participants make diary recordings about intervening events and mood several times during the day at standard intervals (signaled by special wristwatch). It should be mentioned that, unlike the studies conducted by Bolger and associates, we did not focus exclusively on interpersonal conflicts; participants were asked to note any problems that occurred during the recording interval.

In both studies, the occurrence of problems in the preceding hour tended to contribute to a poorer mood among all participants. However, even after adjusting for prior mood, more neurotic individuals exhibited hyperreactivity (that is, a larger change in negative mood) after minor, daily problems occurred. These results provide evidence that neurotic individuals are indeed more emotionally hyperreactive to daily problems, and their elevated negative "baseline" alone does not account for the distress that they experience. Clarity about the terms *problem* and *stressor* should be provided at this point. Some life events' researchers have proposed that interpersonal conflicts are the most potent sources of stress in daily life and have been the focus of their attention (Bolger, DeLongis, Kessler, & Schilling, 1989). However, in my research, I have found that a wide range of problems engender distress. Although many of the neurotic's problems are interpersonal in nature, by no means all are (Magnus, Diener, Fujita, & Pavot, 1993). Furthermore, I found no evidence that hyperreactivity was restricted only to conflicts (Suls, Martin, & David, 1998). It is also worth mentioning that Suls et al. (1998) also measured the other four dimensions of the Big Five; the effect of neuroticism persisted even after controlling for participants' standing on the other dimensions. Perhaps of greater note, none of the other dimensions of the FFM showed significant associations with reactivity. As our reasoning suggested, neuroticism seems to be the only dimension linked to oversensitivity to any kind of stressor.

Results also showed that other factors probably also contributed to the neurotic's negative mood. Neurotic individuals reported having more frequent daily and life problems (see also Bolger & Zuckerman, 1995; Headley & Wearing, 1989). A lower threshold for defining events as problems may be responsible (see later in this chapter), but in addition, other investigators (Magnus et al., 1993) have found that even when life events are measured objectively, neurotics experience more stressors. One interpretation is that people seek out or create particular environments as a function of disposition (Diener, Larsen, & Emmons, 1984). Increased *exposure* to problem events, as well as hyperreactivity, probably contributes to the daily distress of neurotic individuals.

In addition, our studies also found two other contributing factors. A prior "bad mood" lasted longer for the more neurotic individuals. It has been previously established that prior mood tends to exhibit a lag effect, at least within the same day (e.g., Williams, Suls, Alliger, Learner, & Wan, 1991). However, the stronger lag effect exhibited by neurotic persons suggests that they suffer from a form of "affective inertia." A fourth result emerged when we considered whether reported problems were "new" or represented the recurrence of a problem. Neurotic individuals tended to more affected by old problems. Both neurotic and nonneurotic individuals were perturbed comparably by new problems. This may have implications for the kinds of appraisals and coping strategies neurotic persons use (see later in this chapter).[2]

---

[2]Analyses in which all Big Five dimensions were entered simultaneously confirmed that the old versus new problem effect and increased exposure varied only as a function of neuroticism. There was some indication that agreeableness may be related to less affective inertia and neurotism to more affective inertia.

Taking together the results of naturalistic experiments and other research, four distinct elements appear to characterize the life experience of neurotics: (a) hyperreactivity, (b) exposure to more problems, (c) negative affective inertia, and (d) inability to adjust when old problems recur. Because all four elements seem to represent a confluence of "forces" with the consequence of creating an all-pervasive negative affect, I refer to these as the *neurotic cascade*.

PROCESSES CONTRIBUTING TO THE NEUROTIC CASCADE

Four aspects of the affective experience of neurotic individuals have been described, but discussion to this point has been mainly descriptive. What specific processes make neurotics more prone to these tendencies? One explanation, advanced originally by Eysenck (1967), was that neurotics have a constitutional reactivity to stressors as a function of a more labile sympathetic nervous system (see Suls & Rittenhouse, 1990, for additional discussion of constitutional explanations for vulnerability to stress). Although there is little consistent evidence linking neuroticism with greater limbic system activity (e.g., Schwebel & Suls, 1999), considerable support for the heritability of neuroticism has been reported (Tellegen, Lykken, Bouchard, Wilcox, & Rich, 1988). A physiological mechanism may account for the heightened emotionally reactivity of neurotic individuals, but this explanation seems less plausible for some other aspects of their experience—greater exposure to life events, affective inertia, and exaggerated reactivity to old problems, but not to new ones.

Another, nonmutually exclusive explanation is that neurotics appraise major and minor life events in more negative terms. As illustrative evidence, Hemenover and Dienstbier (1996) and Gallagher (1990) reported that more neurotic college students approach college stressors, such as examinations, with greater worries and fears and lower confidence. This suggests that neurotics are more likely to perceive stressors as threats to self-esteem or well-being than as challenges to be overcome. Such negative cognitive appraisals are consistent with other evidence that neurotics accentuate the negative. They tend to be better at recognizing, recalling, and relearning stimuli that have been associated with failure (e.g., Eriksen, 1954), interpret ambiguous stimuli more negatively (e.g., Goodstein, 1954), and accept negative information about themselves more readily (Watson &

Clark, 1984; Swann, Griffin, Predmore, & Gaines, 1987; see also Rusting, chap. 17, this volume).

Such evidence suggests that neurotic persons have a lower threshold for assessing life events as stressors. Other evidence indicates, however, that neurotic individuals actually do experience more objectively negative events so a lower threshold or a perceptual bias is unlikely to furnish a complete explanation (Magnus et al., 1993). A plausible explanation for differential exposure is that the neurotic's negative view of him-herself and others (Epstein, 1990) leads to behavior that creates problematic situations (Swann et al., 1987). For example, a person with low feelings of self-worth may continually seek positive approval from a romantic partner and question the partner's affection for them because the self feels unworthy. As a consequence, the partner may eventually withdraw from the relationship (see Sedikides & Green, chap. 7, this volume). In addition, a preexisting high level of negative affect may create problems, especially interpersonal conflicts (Magnus et al., 1993; Bolger & Zuckerman, 1995).

A third explanation, the "differential coping hypothesis," is that neurotic individuals use less-than-optimal coping strategies in dealing with life events (Bolger & Zuckerman, 1995; Watson & Hubbard, 1996). A related explanation, the "coping effectiveness hypothesis" (Bolger & Zuckerman, 1995), is that certain strategies work less effectively for more neurotic individuals. With respect to the first hypothesis, retrospective accounts of coping use indicate that neurotic persons report more frequently responding to stress by giving up (behavioral disengagement), daydreaming, or engaging in substitute activities to take their mind off the problems (mental disengagement), expressing their negative feelings openly (venting of emotions), and pretending their problems are not real (denial; McCrae & Costa, 1986; Watson et al., 1999). These forms of coping have been characterized as passive and maladaptive by many authors because they emphasize emotion-focused rather than problem-focused strategies. As noted earlier, however, retrospective accounts of coping are susceptible to recall biases and may reflect one's theory about what one has done rather than actual behavior (Pietromonaco & Feldman-Barrett, 1997; Stone et al., 1998). Prospective studies and diary studies, fortunately, reveal similar patterns in coping. For example, in a prospective study, Bolger's (1990) more neurotic subjects were apt to use wishful thinking and fantasy in coping with a stressful and important examination. In a daily diary study with community residents, David and Suls (1999) found that persons high in neuroticism reported using more catharsis and relaxation, both of which are emotion-focused strategies. Also, neurotic participants relied more on emotion-focused strategies, such as distraction and relaxation, even when the stressor was perceived to be relatively minor (compared to less neurotic individuals). In another daily study focusing on the effects of interpersonal conflict (Bolger & Zuckerman, 1995), highly neurotic subjects reported using more self-controlling (e.g., "I tried to keep my feelings to myself"), confrontive, and escape–avoidance coping (surprisingly, they also reported more planful problem solving, a supposedly mature coping strategy). However, in general, neurotics tend to rely on different strategies that, for the most part, tend to be passive, in that they do nothing about the problem itself.

The only evidence (Bolger & Zuckerman, 1995) for differential effectiveness of certain strategies depending on personality was that self-control was ineffective for modifying depressive feelings among high-neuroticism subjects, but effective for low-neuroticism subjects. Escape and avoidance actually exacerbated depression in those low in neuroticism, but had no effect for more neurotic subjects. Confrontive coping was ineffective in terms of reducing angry feelings for persons both high and low in neuroticism. These results should be considered preliminary because they are based only on reactions to social conflicts; however, Bolger's distinction between differential coping choice as a function of personality versus differential effectiveness as a function of personality may prove to be important. It should be acknowledged that both possibilities may be a consequence of the same process. Neurotic individuals, because of their negative expectations, may assume that they can only rely on emotion-focused strategies because they expect to be unable to solve the problem. These low expectations also may prompt them to use strategies with less persistence and competence (Suls & David, 1996). Thus, rather than assuming that certain coping strategies intrinsically are maladaptive, neurotic individuals may not use them appropriately or with sufficient effort.

Adoption of strategies that do not rectify the problem event directly or the inability to execute the strategy appropriately may account for the longer time to recover from a negative mood (the lag effect) (of course, a psychobiological mechanism is possible also). In addition, when an old problem recurs, this may reinforce negative conceptions of one's self as the kind of person to whom "bad things" happen, and signals the failure of past attempts to deal with the problem. Consequently, when the problem recurs, the individual may feel poorly, not just about the problem per se, but also about their previous futile efforts to correct it (i.e., further evidence of unworthiness or incompetence).

PERSONALITY IN THE CONTEXT
OF AFFECTIVE–COGNITIVE NETWORKS

We may better understand why neuroticism is associated with heightened perception, reactivity, exposure to negative events, and use of passive coping strategies by integrating contemporary affect–cognition network approaches and related experiments on mood effects on cognition (Forgas, 1995; Forgas & Bower, 1988; Rusting, 1999) with personality theory. One mechanism is the already-mentioned diathesis, probably constitutional, proposed by Eysenck (1967), Gray (1981), Strelau (1987), and Tellegen (1985), involving a heightened sensitivity to negative events. This tendency need not be hard-wired, however, because socialization experiences and an absence of unconditional positive regard in the early years of development may create a foundation for enduring negative expectations and a negative self-concept (Brown, 1993).

However, this heightened sensitivity seems unlikely to provide a full explanation for the cascade of negative processes observed in neurotics. A more compelling explanation emerges when one appreciates that this sensitivity operates in the general context of affect–cognitive networks (Bower, 1981; Forgas, 1994). According to network theories, memory is composed of networks of associated concepts that include cognitive and emotion nodes. A specific emotion is represented by a particular emotion node within a cognitive network consisting of emotion-related memories and cognitions. When a specific node is activated, this activation is channeled through the network of connections to evoke emotion-related memories and congnitions (Bower, 1981). The ability of affect to prime cognitions (see Bower & Forgas, chap. 5, and Rusting, chap. 17, this volume) has important implications because, as a result, mood states influence the processing of complex and ambiguous social judgments. This occurs through three routes: "priming mood-consistent constructs that influence the interpretation of ambiguous details; (b) facilitating the selective recall of mood-consistent information; and (c) focusing selective attention and learning on mood-consistent details of a complex stimulus" (Forgas, Bower, & Moylan, 1990, p. 810). These priming effects are especially strong regarding thoughts about the self. Most research of this kind has examined the effects of short-term inductions of mood, but mood-contingent processing biases also should apply to chronic affective states, such as experienced by neurotic individuals.

The import of selective affect-cognition priming for the neurotic's experience is that preexisting negative affect should prime the interpretation, recall, and attention to negative aspects of life problems, circumstances, and self-attributes. This means that stressors may be appraised as more threatening and one's personal resources may be judged as inadequate to overcome the problem. As a consequence, individuals who tend toward negative affectivity would rely on passive strategies, such as ruminating about life difficulties or "wishing" them away instead of actively dealing with them. In those rare instances, when a problem-focused strategy is attempted, affect priming may create negative expectations and interpretations even if progress toward a solution is being made. The result is that the individual may relinquish positive efforts and fall back on passive strategies. Thus, a vicious self-perpetuating cycle is set in motion. The combination of an oversensitivity posited by the personalogic tradition with contemporary theorizing about the role of affect on social cognition provide a plausible "hybrid" explanation for the four phenomena documented in individuals high in neuroticism—the affective inertia, reactivity, increased exposure, and exaggerated impact of repeated problems.

PERSON × ENVIRONMENT FIT: THE CASE OF AGREEABLENESS

The emphasis to this point has been on the role of neuroticism in the stress experience. This seems appropriate if we are interested in identifying a generalized susceptibility to all manner of stressors. Standing on other dimensions in the Big Five, however, may be important for understanding reactions to particular kinds of stressors. This is suggested by theories of person × environmental (P-E) fit, otherwise known as *interactional models of behavior*. Lewin (1935) suggested that people react best to situations in which their attributes provide a match to the environment (the situation and other people), and react worse when there is a mismatch. In a contemporary version of P-E fit, such as Diener, Larsen, and Emmon's (1984) situational congruence model, people are thought to experience unpleasant affect when they engage in behaviors or encounter situations discordant with their traits (see also Snyder & Gangestad, 1982). This view typically has been examined only with regard to very specific, lower-level traits such as locus of control orientation (i.e., people who perceive that they have control over their circumstances vs. those who do not). However, one basic dimension of the Big Five, agreeableness, may be an important moderator of emotional reactivity to a specific class of life stressor, interpersonal conflict.

Persons who score high in agreeableness tend to be trusting, sympathetic, and cooperative with others. Their disagreeable counterparts, in contrast, tend to be rude, uncooperative, and manipulative (Costa & McCrae, 1985). Based on these profiles, one might hypothesize that problems involving interpersonal conflict will elicit differential reactivity in persons differing in agreeableness, whereas other types of problems would not. For example, conflict should create more of a mismatch, and, therefore, more distress, for agreeable persons than would problems involving threats to control because interpersonal conflict represents a mismatch with a trusting, cooperative, and sympathetic interpersonal orientation.

This hypothesis has been tested in two naturalistic studies. In an experience sampling study, Moskowitz and Coté (1995) found that people high in agreeableness reported more unpleasant affect when they engaged in behaviors that were sarcastic or quarrelsome than did less-agreeable individuals. A daily diary study found that persons scoring higher in agreeableness experienced more distress when they encountered more frequent interpersonal conflicts during the day than did their less-agreeable counterparts (Suls, Martin, & David, 1998). Interestingly, agreeableness was unrelated to reactivity to frequent nonconflict problems (see Suls et al., 1998, pp. 94–95). Hence, as predicted, emotional hyperreactivity was associated only with problems relevant to the individual's orientation about being cooperative, trusting, and sympathetic. When the role of neuroticism was assessed, however, both conflict and nonconflict problems elicited greater reactivity in the more neurotic individuals. This evidence provides additional evidence that neurotics exhibit an exaggerated sensitivity to any kind of life difficulty, but agreeable–disagreeable persons are reactive differentially only to stressors involving interpersonal conflict.

In further contrast to neuroticism, agreeable persons reported fewer interpersonal conflicts than their disagreeable counterparts and no difference in the frequency of nonconflict problems (see also Graziano, Jensen-Campbell, & Hair, 1996). Neurotics reported both more nonconflict and conflict problems than their nonneurotic counterparts (Suls et al., 1998). It might be inferred then, that exposure does not contribute to the agreeable person's responses to conflict. However, ironically, the occurrence of fewer conflicts for agreeable persons probably makes the conflicts that do occur more salient. In Gestalt terms, conflict probably becomes figural against a nonconflictual background, and, as earlier results indicate, as conflicts add up over the day, agreeable people experience increasingly more distress.

One additional note about agreeableness and reactivity may be appropriate. The results described previously may seem discrepant with other reports that hostile or disagreeable persons are more physiologically reactive to hostile provocation (Smith, 1992; Suarez & Williams, 1989; Suls & Wan, 1993). It is important, however, to distinguish between subjective experience and physiological arousal, because they are not isomorphic (e.g., Rachman, 1980; Schwebel & Suls, 1999). In addition, the agreeableness dimension in the FFM is not the same as the hostility measured in experiments demonstrating differential physiological reactivity to hostile provocation. In particular, the later experiments use personality measures that represent a mixture of different attributes and are not pure measures of agreeableness (see Martin, 1996).

The studies of affective responses to conflict as a function of agreeableness support conceptions of person–environment fit. It remains for future research to determine whether concordance applies to other categories of problems with respect to the remaining three dimensions of the Big Five.

CONCLUSIONS

The main focus of this chapter has been to understand how negative affectivity in social life is produced by a confluence of personality characteristics, cognitive processes, and stressful experiences. I have reviewed evidence indicating that standing on neuroticism, one of the basic personality dimensions of the FFM, is related to suceptibility to heightened reactivity to the occurrence of major and minor life stressors. This hyperreactivity, combined with increased exposure to life stressors, negative affective inertia, and sensitivity to recurrent problems, represents a cascade of processes that contribute to pervasive negative feelings reported by individuals high in neuroticism. A comprehensive model suggests that the negative cascade may be the outcome of a heightened hypersensitivity to stress (either constitutional in nature or acquired through early socialization) operating in the context of normal selective affect–cognition priming.

The neurotic cascade tends to be nonspecific, and appears to apply to all manner of problems; in fact, as described earlier, neurotics may see situations as problematic that other people do not. In contrast, other dimensions of the FFM may be related to emotional hyperreactivity, but only for specific kinds of problems. For example, agreeableness seems to be associated with a distinctive sensitivity to interpersonal conflicts. The exaggerated sensitivity, in this case, is associated with discordances between the individual's dominant orientation and situational factors, but seems unlikely to be the result of constitutional hypersensitivity. Although more research is needed, a sufficient body of theory and evidence on the relationship between affect and cognition has accumulated to identify those individuals most likely to respond with exaggerated affect to life changes. In light of empirical evidence linking personality, stress, affect, and physical disease (Friedman et al., 1995), an integration of personality and social cognition theories may provide an explanation for the mediating processes underlying these links. In any case, sufficient scientific progress has been made to provide a tentative explanation for why, as songwriter Paul Simon said, "Some folks' lives roll right easy. Some folks' lives never roll at all."

The emphasis here has been on negative affectivity, but future researchers may wish to consider the possibility that there are parallel processes operating for persons high in extraversion or positivite affectivity. Perhaps, for example, extraverts exhibit a affective inertia for positive mood states and an exaggerated positive reactivity to pleasurable or positive events. Hence, the phenomenon found for neuroticism may have broader implications for affective–cognitive processes in social life.

ACKNOWLEDGMENTS

The author's research reported in this chapter was supported by NIH grant HL46448. During the writing of this chapter, the author received support from the National Science Foundation. The author also extends his thanks to Joseph Forgas for his suggestions concerning an earlier version of this chapter.

REFERENCES

Allport, G., & Odbert, H. S. (1936). Trait-names: A psycholexical study. *Psychological Monographs, 53*, 337–348.

Blascovich, J., & Tomaka, J. (1996). The biopsychosocial model of arousal regulation. In M. P. Zanna (Ed.), *Advances in experimental social psychology* (pp.1–51). New York: Academic Press.

Bolger, N. (1990). Coping as a personality process: A prospective study. *Journal of Personality and Social Psychology, 59*, 525–537.

Bolger, N., DeLongis, A., Kessler, R. C., & Schilling, E. A. (1989). Effects of daily stress on negative mood. *Journal of Personality and Social Psychology, 57*, 808–818.

Bolger, N., & Schilling, E. A. (1991). Personality and problems of everyday life: The role of neuroticism in response and exposure to stress. *Journal of Personality, 59*, 355–386.

Bolger, N., & Zuckerman, A. (1995). A framework for studying personality in the stress process. *Journal of Personality and Social Psychology, 69*, 890–902.

Bower, G. H. (1981). Mood and memory. *American Psychologist, 36*, 129–148.

Bradley, B. P., & Moog, K. (1994). Mood and personality in recall of positive and negative information. *Behaviour Research and Therapy, 32*, 137–141.

Brown, J. D. (1993). Self-esteem and self-evaluation: Feeling is believing. In J. Suls (Ed.), *Psychological perspectives on the self* (Vol. 4, pp. 27–58). Hillsdale, NJ: Lawrence Erlbaum Associates.

Cattell, R. B. (1945). The principal trait clusters for describing personality. *Psychological Bulletin, 42*, 129–161.

Ciarrochi, J. V., & Forgas, J. P. (in press). The pleasure of possessions: Mood effects on consumer judgments. *Europeon Journal of Social Psychology*.

Costa, P. T., Jr., & McCrae, R. R. (1985). *The NEO Personality Inventory: Manual Form S and Form R*. Odessa, FL: Psychological Assessment Resources, Inc.

David, J. P., Green, P. J., Martin, R., & Suls, J. (1997). Differential roles of neuroticism, extraversion, and event desirability for mood in daily life: An integrative model of top-down and bottom-up influences. *Journal of Personality and Social Psychology, 73*, 149–159.

David, J. P., & Suls, J. (1999). Coping efforts in daily life: Role of Big-Five traits and problem appraisals. *Journal of Personality, 67*, 265–294.

DeLongis, A., Coyne, J., Dakof, G., Folkman, S., & Lazarus, R. (1982). Relationship to daily hassles, uplifts, and major life events to health status. *Health Psychology, 1*, 119–136.

Dembroski, T. M., & Costa, P. T., Jr. (1987). Coronary-prone behavior: Components of the Type A pattern and hostility. *Journal of Personality, 55*, 211–235.

Diener, E., Larsen, R. J., & Emmons, R. A. (1984). Person × situation interactions: Choice of situations and congruence among response models. *Journal of Personality and Social Psychology, 47*, 580–592.

Diener, E., Smith, H., & Fujita, F. (1995). The personality structure of affect. *Journal of Personality and Social Psychology, 47*, 1105–1117.

Digman, J. M. (1990). Personality structure: The emergence of the five-factor model. *Annual Review of Psychology, 41*, 1168–1176.

Epstein, S. (1990). Cognitive-experiential self theory. In L. Pervin (Ed.), *Handbook of personality: Theory and research* (pp. 165–195). New York: Guilford Press.

Eriksen, C. W. (1954). Psychological defenses and "ego strength" in the recall of completed and uncompleted tasks. *Journal of Abnormal and Social Psychology, 49*, 45–50.

Eysenck, H. J. (1967). *The biological theory of personality*. Springfield, IL: Charles C. Thomas.

Eysenck, H. J., & Eysenck, S. B. G. (1975). *Manual of the Eysenck Personality Inventory*. San Diego: Educational and Industrial Testing Service.

Feist, G., Bodner, T., Jacobs, J., Miles, M., & Tan, U. (1995). Integrating top-down and bottom-up structural models of subjective well-being. *Journal of Personality and Social Psychology, 68*, 138–151.

Forgas, J. P. (1995). Mood and judgment: The affect infusion model. *Psychological Bulletin, 117*, 39–66.

Forgas, J. P., & Bower, G. H. (1988). Affect in social and personal judgments. In K. Fiedler & J. P. Forgas (Eds.), *Affect, cognition, and social behavior* (pp. 183–208). Gottingen: Hogrefe.

Forgas, J. P., Bower, G. H., & Moylan, S. J. (1990). Praise or blame? Affective influences on attributions for achievement. *Journal of Personality and Social Psychology, 59*, 809–819.

Friedman, H., Tucker, J., Schwartz, J., Tomlinson-Keasey, Martin, L., Wingard, D., & Criqui, M. (1995). Psychosocial and behavioral predictors of longevity: The aging and death of the "termites." *American Psychologist, 50*, 69–78.

Gallagher, D. J. (1990). Extraversion, neuroticism and appraisal of stressful academic events. *Personality and Individual Differences, 11*, 1053–1057.

Goldberg, L. R. (1981). Language and individual differences: The search for universals in personality lexicons. In L. Wheeler (Ed.), *Review of personality and social psychology* (Vol. 2, pp. 141–165). Beverly Hills, CA: Sage.

Goldberg, L. R. (1992). The development of markers for the Big-Five factor structure. *Psychological Assessment, 4*, 26–42.

Goodstein, L. D. (1954). Interrelationships among several measures of anxiety and hostility. *Journal of Consulting Psychology, 18*, 35–39.

Gray, J. A. (1981). A critique of Eysenck's theory of personality. In H. J. Eysenck (Ed.), *A model for personality* (pp. 246–276). New York: Springer.

Graziano, W. G., Jensen-Campbell, L. A., & Hair, E. C. (1996). Perceiving interpersonal conflict and reacting to it: The case for agreeableness. *Journal of Personality and Social Psychology, 70,* 820–835.

Gross, J. J., Sutton, S., & Ketelaar, T. (1998). Relations between affect and personality: Support for the affect-level and affective–reactivity views. *Personality and Social Psychology Bulletin, 24,* 279–288.

Headley, B., & Wearing, A. (1989). Personality, life events, and subjective well-being: Toward a dynamic equilibrium model. *Journal of Personality and Social Psychology, 57,* 731–739.

Hemenover, S. H., & Dienstbier, R. A. (1996). Prediction of stress appraisals from mastery, extraversion, neuroticism, and general appraisal tendencies. *Motivation and Emotion, 20,* 299–317.

Holmes, T. H., & Rahe, R. (1967). The social adjustment rating scale. *Journal of Psychosomatic Research, 11,* 213–218.

John, O. P. (1990). The "Big Five" factor taxonomy: Dimensions of personality in the natural language and in questionnaires. In L. Pervin (Ed.), *Handbook of personality: Theory and research* (pp. 66–100). New York: Guilford Press.

Lazarus, R. S., & Folkman, S. (1984). *Stress, appraisal, and coping.* New York: Springer.

Lewin, K. (1935). *A dynamic theory of personality.* New York: McGraw-Hill.

McCrae, R. R., & Costa, P. T. (1986). Personality, coping, and coping effectiveness. *Journal of Personalty, 49,* 710–721.

Magnus, K., Diener, E., Fujita, F., & Pavot, W. (1993). Extraversion and neuroticism as predictors of objective life events: A longitudinal analysis. *Journal of Personality and Social Psychology, 65,* 1046–1053.

Marco, C., & Suls, J. (1993). Daily stress and the trajectory of mood: Spillover, response assimilation, contrast, and chronic negative affectivity. *Journal of Personality and Social Psychology, 64,* 1053–1063.

Martin, R. (1996). *The structure of trait anger.* Unpublished doctoral dissertation. University of Iowa, Iowa City, Iowa.

Moskowitz, D. S., & Coté, S. (1995). Do interpersonal traits predict affect? A comparison of three models. *Journal of Personality and Social Psychology, 69,* 915–924.

Norman, W. T. (1963). Toward an adequate taxonomy of personality attributes: Replicated factor structure in peer nomination personality ratings. *Journal of Abnormal and Social Psychology, 66,* 574–583.

Ormel, J., & Wohlfarth, T. (1991). How neuroticism, long-term difficulties, and life situation change influence psychological distress: A longitudinal model. *Journal of Personality and Social Psychology, 60,* 744–755.

Parkes, K. (1994). Personal and coping as moderators of work stress processes: Models, methods, and measures. *Work and Stress, 8,* 110–129.

Pietromonaco, P. R., & Feldman-Barrett, L. (1997). Working models of attachment and daily social interactions. *Journal of Personality and Social Psychology, 73,* 1909–1923.

Rachman, S. (1980). Emotional processing. *Behavioral Research and Therapy, 18,* 51–61.

Russell, J. A., & Carroll, J. M. (1999). On the bipolarity of positive and negative affect. *Psychological Bulletin, 125,* 3–30.

Rusting, C. L. (1998). Personality, mood, and cognitive processing of emotional information: Three conceptual frameworks. *Psychological Bulletin, 124,* 165–196.

Rusting, C. L., & Larsen, R. J. (1998). Personality and cognitive processing of affective information. *Personality and Social Psychology Bulletin, 24,* 200–213.

Scheier, M., & Carver, C. (1987). Optimism, coping and health: Assessment and implications of generalized outcome expectancies. *Health Psychology, 4,* 219–247.

Schwebel, D. C., & Suls, J. (1999). Cardiovascular reactivity and neuroticism: Results from a laboratory and controlled ambulatory stress protocol. *Journal of Personality, 67,* 67–92.

Smith, T. W. (1992). Hostility and health: Current status of a psychosomatic hypothesis. *Health Psychology, 11*, 139–150.

Snyder, M., & Gangestad, S. (1982). Choosing social situations: Two investigations of self-monitoring processes. *Journal of Personality and Social Psychology, 43*, 123–135.

Strelau, J. (1987). Emotion as a key concept in temperament research. *Journal of Research in Personality, 21*, 510–528.

Suarez, E. C., & Williams, R. B., Jr. (1989). Situational determinants of cardiovascular and emotional reactivity in high and low hostile men. *Psychosomatic Medicine, 51*, 404–418.

Suls, J., & David, J. P. (1996). Coping and personality: Third time's the charm? *Journal of Personality, 64*, 993–1005.

Suls, J., Green, P. J., & Hillis, S. (1998). Emotional reactivity to everyday problems, affective inertia, and neuroticism. *Personality and Social Psychology Bulletin, 24*, 127–136.

Suls, J., Martin, R., & David, J. P. (1998). Person–environment fit and its limits: Agreeableness, neuroticism, and emotional reactivity to interpersonal conflict. *Personality and Social Psychology Bulletin, 24*, 88–98.

Suls, J., & Mullen, B. (1981). Life change and psychological distress: The role of perceived control and desirability. *Journal of Applied Social Psychology, 11*, 379–389.

Suls, J., & Rittenhouse, J. D. (1990). Models of linkages between personality and physical disease. In H. Friedman (Ed.), *Personality and disease* (pp. 38–64). New York: John Wiley.

Suls, J., & Wan, C. K. (1993). The relationship between trait hostility and cardiovascular reactivity: A quantitative review and analysis. *Psychophysiology, 30*, 615–626.

Swann, W. B., Jr., Griffin, J. J., Predmore, S., & Gaines, B. (1987). The cognitive–affective crossfire: When self-consistency confronts self-enhancement. *Journal of Personality and Social Psychology, 52*, 881–889.

Tellegen, A. (1985). Structures of mood and personality and their relevance to assessing anxiety, with an emphasis on self-report. In A. H. Tuma & J. D. Maser (Eds.), *Anxiety and the anxiety disorders* (pp. 681–706). Hillsdale, NJ: Lawrence Erlbaum Associates.

Tellegen, A., Lykken, D., Bouchard, T., Jr., Wilcox, K. J., & Rich, S. (1988). Personality similarity in twins raised apart and together. *Journal of Personality and Social Psychology, 54*, 1031–1039.

Watson, D., & Clark, L. A. (1984). Negative affectivity: The disposition to experience aversive emotional states. *Psychological Bulletin, 96*, 645–690.

Watson, D., & Clark, L. A. (1992). On traits and temperament: General and specific factors of emotional experience and their relation to the five-factor model. *Journal of Personality, 60*, 489–505.

Watson, D., & Clark, L. A. (1997). The measurement and mismeasurement of mood: Recurrent and emergent issues. *Journal of Personality Assessment, 86*, 267–296.

Watson, D., David, J. P., & Suls, J. (1999). Personality, affectivity, and coping. In C. R. Snyder (Ed.), *Coping: The psychology of what works* (pp. 119–140). New York: Oxford University Press.

Watson, D., & Hubbard, B. (1996). Adaptational style and dispositional structure: Coping in the context of the five-factor model. *Journal of Personality, 64*, 737–774.

Watson, D., & Tellegen, A. (1985). Toward a consensual structure of mood. *Psychological Bulletin, 98*, 219–235.

Young, G. C. D., & Martin, M. (1981). Processing information about self by neurotics. *British Journal of Clinical Psychology, 20*, 205–212.

Williams, K. J., Suls, J., Alliger, G. M., Learner, S. M., & Wan, C. K. (1991). Multiple role juggling and daily mood states in working mothers: An experience sampling study. *Journal of Applied Psychology, 76*, 664–674.

19

Emotion, Intelligence, and Emotional Intelligence

John D. Mayer
University of New Hampshire

Putting Emotion and Cognition in Their Place   413
  The Trilogy of Mind   413
  Other Parts of Personality   415
  Emotional Traits   415
  Cognitive Traits   416
  Emotion and Cognition: What Is Intelligence and What Is Not? 417
The Theory of Emotional Intelligence   418
  Emotion as Information   418
  Emotional Perception   419
  Emotional Integration   420
  Understanding Emotion   421
  Management of Emotion   422
Emotional Intelligence as a Standard Intelligence   423
  Measuring Emotional Intelligence as an Ability   423
  A Description of the MEIS   424
  Scoring the MEIS   425
  Findings with the MEIS   425

Address for correspondence: John D. Mayer, Department of Psychology, 10 Library Way, University of New Hampshire, Durham NH 03824, USA. Email: jack.mayer@unh.edu

Discussion and Conclusion 426
References 428

The study of emotional intelligence emerged, in part, from the research area of cognition and affect—an area that was concerned with how emotion changed thought, and vice versa.

The research area of cognition and affect gained in visibility during the years 1978 to 1982 as a consequence of several key publications. First, Isen, Shalker, Clark, and Karp (1978), writing in the *Journal of Personality and Social Psychology*, considered the possibility that there existed a "cognitive loop" connecting mood to judgement. Their "loops" described the possibility that, for example, as a person grew happy, he or she might cognitively judge past social behaviors as more helpful and kinder than otherwise, thereby further improving his or her mood. A downward loop was possible as well, with bad moods leading to negative thoughts and to worse feelings.

Each year, the American Psychological Association awards a Distinguished Scientific Contribution Award to several scientists, each of whom delivers an address that is reprinted in the *American Psychologist*. In one 1980 address, Robert Zajonc (1980) argued that feelings were more important than cognition in determining attitudes. He quoted from ee cummings that

> since feeling is first
> who pays any attention
> to the syntax of things
> will never wholly kiss you
>
> —ee cummings, cited in Zajonc, 1980, p. 151

Gordon Bower, an award winner the following year, examined mood's profound influences on memory. He described a spreading activation model of memory in which happy moods activated happy thoughts and sad moods activated sad thoughts, which helped explain many empirical phenomena in the area (Bower, 1981). The next year saw publication of Clark and Fiske's (1982) edited volume, *Affect and Cognition*, which brought together much work in the area.

The study of emotion and thought by cognitive psychologists (and allied social and personality psychologists) marked a departure from much research on emotion–cognition interactions. Sigmund Freud's concept of defense mechanisms emphasized interactions between emotion and thought, but with a distinct emphasis on the pathological (e.g., S. Freud, 1940/1949; A. Freud, 1937/1966). Thereafter, Aaron T. Beck (1967) suggested that depression was caused by negative cognitions that exaggerated failure and incompetence (e.g., Beck, Rush, Shaw, & Emery, 1979).

When the cognition and affect literature emerged, it inherited the view that emotions biased and disrupted thought. Some early research in the area freely induced "depressed" and "elated" mood states and examined the thought processes of mood-disordered patients. The emphasis of mostly cognitively trained psychologists, however, was on extending such findings to normal people undergoing emotional episodes. Thus, mood inductions in the area emphasized "happy" and "sad" moods rather than pathological states (e.g., Bower, 1981; Fiske & Taylor, 1991; Forgas, 1995; Salovey & Birnbaum, 1989). Ultimately, mood influences were examined in everyday people going through everyday moods and mood changes (e.g., Espe & Schulz, 1983; Forgas & Moylan, 1987; Mayer & Bremer, 1985; Mayer, Gaschke, Braverman, & Evans, 1992; Mayer & Hanson, 1995; Mayer, McCormick, & Strong, 1995). As research on emotions and thought moved from an emphasis on psychopathology to everyday moods and thoughts, the idea that emotions might be adaptive for thought coexisted with the idea that they caused bias. Ketelaar and Clore (1997, p. 357) observed: "Although most psychologists view demonstrations of emotional influence as evidence of bias and distortion, some others are beginning to focus on functional rather than dysfunctional relationships between emotion and cognition . . . "

One outcome of this development was the concept of emotional intelligence—the idea that emotions and intelligence can combine to perform more sophisticated information processing than either is capable of alone (Mayer, DiPaolo, & Salovey, 1990; Salovey & Mayer, 1990). The purpose of this chapter is to introduce workers in cognition and affect to the area of emotional intelligence. To do this, the nature of emotion and cognition are briefly described in the second section of this chapter. Emotional intelligence is then defined and described in the third section. Research in the area, and the implications of emotional intelligence for cognition and affect are examined in the fifth, "Conclusion" section.

There are really "two" emotional intelligences in the literature nowadays. One is the popular emotional intelligence, which is defined in various different ways, is said to be readily acquired, to outpredict intelligence, and to be the best predictor of success in life. The other emotional intelligence is the scientific concept to be examined here. Elsewhere, my colleagues and I have made a concerted effort to take the popularized versions of our emotional intelligence theory seriously, to see if they make sense. The interested reader is invited to refer to our own and others' various comparisons of the approaches (e.g., Epstein, 1998; Mayer, Salovey, & Caruso, 1999; Mayer & Cobb, 2000). Here, I examine the more research-based concept of emotional intelligence, for that is the one my colleagues and I conclude has the most potential to contribute to scientific psychology.

PUTTING EMOTION AND COGNITION IN THEIR PLACE

The Trilogy of Mind

Emotion and *cognition* are often said to constitute two parts of a trilogy of mind (Hilgard, 1980; Mayer, Chabot, & Carlsmith, 1997). The full trilogy also includes *conation*, which is usually interpreted as denoting motivation.[1] The conation–affect–cognition trilogy (Table 19.1) dates from the 18th century and has gradually been updated with the times.[2] Hilgard (1980) argued that the full trilogy provides a relatively complete view of the mind, and that when our psychological science treats all three, it is balanced; our models become unbalanced through neglect of one or another area.

The three parts of the trilogy are arranged from the smaller, more biologically driven system of motivation, to the larger, broader one of cognition. Broadly speaking, the motivational system is the portion of the trilogy responsible for inward, bodily monitoring that signals important biologic needs and urges to the rest of the mind. For example, motives translate bodily needs into psychological urges: the body's need for food into hunger; the need for water into thirst, and the need for self-defense into urges for safety or attack.

Emotions, too, are internal in the sense that feelings can be private, and that emotions arise in response to internal models of relationships with other people and situations. It is worth stressing this internal quality of

---

[1] A more historical intepretation is that conation refers to "will" or "conscious will." Sometimes the trilogy is expanded to a quaternity by adding "consciousness."

[2] Although the trilogy dates at least from the 18th century, the trilogy of mind has gradually changed to keep up with the theoretical times, as it were. Over the years, the trilogy has been viewed increasingly as (a) psychologically internal and closely associated with a brain area or areas; (b) defined so as to include an arguably unitary group of functions; (c) close to automatic, biologic, and unlearned processes; and, finally, the entire trilogy is (d) recognized as spanning important parts of the mind rather than being a comprehensive description of the entire mind.

TABLE 19.1
An Overview of Conation, Affect, and Cognition

Characteristic	*Conations*	*Affects*	*Cognitions*
RELATIVELY SIMPLER, PURE EXAMPLES:	Hunger pangs, urge for physical contact	Basic happiness, anger, sadness, fear	Sensorimotor operations, learning, associations
RESPONDS TO:	Internal body states	Changed relationships	Either internal or external states
OVER TIME:	Precedes action, rises and falls rhythmically or cyclically	Respond to events and follow specific timelines	Occurs any time
INFORMS US ABOUT:	What is lacking and what must be done	A class of events that must be addressed	Specific or general, depending on problem REQUIREMENTS, ETC.
ASSOCIATED MAJOR BRAIN AREAS ARE:	The brain stem and limbic system	The limbic system	The association and cerebral cortex

Adapted from Mayer, J. D., Chabot, H. F., & Carlsmith, K. M. (1997). Conation, affect, and cognition in personality. In G. Matthews (Ed.), *Cognitive science perspectives on personality and emotion* (pp. 31–63). New York: Elsevier.

emotions. One responds directly to relationships one believes one has, and only indirectly to the actual relationships. Most of the time we do not pay too much attention to this distinction because the internal models match the external world fairly closely. Sometimes, however, we learn from friends and relatives—who are often anxious to correct us—that what we believed was going on in our relationship with them in fact was not. In such cases, we discover that our own internal model of the relationship was wrong, and what actually had gone on was something we had not dreamt of!

Each emotion signals a different relation. Some emotions signal relations jointly with motivations, so as to amplify them. For example, anger signals injustice and often accompanies the motive to aggress and amplifies it. An altruistic motive is amplified by happiness, which signals harmonious-ness (Salovey, Mayer, & Rosenhan, 1991). Fear signals the presence of threat and cooccurs with the need for avoiding harm. Sadness signals loss and a need for reflection and isolation. Although some emotions cooccur with motives, others are more independent of the motivational system. For example, acceptance, regret, and contempt are less readily equated with specific motives.

The third, cognitive, system is the most independent of the person, and the most integrated with and beholden to outside influences. On the one hand, cognition serves motivation and emotion, solving problems so that motivational needs may be met and emotions maintained at an acceptable level of positivity over time. On the other hand, cognition is outward looking, actively learning about the external world, problem solving, and imagining new environments that can be created through actions.

Other Parts of Personality

The three parts serve as features or aspects of the mind, but they do not define the full activities of human personality. Rather, they play supportive or embedded roles in learning and acting (Mayer, 1995, 1998). Each individual must create models or maps of him- or herself, of the world, and of him- or herself in the world. These learned models interact with the trilogy of mind. Consider models of the world of dinosaurs. As a child learns about the *Giganotosaurus*—the largest dinosaur discovered thus far—that learning includes attaching motivations to it, such as imagining fleeing from it, or wanting to be strong and dangerous. It also involves attaching feelings to it, such as fear and awe, as well as simple information such as that *Giganotosaurus* lived 90 million years ago and that the name means "giant reptile of the south."

Personality traits emerge from the motives, feelings, and thoughts that permeate the learned models of the self and world. As learning takes place, motives, feelings, and thoughts are embedded in concepts. For example, a need for excitement may become attached to mental models of adventure novels as well as to judgments of that material (e.g., judging it according to how fast-paced it is). The same need for excitement might generate interest in the *Star Wars* music of John Williams, in preference to calmer pieces. As these motives and emotions become distributed over many learned concepts, they may reach a critical mass and work together thematically. Traits can be thought of as such thematically related features of personality (Mayer, 1995, 1998).

Emotional Traits

There exist many traits related to emotionality: aggressiveness, empathy, emotionality, emotional intensity, and so forth. One useful conceptual breakdown of the two most central emotional traits refers to: (a) an average mood level, which denotes the degree to which a person is typically feeling pleasant (e.g., happy) or unpleasant (e.g., sad, angry, afraid); and (b) a degree of mood variability, which denotes whether a person's mood is fairly consistent, unchanging, and nonreactive, versus whether a person's mood is variable, changeable, and highly reactive. Individual differences in the first emotional trait, mood level, begin at the low point of the deeply depressed; move up to the person we might describe as a melancholic pessimist; to the happy-go-lucky optimist; and then, to the pathological extremes of a manic personality. Individual differences in mood variability are equally big, ranging from the individual who manifests virtually no mood at all (sometimes referred to as *alexithymic*; e.g., Taylor, 1984); to the merely stable and calm; to the person with reactive, intense mood swings and ready emotional responsiveness (e.g., Larsen & Diener, 1987) to the clinical extremes of the cyclothymic personality disorder; and finally to the Bipolar I and II affective disorders (formerly known as *manic depression*). This continuum has been mapped by Goodwin and Jamison (1990; cf. Carson, Butcher, & Mineka, 1996, p. 213).

Mood level and mood variability are somewhat related. People with stable nonreactive moods also tend to express more pleasant mood levels, and in contrast, people with mood variability tend to experience more negative, unpleasant moods. A dimension describing negative, variable emotionality, on the one hand, and pleasant, stable mood, on the other is Hans Eysenck's dimension of *emotionality–stability*, (which is also called *neuroticism–stability*, a regrettable name given its pathological connotations). *Emotionality/neuroticism–stability* is one of five central traits known as the Big Five that lay people use to describe one another. In the NEO-PI, which measures the Big Five, emotionality-stability is subdivided into smaller factors, three of which refer to mood level (anxiety, angry hostility, and depression), and three of which refer to instability (self-consciousness, impulsiveness, and vulnerability; Costa & McCrae, 1992).

Cognitive Traits

Just as there are differences in emotional dimensions of personality, so too, are there cognitive differences. A major individual difference variable in cognition is general intelligence, of course, although there are plenty of other cognitive traits as well; for example, field dependence–independence, reflectivity–impulsivity, creativity, and the like. General intelligence, in turn, can be divided into fluid and crystallized intelligence, and a number of smaller group intelligences (Carroll, 1993). Three national conferences on intelligence in the 20th century have identified the *sine qua non* of intelligence as the capacity to carry out abstract reasoning, and these same conferences also identify adaptation as of some importance (Neisser et al., 1996). A review of 20th century intelligence theories suggests that most specify some form of information that is input to a central processing area, the creation of expert information to reference (e.g., crystallized intelligence), and the output of accurate information (Mayer & Mitchell, 1998).

Emotion and Cognition: What Is Intelligence and What Is Not?

Many effects within the cognition and affect literature are independent of intelligence per se. For example, *mood congruence* refers to the idea that happy people have happy thoughts, whereas sad people have depressed thoughts. More specifically, the effect states that: "An affective match between a person's moods and ideas increases the judged merit, broadly defined, of those ideas. For example, mood-congruent concepts will be judged richer in associations, mood-congruent attributes will be judged as more applicable, mood-congruent examples of categories will be judged as more typical, and mood-congruent causes and outcomes will be judged more probable" (Mayer et al., 1992, p. 129).

Mood-congruence effects, including happiness-induced optimism and sadness-induced pessimism are biases—unrelated to intelligence. If mood congruence leads a happy person to think that good weather is on the way and Paris is a good example of a city, and if mood congruence leads a sad person to think that bad weather is on the way and that overcrowded Calcutta is a good example of a city, neither person is more correct on average. Rather, each is using a different, legitimate perspective. The proverbial glass is no more half full than it is half empty.

Some cognition and affect researchers have looked for ways in which emotion might facilitate thought. One idea they investigated was whether certain emotional states in particular might render intelligence more effective than other states. So, researchers suggested variously that moderate happiness might enhance recall relative to other feelings (Ellis & Ashbrook, 1988); enhance creativity (Isen, Daubman, & Nowicki, 1987); or enhance the global processing, such as inductive reasoning (Palfai & Salovey, 1994).

Although happiness appeared good for some types of thoughts, sadness had its own champions as well. Alloy and Abramson (1979) suggested the possible existence of "depressive realism"—that depressives more accurately comprehend the world than happy people. The researchers had studied college students who estimated their degree of control over a green light that went on only sometimes after they pressed a button. Over experimental conditions, pushing the button was varied in terms of its control over the light—from no control to moderate levels of control (Alloy & Abramson, 1988, p. 22; Benassi & Mahler, 1985; Martin, Abramson, & Alloy, 1984). Depressed people's sensitivities to actual control were more realistic much of the time. Furthermore, depression may assist more detailed processing. Palfai and Salovey (1994) argued that although inductive reasoning was better in good moods, deductive reasoning was better in sad moods.

The area of cognition and affect perhaps came closest to the idea of emotional intelligence at its interface with cognitive science and artificial intelligence. There, computer scientists had begun to develop software that could unravel the secrets of understanding emotional episodes (Dyer, 1983). As they understood the informative nature of emotional stories, they wondered whether giving computers emotions would enhance the computers' function in some ways. Some argued that computers and robots should have emotions, because those feelings would help them think through certain problems (Mayer, 1986; Sloman & Croucher, 1981); this theme is currently receiving renewed interest in computing circles (e.g., Picard, 1997).

THE THEORY OF EMOTIONAL INTELLIGENCE

Emotion as Information

To some, emotion and intelligence seem as different as oil and water. In fact, the very term *emotional intelligence* appears to be an oxymoron— expressing a contradiction not much different than those found in such phrases as a "small crowd," "peace force," or a "definite maybe." Thought of this way, emotional intelligence may be "clearly misunderstood!" The assumption that renders emotional intelligence sensible is that emotions themselves convey information that can and ought to be processed—they signal relations.

Since at least the writings of Aristotle (384–322 BCE), philosophers have read meanings into emotions. Spinoza's *Ethics* (Part III) is entitled, "On the Origin and Nature of Emotions" and provides a glossary of emotion meanings. Each emotion defines a person's relationship to his or her own self and to other people. Approval is "love towards one who has done good to another" (cited in Calhoun & Solomon, 1984, p. 81). Moreover, emotional meanings are regular and often universal. In the 19th century, Darwin argued that the language of emotion was anchored by specific facial and postural expressions and signs, across species and among humans around the world. Thus, contented expressions in the dog should be recognizable to other dogs as well as to people, just as contended expressions in people could be interpreted by dogs. This work was extended and verified over a century of research (e.g., Ekman, 1973).

The mantle of deciphering the universal meanings of emotion was taken up by cognition and affect researchers in the mid-1980s. Roseman (1984) outlined an elegant system that defined joy as the positive feeling that follows certainty that reward is present, and contrasted it with relief, defined as the positive feeling that punishment is absent. Ortony, Clore, and Collins (1988) took a similar approach, defining joy as a "well-being" emotion that involves the self's reaction to desirable events. The information these emotions convey is what is processed in emotional intelligence.

In 1990, my colleague, Peter Salovey, and I published two articles on emotional intelligence. One provided the first formal definition of the concept (Salovey & Mayer, 1990), and the other provided a demonstration study that aspects of the concept could be measured as an ability (Mayer, DiPaolo, & Salovey, 1990). A revision of that earlier model divides emotional intelligence into four branches of abilities: (a) the perception and expression of emotion, (b) the integration of emotion in thought, (c) understanding emotions, and (d) managing emotions (Mayer & Salovey, 1997). Each of these four classes of abilities are integral to the overall theory, and are described in turn in the following subsections.

Emotional Perception

The processing of emotional information begins with its accurate perception. An emotional perception system is likely "built-in" through evolution, to promote communication between infant and parent. The mother mirrors the infant's smiles in her smiles, the infant's coo's in her coo's, and the infant's pain in her own furrowed brow. This empathic mirroring takes place between parent and healthy child, and helps the child learn about emotions. The growing person learns to generalize patterns of emotional manifestations so they can be identified in other people, artwork, and ultimately, objects. For example, an individual may learn that a relaxed-shouldered posture accompanies calmness, and that curtains are often thought to hide emotional secrets. Both these ideas may be echoed in a good theater, by the relaxed hanging curtain that calmly covers the stage's secrets—secrets to be revealed only as the performance begins.

Buck's (1984) landmark review of the area of nonverbal communication research examined several measures of interpersonal communication that arguably involved considerable emotional information. He concluded that the measures were not terribly reliable and, despite superficial similarities, measured different things. In 1990, our (Mayer, DiPaolo, & Salovey, 1990) first empirical paper on emotional intelligence examined measurement of emotional perception across a variety of stimuli. We suggested that small modifications in tasks, such as those reviewed by Buck, would make them far more reliable, which turned out to be the case. We also studied emotional perception not only in faces but, drawing on the aesthetics literature, added color and abstract designs among our stimuli. Individual differences in emotional perception formed a single factor that was correlated with empathy. In its own way, the emotional perception subfactor of emotional intelligence has been the easiest to measure. Subsequent studies indicate that the same factor accounts for perceiving voice timbre, music, designs, landscapes, faces, and many other stimuli (Davies, Stankov, & Roberts, 1998, Study 1). This contrasts with the second factor of emotional intelligence, which is much more complex.

Emotional Integration

After emotion is perceived, emotion may facilitate the cognitive system at basic levels of processing. The "emotional integration" branch focuses on emotion's basic contributions to reasoning. There are several central suggestions as to how emotion may help cognition.

First, emotion may provide interrupts and prioritizations of problems (Easterbrook, 1959; Mandler, 1975; Simon, 1982). Consider a student deep in concentration in the library. His concentration is so powerful that he mentally leaves behind the linoleum floor, the surrounding stacks, and the flourescent lights. Nonetheless, he may sense a slowly mounting anxiety and, on hearing the ring of a distant office telephone, remember that he promised to call his parents at about that time. That interrupting anxiety represents, in some sense, a second processing system that operates independently of the central cognitive system—allowing cognition to commit a large array of resources to a logical problem until and unless the urgently competing response is plainly noticeable.

A second, allied way emotion facilitates cognition is, arguably, by operating as a second memory store about emotion itself. For example, if a visual artist wants to communicate regret in a painting or photograph, he or she may recall an experience of regret and recreate the feeling as an "on-line" experience. The heavy, dark feeling of having made a wrong choice, combined with the light, airy feeling of the many alternatives of life, could be used to construct a highly communicative contrast in light and dark that represents the feeling better than if it were not recreated as a mental experience to be examined in all its detail.

A third way in which emotion may contribute to intelligence is through the act of mood shifting or cycling. Each mood change refreshes or resets the cognitive system, so that over time all its tools are brought to bear on a problem. This may be true especially for people high in emotionality—those who rapidly alternate between moods. The consequent shifts in judgment may enhance functioning by increasing motivational direction. For example, when things are going well, goals appear more positive and desirable, thus keeping up motivation to continue as in the past. When things go poorly, however, goals are reduced in attractiveness. Moreover, in bad moods, detailed processing is enhanced, perhaps so as to encourage new learning and new perspectives (Ketalaar & Clore, 1997, p. 364; Palfai & Salovey, 1994). The cycling between different moods also leads to different perspectives on problems and, as a consequence, appears related to creating a wider and perhaps more creative set of plans (Mayer, 1986; Mayer & Hanson, 1995).

A fourth way mood can assist thought is by representing implicit information about earlier experiences. Many of us have listed the pros and cons of a decision, only to remain unsure of which alternative is better. In such a case, it makes sense to check one's feelings about which alternative one wants to choose. Feelings about alternatives may provide a summary of the emotional memories associated with alternatives, in cases where the individual memories are no longer available. Feelings toward these alternatives may summarize past experiences—real and imagined—in such settings. The feeling intensity reflects an associative networks of memories that convey information (Bower, 1981; Schwarz & Clore, 1988, p. 46); this is done by retrieving relevant cognitive schemas and other knowledge structures about the alternatives without any necessary conscious recall of them (Banaji & Greenwald, 1995). For example, the fact that one prefers summer barbecues over a visit to the dentist may not require the retrieval of individual instances. This principle may apply to choosing between a career in law versus one in education, in which one's feeling may summarize many emotional encounters with courtrooms and arguments on the one hand, and classrooms and lectures on the other.

Understanding Emotion

Understanding emotion is the branch closest to that of a traditional intelligence. We hypothesize that a mental processor exists that specializes in understanding, abstracting, and reasoning about emotional information. This processing involves labeling feelings, understanding the relations they represent, how they blend together, and the transitions they go through over time. For example, a person must label a feeling they feel, such as "joy." Having labeled it, they must also be able to discern that joy generally reflects a harmonious relationship with others. If the joy is coupled with feelings of acceptance, then it might describe love. Knowing this involves expert knowledge. Similarly, understanding emotional transitions and progressions means recognizing, for example, that joy, acceptance, excitement, and surprise may describe the early stages of falling in love, whereas those feelings are likely to give way to some inevitable disappointments and frustrations thereafter, followed by a more stable joy and acceptance later, often coupled with admiration and thankfulness. Emotional understanding involves comprehending many such possible emotional relations, transitions, and progressions.

Management of Emotion

The last branch of the 1997 emotional intelligence model involves the management of emotion for personal growth. The management of emotion begins with being open to emotion. If emotions are informative, then opening oneself to such information will enable one to know more about the surrounding world—particularly the world of relationships—than if one were closed. People open to anger better identify personal injustices; people open to sadness better understand helpless losses that all humanity must face. Such openness also enhances the good: Who can truly appreciate life's blessings without understanding life's injustices and losses?

Management does not end with openness, of course. The open-to-feeling person must use the knowledge gained from the perception, integration, and understanding of emotion (the first three branches) in order to manage emotion optimally. Only by perceiving and understanding emotions can one understand the outcomes of experiencing them or cutting them off. For example, if a loved-one dies, good emotional management involves allowing a grief reaction to the death, and not trying to cover it up all the time at work. Rather, one would manage around it. For example, explaining to coworkers what is going on and making arrangements at work to any degree possible. Similarly, if one were angry, it would be important to determine from what, and if possible, address it. If it were impossible or unreasonable to address the anger, one might choose to mask it from others, but one would not want to disconnect from it, because it serves as a source of information about oneself and about the target of anger. Rather, one would want to keep it, if real, and if lucky, transfom it somehow, through personal activity and understanding.

The exact manner in which emotions are managed with emotional intelligence is left open in the theory. Intelligences permit plasticity, and allow a person to imagine and evaluate new possibilities with their own aims in mind. Although one hopes most may manage their emotions well—for both their personal and the common good—some emotionally intelligent people may manage their feelings in more negative ways: to manipulate, control, and exploit themselves and others.

EMOTIONAL INTELLIGENCE AS A STANDARD INTELLIGENCE

Measuring Emotional Intelligence as an Ability

The development of emotional intelligence involved both the construction of the theoretical model previously discussed and of measurement procedures to accompany them (e.g., Mayer, DiPaolo, & Salovey, 1990; Mayer & Geher, 1996). Intelligence is assessed almost entirely by ability tests. People who take ability tests perform relevant mental tasks in a controlled setting so as to gauge their optimal mental performance. Ability tasks measure something different than a person's self-report or self-conception of intelligence. Although self-report tests are relatively briefer and easier for participants to take than ability tasks, they show very low test-to-test relationships with ability scales (e.g., $R = .15$–$.30$; Paulhus, Lysy, & Yik, 1998). For these reasons, ability tests are viewed as the standard in the field of intelligence.

Emotional intelligence, too, can be measured as an ability. Although self-report scales of the concept exist and measure important outcomes, they perform quite differently than ability measures. For example, they correlate with overall mood and social desirability, and do not relate to other intelligence measures (e.g., Mayer & Stevens, 1994; Salovey, Mayer, Goldman, Turvey, & Palfai, 1995; see Mayer, Salovey, & Caruso, 2000, for a review).

A number of early tests of individual abilities at emotional intelligence exist, both under that label (e.g., Davies, Stankov, & Roberts, 1998; Mayer, DiPaolo, & Salovey, 1990; Mayer & Geher, 1996), and other names such as *emotional creativity* (e.g., Averill & Nunley, 1992), *emotional awareness* (Lane et al., 1996), and others (e.g., Simon, Rosen, & Pomipom, 1996). Most of these early studies examined just one emotional intelligence task at a time—for example, examining the ability to perceive emotion in faces.

The establishment of an intelligence, however, requires examining many different skills to which the intelligence may contribute. That is because, for an intelligence to exist, its skills must be intercorrelated, the intelligence must be related to but distinct from general intelligence, and it must develop with age. Demonstrating these characteristics requires examining many tasks together, as they are performed by people of different ages.

A Description of the MEIS

To understand whether emotional intelligence exists, my colleagues and I have developed the Multifactor Emotional Intelligence Scale MEIS (Mayer, Salovey, & Caruso, 1999), and a successor scale, the Mayer-Salovey-Caruso Emotional Intelligence test MSCEIT (Mayer, Salovey, & Caruso, 1999). Research work to date has focused on the MEIS, with the MSCEIT being so new that information about it is only now beginning to come in. For that reason, I focus here on findings with the MEIS.

The MEIS is composed of 12 tasks believed, on the basis of our revised theory (Mayer & Salovey, 1997), to assess the four broad areas of emotional intelligence just described in the previous section.

The first group of MEIS tasks, Emotional Perception, asks people to identify emotions that are present in a variety of stimuli. For example, there are subscales concerned with identifying emotions in faces, music, abstract designs, and stories. A group of items from this section might ask people to identify how much happiness, anger, fear, and other feelings might be present in a face. Each emotion is followed by a 5-point scale (with 1 anchored by "none" and 5 anchored by "an extreme amount") to which the participant responds.

The second group of tasks, Emotional Integration, of the MEIS asks people to compare emotional sensations with other mental phenomena, as well as to understand how emotions might change thought. For example, the Synesthesia task asks people what color "Anger" is, as well as how "Sweet" it is, and so on.

The third group of tasks, Understanding, asks people a number of questions about their understanding of feelings. For example, the "Blends" task asks people such questions as the following:

Contempt most closely combines which two emotions?
(1) anger and fear
(2) fear and surprise
(3) disgust and anger
(4) surprise and disgust

And the "Progressions" task asks such questions as the following:

> If you feel guiltier and guiltier, and begin to question your self-worth, you feel:
> (1) depression
> (2) fear
> (3) shame
> (4) pity

The fourth group of tasks, Managing Emotions, presents people with a situation and asks them what is the best social response for managing the feelings of the situation. For example, in the "Managing Others" task, items describe a social situation to which the test-taker must respond. In one such item, for example, a coworker says he lied on his job application to get a job, and it has been bothering him. The test-taker is asked to evaluate various alternatives for handling the situation so that the coworker's emotional difficulties are properly managed.

Scoring the MEIS

Scoring of the MEIS tasks can be performed according to different approaches. Our research (Mayer & Geher, 1996; Mayer, Caruso, & Salovey, 1999) indicates that the best way to do this is to use consensus scoring. According to this method, the individual obtains an item score based on the proportion of people in the standardization sample who agree with the answer. For example, on the Progressions question above (e.g., if a person felt guiltier and guiltier and questioned his or her self-worth...), if .37 of the sample said that "depression" (answer "1") was the correct answer, then a person responding that way would receive a .37 for that answer. If they answered "fear" (answer "2") and only .05 of the sample responded that way, they would be credited with .05 for that answer.

Findings with the MEIS

Findings with the MEIS strongly support the existence of an emotional intelligence that can be measured reliably. Factor analyses of the MEIS scale indicate that it can be modeled in two complementary fashions. First, a single general factor can be used to describe the test. From this perspective, the test measures a single General Emotional Intelligence factor, which represents considerable variance of each of the 12 specific tasks. (This general factor is similar to the first factor of a principal axis extraction.) The complementary, more fine-tuned approach, breaks the scale down into three or four intercorrelated factors. The three strongest factors are (a) Emotional Perception, (b) Emotional Understanding, and (c) Emotional Management. These factors correspond very closely to three of the four areas of skill proposed in the central theory of emotional intelligence (Mayer & Salovey 1997). Covariance structural modeling suggests the possibility that a fourth factor reflecting (d) Emotional Integration might also be possible to measure. Details on how to obtain each factor model can be found in our empirical report (Mayer, Caruso, & Salovey, 1999).

Such results indicate that it makes sense to talk about an overall emotional intelligence level as well as to break it down into abilities at emotional perception, understanding, and management. All the individual subscales as well as the overall test are highly reliable. The overall test has an alpha reliability of $r = .96$; those for the subscales range from between $r = .81$ to .96. Overall emotional intelligence, measured as shown previously, correlates $r = .36$ with a measure of Verbal IQ, and about $r = .33$ with a measure of self-reported empathy. Such results suggest that emotional intelligence is sufficiently related to preexisting intelligences to qualify as an intelligence while being sufficiently distinct to be worth measuring on its own. In addition, developmental studies have shown that there is a temporal progression to emotional intelligence, as with general intelligence, wherein adolescents are outperformed by young adults. This appears to qualify emotional intelligence as a standard intelligence.

One study with the MEIS replicated many of the previously described findings. In addition, the MEIS was related to life satisfaction, even after controlling for IQ and personality traits. The MEIS was also related to people's ability to manage their moods (Ciarrochi, Chan, & Caputi, 2000). These findings, and others presently being obtained, suggest that the EI construct is distinctive and useful. Moreover, it may predict important aspects of good behavior that have been difficult to assess before (Mayer, Caruso, Salovey, in press).

DISCUSSION AND CONCLUSION

The field of cognition and affect provided some of the foundation for a new theory of emotional intelligence. As cognition and affect researchers examined how emotion changed thought, they took over the mantle from clinical researchers who had stressed how emotions pathologized thought.

Researchers in cognition and affect began to normalize such phenomena, finding them in everyday behavior. Emotional intelligence focused especially on how emotion and intelligence mutually facilitate one another to create a higher level of thought, information processing of emotion, and, potentially, to improve feelings as well.

During the 1990s, a central model of emotional intelligence was developed that viewed it as an intelligence that processes emotional signals about relationships. Emotional intelligence involved the capacity to reason with emotions, particularly to perceive, integrate, understand, and manage emotions (Mayer & Salovey, 1997; 1993; Salovey & Mayer, 1990). Measures of emotional intelligence were developed concurrently, and these show great promise for assessing and validating the theoretical model (Mayer, DiPaolo, & Salovey, 1990; Mayer, Caruso, & Salovey, 1999).

Exactly what emotional intelligence predicts is presently a matter of considerable research interest. Findings with ability tests are as-of-yet sparse, and include positive correlations with empathy and intelligence scales (at about $r = .35$ levels), as well as with retrospective reports of parental warmth. It also appears related to well-being and the ability to regulate one's mood. The level of ongoing research now taking place suggests that various predictive studies are forthcoming.

In addition, very little is understood about the mental processes underlying emotional reasoning. There are many opportunities for the experimental study of mental processes underlying emotional reasoning. For example, researchers may wonder whether emotional reasoning is improved or impaired by different mood states, and if so, how? They may wish to study whether experimental analogs of mood swings (e.g., happy–sad–happy–sad mood inductions) can indeed improve or broaden a person's plans, or how physiological states correspond to self-reports among those who are high versus low in emotional intelligence. There are already many studies of expert knowledge related to emotion. In fact, much of the area of cognition and affect (and of emotions research) is creating and synthesizing such expert knowledge. In the future, researchers may wish to know more about how expert knowledge of emotion develops and is stored. Still other researchers may wish to turn to emotional intelligence itself—how it relates to other intelligences, and what it might predict in regard to personal and social outcomes.

Although we do not yet know much about what emotional intelligence might predict, its very existence promises a changed perspective on some matters. It promises that, among some people whom we call warm-hearted or romantic, some sophisticated information processing is going on.

At the outset, I noted that one of the contributions of the area of cognition and affect was to view emotions and cognition as interacting in normal rather than pathological ways. There is also the opportunity to apply what is learned to clinical populations. In the case of emotional intelligence, it is apparent that people's emotional afflictions are sometimes a consequence of improper perceptions, integrations, and understandings of emotions. Given such troubles, it is little wonder such people find it difficult to manage their feelings. Perhaps some of the previously described research will be useful to better help people construct a more accurate understanding of their emotions, and to build a better approach to managing their feelings. In the long run, such understandings could improve all our lives.

REFERENCES

Alloy, L. B., & Abramson, L. Y. (1979). Judgment of contingency in depressed and non-depressed students: Sadder but wiser? *Journal of Experimental Psychology, 108*, 441–485.

Alloy, L. B., & Abramson, L. Y. (1988). Depressive realism: Four theoretical perspectives. In L. B. Alloy, et al. (1988). *Cognitive processes in depression*, (pp. 223–265). New York: Guilford Press.

Averill, J. R., & Nunley, E. P. (1992). *Voyages of the heart: Living an emotionally creative life*. New York: Free Press.

Banaji, M. R., & Greenwald, A. G. (1995). Implicit social cognition: Attitudes, self-esteem, and stereotypes. *Psychological Review, 102*, 4–27.

Beck, A. T. (1967). *Depression: Clinical, experimental, and theoretical aspects*. New York: Harper & Row.

Beck, A. T., Rush, A. J., Shaw, B. F., & Emery, G. (1979). *Cognitive therapy of depression*. New York: Guilford Press.

Benassi, V. A., & Mahler, H. I. M. (1985). Contingency judgments by depressed college students: Sadder but not always wiser. *Journal of Personality and Social Psychology, 49*, 1323–1329.

Bower, G. H. (1981). Mood and memory. *American Psychologist, 36*, 129–148.

Buck, R. (1989). *The communication of emotion*. New York: Guilford Press.

Calhoun, C., & Solomon, R. C. (Eds.) (1984). *What is an emotion? Classic readings in philosophical psychology*. New York: Oxford University Press.

Carroll, J. B. (1993). *Human cognitive abilities: A survey of factor-analytic studies*. New York: Cambridge University Press.

Carson, R. C., Butcher, J. N., & Mineka, S. (1996). *Abnormal psychology and modern life* (10th ed.). New York: HarperCollins.

Ciarrochi, J. V., Chan, A. Y. C., & Caputi, P. (2000). A critical evaluation of the emotional intelligence construct. *Personality and Individual Differences, 28*, 539–561.

Clark, M. S., & Fiske, S. T. (1982). *Affect and cognition: The 17th annual Carnegie Symposium on Cognition*. Hillsdale, NJ: Lawrence Erlbaum Associates.

Costa, P. T., & McCrae, R. R. (1992). *Revised NEO Personality Inventory*. Odessa, FL: Psychological Assessment Resources, Inc.

Davies, M., Stankov, L., & Roberts, R. D. (1998). Emotional intelligence: In search of an elusive construct. *Journal of Personality and Social Psychology, 44*, 113–126.

Dyer, M. G. (1983). The role of affect in narratives. *Cognitive Science, 7*, 211–242.

Easterbrook, J. A. (1959). The effects of emotion on cue utilization and the organization of behavior. *Psychological Review, 66*, 183–200.

Ekman, P. (1973). *Darwin an facial expression: A century of research in review*. New York: Academic Press.

Ellis, H. C., & Ashbrook, P. W. (1988). Resource allocation model of the effects of depressed mood states on memory. In J. Forgas & K. Fiedler (Eds.). *Affect, cognition, and social behavior*. Toronto, Canada: Hogrefe.

Epstein, S. (1998). *Constructive thinking: The key to emotional intelligence*. Westport, CT: Praeger Publishers/Greenwood Publishing Group.

Espe, H., & Schulz, W. (1983). Room evaluation, moods, and personality. *Perceptual and Motor Skills*, *57*, 215–221.

Fiske, S. T., & Taylor, S. E. (1991). *Social cognition* (2nd ed.). New York: McGraw-Hill.

Forgas, J. P. (1995). Mood and judgment: The affect infusion model (AIM). *Psychological Bulletin*, *117*, 39–66.

Forgas, J. P., & Moylan, S. J. (1987). After the movies: Transient mood and social judgments. *Personality and Social Psychology Bulletin*, *13*, 467–477.

Freud, A. (1966). *The ego and the mechanisms of defense* (C. Baines, Trans.) (Rev. Ed.). New York: International Universities Press. (Original work published 1937.)

Freud, S. (1949). *An outline of psychoanalysis* (J. Strachey, Trans.) (Rev. Ed.). New York: Norton. (Original work published 1940.)

Goodwin, F. K., & Jamison, K. R. (1990). *Manic–depressive illness*. New York: Oxford University Press.

Hilgard, E. R. (1980). The trilogy of mind: Cognition, affection, and conation. *Journal of the History of the Behavioral Sciences*, *16*, 107–117.

Isen, A. M., Daubman, K. A., & Nowicki, G. (1987). Positive affect facilitates creative problem-solving. *Journal of Personality and Social Psychology*, *52*, 1122–1131.

Isen, A. M., Shalker, T., Clark, M., & Karp, L. (1978). Positive affect, accessibility of material in memory and behavior: A cognitive loop? *Journal of Personality and Social Psychology*, *36*, 1–12.

Ketelaar, T., & Clore, G. L. (1997). Emotion and reason: The proximate effects and ultimate functions of emotion. In G. Mathews (Ed.). *Cognitive science perspectives on personality and emotion* (pp. xxx) Amsterdam, The Netherlands: Elsevier Science.

Lane, R. D., Sechrest, L., Reidel, R., Weldon, V., Kascniak, A., & Schwartz, G. E. (1996). Imparied verbal and nonverbal emotion recognition in alexithymia. *Psychosomatic Medicine*, *58*, 203–210.

Larsen, R. J., & Diener, E. (1987). Affect intensity as an individual differences characteristic: A review. *Journal of Research in Personality*, *21*, 1–39.

Mandler, G. (1975). *Mind and emotion*. New York: Wiley.

Martin, D. J., Abramson, L. Y., & Alloy, L. B. (1984). The illusion of control for self and others in depressed and nondepressed college students. *Journal of Personality and Social Psychology*, *46*, 125–136.

Mayer, J. D. (1986). How mood influences cognition. In N. E. Sharkey (Ed.), *Advances in cognitive science* (pp. 290–314). Chichester, West Sussex, England: Ellis Horwood Limited.

Mayer, J. D. (1995). A framework for the classification of personality components. *Journal of Personality*, *63*, 819–878.

Mayer, J. D. (1998). A systems framework for the field of personality. *Psychological Inquiry*, *9*, 118–144.

Mayer, J. D., & Bremer, D. (1985). Assessing mood with affect-sensitive tasks. *Journal of Personality Assessment*, *49*, 95–99.

Mayer, J. D., Caruso, D. R., & Salovey, P. (1999). Emotional intelligence meets traditional standards for an intelligence. *Intelligence*, *17*(4), 433–442.

Mayer, J. D., Caruso, D. R., & Salovey, P. (in press). Choosing a measure of emotional intelligence: The case for ability scales. In R. Ban-On *Handbook of Emotional Intelligence*, Guilford.

Mayer, J. D., Chabot, H. F., & Carlsmith, K. M. (1997). Conation, affect, and cognition in personality. In G. Matthews (Ed.), *Cognitive science perspectives on personality and emotion* (pp. 31–63). New York: Elsevier.

Mayer, J. D., & Cobb, C. D. (2000). Educational policy on emotional intelligence: Does it make sense? *Educational Psychology Review, 12*(2), 163–183.

Mayer, J. D., DiPaolo, M. T., & Salovey, P. (1990). Perceiving affective content in ambiguous visual stimuli: A component of emotional intelligence. *Journal of Personality Assessment, 54,* 772–781.

Mayer, J. D., Gaschke, Y., Braverman, D. L., & Evans, T. (1992). Mood-congruent judgment is a general effect. *Journal of Personality and Social Psychology, 63,* 119–132.

Mayer, J. D., & Geher, G. (1996). Emotional intelligence and the identification of emotion. *Intelligence, 22,* 89–113.

Mayer, J. D., & Hanson, E. (1995). Mood-congruent judgment over time. *Personality and Social Psychology Bulletin, 21,* 237–244.

Mayer, J. D., McCormick, L. J., & Strong, S. E. (1995). Mood-congruent recall and natural mood: New evidence. *Personality and Social Psychology Bulletin, 21,* 736–746.

Mayer, J. D., & Mitchell, D. C. (1998). Intelligence as a subsystem of personality: From Spearman's g to contemporary models of hot-processing. In W. Tomic & J. Kingma (Eds.), *Advances in cognition and educational practice (Vol. 5: Conceptual issues in research in intelligence)* (pp. 43–75). Greenwich, CT: JAI Press.

Mayer, J. D., & Salovey, P. (1993). The intelligence of emotional intelligence. *Intelligence, 17*(4), 433–442.

Mayer, J. D. & Salovey, P. (1997). What is emotional intelligence? In P. Salovey & D. Sluyter (Eds.). *Emotional development and emotional intelligence: Implications for educators* (pp. 3–31). New York: Basic Books.

Mayer, J. D., Salovey, P., & Caruso, D. R. (2000). Competing models of emotional intelligence. In R. J. Sternberg (Ed.), *Handbook of intelligence* (396–420). New York: Cambridge.

Mayer, J. D., Salovey, P., & Caruso, D. R. (1999). *MSCEIT Item Booklet (Research Version 1.1)*. Toronto, Ontario: Multi-Health Systems Inc.

Mayer, J. D., & Stevens, A. (1994). An emerging understanding of the reflective (meta-) experience of mood. *Journal of Research in Personality, 28,* 351–373.

Neisser, U., Boodoo, G., Bouchard, T. J., Boykin, A. W., Brody, N., Ceci, S. J., Halpern, D. F., Loehlin, J. C., Perloff, R., Sternberg, R. J., & Urbina, S. (1996). Intelligence: Knowns and unknowns. *American Psychologist, 51,* 77–101.

Ortony, A., Clore, G. L., & Collins, A. (1988). *Cognitive structure of emotions.* New York: Cambridge.

Palfai, T. P., & Salovey, P. (1994). The influence of depressed and elated mood on deductive and inductive reasoning. *Imagination, Cognition, and Personality, 13,* 57–71.

Paulhus, D. L., Lysy, D. C., & Yik, M. S. M. (1998). Self-report measures of intelligence: Are they useful as proxy IQ tests? *Journal of Personality, 66,* 525–554.

Picard, R. W. (1997). *Affective computing.* Cambridge, MA: MIT Press.

Roseman, I. J. (1984). Cognitive determinants of emotion: A structural theory. In *Review of Personality and Social Psychology (Vol. 5)* (pp. 11–36). Beverly Hills, CA: Sage Publications.

Salovey, P., & Birnbaum, D. (1989). The influence of mood on health-relevant cognitions. *Journal of Personality and Social Psychology, 57,* 539–551.

Salovey, P., & Mayer, J. D. (1990). Emotional intelligence. *Imagination, Cognition, and Personality, 9,* 185–211.

Salovey, P., Mayer, J. D., Goldman, S., Turvey, C., & Palfai, T. (1995). Emotional attention, clarity, and repair: Exploring emotional intelligence using the Trait Meta-Mood Scale. In J. W. Pennebaker (Ed.), *Emotion, disclosure, and health* (pp. 125–154). Washington, DC: American Psychological Association.

Salovey, P., Mayer, J. D., & Rosenhan, D. (1991). Mood and helping: Mood as a motivator of helping and helping as a regulator of mood. *Review of Personality and Social Psychology, 12,* 215–237.

Schwarz, N., & Clore, G. L. (1988). How do I feel about it? The informative function of affective states. In K. Fiedler & J. Forgas (Eds.), *Affect, cognition, and social behavior* (pp. 44–62). Toronto, Canada: C. J. Hogrefe.

Simon, E. W., Rosen, M., & Pompipom, A. (1996). Age and IQ as predictors of emotion identification in adults with mental retardation. *Research in Developmental Disabilities, 17,* 383–389.

Simon, H. A. (1982). Comments. In M. S. Clark & S. T. Fiske (Eds.), *Affect and cognition* (pp. 333–342). Hillsdale, NJ: Lawrence Erlbaum Associates.

Sloman, A., & Croucher, M. (1981). Why robots will have emotions. In T. Dean (Ed.), *Proceedings of the Seventh International Joint Conference on Artificial Intelligence, Vol. 1.* San Francisco, CA: Morgan Kaufmann.

Taylor, G. J. (1984). Alexithymia: Concept and measurement. *The American Journal of Psychiatry, 141,* 725–732.

Zajonc, R. B. (1980). Feeling and thinking: Preferences need no inferences. *American Psychologist, 35,* 151–175.

Author Index

A

Abbott, R. A., 367
Abele, A., 12, 22, 102, 117, 146, 157, 158, 331,
   338, 346, 363
Abelson, R. P., 53, 60, 70, 96, 117
Abend, T. A., 159, 221, 230
Abramson, L. Y., 170, 417, 418, 428, 429
Achee, J. W., 129, 143, 334, 341
Adolphs, R., 2, 3, 13, 14, 27, 34, 35, 40, 41, 42,
   48, 58, 70, 96, 294, 320
Adorno, T. W., 325, 338
Aerts, J., 48
Affleck, G., 351, 364
Ahleman, S., 349, 350, 366
Ajzen, I., 102, 122, 142, 217,
   222, 229
Alkire, M. T., 46
Alliger, G. M., 398, 409
Alloy, L. B., 170, 417, 418, 428, 429
Allport, G., 281, 289, 338, 394, 406
Allport, G. W., 322
Allred, K. D., 388

Amir, Y., 322, 338
Anastasio, P. A., 323, 340
Anderson, A. K., 34, 45, 49
Anderson, J. R., 88, 90, 100, 117, 222,
   228, 368
Anderson, N. B., 51, 70
Anderson, N. H., 58, 70, 102, 117,
   122, 141
Anderson, S. W., 38, 46, 48
Angier, R. P., 75, 90
Arbisi, P., 58, 71
Aristotle, 2, 418
Arnold, M. B., 76, 77, 78, 79, 84, 90
Aronson, E., 244, 253
Asbeck, J., 76, 90, 165, 335, 340
Ashbrook, P. W., 171, 177, 183, 417, 429
Aspinwall, L. G., 258, 261, 262, 271,
   272, 273
Asuncion, A. G., 230
Audrain, P. C., 125, 142
Austin, G. A., 98, 117
Averill, J. R., 428
Aziza, C., 247, 252, 255

433

B

Babinsky, R., 34, 35, 45, 46
Bach, J. S., 152
Bachman, B. A., 323, 340
Baker, K. H., 350, 364
Baker, S. M., 213, 216, 221, 231
Baldwin, M. W., 287, 289
Banaji, M., 66, 70, 332, 342, 421, 428
Bandura, A., 347, 363
Bargh, J. A., 63, 70, 74, 86, 90, 127, 141, 143, 328, 329, 338
Baron, R. S., 218, 228, 332, 338
Barron, K. E., 242, 253
Barter, J., 53, 54, 74
Bartlett, F. C., 131, 132, 141
Bartlett, J. A., 350, 365
Bartolic, E. I., 44, 46
Bassili, J. N., 197, 208
Basso, M. R., 44, 46
Batra, R., 221, 228
Batson, C. D., 324, 338
Baumeister, R. F., 151, 158, 361, 362, 363, 366
Beattie, M., 48
Beauvois, J. L., 238, 253
Bechara, A., 33, 37, 38, 39, 45, 46
Beck, A. T., 412, 428
Beck, K. H., 218, 228
Becker, M. H., 347, 363, 365
Bedell, B. T., 5, 20, 315, 344
Bednar, L. L., 338
Bell, D. W., 60, 70
Benassi, V. A., 418, 428
Bentham, J., 276, 289
Berkman, L. F., 359, 363
Berkowitz, L., 11, 22, 110, 117, 175, 183, 247, 249, 253, 254, 358, 363
Berntson, G. G., 51, 52, 53, 54, 55, 56, 59, 61, 70, 71, 194, 208
Berridge, K. C., 61, 70, 72
Berry, D. S., 54, 70
Biernat, M., 324, 327, 338, 339
Birnbaum, D., 346, 347, 348, 367, 412, 430
Black, J. B., 97, 117
Black, P. H., 365
Blaney, P. H., 111, 117, 136, 138, 141, 143, 372, 373, 385, 388
Blanz, M., 54, 70
Blascovich, J., 83, 92, 393, 406
Bless, H., 18, 22, 129, 130, 134, 141, 145, 159, 165, 169, 170, 173, 177, 180, 183,
184, 213, 223, 224, 228, 232, 270, 272, 295, 299, 311, 312, 313, 329, 331, 333, 334, 335, 338, 339, 342
Blessum, K. A., 331, 339
Blisset, S. E., 350, 366
Block, L. G., 218, 230
Bodenhausen, G. V., 5, 14, 20, 129, 141, 146, 164, 315, 319, 320, 321, 322, 325, 327, 328, 329, 330, 331, 332, 333, 334, 336, 339, 341, 342
Bodner, T., 392, 407
Bohner, G., 165, 170, 183, 213, 223, 224, 228, 232, 270, 272, 329, 331, 338, 342
Bolger, N., 397, 398, 400, 401
Bond, R. N., 196, 209
Boniecki, K. A., 324, 339
Bonneau, R., 365
Boodoo, G., 430
Boster, F. J., 217, 229
Bouchard, T., Jr., 399, 409, 430
Bower, G. H., 4, 13, 14, 15, 17, 18, 22, 23, 76, 86, 90, 95, 97, 99, 100, 101, 103, 104, 105, 106, 107, 108, 109, 110, 114, 115, 116, 117, 118, 122, 136, 137, 138, 139, 141, 167, 168, 169, 170, 171, 173, 183, 184, 221, 222, 228, 229, 261, 270, 272, 278, 289, 298, 301, 302, 316, 317, 318, 327, 340, 359, 372, 388, 402, 406, 407, 411, 412, 421, 428
Boykin, A. W., 430
Boysen, S. T., 61, 70
Bradburn, N. M., 54, 70
Bradley, B. P., 396, 406
Bradley, M. M., 34, 46, 57, 63, 73
Bradley, P. P., 109, 117
Braverman, D., 119, 159, 222, 230, 318, 348, 366, 385, 390, 412, 430
Breckler, S. J., 221, 229
Brehm, J., 57, 70, 238, 239, 240, 241, 253, 254, 255
Brehm, S. S., 378, 389
Breiter, H. C., 40, 46
Brekke, N., 336, 343
Bremer, D., 412, 429
Brendl, C. M., 198, 208
Brewer, M. B., 54, 70, 322, 331, 339
Brickman, P., 258, 274
Bridges, M. W., 367
Brioni, J. D., 31, 46
Britt, T. W., 324, 339
Brock, B. M., 347, 364
Brock, T. C., 224, 231

Brody, N., 430
Broks, P., 40, 46, 49
Brown, J. D., 152, 153, 158, 257, 272, 358, 368,
  382, 388, 391, 402, 407
Brown, L. M., 324, 339
Brownbridge, G., 53, 54, 74
Browning, R. A., 37, 47
Bruner, J. S., 13, 22, 98, 117, 165, 183, 206, 210
Buck, R., 419, 428
Buckner, R., 46, 67, 70
Bucy, P. C., 40, 48
Buechel, C., 33, 46
Buehler, R., 158, 159
Bunney, B. S., 31, 48
Burke, A., 34, 46
Burke, M., 107, 109, 117
Burnham, D. K., 373, 389
Burris, C. T., 251, 253
Bush, L. E. II., 188, 208
Bushman, B. J., 347, 365
Buss, A. H., 357, 363
Butcher, J. N., 416, 428
Byrne, D., 10, 11, 17, 18, 22, 123, 141

C

Caccioppo, J. T., 2, 3, 13, 14, 16, 50, 51, 52, 53,
  54, 55, 56, 59, 61, 62, 63, 64, 65, 66, 70, 71,
  72, 76, 91, 194, 208, 213, 214, 215, 220, 221,
  229, 231, 244, 245, 248, 253, 254, 294, 311,
  365, 394
Cahill, L., 31, 32, 34, 35, 36, 45, 46, 48, 49, 96,
  117, 119
Calder, A. J., 40, 45, 46, 48
Calhoun, C., 418, 428
Campbell, J. D., 151, 158, 283, 289
Cane, D. B., 378, 389
Canli, T., 36, 47
Cannon, W. B., 79, 90, 345, 363
Cantor, N., 323, 341
Caputi, P., 426, 428
Carlsmith, M., 239, 253, 413, 414, 429
Carlston, D. E., 58, 74
Carrell, S. E., 287, 289
Carrillo, M., 257, 258, 273
Carroll, J., 53, 73, 394, 408, 416, 428
Carson, R. C., 416, 428
Caruso, D. R., 413, 424, 425, 426, 429, 430
Carver, C. S., 19, 22, 130, 141, 156, 159, 187,
  208, 351, 358, 363, 364, 367, 393, 408

Carver, S. C., 258, 272
Castelli, L., 329, 341
Catanzaro, S. J., 282, 289, 355, 364, 365,
  382, 388
Cattell, R. B., 394, 407
Ceci, S. J., 430
Cejka, M. A., 327, 343
Cerkovnik, M., 361, 364
Cervone, D., 155, 158
Cezayirli, E., 46
Chabot, H. F., 413, 414, 429
Chaiken, S., 63, 70, 206, 208, 213, 214, 218,
  221, 229, 230, 267, 273, 330, 339
Chan, A. Y. C., 426, 428
Chaudhary, B., 359, 367
Chee, M., 365
Chen, W. K., 213, 229
Chiba, A. A., 37, 49
Christianson, F. A., 99, 117
Church, M. A., 54, 71
Cialdini, R. B., 283, 289
Ciarrochi, J. V., 20, 22, 244, 249, 253, 310, 314,
  315, 316, 318, 395, 407, 426, 428
Cicchetti, P., 30, 48, 58, 73
Cicero, M. T., 212, 229
Claeys, W., 372, 389
Claparède, E., 75, 90
Clark, K. B., 37, 47
Clark, K. C., 363
Clark, L. A., 53, 74, 188, 211, 356, 368, 375,
  391, 391, 394, 395, 396, 400, 409
Clark, M., 17, 18, 19, 22, 103, 115, 117, 119,
  122, 136, 142, 168, 184, 222, 230, 276, 289,
  298, 299, 317, 372, 389, 411, 428, 429
Clore, G. L., 4, 10, 11, 13, 15, 16, 17, 18, 22, 23,
  51, 73, 76, 77, 91, 92, 102, 112, 118, 121,
  122, 123, 124, 125, 126, 127, 129, 130, 131,
  132, 134, 135, 137, 139, 141, 142, 143, 144,
  145, 155, 158, 164, 166, 168, 169, 170, 171,
  174, 175, 177, 180, 183, 185, 187, 210, 214,
  215, 220, 224, 226, 227, 232, 247, 258, 270,
  272, 273, 295, 296, 298, 302, 317, 318, 320,
  331, 338, 339, 412, 419, 421, 429, 430
Cobb, C. D., 413, 430
Coffey, P. J., 46
Cogan, D., 350, 364
Cogan, R., 350, 364
Cohen, A. R., 239, 241, 253
Cohen, P. R., 103, 116, 117, 171, 173, 183
Cohen, S., 356, 357, 359, 360, 361, 364
Coles, M. G. H., 59, 64, 70, 71

Collins, A., 51, 73, 77, 91, 124, 143, 187, 210, 419, 430
Collins, P., 58, 71
Comer, R., 249, 254
Commons, M. J., 282, 286, 289
Conway, M., 11, 22, 102, 118, 122, 141, 145, 158, 164, 183, 298, 317, 320, 339
Cook, W. A., 346, 365
Cooper, J., 226, 229, 233, 242, 243, 245, 248, 253, 255, 321, 339
Cornelius, R., 89, 90
Cornell, D. P., 250, 255, 257, 273
Costa, P. T., 54, 71, 310, 317, 375, 389, 400, 408, 416, 428
Costa, P. T., Jr., 356, 364, 393, 394, 404, 407
Coté, S., 404, 408
Coury, A., 57, 71
Cousins, N., 350, 364
Cox, S., 362, 368
Coyne, J., 393, 407
Criqui, M., 407
Crisson, J. E., 346, 365
Critchlow, B., 249, 255
Crites, S. L., 59, 70, 71, 215, 229
Crocker, J., 258, 272
Crouch, J. G., 362, 364
Croucher, M., 418, 431
Crow, K., 223, 228
Crowe, E., 192, 193, 194, 207, 208, 209
Crowson, J. J., Jr., 353, 365
Croyle, R. T., 346, 364
Crystal, B., 277
Cummings, K. M., 347, 364
Cuniff, M., 384, 390
Cuthbert, B. N., 57, 63, 73

D

Dakof, G., 393, 407
Damasio, A. R., 2, 3, 13, 14, 16, 22, 27, 28, 37, 38, 39, 40, 41, 42, 45, 46, 47, 48, 58, 70, 96, 125, 141, 294, 317, 320, 339
Damasio, H., 37, 38, 39, 40, 45, 46, 47, 58, 70
Darke, S., 323, 339
Darley, J. M., 217, 229
Darrow, C. W., 75, 90
Darwin, C., 214, 253, 418
Daubman, K. A., 170, 184, 328, 341, 417, 429
Daubman, L. A., 129, 142

David, J. P., 392, 394, 395, 398, 400, 401, 404, 407, 409
Davidson, R. J., 44, 47, 72
Davies, M., 420, 423, 428
Davis, M., 30, 31, 33, 40, 47, 48, 58, 71, 72
Degueldre, C., 48
DeHart, T. L., 381, 391
Delfiore, G., 48
DeLongis, A., 359, 364, 393, 398, 406, 407
Demb, J. B., 67, 72, 74
Dember, W. N., 164, 183
Dembroski, T. M., 393, 407
Denny, E. B., 385, 389
Depue, R. A., 58, 71
Derry, P. A., 385, 389
Derryberry, D., 76, 90, 134, 141, 377, 389
Descartes, R., 2, 6
Desmond, J., 36, 47
Desmond, J. E., 67, 72, 74
DeSousa, R. J., 3, 16, 22
DeSteno, D., 4, 164, 158, 212, 222, 227, 229, 302
Detweiler, J. B., 5, 20, 315, 344
Devine, P. G., 65, 66, 68, 71, 242, 244, 245, 246, 251, 253, 323, 324, 337, 339, 340
Diener, E., 52, 53, 54, 71, 73, 157, 159, 187, 188, 208, 209, 357, 364, 366, 393, 395, 398, 403, 407, 408, 416, 429
Dienes, B. P. A., 129, 133, 135, 141, 170, 183
Dienstbier, R. A., 399, 408
Digman, J. M., 394, 407
Dijker, A. J., 321, 340
Dillon, K. M., 350, 364
DiPaolo, M. T., 229, 412, 419, 423, 427, 430
Ditto, P. H., 217, 335, 342
Dodson, J. D., 164, 185
Dolan, R. J., 33, 46, 48
Dollard, J., 325, 340
Donaghue, E. F., 363
Donchin, E., 64, 71
Doob, L., 325, 340
Doren, B., 182, 184, 373, 389
Dovidio, J. F., 66, 71, 321, 323, 328, 340
Doyle, W. J., 364
Drake, C. A., 318
Drevets, W. C., 44, 47
Droppleman, L., 347, 366
Drysdale, E., 34, 49
Duncan, B. L., 331, 340
Dunn, M., 329, 343
Dunning, D., 147, 158

Dunton, B. C., 63, 71
Dutton, K. A., 257, 272
Duval, S., 358, 364
Dyck, D. G., 379, 390
Dyer, J. B., III., 362, 364
Dyer, M. G., 418, 428

E

Eagly, A. H., 206, 208, 213, 215, 229
Easterbrook, J. A., 164, 183, 420, 428
Ebmeier, K. P., 34, 49
Eckenrode, J., 361, 364
Edwards, J. A., 332, 340
Edwards, K., 76, 91, 216, 218, 229, 325, 341
Eich, E., 17, 22, 37, 47, 107, 108, 109, 116, 118, 169, 171, 180, 183
Einhorn, H. J., 154, 158
Eitel, P., 346, 365
Ekman, P., 76, 90, 124, 142, 253, 419, 429
Elkin, R. A., 241, 245, 251, 253
Elliot, A. J., 54, 71, 242, 244, 245, 251, 253, 337, 340
Elliott, T. R., 352, 364
Ellis, H. C., 171, 177, 183, 417, 429
Ellsworth, P. C., 51, 74, 76, 79, 80, 81, 90, 91, 92, 187, 210, 325, 341
Elster, J., 2, 22
Ely, T. D., 36, 48
Emerson, R. W., 371
Emery, G., 412, 428
Emmerich, S., 48
Emmons, R. A., 53, 54, 71, 187, 208, 357, 366, 398, 403, 407
Epstein, S., 158, 159, 217, 229, 400, 407, 413, 429
Erb, H. P., 223, 228
Erber, M. W., 5, 14, 18, 19, 136, 142, 156, 225, 275, 278, 280, 282, 289, 290, 295, 298, 313, 330, 354, 373, 389
Erber, R., 5, 14, 18, 19, 136, 142, 156, 225, 275, 276, 277, 278, 280, 282, 284, 285, 286, 289, 290, 295, 298, 313, 330, 354, 373, 389
Eriksen, C. W., 399, 407
Espe, H., 412, 429
Esses, V., 60, 70, 157, 159, 321, 332, 340, 341
Etcoff, N. L., 46, 74
Evans, T., 119, 159, 222, 230, 318, 348, 366, 385, 390, 412, 430
Everitt, B. J., 30, 32, 47

Evett, S. R., 323, 339
Ewing, J. H., 362, 364
Eysenck, H. J., 394, 395, 399, 402, 407, 416
Eysenck, M. W., 375, 376, 389
Eysenck, S. B. G., 394, 407

F

Fabre-Thorpe, M., 30, 47
Fabrigar, L. R., 215, 216, 229
Fahey, J. L., 349, 352, 365, 368
Fallon, J., 46
Fay, D., 165, 181, 184
Fazio, R. H., 63, 66, 71, 102, 118, 197, 208, 214, 226, 229, 243, 248, 253, 327, 343
Fein, S., 329, 343
Feist, G., 392, 407
Feldman Barrett, L., 53, 73, 188, 200, 203, 204, 209, 400, 408
Fenz, W. D., 158, 159
Ferguson, M., 4, 256
Feshbach, S., 9, 11, 12, 22, 164, 184, 217, 219, 230, 295, 317
Festinger, L., 226, 229, 238, 239, 240, 246, 253
Fibiger, H. C., 57, 71
Fiedler, K., 3, 4, 12, 13, 14, 15, 18, 22, 76, 90, 111, 114, 115, 118, 134, 142, 145, 159, 163, 164, 165, 166, 167, 168, 169, 170, 171, 173, 176, 177, 178, 179, 180, 181, 183, 184, 295, 297, 299, 302, 311, 312, 317, 318, 332, 334, 335, 338, 340, 358
Fine, B. J., 213, 233
Fiorini, D. F., 57, 71
Fireman, P., 364
Fischer, G. W., 65, 73
Fishbein, M., 102, 118, 122, 142, 217, 222, 229
Fishkin, S., 318
Fiske, S. T., 53, 58, 70, 71, 322, 331, 335, 340, 411, 412, 428, 429
Fitzgerald, T. E., 351, 364
Fladung, U., 166, 170, 184
Fleetwood, R. S., 323, 342
Fogarty, S. J., 107, 120
Folkman, S., 258, 273, 359, 364, 393, 407, 408
Fong, C., 329, 343
Ford, T. E., 215, 321, 232, 343
Forgas, J. P., 1, 3, 4, 5, 12, 13, 14, 15, 17, 18, 19, 20, 21, 22, 23, 51, 65, 71, 72, 76, 90, 95, 96, 97, 98, 107, 109, 110, 111, 112, 113, 114, 115, 116, 118, 137, 142, 145, 146, 147, 159,

164, 166, 167, 168, 169, 171, 172, 173, 174, 176, 180, 184, 213, 221, 222, 230, 244, 247, 248, 249, 252, 253, 261, 270, 271, 272, 276, 281, 290, 293, 295, 296, 297, 298, 299, 300, 301, 302, 303, 304, 305, 306, 307, 308, 309, 310, 311, 312, 313, 314, 315, 316, 317, 318, 326, 327, 332, 334, 340, 348, 359, 364, 372, 373, 380, 386, 389, 395, 402, 407, 412, 429
Forster, J., 54, 71, 194, 202, 209, 335, 340
Fox, B. H., 365
Franck, G., 48
Frandsen, K. J., 351, 365
Frank, J. D., 353, 364
Frank, R., 38, 47
Fredrickson, B. L., 380, 390
Freeman, D. H., 353, 366
French, C. C., 378, 391
Frenkel, A., 218, 228
Frenkel-Brunswik, E., 325, 338
Freud, A., 412, 429
Freud, S., 2, 6, 8, 9, 164, 184, 325, 340, 365, 411, 412, 429
Fricke, K., 336, 341
Friedman, H., 406, 407
Friedman, R., 197, 209
Friend, R., 346, 365
Frijda, N. H., 51, 72, 79, 80, 91, 164, 184, 187, 200, 208, 209, 241, 253, 320, 340, 380, 389
Friston, K. J., 33, 46
Frith, C. D., 48
Fujita, F., 393, 398, 407, 408
Fuller, R., 109, 120
Futterman, A. D., 349, 365

G

Gabriel, S., 5, 146, 164, 315, 319, 327, 342
Gabrieli, J. D. E., 36, 47, 67, 72, 74
Gaertner, S. L., 321, 323, 328, 340
Gaes, G. G., 245, 253
Gaffan, D., 30, 37, 47
Gage, P., 38
Gaines, B., 400, 409
Galaburda, A. M., 38, 47
Gallagher, D. J., 399, 407
Gallagher, M., 31, 32, 37, 47, 48, 49
Gangestad, S., 403, 409
Gannon, K., 331, 343
Gannon, L., 54, 72
Gardner, W. L., 53, 54, 59, 70, 71, 72, 244, 253

Garvin, E., 4, 121, 138, 139, 142, 155, 164, 220, 302
Gaschke, Y. N., 119, 222, 230, 318, 348, 385, 390, 412, 430
Gasper, K., 4, 121, 124, 126, 131, 132, 134, 135, 141, 142, 155, 159, 164, 170, 183, 220, 302, 366
Gatenby, J. C., 33, 48
Gaurnaccia, C. A., 54, 74
Gayle, M. C., 372, 384, 389, 390
Gazzaniga, M. S., 61, 66, 72
Geen, T. R., 215, 229
Geher, G., 423, 425, 430
Gendolla, G. H. E., 331, 338
Genevie, L. E., 364
Gentner, D., 205, 310
Gerard, H. B., 240, 254
Gergen, K. J., 147, 159
Gerrard, M., 347, 365
Gervey, B., 263, 266, 271, 274
Gewirtz, J. C., 30, 48
Giannopoulos, C., 183
Gibb, J., 368
Gibbons, F. X., 347, 365
Gibbs, R., 304, 318
Gilbert, D. T., 313, 318, 326, 329, 341
Gilboa, E., 375, 389
Gilligan, S., 104, 105, 117, 122, 136, 139, 141, 167, 168, 183, 278, 289
Giorgi, R. G., 365
Glaser, R., 360, 365
Glauser, T., 44, 46
Gleicher, F., 213, 216, 218, 221, 230, 231
Glenn, N. D., 360, 365
Glover, G., 36, 47, 67, 72, 74
Glowalla, U., 373, 391
Goffman, E., 284, 290
Gohm, C., 124, 141, 142, 170, 183
Goldberg, J. D., 359, 367
Goldberg, J. H., 334, 341
Goldberg, L. R., 393, 394, 407
Goldman, S., 423, 430
Goldman, S. L., 124, 143, 187, 209, 354, 365, 367
Goldsamt, L. A., 280, 290, 358, 368
Goldstein, L. D., 407
Goldstein, L. E., 31, 48
Goldstein, M. D., 54, 72
Golisano, V., 177, 331, 141, 183, 338
Gollwitzer, P. M., 282, 258, 272, 290
Gonzalez, P., 107, 119

Goodnow, J. J., 98, 117
Goodstein, L. D., 399
Goodwin, F. K., 416, 429
Gore, J. C., 33, 48
Gormly, J. B., 123, 141
Gotlib, I. H., 378, 389
Gottleib, G., 52, 72
Gouaux, C., 10, 11, 23, 110, 118, 219, 230
Govender, T., 63, 70
Grabowski, T., 38, 47
Graesser, A. C., 97, 118
Graf, P., 181, 185
Grafton, S. T., 36, 48
Grant, H., 189, 198, 205, 209
Gray, J. A., 376, 389, 402, 408
Graziano, W. G., 404, 408
Green, D. P., 187, 209, 347, 365
Green, J., 4, 221, 230
Green, J. D., 145, 159, 400
Green, P. J., 397, 392, 407, 409
Greenberg, J., 246, 254, 257, 273, 358, 367, 368
Greenwald, A. G., 66, 72, 421, 428
Greenwald, M. K., 34, 46
Greenwood, G., 364
Griffin, D. W., 60, 74
Griffin, J. J., 400, 409
Griffin, K. W., 346, 365
Griffitt, W., 10, 17, 23, 295
Griffitt, W. B., 219, 230
Grill, H. J., 61, 72
Griner, L. A., 80, 85, 91, 92
Gross, J. J., 54, 72, 396, 407
Gschneidinger, E., 127, 144
Guerra, P., 340
Gunawardene, A., 303, 304, 318
Gustafson, R., 362, 365
Gwaltney, J. M., 364

H

Haarman, A., 384, 390
Haddock, G., 157, 159, 321, 341
Hadley, D., 46
Haefner, D. P., 347, 363, 364
Hafen, B. Q., 351, 365
Haier, R. J., 46
Hair, E. C., 404, 408
Halberstadt, J., 97, 98, 119
Halgren, E., 58, 72
Halpern, D. F., 430

Hamann, S. B., 34, 36, 45, 48
Han, J.-S., 32, 48
Hanley, J. R., 49
Hansen, J. S., 54, 70
Hanson, E., 412, 421, 430
Hänze, M., 331, 341
Harackiewicz, J. M., 54, 71, 334, 341
Hardin, C., 66, 70
Harmon-Jones, C., 252
Harmon-Jones, E., 4, 14, 19, 226, 230, 237, 238,
    239, 240, 242, 243, 244, 245, 246, 251, 253,
    254, 302, 338
Harney, P., 368
Harris, C., 368
Harris, S. D., 363
Hartman, G. W., 213, 230
Hasher, L., 182, 184, 372, 373, 389
Haslam, S. A., 327, 342
Hass, R. G., 54, 60, 72
Hassert, D. L., 47
Haugtvedt, C., 228, 231
Headley, B., 398, 408
Hearst, E., 154, 159, 200, 209
Hebb, D. O., 138, 142
Heberlein, A. S., 41, 43, 48
Heckhausen, H., 282, 290
Heeren, T. C., 365
Heesacker, M., 231
Heider, F., 19, 23, 41, 48, 128, 142, 300,
    313, 318
Heine, S. J., 158, 289
Hellawell, D. J., 49
Hemenover, S. H., 399, 408
Hepburn, L., 375, 389
Herman, C. P., 283, 289
Hermer, P., 146, 157, 346, 158, 363
Herndandex, L., 58, 72
Herrick, S., 352, 364
Hertel, G., 170, 184
Hesse, F. W., 331, 341
Hetherington, M. M., 361, 362, 366
Heuer, F., 34, 46, 48, 49
Higgins, E. T., 4, 14, 18, 54, 72, 127, 143, 179,
    186, 189, 192, 193, 194, 195, 196, 197, 198,
    202, 205, 206, 207, 208, 209, 210, 211, 245,
    251, 254, 257, 272, 335, 340
Hilgard, E. R., 6, 7, 12, 13, 23, 115, 119, 294,
    318, 413, 429
Hillis, S., 397, 409
Hinton, G. E., 222, 230
Hippocrates, 345

Hirt, E. R., 170, 185, 326, 334, 341
Hitchberger, L., 338
Hitchcock, J. M., 58, 72
Hixon, J. G., 326, 329, 341
Hodges, J. R., 46
Hoebel, B. G., 58, 72, 131, 142
Hoffman, J., 54, 74
Hoffman, J. T., 352, 364
Hogarth, R. M., 154, 158
Holbrook, A. L., 53, 72
Holland, P. C., 32, 48
Holleran, S. A., 368
Holmes, T. H., 393, 408
Hovland, C. I., 215, 232
Howard, A., 66, 71
Hubbard, B., 400, 409
Hubbard, C., 133, 143, 331, 342
Hugdahl, K., 44, 47
Hughes, J., 365
Hunt, R. R., 385, 389
Hyman, S. E., 46
Hymes, C., 192, 209

I

Idson, L. C., 54, 72, 194, 202, 209
Imhoff, H. J., 338
Ingram, R. E., 358, 365, 378, 389
Inman, M. L., 218, 228, 332, 338
Irving, L. M., 353, 365, 368
Irwin, W., 58, 72
Isaac, C., 46
Isbell, L., 123, 129, 130, 133, 135, 141, 142,
    144, 170, 183
Isen, A. M., 3, 17, 18, 19, 22, 23, 103, 115, 117,
    119, 122, 129, 133, 136, 137, 142, 165, 167,
    168, 169, 170, 171, 177, 182, 184, 222, 230,
    250, 254, 262, 269, 270, 272, 276, 278, 279,
    289, 290, 298, 299, 317, 323, 328, 331, 335,
    340, 341, 372, 373, 380, 389, 411, 417, 429
Isenberg, N., 41, 48
Ito, T. A., 2, 3,13, 14, 16, 50, 51, 59, 64, 65, 66,
    70, 72, 74, 294, 394
Izard, C. E., 7, 8, 23, 24, 76, 79, 80, 84, 89, 91,
    241, 254

J

Jackson, J. R., 63, 71
Jackson, L. A., 321, 341

Jacobs, J., 392, 407
Jaffee, S., 22, 117, 175, 183
James, W., 14, 23
Jamison, K. R., 416, 429
Janis, I. L., 164, 184, 213, 217, 219, 230
Janz, N. K., 347, 365
Jemmott, J. B., 217, 229
Jenike, M. A., 74
Jensen, R. A., 37, 47, 49
Jensen-Campbell, L. A., 404, 408
Jepson, C., 218, 230
Jette, A. M., 347, 364
Jo, E., 11, 22, 175, 183
John, O. P., 54, 65, 72, 73, 394, 408
Johnson, B., 66, 71
Johnson, C., 66, 71
Johnson, E., 167, 168, 184, 222, 230, 348, 365
Johnson, M., 49, 100, 119
Johnson, M. M. S., 165, 170, 184
Johnson, R., 249, 253, 314, 315, 318
Johnson, W., 378, 391
Jones, D. E., 76, 91, 384, 390
Jones, E. E., 240, 254
Jones, J. M., 323, 341
Jones, W. H., 242, 254
Josephson, B. R., 379, 389
Joule, R. V., 238, 253
Judd, C. M., 63, 74, 329, 343
Jussim, L., 321, 341

K

Kahn, S., 356, 366
Kahneman, D., 58, 72, 131, 144
Kant, I., 2, 6, 7, 14
Kao, C. F., 218, 228, 332, 338
Kaplan, M. F., 12, 23, 129, 142
Kaplan, S. R., 364
Kapp, B. S., 31, 47
Kardes, F. R., 63, 71, 102, 118
Karp, L., 119, 122, 136, 142, 168, 184, 222, 230,
    372, 389, 411, 429
Karren, K. J., 351, 365
Kascniak, A., 429
Kasimatis, M., 346, 366
Kasl, S. V., 363
Kasmer, J. A., 76, 91
Katon, W., 346, 365
Katz, D., 215, 230
Katz, I., 54, 60, 72, 158, 289
Katz, P. A., 321, 341

Kawakami, K., 66, 71
Kaye, D., 213, 230
Keating, J., 223, 230
Keator, D., 46
Kedem, P., 207, 210
Keefe, F. J., 346, 365
Keller, P. A., 218, 230
Keller, S. E., 350, 365
Kelsey, R. M., 83, 92
Keltner, D., 76, 91, 125, 142, 325
Kemeny, M. E., 349, 352, 365, 367, 368
Kemmelmeier, M., 334, 339
Kemmerer, D., 48
Kennedy, J. F., 34
Kennedy, S., 365
Kennedy, W. A., 46
Kernis, M. H., 151, 159
Kesner, R. P., 31, 48
Kessler, R. C., 398, 406
Ketcham, A. S., 363
Ketelaar, T., 127, 141, 375, 376, 390, 396, 408,
    412, 421, 429
Khan, S. R., 336, 341
Kickul, J., 129, 142
Kidd, R. F., 249, 254
Kiecolt-Glaser, J. K., 360, 365
Kiesler, C. A., 213, 233, 321, 343
Kihlstrom, J., 118
Kilts, C. D., 36, 48
Kim, J. G., 362, 367
Kim, J. K., 100, 119
Kimble, G. A., 178, 185
Kimchi, R., 134, 142
Kinder, D. R., 53, 70
King, K. C., 54, 74
Kirby, L. D., 3, 14, 15, 16, 23, 75, 80, 85, 88, 91,
    92, 104, 116, 119, 169
Kirsch, I., 355, 365
Kirschner, P., 213, 230
Kirscht, J. P., 363
Klein, D. J., 232
Klein, R., 196, 209
Klein, T. R., 338
Kluver, H., 40, 48
Knapp, P. H., 349, 365
Knasko, S. C., 346, 366
Kobasa, S. C., 355, 356, 366
Koehnken, G., 34, 48
Koestler, A., 2, 23
Koivumaki, J., 146, 159
Kopp, D. A., 155, 158
Kothandapani, V., 215, 230

Kowalski, D. J., 97, 118
Kraemer, D. T., 354, 365
Kramer, G. P., 129, 141, 325, 331, 339
Krantz, S., 17, 22, 110, 118, 301, 317
Krosnick, J. A., 53, 72
Krug, C., 165, 181, 184
Kruger, G., 361, 364
Kuhl, J., 258, 273
Kuiper, N. A., 385, 389
Kuipers, P., 80, 91, 187, 209
Kulik, J. A., 347, 366
Kumpf, M., 125, 143
Kunda, Z., 119, 327, 331, 341, 342
Kunst-Wilson, W. R., 27, 49
Kuykendall, D., 223, 230
Kwiatkowski, S. J., 373, 390

L

LaBar, K. S., 33, 34, 48, 49
Labott, S. M., 349, 350, 366
Lachnit, H., 165, 181, 184
Laird, J. D., 245, 255, 384, 390
Lambert, A. J., 336, 341
Lane, R. D., 423, 429
Lang, P. J., 34, 46, 57, 63, 73, 200, 209
Langelle, C., 368
Lapp, L., 36, 49
Larsen, J. R., 54, 73
Larsen, J. T., 51, 59, 70, 72
Larsen, R. J., 53, 73, 157, 159, 187, 188, 209,
    346, 357, 366, 375, 376, 390, 391, 396, 398,
    403, 408, 416, 429
Launier, R., 77, 91
Lavallee, L. F., 158, 289
Laws, H., 152
Lazarus, R. S., 14, 16, 23, 77, 78, 79, 80, 81, 82,
    83, 84, 88, 89, 91, 92, 258, 273, 359, 364,
    393, 407, 408
Learner, S. M., 398, 409
LeDoux, J. E., 30, 33, 40, 48, 49, 58, 61, 66,
    72, 73
Lee, G. P., 46
Lee, M. B., 74
Lee, Y., 33, 47
Lefcourt, H. M., 350, 366
Lefebvre, R. C., 367
Lehman, D. R., 158, 289
Leippe, M. R., 241, 245, 251, 253
Leith, K. P., 361, 366
Leitten, C. L., 83, 92

Lemm, K. M., 198, 208
Leon, A., 48, 58, 71
Lepper, M. R., 57, 73
Lerner, J. S., 334, 341
Leveille, E., 57, 73
Levenbeck, S., 283, 289
Leventhal, H., 79, 80, 84, 85, 86, 91
Levin, J. S., 353, 354, 366
Levine, G. M., 326, 341
Levine, S. R., 159
Levinger, G., 295, 318
Levinson, D., 325, 338
Levy, E. M., 365
Levy, A., 283, 289
Lewin, K., 194, 209, 403, 408
Lewinsohn, P. M., 107, 119
Liberman, A., 193, 211, 213, 229, 267, 273
Liberman, N., 202, 209
Lickel, B. A., 336, 341
Lightner, J. M., 359, 367
Lindsley, D. B., 187, 209
Linville, P. W., 65, 73
Lippa, R., 218, 231
Lishman, W. A., 107, 119
Lloyd, G. G., 107, 119
Lobel, M., 346, 365
Locke, K. D., 125, 142
Loehlin, J. C., 430
Loftus, E., 34, 48, 302, 318
Logan, H., 218, 228, 332, 338
Lombardi, W. J., 127, 143
Lopez, D. F., 217, 229, 287, 289
Lord, C. G., 332, 339
Lorr, M., 347, 366
Losch, M. E., 245, 248, 254
Lowe, M. J., 72
Lowenstein, G., 137, 142, 258, 273
Lowrance, R., 328, 340
Luchetta, T., 54, 72
Luchins, A. S., 131, 143
Luciana, M., 58, 71
Luxen, A., 48
Lykken, D., 399, 409
Lysy, D. C., 423, 430
Lyubomirsky, S., 381, 390

M

Maass, A., 34, 48
Macauley, D., 17, 22

Macauley, E., 107
Macdiarmid, J. I., 361, 362, 366
MacDonald, M. R., 385, 389
MacDonald, T. K., 60, 73
Mackie, D. M., 170, 176, 177, 185, 213, 219,
     223, 224, 233, 299, 318, 329, 331, 333,
     341, 343
MacLeod, C., 109, 377, 390
Macrae, C. N., 327, 328, 329, 330, 331, 333,
     336, 339, 341, 342
Macrae, R. R., 54, 71, 310
Maddi, S. R., 356, 366
Maddox, G. L., 346, 366
Magnus, K., 398, 400, 408
Magnusson, D. E., 97, 119
Magovern, G. J., 367
Maheswaran, D., 221, 229, 331, 339
Mahler, H. I. M., 347, 366, 418, 428
Maiman, L. H., 363
Major, B., 258, 272
Malarkey, W., 365
Malavade, K., 48
Malone, P. S., 313, 318
Mamberg, M. H., 385, 390
Mandler, G., 187, 209, 420, 429
Manheimer, E. D., 353, 366
Manis, M., 321, 338, 341
Mankowski, T. A., 152, 153, 158, 382, 388
Mao, H., 365
Maquet, P., 36, 48
Maratos, E. J., 46
Marco, C., 397, 408
Mark, G. P., 58, 72, 142
Mark, M. M., 129, 135, 144, 232, 331, 343
Markman, A. B., 205, 210
Markowitsch, H. J., 34, 46
Markus, H., 147, 159, 215, 233, 320, 343
Marshall-Goodell, B. S., 62, 71, 229
Martin, D. J., 418, 429
Martin, L. L., 3, 12, 18, 23, 123, 129, 130, 136,
     143, 159, 164, 185, 221, 227, 230, 257, 273,
     288, 290, 326, 334, 341, 407
Martin, M., 396, 409
Martin, R., 392, 398, 404, 405, 407,
     408, 409
Martin, R. A., 350, 366
Martin, R. B., 349, 350, 366
Mathews, A., 377, 390
Mathews, A. M., 107, 109, 117, 119, 120
Matthews, A., 327, 342
Matthews, K. A., 367

Mayer, J. D., 3, 5, 8, 13, 14, 21, 109, 116, 119, 122, 124, 136, 141, 143, 159, 170, 171, 183, 185, 222, 230, 299, 310, 314, 315, 318, 348, 354, 366, 367, 373, 384, 385, 390, 410, 412, 413, 414, 415, 417, 418, 419, 421, 423, 424, 425, 426, 427, 429, 430
Mayes, A. R., 46
McBride, T. J., 362, 364, 366
McClain, T. M., 380, 391
McClelland, J. L., 222, 230
McCormick, L. J., 373, 390, 412, 430
McCrae, R. R., 317, 356, 364, 375, 389, 393, 394, 400, 404, 407, 408, 416, 428
McCue, M., 350, 364
McDonald, H. E., 326, 334, 341
McDougall, W., 164, 185
McFarland, C., 158, 159
McGaugh, J. L., 31, 32, 34, 46, 48, 49, 96
McGaugh, M. C., 119
McGhee, D. E., 66, 72
McGregor, H., 254
McGuire, W. J., 213, 230, 231
McHugo, G. J., 86, 91
McInerney, S. C., 74
McLeod, C., 119, 399
McMahan, R. W., 32, 48
McNair, D., 347, 366
McNaughton, B., 36, 49
Means, B., 3, 23, 165, 169, 177, 184, 331, 341
Means, J., 282
Mearns, J., 289, 355, 364, 365, 382, 388
Mechanic, D., 346, 368
Meehan, M. E., 384, 390
Melburg, V., 245, 253
Melton, R. J., 326, 329, 334, 341, 342
Mendelssohn, M., 6
Mendez, A. A., 362, 364
Mertz, E., 165, 170, 184
Metcalf, J., 258, 273
Mewborn, C. R., 218, 232
Meyer, G. J., 375, 390
Meyer, H. A., 331, 341
Miezen, F. M., 67, 70
Mikulincer, M., 207, 210
Miles, M., 392, 407
Millar, K. U., 216, 231
Millar, M. G., 216, 231
Miller, G. A., 51, 66, 73
Miller, N., 74, 194, 210, 322, 325, 339
Mills, J., 230, 238, 242, 254
Milne, A. B., 327, 329, 336, 339, 341

Minchoff, B., 350, 364
Mineka, S., 416, 428
Mischel, W., 258, 273
Mitchell, D. C., 417, 430
Mitchener, E. C., 338
Mladinic, A., 215, 229
Mock, B. J., 72
Moffat, F. L., 363
Mongeau, P., 217, 229
Montaldi, D., 46
Monteiro, K. P., 104, 105, 117, 122, 136, 139, 141, 167, 168, 183, 278, 289
Monteith, M. J., 337, 340, 342
Moog, K., 396, 406
Moreland, R. L., 382, 390
Moreno, K. N., 5, 146, 164, 315, 319, 322, 339, 342
Morris, J., 33, 40, 46, 48
Morris, W. N., 380, 390
Morrow, J., 366, 380, 390
Moser, C. G., 379, 390
Moskowitz, D. S., 404, 408
Mowrer, O. H., 325, 340
Moylan, S. J., 110, 114, 118, 213, 222, 230, 295, 298, 301, 311, 315, 316, 318, 348, 364, 402, 407, 412, 429
Muhlbaier, J. H., 346, 365
Muhlin, G. L., 364
Mullen, B., 393, 409
Mullis, J., 218, 231
Mummendey, A., 54, 70
Munro, G. D., 335, 342
Murphy, S. T., 63, 73, 127, 143
Murray, E. A., 30, 37, 47
Murray, H. A., 8, 23
Murray, N., 170, 185
Mussweiler, T., 5, 146, 164, 315, 319, 327, 336, 342

N

Nagahara, A. H., 31, 46
Naparstek, J., 378, 391
Naritoku, D. K., 37, 47
Nasby, W., 146, 154, 155, 157, 159, 372, 390
Neisser, U., 13, 23, 34, 49, 122, 143, 417, 430
Nelson, D. E., 254
Nelson, T. E., 321, 341
Neter, E., 257, 258, 261, 271, 274, 284, 290

Neuberg, S. L., 331, 335, 340
Newman, J., 154, 159
Newman, J. R., 380, 391
Newsom, J. T., 364
Newton, I., 281, 288
Newton, T., 365
Nezu, A. M., 350, 366
Nezu, C. M., 350, 366
Nickel, S., 76, 90, 165, 335, 340
Niedenthal, P. M., 17, 76, 91, 97, 98, 118, 119,
    139, 143, 178, 185, 323, 341, 384, 390
Nisbett, R. E., 61, 66, 73, 247, 254
Nolen-Hoeksema, S., 358, 359, 366, 380, 381,
    390, 391
Noriega, V., 363
Norman, W. T., 394, 408
Nowicki, G., 417, 429
Nowicki, G. P., 169, 177, 184
Nunley, E. P., 428

O

O'Carroll, R. E., 34, 49
O'Connor, K. J., 34, 49
O'Hara, M. W., 196, 210
O'Leary, A., 318
Oakes, P. J., 327, 342
Odbert, H. S., 394, 406
Öhman, A., 86, 91, 321, 342
Öhmann, A., 86
Oktela, C., 282, 290
Olinger, L. J., 385, 389
Olson, J. M., 247, 254
Onesto, R., 278, 290
Ormel, J., 375, 390, 397, 408
Ortony, A., 51, 73, 77, 81, 91, 124, 127, 141,
    143, 187, 210, 419, 430
Osgood, C. E., 146, 159, 204, 210
Ostrom, T. M., 215, 231
Ottati, V., 133, 143, 331, 342
Otten, S., 54, 70
Otto, S., 215, 229
Owens, J. F., 367
Oxman, T. E., 353, 366

P

Packard, M. G., 32, 49
Paivio, A., 88, 91

Palfai, T., 124, 143, 354, 367, 418, 421, 423, 430
Palmer, S. E., 134, 142
Panksepp, J., 28, 43, 49, 124, 143
Parish, T. S., 323, 342
Park, B., 63, 74, 329, 343
Park, J., 332, 342
Parkes, K., 393, 408
Parkinson, S. R., 373, 390
Parrott, W. G., 111, 119, 127, 141, 143, 373,
    380, 390
Pascal, B., 2, 3, 23
Pascoe, J. P., 31, 47
Patrick, R., 169, 177, 184
Paul, B. Y., 66, 74
Paulhus, D. L., 423, 430
Pavelchak, M. A., 322, 340
Pavot, W., 398, 408
Paz, D., 207, 210
Peck, H. B., 364
Pelham, B. W., 147, 159
Pellicoro, P., 121
Pendry, L. F., 328, 342
Pennebaker, J. W., 252, 254, 356, 359, 367, 368
Peplau, L. A., 360, 367
Perie, M., 147, 158
Perloff, R., 430
Perrett, D. I., 46, 48
Persson, L.-O., 346, 367
Pervin, L. A., 97, 119
Peters, J.-M., 48
Peters, M. D., 53, 70
Petersen, S. E., 67, 70
Petrovich, G. D., 31, 49
Petry, M. C., 34, 46
Petty, R. E., 4, 14, 15, 18, 60, 62, 71, 73, 76, 91,
    110, 119, 136, 144, 151, 152, 153, 160, 164,
    170, 174, 185, 212, 213, 214, 215, 216, 218,
    219, 220, 221, 222, 223, 224, 225, 227, 228,
    229, 230, 231, 232, 233, 262, 270, 272, 274,
    276, 282, 290, 302, 336, 343, 382, 391
Petzold, P., 12, 22, 102, 117, 331, 338
Pham, M. T., 325, 342
Phelps, E. A., 33, 34, 45, 48, 49
Phillips, A. G., 57, 71
Piaget, J., 179, 185
Picard, R. W., 418, 430
Pietromonaco, P. R., 400, 408
Pilkonis, P. A., 213, 233, 321, 343
Pitkanen, A., 30, 49
Plato, 2, 6
Plomin, R., 357, 363

Plutchik, R., 76, 91
Poehlmann, K. M., 51, 70
Polonsky, W., 349, 365
Polycarpou, M. P., 338
Pomerantz, E. M., 271, 274
Pompipom, A., 423, 431
Popper, K., 9
Pothos, E., 58, 72, 142
Powell, M. C., 63, 71, 102, 118
Pozo, C., 363
Pransky, G. S., 351, 364
Pratto, F., 63, 65, 70, 73
Predmore, S., 400, 409
Pribram, K. H., 187, 210
Priester, J. R., 60, 73, 194, 208, 220, 231
Prins, B., 34, 46
Pyszczynski, T., 246, 247, 252, 254, 257, 273, 358, 367

R

Rabe, C., 177, 331, 141, 183, 338
Rachman, S., 405, 408
Rada, P. V., 142
Raghunathan, R., 4, 256, 267, 268, 270, 271, 273, 325, 342
Rahe, R., 408
Raichle, M. E., 44, 47, 67, 70
Rapp, P. R., 31, 47
Rasmusson, A. M., 31, 48
Ratcliff, R., 102, 119
Rauch, S. L., 46, 74
Rayner, R., 164, 185
Razran, G. H. S., 7, 17, 23, 219, 231
Reed, G. M., 352, 367
Reed, M. A., 134, 141, 377
Reed, M. B., 258, 261, 273, 389
Reich, J. W., 54, 74
Reidel, R., 429
Reilly, N. P., 380, 390
Reisberg, D., 34, 46, 48, 49
Reisenzein, R., 125, 143, 188, 210
Reither, A., 129, 142
Rempel, J. K., 215, 233
Renne, K. S., 360, 367
Repetti, R. L., 346, 367
Revelle, W., 375, 389
Rhodes, K., 54, 72
Rhodewalt, F., 245, 249, 254
Rich, S., 399, 409

Richards, A., 378, 391
Richman, S., 231
Ricks, D. F., 8, 24
Riecken, H. W., 240, 253
Riff, G., 100, 119
Rinck, M., 373, 391
Rinn, W. E., 62, 73
Rippetoe, P. A., 218, 231
Riskind, J. H., 138, 143
Rittenhouse, J. D., 399, 409
Robbins, T. W., 30, 32, 47
Roberts, N., 46
Roberts, R. D., 420, 423, 428
Robinson, D. S., 363
Robinson, G., 165, 170, 184
Robinson, M. D., 84, 91
Rockland, C., 46
Rodin, G., 346, 367
Rodin, J., 347, 358, 367
Rogers, R. W., 213, 218, 231, 232
Rolls, E. T., 30, 49
Romanski, L. M., 30, 48, 58, 73
Rompre, P. P., 57, 58, 74
Roney, C., 192, 209, 210
Roney, C. J. R., 198
Roozendaal, B., 31, 48
Rosch, E., 326, 342
Rose, K. C., 182, 184, 373, 389
Roseman, I. J., 80, 81, 91, 187, 200, 210, 419, 430
Rosemary, P., 217, 229
Rosen, B. R., 46
Rosen, M., 423, 431
Rosen, S., 279, 290
Rosenbaum, M., 10, 107, 119
Rosenberg, M. J., 215, 232
Rosenberg, S., 147, 159
Rosenhan, D., 414, 430
Rosenstock, I. M., 363
Rosenthal, R., 146, 159
Rosenzweig, A. S., 129, 133, 142
Ross, L., 200, 210
Rosselli, F., 230
Roth, R. H., 31, 48
Rothkopf, J. S., 138, 143
Rothman, A. J., 347, 367
Rowland, D., 46, 48
Ruberman, W., 359, 367
Rucker, D., 164, 212, 222, 227, 229, 303
Rudolph, D. L., 362, 367
Rudy, T. E., 346, 347, 368

Ruiz Caballero, J. A., 107, 119
Rumelhart, D. E., 222. 230
Rush, A. J., 412, 428
Rusker, D., 4
Russell, D., 242, 254
Russell, J. A., 41, 46, 53, 73, 82, 91, 187, 188, 200, 203, 204, 209, 210, 394, 408
Rust, M. C., 323, 340
Rusting, C. L., 3, 5, 13, 14, 20, 21, 54, 73, 111, 119, 151, 299, 310, 314, 371, 372, 373, 375, 377, 380, 381, 384, 385, 386, 391, 396, 400, 402, 408

S

Sabini, J., 111, 119, 143, 373, 380, 390
Salovey, P., 5, 14, 20, 21, 65, 73, 122, 124, 143, 158, 171, 185, 187, 209, 280, 290, 315, 318, 338, 344, 346, 347, 348, 354, 358, 365, 367, 368, 372, 373, 379, 380, 389, 391, 412, 413, 414, 418, 419, 421, 423, 424, 425, 426, 427, 429, 430
Saltzberg, J. A., 280, 358, 290, 368
Sanbonmatsu, D. N., 63, 71, 102, 118
Sanford, R. N., 325, 338
Sanft, H., 182, 184, 373, 389
Savander, V., 30, 49
Schachter, S., 187, 210, 240, 247, 253, 254, 295, 318
Schacter, D. L., 33, 49
Schaufeli, W. B., 375, 390
Schaumann, L., 155, 158
Schefft, B. K., 44, 46
Scheier, M. F., 19, 22, 130, 141, 156, 159, 258, 272, 350, 351, 358, 363, 364, 367, 393, 408
Schelling, T., 258, 273
Scherer, K. R., 29, 49, 51, 73, 76, 78, 79, 80, 81, 84, 85, 86, 88, 91, 92, 146, 159, 187, 200, 210
Schiffenbauer, A. I., 109, 119
Schiller, F., 353
Schilling, E. A., 397, 398, 406
Schleifer, S. J., 350, 365
Schlosberg, H., 187, 188, 210, 211
Schneider, K., 373, 391
Schoenbaum, G., 37, 49
Schul, R., 34, 35, 45
Schultz, T. R., 57, 73
Schultz, W., 37, 49, 412, 429
Schulz, R., 367
Schumann, D., 231

Schwartz, G. E., 429
Schwartz, J., 407
Schwartz, J. L. K., 66, 72
Schwarz, N., 11, 18, 22, 23, 51, 65, 73, 76, 92, 102, 112, 118, 119, 122, 123, 125, 127, 130, 131, 134, 139, 141, 143, 144, 145, 156, 158, 159, 160, 164, 165, 168, 170, 171, 174, 175, 177, 183, 185, 213, 214, 215, 220, 223, 224, 226, 227, 228, 232, 247, 254, 261, 270, 272, 273, 295, 296, 298, 318, 320, 328, 329, 331, 332, 333, 334, 336, 337, 338, 339, 342, 421, 430
Schwebel, D. C., 399, 405, 408
Scott, D. G., 362, 364
Scott, H. S., 85, 92
Scott, J., 121, 143
Scott, L., 196, 210
Scott, P. A., 51, 70
Scott, W. D., 155, 158
Sears, R. R., 325, 340
Sechrest, L., 429
Sedikides, C., 3, 4, 12, 13, 18, 23, 110, 119, 145, 146, 147, 148, 153, 156, 159, 160, 221, 230, 257, 273, 295, 296, 313, 315, 318, 358, 368, 373, 380, 391, 400
Seeman, T. E., 359, 368
Segerstrom, S. C., 352, 368
Servay, W., 125, 143
Setterlund, M. B., 76, 91, 139, 143, 178, 185, 384, 390
Shack, J. R., 375, 390
Shaffer, D. R., 242, 254
Shah, J., 189, 197, 198, 205, 206, 209, 210
Shajahan, P., 34, 49
Shalker, T., 230, 411, 429
Shalker, T. E., 119, 122, 136, 142, 372, 389
Shapiro, D., 349, 365
Shapiro, P. N., 323, 343
Shaw, B. F., 385, 389, 412, 428
Sheehan, K., 384, 390
Sheppard, L. A., 325, 339
Sherman, J. W., 331, 333, 339, 342
Sherman-Williams, B., 331, 341
Shiflett, S. C., 350, 365
Showers, C. J., 54, 74
Shulman, D., 384, 390
Sia, T. L., 332, 339
Sideris, J., 246, 254
Siemer, M., 125, 143
Sigmon, S. T., 368
Silbersweig, D., 48

Simmel, M., 41, 48
Simmonds, S., 269, 272
Simon, E. W., 423, 431
Simon, H. A., 122, 144, 187, 210, 420, 431
Simon, L., 254
Sinclair, L., 342
Sinclair, R. C., 129, 135, 144, 232, 327, 331, 343
Singer, J. A., 367, 372, 373, 379, 380, 389, 391
Singer, J. E., 187, 210, 247, 254
Singer, R. D., 9, 11, 12, 22, 295, 317
Sjoberg, L., 346, 367
Skoner, D. P., 364
Skowronski, J. J., 58, 74
Slack, A. K., 375, 391
Slamecka, N. J., 181, 185
Sloman, A., 86, 92, 418, 431
Smith, C. A., 3, 13, 14, 15, 16, 23, 36, 49, 51, 74, 75, 77, 78, 79, 80, 81, 82, 83, 84, 85, 86, 88, 89, 90, 91, 92, 104, 116, 119, 169, 187, 210
Smith, D. A., 97, 118
Smith, D. C., 37, 47
Smith, E. R., 215, 222, 232, 327, 343
Smith, H., 393, 407
Smith, M. B., 206, 210, 232
Smith, N. K., 59, 72
Smith, N. L., 351, 365
Smith, S. M., 110, 119, 136, 144, 151, 152, 153, 160, 213, 225, 228, 231, 233, 276, 282, 290, 382, 391
Smith, S. S., 174, 185
Smith, T. W., 358, 365, 368, 378, 388, 389, 405, 409
Snyder, M., 106, 120, 167, 185, 403, 409
Snyder, C. R., 352, 353, 365, 368
Soffin, S., 321, 341
Solomon, R. C., 418, 428
Solomon, S., 246, 254
Sorenson, J. A., 72
Southwick, L. L., 249, 255
Spencer, D. D., 33, 48
Spencer, S. J., 329, 330, 343
Squire, L. R., 34, 48
Srull, T. K., 138, 139, 144, 232
Staats, A. W., 219, 232
Staats, C. K., 219, 232
Stangor, C., 215, 232, 321, 343
Stankov, L., 420, 423, 428
Stayman, D. M., 221, 228
Steblay, N. M., 34, 49
Steele, C. M., 243, 244, 249, 250, 255, 257, 273

Steiner, J. E., 61, 74
Steller, B., 282, 290
Stephan, C. W., 323, 343
Stephan, W. G., 323, 343
Steptoe, A., 362, 368
Stern, E., 48
Sternberg, R. J., 430
Stevens, A., 423, 430
Steward, W. T., 5, 20, 315, 344
Stickgold, R., 49
Stieg, R. L., 346, 368
Stone, J. A., 244, 255, 400
Stone, M. V., 72
Story, A. L., 147, 158
Stotland, E., 215, 230
Strack, F., 127, 144, 165, 170, 183, 194, 208, 209, 213, 223, 228, 270, 272, 331, 335, 336, 340, 342, 343
Strathman, A. J., 231
Strauman, T. J., 196, 205, 207, 209, 211
Strauss, M. M., 46
Strelau, J., 376, 391, 402, 409
Stretton, M., 318, 368
Stroebe, M., 359, 360, 368
Stroebe, W., 359, 360, 368
Stroehm, W., 167, 171, 176, 178, 184
Strong, S. E., 373, 390, 412, 430
Strube, M. J., 54, 72, 148, 160, 257, 273
Struening, E. L., 364
Strum, G., 384, 390
Stryker, S., 147, 160
Stubing, M. J., 246, 254
Suarez, E. C., 405, 409
Suci, G. J., 146, 159
Sujan, H., 170, 185
Sujan, M., 170, 185
Sullivan, L. A., 215, 321, 341, 343
Suls, J., 5, 14, 21, 232, 299, 392, 393, 394, 397, 398, 399, 400, 401, 404, 405, 407, 408, 409
Summerfield, A. B., 200, 210
Summers, K., 11, 23, 110, 118
Süsser, K., 129, 141, 331, 339
Sutton, S., 396, 408
Sutton, S. R., 218, 232
Swann, W. B., Jr., 148, 160, 400, 409
Swanson, L. W., 31, 49
Swartz, T. S., 200, 210
Sweeney, P. D., 382, 390
Swets, J. A., 193, 211
Syme, S. L., 359, 360, 361, 364, 368

T

Tan, U., 392, 407
Tang, C., 46
Tannenbaum, P. H., 146, 159
Tanner, W. P. Jr., 193, 211
Tarpley, W. R., 251, 253
Tassinary, L. G., 62, 71, 229
Tauer, J. M., 242, 253
Taylor, G. J., 416, 431
Taylor, S. E., 257, 258, 272, 273, 276, 278, 290,
    352, 358, 367, 368, 382, 391, 412, 429
Teasdale, J. D., 107, 120
Teather, L. A., 32, 49
Tedeschi, J. T., 245, 253
Tellegen, A., 53, 54, 74, 79, 82, 92, 188, 211,
    356, 368, 375, 391, 394, 399, 402, 409
Tennen, H., 351, 364
ter Schure, E., 80, 91, 187, 209
Terkildsen, N., 133, 143, 331, 342
Tesser, A., 250, 255, 257, 273, 276, 279,
    280, 290
Tessler, R., 346, 368
Tetlock, P. E., 334, 341
Thaller, R. H., 258, 273
Thayer, R. E., 188, 211, 380, 391
Therriault, N., 277, 278, 282, 285, 290
Thompson, M. M., 60, 74
Thorne, T. M. J., 329, 341
Titanic-Schefft, M., 44, 46
Titchener, E. B., 7, 14
Tomaka, J., 83, 92, 393, 406
Tomkins, S. S., 76, 92
Tranel, D., 38, 39, 40, 41, 42, 45, 46, 47, 48,
    58, 70
Trapnell, P. D., 158, 289
Tremblay, L., 37, 49
Trimboli, C., 373, 389
Troccoli, B. T., 11, 22, 117, 175, 183,
    358, 363
Trope, Y., 4, 14, 19, 193, 211, 256, 257, 258,
    261, 263, 266, 267, 268, 270, 271, 273,
    274, 284, 290
Truax, K. M., 347, 365
Tucker, D. M., 76, 90
Tucker, J., 407
Turk, D. C., 346, 347, 368
Turner, J. C., 327, 342
Turner, T. J., 97, 117
Turski, P. A., 72
Turvey, C., 124, 143, 354, 367, 423, 430

Tversky, A., 58, 72, 131, 144, 167, 168, 184,
    222, 230, 348, 365
Tykocinski, O., 192, 207, 209

U

Urbina, S., 430
Uretsky, M. D., 346, 364

V

Vaidya, C. J., 72
Vallacher, R. R., 134, 144
van Reekum, C. M., 88, 92
Vance, K. M., 242, 253
Vanman, E. J., 66, 68, 74
Vargas, P. T., 316
Vasquez-Suson, K. A., 323, 339
Vaux, A., 54, 72
Velten, E., 152, 154, 157, 160
Vescio, T. K., 324, 327, 338, 339
Visscher, B. R., 352, 367
Visser, P. S., 53, 72
Volanth, A. J., 109, 119, 348, 366, 385, 390
von Hippel, W., 216, 229
Voshart, K., 346, 367

W

Wagner, A. D., 67, 72, 74
Wahler, H. J., 347, 368
Walbott, H. G., 200, 210
Walker, D. L., 33, 47
Walker, L. M., 375, 391
Waltz, W., 350, 364
Wan, C. K., 398, 405, 409
Wang, H. J., 352, 367
Ward, D. W., 129, 143, 334, 341
Warr, P., 53, 54, 74
Waschull, S. B., 151, 159
Watkins, T., 109, 120
Watson, D., 53, 54, 74, 79, 82, 92, 188, 211,
    356, 375, 368, 391, 394, 395, 396, 400, 409
Watson, J. B., 9, 10, 3, 21, 164, 185
Wayment, H. A., 257, 258, 273
Wearing, A., 398, 408
Weary, G., 328, 331, 332, 337, 340, 343
Weaver, C. N., 360, 365

Webb, J. R., 316
Weber, M., 34, 46
Wegener, D. T., 136, 144, 174, 185, 213, 214, 215, 221, 222, 223, 224, 225, 227, 228, 229, 231, 232, 233, 262, 270, 272, 276, 274, 290, 336, 343
Wegner, D. M., 63, 74, 134, 141, 282, 285, 290
Wehmer, G., 7, 24
Weinblatt, E., 359, 367
Weiner, B., 257, 274
Weinstein, N. D., 347, 368
Weiskrantz, L., 40, 49
Weiss, W., 213, 233
Weldon, V., 429
Wells, G. L., 224, 231
Wessman, A. E., 8, 24
Whalen, P., 32, 46, 49, 58, 74
White, P., 106, 120, 167, 185, 227, 231
White, R. W., 206, 210
Wicklund, R. A., 238, 255, 358, 364
Wieland, R., 331, 339
Wiest, C., 200, 210
Wiggins, E. C., 222, 229
Wilcox, K. J., 399, 409
Wilder, D. A., 323, 343
Wilkins, R. H., 346, 365
Williams, C., 37, 49
Williams, C. J., 63, 71
Williams, J., 378, 391
Williams, K. J., 398
Williams, R., 277
Williams, R. B., Jr., 405, 409
Williamson, D. A., 109, 120
Wills, T. A., 361, 364
Wilson, M., 36, 49
Wilson, T. D., 61, 66, 73, 247, 254, 336, 343
Wingard, D., 407
Winkielman, P., 127, 144
Winograd, E., 34, 49
Wise, R. A., 57, 58, 74
Witte, K., 218, 233
Wittenbrink, B., 63, 66, 74, 329, 343
Witty, T. E., 352, 364
Wixon, D. R., 245, 255
Woelk, M., 141, 177, 183
Wohlfarth, T., 397, 408
Wolever, M. E., 349, 350, 366
Wolfe, C. T., 329, 343

Wolff, C., 6
Wolff, W. T., 154, 159
Wölk, M., 331, 338
Woll, F. B., 97, 118
Wood, J. V., 280, 290, 358, 368
Woodworth, R. S., 188, 211
Worth, L. T., 170, 176, 177, 185, 213, 219, 223, 224, 230, 233, 299, 318, 329, 331, 333, 341, 343
Wu, J., 46
Wundt, W., 7, 14, 187, 211
Wyer, R. S., 123, 129, 130, 136, 137, 138, 139, 141, 142, 143, 144, 159, 183, 170, 330, 334, 339, 341

X

Xagoraris, A., 30, 48, 58, 73

Y

Yando, R., 372, 390
Yerkes, R. M., 164, 185
Yik, M. S. M., 423, 430
Yoshinobu, L. R., 368
Young, A. W., 40, 45, 46, 48, 49
Young, G. C. D., 396, 409
Young, M. J., 129, 133, 142
Young, P. T., 75, 92

Z

Zacks, R. T., 182, 184, 373, 389
Zajonc, R. B., 13, 16, 24, 27, 49, 63, 73, 80, 84, 92, 98, 99, 101, 120, 127, 143, 144, 215, 233, 411, 320, 324, 343, 431
Zanna, M. P., 60, 73, 74, 157, 159, 213, 215, 219, 226, 233, 242, 245, 247, 248, 252, 254, 255, 321, 332, 340, 341, 343
Zautra, A. J., 54, 74
Zevon, M. A., 53, 54, 74
Zhao, Z., 36, 47
Zillmann, D., 187, 211, 220, 233
Zimbardo, P. G., 238, 255
Zuckerman, A., 397, 398, 400, 401, 406
Zuwerink, J. R., 337, 340

Subject Index

A

accommodation, *see* assimilation vs. accommodation

activation, 187–188, 199, 203–204

affect
  and attitude change, 212–228
  and cognition, 2, 3, 8–9, 12–15, 16, 21–22, 28–30, 44–45, 99–103, 294, 296, 411–412, 417–419
  and conditioning, 9–12
  and health, 5, 344–368
  and memory, 13, 14, 16, 30–32, 33–37, 95–115
  and personality, 5, 20–21, 147, 151, 153, 157, 371–387, 392–405
  and processing strategies, 312–314, 329, 333, 334, 335, 336, 337
  and self-concept, 145–157
  and self-discrepancy, 186–207
  and social episodes, 96–99
  and social motivation, 4–5, 19
  and stereotyping, 319–343
  and stress, 392–405
  and the immune system, 349–351, 352, 360
  appraisal of, 75–90
  as a resource, 256–272
  as information, 121–139
  congruence, 7–8, 17–18, 164, 166, 295, 314, 315. *See also* mood congruence
  control, 248, 315
  integral vs. incidental, 320–324, 333, 337, 338

Affect Infusion Model (AIM), 20, 112–116, 146, 147, 150–157, 172–182, 296–316, 326, 386

affect infusion, 12, 14, 20, 113, 116, 148, 173, 174, 177, 178, 221, 248, 249, 294, 296, 297–299, 301, 306–308, 312, 314, 315

affect intensity, 157–158, 357–358

affect management, *see* affect regulation

affect modulation in animals, 30–33

affect priming, 4, 13, 17, 102–103, 107, 110–116, 402–403, 405

affect regulation, 5, 14, 19, 313–314, 354–355, 380–382, 383

affect-as-information model, 2, 4–6, 8, 10–17, 18–20, 24, 25, 102, 174, 296–297
affective disorders, 107, 109, 110
affective inertia, 398, 403
affective influences on
  behavior interpretation, 300–302, 314
  decision making, 3, 17, 37–40
  eyewitness memory, 302–303, 315
  persuasive communication, 311–312
  requests, 304–307, 315
  responding to social situations, 307, 308
  self concept, 4, 12–15, 18–19, 21
  social behavior, 5, 19–20, 294–295, 304–306, 314
  social judgment, *see* social judgment
  spontaneous interaction, 303–304, 314
affective recall without factual recall, 99–103
affective valence, 146, 148, 149, 150
affective-cognitive network and neurotic cascade, 402–403
affect-priming theory, 99–105, 296. *See also* associative network model
affirmative vs. nonaffirmative judgment, 154–155
agitation, 187–189, 195–199, 200, 202, 203, 204, 205, 207
agreeableness, 305, 404–405
AIDS, 352
alcohol, 249, 362
amygdala, 29, 30–33, 34–36, 40–43, 58, 96
anger, 28–29, 82, 83, 89, 166, 374, 378, 379, 401
anxiety, 7, 20, 78, 107, 109, 196, 207, 244, 245, 248, 278, 295, 310–311, 325, 332, 374, 377, 395
appetitive situations, 178, 179, 180
appraisal theory of emotion 4, 6, 16, 24, 75–90
  components of, 80, 81–83
  detectors, 85, 86, 87
  function of, 77–78, 79
  process model of, 80, 84–89
  properties of, 78–79
  structural model of, 80–84
approach vs. avoidance motivations, 194
arousal, 31, 34, 187–188, 203–204
artificial intelligence, 418
assimilation vs. accommodation, 4, 165, 166, 177, 178, 179, 180, 181, 183
associative network model, 4, 13, 17, 102–103, 104–110, 115, 169, 170, 175, 372, 380, 402
associative processing , 84, 85, 86–87, 88

attention, 5, 12, 14, 18, 25, 250, 329, 333, 358–359, 396
attitude change, 212–228, 238, 239, 242–247, 249, 250, 251
attitudes, 3, 10, 100, 106, 206, 214, 215, 269–270
attribution, 4, 6–11, 16, 18, 24, 43
autobiographical memory, 99, 107, 111, 146, 147, 150, 207, 305, 373
aversive situations, 178, 179, 180

B

bargaining strategies, 146, 309–310
basal forebrain, 32, 33
behavior change, 238, 239, 240, 241, 242, 252, 301
behavioral activation and inhibition system, 376
behavioral intentions, 269–270
behaviorism, *see* conditioning theories
belief-disconfirmation paradigm, 238, 240, 251
Big Five, *see* Five-Factor Model of Personality
bottom-up processing, *see* top-down vs. bottom-up processing
brain imaging, 36, 40, 44
brainstem, 29
bulimia nervosa, 362

C

capacity theories, 176–177
category identification, 326–328, 338
cheerfulness, 186–189, 191, 195, 197–199, 200–203, 204, 205, 207
cholinergic system, 32, 37
classical conditioning, 219–220
cognition and affect, *see* affect and cognition
cognitive change, 241, 242, 244, 247, 252
cognitive dissonance, 18, 226, 238, 242
  action-based model of, 240
  and commitment 249
  and negative affect, 240, 241–252
  role of aversive consequences in, 243
cognitively taxing tasks, 281, 282
conditioning theories, 5, 9–12, 18, 321, 323
constructive processing, 301, 305, 309, 312. *See also* substantive processing
consumer preferences, 315

contact hypothesis, 322, 323
context and mood, 279, 281, 282, 285, 286
coping strategies, 330, 440
correction effects, 226–228
creativity, 207

D

decision making, 28, 37–40, 76, 169
declarative memory, 33–37. *See also* memory
defensiveness, 217, 257–261
depressed mood, 174, 177, 187–189, 195–205,
    207, 245, 378–379, 395, 401
depressive realism, 417
differential coping hypothesis, 400
differential sensitivity hypothesis, 149
direct access processing, 147, 148, 172, 173,
    182, 297, 315, 316.
disgust, 166
dissonance, *see* cognitive dissonance
distraction and mood repair, 278, 380–382, 383
dopamine, 57–58

E

eating, 361–362
Elaboration Likelihood Model (ELM), 214,
    218–228
electrodermal activity, 241, 245, 248, 251, 252.
    See also psychophysiology
emotional intelligence, 2, 5, 21, 410–427
emotional memory, 31–32, 34–37, 95–115;
    See also memory
emotional traits, 374, 378. *See also* personality
emotion-focused coping potential, 81, 82, 83
emotions, 104
    adaptive functions of, 77, 79, 83
    appraisal of, 75–90, 206
    elicitation of, 76–77, 89–90
    experiences of, 186–189, 199, 201, 204
    meaning of, 418–419
    regulation of, 19, 380–381. *See also* affect
        regulation
    vs. mood, 15
empathy, 324
encoding and retrieval mood effects, 168
endocrine and neuroendocrine function, 29
envy, 166

escape-from-self, 362
ethnic minorities, 332–333
Evaluative Space Model (ESM), 54–57, 60
event-related brain potentials (ERPs), 59, 64–65
evolution, 2, 3,
exercise and mood, 277
expectancy-value model, 218, 222–223
extraversion, 5, 21, 374, 375–378, 379, 387,
    388, 394–395
eyewitness memory, 34, 302–303, 312,
    313, 315

F

facial expression, 40, 41, 44, 62, 249
faculties of mind, 6–7, 14, 294, 414
fear, 5, 8, 22, 83, 89, 166, 244, 295, 395.
    See also anxiety
fear appeals, 217–218
fear conditioning, 30, 33, 40
feedback-seeking, 257–270
    and accuracy of feedback, 266
    and emotional cost, 257–258, 264–265
    and informational benefits, 257–258, 264
feelings-as-information, *see*
        affect-as-information model
field experiments, 307, 313
Five-Factor Model of Personality, 393, 394, 395,
    398, 403, 405
flashbulb memory, 33
flexible correction model, 227
focal awareness, 84, 85
forced compliance paradigm, *see* induced
        compliance paradigm
forgetting, 246, 250. *See also* memory
free choice paradigm, 239
frustration-aggression hypothesis, 324–325
fundamental attribution error, 312–313, 315
future expectancy, 81, 82, 83

G

Gestalt psychology, 11
global-local focus, 17, 18, 25
goal-looms-larger effect, 194, 195
goals, 81, 262–269
guided imagery mood induction, 149, 157
guilt, 83

H

hardiness, 355–356
health, 5, 20, 89, 267–270, 315
heart rate, 29
hedonic contingency model, 174, 224–226
hedonism, 273, 277, 278, 280, 285, 286, 288
heuristic processing, 13–15, 114, 147, 165, 168, 169–174, 177, 178, 180–182, 297–299, 313
heuristics, 11, 330, 331, 332
heuristic-systematic model, 214. *See also* Elaboration Likelihood Model
high vs. low elaboration processing, 4, 219–223
hippocampus, 32, 34
history, 2–12
hope, 83, 166, 352–353
hostility, 374, 379, 405
how-do-I-feel-about-it heuristics, 102, 174, 296–297. *See also* affect-as-information model
hydraulic principle, 6, 8–9
hyperreactivity, *see* reactivity
hypnotically induced moods, 105–106

I

immediacy principle, 8, 11, 24
immune system, 349–351, 352, 360
implicit evaluations, 63–67
impression formation, *see* social judgments
incidental affect, 249, 321, 324–326, 333, 338
individual differences, *see* personality; affect and personality
individuation, 331, 335
induced compliance paradigm, 239–243, 245, 246, 247–250
information principle, 5, 6, 24
information processing strategies, 112–114, 164, 169–170, 172, 295–296, 331, 333–335
integral vs. incidental affect, 320–324, 333, 337, 338
intelligence, 38. *See also* emotional intelligence
intergroup behavior, 5, 20, 146, 320–324, 328, 337
intimate relationships, 300, 301
introspectionism, 7, 14

J

judgments, *see* social judgments

K

Korsakoff's syndrome, 100

L

lag effect of mood, 398, 401
late-positive potential (LPP), 59, 64–65
laughter, 350–351
learning as a goal, 265–267
Lewinian field theory, 288
Life Orientation Test (LOT), 351–352
life stressors, 393, 396–403, 405
locus of control, 393, 403
loneliness, 360

M

machiavellianism, 111, 310
memory, 3, 4, 13, 14, 16, 28, 30–33, 34–37, 44, 76, 86–87, 95–116, 147, 148, 152, 154, 157, 164, 165, 168, 169, 171, 173, 176, 180, 192, 193–194, 207, 302–303, 315, 378–379, 383, 396
methodological issues, 373, 384, 386, 387
midbrain, 29
misattribution, 8, 11, 12, 18, 24, 88, 175, 220, 245, 247, 248, 250
mood
  and goals, 257, 262–263
  and judgments, *see* social judgments
  and memory, 2, 3, 20–23, 25, 104–108, 169, 267–268, 374, 378–379, 383
  and persuasion, 267–270
  and processing, 108–110, 115–116
  and self-assessment, 146, 258–267
  and self-focus, 282, 283
  as a resource, 257–262
  as information, 175, 182; *See also* affect-as-information model
  as input, 334
  congruence, 146–148, 152–155, 157, 158, 168–173, 176, 178, 180–182, 276, 279, 280, 282, 284, 285, 287, 288, 327,

372–388, 396, 402, 417. *See also* affect congruence

incongruence, 258–261, 278, 281, 282, 284, 285, 287, 288 295–296, 313–314

induction, 149, 152–153, 157, 167–168, 276, 277, 282, 287, 346–348, 384–385, 387

maintenance, 262–264

priming, 280, 281, 287. *See also* associative network models

regulation, 19, 281–285, 287, 288, 313–314, 354–355, 380–382, 383. *See also* affect regulation

repair, 156, 171, 174, 263, 276, 277, 278, 279, 282, 283, 286, 374, 386. *See also* affect regulation

vs. emotion, 15

motivated processing, 110, 147, 172, 173–174, 182, 241, 248, 249, 297–299, 310, 312, 314, 315, 316. *See also* Affect Infusion Model

motivation and mood congruency, 379–380, 382, 385–387

motivation and cognitive dissonance, 240, 242

motivational states, 79, 83, 89, 173, 174, 189, 191, 192, 194, 195, 199, 200–203, 206, 208, 271, 328, 334, 335, 374, 379, 380, 382, 385, 387

multiple determinism, 52

music and mood induction, 152–153, 157

N

natural mood states, 385

need for approval, 310

negative affect, 241, 247, 249–250, 356–357

and dissonance reduction, 240, 241–243, 246–251,

and psychological discomfort, 241, 242

and self-esteem, 242, 244, 247, 252, 280

and stereotyping, 332–333, 335–337

awareness of, 61, 63–67

classical conditioning of, 62, 63, 65–67

misattribution of, 245, 247, 248, 250

need to reduce, 240, 241, 247, 248, 249

neural representation of, 57–58, 60–69

suppression of, 247, 252

vs. positive affect, 52–60, 69, 244

negativity bias, 58–59, 65

negotiating strategies, 309–310

network models, *see* associative ne

neuropsychology, 14, 16, 241, 248

neuroscience, 3, 14, 27–45

neurotic cascade, 399

neuroticism, 5, 21, 356, 374, 375–378, 379, 388, 393–406

neurotransmitters, 31, 37

neutral mood, 283, 284, 286

New Look, 13

Newton's First Law, 281, 288

non-emotional motivational states, 189, 192–195, 199–200, 203, 206, 208

nonverbal communication, 299, 302

nurturance vs. security, 189, 191

O

object appraisals, 206

openness to experience, 394–395

openness to feeling, 310

optimism, 351–352

orbitofrontal cortex, 30

organizational behavior, 315

other-accountability, 81, 82

P

perception, 76, 164, 396

performance outcomes, 155–156

person X environment fit, 403

personality, 5, 20–21, 38, 89, 393, 394

and affect, 371–388

and cognition, 413–414, 416–417

and emotional traits, 415–416

components of, 413–415

persuasion, 4, 169–170, 212–228, 311–312

and attitudes, 269–270

and health, 268–271

and mood 267–270

high vs. low elaboration in, 219–223

philosophy, 2, 5, 6–7, 9

physiological arousal, 241, 250, 251, 252

positive affect

and stereotyping, 331–335

awareness of, 61, 63–67

neural representation of, 57–58, 60–69

vs. negative affect, 52–60, 69

Positive and Negative Affect Schedule (PANAS), 53

prejudice, 5, 65–68, 324. *See also* affect and stereotyping
primary appraisal, 82, 83
priming, 9, 10, 16, 21, 23, 26, 164, 168, 169, 175. *See also* associative network models
problem-focused coping potential, 81, 82, 83
processing motivation and affect, 329, 334, 336, 337
processing principle, 12–14, 16, 23, 25
processing style, 170, 176
projection, 9, 11
promotion vs. prevention focus, 4, 18, 54, 189–198, 201–207
psychoanalysis, 6, 8–9, 17
psychoneuroimmunology, 349–351
psychophysiology, 241, 248
psychoticism, 394
punishment, 376–377

Q

quiescence, 186–189, 191, 195, 197–199, 200–203, 204, 205, 207

R

reactivity, 393, 395, 396–398, 403
reasoning, 76, 86, 87–88
recall, *see* memory
regret, 244
regulatory focus, 187–208
relaxation as a coping strategy, 400–401
religiosity, 353–354
REM sleep, 36
repression, 247, 252
requesting, 146, 176, 304–307, 315
reward and punishment, 37, 376–377
right brain hemisphere, 30
risk, 5, 7, 23, 348
rumination, 358–359, 381–382, 383, 388

S

sadness, *see* depressed mood
scapegoating, 325, 330
scripts, 96, 331
secondary appraisal, 82–83

self-accountability, 81, 82, 83
self-affirmation theory, 244, 250
self-concept, 4, 20, 146, 147, 157, 158, 242, 244, 362
    and AIM, 147–151, 153, 158
    central vs. peripheral, 147–148, 149, 150, 151, 153, 157
self-discrepancy theory and affect, 186–207, 244
self-esteem, 20, 111, 151–153, 157, 158, 257, 314, 325, 329, 347, 374, 382–383, 399, 400
self-focused attention, 358–359
self-induced mood, 261–262
self-regulation, 189, 190, 191, 192, 193, 196–197
    and mood, 202, 262–263. *See also* affect regulation
    effectiveness of, 187, 189, 198, 199, 200–202
self-relevant information processing, 257–270
Selves Questionnaire, 196
semantic opposites, 204–205
shame, 83
S-IgA, 349–350
skin conductance, 33, 195
sleep, 36
social appropriateness, 282, 284, 286, 287, 288
social cognition, 2, 3, 4, 5, 8–9, 12–15, 16, 21–22, 28–30, 44–45, 99–103, 294, 296, 411–412, 417, 418–419
    and emotional intelligence, 419–422
    and personality processes, 413–414
    future research in, 427
social constraints model of mood regulation, 279–284, 285
social desirability, 111
social episodes, 96–99
social influence and persuasive communication, 212–228
social interaction, 302–304, 307, 308–310, 315
social judgments, 3–11, 13, 14, 16, 20, 22, 24, 28, 40–43, 44, 107–108, 147, 154–155, 156, 157, 158, 171, 338, 386
social neuroscience, 51–52, 69
social support, 359–361
socialization, 190
somatic marker hypothesis, 29, 30, 40
startle eyeblink modification, 62–63
stereotypes, 5, 12, 16, 17, 20, 25, 89, 165, 324, 325, 326–338
    activation of, 326, 328–330
    and affect, 319–338

application of, 326, 330–335
correction of, 326, 336–337
stigmatized social groups, 324, 325
stress, 5, 21, 31, 82, 83, 89, 392–406
subliminal priming, 8, 9, 16
substantive processing, 113, 147, 151, 172, 173,
    175, 176, 178, 181, 182, 297–299, 307,
    308, 314, 315, 316, 386. *See also* Affect
    Infusion Model
sympathetic nervous system activity, 241, 248,
    324, 399. *See also* neuropsychology;

T

temperament, 357–358
tolerance for dissonance, 246, 250
top-down vs. bottom-up processing, 165, 169,
    179, 180, 299–302, 313, 331, 392–393

trait anxiety, 310, 374, 377–378
Trait Meta-Mood Scale (TMMS), 355
trilogy of mind *see* faculties of mind
two-dimensional conceptions of emotion,
    79, 82
Type A personality, 393, 379

V

Velten procedure, 154
ventral striatum, 30, 31
ventromedial frontal cortex, 29, 37–40
voodoo death, 345

W

weapons effect, 34